SAP SuccessFactors Talent: Volume 1

A Complete Guide to Configuration, Administration, and Best Practices: Performance and Goals

Susan Traynor
Michael A. Wellens
Venki Krishnamoorthy

Apress®

SAP SuccessFactors Talent: Volume 1: A Complete Guide to Configuration, Administration, and Best Practices: Performance and Goals

Susan Traynor
California, CA, USA

Michael A. Wellens
North Carolina, NC, USA

Venki Krishnamoorthy
Pennsylvania, PA, USA

ISBN-13 (pbk): 978-1-4842-6599-4
https://doi.org/10.1007/978-1-4842-6600-7

ISBN-13 (electronic): 978-1-4842-6600-7

Managing Director, Apress Media LLC: Welmoed Spahr
Acquisitions Editor: Divya Modi
Development Editor: Matthew Moodie
Coordinating Editor: Divya Modi

Cover designed by eStudioCalamar

Cover image designed by Pixabay

Distributed to the book trade worldwide by Springer Science+Business Media New York, 1 New York Plaza, New York, NY 10004. Phone 1-800-SPRINGER, fax (201) 348-4505, e-mail orders-ny@springer-sbm.com, or visit www.springeronline.com. Apress Media, LLC is a California LLC and the sole member (owner) is Springer Science + Business Media Finance Inc (SSBM Finance Inc). SSBM Finance Inc is a **Delaware** corporation.

For information on translations, please e-mail booktranslations@springernature.com; for reprint, paperback, or audio rights, please e-mail bookpermissions@springernature.com.

Apress titles may be purchased in bulk for academic, corporate, or promotional use. eBook versions and licenses are also available for most titles. For more information, reference our Print and eBook Bulk Sales web page at http://www.apress.com/bulk-sales.

Any source code or other supplementary material referenced by the author in this book is available to readers on GitHub via the book's product page, located at www.apress.com/978-1-4842-6599-4. For more detailed information, please visit http://www.apress.com/source-code.

Printed on acid-free paper

Dedicated with gratitude to

Jeffrey S. Kob and Randall M. Kob

and

Sheila McGovern who gave Michael the
opportunity to jump into the world of SAP SuccessFactors

and

Venki's mom, Thiripurasundari, who was
his guide and dear friend

Table of Contents

About the Authors

Susan Traynor, M.A., is an SAP SuccessFactors certified professional with more than 21 years of progressive experience in SAP HCM and SuccessFactors. She has considerable experience working on full-lifecycle project implementations, as well as supporting upgrades and integration projects. You can follow her on LinkedIn.

Michael A. Wellens, M.S., is a certified SAP SuccessFactors consultant with over 15 years of human resources (HR) information systems implementation experience. He has successfully launched a variety of core HR and talent management solutions across a number of Fortune 500 companies around the world. You can follow him on LinkedIn or on Twitter at @mike_wellens.

Venki Krishnamoorthy is an SAP SuccessFactors consultant. He has over 15 years of experience as a functional lead, project manager, and program manager in HCM transformation projects. Venki has completed over 35 full-lifecycle implementations of SuccessFactors projects across multiple modules. You can follow him on LinkedIn or on Twitter at `@venki_sap`.

About the Technical Reviewer

Gaye Bowles is an SAP SuccessFactors certified consultant with 16+ years of technical and functional experience in SuccessFactors and HR applications. With over 25 full-lifecycle global implementations including large transformation and conversion projects for Fortune 500 companies, she has also supported both commercial and national security (NS2) clients. You can follow her on LinkedIn.

About the Technical Reviewer

Acknowledgments

Special thanks to Jeremy Masters for bringing us all together.

CHAPTER 1

An Introduction to SAP SuccessFactors Talent Modules

Welcome!

Welcome to *SAP SuccessFactors Talent*! SAP SuccessFactors is a grouping of cloud-based modules across a common platform that spans the entire realm of HCM data storage, management, and reporting. Modules include Employee Central (EC) which acts as a core Human Resources Information System (HRIS), Onboarding (ONB), Learning Management System (LMS), Recruiting (RCM/RMK), Analytics and Planning (WFA/ WFP), Compensation and Variable Pay (CMP/VarPay), and Jam, as well as a variety of Talent Management modules. SAP SuccessFactors Talent modules provide a grouping of state-of-the-art tools built on the SuccessFactors cloud platform for customers interested in storing and managing talent information in real time from anywhere in the world. These modules include Job Profile Builder (JPB), Goal Management (GM), Performance Management (PM), 360, Continuous Performance Management (CPM), Calibration, Career Development Planning (CDP), and Succession Management (SCM). Using these cloud-based tools, customers are able to quickly request an instance and work with SAP and/or a certified SAP SuccessFactors partner to configure that instance specifically to their needs. Since an instance is a fully operational system that only needs to be configured without coding, the cloud solution gets you up and running in less time and for much less capital investment than traditional on-premise solutions. This book will guide you through each module configuration, as well as using the configured modules so you can realize your talent solution quickly and effectively.

© Susan Traynor, Michael A. Wellens and Venki Krishnamoorthy 2021
S. Traynor et al., *SAP SuccessFactors Talent: Volume 1*, https://doi.org/10.1007/978-1-4842-6600-7_1

What Will We Cover?

This two volume title covers only SAP SuccessFactors Talent modules. Each chapter or group of chapters is dedicated to a single module or cross-module area of the system. The chapters walk you through the configuration and use of each module so you are empowered to implement and use it quickly! The order of chapters follows a logical progression of module configuration. We do our best in each chapter to live up to being "the complete guide." We cover all of the available configuration options while still pointing you to recommended options based on our collective real-life experiences implementing SAP SuccessFactors for a variety of organizations.

Chapter 2 starts us out with Talent Profile. When we refer to the "Talent Profile," we are referring to the talent-related components of the People Profile and Succession Data Model (SDM). In this chapter, we will discuss the different talent management–related portlets that can be configured and displayed in Talent Profile. We will share how SAP SuccessFactors delivered portlets are updated automatically with the data from Talent modules. We will also discuss how to develop custom portlets, how to import/export data to these portlets, and how changes to data in these portlets are carried over to downstream processes such as Succession Management and Calibration.

Chapter 3 continues with Job Profile Builder (JPB). Job Profile Builder is an important tool that can be key to creating a well-structured job catalog. We will discuss how to create job profile templates and how to import job data into the instance. We will also highlight how the JPB is integrated with other SAP SuccessFactors Talent modules acting as a cornerstone for job-related data and functionality.

Chapters 4 and 5 will cover Goal Management (GM). Goal Management is an important process in talent strategy which aligns employees to your organization's business objectives. In this chapter, we will review how goals are set and managed in SAP SuccessFactors. We start in Chapter 4 by walking through all the steps needed to configure and use a very basic Goal Management implementation. Then Chapter 5 takes us into alternative goal management functionalities which are less commonly used but can help meet the specific business needs of certain customers.

Chapters 6–13 dive into Performance Management (PM). These chapters will discuss the components of the Performance Management module and how to make the employee evaluation process meaningful for your organization. Chapters 6 and 7 will walk through the steps needed to configure a basic performance form. Once your performance form is configured, Chapter 8 steps through how to administer the form through the performance review process. Chapter 9 then takes on the end user perspective as we go through the performance review. After that, Chapter 10 jumps into more advanced performance management, showing you some features you can only configure through the XML, as well as the translation process. Chapter 11 then covers the Ask for Feedback, Get Feedback, Add Modifier, and Add Signer features that can help facilitate getting performance input outside of a regular route map. In Chapter 12, we will also explore options for getting performance feedback from a wider audience using 360 forms. Chapter 13 wraps up with Continuous Performance Management which has seen increasing adoption as an alternative and/or supplement to annual performance forms in recent years.

Chapters 14 and 15 take us into the next step that typically occurs at the end of a performance review: Calibration. In Chapter 14, we will discuss how to integrate Calibration into the performance review process, as well as options to integrate talent fields and Succession data into the calibration tool. We will discuss how to configure Calibration including the revisions needed to the PM form and route map. We will also share updates to make to the Succession Data Model in order to use performance and potential ratings. Then in Chapter 15, we take a walk through a calibration session.

Finally, we wrap up in Chapter 16 with the Conclusion. The Conclusion reviews the concepts and lessons learned in each chapter. It will help the reader summarize the realized goals of each chapter and understand the overall business value of the final solution before leading the user to next steps after the system is launched.

Volume 2 will jump into the Development module, Career Worksheet, and mentoring (also known as the Career Development Planning, or CDP, module) followed by Succession Management (SCM).

Key Concepts

Before we begin, let us cover a few key concepts that will help prepare us for the chapters ahead.

Instance/Company

An "instance" or "company" refers to a unique configurable partition of the SuccessFactors system on a particular data center. An organization may have multiple instances, for example, most companies will have a test system on the preview data center where they can test their configurations during implementation and also postproduction to test out new and upcoming release features as well as a production instance. Each instance or company is assigned a unique company id to distinguish it. Data and configuration is not shared between instances, so that the organizations' data is secure and accessible only to themselves. However, there are ways to import/export data and sync configurations within a company.

Provisioning

Provisioning is an area of the SAP SuccessFactors system that only SAP or certified SAP SuccessFactors partners can access. It allows these resources to turn on certain functionality, schedule jobs, and perform certain configurations. Throughout the book, we will indicate if a certain configuration requires provisioning access.

Role-Based Permissions

When SuccessFactors was first created prior to the merger with SAP, permissions were assigned to individual users. Later, SuccessFactors introduced the concept of permission roles to align better with enterprise-wide system expectations. Role-based permissions (RBPs) allow administrators to create roles that represent a set of permissions that allow access to features and functionality as well as information about a specific set of users. Roles can be assigned to permission groups which are the users to whom the roles are assigned. Permission groups can also represent the target populations which are the set of data the permission group can view, edit, and so on.

Search Bar

The search bar allows users to quickly access different functionalities throughout the system without the use of the more traditional menu navigation system. Simply start typing the name of the screen or feature using the type-ahead functionality, and the system will start showing navigation options relevant to your security settings that match your text search. You can then click any of the search results that start appearing in the type-ahead list to navigate to that screen. The search bar is found at the top of the screen.

Note   The search bar can also be used in the same fashion to search for users in the system and display their profile.

User Data File

The user data file (UDF) allows customers to enter employee data in the system so that the Talent modules can access it. It is a comma-separated value (.csv) flat file where each column represents one of the standard or custom fields that can be loaded. You can download the .csv template and import data by typing and selecting "Import Employee Data" in the search bar. Note that some of the columns in this template may appear slightly different depending on your Succession Data Model configuration.

Note   EC customers would not directly load the user data file using the employee import screen since this data is created by the EC HRIS internally or integrated from the recruiting or onboarding modules. EC data can also be loaded in the import and export data screen. EC data is mapped to the UDF and automatically synchronized into the UDF from EC. We will not cover this process in detail. For more information, see SAP note 2080728.

Check Tool

We do our best in each chapter to guide you through configuration steps in a logical order to avoid any configuration mistakes. However, mistakes do happen! If you get stuck, SAP has introduced the "Check Tool" to help you out! Since this tool covers most modules, we don't dive into it in any particular chapter. It is good to know it exists to help you out in a bind! You can check out SAP note 2472648 for more information.

DTDs

When editing XMLs on your local machine, there are Document Type Definition (DTD) files available from SAP. These can be helpful to check the structure of the XML that you are editing before attempting to load it in provisioning. While these are not a must-have (the system will warn you anyway if your XML is not structured correctly when uploading in provisioning), they are worth mentioning. Since every XML has a DTD, we do not cover them in any particular chapter. For more information on DTDs, see SAP note 2292731.

Text Replacement and Manage Languages

Throughout the book, we cover how to provide typical translations within each module. However, there are some areas that don't look like they can be translated because they are part of the overall platform. Some basic words like "employee" can be replaced using the Text Replacement feature. For info on Text Replacement, see SAP note 2089472. For words not available in Text Replacement, the Manage Languages feature can be used to replace words. For more information, see SAP note 2576546.

Mobile

For the sake of brevity, we do not cover mobile features and functions of each module in depth. Furthermore, mobile application release schedules are completed in a matter of weeks rather than the semiannual release schedules of the main SuccessFactors application – so any specifics we would give in this book would be quickly out of date!

Mobile applications can be downloaded via the Apple App Store and Android Market. They have a demo mode you can try out for free if you are curious after downloading. In general, the capabilities are the same as the main application, but reduced. For more information on specific capabilities across all modules, please reference the mobile capabilities matrix which can be found here:

```
https://help.sap.com/viewer/c3cbc8ddf8ef421d81d4b71a6f88a7a3/latest/en-US
```

Let's Get Started!

We hope this chapter has prepared you well for your upcoming journey through the various modules of SAP SuccessFactors Talent Management. We've given you an overview of what SAP SuccessFactors is and what comprises the Talent Management portion of the overall solution. We've also discussed which modules are covered in which chapters along with an overview of what will be covered in each. Additionally, we've covered some key concepts that will help prepare you to understand these chapters. Let's get started!

CHAPTER 2

Talent Profile

The People Profile in SuccessFactors displays the employee data as different portlets. These portlets provide employees and managers with self-services functionality. What data is displayed in the portlets can be controlled through permissions; the view of the portlet can be controlled through permissions as well. Typically, the People Profile contains portlets such as Personal Information, Address, and Contact Details. If you have implemented the SAP SuccessFactors HRIS offering called Employee Central, then you can configure additional portlets such as Payroll, National ID, and more.

The Talent Profile is a subsection of the People Profile in SAP SuccessFactors. the Talent Profile consists of portlets such as Performance, Potential, Compensation, and Succession Management.

In this chapter, we will discuss the Talent Profile in detail, including how to configure the Talent Profile with portlets that provide employee and manager self-service capabilities, how to populate the portlets, and how to set the permissions for the portlets for edit or display only.

Note When you configure SuccessFactors and import employees to the instance, SuccessFactors will create a People Profile by default for all employees. You can add portlets to the People Profile. These portlets can be a combination of delivered portlets and customer-built portlets.

The blocks in the Employee Profile that display employee-related data are referred to as *portlets*.

© Susan Traynor, Michael A. Wellens and Venki Krishnamoorthy 2021
S. Traynor et al., *SAP SuccessFactors Talent: Volume 1*, https://doi.org/10.1007/978-1-4842-6600-7_2

People Picker in the People Profile

People Picker is a drop-down in the People Profile (see Figure 2-1) that displays the employee's manager, direct reports, and peers. The user can select from the names to view the specific employee's profile. When you click the drop-down, the system displays a search box. You can also use the search box to search for employees.

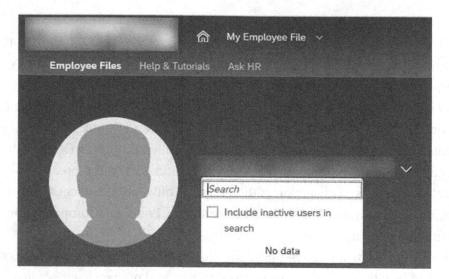

Figure 2-1. *People Picker in the People Profile*

Customers sometimes have a business need to hide peers in the People Picker. There is a setting in the Admin Center, where you can hide the peers in the People Picker drop-down. Note that this setting is universal and cannot be restricted to a specific group of employees.

To hide the peer details in People Picker, go to the Admin Center and click Platform Feature Settings. On the displayed configuration page, select the setting called Hide Peers. Save your configuration.

Talent Profile

The Talent Profile displays portlets related to talent solutions (see Figure 2-2). When the SuccessFactors talent solutions such as Performance Management, Succession Management, Compensation, and Learning Management Systems are installed, the portlets related to these solutions are activated and available in the system.

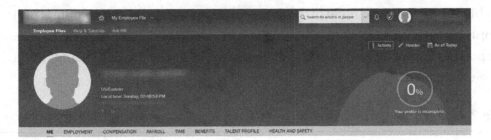

Figure 2-2. *Talent Profile*

Note   You can access the Employee Profile by going to the SuccessFactors home page, clicking the Home drop-down, and selecting My Employee File (Figure 2-3) for the Employee File in the SuccessFactors demo instance. The Employee Profile will display various headings. Clicking the heading will navigate you to the particular portlet in the Employee Profile.

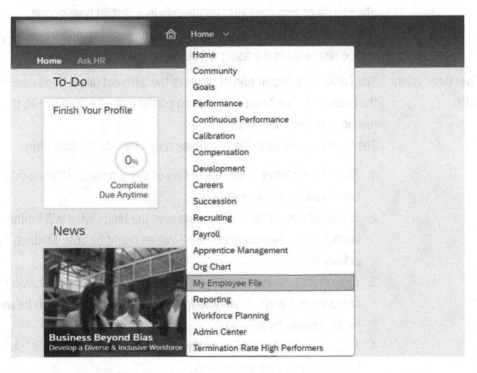

Figure 2-3. *Navigating to My Employee File*

Table 2-1 provides a sample of the portlets you will see in a talent profile. This is not a comprehensive list, and a customer might have configured some of these or several other portlets. Some of these portlets might be referred to by different names in the customer instance.

Table 2-1. *Sample Portlets in the Talent Profile*

Portlet	Description
Badges	Organizations assign badges to an employee to recognize an employee's outstanding work effort.
	For example, an employee might receive a "Team Player" badge to recognize the employee as an outstanding team player. The employee can display this badge for a certain period of time.
	There are other badges that might not be tied to an employee's work efforts; rather, a badge can be a reflection of the employee work culture. For example, a badge might recognize an employee's 100 percent attendance or zero customer complaints in a certain time period.
	Badges are typically a way to denote peer recognition, and these badges can be displayed in the assigned portlet in the Talent Profile.
Talent Overview: Talent Information	The Talent Information portlet displays the different talent flags used in the enterprise. The Talent Information portlet can be edited by HR, the manager, or the Talent team.
	The flags configured in the enterprise might include the following:
	1. *Risk of Loss*: What is the risk of loss of this employee? Values might be Low, Medium, High, or Very High.
	2. *Impact of Loss*: If this employee leaves the team, what will be the impact on the team/organization? Values might be Low, Medium, High, or Very High.
	3. *Reason for Leaving*: A comment box, where the reason for leaving is captured or a drop-down (also known as picklist values) can be used for the reason for leaving.
	4. *Future Leader*: Does this employee have the potential to be a leader? Possible values are Yes and No.

(continued)

Table 2-1. (*continued*)

Portlet	Description
	5. *Diversity Candidate*: Is this employee a diversity candidate? The meaning of *diversity* can be different from country to country or from geography to geography.
	6. *New to Position*: If the employee is new to position, this flag might be set to Yes. An enterprise might use this flag for the first 180 or 365 days. This flag might be used to trigger downstream activities such as initiating 30/60/90-day goals.
	These flags might have binary (Yes/No) or multiple values. What values are used depends on the business, and these can be discussed and captured in a workshop.
	The customer enterprise may not use all of these flags, or some of these flags might be repurposed to align with the enterprise culture. The customer can use customer flags as well.
Talent Overview: Overview	This portlet will display the overall performance score, potential ranking, competency ranking, and goal score.
	The portlet will also display the Performance versus Potential nine-box matrix.
Skill Profile	The employee (or anybody who has the right permission) can add skills in this portlet.
Performance and Competencies: Performance History	The portlet displays the performance ratings of the employee within the configured date range and processes.
	This portlet is delivered and has predefined fields. Therefore, it is not possible to make changes to this portlet.
Performance and Competencies: Competencies	This portlet displays the competency ratings the employee has received in their annual performance form, within the configured date range and processes.

(*continued*)

Table 2-1. (*continued*)

Portlet	Description
Promotability and Performance: Promotability (Manager View Only)	In this portlet, the manager will enter details of the job role, whether the employee is ready to be promoted, and the time frame when the employee might be ready for the role. There is an optional comments field, where the manager can enter their comments.
Potential and Performance Views: Potential (Manager View Only)	In this portlet, the manager will enter the potential rating for the employee.
Objective-Competency Historical Matrix Grid Placement	The portlet will display the nine-box grid matrix of the objective versus competency ratings. These ratings are derived from the annual performance form within the configured date range and processes.
Successors: Successor portlet	This portlet displays the successors nominated to the employee's position.
Successors: Nomination portlet	This portlet displays the positions where the employee is nominated as a successor.

A customer can configure many different portlets to align with their culture and business needs. It is important for the consultants or in-house SuccessFactors team to understand what the business needs are and configure the portlets accordingly.

Tip   It is a suggested practice to use the default portlets where possible. One distinct advantage of using a default portlet is that if there is an upgrade from SuccessFactors, these portlets are automatically upgraded with no required effort from the customer team. For portlets containing data from talent solutions, the default portlets are automatically updated with ratings from the latest forms or objects.

In the next section, we will dive deep into the configuration of the Talent Profile in the different portlets. We will also look at what configurations need to be done in the Succession data model using XML. While exploring the configurations, we will take a peek at the configuration step called Manage Business Configuration.

Building Custom Portlets

The Talent Profile can contain a combination of default portlets, as well as customer-specific portlets. We can configure the portlets in the Succession data model, which is XML based. If you do not have access to the data model, you can configure the portlets in the Admin Center.

In this section, we will discuss how to create background elements in the Admin Center UI, and later we will discuss how to create a background element in XML.

Note   If you are comfortable configuring XML, you can download the Succession XML file from Provisioning. Customers do not have access to Provisioning. Only certified consultants who are provided access to Provisioning have access to it.

Creating a Background Element in UI

Custom portlets in the People Profile are referred to as *background elements*.

Enter the configuration step **Manage Business Configuration** in the search box (see Figure 2-4). On the Manage Business Configuration screen, scroll down to the section Employee Profile, and expand Background Elements. We will create a custom background element in this section. Scroll down and click Create New.

Figure 2-4. Action search box

On the displayed page (see Figure 2-5), you are required to fill in the fields. Table 2-2 describes the different fields and what each field means.

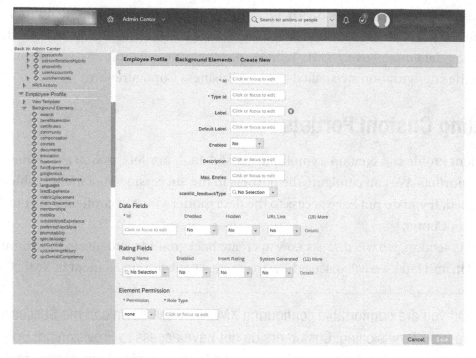

Figure 2-5. *Creating a background element*

Note   If the search does not take you to the Manage Business Configuration page, then review the next section, "Enabling the Business Configuration UI." Otherwise, jump to the section "Block Settings."

Enabling the Business Configuration UI

Customers and implementation teams use the Business Configuration UI (BCUI) to perform the following actions:

7. Add/maintain the custom background elements

8. Maintain standard userinfo objects

9. Add/change labels

10. Add/change translations

11. Enable fields

12. Change the visibility of fields

13. Make fields required

Prerequisites

You need to ensure the Succession data model is available in Provisioning. The Manage Business Configuration (also referred to as BCUI) is an admin tool available in SuccessFactors to create and maintain objects that are typically maintained in the XML data model.

If the Succession data model, then open a ticket under the component LOD-SF-PLT-PPRV, and request support to import the Succession data model to your company ID.

Enabling the BCUI in Your Instance

In Provisioning, verify that the config switch Enable Generic Objects is checked. If it is not checked, you are required to check it. Once Enable Generic Objects is enabled, in the Admin Center select Enable Business Configuration. Once this is enabled, you are required to execute the BCUI sync job, called Synchronize Business Configuration, in Provisioning (see Figure 2-6). This job is executed once only.

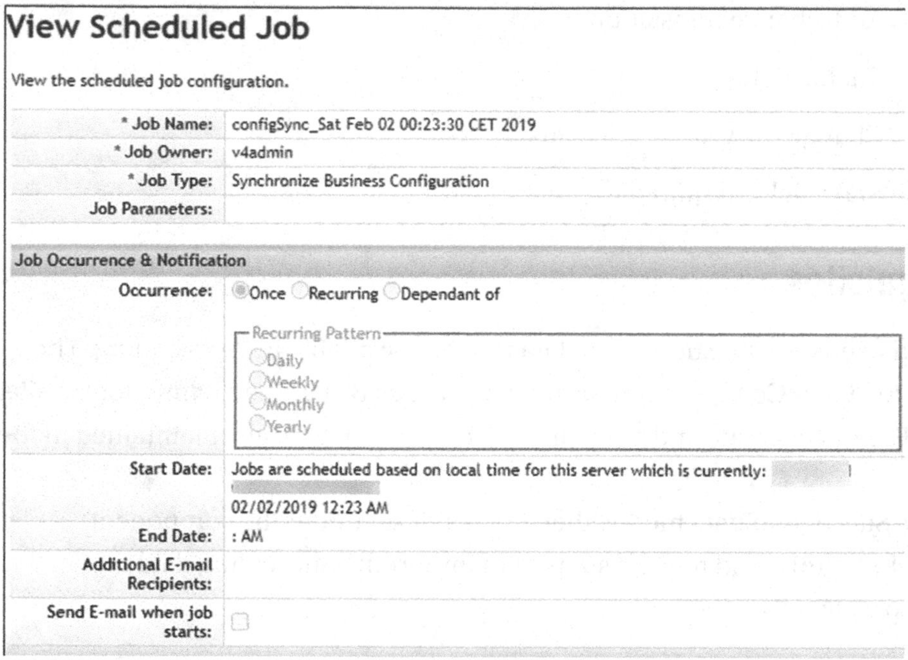

View Scheduled Job

View the scheduled job configuration.

* Job Name:	configSync_Sat Feb 02 00:23:30 CET 2019
* Job Owner:	v4admin
* Job Type:	Synchronize Business Configuration
Job Parameters:	

Job Occurrence & Notification

Occurrence:	⦿Once ◯Recurring ◯Dependant of
	┌─Recurring Pattern─────────────────────────┐
	◯Daily
	◯Weekly
	◯Monthly
	◯Yearly
Start Date:	Jobs are scheduled based on local time for this server which is currently: ▨
	02/02/2019 12:23 AM
End Date:	: AM
Additional E-mail Recipients:	
Send E-mail when job starts:	☐

Figure 2-6. *Configuring Synchronize Business Configuration*

In Provisioning, click Manage Scheduled Jobs. On the displayed page, create a job of job type Synchronize Business Configuration. After configuring the job, execute the job once only.

Note   While the job is running, the config step Manage Business Configuration is locked. During this time, making any changes to the Succession data model may cause differences between the BCUI and the Succession data model.

After the job is executed, any changes you make to the Succession data model via Manager Business Configuration will automatically trigger this job.

Permissions for the BCUI

For the permissions group/permission roles that need access to Manage Business Configuration, you are required to assign permissions to access and maintain objects in Manage Business Configuration. In the Admin Center, the Manage Permission Roles item assigns the permissions described in this section.

In the Administrator Permissions section's Metadata Framework permission group, select the following:

- Manage Data

- Read/Write Permission on Metadata Framework

- Import Permission on Metadata Framework

- Admin Access to the OData API

- Manage Configuration UI

In the Administrator Permissions section's Manage Business Configuration permission group, do the following:

- Select the visibility and actions for the listed objects.

  - Selecting Visibility for an object means that the object will appear in the BCUI.

  - Actions denote the operations that can be performed on that particular object.

- Click Done to save your settings.

Block Settings

Configure the settings in Table 2-2 to configure the background element.

Table 2-2. *Fields in a Background Element*

Field	Comments
Type Id	The Type Id value identifies the background element. Hence, the Type Id value should be unique and an integer, for example 10.
ID	You enter the ID of the background element in this field. The ID should be unique and not be used by any other element. The ID should not contain any spaces as this is not supported, for example custWillingToRelocate. It is a suggested practice to start the ID with a lowercase letter, followed by other capitalized words with no spaces. *Note: You will notice that some SuccessFactors-delivered background elements start with* sys. *These portlets have restrictions that need to be considered while modifying such portlets.*
Label	This is the name of the field that will be displayed in the People Profile. You can add language translations by clicking the icon displayed next to the field.
Default Label	This is the label that will be displayed for languages where the label is not configured.
Enabled	The values for Enabled are Yes/No. If you want the field to be displayed in the People Profile, then choose the value Yes. *Note: Displaying a portlet in the People Profile is a two-step process.* *Step 1: Enable the portlet in the configuration.* *Step 2: Give the portlet permissions to view/edit in the role-based permissions.*
Description	This entry is displayed in the block. The field is for reference only.
Max Entries	This is the maximum number of entries that can be created in this background element. The maximum number of entries is valid for ESS/MSS only. The maximum number of entries is overridden when the portlet is populated through a flat-file import.
Scale Id (Feedback Type)	Enter the rating scale that you plan to use in this portlet. For example, if the portlet is used to capture the employee's interest to relocate and if the interest is captured on a scale of 1 to 3, you will use a rating scale that has 1, 2, 3.

Data Fields

In this section, you fill in the details for the fields that are displayed in the background portlet. As you can see in Figure 2-5 the first four fields are visible on the screen. To view other fields that need to be filled in, you are required to click Details. Table 2-3 describes the fields.

Note   As a suggested practice, fill out the settings under Block Settings before filling in these fields.

Table 2-3. *Data Fields in a Background Element*

Field	Comments
Id	This is the ID of the background data field. It should be unique and cannot be repeated for any other data field in this particular background element.
Enabled	The values are Yes and No. If you want the field to be displayed in the background element, then choose the value Yes.
Hidden	If you do want the field to be rendered in the People Profile, then select the value Yes. Otherwise, the value should be No.
URL Link	The value entered in the field will be displayed as a link. The default values are Yes and No. If you do not want the value to be displayed as a link in the UI, then select No.
Field Name	This is the database field name. The supported values are as follows: **VARCHAR (text) field (vfld1 to vfld13)**: You can use this if the field displays text and if it is a drop-down. You can use values from vfld1 to vafld13. *Note: Within a particular background element, you cannot reuse a field name. If you have a field with the field name vfld1, then the next time you have a text/picklist field, you have to use vfld2, for example.*

(continued)

Table 2-3. (*continued*)

Field	Comments
	DATE fields (dfld1 to dfld5): If the field is a date field, then name the field from dfld1 to dfld5. When you use this field name, the field will display a "calendar" button that you can use to select a date.
	Note: *Similar to the Varchar field name, you cannot reuse the date field name in the same background element. Hence, if you name a data field as dfld1, then the next date field will be dfld2. There is a system restriction that you can have a max of five date fields in a particular background element.*
	Start date and end date (*startDate, endDate*): These are date fields. If you use this date name, then make both fields required so that both the start date and end date fields are filled. This field is typically used to ensure the start date and end date values are in sync. In other words, the value of the end date is not earlier than the start date.
	Note: *You can use only a start date/end date in a particular background element. Making the start date and end date fields required ensures that both the fields are filled, and one or the other is not left blank.*
	INTEGER fields (ifld1 to ifld4): This supports integers ranging from -2,147,483,648 to 2,147,483,647. If you plan to use this field name, the values need to be in the range ifld1 to ifld4. The field name used for this field cannot be reused for a different field in the same background element.
	Note: *If the field is used to capture phone numbers, it is suggested you use the field as a text field; in other words, the field name can be from vfld1 to vfld15.*
	FLOAT (real number) fields (ffld1 - ffld4): Use this field name if you plan to use the field to enter floating numbers. The field names need to be in the range from ffld1 to ffld4.
	Last Modified Date (lastModified): This field displays the date when the portlet line item was last modified.
	Note: *Do not use this field name if you are planning to import values to this field. This field is not supported during imports.*
	Attachment Field (ATTACHMENT_ID): Use this field name if you are planning to use this field to upload/import attachments.
	Note: *You can have only one attachment field in a background element.*

(*continued*)

Table 2-3. (*continued*)

Field	Comments
Number Format Ref.	You can leave this data field empty. *Note: SuccessFactors has created this field as a placeholder for future product development. Even though the field is displayed, it is currently not available for any configuration.*
Field Display Format Ref.	You can leave this data field empty. *Note: Similar to Number Format Ref., this field is displayed in the configuration UI as a placeholder for a future SuccessFactors product.*
Masked	If the data in the field needs to be protected from display in the People Profile UI, then select Yes. The available values are Yes and No. *Note: When you select Yes, the data in the field will be masked with asterisks and displayed as ******. You are required to click the asterisks to view the value.*
Document Type Id	If you are using this background element to upload attachments, you can use this data field to classify the attachment. This field is a picklist, and it provides the following values: • 360 multi-rater attachments • Application interview attachments • Attachments • Candidate history • Certifications • Cover letter • Generic object attachment • HRIS attachment • Performance assessments • Performance attachment • Publications • Resume • User defined *Note: This field needs to be filled in only if the field type is Attachment_ID.*

(*continued*)

Table 2-3. (*continued*)

Field	Comments
Max. File Size KB	This is the max file size of the attachment that can be uploaded to this field in the background element. *Note: The file size specified here should be less than or equal to the attachment's max file size configured in Provisioning (see Figure 2-6).* *You should be a SuccessFactors-certified consultant to have access to Provisioning. Currently customers are not provided access to Provisioning.*
File Formats	If the field type is Attachment, you can define what file formats are supported in this data field for this background element. The supported file formats are as follows: DOC, PDF, CSV, HTM, PPT, XLS, GIF, PNG, JPG, JPEG, HTML, RTF, BMP, XLSX, DOCX, PPTX, TXT, XML, MSG, DOCM, TIF, and MP4.
HRIS Fields Mapping value	You can leave this data field empty.
Earning Data Mapping Value	You can leave this data field empty.
Text Area Enabled	If the field name is a VarChar, you can select Yes if you want multiple lines of text to be supported in this field. The valid values for this data field are Yes and No.
Merge	The default value is Yes. Do not change this value.
Label	This is the name that will be displayed in the UI and within the SuccessFactors instance. In this data field, you can configure language translations by clicking the icon displayed in the field.
Default Label	This is the label that will be displayed for the language for which you have not configured the label. *Example: If Chinese is one of the languages in the instance and if you have not configured the label for the Chinese language (see the field Label for details), then the value configured in this data field will be displayed if your language is Chinese.*

(*continued*)

Table 2-3. (*continued*)

Field	Comments
Picklist	If your field is a picklist, then select the picklist that will be displayed in this data field for this particular background element. *Note: Picklists should be configured and exist in the instance prior to the picklist being selected in this field.*
Parent Picklist Id	If you want this field to be a picklist and if it uses another field as a parent field, then enter the ID of the parent field. *Example: In this background element, you are capturing to which country and state the employee is open to relocate to if there is an opportunity. You have two fields, Country and State. So, if you select USA in the Country field, the state field will display all the states in the United States. If you select Canada in the parent field, the state field will display all the states in Canada. When you configure the Country field, in the picklist data field you will select the Country picklist. When you configure the State field, in the picklist data field you will select the State picklist. In the State field, in the parent picklist ID data field, you will enter the ID of the Country field.*
Required	If you want this field to be required, then select Yes. Selecting No will make the field optional. The valid values are Yes and No.
Max Length	In this data field, you can configure the maximum length of the field. The valid values are as follows: • vfld1 to vfld15 (4,000 characters) • Start date: date • End date: date • dfld1 to dfld3: date • ifld1 to ifld5: integer -2147483648 to 2147483647 • ffld1 to ffld4: float 1.40129846432481707e-45 to 3.40282346638528860e+38 positive or negative
Display Size	This data field is not being used. You can leave it blank.

Configuring a Background Element Using XML

You can configure background elements in XML. You can download a copy of the Succession data model from Provisioning. In Provisioning, the Succession data model is available in the Succession Management section; click the Import/Export Data Model link (see Figure 2-7). On the displayed page, select the option Export file (select Save, not Open) and click Submit.

Note   You need an editor to edit XML files. There are a few freeware editors that are available on the internet. Notepad++ and XMLPad are two of the more popular editors.

Open the XML file using any editor of your choice. Scroll down to the section where there is XML code for the background element.

As an exercise, we will create a background element using XML. In the background element, the employee will enter their top five favorite travel destinations. They will rank the destinations on a scale of 1 to 5, and a maximum of five records can be created.

The structure of the background element will be as follows:

- Name of the travel destination (text field)

- Description of why this travel destination is their favorite (text area field)

- A rating for the travel destination (picklist)

- Date last visited (date)

- Attachment (upload a picture of the travel destination)

The structure of the background element should be enclosed within the tags <background-element> and </background-element>. You should never build a new background element within another background element structure; in other words, nested background elements are not supported.

Listing 2-1 shows the XML code of the provided background element insideWorkExperience available within the Succession data model.

Listing 2-1. XML Code of a Background Element

```
<background-element id="insideWorkExperience" type-id="1">
  <label>Inside Work History</label>
  <label xml:lang="en-US">Inside Work History</label>
  <data-field id="startDate" field-name="startDate" required="true"
  max-length="999" max-file-size-KB="1000">
    <label>From Date</label>
    <label xml:lang="en-US">From Date</label>
  </data-field>
  <data-field id="endDate" field-name="endDate" required="true"
  max-length="999" max-file-size-KB="1000">
    <label>End Date</label>
    <label xml:lang="en-US">End Date</label>
  </data-field>
  <data-field id="title" field-name="vfld1" required="true"
  max-length="4000" max-file-size-KB="1000">
    <label>Title</label>
    <label xml:lang="en-US">Title</label>
  </data-field>
  <data-field id="Insidedepartment" field-name="vfld2" required="true"
  max-length="4000" max-file-size-KB="1000">
    <label>Department</label>
    <label xml:lang="en-US">Department</label>
  </data-field>
</background-element>
```

Refer to Tables 2-2 and 2-3 to gain a better understanding of this XML code. If you are new to XML, an easy way to develop a new background element is to copy an existing background element and make changes to it.

Tip   To build our new background element, we will copy this provided background element and make changes to it. We will label the background element Favorite Travel Destinations, and the ID will be favTravelDestinations. For the type ID, we will start with 90. You can use any ID that is not used in your XML file. Typically, for custom background elements, I start at 90. So, the first custom element will be 90, followed by 91, etc. Ensure the ID you are using is not used by any other background element. Duplicate IDs are not supported.

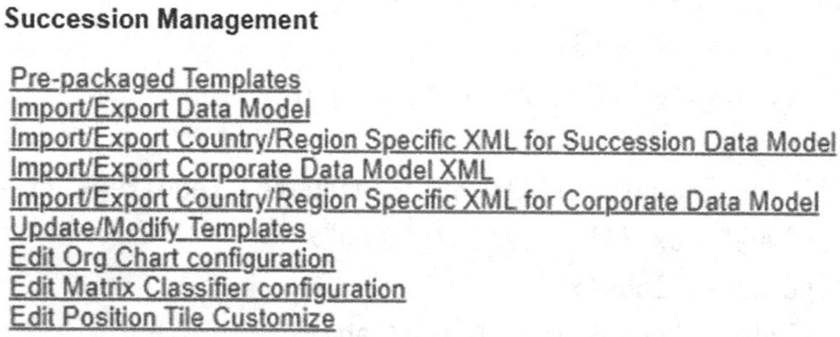

Succession Management

Pre-packaged Templates
Import/Export Data Model
Import/Export Country/Region Specific XML for Succession Data Model
Import/Export Corporate Data Model XML
Import/Export Country/Region Specific XML for Corporate Data Model
Update/Modify Templates
Edit Org Chart configuration
Edit Matrix Classifier configuration
Edit Position Tile Customize

Figure 2-7. *Downloading the Succession data model*

Listing 2-2 shows the XML code for the background element Favorite Travel Destinations.

Listing 2-2. XML Code of Custom Background Element

```
<background-element id="favTravelDestinations" type-id="90"
max-entries="5">
 <label xml:lang="en-US">Favorite Travel Destinations</label>
 <label>Favorite Travel Destinations</label>
 <description>Test</description>
 <data-field id="destName" field-name="vfld1" required="true"
max-length="4000" max-file-size-KB="1000">
   <label xml:lang="en-US">Name of destination</label>
   <label>Name of destination</label>
 </data-field>
 <data-field id="destDesc" field-name="desc" max-length="1024"
max-file-size-KB="1000" text-area-enabled="true">
   <label xml:lang="en-US">Desc why this is your fav destination?
   </label>
   <label>Desc why this is your fav destination?</label>
 </data-field>
```

```
<data-field id="rateTraveDest" field-name="vfld11" max-length="4000"
max-file-size-KB="1000">
   <label xml:lang="en-US">Rate travel destination</label>
   <label>Rate travel destination</label>
   <picklist id="rateDestination"/>
</data-field>
<data-field id="endDate" field-name="endDate" max-length="999"
max-file-size-KB="1000">
   <label xml:lang="en-US">Date last visited</label>
   <label>Date last visited</label>
</data-field>
<data-field id="uploadPics" field-name="attachment1" max-length="999"
document-type-id="ATTACHMENTS" max-file-size-KB="1000">
   <label xml:lang="en-US">Post PICS if any</label>
   <label>Post PICS if any</label>
</data-field>
</background-element>
```

Now, let's review the XML code we configured. You will notice that the background element is enclosed within the tags <background-element> and </background-element>. All the configurations related to favTravelDestination are enclosed within these tags.

- The ID of the background element favTravelDestination is mentioned in the field called id. The type ID is mentioned in the field type-id. We discussed that the employee can enter a maximum of five entries only. This is mentioned in the field max-entries. We have labeled the background element as Favorite Travel Destinations.

```
<background-element id="favTravelDestinations" type-
id="90" max-entries="5">
<label xml:lang="en-US">Favorite Travel Destinations
</label>
<label>Favorite Travel Destinations</label>
<description>Test</description>
```

27

- The individual fields in the background element are enclosed in the
  tags <data-field> and </data-field>. We configured the name of the
  destination as a text field, so the field name is vfld1. The field ID is
  destName. The label of the field is "Name of destination."

  ```
  <data-field id="destName" field-name="vfld1"
  required="true" max-length="4000" max-file-size-
  KB="1000">
  <label xml:lang="en-US">Name of destination</label>
  <label>Name of destination</label>
  </data-field>
  ```

- We want the employee to describe why this is their favorite travel
  destination. The field needs to be a text area so that the entries are
  displayed in a larger text field and so we can scroll the field. You
  can notice the XML code text-area-enabled is true. If we do not
  set this, the field will be displayed as a text field. Since the field is a
  description, here is what it looks like:

  ```
  <data-field id="destDesc" field-name="desc" max-
  length="1024" max-file-size-KB="1000" text-area-
  enabled="true">
  <label xml:lang="en-US">Desc why this is your fav
  destination?</label>
  <label>Desc why this is your fav destination?</label>
  </data-field>
  ```

- We want the employee to rate the travel destination on a scale of 1 to
  5. For this, the field should be configured as a picklist, and we also
  need to configure a picklist and assign it to the field. If you look at the
  XML code, you will see the field name is vfld11. We have already used
  the field name vfld1 for "Name of destination." As discussed earlier,
  the field name should be unique for each background element. You
  will notice the XML code <picklist id>. This denotes that the field is a
  picklist field. The picklist ID denotes the picklist that is configured to
  this field.

```
<data-field id="rateTraveDest" field-name="vfld11"
max-length="4000" max-file-size-KB="1000">
<label xml:lang="en-US">Rate travel destination</label>
<label>Rate travel destination</label>
<picklist id="rateDestination"/>
</data-field>
```

- We want to configure a date field to capture the last time the employee has visited the destination. Since the field is a date field, the field id value is endDate, and the field name is endDate.

```
<data-field id="endDate" field-name="endDate"
max-length="999" max-file-size-KB="1000">
<label xml:lang="en-US">Date last visited</label>
<label>Date last visited</label>
</data-field>
```

- We want to configure a field for the employee to upload travel pictures if they want to share them. We have configured field-name as attachment1, and document-type-id is Attachments.

```
<data-field id="uploadPics" field-name="attachment1"
max-length="999" document-type-id="ATTACHMENTS" max-
file-size-KB="1000">
<label xml:lang="en-US">Post PICS if any</label>
<label>Post PICS if any</label>
</data-field>
```

Tip   As you can see, it is lot easier to configure background elements in the UI, using the Admin Center. That is my preferred method to configure background elements anyway. As a product road map, SuccessFactors is moving more and more configuration tasks from Provisioning to the Admin Center so that customers can configure and maintain their applications in the UI.

Configuring Picklists

While configuring picklists is beyond scope of this book, we will take a brief look at how to configure them, since we have used a picklist while configuring a custom background element. In this section, we will see how we create a picklist in the Picklist Center.

Note SAP has announced that all SuccessFactors customers will be migrated to the Picklist Center. Hence, in this section, we will review how to create picklists in the Picklist Center.

Enter the config step **Picklist Center** in the Action search box. On the displayed page (see Figure 2-8), click the + icon to create a new picklist. If a picklist is already created and you want to maintain the picklist, enter the name of the picklist in the search box.

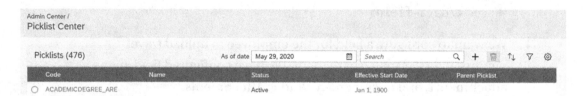

Figure 2-8. Configuring picklists

A dialog box is displayed to create the picklist (see Figure 2-9). In the dialog box, configure these settings:

- *Code*: Enter the code of the picklist. This code should be unique.

- *Name*: This is the label for the picklist you are creating. This label will be displayed in the picklist field UI.

- *Status*: The picklist status needs to be Active to be able to use the picklist. If you no longer need the picklist, then change the status to Inactive.

- *Effective Start Date*: This is the date on which the picklist will be active and be available in the instance. As a practice, we configure this date to be 01/01/1900.

- *Display Order*: By default, the display order is Alphabetical. The other values are Numeric and Custom.

- *Parent Picklist*: If the picklist you are creating is a child picklist, enter the name of the parent picklist.

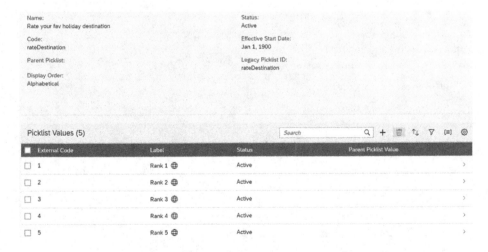

	Create a New Picklist	
*Code:		
Name:		
Status:	Active	⌄
Effective Start Date:	May 30, 2020	📅
Display Order:	Alphabetical	⌄
Parent Picklist:		⎘
	Save Cancel	

Figure 2-9. *Creating a new picklist*

Click Save to create the new picklist. Now we will add values to this picklist. See Figure 2-10.

Name:
Rate your fav holiday destination

Status:
Active

Code:
rateDestination

Effective Start Date:
Jan 1, 1900

Parent Picklist:

Legacy Picklist ID:
rateDestination

Display Order:
Alphabetical

Picklist Values (5)   Search 🔍 + 🗑 ↕ ▽ [≡] ⚙

External Code	Label	Status	Parent Picklist Value	
☐ 1	Rank 1 ⊕	Active		>
☐ 2	Rank 2 ⊕	Active		>
☐ 3	Rank 3 ⊕	Active		>
☐ 4	Rank 4 ⊕	Active		>
☐ 5	Rank 5 ⊕	Active		>

Figure. 2-10. *Adding values to picklist*

On the displayed page, click the + icon. Then enter these values for the settings:

- *External Code*: All modules in SuccessFactors communicate through external code. The setting External Code is the ID for this particular picklist value. Within a picklist, ensure the external code is unique.

- *Label*: This is the label of the picklist value. This label will be displayed in the picklist UI. As a suggested practice, the label should be meaningful and communicative.

- *Status*: If you want the picklist value to be displayed, the status should be Active. If the value is no longer being used, the status of the value will be InActive.

- *Non-unique External Code*: By default, the system copies the value from the field External Code. This field is retained to maintain the external code of legacy picklists after they are migrated. Do not make changes to the value displayed in this field.

Click Save to save the values. In a similar manner, enter the other values for this picklist (see Figure 2-11).

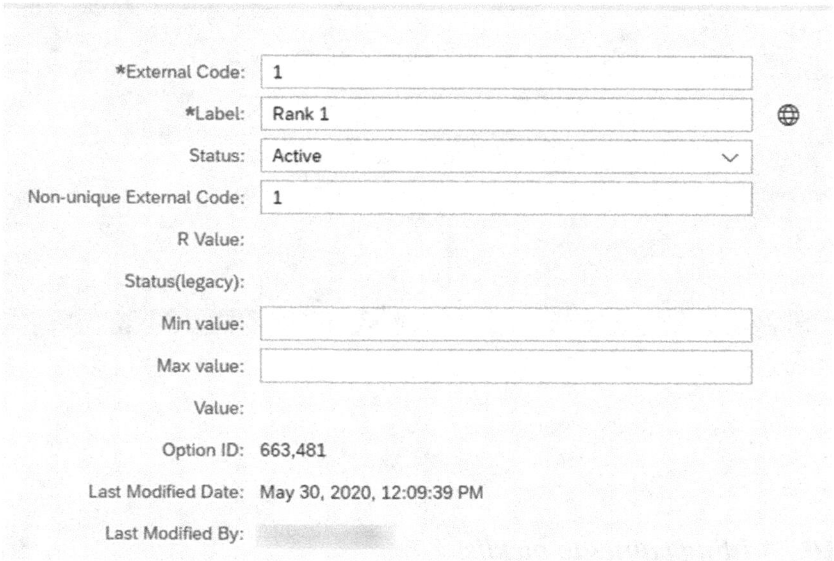

*External Code:	1
*Label:	Rank 1
Status:	Active
Non-unique External Code:	1
R Value:	
Status(legacy):	
Min value:	
Max value:	
Value:	
Option ID:	663,481
Last Modified Date:	May 30, 2020, 12:09:39 PM
Last Modified By:	

Figure 2-11. *Configuring the picklist values*

Tip   After creating the picklist, if you do not see the newly created picklist in the picklist field, then in the Action search box, enter the config step **OData API Metadata Refresh And Export**. On the displayed page, click the Refresh button next to the Cache field (see Figure 2-12).

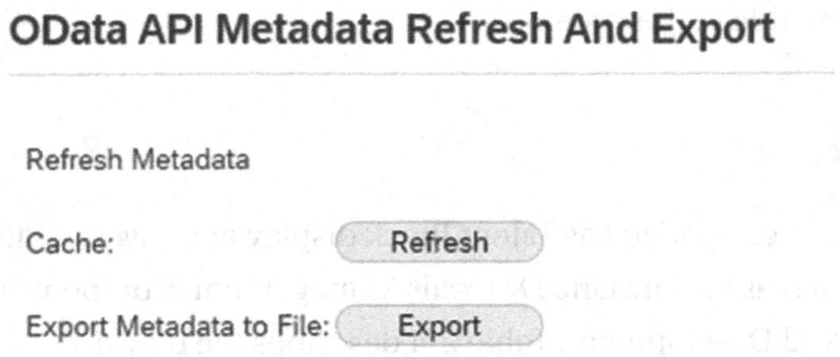

OData API Metadata Refresh And Export

Refresh Metadata

Cache: (Refresh)

Export Metadata to File: (Export)

Figure 2-12. *OData API metadata refresh*

This refreshes the cache. After the refresh, you will see the newly created picklist in the picklist values.

Having created the background element, in the next section we will discuss how to add the background element to the Employee Profile.

Configuring Talent Profile

The background element that we configured needs to be displayed in the People Portal. Displaying a background element in the People Profile is a two-step process.

1. Assign the background element to a section and block in the configuration step Configure People Profile.

2. Assign the required permissions so the background element is displayed in the People Profile.

In the next section, we will discuss how to assign the background element to a block.

People Profile Blocks

If you want to display a background element in the People Profile, the background element needs to be assigned to a block. This assignment is done in the configuration step Configure People Profile. You can access the configuration step by going to the Admin Center and clicking Configure People Profile.

Prior to discussing the configuration step, in this section we will review the different blocks that are available in the system.

Talent Block

The provided blocks categorized as Talent Block display employee-related data from talent solutions such as Performance & Goals Management, Compensation & Variable Pay, Succession, and Development. Table 2-4 describes the blocks.

Table 2-4. Talent Blocks

Block Name	Description of the Block
Live Profile Trend Information	This block is used to display the rating information, such as overall performance ratings, of the employee. When you use this block, you can select which rating information you want to display. The different options are as follows: Performance **Manager view only Potential **Manager view only Overall Objective Overall Competency
Competency-Behavior Breakdown	This block is used to display the behavior ratings collected in SuccessFactors Performance Management forms.
Competencies	This block is used to display the competency ratings collected in SuccessFactors Performance Management forms.
Development Goals	This block is used to display the development goals information captured in SuccessFactors Development Goal Plan.
Goal Ratings	This block is used to display the goal ratings captured in SuccessFactors Performance Management forms.

(*continued*)

Table 2-4. (*continued*)

Block Name	Description of the Block
Overview	This block is used to display the latest ratings of Performance versus Potential or How versus What.
Performance History	This block is used to display the performance ratings of the employees.
Successors	This block is used to display the employees who are nominated as successors to the employee's current position.
Position	The employee's current positions details are displayed in this block.
Performance-Potentials Historical Matrix Grid Placement Trend	Performance versus potential ratings are displayed in this block.
Current Nominations	The positions where the employee is nominated as a successor is displayed in this block.
How vs What Historical Matrix Grid Placement Trend	Objective versus competency ratings are displayed in this block.
Learning History	This block displays the list of learning items completed by your employee.
Curricula Status	The curriculum assigned to the employees and the completion status are displayed in this block.
Variable Pay Individual View	The employee's variable pay is displayed in this block.
History	All the forms in the system such as completed performance, 360-degree review forms, and active goal forms are displayed in this block.
Personal Variable Pay Statement	The employee's personal variably pay statement is displayed in this block.
Compensation Statement	The employee's compensation statement is displayed in this block.
Bonus Assignment Statement	The employee's bonus assignment statement is displayed in this block.

(*continued*)

Table 2-4. (*continued*)

Block Name	Description of the Block
Skill Profile	The skills assigned to the employee and their expected/current ratings are displayed in this block. In the People Profile, this block can be edited by the employee to add new skills and provide their ratings.
Personal Combined Statement	The personal combined statement of the employee is displayed in this block. This is a compensation-specific portlet.
Objective	In this block, you can create and edit goals. *Note: In SuccessFactors, goals are interchangeably referred to as objectives.*

Note   We are not discussing the Employment Information block, since this block is used to display data from Employee Central.

Personal Information

These blocks display personal data that is collected in standard elements and userinfo elements defined in the Succession data model. Table 2-5 describes the blocks.

Note   Standard elements are data elements that are delivered by SuccessFactors. Examples of standard elements are username, userid, firstname, lastname, address fields, ssn, etc.

Table 2-5. *Personal Information*

Block Name	Description of the Block
Biographical Information	This block captures the person information of the employee, such as personID, date of birth, and country of birth. *Note: The personID is typically used to capture the employee's ID in the system. Depending on the business need, the personID can be used to maintain the legacy ID (from the prior HRIS application) of the employee. During the business requirements gathering workshops, understand the needs and how this field can be used in SuccessFactors.*
Personal Information	This block displays the personal information of the employee. Details such as name, marital status, nationality, title, preferred name, etc., are captured in the block. If Employee Central is implemented, this block also displays the global information details of the employee. When you select the country where the employee is residing, the system will display the country-specific fields. For example, if you select USA, the country-specific fields such ethnic group, veteran status, and disability details are displayed for the employee to fill in. *Note: Customers used Preferred Name to capture the preferred name of the employee. Many employee's use nicknames in the workplace and are known by that name among co-workers. This field can be used to capture the preferred name of the employee.*
Contact Information	This block contains the contact information such as email and phone numbers. For both email and phone numbers, you can capture the busines, personal, and any customer-defined contact information.
Address Information	This block is used to maintain the address information of the employee. The typical options for address type are home, mailing, payroll, etc. Your customer can have different options than these.
National ID Information	This block is used to capture the national ID of the employee. If an employee has multiple national IDs (common with employees who carry dual citizenships or are working as expats), these can be captured as well in this block.

(*continued*)

Table 2-5. (*continued*)

Block Name	Description of the Block
Work Eligibility	This block displays the work permit details of the employee. This block is typically filled out if the employee is an immigrant or an expat. Details such as the country that issues the work permit, document type, document number, date issued, and date of expiry are captured in this block. *Note: Customers have questions on how should maintain this block or how will HR be notified if a work permit is nearing the expiration date. If you have Employee Central, you can configure alerts so that HR (or whoever needs to be notified) can be notified "n" days before a work permit is nearing expiration.* *If you do not have Employee Central in the landscape, currently there is no functionality to inform HR of an upcoming work permit expiration. The workaround will be to develop a report to identify all employee whose work permits are nearing expiration.*
Emergency Contact	The emergency contact details of the employee are captured in this block. The relationship of the employee to the emergency contact is also maintained in this block. *Note: During the business requirements gathering workshops, check with the customer what their culture is, while capturing the emergency contacts of the employee. At times, customer would like to maintain only one emergency contact and maintain just the phone number of the contact and not the email address.* *If the customer has SuccessFactors Onboarding, the emergency contact information is typically captured in the onboarding process. In that scenario, the information captured during the onboarding process should be displayed in this block.*
Dependents	The dependents details of the employee, and their relationship to the employee, are maintained in this block.

Compensation Information

Data from SuccessFactors Compensation are displayed in these blocks. See Table 2-6.

Table 2-6. Compensation Information

Block Name	Description of the Block
Compensation Information	The compensation details of the employee such as the pay type, pay group, pay grade, bonus target, compa ratio, and penetration rate are displayed in this block.
Pay Component Non-Recurring	Non-recurring pay components such bonus are displayed in this block.
Alternative Cost Distribution	If an employee is assigned to multiple cost centers, those details are displayed in this block.
One Time Deduction	Single deductions of an employee are displayed in this block.
Eligibility For Advances	Eligibility details for salary advances are displayed in this block.
Current Advances	Salary advances taken by the employee are displayed in this block.
Payroll Information	The employee's payroll details are displayed in this block. *Note: If the payroll is outsourced to a third-party payroll provider, then does not enable this block.*
Total Compensation History	This is a widget. The widget displays the compensation history of the employee in graphical format.
Recurring Deduction	Recurring deductions against an employee's salary are displayed in this block.

Custom Blocks

Custom blocks (see Table 2-7) contain objects that capture data from employees and are independent of any SuccessFactors modules. For example, details about managerial experience will be captured in a background element and displayed in a Live Profile Background Information block.

Table 2-7. *Custom Blocks*

Block Name	Description of Block
Live Profile Background Information	This block displays the data in the background elements. The background elements can be custom built or delivered by SuccessFactors.
Live Profile User Information	The basic details of the employee, such as FirstName, LastName, etc., are displayed in the block.
Badges	This block displays the badges the employee has received. Both custom and system-delivered badges are displayed in this block. *Note: If needed, you can configure custom badges that are aligned to your organization's culture.*
Tags	You can tag an employee for specific skills, experience, or interests, etc. You can use these tags to search for employees who have specific skills or interests.
Notes	This is a text area block, where notes can be entered and displayed. Typically, the Notes block is used by HR or a manager to enter notes related to the employee. If the Notes block is used by HR or a manager, then typically the employee is not permissioned to view the Notes block (i.e., the block will be hidden from the employee's view).
Org Chart	The reporting line relationship between the employee and their manager is displayed in this block. If the employee has direct reports, then the direct reports of the employee are displayed as well. When you click the displayed picture, the system will take you to the People Profile of that particular employee.
LinkedIn	This block is a widget that displays the LinkedIn profile of the employee. You can configure an integration between the People Profile and LinkedIn to dynamically display the LinkedIn profile in the People Profile.
Live Profile Trend Information	This block displays the rating information of the employee. The rating information is gathered from performance ratings, objectives ratings, and data such as performance versus potentials ratings.

Adding a Section

In the People Profile, a section allows you to group different portlets logically. A section consists of a section title and subsections. A section can contain any number of subsections.

A People Profile can contain any number of sections.

In Figure 2-13, the titles Benefits and Talent Profile are sections. As you see in the figure, by categorizing the People Profile into sections and adding subsections containing background elements, the user is presented with a cleaner, user-friendly People Profile.

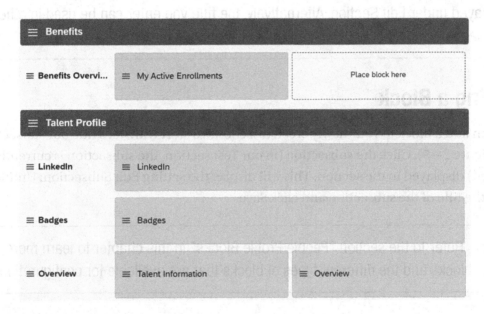

Figure 2-13. *Sections/subsections*

To create a section, go to the Admin Center and select Configure People Profile. On the displayed page, scroll to the bottom of the page. Click the "Add a new section" button.

A new section (see Figure 2-14) is created. Under Edit Section: Untitled, enter the name of the section, and click Save.

Figure 2-14. *Creating a section*

Tip   You can add section title in multiple languages by clicking the globe icon displayed under Edit Section. Alternatively, the title you enter can be used in other languages when you click the Apply to All Languages button.

Adding a Block

You can add a block to your newly created section. To start with, let's title our subsection (see Figure 2-15). Click the subsection (in our Test section, the subsection is currently untitled) displayed in the section. This will display the setting Edit Subsection: Untitled. Enter the title of the subsection and click Save.

Note   Refer to the section "People Profile Blocks" in this chapter to learn more about blocks and the different types of blocks that are available for configuration.

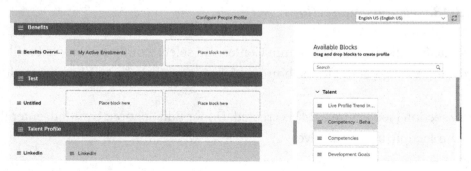

Figure 2-15. *Creating a block*

To add a block to a subsection, scroll through the available blocks to identify the block you want to add. Drag the block to the subsection where you want to display it.

If the subsection is filled (i.e., if two blocks are already configured in that subsection), hover the block between the two blocks or between the block and the next subsection. The system will automatically create a new subsection.

Tip   When you move a block to a subsection, if you see a red tick in the block, it means the system does not have sufficient space to drop the block in that particular subsection. When the system is able to drop a block in a subsection, you will notice a green tick in the upper-right corner of the block.

When you move the block to a subsection, you will notice you are required to add details such as a block title and description, as well as an option for how you want ratings to be displayed (see Figure 2-16). The title is a required field and is displayed in the People Profile. The description you enter in the configuration is displayed as contextual help text in the People Profile. Save your configuration.

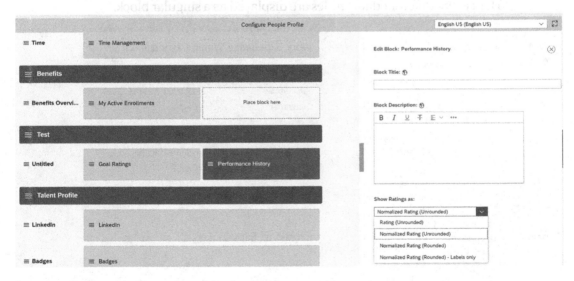

Figure 2-16. *Configuring a block*

When you configure a Live Profile Background Information block, you will notice there are additional configurations that are required.

- *Background Element*: The system displays a listing of all background elements' configuration settings that are available in the system. You select the background element that you want to display in the People Profile.

- *Title for Repeating Entries*: In a background element block, the user can create multiple data entries. You can choose if you want to title each individual entry. The columns configured in that background element are available for you to choose from. Alternatively, you can choose None. If you choose None, then the system will display the multiple data entries as one singular block, with no titles. In Figure 2-17 we have two different subsections displaying background elements: Work Experience Within Organization and Functional Experience. In the background element Work Experience Within Organization, we have the column Title as the title for repeating entry, whereas in the background element Functional Experience, choose None as the title for repeating entry. Hence, the different data entries are displayed as a singular block.

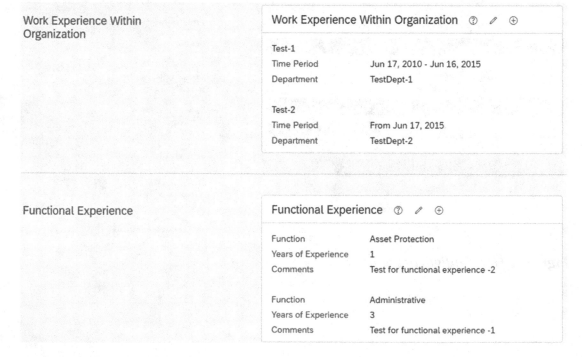

Figure 2-17. *Repeating entries*

- *Block Size*: The options are Small and Large. When you choose Small, the background element is displayed in one column of the subsection. When you choose Large, the background element is displayed in two columns of the subsection.

- *Block Layout*: The options are List View and Table View. The background element displayed in Figure 2-17 is in list view. The entries in the background element are displayed as a rolling list. The background element in Figure 2-18 is displayed in table view. In a table view, the columns of the background element are displayed as column headers, and the different entries are displayed in individual lines.

Functional Experience	Functional Experience ⓘ ✎ ⊕		
	Function	Years of Experience	Comments
	Asset Protection	1	Test for functional experience -2
	Administrative	3	Test for functional experience -1

Figure 2-18. *Background element displayed in table view*

You can add as many blocks as you want in a section. New subsections are automatically created as you add blocks to a section. As you can see in Figure 2-16 each subsection displays two columns; hence, you can configure two blocks in each subsection. There are blocks such as LinkedIn and Badges, which are wide and occupy two columns. Hence, in those subsections, you can configure one block only.

Tip   When you are configuring a section or a subsection, if you want to return to the available blocks, click the X icon displayed in the top-right corner of the Edit Section/Edit Subsection config view. The available blocks config view will now be displayed.

Configuring General Settings

On the Configure People Profile config page, at the top of the page you will see a section called General Settings. You can enable and disable these settings by checking/unchecking the options (see Figure 2-19).

Table 2-8 summarizes each of these options.

Table 2-8. *General Settings Configuration Options*

Configuration Settings	Description
Allow employees to edit background images	When you enable this option, the employees can upload their own background image to the profile header.
Manager background image library	The image library maintains the repository of images that are available for employees to choose from. As an administrator, you can maintain the images that are available to employees.
Allow employees to record pronunciation of name	If checked, the employees are provided access to My Name in the People Profile. Users can use this feature to record a short audio clip on how to pronounce their name. The users can enter their phonetic spelling as well. Note: Below the checkbox, you will notice a link to Read My Name Agreement. The agreement says that all media content is stored in the SAP data center in Germany. This link/agreement is not made available to users.
Allow employees to record About Me video	If checked, the employees are provided access to About Me in the People Profile. Users can use this feature to record a short a video clip about themselves. The video clip is made available in that employee's profile header, in the People Profile. Note: Below the checkbox, you will notice a link called Read About Me Agreement. The agreement says that all media content is stored in SAP data center in Germany. This link/agreement is not made available to users.
Allow employees to enter introductory text	When you enable this option, the employees can enter an introductory text about themselves, up to a maximum of 500 characters. The introductory text is made available in that employee's profile header in the People Profile.
Show percent complete	If this option is enabled, the end user will see an icon displaying percentage of completion in their People Profile. The employee can use the profile completion wizard to complete their profile. Note: The show percent complete is visible to that particular employee only (in other words, when they view their People Profile as Self) and is not visible to any other users/roles, including the role of an administrator.

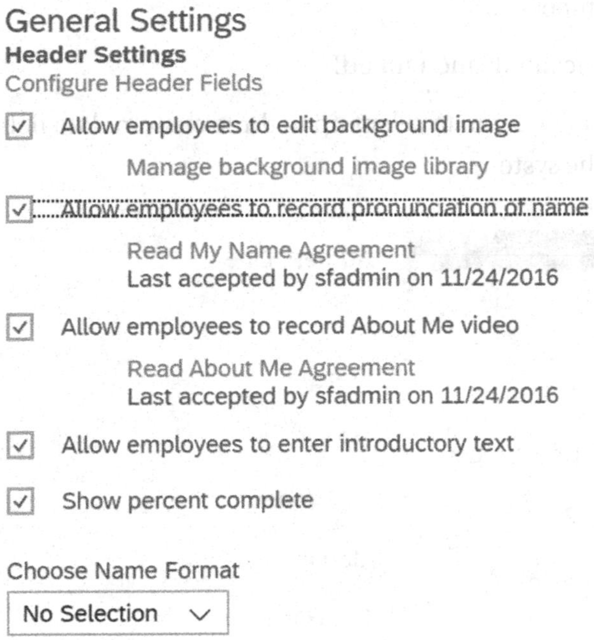

General Settings
Header Settings
Configure Header Fields

☑   Allow employees to edit background image

   Manage background image library

☑   Allow employees to record pronunciation of name

   Read My Name Agreement
   Last accepted by sfadmin on 11/24/2016

☑   Allow employees to record About Me video

   Read About Me Agreement
   Last accepted by sfadmin on 11/24/2016

☑   Allow employees to enter introductory text

☑   Show percent complete

Choose Name Format
┌─────────────────────┐
│ No Selection   ∨   │
└─────────────────────┘

Figure 2-19. *People Profile: General Settings configuration*

Configuring Header Fields

As shown in Figure 2-20, you can click the link Configure Header Fields to configure what data fields should be displayed in the People Profile header.

By default, the following fields are available for display in the profile header:

- Photo of the employee

- Name of the employee

- User ID

- Position title

- Employee's organization details such as department, division, location

- Time zone (as selected by the employee)

- Local time (in the employee's time zone)

- Email

- Phone numbers

- Logos of Facebook and LinkedIn

The system also allows you to select up to three custom data fields that you might have configured in the system.

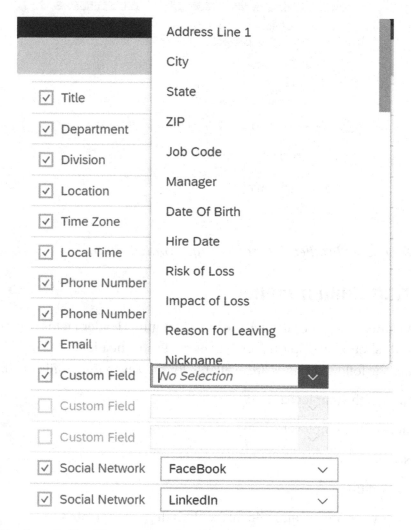

Figure 2-20. *People Profile: configuring header settings*

When you click the link Configure Header Fields, the fields that are available for configuration are displayed (see Figure 2-20). On the displayed page, you can check/uncheck the fields that you want to be displayed in the People Profile header.

To configure a custom field, you are required to check Custom Field. Once it is checked, the picklist is enabled. You can choose any of the available fields in the picklist to display in the profile header.

Note   An employee will need to be permissioned to be able to view a field in the People Profile header. What we are doing in this configuration as an administrator is to enable the fields that can be edited/made visible in the People Profile and profile header. To be able to view or edit a field, an employee will need to be provided the appropriate permissions as Self. Other roles such as Manager, 1 Up Manager, HR, and Peers need to have the appropriate permissions as well. For example, you might have a requirement where Facebook should be visible to an employee and HR only (the role is Self). In this scenario, you will provide the permissions to Self and HR only. Other roles (such as Manager, 1 Up Manager, HR, and Peers) will not have the permissions to view or edit.

Configuring Talent Data Settings

In the Talent Data Settings area (see Figure 2-21), you can configure the date ranges for when the ratings should be displayed in the People Profile. You can also configure the sources for these ratings. The sources will be the different forms that are configured and available in the system. You can also include in-flight forms as a data source.

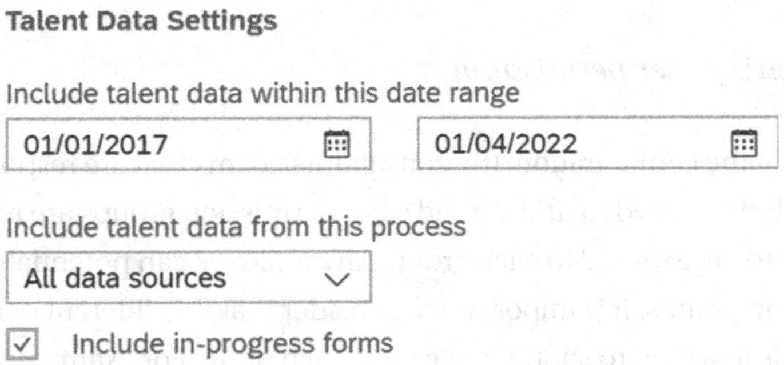

Talent Data Settings

Include talent data within this date range

| 01/01/2017 | 📅 | | 01/04/2022 | 📅 |

Include talent data from this process

All data sources ⌄

☑ Include in-progress forms

Figure 2-21. *People Profile: configuring talent data settings*

Tip   It is recommended you select all the data sources. This way you can view an employee's ratings over the years.

Set Permissions on the Portlet

We need to set the permission for edit/view functionality of the different portlets and data fields in the People Profile for different roles such as employee (Self), HR, Manager, 1 Up and above Managers. In the next section, we will review how to permission for the different roles.

Manager Permissions Roles

You assign permissions to a role and assign that role to a permission group (see Figure 2-22 where you can access the permission-related configuration steps). An employee needs to be assigned to a permission group to be able to navigate in SuccessFactors.

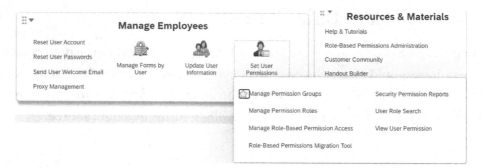

Figure 2-22. *Setting user permissions*

Prior to starting the configuration, the consultants/teams that are responsible for configuring permissions need to understand what permission groups are required, and permissions need to be assigned to each group. An employee can potentially be assigned to multiple permission groups. It is important to consider that the different permissions groups that an employee is assigned to should not cancel each other. For example, say an employee is assigned to a group where they do not have permissions to view other employees' performance ratings and assigned to a group that has permissions to view other employee's performance ratings. In this scenario, the system will determine that the group that has view permissions will have priority over the group that does not have view permissions.

Customers typically have questions about how HR, managers, or the HR support desk will be aware if the employee make updates to their information in the People Profile. For example, if an employee changes their name or dependent details, HR needs to be made aware of this change so downstream processes can be supported. Without Employee Central in the landscape, it is not possible for HR to be notified of any name change. Hence, in this particular scenario, the business needs to be made aware that names will be viewed only for the employee (Self), and only HR will have edit capabilities.

While reviewing the permissions of the blocks, you need to check with business about who will be maintaining the data in the blocks. You should meticulously fill in the permissions workbook and identify the actors (HR, Manager, Manager +1, etc.) and what their permissions (edit/ view) will be for each block.

Tip   There are delivered reports in SuccessFactors that you can execute to support you during role-based permissions (RBP) configurations. The reports are as follows:

- *RBP User to role report*: This report lists all the permission roles a user is granted, as well the target population assigned to that permission role.

- *RBP Permission to user report*: This report lists all the permissions and the users who are granted the particular permission.

- *RBP User to group report*: This report lists the users and the permission groups they are assigned to.

- *RBP Permission roles report*: This report lists the permission roles that are granted and the assigned target populations.

Permissions to Be Assigned

The People Profile is possibly the most important object in SuccessFactors. It is the one object that will be viewed/edited more often than any other object in SuccessFactors. Hence, it is important that permissions requirements are captured and configured correctly. Configuring People Profile–related permissions gets more challenging when you have multiple modules in the landscape. When you are configuring permissions, you need to take precautions that you do not end up creating too many permission groups or permission roles than what might be required.

Tip   Typically, permissions workbook are maintained for each individual SuccessFactors module. While this is a standard approach during an implementation, for the security admin this does not provide any insight into how the permissions are being merged with existing permissions groups and roles.

Figure 2-23 shows a snapshot of a permissions workbook that is typically used in my implementations. On the left, we have displayed all the permissions available in the system. On the right, we have identified the different actors such as all users, employee groups, leaders (typically 1 Up Manager and above), etc. We then identify who needs access to which permissions. I have found that maintaining one universal permissions workbook goes a long way in making permissions requirements gathering and configuration less stressful, as well helping the security admin to understand the overall picture of the security architecture for SuccessFactors.

USER PERMISSIONS * = Target needs to be defined	All Users (Includes Contractors, Student, Temp, Casual, Union)		Salaried/Hourly Employees (access to all users data)		Salaried/Hourly Employees (access to own data)		All Employees - Profile Access		Leader (includes contractor-leaders)		HRBP / HR Reporting Analyst *Access is repeated from Salaried/Hourly role for Temp/Contractor users in HR		HRBP / HR Reporting Analyst - Calibration Sessions Only		SYSTEM ADMINISTRATOR	
Calibration	Yes	No	Yes	No	Yes	No	Yes	No	Yes	No	Yes	No	Yes	No	Yes	No
Detailed Calibration Permissions*																
View Calibration Tab																
Goals	Yes	No	Yes	No	Yes	No	Yes	No	Yes	No	Yes	No	Yes	No	Yes	No
Goal Management Access *											x					
New Group Goal Creation *																
Goal Plan Permissions *																

Figure 2-23.   *Permissions workbook*

Note   It is beyond the scope of this book to review the permissions workbook in detail.

In Table 2-9, we will review what permissions need to be assigned to access certain objects in the People Profile.

Table 2-9. *Permissions*

Object to Access	Name of Permission	Description
People Profile	User Permissions ➤ General User Permission ➤ Live Profile Access	This permission should be assigned to all users who will need to access the People Profile.
Sections and Blocks configured in the People Profile	User Permissions ➤ Employee Views	Control visibility of the People Profile sections configured in the People Profile. The different sections configured in the People Profile are listed in Employee Views. You can select/unselect what sections need to be assigned to this permission role.
Data fields in People Profile	User Permissions ➤ Employee Data	The permissions to view employee data are listed in this permission. You can control what fields/background elements can be edited or viewed by which permission role. Note: You can permission individual HRIS field such as First Name, Last Name, Address 1, etc. Background elements (delivered and custom built) can be permissioned as individual background elements only.

Import and Export Data

We can import data to any background element that we configure in the system. Currently the only way to export data from non-MDF background elements are by reports.

To import data to non-MDF background elements, you can go to the Admin Center and click Import Extended User Information.

Note   You can export and import data to MDF-based background elements by going to the Admin Center and clicking Import and Export Data. It is beyond the scope of this book to discuss the MDF-based background element. The MDF-based background elements are used when SuccessFactors Employee Central is in the landscape.

Import Extended User Information

On the landing page of the config step Import Extended User Information (see Figure 2-24), select the option Background Information to import data to background elements.

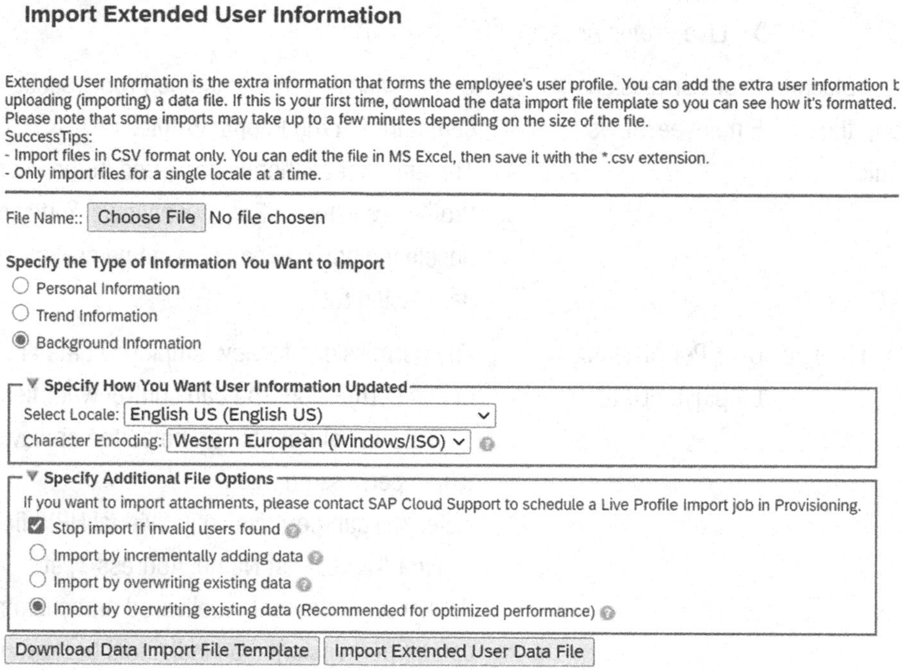

Import Extended User Information

Extended User Information is the extra information that forms the employee's user profile. You can add the extra user information by uploading (importing) a data file. If this is your first time, download the data import file template so you can see how it's formatted. Please note that some imports may take up to a few minutes depending on the size of the file.
SuccessTips:
- Import files in CSV format only. You can edit the file in MS Excel, then save it with the *.csv extension.
- Only import files for a single locale at a time.

File Name:: [Choose File] No file chosen

Specify the Type of Information You Want to Import
- ○ Personal Information
- ○ Trend Information
- ◉ Background Information

┌─ ▼ **Specify How You Want User Information Updated** ───────
│ Select Locale: [English US (English US)   ∨]
│ Character Encoding: [Western European (Windows/ISO) ∨] ⓘ

┌─ ▼ **Specify Additional File Options** ──────────────────
│ If you want to import attachments, please contact SAP Cloud Support to schedule a Live Profile Import job in Provisioning.
│ ☑ Stop import if invalid users found ⓘ
│ ○ Import by incrementally adding data ⓘ
│ ○ Import by overwriting existing data ⓘ
│ ◉ Import by overwriting existing data (Recommended for optimized performance) ⓘ

[Download Data Import File Template] [Import Extended User Data File]

Figure 2-24. *Background Information import data*

Click Download Data Import File Template to download the import template we will use. The template contains structures for all non-MDF background elements in the system. We will use only the background elements for which we will import data. Hence, you are required to delete the structures of the background elements that you will not use for this import.

Figure 2-25 shows the columns of the background element Favorite Travel Destinations that we configured earlier. We will import data for a few employees for this background element only.

We will fill in data in the following format:

- *^UserID*: Enter the UserID of the employee for whom you are importing the data.

Note You can gather the UserID from the UDF file (the "user data file"). You can export the UDF file from the system by going to the Admin Center and clicking Employee Export.

- *^AssignmentID*: You can leave this column blank.

- *favTravelDestinations*: The column will always have the value favTravelDestinations. This value is static.

- *destName*: Enter the name of the destination. For the import, our value will be London,England.

- *destDesc*: This column will hold the description on why this is a favorite destination. Our value will be "I love everything about London."

^UserId	^AssignmentId	googledocs	documentur	documentl	lastmodifieddate		
^UserId	^AssignmentId	sysScoreCardDevelopmentObjectivesPortlet					
^UserId	^AssignmentId	talentPool		talentPoolit	startDate	talentPoolStatu	talentPoolComments
^UserId	^AssignmentId	talentPoolcorp		talentPoolit	startDate	talentPoolStatu	talentPoolComments
^UserId	^AssignmentId	favTravelDestinations	destName	destDesc	rateTraveDest	endDate	uploadPics

Figure 2-25. *Import template to import data*

- *rateTravelDest*: Our value will be Rank 5.

Note In the background element, the field rateTravelDest is a picklist field. You need to review the picklist for the actual values you will use here. You are required to enter the label of the picklist value in this column.

- *endDate*: The label in the UI for this field is Date Last Visited. We will use the value 7/3/2017.

In the config step Import Extended User Information (see Figure 2-25), choose the radio button Background Information. Select the appropriate locale and character encoding. For our discussion here, we will choose English US and Unicode (UTF-8).

In the section Specify Additional File Options, you have these three options:

- *Import by incrementally adding data*: When you choose this option, data in the file is added to the existing data in the employee record. If there is no record for an employee in the import file and there are already existing records in the system, the existing record is not affected.

- *Import by overwriting existing data*: This option will overwrite existing data. Hence, if employee 1000 (UID) has an existing record for this background element, and if they are not present in the import file, their data will be erased. Be cautious when using this option.

- *Import by overwriting existing data (Recommended for optimized performance)*: This option will overwrite data with existing data from the file. If the data in the system is same as data in the file, then that record will be skipped.

For our import, we will choose the option "Import by incrementally adding data." Click Choose File and upload the file. Click Import Extended User Data File to import the file. The system will now display a dialog box. Read the dialog box and click Yes.

Visit the People Profile and review the background element. You will notice that the data is imported successfully.

Scheduled Jobs to Export Data

If you have access to Provisioning, you can configure backend jobs to schedule an export. In Provisioning, go to the configuration step Manage Scheduled Jobs in the section Managing Job Scheduler. In the displayed page, click Create New Job.

Edit Job

Use this page to create a new job. Fields marked with * are required.

Job Definition	
* Job Name:	Test
* Job Owner:	Venki Krishnamoorthy ⊕ Find User...
	The Job Owner will be used to authenticate all submitted jobs. They will also be the default user to receive E-mail notifications.
* Job Type:	Live Profile Export
Job Parameters:	* Live Profile Type:

     ○ Personal Information

     ◉ Background Information (☑ Include Attachment)

     ○ Trend Information (☐ Include form data – only applicable to Export Extended Data with User Attributes)

     Supported Locales: [English US (English US) ∨]

     Character Encoding: [Western European (Windows/ISO) ∨]

     ☐ Valid users only.

     ☐ Exclude Contingent Worker

     ☐ Remove carriage returns and line breaks on export

     * Select what to export:

     ◉ Export Extended Data Only

     ○ Export Extended Data with User Attributes

     ☐ Unzip export file if it is zipped

Figure 2-26. *Scheduling a job to export data*

As shown in Figure 2-26, enter the job name and the owner of the job. In Job Type, select Live Profile Export. In Job Parameters, select Background Information and select Include Attachment. In the section "Select what to export," select Export Extended Data Only.

In Server Access, you are required to enter the SFTP details.

Note   All SuccessFactors customers will have access to SuccessFactors-provisioned SFTP. At times, customers may prefer to use their native SFTP. Check with the customer on their preferences.

In File Access, enter the folder where you want the exported file to be made available.

In Job Occurrence & Notification, configure the job to be executed once.

Save the job. On the job page, submit the job and have it executed immediately. When the job is executed successfully, log into SFTP, and you should see the file exported in the folder you configured in Provisioning.

Tip   You can configure jobs in Provisioning to import data to background elements. Make the import file available in SFTP in a particular folder. Configure and execute the job. The scheduled job will consume the file and update the background elements accordingly.

Exporting Background Elements Data with Integration Center

While the Integration Center is typically used to create data files for integrations, you can also use the Integration Center to export the data of background elements. You can access the Integration Center by going to the Admin Center and clicking Integration Center. On the displayed page, click My Integrations. This will bring up a new page that will display all the integrations that are configured and available in the Integration Center. Click Create and select Scheduled Simple File Output Integration to create a new integration.

In the search box, enter the ID of the background element (see Figure 2-26) whose data you want to export. For our discussion, we will enter **favTravelDestinations**. On the right side of the same page, you will see the fields configured in this background element. Select the fields you want to include in your export file. Click Select. On the next page, you can enter the name of the file, as well the file output format. Click Next. The data in the background element is displayed here. In the displayed page, you also have an option to rename the column headings, as well as the format of the data. If needed, you can also change the order of columns by dragging and dropping in the order you want to see.

Tip   The option to rename column headings or configure the format of the data is not feasible when you export data using scheduled jobs in Provisioning. Hence, some customers prefer to export data using the Integration Center.

In the page where the data is displayed, you can right-click any column heading. This will display the options that are available to configure that specific column.

In Destination Settings option, you can configure the SFTP details, filename, and file folder where you want the generate file to be available. In the Scheduling option, you can configure when and how often you want this job to be executed. See Figure 2-27.

Note   You can also export data by creating table-based reports in Report Center. As you can see, we have multiple options to export data. Which option you prefer depends on what the business needs are. For example, if you need the data exported as a one-time need or as needed, then data export using reports is preferred. If the data export will be consumed by other applications, then you can export data using the Integration Center or by using scheduled jobs in Provisioning. Scheduled jobs in Provisioning are more common and popular since the Integration Center is relatively new, compared to scheduled jobs in Provisioning.

Figure 2-27. *Export of data using the Integration Center*

Case Study

In this section, we will review a case study where we will configure trend elements in the People Profile and import historical data into these elements.

Description

Customer A wants to configure the trend elements in the People Profile and have those elements be viewable and editable by the line manager and HR managers only. The employees will not have access to these trend elements. The customer wants the Performance and Potential blocks to be labeled as Performance **Manager/HR view only and Potential **Manager/HR view only.

Customer A would also like to load historical legacy data to these trend elements.

Solution

The background elements sysOverallObjective, sysOverallCompetency, sysOverallPerformance, sysOverallPotential, sysOverallCustom1, and sysOverallCustom2 are referred to as *trend elements*.

We will configure them in the People Profile similar to other background elements.

Step 1: We will review the structure of the trend elements and enable them if needed. Go to the Admin Center and click Manage Business Configuration.

On the displayed page (see Figure 2-28), click the section Employee Profile, and click Background Elements. Scroll down, and click sysOverallPerformance.

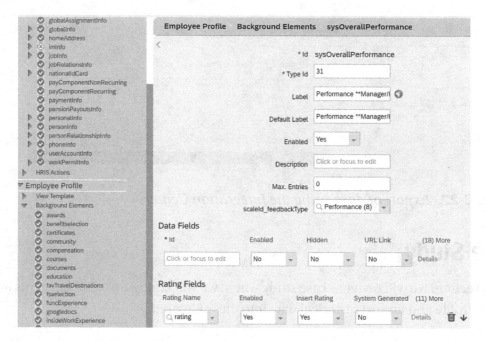

Figure 2-28. *Enabling sysOverallPerformance*

Check if the field Enabled has a value of Yes. If not, select Yes from the drop-down, and click Save. This will enable the trend element.

Note   The section Rating Fields is used for trend elements. These fields display the rating data. In the rating fields, go to the field rating, and click Details. On the displayed page, ensure the field Enabled is Yes and that the field Insert Rating is Yes. Click Save to save your changes.

Similarly, enable the trend element sysOverall Potential and make changes to the Rating Field rating if needed.

Step 2: We will now configure these two trend elements in the People Profile by going to the Admin Center and clicking Configure People Profile. On the displayed page (see Figure 2-29), scroll to the section Talent Profile.

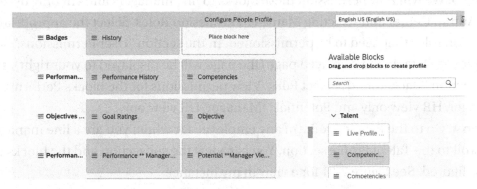

Figure 2-29. *Configuring sysOverallPerformance/sysOverallPotential in the People Profile*

In the Available Blocks list, scroll to the section Talent. The first block in the section is Live Profile Trend Information. Select that block and drop it in the Talent Profile section. This will display the Edit Block properties (see Figure 2-30). On the edit page, in the Trend Element drop-down, select the trend element Performance **Manager view only. This is the block sysOverallPerformance that we reviewed in the previous section. Now, change Block Title to Performance **Manager/HR View only. Change the description to reflect the Block Title setting. Click Save to save your changes.

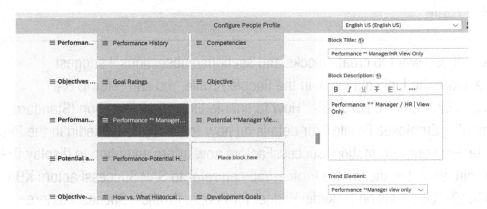

Figure 2-30. *Editing the block sysOverallPerformance*

Similarly, configure the block sysOverallPotential. Change the subsection label to be Performance and Potential Manager / HR view only. Remember to check the option "Show this subsection on the profile." Click Save to save your changes.

Step 3: We will now permission these blocks to line managers and HR only by going to the Admin Center and selecting Manager Permission Roles. Select the appropriate permission roles that need to be permissioned. In the section "User Permissions," scroll to Employee Data. In the displayed page (the page will be displayed to your right), scroll to the section "Background". Select Edit / View permissions for the blocks Performance **Manager/HR view only and Potential **Manager/HR view only.

Step 4: Go to the People Profile of any employee for whom you are a line manager or HR. Scroll to the Talent Profile section. You can view the subsection and the blocks we just configured. See Figure 2-31 for a view in my instance.

Figure 2-31. *sysOverall Performance and sysOverall Potential display in the People Profile*

Note   If you want to create blocks and sections/subsections, I suggest you explore the LinkedIn block in the People Profile. You can refer to SAP SuccessFactors KBA: 2085406, "How to enable LinkedIn Integration (Standard Element) - Employee Profile," for details on how to configure LinkedIn in the People Profile. For your information, SuccessFactors now offers an option to display the LinkedIn widget in the People Profile. You can refer to SAP SuccessFactors KBA: 2507469, "Overview on Linkedin Widget for People Profile - SuccessFactors Employee Profile," on how configure the widget.

Conclusion

In this chapter, we discussed the People Profile and the Talent Profile. Then we discussed how to configure blocks in the People Profile. We looked at the two options that are currently available: configuring them in the Admin Center UI and configuring them in the Succession data model. Which option you should use depends on your own preference. There is no one way or the other. Both options can accomplish the task. Later in the chapter we discussed how to export and import data. We looked at the options to manually do the import available in the Admin Center and to configure scheduled jobs in Provisioning. Later we reviewed how we can export data by configuring an export job in Provisioning. We also discussed the options available in the Integration Center and in the Report Center. Toward the end of the chapter, we looked at a case study where we discussed how to configure trend elements such as sysOverallPerformance and sysOverallPotential.

One thing we did not discuss and I am leaving as an exercise for you is to import data to the newly configured trend elements. As a tip, I suggest you review the section "Import Extended User Information" and Figure 2-24. The process is similar to importing data for background elements.

In the next chapter, we will discuss the Job Profile Builder, where we will review what functionality the Job Profile Builder offers and how it can be leveraged to bring efficiency to your talent strategy.

CHAPTER 3

Job Profile Builder

The Job Profile Builder is a tool within SAP SuccessFactors that is used to maintain the elements of a job. The elements include job descriptions, experiences, qualifications, skills, competencies, behaviors, education, certifications, and skills. The Job Profile Builder (JPB) is based on the SuccessFactors Metadata Framework and can be integrated with the SuccessFactors talent modules such as Recruiting, Performance & Goals Management Career Development, Succession Management, and People Profile.

Note   In this chapter, we will refer to the Job Profile Builder as the JPB.

Using the JPB, you can build content repositories in SuccessFactors for the different content types. The following are the content types available in the JPB:

- Families
- Roles
- Certifications
- Competencies, including behaviors
- Employment conditions
- Education, degree
- Education, major
- Interview questions
- Physical requirements for the job
- Skills, with up to five levels of proficiency
- Relevant industry
- Job responsibility, including duties

© Susan Traynor, Michael A. Wellens and Venki Krishnamoorthy 2021
S. Traynor et al., *SAP SuccessFactors Talent: Volume 1*, https://doi.org/10.1007/978-1-4842-6600-7_3

Once the content is developed in the JPB, you need to create job profile templates where you define the format and sections to include in the job profile. The job profiles are attached to job roles, and the content specific to the job role is derived from the content that you will created or import into the system.

The JPB is built on top of the SuccessFactors Metadata Framework (MDF). The MDF enables you to create and maintain object definitions, relationships between objects, and a hierarchy of objects. The JPB is a successor of the Job Description Manager (JDM), the legacy tool from SuccessFactors. The differentiator between the JDM and the JPB is the MDF. If you are an existing JDM customer, you can upgrade to the JPB by migrating families, roles, and job code to role mappings and competencies to the newly configured JPB framework. You can do the configuration only after configuring the JPB. KBA article 2276692, "Clarification on Migration option from JDM to JPB," is a good reference.

Note   It is beyond the scope of this book to discuss the MDF in detail.

Prior to implementing the JPB, ensure that the customer instance meets these prerequisites:

- The customer should have implemented the SuccessFactors platform.

- The customer should have implemented role-based permissions (RBP).

- The customer should be on the V12 user interface.

Note   The JPB is a component of the SuccessFactors platform, and no additional license fees are required.

Figure 3-1 shows how different SuccessFactors modules leverage the JPB.

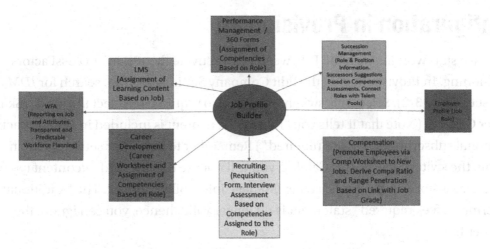

Figure 3-1. *Integrating the JPB with the SuccessFactors talent modules*

Implementing the JPB provides the different job roles in the enterprise with clear insight into the job requirements, skills, and competencies that are required. When the job criteria are defined in the system, an employee can identify what the job requirements are for their job, identify the training needs, work with their supervisors to plan performance goals, and identify what skills and competencies are needed for their next job role in the enterprise. Recruiters can create requisitions using content from the JPB, and compensation planning can be performed by leveraging comparison ratios and range penetrations linked to the job.

Note   Customers use job descriptions, skills, and competencies developed by third-party vendors. We can use the content provided by such third-party vendors and load them into the JPB.

In this chapter, we will discuss how to configure the JPB and how it can be integrated into the SuccessFactors talent modules. We will start by reviewing how to activate JPB in Provisioning. Then we will cover the permissions that need to be set up to get access to the JPB and to different objects, as well as how to configure the visibility settings of the different objects. We will review the different content types, as well as how to import data into the different content types. Toward the end of the chapter, we will look at a case study and see how the JPB can be integrated into the SuccessFactors modules in a realistic scenario. This chapter will provide a good overview of how the JPB can be leveraged in the enterprise talent strategy.

Configuration in Provisioning

Before we start working with the JPB, we need to activate the JPB in SuccessFactors Provisioning. In Provisioning, in the Edit Company Settings section, search for *JDM v2.0* (see Figure 3-2). Select this switch. You are also required to select the switch Skill Master Catalog. (Note that it tells you "Ensure the content is included in the contract. Additional subscription fees are required.") Remember to save your settings. If do not activate the switch Skill Master Catalog, you will not see the link Add <<content type>> from SuccessStore on the config screen Manage Job Profile Content. The "Additional subscription fees required" statement is no longer valid; hence, you can ignore the statement.

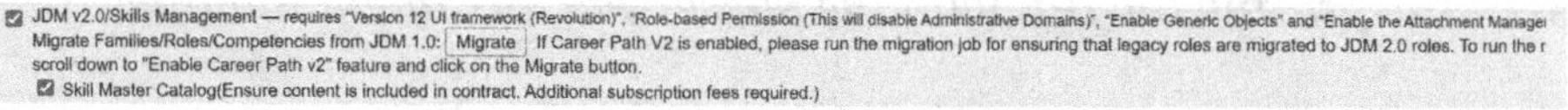

Figure 3-2. *Activating the JPB in Provisioning*

Note   Prior to activating JDM v2.0, you are required to activate these switches:

- Enable Generic Objects
- Enable the Attachment Manager

Setting Up Security Permissions

You need to configure visibility role-based permissions for the following the JPB permissions:

- Job and skills visibility
- Skill profile
- Rated skills

Since the JPB is an MDF-based object, we configure these settings on the admin screen Configure Object Definitions. Follow the steps in the next sections to complete the configurations.

You can view these permissions in Administrator Section ➤ Manage Job & Skill Profile Visibility.

Setting Up Visibility: Job Profile

We need to edit the Job Profile object definition to configure the visibility settings. Go to the Admin Center and click Configure Object Definitions.

On the displayed screen, in the first search box, select Object Definition. Then in the search box, enter **Job Profile** (see Figure 3-3).

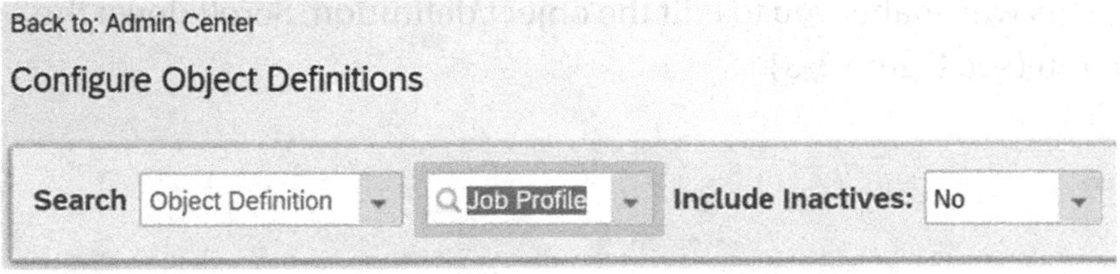

Back to: Admin Center

Configure Object Definitions

Search | Object Definition ▾ | Q Job Profile ▾ | Include Inactives: | No ▾

Figure 3-3. *Job Profile object definition*

The object definition of Job Profile is displayed. Click Take Action ➤ Make Correction. This will enable you to edit the object definition. Scroll down the page to the Security section (see Figure 3-4).

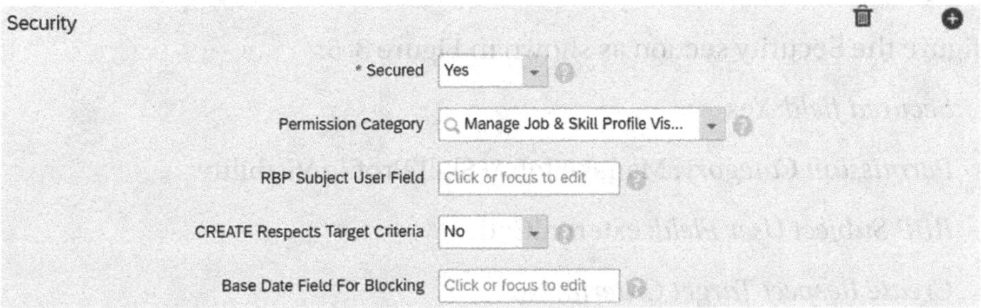

Security

* Secured | Yes

Permission Category | Q Manage Job & Skill Profile Vis...

RBP Subject User Field | Click or focus to edit

CREATE Respects Target Criteria | No

Base Date Field For Blocking | Click or focus to edit

Figure 3-4. *Editing the security settings for the Job Profile object definition*

Configure the Security section as shown in Figure 3-4.

- *Secured field*: Set to Yes.
- *Permission Category*: Set to Manage Job & Skill Profile Visibility.
- *RBP Subject User Field*: Leave it empty.
- *Create Respect Target Criteria*: Set to No.

Click Save to save your settings.

Setting Up Visibility: Skill Profile

We need to edit the Skill Profile object definition to configure the visibility settings. Go to the Admin Center and click Configure Object Definitions.

On the displayed screen, in the first search box, select Object Definition. Then in the adjoining search box, enter **Skill Profile**.

The object definition of Skill Profile is displayed. Click Take Action ➤ Make Correction. This will enable you to edit the object definition. Scroll down the page to the Security section (see Figure 3-5).

Figure 3-5. *Editing the security settings for Skill Profile object definition*

Configure the Security section as shown in Figure 3-5:

- *Secured field*: Yes

- *Permission Category*: Manage Job & Skill Profile Visibility

- *RBP Subject User Field*: externalCode

- *Create Respect Target Criteria*: No

Click Save to save your settings.

Setting Up Visibility: Rated Skills

We need to edit the Rated Skills object definition to configure the visibility settings. Go to the Admin Center and click Configure Object Definitions.

On the displayed screen, in the first search box select Object Definition. Then in the adjoining search box, enter **Rated Skills**.

The object definition of Rated Skills is displayed. Click Take Action ➤ Make Correction. This will enable you to edit the object definition. Scroll down the page to the Security section (see Figure 3-6).

Configure the Security section as shown in Figure 3-6.

- *Secured field*: Yes

- *Permission Category*: Manage Job & Skill Profile Visibility

- *RBP Subject User Field*: external Code

- *Create Respect Target Criteria*: No

Click Save to save your settings.

Figure 3-6. *Editing the security settings for Rated Skills*

Configuring Role-Based Permissions

You are required to grant the permissions shown in Table 3-1 to the roles that require access to the JPB.

Table 3-1. *Permissions for the JPB*

RBP Permission Option	Permissions
General User Permission	Select User Login. Select Live Profile Access.
Metadata Framework	Select All. Note: Select All will select all the permissions available under the Metadata Framework option.
Manage Job Profile Builder	Select All. Note: This permission grants access to managing the job profile and job profile content, as well as importing and exporting the job profile content.

(continued)

Table 3-1. (*continued*)

RBP Permission Option	Permissions
Manage Job & Skill Profile Visibility	Scroll to these permission: Job Profile: Select View, Edit, and Import/Export. JobReqJobProfile: Select View, Edit, and Import/Export. Skill Profile: Select View, Edit, and Import/Export.
Manage Job & Skill Profile Visibility	Skill Profile.Rated Skills (Rated Skills): Select View, Correct, Create, Adjust Order, Delete, and Import/Export. Note: This permission will be visible only if the Skill Profile object is enabled.

Click Done to save your changes.

Figure 3-7 shows the permissions settings that need to be configured to grant view/edit permissions to the Job Profile object.

Figure 3-7. *Configuring RBP for the JPB*

Note   Field Level Overrides provides two options: No Access and Read Only. If a particular role should not have read or should have no access to a specific field in that object, then you can use Field Level Overrides and assign the specific permission.

Job Profile Builder Content

In Table 3-2, we will review the job profile content types.

Table 3-2. *Profile Content Types*

Content Type	Description	JPB Object
Families	Jobs that involve similar types of work can be grouped into families. Typically jobs in a family will require similar types of competencies, skills, and training. Examples: Human Resources (HR), Accounting, etc.	Set Up Families & Roles
Roles	An expected behavior and skills associated with a specific position. In the JPB, a role can be associated with a job code, job classification, family, and position. Example: Accountant.	Set Up Families & Roles
Competency Types	Competency Types helps to organize competencies into different categories. Examples: All competencies tied to the Accountant role can be categorized as Competency Type Accounting. A competency can be assigned to multiple competency types.	Competency Types
Competency	A competency is a defined set of behaviors. Competencies help organizations and employees to identify and evaluate competency gaps that need to be developed. Competencies also help organization and employees to identify competencies that an employee excels in. An employee needs to possess and have experience in the identified set competencies defined for a role. Example: A competency called Accepting Responsibility might have the behavior "Takes accountability for delivering on commitments; demonstrates ownership for tasks and objectives; does not make excuses for poor performance or try to place the blame on others" associated to it. Hence, if the competency Accepting Responsibility is associated to a role, we will expect the employees to demonstrate the behavior "Takes Accountability and Ownership for the tasks they are required to deliver."	Competency

(continued)

Table 3-2. (*continued*)

Content Type	Description	JPB Object
Behaviors	This is a defined set of qualities that a role requires. Examples: The Human Resources Business Partner (HRBP) role might require a competency called Good Listener that might have the associated behavior Empathy. A competency can have multiple behaviors associated to it. A behavior can be associated to multiple competencies.	Assign Behaviors
Skill	Skills are a combination of knowledge and experience required for a job. Employees can develop these skills through experience, learning, mentoring, and shadowing of experienced personnel. Note: A skill is assessed by the proficiency level. Examples: System Design is a skill required for the role of Systems Analyst. The employee can develop this skill from education, experience (from past jobs), learning (through organization-provided learning courses), as well as by shadowing an experienced colleague. System Design is a required skill for the job of Systems Analyst. To be a lead systems analyst, you will need to have a proficiency level of 5 (5/5), while a junior systems analyst requires a proficiency level of 3 only.	Skill
Job Responsibility	Job responsibilities are a listing of tasks, duties, and responsibilities assigned to a job position. Example: As an HR Business Partner (HRBP), your job responsibilities will include maintaining an employee's personnel record in the computer system.	Job Responsibility
Relevant Industry	This is a listing of industries. Certain jobs might require specific industry experience. This listing can be tied to such specific jobs. Example: Systems design of a manufacturing process is different from systems design of an HRIS business process. Hence, the role of a System Analyst might require experience in a manufacturing company.	Relevant Industry

(*continued*)

Table 3-2. (*continued*)

Content Type	Description	JPB Object
Employment Condition	This is a listing of conditions required for employment. These employment conditions can be generic, as well as employment conditions tied to a particular job. Example: A generic employment condition might include business hours in a workday. A specific employment condition might be the requirement to work alternate Saturdays.	Employment Condition
Education – Degree	This is a listing of education levels. Some jobs might require a specific degree level. A listing of degrees might include the following: Finished School, Bachelor's Degree, Master's, Doctorate etc. Example: The position of a scientist in a pharma company might require the employee to have a doctorate degree.	Education – Degree
Education – Major	This is a listing of subjects that were studied while pursuing a degree. A listing of majors might include content such as the following: International Business, Artificial Intelligence, Organic Chemistry etc. Example: The role of Scientist in a pharma company might require the employee to have a doctorate degree in organic chemistry.	Education – Major
Physical Requirement	This is a listing of physical requirements, required to perform a job. Example: A warehouse worker might be required to lift objects up to 20 pounds frequently.	Physical Requirement
Certification	This refers to a listing of assessments by an external agency or a qualification gained by education. Example: A SuccessFactors consultant should be Associate Certified in SuccessFactors Recruiting.	Certification
Interview Question	This is a listing of questions maintained in the system. These questions can be generic or specific to a particular role. Examples: A generic question could be "Are you authorized to work in the United States?" A role-specific question could be, "How many SuccessFactors implementations have you done?"	Interview Question

With this introduction to the JPB, we will start reviewing the configuration of individual content types.

Family

A family is the foundational type of content in the JPB. All other content is built on top of family content or related to family content. In this section, we will review how to build a family in the JPB.

Creating Families Using SuccessStore

We can create families in SAP SuccessFactors by downloading the delivered content from SuccessStore.

Note   It is a best practice to leverage the content available in SuccessStore. If you want, you can also build families and roles by manually building the required content.

Go to the Admin Center and click Manage Job Profile Content. On the displayed page, click the drop-down Select Content Type and select Set Up Families and Roles. On the displayed page, click Add Families from SuccessStore. This will display the Manage SuccessStore Skill Content config page.

Note   The config page Manage Job Profile Content contains two tabs: Families and Roles. Ensure you are on the Families tab. See Figure 3-8.

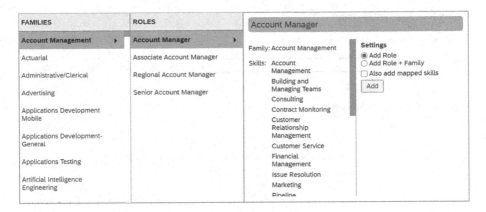

Figure 3-8. *Manage SuccessStore Skill Content page*

On the displayed page, select the family you want to add. This will display all the roles associated with that family. Select the role you want to add. This will display all the skills associated with that role. The options pane provides you with the options Add Role and Add Role + Family. It also has the option "Also add map skills." Click Add to add your selection. Click "I'm done" when you no longer want to add more families. This will take you back to the config page Manage Job Profile Content. On the page Manage Job Profile Content, you will see the new family that you added from SuccessStore.

Creating Families from the UI

You can create families manually from the UI. Go to the config page Manage Job Profile Content by going to the Admin Center and clicking Manage Job Profile Content. On the displayed page, click the drop-down Select Content Type and select Set Up Families and Roles. On the displayed page, click Create Family.

On the next displayed page (see Figure 3-9), enter the name of the family you are creating. (This is a required field.)

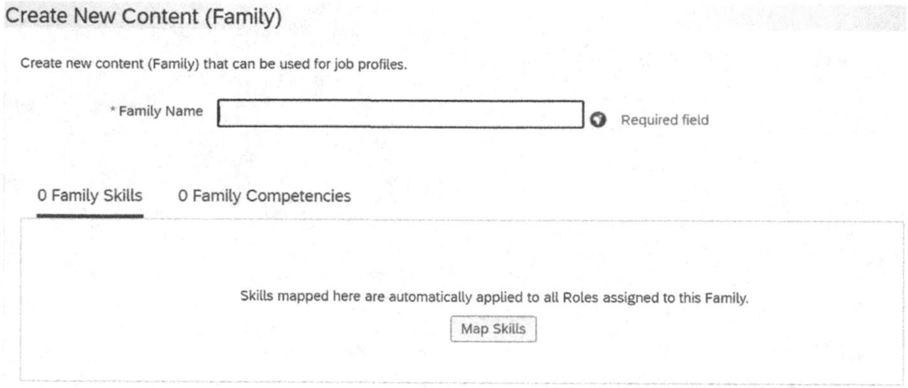

Create New Content (Family)

Create new content (Family) that can be used for job profiles.

* Family Name [   ] ⓘ Required field

0 Family Skills   0 Family Competencies

Skills mapped here are automatically applied to all Roles assigned to this Family.

Map Skills

***Figure 3-9.** Creating a family in the UI*

Click Map Skills to map some skills to the newly created family. On the displayed page (see Figure 3-10), in the drop-down select Unassigned Skills Browsed by Category.

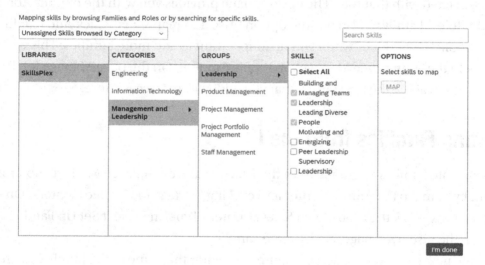

***Figure 3-10.** Mapping skills to a family by selecting Unassigned Skills Browsed by Category*

1. Click the displayed library. This will display the available categories.

2. Select the category you are interested in. This will display groups belonging to the selected category.

3. Select the group you are interested in. This will display skills available to the selected group.

4. Select the skills you are interested in. If you want to map the selected skills to a role, click Map displayed in the options pane.

5. Click "I'm Done" to finish.

This will take you back to the config page Create New Content (Family). You will see the newly added skills are added to the family.

You can add proficiency levels to the newly added skills (see Figure 3-11). Click the drop-down in the Proficiency Level column and select the proficiency level for each skill. Adding a proficiency level to each skill will help managers to assess the proficiency level of their employees against the desired proficiency level of the job. Also, employees can identify any proficiency gap and can attend training programs to fill in the identified proficiency gap.

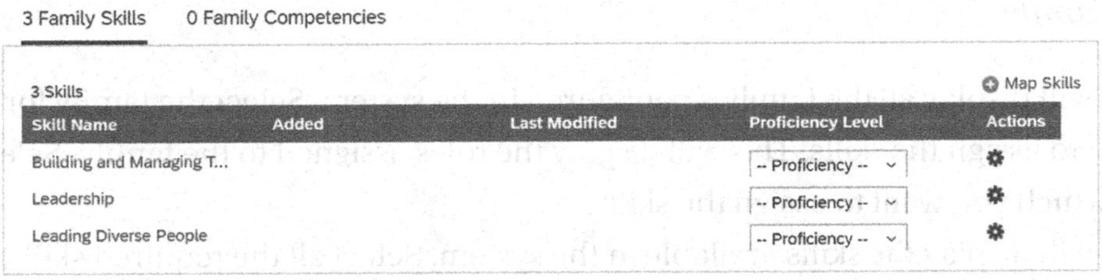

3 Family Skills	0 Family Competencies			
3 Skills				⊕ Map Skills
Skill Name	**Added**	**Last Modified**	**Proficiency Level**	**Actions**
Building and Managing T...			-- Proficiency -- ∨	⚙
Leadership			-- Proficiency -- ∨	⚙
Leading Diverse People			-- Proficiency -- ∨	⚙

Figure 3-11. *Adding proficiencies to newly added skills*

Note   We will cover the skills portlet later in this chapter.

We can also map skills to a family by selecting the option Family-based Skills Browsed by Job Family.

Specifically, to map skills to a family, click the family for which you want to map skills. The roles assigned to the family will be displayed. On the displayed page, click the option Mapped Skills. On the next displayed page, you will see the option Map Skills. On the displayed page, select the option Family-based Skills Browsed by Job Family from the drop-down (see Figure 3-12).

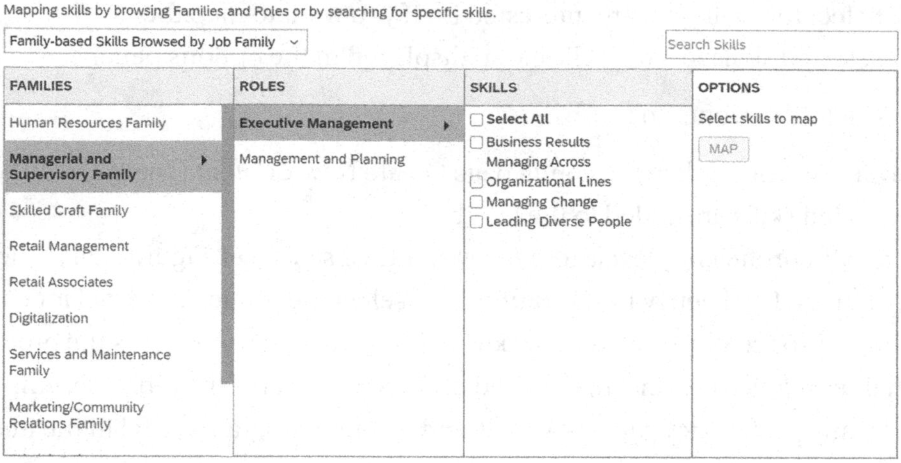

Mapping skills by browsing Families and Roles or by searching for specific skills.

| Family-based Skills Browsed by Job Family ▾ | | | Search Skills |

FAMILIES	ROLES	SKILLS	OPTIONS
Human Resources Family	**Executive Management** ▶	☐ Select All	Select skills to map
Managerial and Supervisory Family ▶	Management and Planning	☐ Business Results Managing Across	MAP
Skilled Craft Family		☐ Organizational Lines	
Retail Management		☐ Managing Change	
Retail Associates		☐ Leading Diverse People	
Digitalization			
Services and Maintenance Family			
Marketing/Community Relations Family			

Figure 3-12. *Mapping skills to a family by selecting Family-based Skills Browsed by Job Family*

This will display all the families configured in the system. Select the family for which you want to assign the skills. This will display the roles assigned to the family. Select a role for which you want to assign the skills.

This will display the skills available in the system. Select all the required skills.

Click Map. This will assign the skills to the particular role.

Click "I'm done."

This will take you to the page where skills assigned to that role and family are displayed (see Figure 3-13).

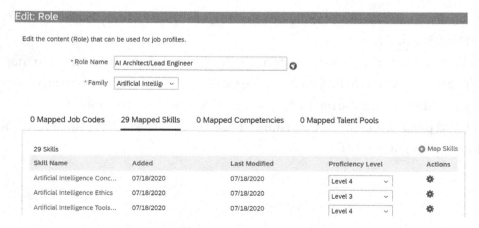

Figure 3-13. *Listing of skills assigned to family and role*

Editing Skills

On the displayed page, click any skill. The new page (see Figure 3-14) will display the content of that skill, as well as a description of the assigned proficiencies.

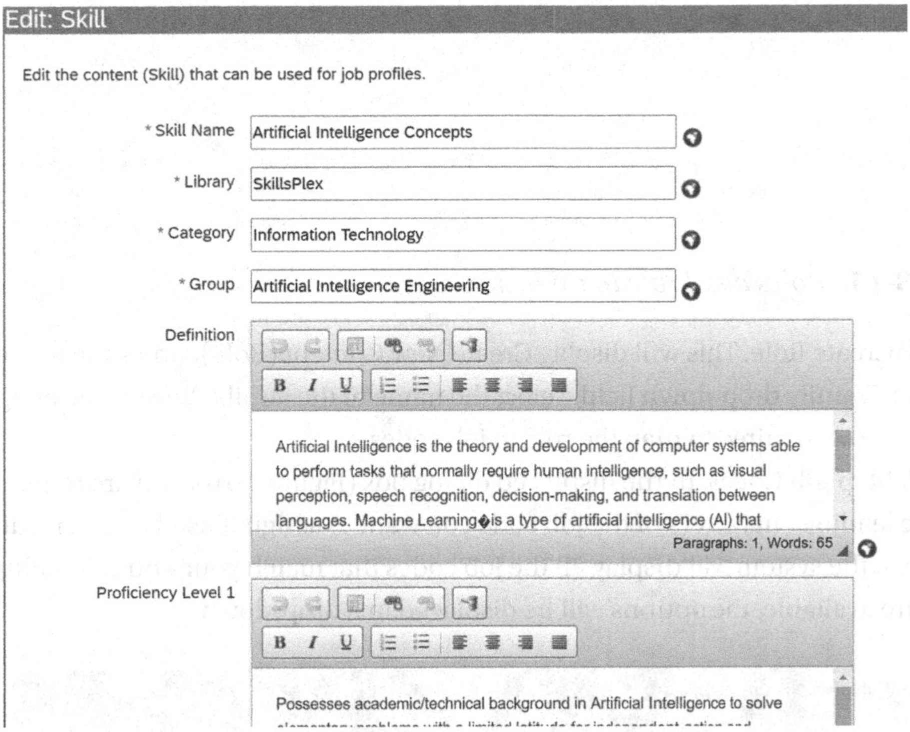

Figure 3-14. *Editing the contents of a skill*

A customer typically purchases third-party tools for skill content and descriptions of the proficiencies. Often, customers want to edit the content to align with the enterprise's culture, as well as the nature of their business. Other times, while importing the content, foreign characters (such as &◆, as shown in Figure 3-14) might get imported, so we have to edit the content to remove them. As the enterprise get familiar with the utility of the JPB and the value-add it brings, the customer might even want to change the category of the skills. You can make such edits on the Edit: Skill page.

Roles

Creating roles in the system is similar to creating families. Go to the Admin Center and click Manage Job Profile Content. On the displayed page, click the Roles tab. The different roles in the system and the family they are assigned to are displayed in the page (see Figure 3-15).

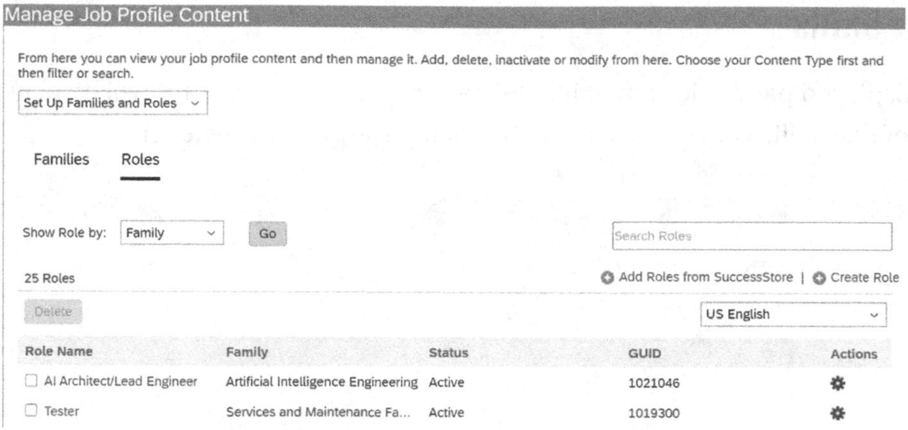

Figure 3-15. *Roles available in an instance*

Click Create Role. This will display Create New Content (Role). Enter the name of the role. In the Family drop-down field, select the name of the family they will be assigned to. We are now required to map the role to job codes.

Click Map Job Codes. In the displayed dialog box (Figure 3-16), you are required to enter the leading characters of the job code you want to assign. Based on the leading characters, the system will display all the job codes that match your entry. If multiple entries are available, the options will be displayed in a drop-down.

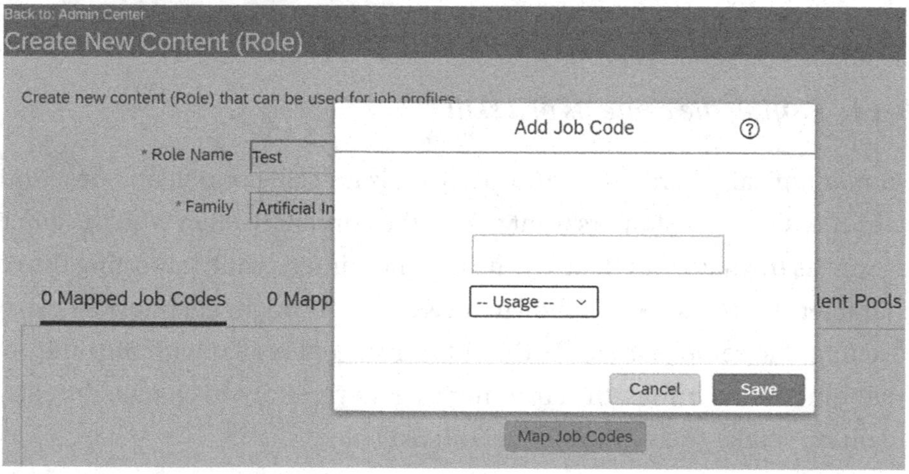

Figure 3-16. *Adding job codes to roles*

After selecting the job code, you are required to select the usage. The available options are Default and Succession. Click Save to add the job code.

If you want to add more job codes, click Add Job Code.

Click Create Role to complete the setup.

If you have Employee Central in your landscape, refer to KBA 2832345, "Difference between mapping a Job Code or Classification to a Role when using JDM or JPB - Employee Profile," to learn how to configure the JPB.

The Manage Job Profile Content page is displayed with the newly created role.

Note   You can add skills, competencies, and talent pools to the newly created role by clicking the respective tabs. The process is similar to adding job codes to the role. When you map the competency, the behaviors and competency type associated to that competency are also mapped to the family. Do note that when you map a talent pool to a role, it is a prerequisite that a talent pool already exists in the system. The process to create a talent pool is similar to creating a competency type, which is discussed later in this chapter.

2) You can create roles using SuccessStore. The process is similar to creating a family using SuccessStore.

Skills

The process of creating a skill in the UI and in SuccessStore is similar to what we discussed for creating a family.

We discussed earlier how to edit the content of a skill, as well as assign proficiencies to a skill and edit the proficiencies assigned to a skill.

Tip   If you have a portlet for skills in the People Profile (see Figure 3-17), you can view the skills assigned to that role.

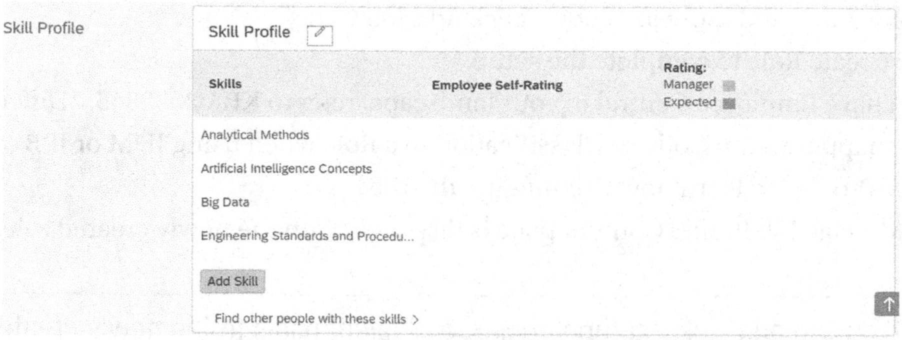

Figure 3-17. Skills portlet in the People Profile

If an employee has the correct permission, they can add skills, as well do a self-rating. The manager's rating is also visible, as well as the expected rating of that skill. This view greatly helps the employee to understand if there are any proficiency gaps in the assigned skills. Understanding the proficiency and the gaps greatly helps the employee with their learning plans. When you click the link "Find other people with these skills," you are returned to the search results of employees who are assigned similar skills. This greatly enhances the employee experience to socialize with their peers and learn from each other's experience.

Competencies and Competency Type

Competency is the ability of an employee to perform a task. Competencies includes identified/defined sets of behaviors and competency types. Competency types are categories of your competencies in the system and can be maintained independently. Assigning competencies to a job code enables organizations to identify competencies that need to be developed for their employees, enables supervisors to identify competencies that need to be invested in, and helps employees to identify competency gaps that need to be filled.

In this section, we will discuss how to create and maintain competencies and competency types in SuccessFactors.

If you have Employee Central in your landscape, refer to KBA 2080013, "How to Manage Families & Roles and Competency Mappings - SuccessFactors Employee Central," for reference.

Note   It is a best practice to leverage the content available in SuccessStore. Or you can create competencies and competency types by manually building the required content.

Competency Type

In SuccessFactors, you can create and maintain competency types in the Manage Data config step. Competency types can also be mass imported into the system from the config step Import and Export Data.

We can create a competency type manually by going to the Admin Center and clicking Manage Data. On the displayed page, for the Create New field, select Competency Type. In Competency Type (see Figure 3-18), enter the name of the competency type. Click Save to save your entry.

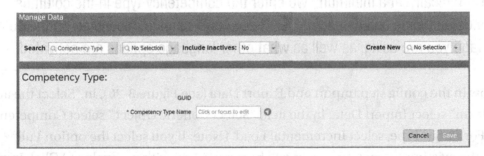

Figure 3-18. Creating a competency type

Note   The GUID is a unique ID and is autogenerated by the system. No configuration is required for a GUID. A GUID will be generated after you have saved the new competency type.

To maintain an existing competency type in Manage Data, in the search box enter **Competency Type**. In the next field, select the competency type you want to maintain. You can change the Competency Type Name field and click Save to save your entries.

Mass Create Competency Type

You can create new competency types by importing the data to the system. Specifically, you can import by going to the Admin Center and clicking Import and Export Data. On the displayed page, in the field "Select the action to perform," select the option "Download template." In the field Select Generic Object, select Competency Type. In the field "Include dependencies," select No. Click Download.

In the template (see Figure 3-19), enter the name of the competency type. You are not required to enter a GUID. Leave column A blank.

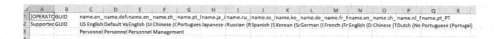

Figure 3-19. *Importing the Competency Type template*

Note   Typically, at a minimum, we enter the competency type in the columns name.defaultValue and name.en_US. These could change depending on the default language you are using, as well as what other language options are activated.

Now in the config step Import and Export Data (see Figure 3-20), in "Select the action to perform" select Import Data. In the field "Select Generic Object," select Competency Type. For Purge Type, select Incremental Load. (Note: If you select the option Full Purge, the existing competency types will be overwritten with new values.) Click Import to import your data. (Note: You can click Validate if you want to validate whether the template is in the correct format. If the validation fails, you can identify what is causing the error, make corrections, and try again.)

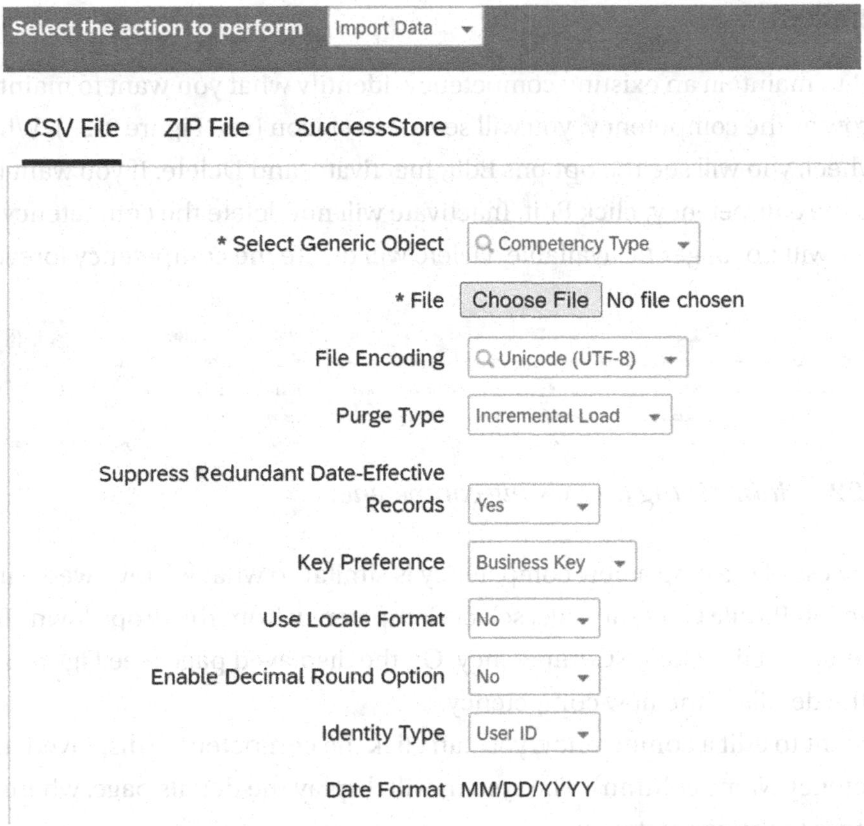

Select the action to perform	Import Data ▼

CSV File   ZIP File   SuccessStore

* Select Generic Object	🔍 Competency Type ▼
* File	Choose File No file chosen
File Encoding	🔍 Unicode (UTF-8) ▼
Purge Type	Incremental Load ▼
Suppress Redundant Date-Effective Records	Yes ▼
Key Preference	Business Key ▼
Use Locale Format	No ▼
Enable Decimal Round Option	No ▼
Identity Type	User ID ▼
Date Format	MM/DD/YYYY

Figure 3-20. *Importing a competency type*

In the config step Monitor Jobs, you can monitor whether the data is imported or whether there are any errors (see Figure 3-21). You can access Monitor Job by going to the Admin Center and clicking Monitor Job. In Monitor Job, if you scroll to the right in the column Job Details, you can see how many records were in the data import template and how many were processed. The column Download Status provides a hyperlink to download the results of the job. The downloaded file will contain error details (if there are any) displayed next to the errored record.

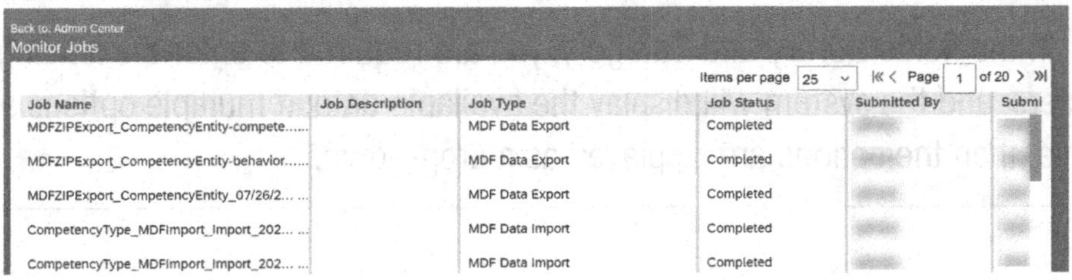

Back to: Admin Center
Monitor Jobs

			Items per page 25 ▼	I< < Page 1 of 20 > >I	
Job Name	**Job Description**	**Job Type**	**Job Status**	**Submitted By**	**Submi**
MDFZIPExport_CompetencyEntity-compete......		MDF Data Export	Completed		
MDFZIPExport_CompetencyEntity-behavior......		MDF Data Export	Completed		
MDFZIPExport_CompetencyEntity_07/26/2... ...		MDF Data Export	Completed		
CompetencyType_MDFImport_Import_202... ...		MDF Data Import	Completed		
CompetencyType_MDFImport_Import_202... ...		MDF Data Import	Completed		

Figure 3-21. *Monitor Jobs screen*

Competencies

If you want to maintain an existing competency, identify what you want to maintain. In the same row as the competency, you will see a wheel icon (see Figure 3-22). When you click the wheel, you will see the options Edit, Inactivate, and Delete. If you want to make changes to the competency, click Edit. Inactivate will not delete the competency, but the competency will no longer be available. Delete will delete the competency forever.

Competency Name	Library	Category	Competency Typ...	Status	GUID	Competenc...	Actio...
☐ Design Architecture	SuccessFactors 2.1 C...	Problem Solving	Project Management	Active	1021118	19903	⚙
☐ Design Engineer	SuccessFactors 2.1 C...	Problem Solving	Personnel Manage...	Active	1021115	19901	Edit
☐ Accepting Direction	SuccessFactors 2.1 C...	SuccessFactors ...	Personnel Manage...	Active	1000030	14349	Inactivate
☐ Inspiring and Motiv	SuccessFactors 2.1 C	SuccessFactors		Active	1000011	14310	Delete

Figure 3-22. *Maintaining an existing competency*

The process of creating a new competency is similar to what we reviewed earlier. On the Manage Job Profile Content page, select Competency from the drop-down. To add a new competency, click Create Competency. On the displayed page (see Figure 3-23), you can enter the details of the new competency.

If you want to edit a competency, you can click the competency (displayed under the Competency Name column). The system will display the details page, where you can make changes to the competency.

When a competency is associated with a job profile, the competency will continue to appear even if you inactivate the competency. If you do not want to use the particular competency and do not want the competency to appear in a job profile, then you need to delete the competency.

On the Edit Competency page (see Figure 3-23), enter the name of the competency and the library and category you want to assign it to. In the Description field, enter the description of the competency. You can select whether the competency is a core competency or not.

Note   In the fields Library and Category, you are required to enter the leading characters, and the system will display the available data. If multiple options are available, then the options are displayed as a drop-down.

After entering the details of the competency, you can define the behaviors for the competency. In the Behaviors section, click Assign Behaviors. In the displayed dialog box, enter the name of the behavior and provide a description. Click OK to save your entries. After the behavior is saved, the system will generate a GUID for the behavior.

Scroll down the page, and in the Competency Type section, you can assign the competency to a competency type. You can assign multiple competency types to a competency. When a competency is assigned to multiple competency types, then on the Manage Job Profile Content (Competency) page, in the Competency Type column, you will notice the first competency type is displayed followed by a hyperlinked plus (+) sign. The plus sign will display the number of additional competency types that are assigned to this competency. Hovering over the + sign will display the assigned competency types.

Note   As a prerequisite, a competency type should be configured in the system and available to assign a competency to a competency type.

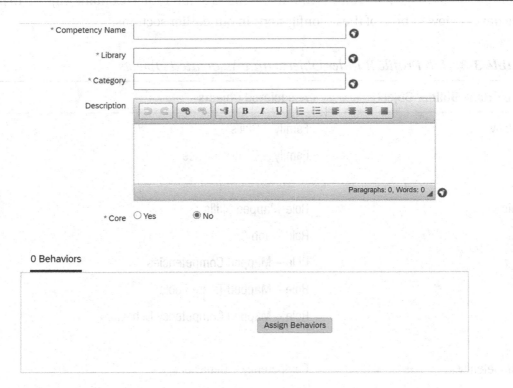

Figure 3-23.   *Creating a new competency*

Tip   You can create new competencies by importing and exporting data (review the section on competency types where we discussed this functionality). We suggest you do this as an exercise on your own: create new competencies and then associate the new competencies to behaviors and competency types.

Note   The process to create content for other JPB objects is similar to what we have discussed so far. We suggest you create the content for other JPB objects as an exercise and become familiar with the process.

Job Profile Object Dependencies

In Table 3-3, we have listed the Job Profile object types and the other Job Profile Builder objects that can be associated with a job profile. You can build the associations in the config steps Manage Job Profile Content and Manage Job Profile Content Import/Export. We have reviewed both of these config steps in our earlier sections.

Table 3-3. Job Profile Builder Objects and Associated Objects

Job Profile Builder Object	Associated Objects
Family	Family – Skills
	Family – Competencies
Role	Role-Mapped Skills
	Role – Job Code
	Role – Mapped Competencies
	Role – Mapped Talent Pools
	Role – Mapped Competency Behaviors
Competency	Competency – Behaviors
	Competency – Competency Types

(*continued*)

Table 3-3. (*continued*)

Job Profile Builder Object	Associated Objects
Education	Education – Degree
	Education – Major
Job Profile	Job Profile – Headers
	Job Profile – Certifications
	Job Profile – Physical Requirements
	Job Profile – Relevant Industries
	Job Profile – Degrees
	Job Profile – Employment Conditions
	Job Profile – Short Descriptions
	Job Profile – Competencies
	Job Profile – Major
	Job Profile – Compensation Data
	Job Profile – Skills
	Job Profile – Long Descriptions
	Job Profile – Footers
	Job Profile – Job Responsibilities
	Job Profile – Interview Questions
Job Template	Job Template – Associated Families
	Job Template – Sections

Manage Job Profile Content Import/Export

We can mass create the content for different Job Profile Builder objects by importing them into the system. You can also export the content of different JPB objects from the same config step. To access the config, go to the Admin Center and click Manage Job Profile Contents Import/Export (see Figure 3-24).

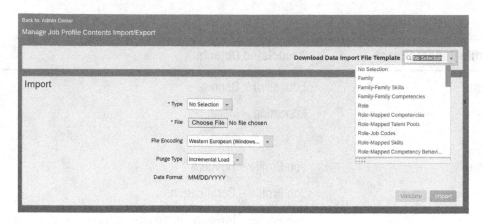

Figure 3-24. *Manage Job Profile Contents Import/Export page*

On the displayed page, in the field Download Data Import File Template, you can download the template for which you want to import content. For our review, we will download the template for the object Role-Mapped Talent Pools and import data for this object.

Note   The Job Profile Builder objects listed in the Download Data Import File Template drop-down are reviewed in the section "Job Profile Object Dependencies."

When you select an object for download, you will have the option to download the template with data or download an empty template. As shown in Figure 3-25, if you select Yes, the template is downloaded with data. Selecting No will download an empty template. If you are new to the JPB configuration, we suggest you download the template with data. You can review how the data is built and use it as a reference when you are filling the template with data. (Note: Remember to delete the downloaded data from the template prior to importing the data.)

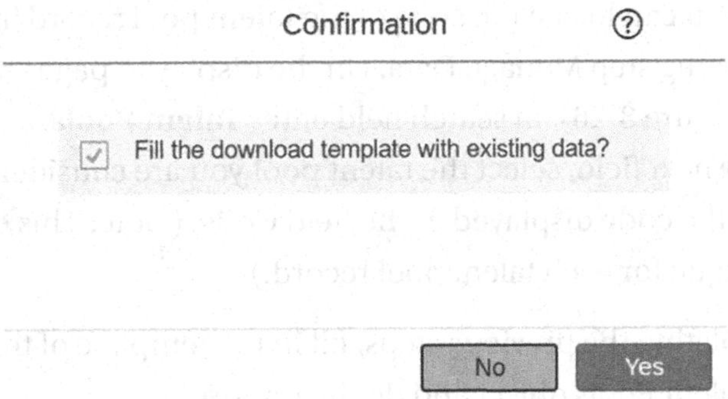

Confirmation   ⑦

☑ Fill the download template with existing data?

No   Yes

Figure 3-25. *Downloading the template*

Note   If you are downloading the template with data, then you need to download the template from the config step Monitor Job. If it is just an empty template, the system will download the template in the config step Manage Job Profile Content Import/Export.

Since JPB objects are based on the MDF, you can have associations between different JPB objects, as well have a parent-children relationship between JPB objects of the same type. Hence, if you are building such associations, it is important that you copy the GUID of the object record you are planning to associate.

As mentioned earlier, for our discussion we are going to import data for the object Role-Mapped Talent Pools. Prior to importing this data, we should review whether the talent pools we are planning to associate the object with exist in the system. If they do not, we need to create those those templates.

Hence, the process for importing data for the object Role-Mapped Talent Pools will be as follows:

1. Create the talent pools.

    a. We discussed earlier that talent pools are created in the config step Manage Data, and to import/export talent pools, we execute the config step Import and Export Data.

    b. After creating the talent pools, we need to note the code of the newly created talent pool. This is needed, since we are associating a role with talent pools.

i. Tip: You can locate the code of the talent pool record in the config step Manage Data. On the displayed page (see Figure 3-26), in search field enter **Talent Pools**. In the next field, select the talent pool you are considering. Note the code displayed in the field Code. (Note: This code is unique for each talent pool record.)

2. After completing the previous steps, fill in the template of the Role-Mapped Talent Pools object and do the import.

3. Verify the import completed successfully.

Figure 3-26. *Talent pool data as viewed in the config step Manage Data*

Job Profile Template

We can use job profile templates to provide a consistent look and feel to the job profiles configured in the system. Job profile templates typically contain sections. You can define which of these sections are required and also define the order that they are displayed in the sections. You can assign a job profile template to a single job family or to multiple job families.

In this section, we will discuss job profile templates, how to configure job profile templates, and how to assign them to job families.

Note   You can have more than one job profile template configured in an instance. You can use one job profile template for all roles in the system or assign different job profile templates for different roles. For example, you can have a job profile template for roles identified as Individual Contributor, a different job profile template for roles defined as Managers, and another job profile for roles defined as Executives.

Configure Job Profile Template

To configure a new job profile template, go to the Admin Center and click Manage Job Profile Templates.

On the displayed page (see Figure 3-27), click Create Template.

Job Profile Templates

Create and manage your job profile templates.

You currently have 2 templates.   Create Template

				US English			∨
Name	**Created On**	**Last Modified ▼**	**Job Families**	**Job Profiles**	**Status**	**Actions**	
Standard Template	Id 2015-09-03 ...	2017-12-15 20:...	Digitalization; Skilled Craft Family; ...	19	Active	✿	
Retail	Id 2017-02-23 ...	2017-05-26 15:...	Retail Associates; Retail Management	7	Active	✿	

Figure 3-27. Managing job profile templates

Tip   If there are existing job profile templates in the system, you have an option to create a new job profile template by copying the existing job profile template. To copy an existing template, click the wheel icon (the wheel icon is displayed in the Actions column) for an existing template. You will see the options Edit, Copy, and Delete. Click Copy to copy the template.

On the displayed page, enter the name of the template. You can add job families that you want to associate to this job profile template. Click Next.

As discussed earlier, a job profile template consists of a section. Each section will contain the data of that job's particular job profile object. Click Add Section to display the different sections that can be added to a job profile template (see Figure 3-28).

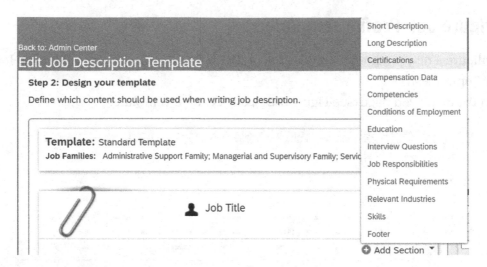

Figure 3-28. *Adding a section to a job profile template*

For our job profile template, we will add sections called Long Description, Short Description, Competencies, Skills, Education, and Interview Questions.

Tip   We can rename the delivered job profile objects to any title that is aligned to our business needs. For example, the Long Description section can be renamed to Job Description, and Short Description can be renamed to Job Summary. To rename a section, click it. The section title is now available for edit. Enter the title you want to use and click "I'm done."

In addition, you can order the sections in a job profile template by dragging and dropping the section to the appropriate place in the job profile template.

You can continue to configure the job profile template (see Figure 3-29).

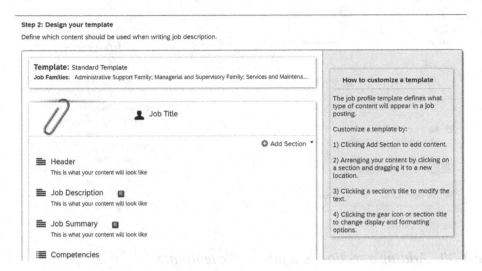

Figure 3-29. *Configuring the job profile template*

When you click a section (see Figure 3-30), the section options are displayed on the right of the section.

The following are the section options that are available:

- *Make this a required section*: If you check this option, then that section is a required section in the job profile template.

Note   When you make a section required, a red *R* is displayed in that section.

- *Section visible to Admins only*: You can make the section visible to the JPB admin only, when they receive job profile acknowledgments.

- *Show in Job Requisition*: Job profile templates can be integrated with SuccessFactors Recruiting. When the integration is configured, checking this section will make the section visible (available) in job requisitions so that resources such as recruiters can see them.

- *Show in external posting*: Checking this option will make the section published in external job postings so that external candidates will see the role requirements formatted according to the template.

- *Show in internal posting*: Checking this option will make the section published in internal job postings so that internal candidates will see the role requirements formatted according to the template.

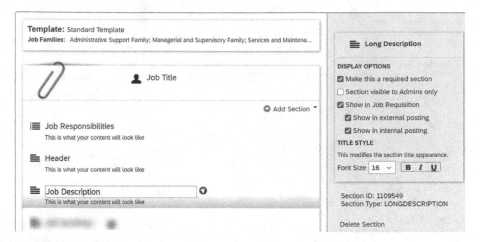

Figure 3-30. Adding a section to a job profile template

Note   When a section is marked as visible to admins only, that section cannot be displayed in job requisitions. Hence, the option Show in Job Requisition will not be available for selection.

You also have options to configure the font style and the different font options (bold, underline, and italics).

Tip   A best practice is to make the font style uniform for all sections in the job profile template.

Now that you understand this background information, we will now discuss job profiles and how to configure job profiles in the system.

Job Profile

The following are the prerequisites to configuring job profiles in the system:

- The content for JPB objects should be available in the system.

- A job profile template is configured and available in the system.

To set up a job profile in the system, go to the Admin Center and click Manage Job Profile.

On the displayed page (see Figure 3-31), you can see the job profiles that are configured and available in the system. You can also filter the job profiles based on the family, roles, or positions they are assigned to.

Figure 3-31.   Managing a job profile

To create a new job profile, click Create Job Profile.

On the displayed page (see Figure 3-32), you can select the job family you want to assign.

All the roles assigned to that job family are displayed. Select the job role you want to assign.

Note   There is a one-to-one relationship between a role and a job profile. In other words, a role can be assigned to one job profile only.

All the positions assigned to that job role are displayed. You can select one or multiple job positions and assign the job profile. After assigning a position or positions to a job profile, click Next.

Create Job Profile

Select one role for your job profile.

10 Job Families	0 Job Role	0 Job Position
Administrative Support Family		
Artificial Intelligence Engineering ❶		
Digitalization		
Human Resources Family		
Managerial and Supervisory Family		
Marketing/Community Relations Family		
Retail Associates		
Retail Management		

Cancel   Next

Figure 3-32. *Creating a job profile*

The job profile template is displayed.

Before we review the sections and add content to the section, we are required to enter a title for the job profile. At top of the job profile, click the field Type Job Profile Name. Here, you are required to enter the title of the job profile. (Note: You will not be able to save your job profile if you do not enter a title.)

Note   If a job profile content (see Figure 3-33) is mapped to that role, then the mapped content is not available for any edits. You can notice that the competencies that are already mapped to this role are displayed as locked (in other words, not available for any edits).

If you want to add new content to the job profile, highlight the section title (in other words, in Figure 3-33), and click Edit. For this job profile, you can add new competencies that are available in the system.

Competencies

Delivering High Quality Work ▾ 🔒

Demonstrating Initiative ▾ 🔒

Inspiring and Motivating Others ▾ 🔒

Setting a Strategic Vision ▾ 🔒

Figure 3-33. *Section not available for edit*

For the JPB objects for which content is not mapped yet, you can add the content directly in the job profile. When you hover your mouse over section title, you will see an Add button. You can click Add to add new content.

Note   The content for the JPB objects should be configured and available in the system.

Click "I'm done" to save your content and changes. (Note: You are required to manually activate the job profile. By default, a new job profile is in Draft status.) This will take you to the configuration page Manage Job Profile. On the displayed page, locate the newly created job profile. Under the Action column, click the wheel icon. This will display the options Edit, Copy, Delete, and Activate. Click Activate to activate the newly created job profile.

Note   In the job profile, if a required section does not have content, you will not be able to activate the job profile. When you try to activate it, you will get an error message (see Figure 3-34). Click Update Job Profile to edit the job profile and to fill in the required section with content.

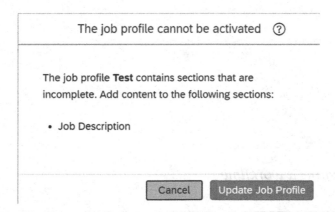

Figure 3-34. *Error message when you try to activate an incomplete job profile*

Note   SuccessFactors does not recommend purging job profile data. When you purge the job profile data, it may impact the data-to-entity mappings. It may also impact the JPB Recruiting Management data.

Job Profile Builder: Workflows

Many organizations want job profiles to be reviewed and approved before they are published. This will ensure that critical stakeholders are aware of the changes, verify whether the correct data is populated in the different sections, and ensure the changes made are aligned with what was discussed.

In this section, we will discuss how to set up workflows and how to configure the workflows to appear in the ToDo tile on the SuccessFactors home page.

Configuring Job Profile Builder Workflow

You can create a workflow by going to the Admin Center and clicking Manage Organization, Pay, and Job Structures. On the displayed page, select Workflow from Create New drop-down.

As shown in Figure 3-35, we have created a workflow called Job Profile Change.

Figure 3-35. *Creating a workflow*

> **Note** A dynamic group is a group of approvers that you have configured, based on certain criteria. When you have a dynamic group as an approver, all members of the group receive workflow approval, comment requests, and workflow completion notices.

The other options for Approver Type are Dynamic Role, Position, and Position Relationship.

To create a dynamic group, go to the Admin Center and click Manage Workflow Groups. On the displayed page (see Figure 3-36), you can click Create New Group to create a new group. You can edit an existing group by clicking the specific group name. You can also copy an existing group by clicking Clone Group.

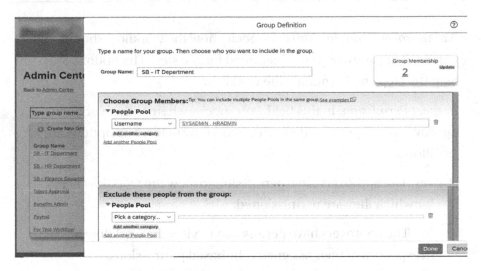

Figure 3-36. *Creating a dynamic group*

- For Approver Type, select Dynamic Group. For Approval Role, select Dynamic Group.

- For Edit Transaction, select Edit without Route Change.

Note   For the field Edit Transaction, you have these options:

- *No Edit*: Approvers cannot edit workflows that are in-flight.

- *Edit with Route Change*: Approvers can edit workflows that are in-flight. The system will automatically recalculate the workflow approval route when it is resubmitted.

- *Edit without Route Change*: Approvers can edit workflows that are in-flight. The system will not recalculate the workflow approval route when it is resubmitted.

- *Edit Attachment Only*: Approvers can edit only the attachments (if any) of the workflow.

- *No Approver Behavior*: You can specify how the workflow should behave if an approver is not identified for the step. The options are Skip the step and Terminate the workflow.

- *Respect Permission*: In this field, you specify whether the workflow approvers have permission to view workflow fields. The options are as follows:

  ✓ *Yes*: The approvers have permission to view the workflow fields for which they are permissioned.

  ✓ *No*: The approvers have permission to view the workflow fields, irrespective of their assigned role-based permissions.

Click Save to save your newly configured workflow.

Having configured the workflow for JPB, in the next section we will review how to make the workflow approval notice appear in the SuccessFactors home page's ToDo tile.

Note   You are required to have the following role-based permissions assigned to be able to set up a workflow in the system:

✓ Manage Workflow Requests

✓ Manage Workflow Groups

You also need to be assigned to a dynamic workflow group.

Job Profile Builder Workflow: Display in ToDo Tile

We will make the configuration change to the Job Profile Draft object definition. To make the change, go to the Admin Center and click Configure Object Definitions.

On the displayed page (see Figure 3-37), select Object Definition in the search box. Select Job Profile Draft from the object definitions list. Click Take Action and then Make Correction.

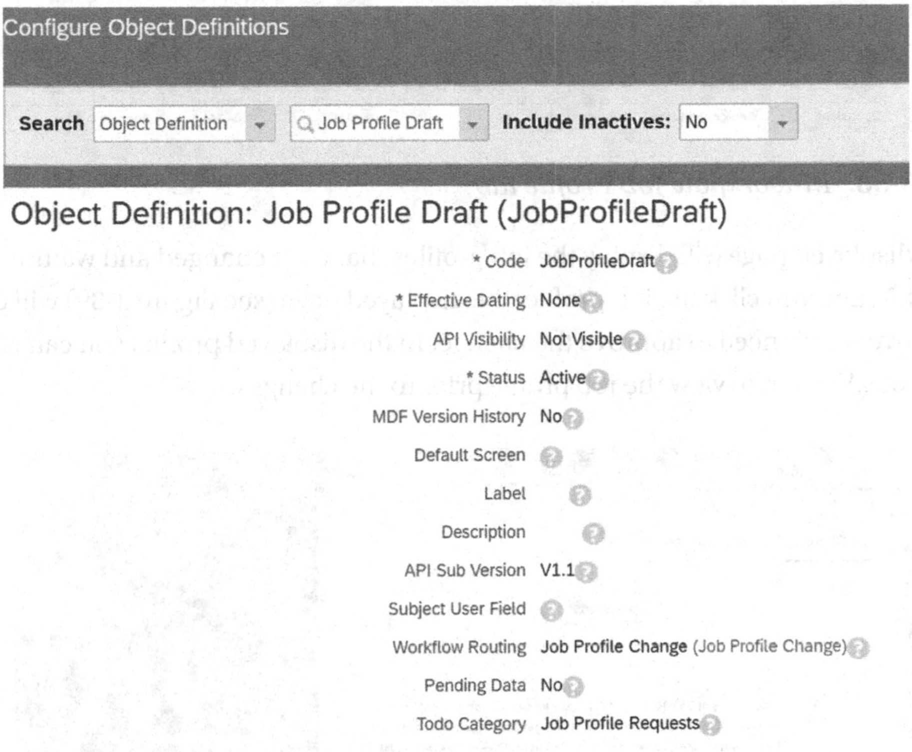

Figure 3-37. *Editing the Job Profile Draft object*

We will make the following changes to the object:

- In the field Workflow Routing, select the workflow (Job Profile Change) that we configured in the section "Configuring the Job Profile Builder Workflow."

- In the field Pending Data, select the option No.

- In the field Todo Category, select the option Job Profile Requests.

Click Save to save your changes.

To view which job profiles and workflows are in-flight, go to the config step Manage Job Profiles. On the displayed page, you will see two tabs: Job Profile and In-workflow Job Profile. To view the workflow, click the tab In-workflow Job Profile (see Figure 3-38).

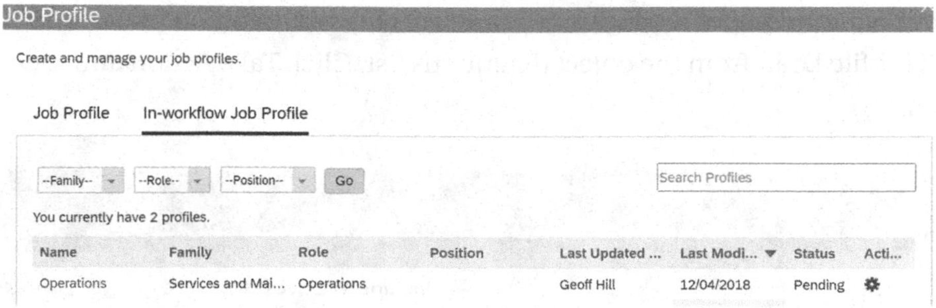

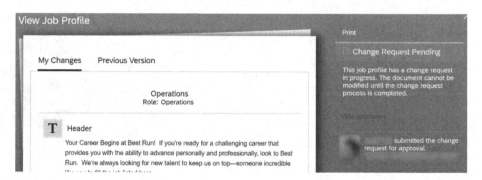

Figure 3-38. *In-workflow Job Profile tab*

The displayed page will display the job profiles that were changed and waiting for approval. When you click the job profile, the displayed page (see Figure 3-39) will display the approvers who need to approve the change. In the displayed profile, you can click the tab Previous Version to view the job profile prior to the changes.

Figure 3-39. *Job profile workflow details*

Job Profile Acknowledgement Settings

In this section, we will discuss how to configure Job Profile Acknowledgement Settings. Certain industries (typically regulated industries such as pharma, healthcare, and so on) require organizations to provide proof that their employees understand the job descriptions of the job they are assigned to. The organization is required to maintain a receipt of this information.

To configure the acknowledgment, go to the Admin Center and click Configure Job Profile Acknowledgement.

Note   If you are not able to access this config step, verify you are assigned the permission Configure Job Profile Acknowledgement Settings. The permission is available in Administrator Permissions under Manage Job Profile Builder.

On the displayed page (see Figure 3-40), you can select the job profile changes that should trigger an acknowledgment. You can trigger an acknowledgment in the following cases:

- A job profile changes

- A job code changes

- A role and job profile mapping changes

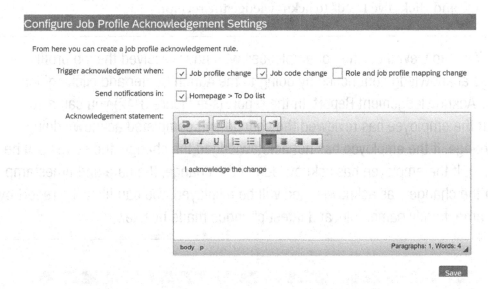

Figure 3-40.   *Configuring the job profile acknowledgment settings*

You can also configure a standard acknowledgment statement.

When you make a change to a job profile, the impacted employees will see the notification in the Job Profile Change tile, displayed in the To-Do list on the SuccessFactors home page (see Figure 3-41).

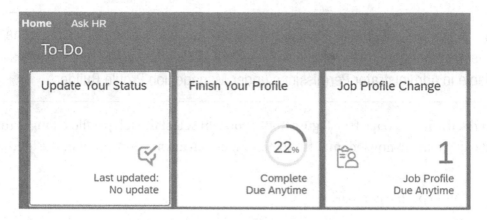

Figure 3-41. *Job Profile Change tile*

Clicking the tile will take users to an acknowledgment page, where they can review the change and click "I've Read" to acknowledge the receipt.

Tip You can view the listing of employees who have received the job profile change acknowledgment notice by going to the Admin Center and clicking Job Profile Acknowledgement Report. In the report (see Figure 3-42) you can also view if the employee has reviewed the change and completed acknowledging the change. If the employee has not acknowledged the change, the status will be Pending. If the employee has acknowledged the change, the date and timestamp when the change was acknowledged will be displayed. You can filter the report by username, family name, role, and latest changes made by user.

Job Profile Acknowledgement Report

Use this page to view the report of acknowledgements including status.

| | | | | | User's name ∨ | USER ∨ |

You currently have 39 Acknowledgements.

User	Family	Role	Job Code	Job Profile	Change Date ▼	Status / Ackno...
Gabriela Alves	Administrative Su...	Professional	50070970	Professional	Sun Aug 09 22:58...	Pending
Anja Klein	Administrative Su...	Professional	50070970	Professional	Sun Aug 09 22:58...	Pending
Martin Snow	Administrative Su...	Professional	50070970	Professional	Sun Aug 09 22:58...	Pending

Figure 3-42. *Job Profile Acknowledgement Report screen*

With this background of the JPB, we will review a case where we are required to integrate the JPB with SuccessFactors Recruiting.

Case Study

In this section, we will review a case study where we will integrate the JPB with SuccessFactors Recruiting Management (RCM).

Description

Customer A has implemented SuccessFactors Recruiting Management. During the current Job Profile Builder implementation, the customer is exploring the possibility of integrating the JPB with RCM. The company would like their consultant to walk them through which config steps need to be completed.

Solution

We will complete the configuration required to integrate Recruiting Management with the JPB.

Step 1: To integrate the JPB with Recruiting, go to the Admin Center and click Manage Recruiting Settings. On the displayed page (see Figure 3-43), scroll to the section Job Requisition. Check the option Use Job Profiles in Requisitions.

Click Save to save your settings.

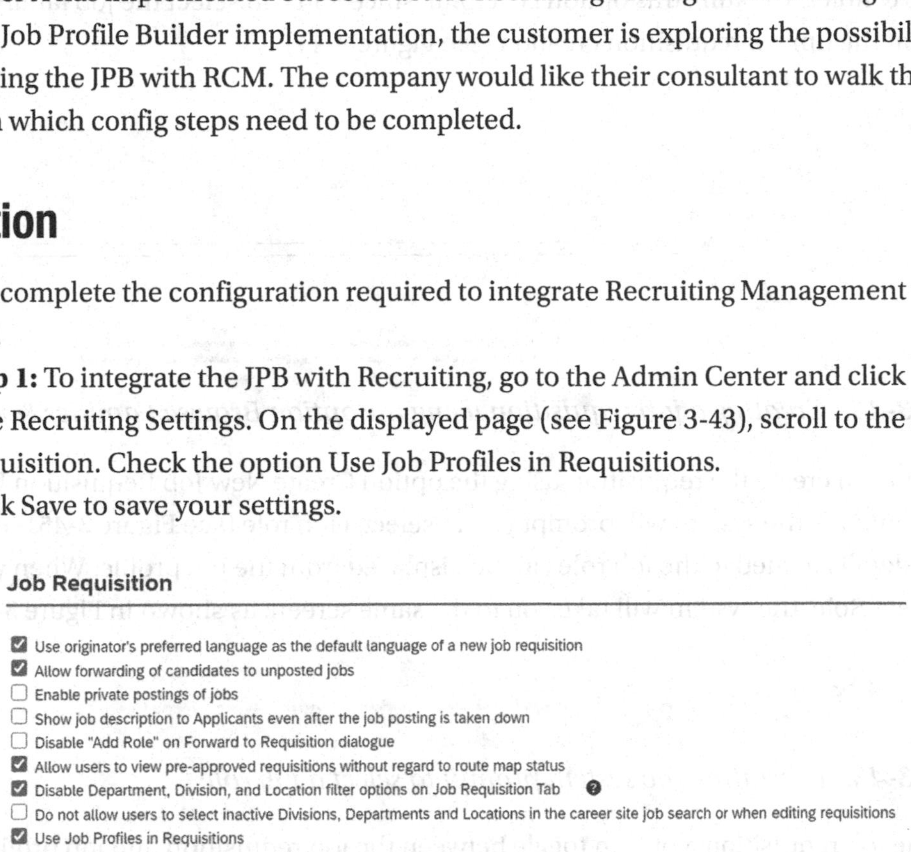

Job Requisition

- ☑ Use originator's preferred language as the default language of a new job requisition
- ☑ Allow forwarding of candidates to unposted jobs
- ☐ Enable private postings of jobs
- ☐ Show job description to Applicants even after the job posting is taken down
- ☐ Disable "Add Role" on Forward to Requisition dialogue
- ☑ Allow users to view pre-approved requisitions without regard to route map status
- ☑ Disable Department, Division, and Location filter options on Job Requisition Tab ❓
- ☐ Do not allow users to select inactive Divisions, Departments and Locations in the career site job search or when editing requisitions
- ☑ Use Job Profiles in Requisitions

Figure 3-43. *Integrating the JPB with RCM*

Step 2: Review the job profile template and verify the sections you want to integrate with the requisition. For such sections, verify you have marked the option Show in Job Requisition. You can check the options "Show in external posting" and "Show in internal posting" if you want the section to be available in job postings.

Tip   Certain sections such as Interview Questions should not be displayed in job postings, but they should be available in the job requisitions. For such sections, you need to select Show in Job Requisition but leave the options "Show in external posting" and "Show in internal posting" unchecked.

Step 3: When you create a new job requisition, you can select the option Browse Families & Roles. Creating this option is helpful, since you can select the job family and the role at the time of requisition creation (see Figure 3-44).

Figure 3-44.   *Creating a job requisition using the option Browse Families & Roles*

When you create the requisition using the option Create New Job Requisition From Blank Template, the system will prompt you to select a job role (see Figure 3-45) so the specific details related to the job role can be displayed from the job profile. When you click Select Role, the system will take you to the same screen, as shown in Figure 3-44.

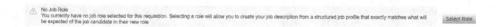

Figure 3-45.   *Recruiting the system prompt to select a job role*

In the job requisition, you can toggle between the job requisition and job profile by clicking the tab Job Profile.

If you want the recruiter or the hiring manager (or any recruiting role) to be able to edit the sections in the job profile, they need to be granted the Edit permission in JobReqJobProfile. You can locate the permission JobReqJobProfile in Administrator Permissions Manage Job & Skill Profile Visibility (see Figure 3-46).

Figure 3-46. *Granting a permission to edit a job profile in a job requisition*

Step 4: When a requisition is integrated with the JPB, if a section is available in the job profile, then that section will be visible on the Job Profile tab. Any changes you make to a job profile in a requisition are local to that requisition and not written back to the master job profile. After a requisition is created, any changes you make to a job profile are not propagated to the requisition.

Conclusion

In this chapter, we started our discussion by reviewing what the Job Profile Builder is and how it is integrated to other SuccessFactors talent modules. We reviewed the permissions that need to be granted to a user so they can access the different JPB-related configuration steps. We saw a listing of JPB content types, and later in the chapter we discussed the dependencies between JPB objects. We had a detailed discussion about how to configure the JPB content and how to import/export the content. Later in the chapter we configured a job profile template, and we used that template to configure a job profile. In the chapter, we discussed how to configure a workflow for the JPB. Toward the end of the chapter, we reviewed how an employee can review and acknowledge the job description of their assigned position. We finished the chapter by discussing how to integrate JPB with RCM.

In the next chapter, we will discuss SuccessFactors Goals Management. The chapter will be a detailed discussion of the configuration options and how an employee and the manager can set their goals.

CHAPTER 4

Basic Goal Management

Goal Management provides SAP SuccessFactors customers with an online means of setting and tracking business objectives across their organization. Furthermore, it provides the starting point for many integrated features in SAP SuccessFactors that allow companies to run smoothly and provide employees positive direction and reward. Customers can configure their goal plan template by identifying the fields used to develop and track each goal. Additionally, customers can decide if employees' goals are individual goals, team goals, and/or group goals. Whichever goal type the customer selects to include on the goal plan, the results can be updated and tracked throughout the year and even incorporated on performance forms.

The abilities of SuccessFactors Goal Management become essential to organizations attempting to execute their business strategy. To illustrate this, let's take the example of two companies. In both companies, high-level business goals are set in the boardroom and communicated to the CEO to execute. In the first company, the CEO gathers their direct reports for a meeting to share the various financial targets and growth figures that comprise the objectives. They then task their direct reports with communicating these down to their various reports. At the end of the quarter, the CFO tasks their team with pulling reports to see if they are on track with their high-level objectives. The CEO's team then reviews the results and orders the direct reports to attempt tracking down where things are going right and where things are going wrong. As the end of the year approaches, performance reviews are conducted offline, and individual employees are given ratings based on individual performance. However, despite a large number of high ratings based on manager observations and relationships, few employees are given raises because of the company's poor performance. When employees ask why there is such a disparity, managers are put in an uncomfortable situation where they are unable to provide a clear answer.

The second company uses SAP SuccessFactors and will serve as our model throughout this chapter. Here, the CEO immediately sets their goals in SAP SuccessFactors following the board meeting. Due to security permissions, the CEO is

113

© Susan Traynor, Michael A. Wellens and Venki Krishnamoorthy 2021
S. Traynor et al., *SAP SuccessFactors Talent: Volume 1*, https://doi.org/10.1007/978-1-4842-6600-7_4

confident only they can see these goals. The CEO then gathers their direct reports into a meeting to discuss how they will distribute some of their goals down into the direct reports' goal plans. The CEO then cascades some of their goals downline to direct reports and creates goals on some other reports and links those goals to their goals. Additionally, the direct reports create some of their own goals. The process then repeats for the direct reports and their direct reports in turn. The process continues as such down to the last goal plan–eligible employee. During regular continuous performance management meetings, employees and managers actively update their goals and status in the system. When Q1 arrives, the CFO delivers the results reports, but this time the CEO's team is able to compare these to the results in the system. The team can navigate from goal plan to goal plan tracking down where in the organization goals are meeting or exceeding targets and where they are not on the individual level and take appropriate action to correct. During continuous performance reviews, these corrective actions are communicated and steer the company in a better direction. At the end of the year, goals are pulled into the annual performance forms and shown as a clear percentage of the overall performance score. This in turn affects the merit-based portion of compensation. This provides managers a clear picture for explaining employee compensation. Furthermore, managers may have the ability to see how their own goals link to the higher goals within the organization, thus helping to explain how individual contributions helped influence overall company performance. Indeed, a well-executed SAP SuccessFactors Goal Management implementation can be highly beneficial to your organization! Let's take a closer look at how to get started!

What Will We Cover?

In this chapter, we will walk you through the steps to setting up Goal Management that will meet the requirements of the majority of organizations. We start by turning on the module in provisioning and assigning configuration permissions. Next, we walk through using the online editor to create and modify a basic goal plan template. Then, we walk through the details of editing the XML generated by that online editor with sample code you can use in real-life applications. We wrap up by taking a quick tour of the end-to-end basic goal process as an end user. In the next chapter, we will cover alternate Goal Management concepts and features that are used less often but can become very powerful in meeting the demands of how different organizations execute their business goals.

Basic Configuration of Goal Management

In this section, we will cover all the steps needed to configure a basic goal plan from beginning to end to allow end users access to a goal plan that fits the simple needs of a company with basic requirements. Often, this type of goal plan is a good start for a first iteration review with real-life customers.

Prerequisites for Configuring Goal Management

Prior to main configuration, there are some steps required to ensure the Goal Management features are turned on and appropriate permissions are given to access the screens needed to perform configurations.

Provisioning Configuration

The first step in setting up Goal Management is to edit your provisioning settings so that the screens and permissions become available in SAP SuccessFactors. Follow these steps:

1. Log in to provisioning and select your company id.

2. Click "Company Settings."

3. Check the box next to "Goal Management Suite" and select "Total Goal Management" in the dropdown as shown in Figure 4-1.

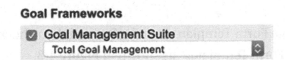

Figure 4-1. Goal Management Settings in Provisioning

Assigning Permissions to Configure and Administer Goal Management

Here, we will assign role-based permissions that enable you to configure and administer Goal Management. Follow these steps:

Note   We assume throughout this chapter that role-based permissions have been turned on in provisioning and that you have access to edit permission roles. Please also note sometimes it takes time for provisioning settings to take effect in the system. If you do not see the permissions appear immediately, log off and log back in an hour or so later. Changes should not take more than overnight to take effect.

1. Type and select "Manage Permission Roles" in the search bar.

2. When the screen loads, click the role you wish to modify. Then click "Permission...:"

3. Click "Manage Goals" on the left and then check the boxes next to "Import Goals," "Import/Export Goals library," and "Goal Management Feature Settings" as shown in Figure 4-2.

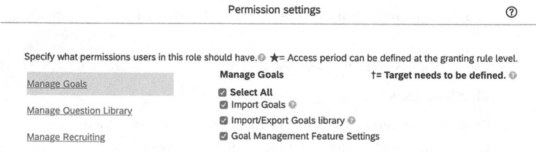

Figure 4-2. Manage Goals Permissions

4. Click "Manage Form Templates" on the left and then check the box next to "Form Templates" as shown in Figure 4-3.

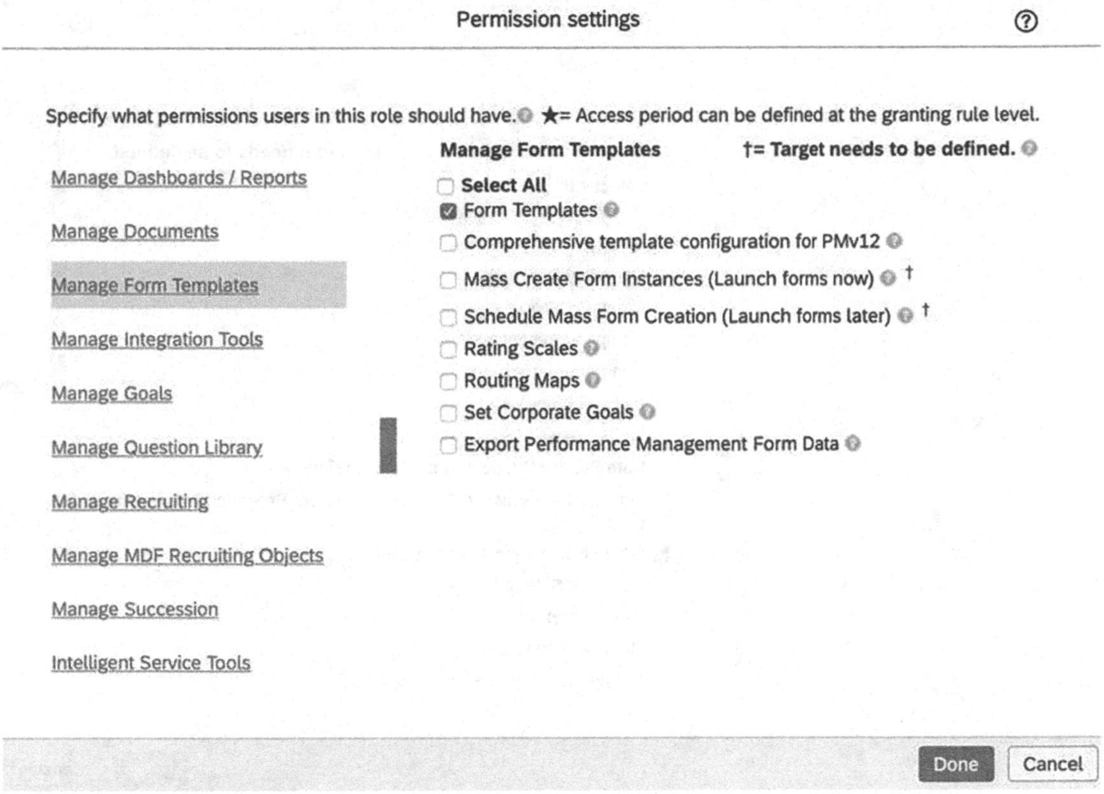

Permission settings   ⑦

Specify what permissions users in this role should have.⑦ ★= Access period can be defined at the granting rule level.

Manage Dashboards / Reports

Manage Documents

Manage Form Templates

Manage Integration Tools

Manage Goals

Manage Question Library

Manage Recruiting

Manage MDF Recruiting Objects

Manage Succession

Intelligent Service Tools

Manage Form Templates   †= **Target needs to be defined.** ⑦

☐ **Select All**
☑ **Form Templates** ⑦
☐ Comprehensive template configuration for PMv12 ⑦
☐ Mass Create Form Instances (Launch forms now) ⑦ †
☐ Schedule Mass Form Creation (Launch forms later) ⑦ †
☐ Rating Scales ⑦
☐ Routing Maps ⑦
☐ Set Corporate Goals ⑦
☐ Export Performance Management Form Data ⑦

Done   Cancel

Figure 4-3. *Assigning Permission to Manage Form Templates*

5.   Click "Manage System Properties" on the left and then check
     the boxes next to "Mobile Settings" and "E-Mail Notification
     Templates Settings" as shown in Figure 4-4.

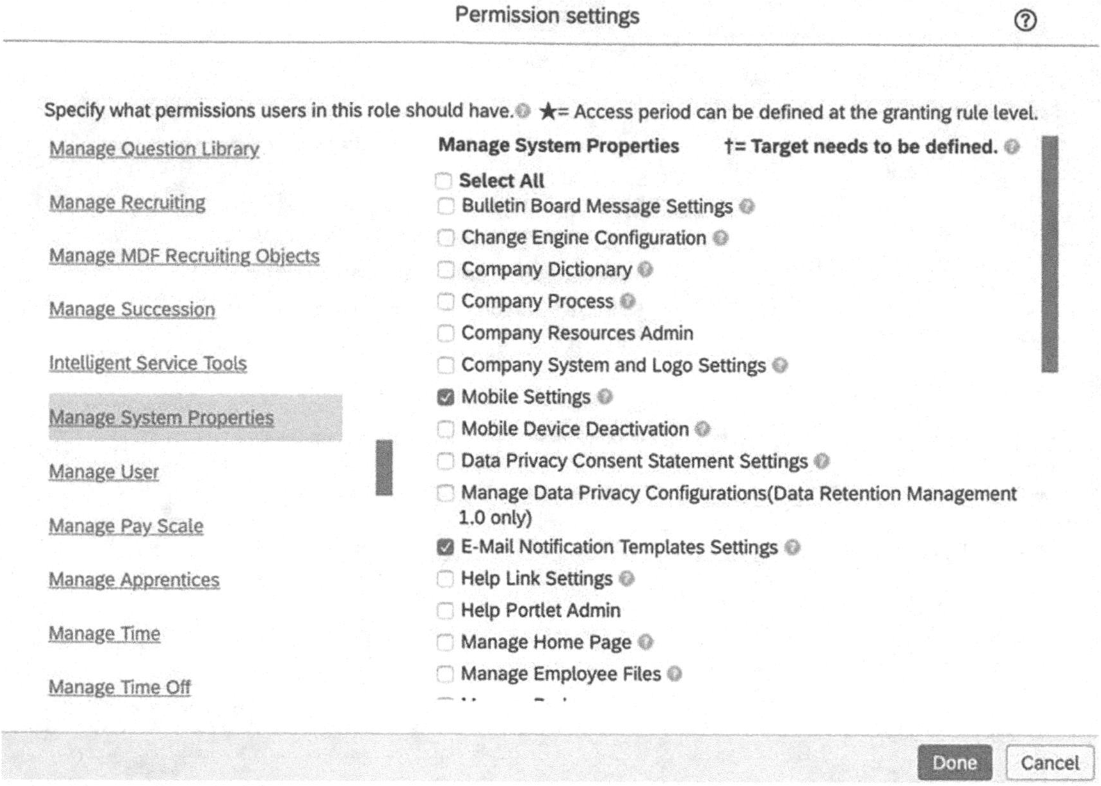

Permission settings   (?)

Specify what permissions users in this role should have.(?) ★= Access period can be defined at the granting rule level.

Manage Question Library   **Manage System Properties**   †= Target needs to be defined. (?)

Manage Recruiting   ☐ **Select All**
                                           ☐ Bulletin Board Message Settings (?)
Manage MDF Recruiting Objects   ☐ Change Engine Configuration (?)
                                           ☐ Company Dictionary (?)
Manage Succession   ☐ Company Process (?)
                                           ☐ Company Resources Admin
Intelligent Service Tools   ☐ Company System and Logo Settings (?)
                                           ☑ Mobile Settings (?)
Manage System Properties   ☐ Mobile Device Deactivation (?)
                                           ☐ Data Privacy Consent Statement Settings (?)
Manage User   ☐ Manage Data Privacy Configurations(Data Retention Management
                                             1.0 only)
Manage Pay Scale   ☑ E-Mail Notification Templates Settings (?)
                                           ☐ Help Link Settings (?)
Manage Apprentices   ☐ Help Portlet Admin
                                           ☐ Manage Home Page (?)
Manage Time   ☐ Manage Employee Files (?)

Manage Time Off

                                                                    [Done] [Cancel]

Figure 4-4. *Manage System Properties Permissions*

6. Click "Done" and then "Save Changes" on the main permission
    role screen.

Primary Configuration of Goal Management

Now that we have the Goal Management module activated and we have permissions to
the needed screens to conduct our configurations, let's get started! This section will walk
you through the basic steps of configuring a simple goal plan, as well as covering the
screens to modify the primary template and administer the process.

Goal Template Configuration

Here, we will take a look at how to create and edit a goal template. Goal templates are
also commonly referred to as goal plans. Typically each year or cycle, a new template
is created; therefore, it is common to include the year in the name of the template, for

example, "2020 Goal Plan" (don't worry; creating a new goal plan is as simple as copying the old one and renaming it). In our example, we will use the "Manage Templates" online editor screen. This is a great way to get started with a basic template and is also available for customers without provisioning access. There are some features of goal templates that are not available for editing in the online editor that must be done directly in the template's underlying XML and then uploaded into the system via provisioning. We will cover those separately. To get started, follow these steps:

1. In the search bar, type and select "Manage Templates." The screen will appear as shown in Figure 4-5.

Admin Center > Manage Templates

Watch a 2-minute Tutorial

| Welcome | Performance Review | Goal Plan | 360 Multi Rater | Development | Recruiting Management |

This is your list of Goal Plan templates.⊞ More

☑ Show Active Templates Only

⊕ Add A New Template				Items per page 10 ∨		< < Page 1 of 1 > >	
Template Name ⊙	Default ⊙	Active ⊙	Updated On ⊙	Date Range ⊙	Sort Order ⊙
2019 Goal Plan Extended	○	☑	01/17/2020	01/01/2019 - 12/31/2019	⬆ ⬇
2019 Goal Plan	○	☑	10/10/2019	01/01/2019 - 12/31/2019	⬆ ⬇
2020 Goal Plan	⊙	☑	12/11/2019	01/01/2020 - 12/31/2020	⬆ ⬇

Figure 4-5. *The Manage Templates Screen*

2. Click "Add A New Template." In the popup, select a template from SuccessStore such as "Extended Goal Plan." This will be a starter template for you to edit. Click "Add to My Instance."

3. Type a name for your template such as "2020 Goal Plan" and click "Save." The editor will appear as seen in Figure 4-6 showing the "Preview" page.

Note   While the Preview can provide a general idea of what fields will show on the template, it is not a 100% true representation of how the form will look on-screen. We recommend testing with a test user instead.

Figure 4-6. *Goal Plan Editor "Preview" Page*

4. Click "General Settings" on the left. The screen will update with
    the General Settings page as shown in Figure 4-7. Start by making
    sure you are on the "default" language in the "Change Language"
    dropdown at the top of the screen. If you are performing a global
    implementation, you can choose a language from the dropdown
    to provide needed translations.

Note   We recommend always configuring the form first using the default
language on every page of the online editor. This will automatically fill in the
values for the remaining languages active for your system (if you need to edit the
available languages, these are activated in provisioning under company settings).
Thus, if you only use US English (en_US) and fill in all of the default values in US
English, you will not have to change languages at all.

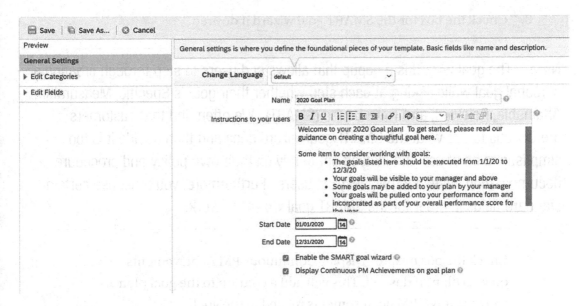

Figure 4-7. Goal Template General Settings

5. Use the "Name" field to change the title of your goal plan as needed.

6. Enter any instructions you would like to provide in the "Instructions to your users" field.

Note   This is an online html editor. We find that some customers like to provide links to technical help documentation and policy documents that provide context of creating SMART goals beyond the online wizard provided by SAP.

---

7. Enter a start and end date.

Note   These are the dates that the goals will be executed by the employee on whose plan they reside. Typically, we find these align to year start and end or fiscal year start and end. If goal plans are due at the end of the first quarter, it is not uncommon for the start date to be in the past.

---

8. Check the box for the SMART goal wizard if desired.

Note   The goal wizard is a popup that allows end users to step through creating a personal goal while asking at each step whether their goal is Specific, Measurable, Attainable, Relevant, and Time-bound (SMART). We often find that customers are curious to see what the SMART goal wizard does and then decide it is too simplistic to be of use and instead opt to rely on their own policy and procedure documentation instead to help instruct users. Furthermore, you must use certain standard fields in order for the SMART goal wizard to work.

---

9. Check the box next to "Display Continuous PM Achievements on goal plan" if desired. This will add a column to the goal plan showing any CPM achievements related to the goal.

Note   We recommend using this feature as it can be helpful to remind users of their achievements. You must have implemented Continuous Performance Management (CPM) for this feature to work. We will cover CPM in more detail in chapter 13.

---

10. Click "Edit Categories" (you may want to click "Save" periodically as well before continuing on to the next page). This will expand to show the standard categories that come with the template you downloaded as seen in Figure 4-8. You can rename these categories, delete them, or add additional categories as needed.

Note   "Categories" are unique as opposed to the remaining areas of goal plan configuration that are "fields." Categories will show up as sections on your end users' goal plans that visually divide each goal. They can also be important for reporting as they may align with major pillars of the overall business plan. To remove the use of categories entirely, you will need to delete them all in the XML template (see the "Downloading, Editing, and Uploading the XML" section later in this chapter).

---

    a. To add a category, click "Add a New Category," and the category will appear on the list.

    b. To edit the name of a category, click the category and type the new name of the category in the field that appears to the right (after making a language selection).

    c. To delete a category, click the trash can icon.

Note   We do not recommend deleting a category after the form is put to use by end users as this can corrupt data! Also, many companies request "Select a Category" be added to the category dropdown. However, if one of the dropdown categories is "Select a Category," this is considered a category as a section on your end users' goal plan. Therefore, we do not recommend adding such a value in the dropdown.

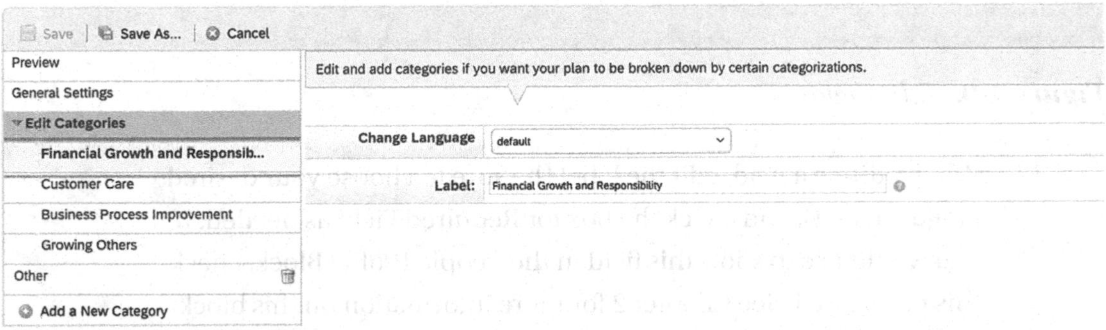

Figure 4-8. Edit Categories

11. Click "Edit Fields." The area will expand showing the fields included in the template you downloaded from SuccessStore as shown in Figure 4-9. You can mouse over a field and click the trash can icon to delete it. You can drag and drop fields to change the order the fields appear in the goal plan. Click "Add a New Field" to add one, or click an existing field to edit it.

Note   You may not delete the "name," "metric," "start," and "due" fields in the online tool. We recommend using these as well since they tie standard functionality such as the goal wizard.

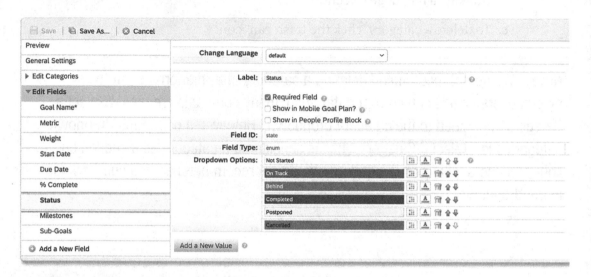

Figure 4-9. *Edit Fields*

12.   When editing a field, edit the label (be sure to choose your desired language first), and check the box for Required Field as needed. If you would like to show this field in the People Profile Block, check this box as well. See Chapter 2 for more information on this block. The "done" and "state" fields also allow you to show these fields on the mobile version of the plan as well. Reference Tables 4-1 and 4-2 to add, edit, and delete standard and custom fields as desired for your organization's business needs.

Table 4-1. *Goal Plan Standard Fields and Options*

Technical Field Name	Field Type	Description	Configuration Options
name	textarea	This is the primary field used to identify the goal, for example, "Increase sales revenue by 5% by end of the year." This field cannot be removed.	Label, Required Field, Show in People Profile Block.
metric	textarea	Used to identify how the goal will be measured. This field cannot be removed.	Label, Required Field, Show in People Profile Block.
weight	percent	This field is often used by organizations that incorporate goals into their performance forms. It will dictate the percentage of the total goal section score this individual goal score will count. We recommend using this field if using performance forms and you feel some goals such as company-mandated goals should hold greater weight than personal goals. Otherwise, all goals will be treated equally.	Label, Required Field, Show in People Profile Block.
start	date	Field used to indicate the begin date of when the goal will be executed. This field cannot be removed.	Label, Required Field, Show in People Profile Block.
due	date	Field used to indicate the end date of when the goal will be executed. This field cannot be removed.	Label, Required Field, Show in People Profile Block.

(continued)

125

Table 4-1. (*continued*)

Technical Field Name	Field Type	Description	Configuration Options
done	percent	Field used to indicate the percentage of goal completion. We recommend using this field as it is helpful in reporting.	Label, Required Field, Show in People Profile Block, Show in Mobile Goal Plan.
state	enum	Used to indicate whether a goal is on track or needs attention. We recommend including this field since it is important for the Execution Map.	Label, Required Field, Show in People Profile Block, Show in Mobile Goal Plan. As an enumeration field, it also requires you to define the list of possible entries, as well as a background and foreground color label for each.
milestones	table	This field is used to track when a specific milestone to help achieve the goal will be targeted for completion vs. when it was actually completed. In our experience, most customers do not use this field because it starts to become too detailed.	Label, Required Field. As a table, you will also need to define the column headers for the table. Default labels are "Target Date," "Milestone," and "Actual Date."
tasks	table	Even though the technical field name is "tasks," this field's default label is "Sub-Goals." In our experience, most customers do not use this field because it starts to become too detailed.	Label, Required Field. As a table, you will also need to define the column headers for the table. The default column labels are "Sub-Goal Description" and "Percent Complete."

(continued)

Table 4-1. (*continued*)

Technical Field Name	Field Type	Description	Configuration Options
targets	table	Even though the technical name is "targets," the default label for this field is "Tasks." The idea is to detail out multiple individual tasks that build to the achievement of the larger goal. In our experience, customers do not use this as it gets into too much unneeded detail.	Label, Required Field. As a table, you will also need to define the column headers for the table. The default header labels are "Target Date" and "Task."
desc	textarea	Used to describe the goal in more detail. We recommend not using this field as it sometimes leads to confusion with what to put in the name field.	Label, Required Field, Show in People Profile Block.

Table 4-2. *Available Custom Field Types and Configuration Options*

Field Type	Configuration Options
text	Required Field, Show in People Profile Block.
textarea	Required Field, Show in People Profile Block.
enum	Required Field, Show in People Profile Block. As an enumeration field, it also requires you to define the list of possible entries, as well as a background and foreground color label for each.
date	Required Field, Show in People Profile Block.
percent	Required Field, Show in People Profile Block.
number	Required Field, Show in People Profile Block.
link	Required Field, Show in People Profile Block.

13. Click "Save."

14. Back on the Manage Templates main screen, you may also want to move your latest template to the top and make it default so that it is the first template users see on the goal plan page.

Congratulations! You have now set up a basic goal plan template! Referencing our model organization, we can see how this template will help the company to record goal data using a variety of fields that can be added, removed, and configured to suit the needs of the organization. We've also shown you which fields can be used to integrate with annual performance reviews and Continuous Performance Management to further incentivize and track employee progress toward these business goals. Next, we will take a look at how the goal library can help guide employees with example well-stated goals and how the Execution Map and Alignment Chart can help give a bigger picture of how well goals are being executed across the organization.

Goal Library

The goal library provides a set of example goals end users can reference. These can be very helpful if employees are new to the concept of goal setting and need concrete examples of how to craft a well-formed goal. SAP SuccessFactors provides a standard goal library that is referenced when you use a goal plan template from SuccessStore. This library can be modified, or a new library can be built from scratch.

Note   While the standard goal library provides some good examples, the categories and specific goals provided may not all be relevant to your organization. Furthermore, the standard library only prepopulates the name and metric fields. If you have other fields you wish to populate, you will need to create a new one (you can simply copy the existing library as a start if needed, but we recommend creating it as a new library with a unique identifier). If you create a custom library, you will also need to perform a mapping in your goal plan template XML to map the fields you uploaded to corresponding fields on the goal plan template. We will cover how to do this in the "Downloading, Editing, and Uploading the XML" section.

To import a goal library, follow these steps:

1. Type and select "Import/Export Goals library" in the search bar.
    The screen will display as shown in Figure 4-10.

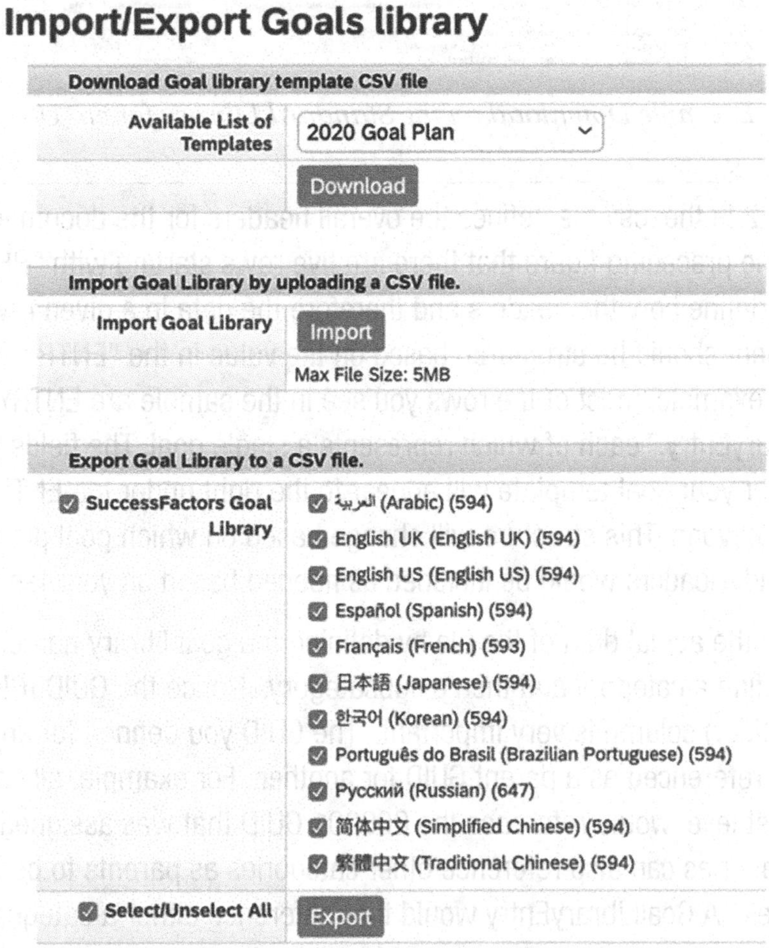

Import/Export Goals library

Download Goal library template CSV file

Available List of Templates	2020 Goal Plan ⌄
	Download

Import Goal Library by uploading a CSV file.

Import Goal Library	Import
	Max File Size: 5MB

Export Goal Library to a CSV file.

☑ SuccessFactors Goal Library

- ☑ العربية (Arabic) (594)
- ☑ English UK (English UK) (594)
- ☑ English US (English US) (594)
- ☑ Español (Spanish) (594)
- ☑ Français (French) (593)
- ☑ 日本語 (Japanese) (594)
- ☑ 한국어 (Korean) (594)
- ☑ Português do Brasil (Brazilian Portuguese) (594)
- ☑ Русский (Russian) (647)
- ☑ 简体中文 (Simplified Chinese) (594)
- ☑ 繁體中文 (Traditional Chinese) (594)

☑ Select/Unselect All   Export

Figure 4-10. *The Import/Export Goals library Screen*

2. You may wish to better understand how the SuccessFactors
    goal library is structured first prior to starting your own. To
    download the SuccessFactors library, click the checkbox next to
    "SuccessFactors Goal Library," as well as the desired language(s)
    you wish to download. Click "Export." You can open the file to
    view and edit the information as shown in Figure 4-11.

	A	B	C	D	E	F	G	H	I	J	K
1	TYPE	Goal Library	VERSION		2						
2	ACTION	ENTRY_TYPE	GUID	PARENT_GUID	LOCALE	ENTRY_NAME					
3	HEADER	GoalLibraryEntry	GUID	PARENT_GUID	LOCALE	name	metric	desc	start	due	done
4	HEADER	Milestone	GUID	PARENT_GUID	LOCALE	target	actual	desc	start	due	completed
5	HEADER	Task	GUID	PARENT_GUID	LOCALE	target	actual	desc	start	due	done
6	HEADER	Target	GUID	PARENT_GUID	LOCALE	target	actual	desc	start	due	done
7	HEADER	MetricLookupEntry	GUID	PARENT_GUID	LOCALE	description	rating	achievement			
8	UPDATE	GoalLibrary	600001		en_US	SuccessFactors Goal Library					
9	UPDATE	Category	660000	600001	en_US	IT					
10	UPDATE	Category	660100	660000	en_US	Application Development					
11	UPDATE	GoalLibraryEntry	660108	660100	en_US	Provide work estimates for programming tasks that are accurate within __% of actuals	Work estimate accuracy rate				
12	UPDATE	GoalLibraryEntry	660101	660100	en_US	Achieve __% bug-free code for delivery to production	Bug rates				
13	UPDATE	GoalLibraryEntry	660110	660100	en_US	Reduce mean time to repair failures __% by (date)	Time to repair rate				
14	UPDATE	GoalLibraryEntry	660106	660100	en_US	Increase mean time to failure __% by (date)	Mean time to failure rate				
15	UPDATE	GoalLibraryEntry	660102	660100	en_US	Decrease defect rate __% by (date)	Defect rate				

Figure 4-11. *Example Download on the Standard Library for en_US Locale*

Note   Row 2 in the .csv file defines the overall headers for the document. You will observe in the preceding figure that there are five rows starting with "HEADER." These each define how the headers and therefore the data in a given row of the .CSV document should be structured based on the value in the "ENTRY_TYPE" column. For example, most of the rows you see in the sample are ENTRY_TYPE of "GoalLibraryEntry," each of which represents a single goal. The fields you have configured for your goal template will appear to the right under the ENTRY_NAME column and beyond. This structure will change based on which goal plan template you download. Headers would be included as needed based on your template.

Row 8 starts the actual data of the file by defining the goal library name. The next two rows define a category and then a subcategory. Notice the GUID (Globally Unique Identifier) column is very important. The GUID you defined for an entry can then be referenced as a parent GUID for another. For example, all categories at the highest level would reference the 600001 GUID that was assigned to the library. Categories can also reference other categories as parents to become subcategories. A GoalLibraryEntry would then reference either a category or subcategory. Milestone, Task, Target, and MetricLookupEntry would each reference a GoalLibraryEntry as their parent.

If you are updating the library, be sure to change the "ADD" in the ACTION column to "UPDATE." You must perform a full load of the library every time; you cannot just update one entry. You can also use the "DELETE" action to remove entries. It is very easy to corrupt the standard library – we recommend instead copying the library entries you wish to keep into a new library.

3. To start a library from scratch, select the goal template for which you want to download the .CSV import file template and click "Download."

4. Open the file and make entries per the instructions in the preceding note. Save the file and then click "Import" to choose the file to upload. Use any error messages to troubleshoot any mistakes; otherwise, your new library will appear under the "Export Goal Library to a CSV file" section.

5. Note that if you created a new library, you will need to change the goal template XML. Instructions on how to do this can be found in the "Downloading, Editing, and Uploading the XML" section of this chapter.

Email Notifications

Goal Management provides notifications designed to keep employees and managers up to date about modifications to goal plans. Follow these steps to configure these emails:

Note   Many customers tend to find that too many emails start to fatigue users. We recommend limiting which emails are turned on. Often, customers do not elect to turn on any of these notifications. Instead, many rely on reporting to manage if employees and managers have filled out their goals and manually notify those who appear inactive.

---

1. Type and select "E-Mail Notification Templates Settings" in the search bar. The screen will appear as shown in Figure 4-12.

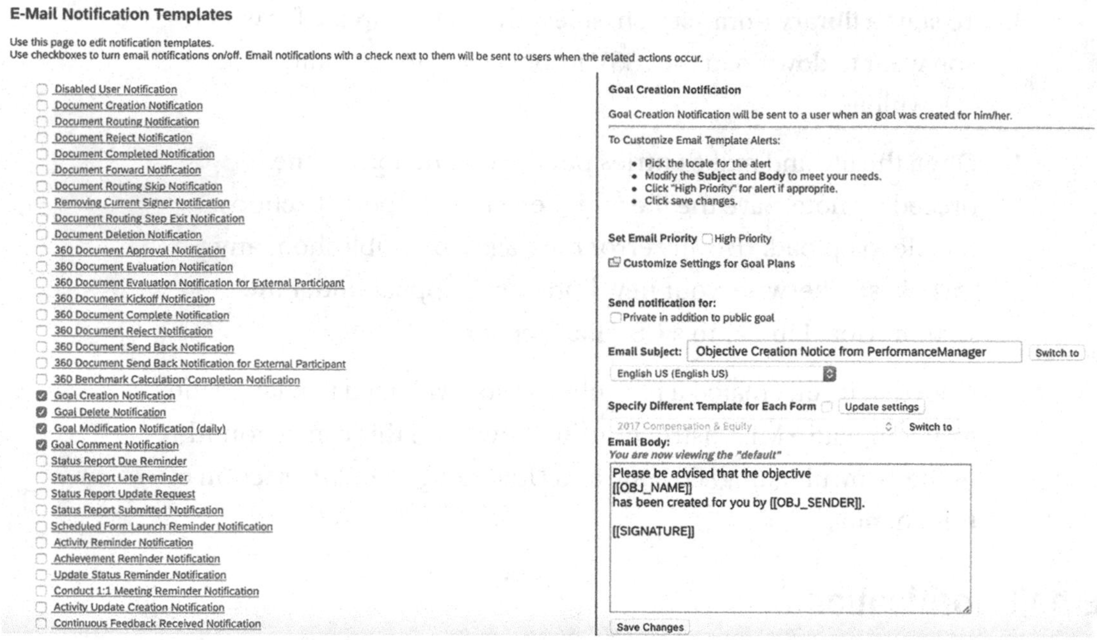

E-Mail Notification Templates

Use this page to edit notification templates.
Use checkboxes to turn email notifications on/off. Email notifications with a check next to them will be sent to users when the related actions occur.

☐ Disabled User Notification
☐ Document Creation Notification
☐ Document Routing Notification
☐ Document Reject Notification
☐ Document Completed Notification
☐ Document Forward Notification
☐ Document Routing Skip Notification
☐ Removing Current Signer Notification
☐ Document Routing Step Exit Notification
☐ Document Deletion Notification
☐ 360 Document Approval Notification
☐ 360 Document Evaluation Notification
☐ 360 Document Evaluation Notification for External Participant
☐ 360 Document Kickoff Notification
☐ 360 Document Complete Notification
☐ 360 Document Reject Notification
☐ 360 Document Send Back Notification
☐ 360 Document Send Back Notification for External Participant
☐ 360 Benchmark Calculation Completion Notification
☑ Goal Creation Notification
☑ Goal Delete Notification
☑ Goal Modification Notification (daily)
☑ Goal Comment Notification
☐ Status Report Due Reminder
☐ Status Report Late Reminder
☐ Status Report Update Request
☐ Status Report Submitted Notification
☐ Scheduled Form Launch Reminder Notification
☐ Activity Reminder Notification
☐ Achievement Reminder Notification
☐ Update Status Reminder Notification
☐ Conduct 1:1 Meeting Reminder Notification
☐ Activity Update Creation Notification
☐ Continuous Feedback Received Notification

Goal Creation Notification

Goal Creation Notification will be sent to a user when an goal was created for him/her.

To Customize Email Template Alerts:

- Pick the locale for the alert
- Modify the **Subject** and **Body** to meet your needs.
- Click "High Priority" for alert if appropriate.
- Click save changes.

Set Email Priority ☐ High Priority

☑ Customize Settings for Goal Plans

Send notification for:
☐ Private in addition to public goal

Email Subject: [Objective Creation Notice from PerformanceManager] Switch to

[English US (English US)]

Specify Different Template for Each Form ☐ Update settings
2017 Compensation & Equity   Switch to
Email Body:
You are now viewing the "default"

Please be advised that the objective
[[OBJ_NAME]]
has been created for you by [[OBJ_SENDER]].

[[SIGNATURE]]

Save Changes

Figure 4-12. *The "E-Mail Notification Templates" Screen*

2. Reference Table 4-3 to make decisions on which templates to activate and/or edit. Click the checkboxes next to the emails you would like to activate, and click "Save Notification Settings" on the bottom left. To edit the individual settings or contents of any particular notification, click the name of the notification on the left and the screen with update on the right. Click "Save Changes" to save the edits made to that individual notification.

a. To modify messages for different languages, select the language from the dropdown and click "Switch to" prior to making your edits.

b. While modifying the email contents, you can insert tokens to pull text data from the relevant goal plan. Available tokens are listed in Table 4-3.

Table 4-3. *List of Goal Management Notifications*

Notification	Comments
Goal Creation Notification	Sends an alert to the owner of the goal plan when a goal has been added. This may be useful in scenarios when a manager updates a plan for an employee. You can choose to include or exclude private goals. Available tokens are [[OBJ_NAME]] [[OBJ_SENDER]] [[SIGNATURE]].
Goal Delete Notification	Sends an alert to the owner of the goal plan when a goal has been removed. This may be useful in scenarios when a manager updates a plan for an employee. You can choose to include or exclude private goals. Available tokens are [[OBJ_NAME]] [[OBJ_SENDER]] [[SIGNATURE]].
Goal Modification Notification (daily)	Sends email notifications in batch every 24 hours to both the employee and manager if any goals were modified. Available tokens are [[LAST_EMAIL_DATE]] [[GOAL_OWNER]] [[OBJ-PLAN-NAME]] [[OBJ_LIST]] [[SIGNATURE]. You can choose to include or exclude private goals. Note that you can also exclude notifications on actions to linked goals, unlinking a goal, and actions to cascaded goals. You can also exclude deletions so that the messages are not redundant with the Goal Delete Notification. You can also choose if a matrix manager will receive notifications for their matrix reports. Furthermore, you can consolidate emails by employee so that managers only get one message per employee goal plan for all changes to that plan. After configuring this notification, you will need to log into provisioning for your company instance and set a scheduled job to send the notifications. Follow these steps: 1. Click "Manage Scheduled Jobs." 2. In the new screen that appears, click "Create New Job" and enter a name such as "Goal Modification Notification." 3. For "Job Type," choose "Goal notification email," and select "Today" for Job Parameters. Select "Recurring" for Occurrence and choose "Daily." Select 23:00 hours as the time (the job works by gathering all modifications since 0:00, so this maximizes capturing all of the modifications).

(continued)

Table 4-3. (*continued*)

Notification	Comments
	4. For Start Date, choose today's date and a time about 5 minutes following the current time.
	5. Click "Create Job."
	6. In the main screen that appears, click the "Actions" menu and select "Submit." Your job will start running at 23:00 daily!
	Also, if you'd like to enable a direct link to the goal plan in this notification, follow these steps:
	1. Make sure the "Consolidate by employee" option is selected for the notification.
	2. Type and select "Company System and Logo Settings" in the search bar.
	3. Click the checkbox next to "Enable HTML notifications."
	4. Click "Save Company System Setting."
Goal Comment Notification	Sends a notification to the employee and manager when comments are added to a goal. If the manager comments, the employee gets the notification. If the employee responds, the manager gets the notification. If anyone else posts a comment, then both get the email.
	Available tokens are [[OBJ_RECIPIENT]], [[OBJ_SENDER]], [[OBJ_NAME]], [[OBJ-PLAN-NAME]], [[OBJ_COMMENT]][[OBJ_COMMENT_HERE]].

Enable Mobile Features

Mobile goals allow employees and managers access to view and edit basic goal information such as name, description, and status. Alternate or advanced features such as group goals, team goals, metric lookup tables, and so on are not supported.

Note   Due to the simplistic nature of the mobile app, we will not cover using the app. We invite you to go to the Apple App Store or Android Market and search for "SuccessFactors" to download the app. Once it is downloaded, you can click "Demo" in the upper right-hand corner to take a tour of the app. If you want to associate your app with a specific user on your instance to use real data, you will need to walk through the on-screen registration process. To see the list of features supported and not supported, please reference SAP note 2475032.

To enable mobile features, follow these steps:

1. Type and select "Enable Mobile Features" in the search bar. The Mobile Settings screen will appear.

2. Click "Modules" on the left. Then click the checkbox next to "Goal Management" as shown in Figure 4-13. The changes will take effect immediately.

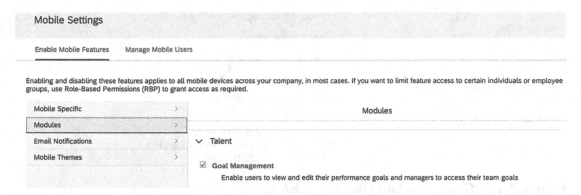

Figure 4-13. *Activating Goal Management in Mobile Settings*

Assigning Goal Form Permissions to End Users

Before we dive into configuring our goal plan further by editing the XML, it is wise to assign permissions to end users (e.g., just a test user) in our test instance so that we can see the results of our XML configurations and troubleshoot as needed. To assign permissions to end users, follow these steps.

Create an Employee Role

1. Type and select "Manage Permission Roles" in the search bar. Click the name of the permission role you want to edit (or create a new one by clicking "Create New") and then click "Permissions...."

2. Click "Goals" on the left-hand side of the popup and click the checkboxes next to "Goal Management Access" (which gives the user the ability to navigate to the Goals section of the system) and "Goal Plan Permissions." Click the "Others" radio button and highlight the particular goal plan(s) to which you wish to give the user permission. An example final result is shown in Figure 4-14.

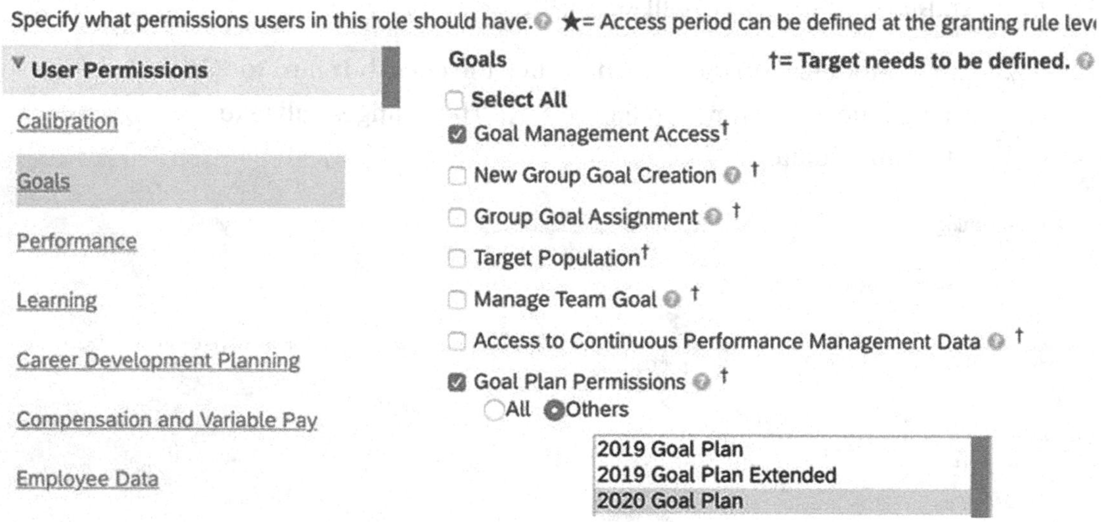

Specify what permissions users in this role should have. ⊘ ★= Access period can be defined at the granting rule lev

Goals   †= Target needs to be defined. ⊘

˅ User Permissions

Calibration

Goals

Performance

Learning

Career Development Planning

Compensation and Variable Pay

Employee Data

☐ Select All
☑ Goal Management Access†
☐ New Group Goal Creation ⊘ †
☐ Group Goal Assignment ⊘ †
☐ Target Population†
☐ Manage Team Goal ⊘ †
☐ Access to Continuous Performance Management Data ⊘ †
☑ Goal Plan Permissions ⊘ †
　　◯All ◉Others

2019 Goal Plan
2019 Goal Plan Extended
2020 Goal Plan

Figure 4-14. *Goal Plan End User Permissions*

3. Click "Done."

4. On the main role screen, you will then need to define the target. Typically for the employee role, this target is only the employee themself. Thus, they can only see and edit their own goal plan. Scroll to the bottom of the role and click "Add...." For "Grant role to:" choose the population to whom the role will be assigned. Under Target population, choose the "Target population of" radio button and then click the checkbox next to the dropdown and choose "Granted User (Self)." See Figure 4-15.

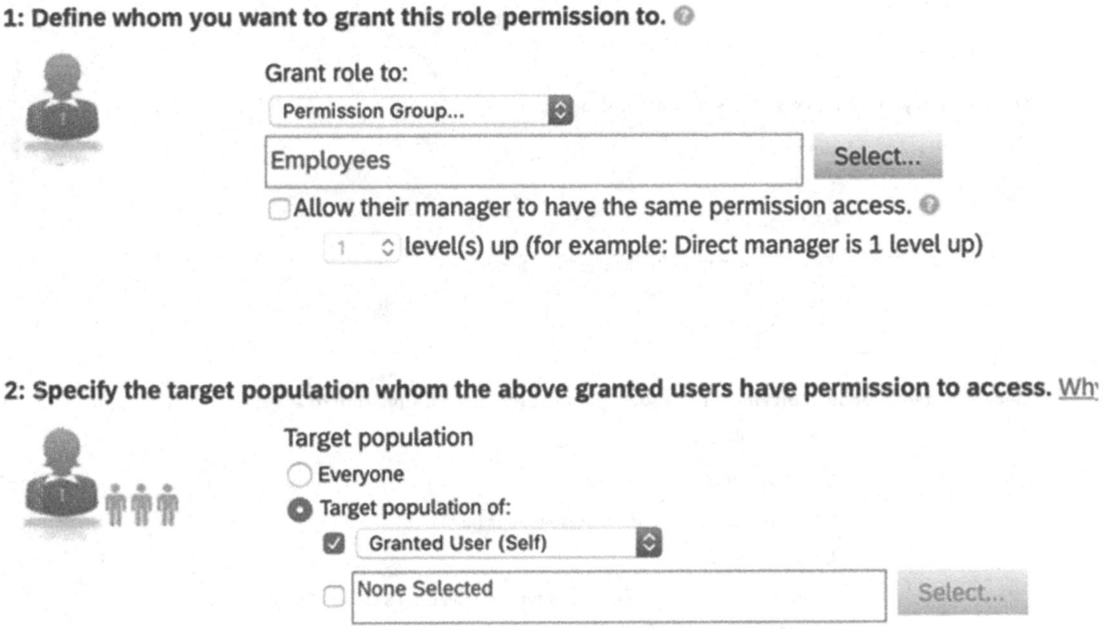

1: Define whom you want to grant this role permission to. ⊘

Grant role to:

Permission Group... ◇

| Employees | Select... |

☐ Allow their manager to have the same permission access. ⊘

1 ◇ level(s) up (for example: Direct manager is 1 level up)

2: Specify the target population whom the above granted users have permission to access. Wh⟩

Target population

○ Everyone

● Target population of:

☑ Granted User (Self) ◇

☐ None Selected | Select... |

Figure 4-15. *Defining the Target Population for Goal Plan Access*

5. Click "Done" and then on the main role screen click "Save Changes."

Note   Permissions here only control access to get to the goal plans for particular employees. Actions that can be taken on goals and visibility of public vs. private goals are defined in each goal plan template XML. Some organizations promote transparency and may wish to allow access to goal plans across the whole organization to everyone but control what actions can be taken so that only employees and managers can edit goals.

Create A Manager Role/HR Role

To create a manager role, repeat the steps provided earlier for the manager role. On step 4, for the "Grant role to:" select "All Managers," or choose a specific group of managers. Also, under "Target population," choose "Granted User's Direct Reports." Check the box for "Include access to the Reports of the Granted User's Direct Reports" and choose how far down the hierarchy you would like the manager to have access. An example final result is shown in Figure 4-16.

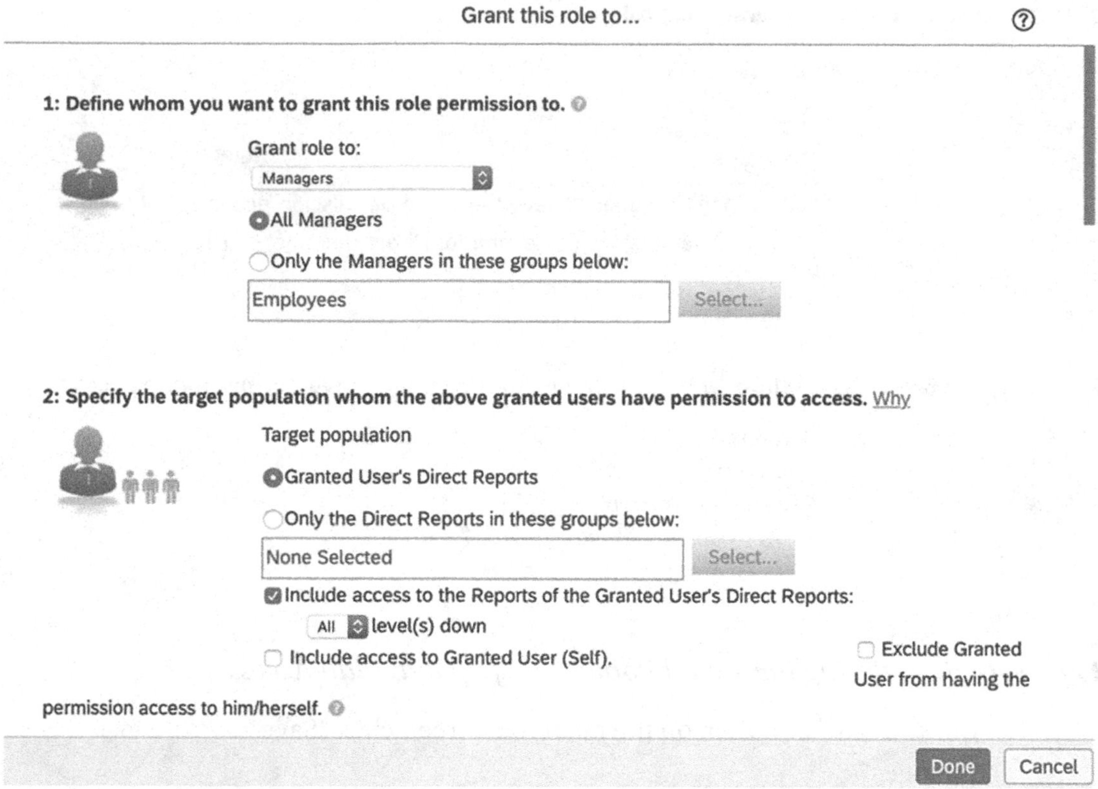

Grant this role to...   ⑦

1: Define whom you want to grant this role permission to. ❷

Grant role to:

| Managers | ⬍ |

● All Managers

○ Only the Managers in these groups below:

| Employees | | Select... |

2: Specify the target population whom the above granted users have permission to access. Why

Target population

● Granted User's Direct Reports

○ Only the Direct Reports in these groups below:

| None Selected | | Select... |

☑ Include access to the Reports of the Granted User's Direct Reports:

    | All | ⬍ | level(s) down

☐ Include access to Granted User (Self).   ☐ Exclude Granted
                                            User from having the

permission access to him/herself. ❷

| | Done | Cancel |

Figure 4-16. *Defining Goal Plan Target Population Access for Managers*

Note   In our experience, you may also want to repeat this process for a separate role for HR admins as well by choosing "HR Managers" in the first dropdown.

Basic Goal Plan Features Requiring XML Configuration

Now that we have a basic goal plan built and assigned to a sample population we can use to troubleshoot, we can begin digging into the less straightforward XML configuration.

Downloading, Editing, and Uploading the XML

In order to edit the XML, we first need to download it. An XML is automatically created when you create the goal plan template using the online tool shown in the prior sections of this chapter. We will now log into provisioning to download the template so we can edit it. Follow these steps to download the template, modify it, and re-upload it:

1. Log in to provisioning for your company and click "Import/ Update/Export Objective Plan Template."

2. Click the icon beneath the "Export" column as shown in Figure 4-17. Your web browser will download the file to your local machine.

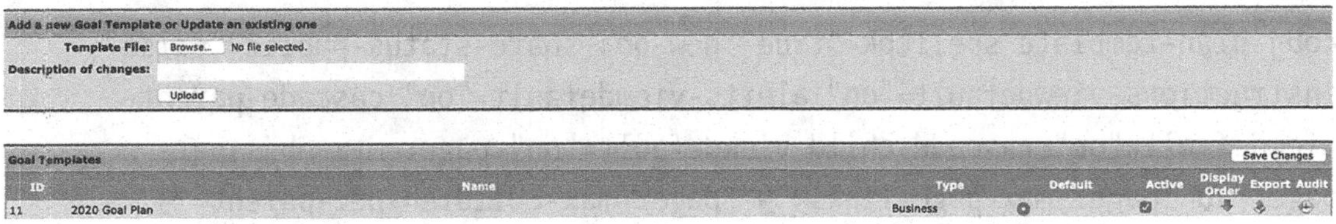

Figure 4-17. Uploading and Downloading Goal Plan XML Templates

3. Open the file using an XML editor and make your edits and click SAVE.

4. Go back to provisioning to upload the goal plan "Import/Update/ Export Objective Plan Template" this time you will upload.

5. Click the "Browse..." button and select your XML file.

6. Click "Upload." The system will process the file and either give you a success message or an error message you can use to troubleshoot the changes you performed.

Note   We recommend changing only a handful of settings at a time and saving each set of changes as a new file name on your local computer to assist with narrowing down the number of possible issues. In a worst case, you can revert to your last succession version of the file.

Goal Plan XML Format

In this section, we step through each area of the XML in order and describe the configuration options including example code segments. By piecing together each of these example code segments in order, you can upload a fully functioning goal plan.

<obj-plan-template> Tag

The <obj-plan-template> tag is the highest-level tag in the XML structure. It defines a series of options that can be turned on or off or adjusted to turn on/off features or adjust them.

An example code segment is shown in the following:

```
<obj-plan-template spellchk="true" new-obj-share-status-public="false"
instructions-viewdefault="on" alerts-viewdefault="on" cascade-parent-
viewdefault="on" cascade-child-viewdefault="on" pager-max-objs-per-
page="10" pager-max-page-links="9" pager-max-children-per-parent="3"
display-alignment-format="goals" more-details-child-format="goal-plan"
share-confirm="true" unshare-confirm="true" allow-group-goal="false"
goal-tree-link="true" expand-collapse-categories="false" use-text-for-
privacy="true" cws-people-role="true" overwrite-target-population="false"
swap-goal-link="false" learning-activity-deep-link="false" show-total-
goalscore="false" show-goal-id="false">
```

Reference Table 4-4 to change the attribute values as desired.

Table 4-4. *<obj-plan-template> Attributes*

Attribute	Description
spellchk	For any textarea fields, a spell-check link is displayed if the value is set to "true"; else, the link is not shown.
new-obj-share-status-public	All new goals default to public when set to "true"; else, they are set to private. If you choose to only allow users to have one type of goal and hide that there can be public vs. private goals, it is important to set this to "true" and remove all private-access permissions. See SAP note 2514964 for more information.

(*continued*)

Table 4-4. (*continued*)

Attribute	Description
instructions-viewdefault	This is no longer used and ignored by the system.
alerts-viewdefault	Defaults the end user's display options to view alerts. Alerts show the user if someone else has modified a goal or linkage/alignment.
cascade-parent-viewdefault	This is no longer used and ignored by the system.
cascade-child-viewdefault	This is no longer used and ignored by the system.
expand-collapse-categories	If "true," then users can expand or collapse each category.
share-confirm	If "true," a popup will display asking for confirmation that the user wishes to share a goal; else, this is not shown.
unshare-confirm	If "true," a popup will display asking for confirmation that the user wishes to unshare a goal; else, this is not shown.
allow-group-goal	If you choose to use group goals, then set this to "true." We will cover group goals in Chapter 5.
goal-tree-link	If "true," then an icon appears for linked goals that users can click to see the Goal Alignment Spotlight report.
pager-max-objs-per-page	Accepts an integer value. Creates pagination based on the number of goals entered here. If set to "0," then all goals are shown on one page. We recommend setting this to "0."
pager-max-page-links	This is no longer used and ignored by the system.
pager-max-children-per-parent	This is no longer used and ignored by the system.
more-details-child-format	If "goal-plan" is entered, then aligned-down goals show as a mini version of what is shown on the goal plan. If not set or set to "original," then only the full name, username, and goal name are shown.

(*continued*)

Table 4-4. (*continued*)

Attribute	Description
show-goal-id	If set to "true," then a goal ID column is added to the goal plan.
display-alignment-format	If set to "names," then the goal owner name is shown with a link to view the goal on their plan. If set to "goals," then the owner name and goal name and other fields are shown instead of a link.
use-text-for-privacy	If set to "true," then the user can select from a dropdown of "Public" and "Private" options. Else, an icon (sunglasses) is used to indicate if the goal is private. Remove this attribute entirely if you will not use private vs. public goals. See SAP note 2514964 for more information.

<obj-plan-id> Element

The first element underneath the <obj-plan-template> tag is the <obj-plan-id>. It sets the unique numeric identifier of the goal plan in the system. This is automatically assigned by the system if you create a plan using the online editor tool. Otherwise, you can pick a number not yet used. You can look in provisioning on the "Import/Update/Export Objective Plan Template" screen at the existing templates and choose a new id. If you upload a plan with the same id of an existing plan, it will overwrite that plan.

An example code segment is shown here:

```
<obj-plan-id>11</obj-plan-id>
```

The number you choose is important as different numbers correspond to different types of goal plans that use the same XML format. The number ranges are shown in the following table:

Number Range	Template Type
1–1000	Goal plans
2001–3000	Development plans
4001–5000	Learning activities
5001–5099	Career worksheets

<obj-plan-type> Element

The <obj-plan-type> element defines whether the plan is a goal plan, development plan, learning activity, or career worksheet. Use "Business" to define the plan type as a goal plan.

An example code segment is shown here:

```
<obj-plan-type>Business</obj-plan-type>
```

<obj-plan-name> Element

This will be the title of the goal plan as you set it using the online tool that appears for end users. The first line defines the default. You can set the name for each active locale in your instance below that.

An example code segment is shown in the following:

```
<obj-plan-name>2020 Goal Plan</obj-plan-name>
<obj-plan-name lang="en_US">2020 Goal Plan</obj-plan-name>
```

<obj-plan-desc> and <obj-plan-lastmodified> Elements

The description and last modified are shown only to those configuring the goal plan in the XML or the online tool. The last modified is updated automatically when you save in the online tool or when you upload the XML in provisioning.

An example code segment is shown in the following:

```
<obj-plan-desc><![CDATA[ Basic Goal Plan for 2020]]></obj-plan-desc>
<obj-plan-lastmodified>6/20/20 3:16 PM</obj-plan-lastmodified>
```

<obj-plan-start> and <obj-plan-due> Elements

The start and due dates define the period for which the goals are achieved. These should have been set up in the online tool. These also act as the default start and end dates when the user creates goals.

An example code segment is shown in the following:

```
<obj-plan-start>01/01/2020</obj-plan-start>
<obj-plan-due>12/31/2020</obj-plan-due>
```

<obj-plan-numbering> Element

Goals can be organized into sub-goals by adding a goal to the plan underneath another goal and then indenting it. In order to turn this feature on, you must define a numbering scheme via this element. Typically, we find if customers want numbering, then they would like a 1.1.1 notation where the first number is the number order of the category, the second number is the number of the goal within the category, and the third is an indented goal:

```
<obj-plan-numbering>
 <obj-plan-number-format><![CDATA[#.]]></obj-plan-number-format>
 <obj-plan-number-format><![CDATA[#.]]></obj-plan-number-format>
 <obj-plan-number-format><![CDATA[#.]]></obj-plan-number-format>
</obj-plan-numbering>
```

To remove numbering, simply remove the three lines of code from this element. To disallow indenting, remove only the last line. To make the numbering automatic based on the sorting the user uses by column, remove two lines.

<switches> Element

The switches element is where you can list various features you wish to turn on or off for the goal plan. In the following example, we only cover those switches relevant for goal plans (others exist for development plans which are covered in Volume 2, Chapter 1).

Reference Table 4-5 to make decisions on which switches to turn off or on.

Table 4-5. *Available Goal Plan XML Switches*

Switch	Description
cascader-role	If you plan on allowing managers or other users to cascade goals, it is important to realize that, by default, the cascader will have write permission to all fields on the target employee's goal. If your requirements are different, you will need to enable this special cascader role which can define different permissions. For more information, see SAP note 2072029.
cws-dispoption-competency-desc	If you link competencies to your goals, turning this on will show the competency description by default on the goal plan.

(continued)

Table 4-5. (*continued*)

Switch	Description
turnoff-add-personal-goal-button	This turns off the ability for users to create personal goals. It essentially forces users to either use a library goal or goals that have been imported onto their plan by an administrator. It is only recommended for organizations that do not allow end users to create ad hoc goals outside of the library or goals that have been placed on their plan by an administrator.
percentage-value-over-100	Turning this switch on allows someone to enter a value over 100 in any percentage field such as the weight field. We recommend leaving this off unless you have a custom percentage field where this could be relevant (e.g., an achievement above 100%).
threaded-feedback	This allows comments on goals to be displayed in a threaded style, whereas before they used to be shown in a table. We recommend turning this feature on. If you plan on adding goals and wish to display the comments on the performance form, follow the instructions in SAP note 2459850.
continuouspm-integration	This switch corresponds to the checkbox in the online tool that enables integration with Continuous Performance Management. This will add a column to the goal plan showing any CPM achievements related to the goal. We recommend turning this on if you have implemented CPM.

An example code segment with our recommendations is shown in the following:

```
<switches>
  <switch for="cascader-role" value="off" />
  <switch for="cws-dispoption-competency-desc" value="off" />
  <switch for="turnoff-add-personal-goal-button" value="off" />
  <switch for="percentage-value-over-100" value="off" />
  <switch for="threaded-feedback" value="on" />
  <switch for="continuouspm-integration" value="on" />
</switches>
```

\<add-wizard> Element

As stated earlier, when creating a template in the online tool, the goal wizard is a popup that allows end users to step through creating a personal goal while asking at each step whether their goal is Specific, Measurable, Attainable, Relevant, and Time-bound (SMART). If you chose to add that feature, you will see this element added to your goal plan template. While you can turn the wizard on and off via the online tool, an extra feature to include goal alignment as part of the wizard can only be added via XML. To add this extra feature, simply add the \<include-goal-align> as in the following example.

Our example code segment is shown in the following (though we recommend not including this based on customer feedback):

```
<add-wizard mode="smart goal">
<include-goal-align/>
</add-wizard>
```

\<text-replacement> Elements

In this area of the XML, you can define a series of elements that are replacement for specific standard text elements on the goal plan screen. SAP note 2072180 defines the available options that can be placed in the "for" attribute. Of important note, you will see the instructions you defined in the online tool appear here.

The following is our example which includes instructions from the online tool:

```
<text-replacement for="Instructions">
<text><![CDATA[Welcome to your 2020 Goal plan!  To get started,
please read our guidance on creating a thoughtful goal <a href="http://
google.com">here</a>.<div><br></div><div>Some item to consider working
with goals:</div><div><ul><li>The goals listed here should be executed
from 1/1/20 to 12/3/20</li><li>Your goals will be visible to your
manager and above</li><li>Some goals may be added to your plan by your
manager</li><li>Your goals will be pulled onto your performance form
and incorporated as part of your overall performance score for the
year</li></ul></div>]]></text>
<text lang="en_US"><![CDATA[Welcome to your 2020 Goal plan!  To
get started, please read our guidance on creating a thoughtful goal
<a href="http://google.com">here</a>.<div><br></div><div>Some item to
```

consider working with goals:</div><div><ul><li>The goals listed here should be executed from 1/1/20 to 12/3/20</li><li>Your goals will be visible to your manager and above</li><li>Some goals may be added to your plan by your manager</li><li>Your goals will be pulled onto your performance form and incorporated as part of your overall performance score for the year</li></ul></div>]]></text>
</text-replacement>

<obj-library> Element

In order to associate a goal library to a goal plan, a mapping needs to be defined in the XML. The standard goal template you downloaded from SuccessStore will already have a mapping to the SuccessFactors goal library. You can replace it with your own mapping such as the one shown in the following example. Simply list all of the library field ids along with all the goal plan XML field names you wish to map.

Our following example maps "Name" in the library to "name" in the goal plan template XML:

```
<obj-library name="Demo Library" id="900000">
<field-mapping src-library-field-id="Name" dst-field-id="name"/>
<field-mapping src-library-field-id="Data1" dst-field-id="metric"/>
</obj-library>
```

Figure 4-18 illustrates how the mapping flows from the library upload, which was covered earlier in this chapter, through the mapping defined in the XML and finally to the end user screens.

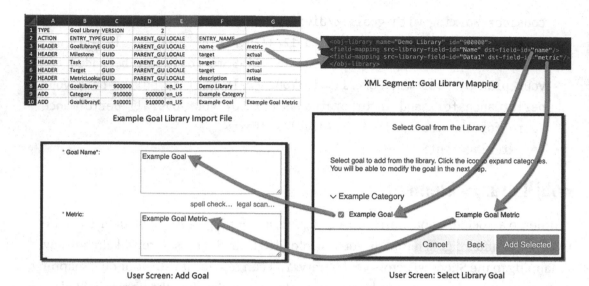

Figure 4-18. *Illustration of Field Mapping Flow from Library Upload to End User Screens*

\<category\> and \<default-category\> Elements

This section of the XML is where your goal categories are defined. We recommend you define your categories using the online tool, and they will populate automatically here. If you do not want your plan divided into categories at all, then remove this section entirely (as well as the default category and permissions for the category field). Note that the order of the categories you define here will define the order they show to the user. The default category must be last.

Our example code segment is shown in the following:

```
<category id="Financial">
  <category-name>Financial Growth and Responsibility</category-name>
  <category-name lang="en_US">Financial Growth and Responsibility
  </category-name>
</category>
<category id="Customer">
  <category-name>Customer Care</category-name>
</category>
<category id="Internal Business Processes">
  <category-name>Business Process Improvement</category-name>
```

```
  <category-name lang="en_US">Business Process Improvement</category-name>
</category>
<category id="Learning and Growth">
  <category-name>Growing Self and Others</category-name>
  <category-name lang="en_US">Growing Self and Others</category-name>
</category>
<default-category id="Other">
  <category-name>Other</category-name>
  <category-name lang="en_US">Other</category-name>
</default-category>
```

<field-definition> Elements

The field definitions are how individual fields are added to the goal plan. They set the name of the field, the type of the field, whether it is required, and so on. We recommend creating all of your fields in the online editor. This is because whenever you add a field, the online tool will automatically make updates to the <field-definition>, <field-permissions>, <plan-layout>, and <form-layout> elements. After the field is added in the online tool, you can then make edits as desired for individual settings that cannot be made in the online tool. There are only a few standard fields and types the online tool cannot create which we need to cover here as a supplement. The first is any "bool"-type field which shows as a checkbox and is rarely used. The second is the standard "comments" field (both id and type="comments") which customers may or may not want to include (we include these in the example so you can see what they look like). The third is standard field id "obj-plan-field1" (type="text") which is used as a mission statement for assigned goals and is rarely used. The last two are "group-rating" and "group-rating-comments" of type "rating" which we will discuss more in Chapter 5.

If you choose to create or manually edit fields, reference Table 4-6 to understand what each attribute of the field definition means.

Table 4-6. *Goal Plan Field Attributes*

Attribute	Description
required	Set "true" or "false" to make the field required or not.
viewdefault	Set to "off" if you want to not display this field by default (the user would have to select it from display options to see); otherwise, this is on by default.
showlabel	When you later define the layout of the plan, this will make more sense – it determines if the label of the field is shown. If the field is on the first row of the layout and therefore shows below the column header, we recommend you turn this to "off"; otherwise, turn it to "on."
reportable	If you set to "true," the field will be added to the standard Objective List report. You can choose at most 20 fields, and they must match by id and type between objective plans. In our experience, most companies do not use this legacy report. It is also important to note that any custom fields must be set to reportable for a manager to see them on an employee's plan when they have cascaded them down.
field-show-coaching-advisor	Only used with field type "textarea." This is really only used on development plans and advises how to write coaching points for making comments when employees are not meeting or meeting or exceeding expectations for a competency.
spellchk	Only used with field type "textarea" to show a spell-check icon that runs a spell-check on the field.
cascade-update	If set to "push-down," then only a group/team goal owner can edit the field. If "regular," then anyone assigned can edit it. We will cover this more in Chapter 5.

Our following example shows only a few sample fields (for the sake of brevity) created as a result of using the online editor, plus we added the comments field manually to give you a solid understanding of how fields of each type are structured:

```
<field-definition id="name" type="textarea" required="true" detail="false"
viewdefault="on" showlabel="false" default-calc-type="step" field-show-
coaching-advisor="false" cascade-update="push-down">
    <field-label>Goal Name</field-label>
    <field-label lang="en_US">Goal Name</field-label>
    <field-description>Goal Name</field-description>
    <field-description lang="en_US">Goal Name</field-description>
</field-definition>
```

```
<field-definition id="metric" type="textarea" required="true"
detail="false" viewdefault="on" showlabel="false" default-calc-type="step"
field-show-coaching-advisor="false" cascade-update="push-down">
   <field-label>Metric</field-label>
   <field-label lang="en_US">Metric</field-label>
   <field-description>Metric</field-description>
   <field-description lang="en_US">Metric</field-description>
</field-definition>
<field-definition id="weight" type="percent" required="true"
detail="false" viewdefault="on" showlabel="true" default-calc-type="step"
field-show-coaching-advisor="false" cascade-update="push-down">
   <field-label>Weight</field-label>
   <field-label lang="en_US">Weight</field-label>
   <field-description>Weight</field-description>
   <field-description lang="en_US">Weight</field-description>
   <default-value>0.0</default-value>
</field-definition>
<field-definition id="start" type="date" required="true" detail="true"
viewdefault="on" showlabel="true" default-calc-type="step" field-show-
coaching-advisor="false" cascade-update="push-down">
   <field-label>Start Date</field-label>
   <field-label lang="en_US">Start Date</field-label>
   <field-description>Start Date</field-description>
   <field-description lang="en_US">Start Date</field-description>
</field-definition>
<field-definition id="due" type="date" required="true" detail="true"
viewdefault="on" showlabel="false" default-calc-type="step" field-show-
coaching-advisor="false" cascade-update="push-down">
   <field-label>Due Date</field-label>
   <field-label lang="en_US">Due Date</field-label>
   <field-description>Due Date</field-description>
   <field-description lang="en_US">Due Date</field-description>
</field-definition>
```

```
<field-definition id="done" type="percent" required="false" detail="false"
viewdefault="on" showlabel="false" default-calc-type="step" field-show-
coaching-advisor="false" cascade-update="push-down">
   <field-label>% Complete</field-label>
   <field-label lang="en_US">% Complete</field-label>
   <field-description>% Complete</field-description>
   <field-description lang="en_US">% Complete</field-description>
   <default-value>0.0</default-value>
</field-definition>
<field-definition id="state" type="enum" required="true" detail="false"
viewdefault="on" showlabel="false" default-calc-type="step" field-show-
coaching-advisor="false" cascade-update="push-down">
   <field-label>Status</field-label>
   <field-label lang="en_US">Status</field-label>
   <field-description>Status</field-description>
   <field-description lang="en_US">Status</field-description>
   <enum-value value="Not Started" style="background:white;color:black;">
     <enum-label>Not Started</enum-label>
     <enum-label lang="en_US">Not Started</enum-label>
   </enum-value>
   <enum-value value="On Track" style="background:green;color:white;">
     <enum-label>On Track</enum-label>
     <enum-label lang="en_US">On Track</enum-label>
   </enum-value>
   <enum-value value="Behind" style="background:red;color:white;">
     <enum-label>Behind</enum-label>
     <enum-label lang="en_US">Behind</enum-label>
   </enum-value>
   <enum-value value="Completed" style="background:blue;color:white;">
     <enum-label>Completed</enum-label>
     <enum-label lang="en_US">Completed</enum-label>
   </enum-value>
   <enum-value value="Postponed" style="background:yellow;color:black;">
     <enum-label>Postponed</enum-label>
     <enum-label lang="en_US">Postponed</enum-label>
   </enum-value>
```

```
  <enum-value value="Cancelled" style="background:gray;color:black;">
    <enum-label>Cancelled</enum-label>
    <enum-label lang="es_ES">Cancelled</enum-label>
  </enum-value>
</field-definition>
<field-definition id="milestones" type="table" required="false"
detail="false" viewdefault="on" showlabel="true" default-calc-type="step"
field-show-coaching-advisor="false" cascade-update="push-down">
  <field-label>Milestones</field-label>
  <field-label lang="en_US">Milestones</field-label>
  <field-description>Milestones</field-description>
  <field-description lang="en_US">Milestones</field-description>
  <table-row-label>Milestones</table-row-label>
  <table-row-label lang="en_US">Milestones</table-row-label>
  <table-column id="start" type="date" required="true" validate-start-
  before-due="false" cascade-update="push-down">
    <column-label>Target Date</column-label>
    <column-label lang="en_US">Target Date</column-label>
    <column-description>Target Date</column-description>
    <column-description lang="en_US">Target Date</column-description>
  </table-column>
  <table-column id="desc" type="textarea" required="true" cascade-
  update="push-down">
    <column-label>Milestone</column-label>
    <column-label lang="en_US">Milestone</column-label>
    <column-description>Milestone</column-description>
    <column-description lang="en_US">Milestone</column-description>
  </table-column>
  <table-column id="due" type="date" required="false" cascade-
  update="push-down">
    <column-label>Actual Date</column-label>
    <column-label lang="en_US">Actual Date</column-label>
    <column-description>Actual Date</column-description>
    <column-description lang="en_US">Actual Date</column-description>
  </table-column>
</field-definition>
```

```
<field-definition id="comments" type="comment" required="false"
detail="false"
   viewdefault="on" showlabel="false">
<field-label>Comments</field-label>
<field-description>Comments</field-description>
</field-definition>
```

`<permission>` Elements

The `<permission>` elements section lists out each of the actions that can be performed in a goal plan and assigns who can perform those actions (as defined by the standard goal management roles). One of the major disadvantages of the online editor is that you cannot edit action permissions using the editor. Luckily, when you create a template, it does give some standard permissions that can be modified in the XML. Reference Tables 4-7 and 4-8 to understand what each action is, who is included in each role, and what actions can be committed by what roles. Remember when thinking of roles and permissions, the starting reference point is always the employee whose goal plan you are viewing.

Table 4-7. Goal Plan Permission Roles

Role	Description	Supported Actions
*	Everyone.	private-access, create, delete, delete-group-goal, cascade-pull, cascade-push, cascade-align, create-row, delete-row, move-row
E	Employee (the person whose goal plan it is).	private-access, create, delete, delete-group-goal, move, share, cascade-pull, cascade-push, cascade-align, unalign-parent, unalign-child, create-row, delete-row, move-row
EM	Employee's manager as defined in the user data file.	private-access, create, delete, delete-group-goal, share, cascade-push, cascade-align, create-row, delete-row, move-row
EMM	Employee's manager's manager.	private-access, delete, delete-group-goal, share, cascade-push, cascade-align, create-row, delete-row, move-row

(continued)

Table 4-7. (*continued*)

Role	Description	Supported Actions
EM+	Employee's manager and everyone in the reporting chain above that manager.	Same as the preceding actions
ED	Employee's direct reports.	Same as the preceding actions
EDD	Direct report of the employee's direct report.	Same as the preceding actions
ED+	Employee's direct report and all reports down the hierarchy.	Same as the preceding actions
EMD	Employee's manager's direct reports (basically co-workers under the same manager).	Same as the preceding actions
EX	Employee's matrix manager as defined in the user data file.	Same as the preceding actions
EY	Employee's direct report as a matrix manager.	Same as the preceding actions
EH	Employee's HR manager as defined in the user data file.	private-access, share, cascade-align, create-row, delete-row, move-row
F	Form reviewer. If you have pulled goals into a performance form and notice some people reviewing the performance form cannot view the goals because they have no direct reporting relationship to the employee, you may need to use this role. For a full explanation, see SAP note 2077256.	private-access, create, share, cascade-align, create-row, delete-row, move-row
OP	Objective Parent role. This is only relevant if you are using team goals (which will be covered in Chapter 5). It refers to the person who pushed down this goal onto the employee's plan.	private-access, delete

(*continued*)

Table 4-7. (*continued*)

Role	Description	Supported Actions
OC	Objective Child role. This is only relevant if you are using team goals (which will be covered in Chapter 5). It refers to the person who had a goal pushed down from this goal onto their own.	private-access
Cascader	Person who cascaded the goal onto the employee's plan. Remember this will only become active if the cascader-role switch is turned on.	create-row, delete-row, move-row (only used for field/table-level permissions)

Note   The preceding table is not a comprehensive list of all roles available in SAP SuccessFactors, but only those supported in Goal Management. For a complete listing across all modules, see SAP note 2087940.

Table 4-8. *Goal Plan Actions*

Action	Description
private-access	If a goal is set to private, the roles defined can view it.
create	Who can create a goal in the goal plan.
delete	Who can remove a goal from the plan. Note that for group goals, the creator can always delete regardless of this permission.
delete-group-goal	Who can remove a group goal from the goal plan.
move	Who can indent or move a goal up or down.
share	Who can make goals public or private.
cascade-pull	Who can pull goals from another plan into the current one (can only be * or none).
cascade-push	Who can push goals from the current plan into another one.

(*continued*)

Table 4-8. (*continued*)

Action	Description
cascade-align	Who can link two different goals from this plan to another.
unalign-parent	Who can unlink a goal that is pushed onto the goal plan.
unalign-child	Who can unlink a goal that is pushed onto another goal plan.
create-row	Who can create a row in a field that is type="table".
delete-row	Who can delete a row in a field that is type="table".
move-row	Who can move a row in a field that is type="table".

The following example shows the standard permissions given when creating a template from SuccessStore. In our experience, you will most likely need to modify these to adjust to your organization's needs:

```
<permission for="cascade-pull">
  <description><![CDATA[Anyone may cascade a goal from anyone else's
  plan.]]></description>
  <role-name><![CDATA[*]]></role-name>
</permission>
<permission for="cascade-push">
  <description><![CDATA[Anyone may cascade a goal to anyone.]]>
  </description>
  <role-name><![CDATA[*]]></role-name>
</permission>
<permission for="cascade-align">
  <description><![CDATA[Anyone may align a goal to anyone.]]>
  </description>
  <role-name><![CDATA[*]]></role-name>
</permission>
<permission for="create">
  <description><![CDATA[Only the employee, manager and form reviewer may
  create goals in a user's plan.]]></description>
  <role-name><![CDATA[E]]></role-name>
  <role-name><![CDATA[EM]]></role-name>
```

```
    <role-name><![CDATA[F]]></role-name>
  </permission>
  <permission for="delete">
    <description><![CDATA[Only the employee and manager may delete goals in
    his/her own plan.]]></description>
    <role-name><![CDATA[E]]></role-name>
    <role-name><![CDATA[EM]]></role-name>
  </permission>
  <permission for="unalign-parent">
    <description><![CDATA[Only the employee may unalign a parent goal from
    his/her own plan.]]></description>
    <role-name><![CDATA[E]]></role-name>
  </permission>
  <permission for="unalign-child">
    <description><![CDATA[Only the employee may unalign a child goal from
    his/her own plan.]]></description>
    <role-name><![CDATA[E]]></role-name>
  </permission>
  <permission for="move">
    <description><![CDATA[Only the employee and manager may move and indent
    goals in a user's plan.]]></description>
    <role-name><![CDATA[E]]></role-name>
    <role-name><![CDATA[EM]]></role-name>
  </permission>
  <permission for="share">
    <description><![CDATA[Only the employee and manager may share and
    unshare goals in his/her own plan.]]></description>
    <role-name><![CDATA[E]]></role-name>
    <role-name><![CDATA[EM]]></role-name>
  </permission>
  <permission for="private-access">
    <description><![CDATA[Employees and their managers up the hierarchy as
    well as HR may view unshared/private goals.Parents of cascaded private
    goals can see the children.]]></description>
    <role-name><![CDATA[E]]></role-name>
    <role-name><![CDATA[EM]]></role-name>
```

```
  <role-name><![CDATA[EM+]]></role-name>
  <role-name><![CDATA[EH]]></role-name>
  <role-name><![CDATA[OP]]></role-name>
</permission>
```

<field-permission> Elements

The <field-permission> elements define permissions for individual fields using the standard roles. The available permissions you can put in the "type" attribute are "None," "Read," and "Write".

Note   Table field permissions can also be defined by individual table columns for table fields; however, we recommend against this as it is not supported in Performance Management (PM) forms.

The following example shows the permissions given by default when you add fields using the online editor. Our example also includes the manually added comments field:

```
<field-permission type="read">
  <description><![CDATA[Everyone may read all fields for everyone.]]></
  description>
  <role-name><![CDATA[*]]></role-name>
  <field refid="name"/>
  <field refid="metric"/>
  <field refid="weight"/>
  <field refid="start"/>
  <field refid="due"/>
  <field refid="done"/>
  <field refid="state"/>
  <field refid="milestones"/>
  <field refid="comments"/>
</field-permission>
<field-permission type="write">
  <description><![CDATA[Theowner and manager may write to all fields for
  the employee's goals]]></description>
  <role-name><![CDATA[E]]></role-name>
```

```
    <role-name><![CDATA[EM]]></role-name>
    <field refid="name"/>
    <field refid="metric"/>
    <field refid="weight"/>
    <field refid="start"/>
    <field refid="due"/>
    <field refid="done"/>
    <field refid="state"/>
    <field refid="milestones"/>
    <field refid="comments"/>
  </field-permission>
```

<plan-layout> Element

The <plan-layout> element controls the order in which fields are shown on the main
goal plan screen. Furthermore, the column weight dictates how much of the screen the
field attempts to take up when the browser window is expanded or contracted (the total
of your weights should equal 100).

Our example is shown in the following:

```
  <plan-layout>
    <column weight="25">
      <field refid="name"/>
      <field refid="milestones"/>
    </column>
    <column weight="25">
      <field refid="metric"/>
    </column>
    <column weight="10">
      <field refid="weight"/>
    </column>
    <column weight="10">
      <field refid="start"/>
    </column>
    <column weight="10">
      <field refid="due"/>
```

```
  </column>
  <column weight="10">
    <field refid="done"/>
  </column>
  <column weight="10">
    <field refid="state"/>
  </column>
</plan-layout>
```

<form-layout> Element

This element controls how goals are displayed in the Goal Details tab within the
Performance Management form (given that you are integrating goals into a performance
form). The entire layout is written in html within the brackets of the CDATA[ ]. You can
see from the following example how each function call corresponds to displaying a
specific field (with corresponding id in the field definitions) within a table cell and how
the column widths are defined again by percentages that should equal to 100.

Our example is shown in the following:

```
<form-layout><![CDATA[
<div align="left">
  <b>Category: ${field.category}</b>
</div>#set ($group = "name-state")
<table width="100%" cellspacing="0" cellpadding="0">
  <tr>
    <td valign="top" width="20%">#if ($display.name) <b>${label.name}:
    </b></br>
     ${field.name} #end</td>
    <td> </td>
    <td valign="top" width="30%">#if ($display.metric) <b>${label.
    metric}:</b></br>
     ${field.metric} #end</td>
    <td> </td>
    <td valign="top" width="10%">#if ($display.weight) <b>${label.
    weight}:</b></br>
     ${field.weight} #end</td>
```

```
<td> </td>
<td valign="top" width="10%">#if ($display.start) <b>${label.start}:
</b></br>
  ${field.start} #end</td>
<td> </td>
<td valign="top" width="10%">#if ($display.due) <b>${label.due}:</b>
</br>
  ${field.due} #end</td>
<td> </td>
<td valign="top" width="10%">#if ($display.done) <b>${label.done}:
</b></br>
  ${field.done} #end</td>
<td> </td>
<td valign="top" width="10%">#if ($display.state) <b>${label.state}:
</b></br>
  ${field.state} #end</td>
</tr>
</table>## turn off grouping for subsequent fields #set ($group = "")
<div style="margin:0.5em 0">
  #if ($display.milestones)
  <div class="objPair" style="display:none" id="${util.newHiddenDivId()}">
    <b>${label.milestones}:</b>${field.milestones}
  </div>#end
</div>]]></form-layout>
```

Note   After the <form-layout> element, you may notice the <pdf-layout> and <details-layout> elements if you created a template from SuccessStore. These are legacy elements no longer used and can be ignored or replaced with "<pdf-layout><![CDATA[[]]]></pdf-layout>

<details-layout><![CDATA[[]]]></details-layout>". If you remove them entirely, the system will throw an error when uploading the XML.

<mobile-field-list> Element

This section controls what fields are shown in the mobile goals list view. If you checked the boxes for the done and state fields in the online tool, they will show here as in our following example:

```
<mobile-field-list>
  <field refid="done"/>
  <field refid="state"/>
</mobile-field-list>
</obj-plan-template>
```

Note   We added the closing of the <obj-plan-template> field here since this is the end of the XML document and the tag needs to be closed.

Wrapping Up Basic Configuration

Congratulations! You have now turned on Goal Management, configured a basic goal plan template using the online editing tool, assigned that form to users, and made modifications to the underlying XML to support any basic requirements of your organization! Now it is time to tour the form we created in the example following an end-to-end goal plan process.

Using Goal Management

In this section, we take a look at the culmination of our configurations by walking through a basic goal setting process based on the sample XML we built in the previous section. First, we will walk through as a manager to create some goals on our own plan and cascade those down to our employees. Then, we will log in as one of those employees to view the goals, make adjustments to our plan, and align goals to our co-workers. Let's get started!

163

Creating and Cascading Goals as a Manager

A typical scenario for managers during the goal setting cycle is to create goals and cascade them down to employees. For the sake of our model company example, this is where the CEO would log into the system and start distributing goals to their team. Let's see how this is accomplished by following these steps:

1. Log into the system or proxy as one of the users you assigned to your manager role.

2. Click the navigation menu in the upper left-hand corner of the screen and choose "Goals." The screen will appear as shown in Figure 4-19. The goal plan selected as the default plan and assigned to managers should appear in the dropdown next to the name of the user. You will notice your chosen categories will appear with no goals yet assigned.

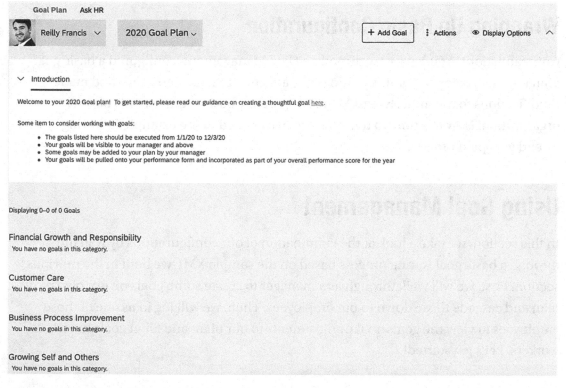

Figure 4-19. *Goal Plan*

3. Click "Add Goal." You will see options to create a new goal, use the goal wizard, or copy from another goal plan.

4. Click "Create a New Goal." You will see options to add a personal goal or a library goal. Click "Library Goal."

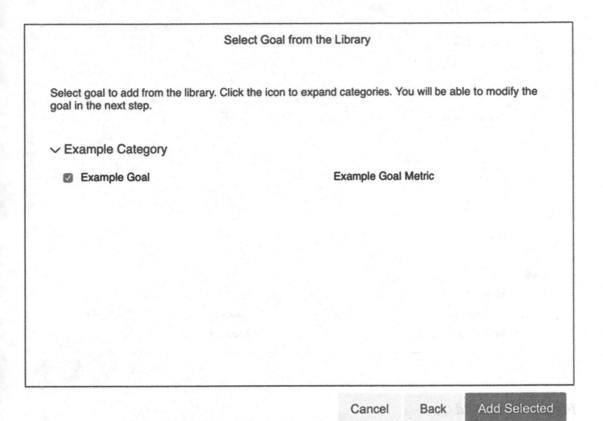

Select Goal from the Library

Select goal to add from the library. Click the icon to expand categories. You will be able to modify the goal in the next step.

∨ Example Category

☑ Example Goal   Example Goal Metric

Cancel   Back   Add Selected

Figure 4-20. *Adding a Library Goal*

5. You will see a listing of the goals you uploaded to the library and associated with the goal plan template in the <obj-library> mapping. Select a goal by clicking the checkbox to the left of it and click "Add Selected." An example is shown in Figure 4-20. The "Add Goal" screen will appear based on the configurations in your <field-definition> elements as seen in Figure 4-21. The mapped library fields will prepopulate as shown in the following figure. The start and due dates will also default to the <obj-plan-start> and <obj-plan-end> dates.

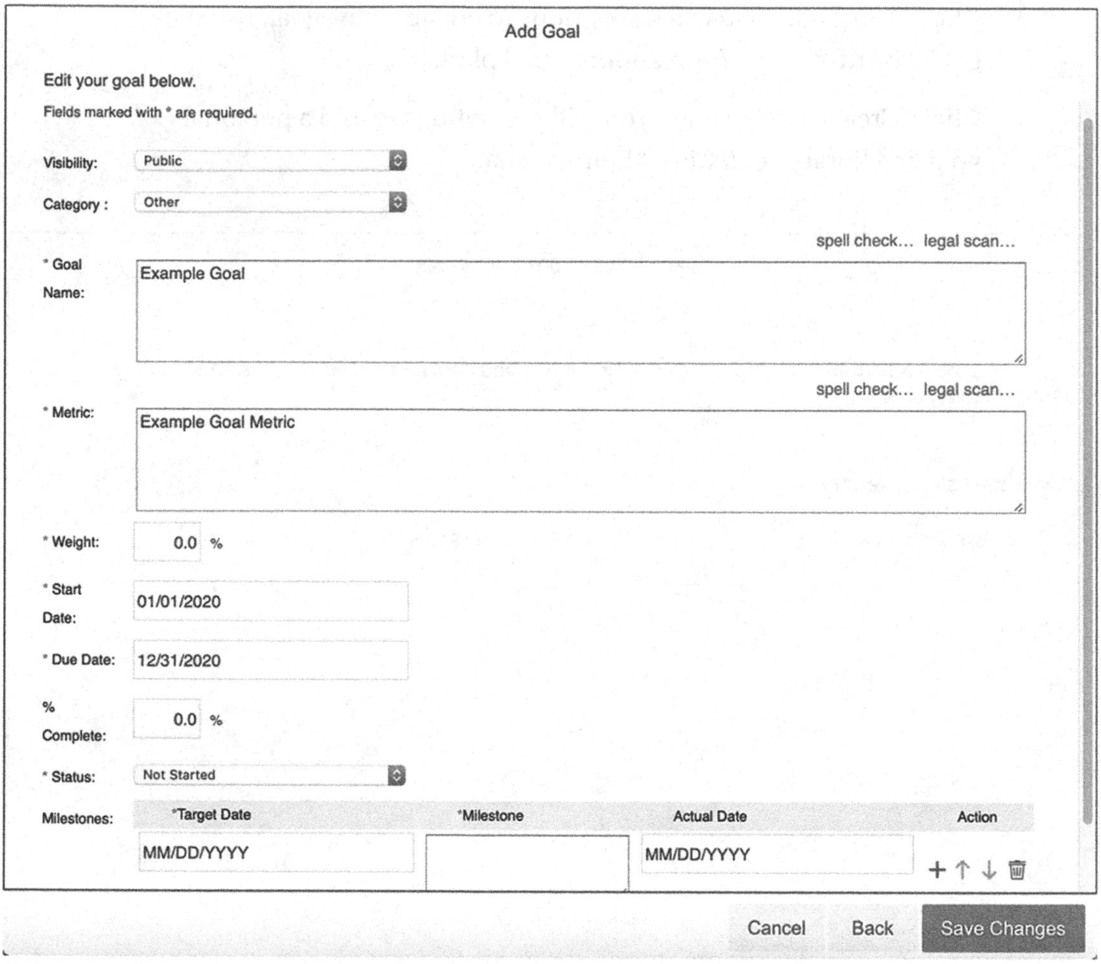

Figure 4-21. *Add Goal*

6. Modify the values in the fields as desired and click "Save Changes."
    The goal will appear as shown in Figure 4-22.

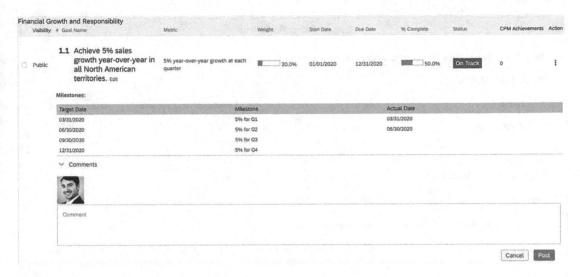

Figure 4-22. *A Goal Shown on the Goal Plan*

7. Click the box next to the goal to select it and then click the three
    dots icon below "Action" at the far right. You will see available
    actions based on your <permission> elements settings. You can
    also click "Actions" at the top of the screen next to "Add Goal" to
    see more actions. Click here and choose "Cascade." The screen
    will show the direct reports of the user as seen in Figure 4-23.

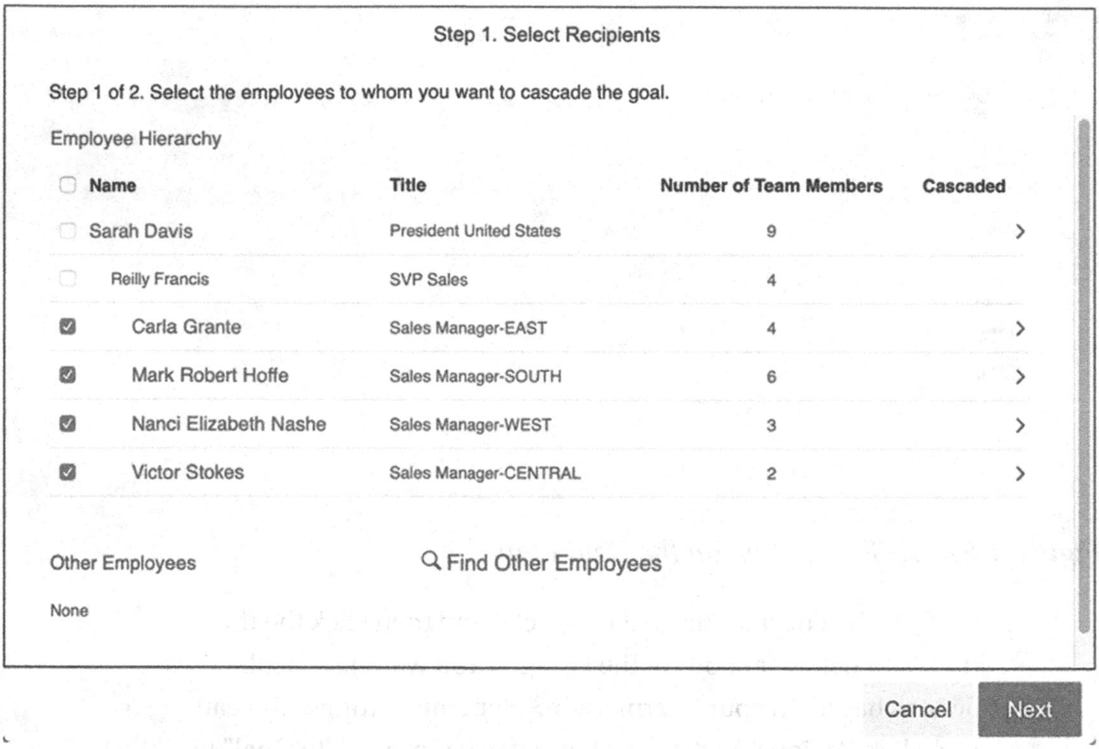

Step 1. Select Recipients

Step 1 of 2. Select the employees to whom you want to cascade the goal.

Employee Hierarchy

	Name	Title	Number of Team Members	Cascaded
☐	Sarah Davis	President United States	9	>
☐	Reilly Francis	SVP Sales	4	
☑	Carla Grante	Sales Manager-EAST	4	>
☑	Mark Robert Hoffe	Sales Manager-SOUTH	6	>
☑	Nanci Elizabeth Nashe	Sales Manager-WEST	3	>
☑	Victor Stokes	Sales Manager-CENTRAL	2	>

Other Employees   🔍 Find Other Employees

None

Cancel   Next

***Figure 4-23.** Cascading a Goal*

8. Given that you have set up permissions correctly, you can click the checkbox next to each of the direct reports for the manager and then click "Next." Confirm the fields are populated as you desire and then click "Cascade."

9. In the success popup, click "Close."

10. Now click the logged-in manager's name in the upper left-hand corner to bring down a listing of direct reports. Click the name of the employee whose plan you want to view. When the plan is loaded, you will see your cascaded goal on the employee's goal plan.

Creating and Aligning Goals as an Employee

Now that we've seen how a manager can create goals and cascade them down to an employee, let's take a look at how an employee can create their own goals using the SMART goal wizard and align them to others. Follow these steps:

1. Log in or proxy as one who is assigned the employee role you created.

2. Click the navigation menu in the upper left-hand corner of the screen and click "Goals." The default goal plan will load.

3. Click "Add Goal." You will see options to create a new goal, use the goal wizard, or copy from another goal plan.

4. Click "Goal Wizard." The "Add a SMART Goal" screen will show as in Figure 4-24. Step through each step of the wizard by entering the required information and clicking "Next." The goal will appear on the goal plan. Make sure the goal is set to public.

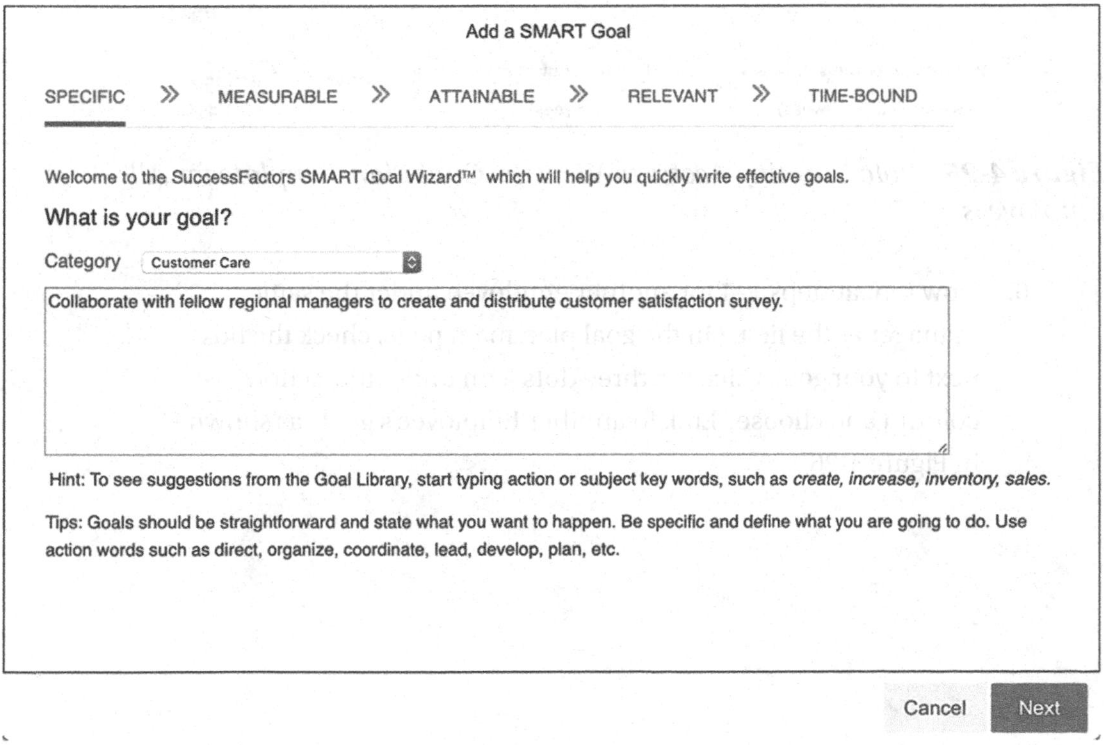

Figure 4-24. Adding a Goal Using the SMART Wizard

5. Log back in as the administrator and follow the steps from the "Create an Employee Role" section, to create a new employee role, but this time give permissions for target users to be "All." The results should look like Figure 4-25.

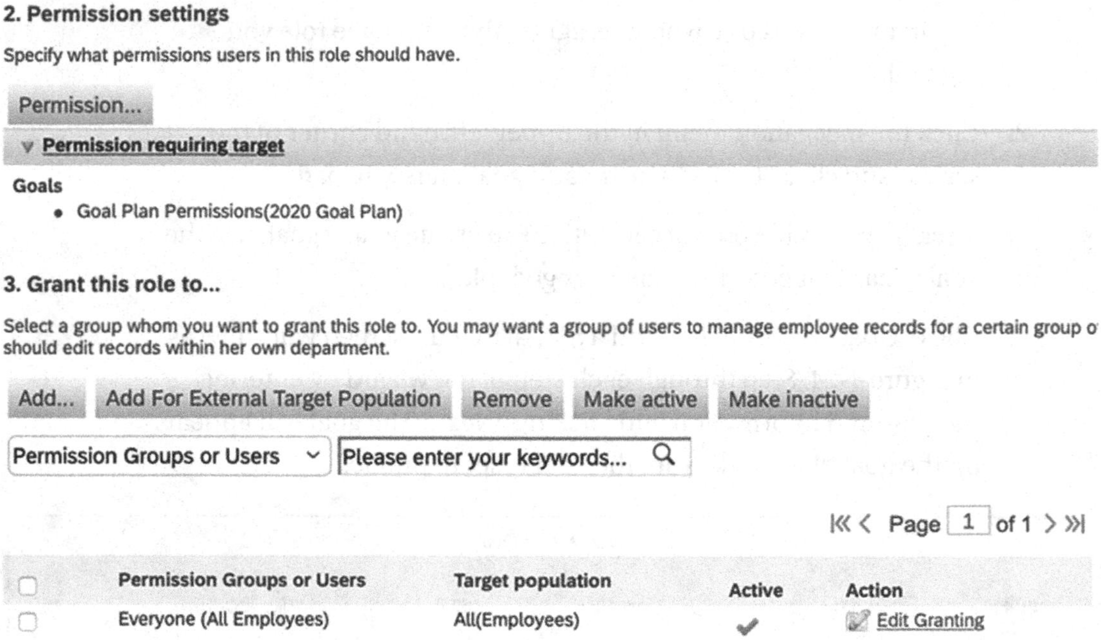

2. Permission settings

Specify what permissions users in this role should have.

Permission...

⋁ **Permission requiring target**

Goals
* Goal Plan Permissions(2020 Goal Plan)

3. Grant this role to...

Select a group whom you want to grant this role to. You may want a group of users to manage employee records for a certain group o should edit records within her own department.

Add...	Add For External Target Population	Remove	Make active	Make inactive

Permission Groups or Users ⌄	Please enter your keywords... 🔍

K⟨ ⟨ Page ☐1 of 1 ⟩ ⟩⟩

	Permission Groups or Users	Target population	Active	Action
☐	Everyone (All Employees)	All(Employees)	✔	📝 Edit Granting

Figure 4-25. *Role Granting Access to View the Goal Plan Template for All Employees*

6. Now repeat steps 1–4 for another employee under the same manager as the first. On the goal plan main page, check the box next to your goal. Click the three dots icon under the Action column and choose "Link to another Employee's goal" as shown in Figure 4-26.

Customer Care
Visibility
Goal Name
Metric
Weight
Start Date
Due Date
% Complete
Status
CPM Achievements
Action
Private
2.1 Achieve team average of "Excellent" rating on customer care survey. Edit
"Excellent" rating or higher.
0.0%
01/01/2020
12/31/2020
0.0%
Not Started
0
Edit goal
View goal detail
Link to another Employee's goal
Goals Alignment Spotlight
Add goal to Outlook
Delete goal
Move goal up
Comments
Comment

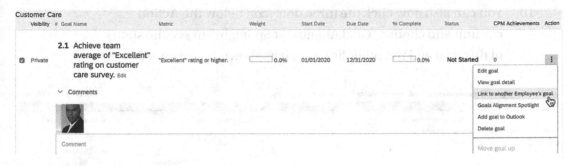

Figure 4-26. Aligning a Goal

7. In the new popup that appears, click the name of the mutual manager of the two employees. You will see the names of the manager's direct reports. Click the radio button next to the user from step 1 and click "Next."
8. Click the radio button next to the goal you created in steps 1–4 and click "Next."
9. In the confirmation screen, click "Link." You should now see the goal aligned to the first goal as shown in Figure 4-27.

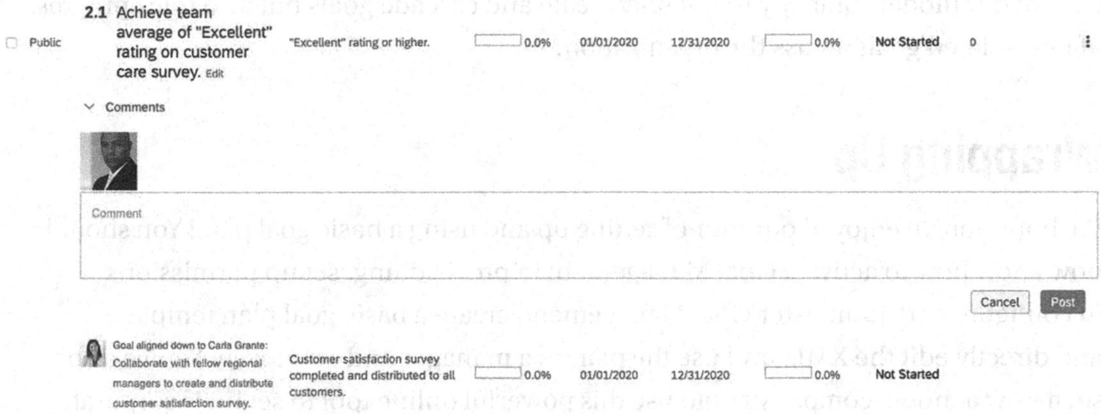

Public
2.1 Achieve team average of "Excellent" rating on customer care survey. Edit
"Excellent" rating or higher.
0.0%
01/01/2020
12/31/2020
0.0%
Not Started
0
Comments
Comment
Cancel
Post
Goal aligned down to Carla Grante: Collaborate with fellow regional managers to create and distribute customer satisfaction survey.
Customer satisfaction survey completed and distributed to all customers.
0.0%
01/01/2020
12/31/2020
0.0%
Not Started

Figure 4-27. Results of Aligning a Goal

10. You can also now click the three dots icon below the Action
     column and choose "Goal Alignment Spotlight" to see the status
     of this goal and the other linked to it as shown in Figure 4-28.

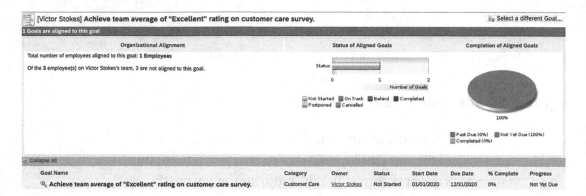

Figure 4-28. *Goal Alignment Spotlight Report*

In the preceding example, we've now shown you the two most common goal plan
scenarios: one where managers set goals for themselves and their employees and
another where employees can also view public goals on other plans and align goals
together with their own plan. We can also relate how the preceding steps would help the
CEO of our model company to not only create and cascade goals but also track progress
of interrelated goals across the organization.

Wrapping Up

We hope you've enjoyed our tour of setting up and using a basic goal plan! You should
now know how to activate Goal Management in provisioning, set up permissions
to configure and administer Goal Management, create a basic goal plan template
and directly edit the XML, and use the plan as a manager and employee. You've also
seen how a model company could use this powerful online tool to set their corporate
objectives and cascade those down level by level within the company so that they are
executed by employees. Furthermore, we can see how employees can use the tool to
collaborate on interrelated goals and how progress on these goals can be tracked across
the company. We've also shown you how employees can draw from a library of example
goals and set up their own personal goals. In the next chapter, we will step through
some alternate goal setting methodologies that take advantage of less common but still
powerful features of Goal Management.

CHAPTER 5

Alternate Goal Management Concepts and Functionality

In our experience, the basic configurations and usage we've covered in the last chapter are what most organizations require for their Goal Management implementations. However, there are other admin tools and configurable features less widely used that can be very powerful. Such functionality is typically only used for organizations that need it to support their unique business processes. In this chapter, we assume you are now familiar with the basic tools to create and use a goal plan and will walk through more specialized scenarios where we can take advantage of some of the lesser-used administration functions and configuration options.

Note We assume you have completed basic configurations outlined in the prior chapter before making any of the additional configurations outlined in this chapter.

Administering Goals Using Mass Update Tools

Many HR administrators will end up administering goals manually by using a permission role granted to them that has access to view and edit goal plans for all employees or for employees where they are the designated HR admins. While this is practical for small groups, a large number of employees would require the use of a mass update tool. The following subsections outline two tools that can be used to perform such mass updates.

173

© Susan Traynor, Michael A. Wellens and Venki Krishnamoorthy 2021
S. Traynor et al., *SAP SuccessFactors Talent: Volume 1*, https://doi.org/10.1007/978-1-4842-6600-7_5

Mass Import and Assigning of Goals

In some organizations where business goal setting is centralized for all employees, the employees will have goals assigned to them en masse by administrators rather than choosing them on their own. This can happen to a varying degree where employees have no self-created goals at all or where some goals are set by the centralized admins and others are self-assigned. For basic goal plans, there are two screens that help mass assign goals: legacy "Import Goals" and "Beta Goal Import" screens.

Prerequisites for Setting Up Import Goals

The legacy "Import Goals" screen is available by default to administrators when you turn on Goal Management in the configuration steps in the previous chapter. To assign permissions to import goals and activate Beta Goal Import, follow these steps:

1. Type and select "Manage Permission Roles" in the search bar.

2. When the screen loads, click the role you wish to modify. Then click "Permission…:"

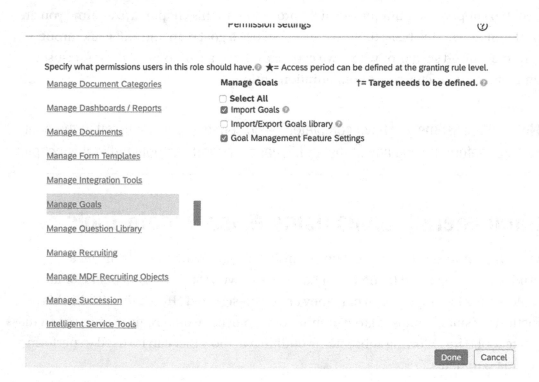

Figure 5-1. Import Goals and Goal Management Feature Settings Permissions

3. Click "Manage Goals" on the left and then click "Import Goals" and "Goal Management Feature Settings" on the right as shown in Figure 5-1.

4. Click "Done." On the main screen, click "Save Changes."

5. Once permissions have been assigned, the "Beta Goal Import" can be activated by typing and selecting "Goal Management Feature Settings" in the search bar, selecting "Goal Import," and clicking "Save."

Note   These two screens are not the only way to mass assign goals. If you implement group goals, there is another method associated with that which we will cover in the next section.

Beta Import Goals

Despite the name, Beta Import Goals is fully functional. It provides the latest functionality SAP has added to the legacy Import Goals. This includes supporting metric lookup tables and comments; scheduling the import as a job; aligning goals; updating goals already added to plans, mission statements, and group goals; and setting goals as read-only. To import goals via the Beta Import Goals screen, follow these steps:

1. Be sure you are logged in as a user that has your email assigned to it, or you will not be able to see the results email at the last step!

2. Type and select "Beta Goal Import" in the search bar. The Beta Import Goals screen will appear as seen in Figure 5-2.

Import Goals

Import Goals by uploading CSV fileThe limit for the total number of goals in a CSV file is up to 30,000. Please don't upload a CSV file containing more than 30,000 goals.

Available List of Templates: 2020 Goal Plan ⌄	Generate CSV Header
Import File: Choose File no file selected	
Character Encoding: Western European (Windows/ISO) ⌄	
Read-only goals ☐ Yes (Check only if you wish to set the imported goals to be read-only)	
Allow Duplicate Assignment of Group Goals ☐	

Import

Figure 5-2. *Beta Import Goals Screen*

3. Select the goal plan template for which you would like to upload goals. Click "Generate CSV Header." The system will download a file containing the fields associated with the goal plan template based on the configuration in the template XML. An example is shown in Figure 5-3.

Figure 5-3. *Example Goal Import Template CSV File with Headers*

4. Add rows to the file.

Note Let's take a minute to look at the example import template shown in the preceding figure. Each row of data you include in the file represents a goal or table field row to be added including at least the minimum required fields on the template along with an assignment of user(s). Columns D, E, and F all represent IDs you give to the goals. Columns G–L all starting with FILTER allow you to use filter criteria to choose who gets the goal. Anyone matching the filter criteria will be assigned the goal. The remaining columns starting with OBJECTIVE are fields according to the XML configuration that will be filled in associated with the goal. Table 5-1 gives specifics on each column.

Table 5-1. *Goal Import File Columns*

Column	Description
TYPE	Specifies whether you are uploading an OBJECTIVE for a normal goal, OBJECTIVE_GROUPV1 or OBJECTIVE_GROUP_V2 depending on the type of group goal (we will cover group goals versions in the next section), or OBJECTIVE_TEAM for team goals (also covered in the next section). You can also specify TASK, MILESTONE, TARGET, METRICLOOKUP, or OBJCOMMENT for table data associated with a goal.
ACTION	Can be ADD, UPDATE, DELETE, ASSIGN, SHARE, UNSHARE, or UNASSIGN. SHARE and UNSHARE are used to assign/unassign owners to team goals. ASSIGN/UNASSIGN simply adds the team goal to the plan.

(continued)

Table 5-1. (*continued*)

Column	Description
ID/SUBID	Not used. SAP will use this field to fill in the automatic internal system ID that is generated for the goal if/when a goal export screen is created.
GUID	Unique ID of a goal that you, the uploader, use to identify the goal to be assigned.
SUBGUID	The unique ID of table data (TASK, MILESTONE, etc.) that you, the uploader, use to identify that table data.
FILTER_*	When you populate these fields, the system will look at the corresponding fields in the user data file (UDF) and only assign the goal/table data to all users that have the same value. The exception is the MGR field which does not work (it was kept in place for future functionality). If you would like to not filter and instead assign the row to all users, input "ALL" into the FILTER_USERNAME column and leave all others blank.
OBJECTIVE_*	These columns will vary depending on the XML definition of the template you chose. They represent each field/table field in the . The PUBLIC field takes a value of "Y" or "N." Date fields should be in the format 3/30/2020.

5. Click "Import File" and choose the file you updated.

6. Choose a character encoding.

Note   We recommend UTF-8 character encoding, particularly for international implementations with a variety of languages to avoid uploading malformed characters.

7. Check the boxes next to "Read-only goals" and "Allow Duplicate Assignment of Group Goals" as desired.

8. Click "Import." You will either get an error message or a success message indicating a job was scheduled, and you will receive an email with the results.

Note   As an alternative to using this screen to upload, you can use the same file template within provisioning to schedule a job to pull the file from a SFTP server. To do this, log into provisioning for your company instance and click "Manage Jobs." Click "Create Job" and choose "TGM FTP Data Import" for the "Job Type" field. You may want to use this in the case of uploading very large files. Note that no matter your method, the system limits you to uploading 30,000 records at a time.

Legacy Import Goals

According to SAP Help documentation, legacy "Import Goals" is used only when "Beta Goal Import" does not support what you want to accomplish – specifically to set the visibility of goal plans and set goals as read-only. However, we've seen in the same documentation that these features are supported in Beta Goal Import. Furthermore, we don't recommend setting visibility of goal plans – this was a legacy activity prior to the existence of role-based permissions which are now used to control access to goal plans. We therefore do not recommend using the legacy "Import Goals." In our personal experience, we have never come across a customer who has needed to use it.

Adding Permission to Import Goals to End Users

In some cases, you may want to make goal import available for end users such as managers. To do this, add the following code segment to the <permission> elements section of the goal plan XML:

```
<permission for="import-goal">
  <description><![CDATA[ Managers can import goals directly on the
  employee's plan ]]></description>
    <role-name><![CDATA[EM]]></role-name>
</permission>
```

The manager will then see the option to import goals from the "Actions" menu in the upper right-hand corner of the goal plan screen as shown in Figure 5-4. The file format is the same as the admin uses; however, only the user filter can be used, and the username must be that of the current goal plan shown on screen.

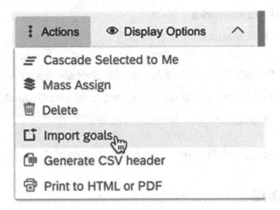

Figure 5-4. *Import Goals from the Actions Menu*

Transferring Goals Between Employees

What happens when an employee leaves or is transferred or their job function changes? In many cases, this results in a shift in business goals where these goals need to be moved from person to person. In order to accomplish this, we can transfer goals between employees. Here, we will walk through the steps needed to set up and use the goal transfer functionality.

Set Up Provisioning

Prior to using the feature, it must be turned on in provisioning. Follow these steps to activate the feature:

1. Log into provisioning and select your company instance.

2. Click "Company Settings."

3. Check the box next to "TGM/CDP Objective Transfer Wizard" as seen in Figure 5-5.

4. Click "Save."

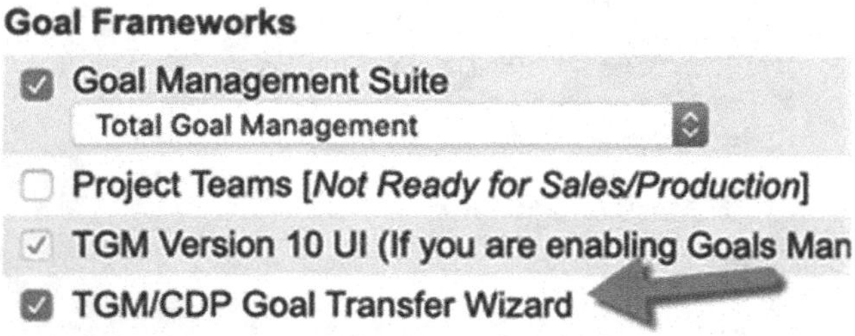

Goal Frameworks

☑ Goal Management Suite
   Total Goal Management ◉
☐ Project Teams [*Not Ready for Sales/Production*]
☑ TGM Version 10 UI (If you are enabling Goals Man
☑ TGM/CDP Goal Transfer Wizard

Figure 5-5. *Turning on Goal Transfer Wizard in Provisioning*

Assign Permissions

Now that the feature is active, it is time to assign permissions to use it:

1. Type and select "Manage Permission Roles" in the search bar.

2. When the screen loads, click the role you wish to modify. Then click "Permission…:"

3. Click "Manage User" on the left and then click "Goal Transfer" on the right as shown in Figure 5-6.

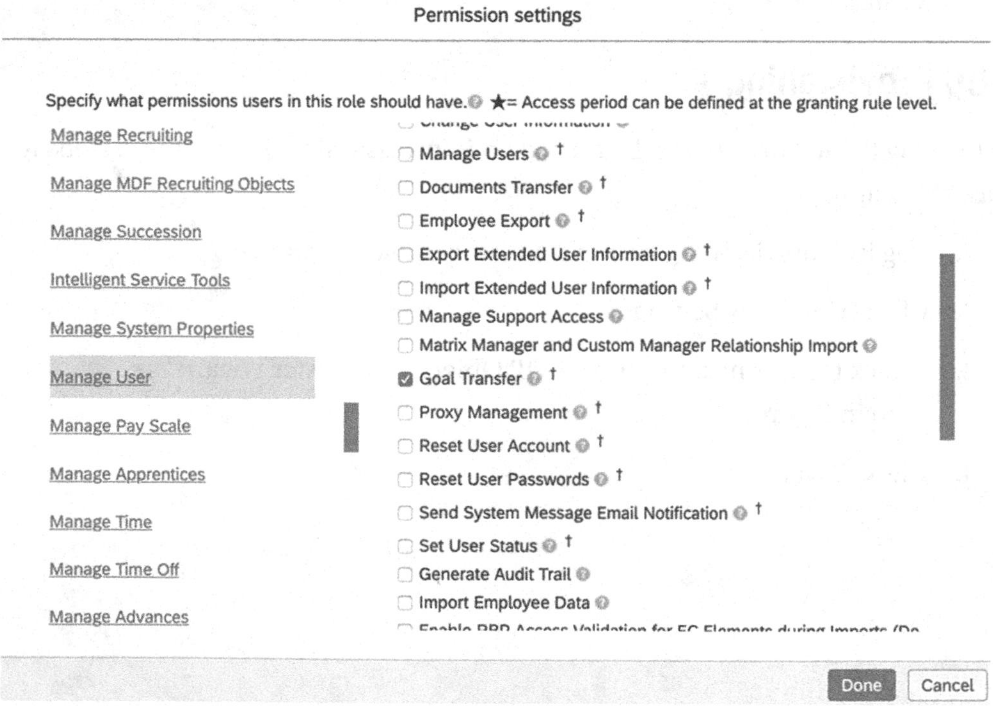

Permission settings

Specify what permissions users in this role should have.◉ ★= Access period can be defined at the granting rule level.

Manage Recruiting	☐ Manage Users ◉ †
Manage MDF Recruiting Objects	☐ Documents Transfer ◉ †
Manage Succession	☐ Employee Export ◉ †
	☐ Export Extended User Information ◉ †
Intelligent Service Tools	☐ Import Extended User Information ◉ †
Manage System Properties	☐ Manage Support Access ◉
	☐ Matrix Manager and Custom Manager Relationship Import ◉
Manage User	☑ Goal Transfer ◉ †
Manage Pay Scale	☐ Proxy Management ◉ †
	☐ Reset User Account ◉ †
Manage Apprentices	☐ Reset User Passwords ◉ †
Manage Time	☐ Send System Message Email Notification ◉ †
	☐ Set User Status ◉ †
Manage Time Off	☐ Generate Audit Trail ◉
Manage Advances	☐ Import Employee Data ◉

Done Cancel

Figure 5-6. *Assigning Goal Transfer Permissions*

4. Click "Done."

5. On the main screen, click "Save Changes."

Using Goal Transfer

Now that the feature is on and we have permissions to use it, let's get started! Follow these steps:

1. Type and select "Transfer Goal Between Users" in the search bar. The screen will appear as shown in Figure 5-7.

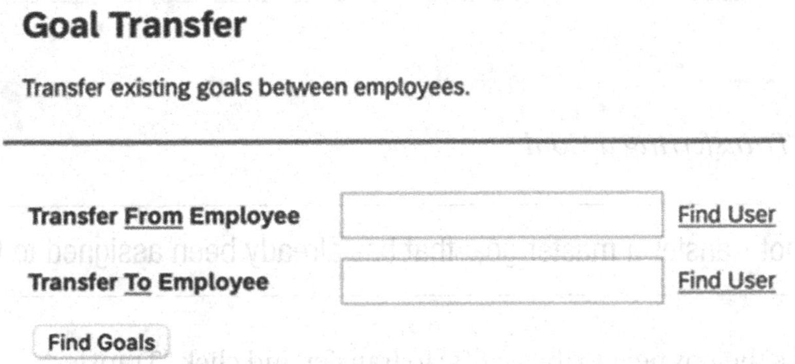

Goal Transfer

Transfer existing goals between employees.

Transfer From Employee [   ]   Find User

Transfer To Employee [   ]   Find User

Find Goals

Figure 5-7. *The "Goal Transfer" Screen*

2. Enter the username of the employee from whom the goal will be transferred or use the "Find User" link to look up the employee.

3. Repeat the preceding step for the employee to whom the goal will be transferred.

4. Click "Find Goals." The goals on the plan will appear as shown in Figure 5-8.

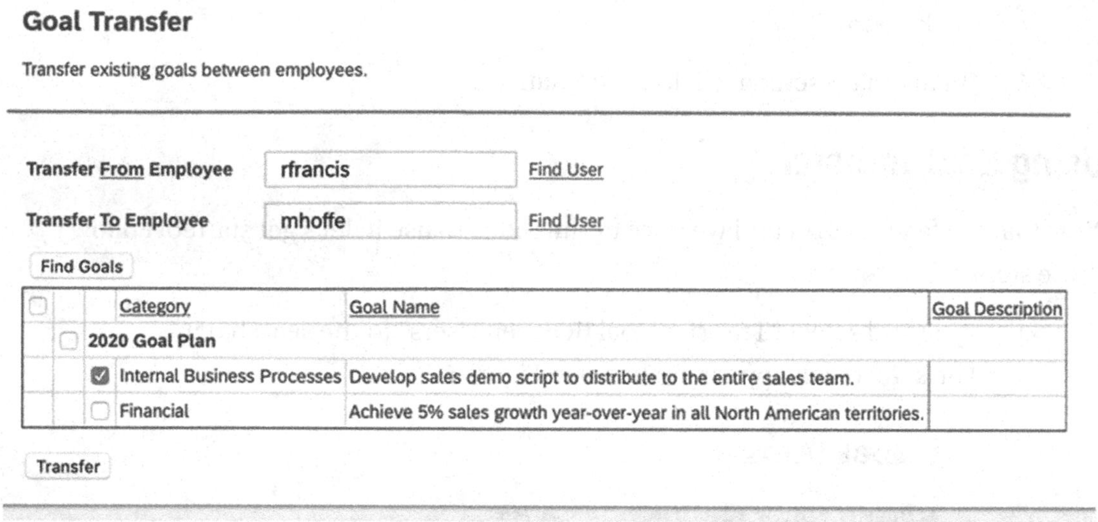

Goal Transfer

Transfer existing goals between employees.

		Category	Goal Name		Goal Description

Transfer From Employee   rfrancis   Find User

Transfer To Employee   mhoffe   Find User

Find Goals

☐		Category	Goal Name		Goal Description
	☐	**2020 Goal Plan**			
	☑	Internal Business Processes	Develop sales demo script to distribute to the entire sales team.		
	☐	Financial	Achieve 5% sales growth year-over-year in all North American territories.		

Transfer

Figure 5-8. *Transferring a Goal*

Note   Do not transfer a master goal that has already been assigned to the user.

5.   Click the box next to the goal(s) to transfer and click "Transfer."

6.   The screen will update telling you the goal was successfully transferred.

Note   Any comments made to the goal will also be transferred along with any linkages to other goals.

Alternate Goal Management Concepts and Features

In this section, we cover functionality that is used less often, but can provide powerful features to meet the more specialized demands of organizations. This includes Goal Execution and Alignment Chart, goal plan state, custom calculations, achievement lookups, group goals, team goals, and initiatives.

Goal Execution/Alignment Chart

Goal Execution provides a way for customers to track progress of goals across the organization in greater depth than the standard percentage complete and status fields. It is intended for organizations that track goal progress frequently and make goal status updates part of their business execution strategies. An example would be an organization that utilizes Management by Objective methodologies and needs a tool to help track progress. Goal Execution consists of three components: the Status Report, Execution Map, and Meeting Agenda. The main concept is that the organization teams closely on their linked goals and provides status reports on a regular basis. In this way, system data is up to date, and the Execution Map or Alignment Chart that shows how linked goals are progressing remains relevant.

Note   The Execution Map is being replaced by the Alignment Chart due to the retirement of Adobe Flash at the end of 2020. Configuration of the two is almost identical, the main technical difference being the underlying user interface technology. We recommend using the new Alignment Chart since the old technology will no longer be supported. Furthermore, end of maintenance is set for the second half of 2019 and end of life is set for the second half of 2020 for Goal Execution features entirely. See SAP note 2071572 for more details. We therefore have kept this section mainly to support existing customers and do not recommend launching a new Goal Execution implementation for new customers.

Goal Execution Prerequisites

There are a few restrictions to note when using this functionality. First, goals must be linked to one another (cascaded or aligned) before the visualization is of any use. Second, the standard fields we will outline in this chapter can only be associated with one active goal plan at a time (this is how the screens know what plan is being executed and to render). Keep in mind as well that permissions come into play here in terms of which goals are public vs. private and therefore who can see them in the Execution Map/Alignment Chart.

Provisioning Settings

To activate Goal Execution in provisioning, follow these steps:

1. Log in to provisioning for your company instance and click "Company Settings."

2. Check the boxes next to "Enable Execution Map – requires 'Version 11 UI framework (ULTRA),'" "Enable Status Report – requires 'Version 11 UI framework (ULTRA),'" and "Enable Meeting Agenda – requires 'Version 11 UI framework (ULTRA).'" An example is shown in Figure 5-9.

3. Click "Save."

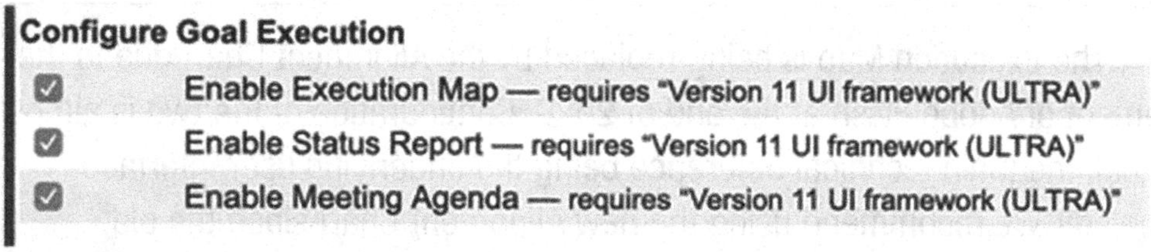

Configure Goal Execution

☑   Enable Execution Map — requires "Version 11 UI framework (ULTRA)"
☑   Enable Status Report — requires "Version 11 UI framework (ULTRA)"
☑   Enable Meeting Agenda — requires "Version 11 UI framework (ULTRA)"

Figure 5-9. *Goal Execution Provisioning Settings*

Configuration Permissions

Follow these steps to assign permissions to configure Goal Execution to your administrator role:

1. Type and select "Manage Permission Roles" in the search bar.

2. Click the name of the role you wish to edit.

3. Click "Permission…:"

4. Click "Manage Goals" on the left.

5. Check the boxes next to "Manage Configuration of Goal Execution" and "Goal Management Feature Settings" as seen in Figure 5-10.

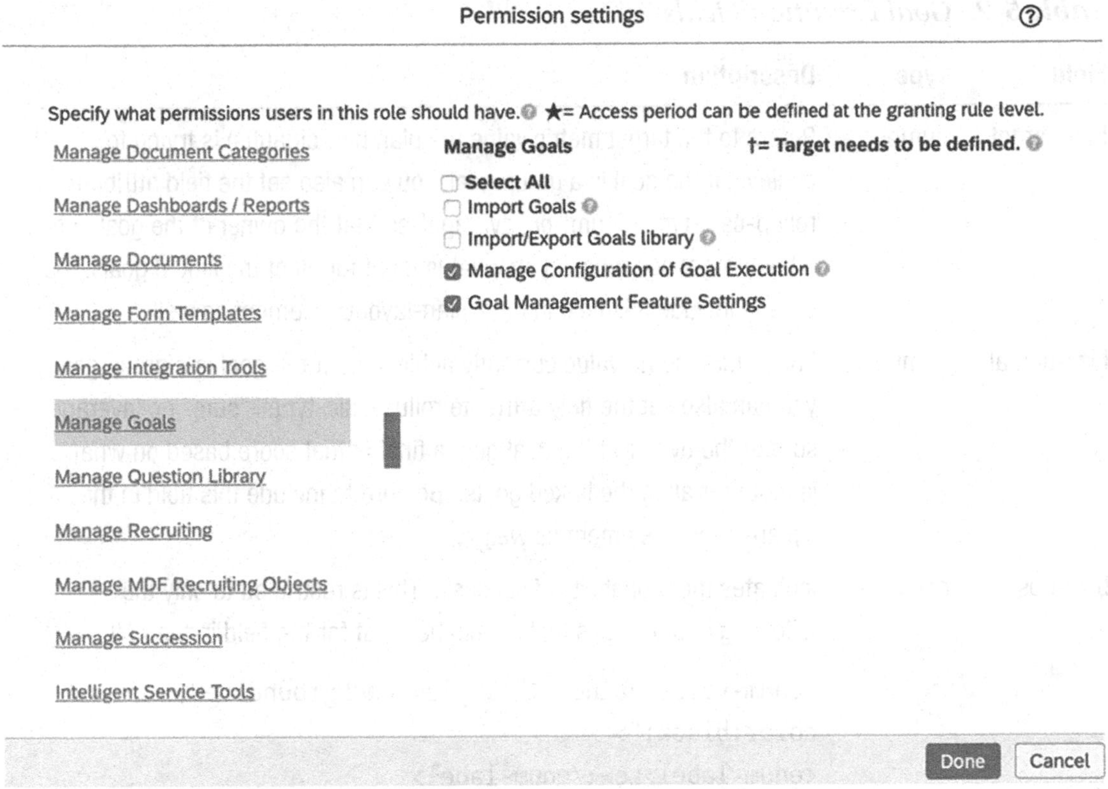

Permission settings   ⑦

Specify what permissions users in this role should have.❶ ★= Access period can be defined at the granting rule level.

Manage Document Categories   **Manage Goals**   †= **Target needs to be defined.** ❶

                                     ☐ **Select All**
Manage Dashboards / Reports   ☐ Import Goals ❶
                                     ☐ Import/Export Goals library ❶
Manage Documents   ☑ Manage Configuration of Goal Execution ❶
                                     ☑ Goal Management Feature Settings
Manage Form Templates

Manage Integration Tools

Manage Goals

Manage Question Library

Manage Recruiting

Manage MDF Recruiting Objects

Manage Succession

Intelligent Service Tools

                                                            Done   Cancel

Figure 5-10. *Managing Goal Execution Permissions*

6. Click "Done."

7. On the main screen, click "Save Changes."

Goal Execution/Alignment Chart Configuration

You will need to implement the following fields in Table 5-2 in your goal plan XML in the <field-definition> elements section before any of the Goal Execution screens will work.

Table 5-2. *Goal Execution Fields*

Field	Type	Description
bizx-target	number	Refers to the target metric value the plan participant(s) is trying to achieve. If the goal is a group goal, you can also set the field attribute rollup-calc-type="sum" or "average" so that the owner of the goal gets a final target score based on what is input for all of the linked goals. Be sure to include this field in the <plan-layout> element as well.
bizx-actual	number	The actual metric value currently achieved. If the goal is a group goal, you can also set the field attribute rollup-calc-type="sum" or "average" so that the owner of the goal gets a final actual score based on what is input for all of the linked goals. Be sure to include this field in the <plan-layout> element as well.

bizx-pos	enum	Indicates the probability of success. This is restricted to only the following enum values that should be input for the field in the XML:
		
		`<enum-value value="1" style="background:red;`
		`color:black;">`
		`<enum-label>Low</enum-label>`
		`</enum-value>`
		`<enum-value value="2" style="background:yellow;`
		`color:black;">`
		`<enum-label>Med</enum-label>`
		`</enum-value>`
		`<enum-value value="3" style="background:green;`
		`color:white;">`
		`<enum-label>High</enum-label>`
		`</enum-value>`
		`<default-value>3</default-value>`
		`</field-definition>`
		
		Be sure to include this field in the <plan-layout> element as well.

(*continued*)

Table 5-2. (*continued*)

Field	Type	Description
bizx-strategic	enum	Yes/no flag for whether or not this is a strategic goal. You can only have the following values defined in the XML:

```
<enum-value value="0" style="background:white;
color:black;">
<enum-label>Non-strategic</enum-label>
</enum-value>
<enum-value value="1" style="background:white;
color:black;">
<enum-label>Strategic</enum-label>
</enum-value>
<default-value>0</default-value>
```

Be sure to include this field in the <plan-layout> element as well.

Field	Type	Description
bizx-effort-spent	enum	Appears in the Execution Map, Status Report, and Meeting Agenda screens (not the main goal plan). The field is limited to the following values you must include in the XML:

```
<enum-value value="0"
style="background:white;color:black;">
        <enum-label>None</enum-label>
    </enum-value>
    <enum-value value="1"
style="background:white;color:black;">
        <enum-label>Very Little</enum-label>
    </enum-value>
    <enum-value value="2"
style="background:white;color:black;">
        <enum-label>A Little</enum-label>
    </enum-value>
```

(*continued*)

Table 5-2. (*continued*)

Field	Type	Description
		```<enum-value value="3"```
		```style="background:white;color:black;">```
		```<enum-label>Some</enum-label>```
		```</enum-value>```
		```<enum-value value="4"```
		```style="background:white;color:black;">```
		```<enum-label>A Lot</enum-label>```
		```</enum-value>```
		```<enum-value value="5"```
		```style="background:white;color:black;">```
		```<enum-label>Really A Lot</enum-label>```
		```</enum-value>```
		```<default-value>0</default-value>```
bizx-status-comments	textarea	Used only for comments on the Status Report view (not the comments on the main goal plan screen).

Once the fields have been added to the XML, you can activate Goal Execution by following these steps:

Note   If you do not add the field prior to this, you will get an error when you try to save your settings!

---

1. Type and select "Goal Execution Settings" in the search bar.

2. In the "Goal Plan" field, choose your active goal plan where you have added the Goal Execution fields.

3. Under "Status Report Settings," consider if you want to add reminders for employees to fill out status reports. In the example shown in Figure 5-11, we set the start date to be the first Friday of the year and set a reminder notification every Friday. If the report is not filled out by Monday, the employee gets another reminder email that the status report is late.

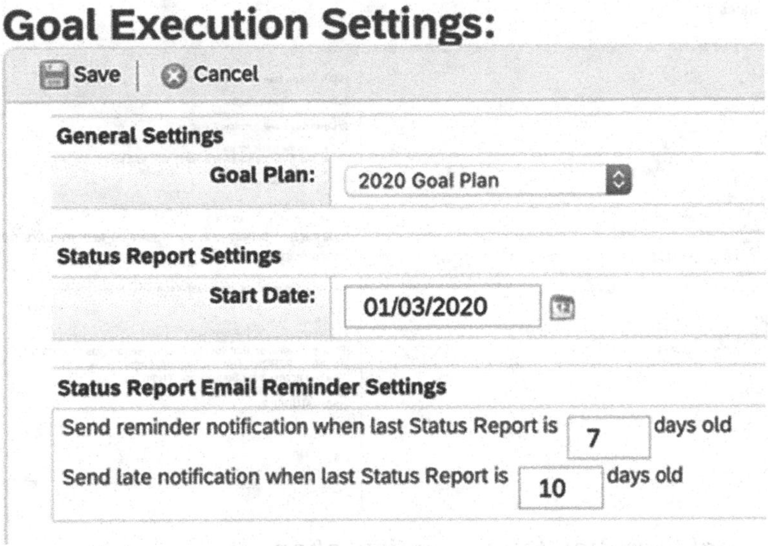

Goal Execution Settings:

💾 Save | ⊗ Cancel

General Settings

Goal Plan: 2020 Goal Plan ⇕

Status Report Settings

Start Date: 01/03/2020 📅

Status Report Email Reminder Settings

Send reminder notification when last Status Report is [7] days old

Send late notification when last Status Report is [10] days old

Figure 5-11. *Goal Execution Settings*

4. Click "Done" to save your changes.

Before the emails will actually be sent out, you will need to complete configuration of the email templates. If you do not want to send email reminders, you will still need to complete the preceding reminder settings; however, you can disable the emails outlined in the next steps. To configure the reminder emails, follow these steps:

1. Type and select "E-Mail Notification Templates Settings" in the search bar.

2. Check the boxes next to "Status Report Due Reminder," "Status Report Late Reminder," "Status Report Update Request," and "Status Report Submitted Notification" as desired and click "Save Notification Settings." An example is shown in Figure 5-12.

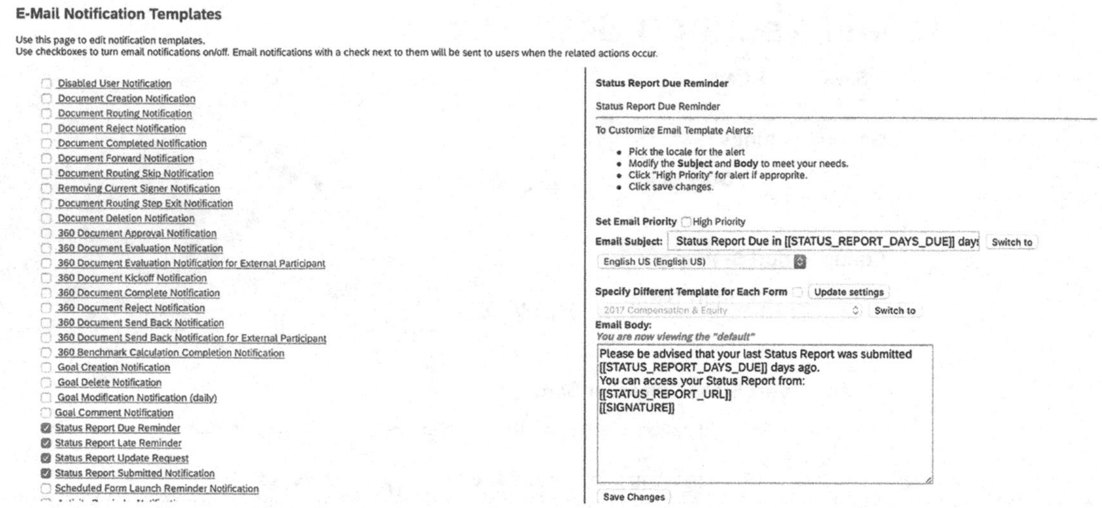

E-Mail Notification Templates

Use this page to edit notification templates.
Use checkboxes to turn email notifications on/off. Email notifications with a check next to them will be sent to users when the related actions occur.

- Disabled User Notification
- Document Creation Notification
- Document Routing Notification
- Document Reject Notification
- Document Completed Notification
- Document Forward Notification
- Document Routing Skip Notification
- Removing Current Signer Notification
- Document Routing Step Exit Notification
- Document Deletion Notification
- 360 Document Approval Notification
- 360 Document Evaluation Notification
- 360 Document Evaluation Notification for External Participant
- 360 Document Kickoff Notification
- 360 Document Complete Notification
- 360 Document Reject Notification
- 360 Document Send Back Notification
- 360 Document Send Back Notification for External Participant
- 360 Benchmark Calculation Completion Notification
- Goal Creation Notification
- Goal Delete Notification
- Goal Modification Notification (daily)
- Goal Comment Notification
- ☑ Status Report Due Reminder
- ☑ Status Report Late Reminder
- ☑ Status Report Update Request
- ☑ Status Report Submitted Notification
- Scheduled Form Launch Reminder Notification

Status Report Due Reminder

Status Report Due Reminder

To Customize Email Template Alerts:

- Pick the locale for the alert
- Modify the **Subject** and **Body** to meet your needs.
- Click "High Priority" for alert if appropriate.
- Click save changes.

Set Email Priority ☐ High Priority

Email Subject: Status Report Due in [[STATUS_REPORT_DAYS_DUE]] days   Switch to

English US (English US)

Specify Different Template for Each Form ☐   Update settings

2017 Compensation & Equity   Switch to

Email Body:
You are now viewing the "default"

Please be advised that your last Status Report was submitted [[STATUS_REPORT_DAYS_DUE]] days ago.
You can access your Status Report from:
[[STATUS_REPORT_URL]]
[[SIGNATURE]]

Save Changes

Figure 5-12. *Goal Execution Email Configuration*

3. Click the email template name you want to edit. When you are finished making your edits, click "Save Changes."

If you would like to use the Alignment Chart instead of the Execution Map, you should also follow these steps after activating all of the preceding notifications:

1. Type and select "Goal Management Feature Settings" in the search bar.

2. Check the box next to "Enable Goal Alignment Chart" as seen in Figure 5-13.

3. Click "Save."

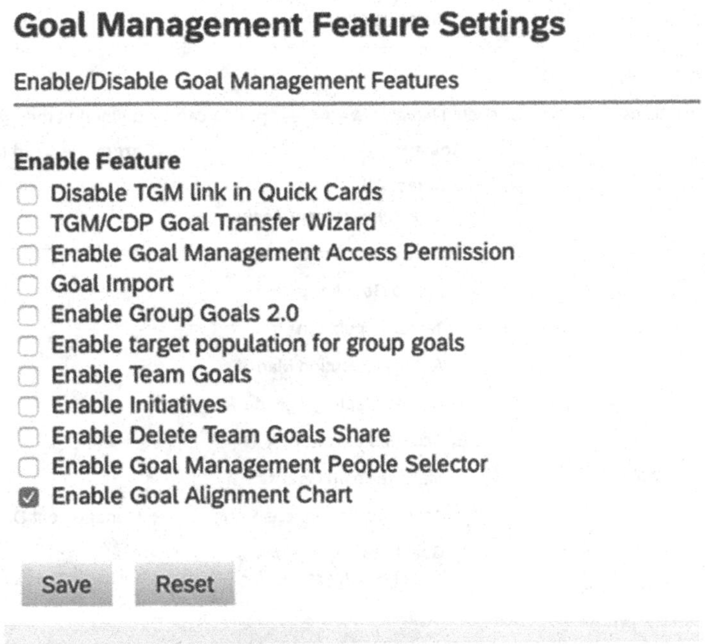

Goal Management Feature Settings

Enable/Disable Goal Management Features

Enable Feature

- ☐ Disable TGM link in Quick Cards
- ☐ TGM/CDP Goal Transfer Wizard
- ☐ Enable Goal Management Access Permission
- ☐ Goal Import
- ☐ Enable Group Goals 2.0
- ☐ Enable target population for group goals
- ☐ Enable Team Goals
- ☐ Enable Initiatives
- ☐ Enable Delete Team Goals Share
- ☐ Enable Goal Management People Selector
- ☑ Enable Goal Alignment Chart

Save   Reset

Figure 5-13. *Enabling Goal Alignment Chart*

Note   We recommend using the new Alignment Chart since Goal Execution will no longer be supported after the year 2020.

Assign End User Permission Roles

Now that we have completed our configurations, we can assign permissions for end users to use the Goal Execution features. Follow these steps:

1. Type and select "Manage Permission Roles" in the search bar.

2. Click the name of the role you wish to edit.

3. Click "Permission…:"

4. Click "Goals" on the left.

5. Check the boxes next to "Access Execution Map," "Access Meeting Agenda," and "Access Status Report" as desired. An example is shown in Figure 5-14.

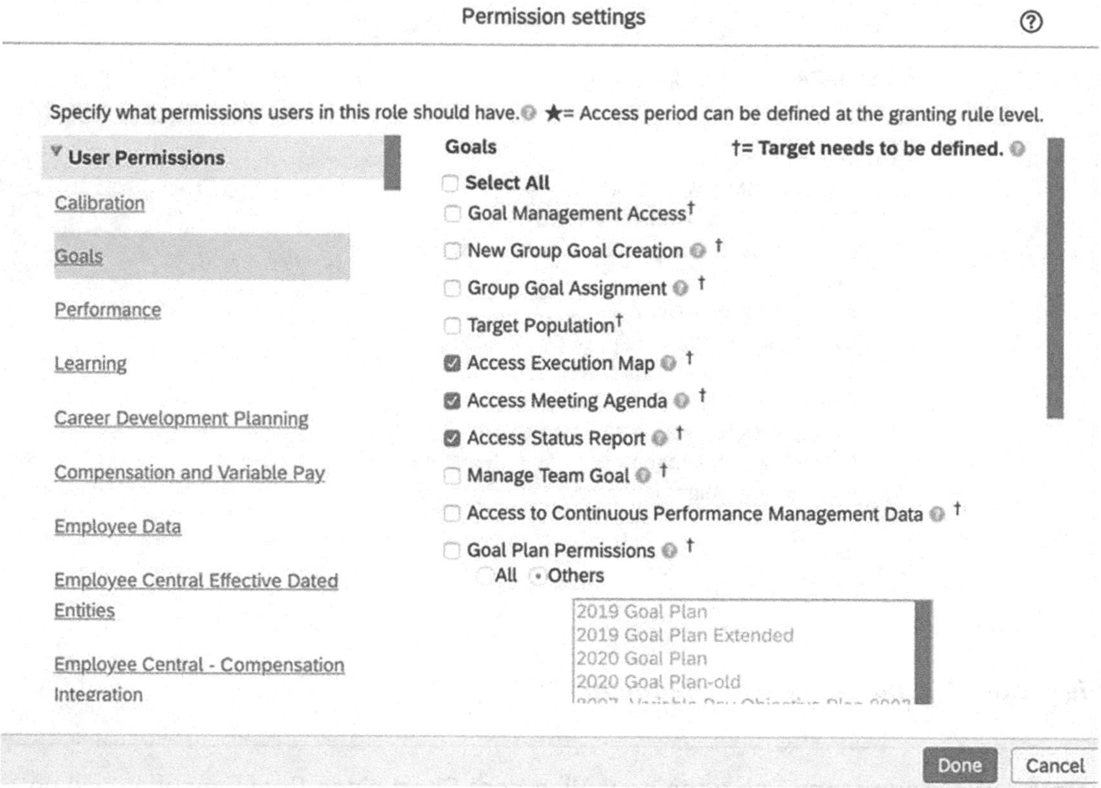

Permission settings   ⑦

Specify what permissions users in this role should have.⑦ ★= Access period can be defined at the granting rule level.

▼ User Permissions	Goals	†= Target needs to be defined. ⑦
Calibration	☐ Select All	
	☐ Goal Management Access†	
Goals	☐ New Group Goal Creation ⑦ †	
	☐ Group Goal Assignment ⑦ †	
Performance	☐ Target Population†	
	☑ Access Execution Map ⑦ †	
Learning	☑ Access Meeting Agenda ⑦ †	
	☑ Access Status Report ⑦ †	
Career Development Planning	☐ Manage Team Goal ⑦ †	
Compensation and Variable Pay	☐ Access to Continuous Performance Management Data ⑦ †	
Employee Data	☐ Goal Plan Permissions ⑦ †	
	○ All ⊙ Others	
Employee Central Effective Dated Entities	2019 Goal Plan 2019 Goal Plan Extended 2020 Goal Plan 2020 Goal Plan-old	
Employee Central - Compensation Integration		

Done   Cancel

Figure 5-14. *Goal Execution End User Permissions*

Note   Typically, the Execution Map is assigned to a manager or executive role, the Meeting Agenda is assigned to a manager role, and the Status Report is assigned to employees.

6.   Click "Done."

7.   On the main permission role screen, click "Save Changes."

Using Goal Execution

Here, we will run through a quick scenario to demonstrate how Goal Execution works:

1.   Log in as an employee who has a goal aligned up to their manager.

2.   Navigate to the goal plan.

3. Under the Action column, click "Edit goal." Fill in values for the new bizx-target, bizx-actual, bizx-pos, and bizx-strategic fields. An example is shown in Figure 5-15.

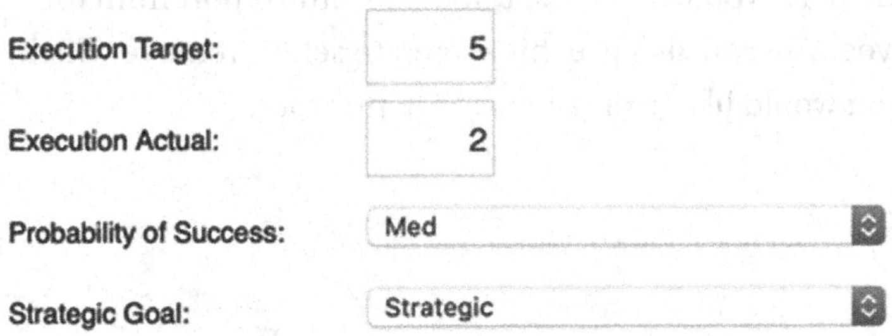

Execution Target:	5
Execution Actual:	2
Probability of Success:	Med
Strategic Goal:	Strategic

Figure 5-15. *Filling in Goal Execution–Specific Fields*

4. Navigate to "Status Report." Fill in values for the bizx-target, bizx-actual, bizx-effort-spent, and bizx-status-comments fields as seen in Figure 5-16. Click "Send Status Update."

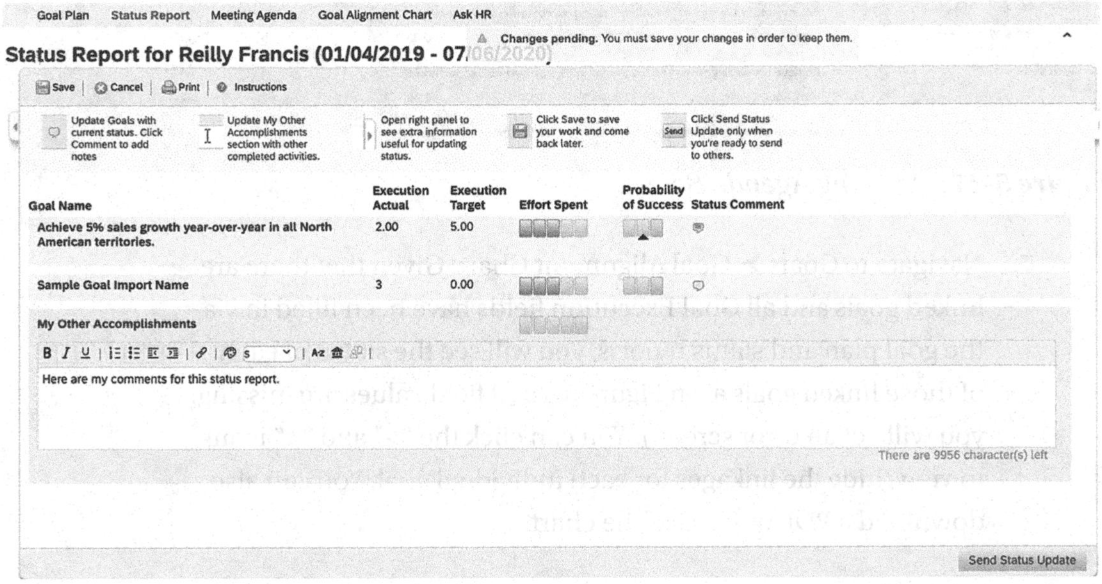

Figure 5-16. *Goal Execution Status Report*

5. Log in as the manager who owns the goal that this goal is aligned up to.

6. Navigate to Goals ➤ Meeting Agenda. The screen will appear as in Figure 5-17. You will see the updated status report from the employee. You can also use this screen to select/remove which goals you would like to create in a PDF printout.

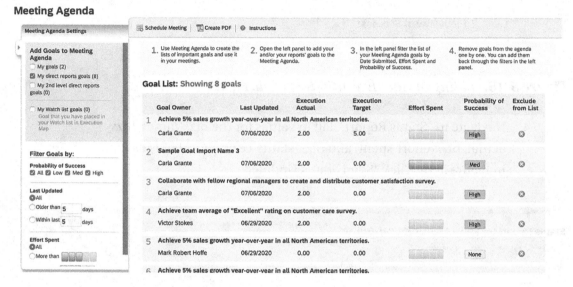

Figure 5-17. *Meeting Agenda Screen*

7. Navigate to Goals ➤ Goal Alignment Chart. Given that there are linked goals and all Goal Execution fields have been filled in via the goal plan and status reports, you will see the status of each of those linked goals as in Figure 5-18 (if field values are missing, you will get an error screen). You can click the ">" and "<" icons to view/hide the linkages for each individual goal. You can also download a PDF or JPEG of the chart.

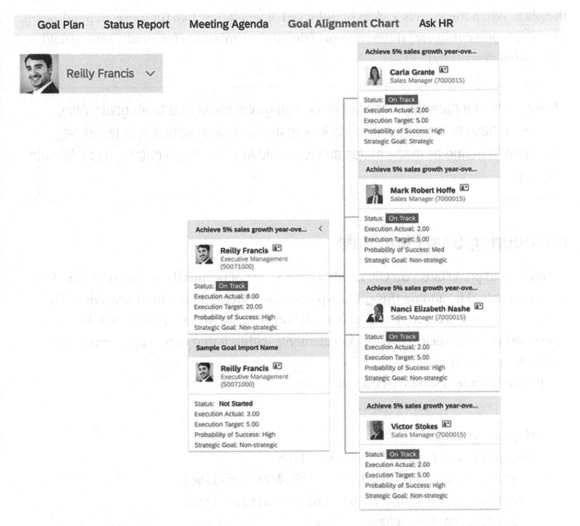

Figure 5-18. *Goal Alignment Chart*

Goal Plan State

In our experience, some organizations request to lock goal plans so that limited or no access is allowed to make further edits to goals. For example, an organization may wish to enforce a goal setting period for the month of January and lock plans thereafter so that goals are not edited later in the year (e.g., to foil any attempt at trying to make it seem the original goal more closely reflects the actual outcome). Since goal plans are not routable forms, the logical way to accomplish this is with the goal plan state. The goal plan state adds a link to the top of the goal plan so that only persons authorized can lock or unlock the plan. When the form is locked or unlocked, it will follow two (or more, depending on how many you configure) different sets of defined permissions (normally setting fields to editable vs. read-only).

Note   This functionality does not work with group goals and team goals. Also, while we have personally only seen locked and unlocked states, it is technically possible to define as many states as you would like. For more details, see SAP note 2072109.

Configuring Goal Plan State

To add a goal plan state, you will need to define a set of permissions for each state. This is accomplished by adding the <object-plan-states> element and then defining each <object-plan-state> element within it. Each <object-plan-state> should include a set of <permission> and <field-permission> elements within it that define the permissions particular to that state.

Example code is shown in the following:

```
...
  <obj-plan-states>
    <obj-plan-state id="A" default="true">
      <state-label lang="en_US">Unlocked</state-label>
      <action-label lang="en_US">Unlock</action-label>
      <permission for="change-state">
        <description><![CDATA[Only Manager and above can change state]]>
        </description>
        <target-state><![CDATA[B]]></target-state>
        <role-name><![CDATA[EM]]></role-name>
      </permission>
<permission for="import-goal">
  <description><![CDATA[ Managers can import goals directly on the
  employee's plan ]]></description>
    <role-name><![CDATA[EM]]></role-name>
</permission>
  ...
```

```
<field-permission type="read">
<description><![CDATA[Everyone may read all fields for everyone.]]></
description>
<role-name><![CDATA[*]]></role-name>
<field refid="name"/>
...
</field-permission>
...
    </obj-plan-state>
<obj-plan-state id="B" default="false">
    <state-label lang="en_US">Locked</state-label>
    <action-label lang="en_US">Lock</action-label>
    <permission for="change-state">
...
    </permission>
...
  <field-permission type="read">
...
  </field-permission>
...
    </obj-plan-state>
    </obj-plan-states>
...
```

Using Goal Plan State

Once the goal plan state is added, users will now see an indicator of the state at the top
of the goal plan as shown in the following. In our example, logging in as the employee,
you will be able to see what the goal plan state is, but you must log in as a manager and
view an employee's goal plan to change its state. The state names and actions will appear
according to how you defined them in the XML configuration. In the example shown
in Figure 5-19, the manager can simply click the "Lock" link and the permissions will
change to those defined for the "Locked" state in our example code.

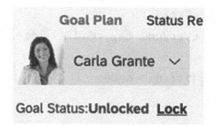

Figure 5-19. *Manager View of the Goal Plan State*

Custom Calculations

It is possible to create fields that are calculations based on the values of other fields. A common example would be a "goal score" field where you multiply the individual goal rating by the total weight of the individual goal.

Configuring Custom Calculations

Using calculations requires adding two new elements (and potentially their own subelements) to the XML. The <calculator> element defines how a calculation is performed (think field a + field b), and the <auto-population> element defines which field gets populated with which calculation(s). Furthermore, the <auto-population> can contain rules. The <rules> element lets you define which <calculator> elements will serve as conditions and which will serve as results. You can even include metric lookup tables (also known as achievement lookups) that will help define what scores meet various conditions and thresholds to be translated into final ratings.

Note   For more information on metric lookup tables, see SAP note 2072202.

When creating calculations and conditions, you can use the standard +, -, *, and / operators. Precedence can also be defined using parentheses (). In addition, functions are also supported using the format FUNC.<functionname>. These standard functions supported are round(number), ceil(number), floor(number), and diff(date1,date2,Unit). Unit can be equal to (MILLISECOND/SECOND/MINUTE/HOUR/DAY/WEEK/MONTH/QUARTER/YEAR). NOW global variable will return the current date and time.

When creating conditions, you can use the standard ==, !=, >, >=, <, <=, &&, ||, and ! operators.

Within tables such as milestones, targets, and tasks, you can use these functions on columns: sum(column), avg(column), add(column1,column2), subtract(column1,column2), multiple(column1,column2), and divide(column1,column2). You can also use the functions gm_sub_goal_rating_of_milestones, gm_sub_goal_rating_of_targets, and gm_sub_goal_rating_of_tasks to calculate a final rating in each of these types of tables.

To calculate a total score for a goal plan, you will need to use the standard field "goal-score" to populate the rating for each individual goal. You can then set the element <obj-plan-template> attribute "show-total-goalscore" to "true." Optionally, you can set a total for each category by setting the same attribute and value in the <category> element.

There are infinite possible examples of how calculations can be used. For the sake of brevity, we've provided a simple but common example in the following to give you an understanding of how calculations are structured so you can create ones specific to your needs. In this example, we calculate a score for each goal and present the total for each category and the final total to the end user.

Our example code is shown in the following:

```
<obj-plan-template ... show-total-goalscore="true"...>
...
  <category id="Financial" show-total-goalscore="true">
...
  </category>
...
<field-definition id="goal-score" type= "number" required= "false " detail=
"false " viewdefault= "on" showlabel= "true " field-show-coaching-advisor=
"false " cascade-update= "regular">
      <field-label>Rating</field-label>
      <field-label lang="en_US">Rating</field-label>
      <field-description>Individual Goal Rating</field-description>
      <default-value>0.0</default-value>
      <field-format>#.#</field-format>
</field-definition>
...
  <field-permission type="read">
   <description><![CDATA[Everyone may read all fields for everyone.]]>
   </description>
```

```
    <role-name><![CDATA[*]]></role-name>
...
    <field refid="goal-score"/>
  </field-permission>
<calculator id="goalScoreCalc">
    <![CDATA[weight*done*1000]]>
</calculator>
<auto-population field="goal-score" mode= "auto">
    <rule><calculated-result calculator-id= "goalScoreCalc"/></rule>
</auto-population>
<plan-layout>
...
    <column weight="5">
      <field refid="goal-score"/>
    </column>
  </plan-layout>
...
```

Note   There are a couple of "gotcha's" here that might frustrate you! First, when you add the goal-score to the plan layout, it won't appear until overnight. Second, if you update the calculation logic, you will need to update the values in each goal as an end user before the new calculation is performed! Many times it is a good idea to simply start with new goals entirely when testing once the calculation logic has changed. Changing the calculation logic mid–goal plan cycle would likely cause calculation errors and confusion.

View Goal Scores as an End User

As an end user, you can now see the goal ratings at the top of the goal plan, at the top of each category, and as a column for each goal as shown in Figure 5-20.

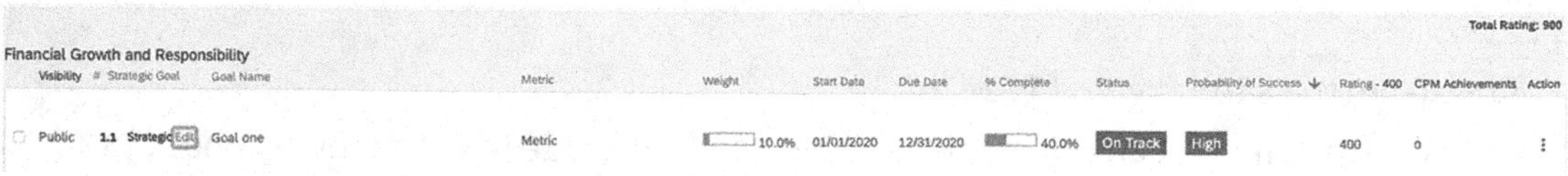

Figure 5-20. *Goal Ratings as Shown to End Users*

Group Goals

Group goals provide two different versions (v1 and v2) for creating, managing, and assigning goals to a specific group of individuals to collaboratively execute. Regardless of the version you choose to use, each goal has a creator (the person who makes the goal), an owner (the person on whose plan the goal was first created), an assigner (the person who assigns the goal to members), and members (users that have the goal assigned). Additionally, in both versions, any changes made to the owner's goal can be pushed down to member goals (which is a key reason for using group goals as opposed to simply linking personal goals). Table 5-3 highlights the differences between v1 and v2 to help you choose which version (if any) might be right for your organization. You must choose one version or the other.

Table 5-3. *Group Goals Versions*

Group Goals Version	Description
v1	Best used when you would like members to be dynamically assigned (e.g., by division, department, location fields) and/or you would like for all members to receive the same rating.
v2	While this version does not support dynamic assignment (all members must be specifically identified but can be changed after the goals are assigned) nor group ratings, it supports newer features such as tasks, targets, milestones, and calculated ratings. Additionally, fields can be made editable by group members. For more information, see SAP note 2072705.

Prerequisites for Configuration

Before configuring group goals, you must decide if you would like to use group goals v1 or v2. If you choose v1, it is already on by default, and you only need to perform XML and permission settings. If you would like to use v2, then you need to turn on your desired version in provisioning. Follow these steps to turn on group goals v2:

1. Log in to provisioning for your company instance.

2. Click "Company Settings."

3. Click "Enable Group Goals 2.0 – requires 'Total Goal Management.'"

4. Click "Save."

Note   If you would like your updates to group goals to also apply to inactive users (e.g., if they are on leave), then click the option shown in the following. Additionally, if you are using role-based permissions and would like to add a permission to the role that also allows end users to define a target population, click the "Enable target population for group goals – requires 'Total Goal Management'" as shown in the following. You can also check the boxes for "Enable target population of Group Goal Assignment permission" and "Enable target population of Group Goal Deletion permission" so that these permissions use the role's target population when granting access. Figure 5-21 points out the location of these options.

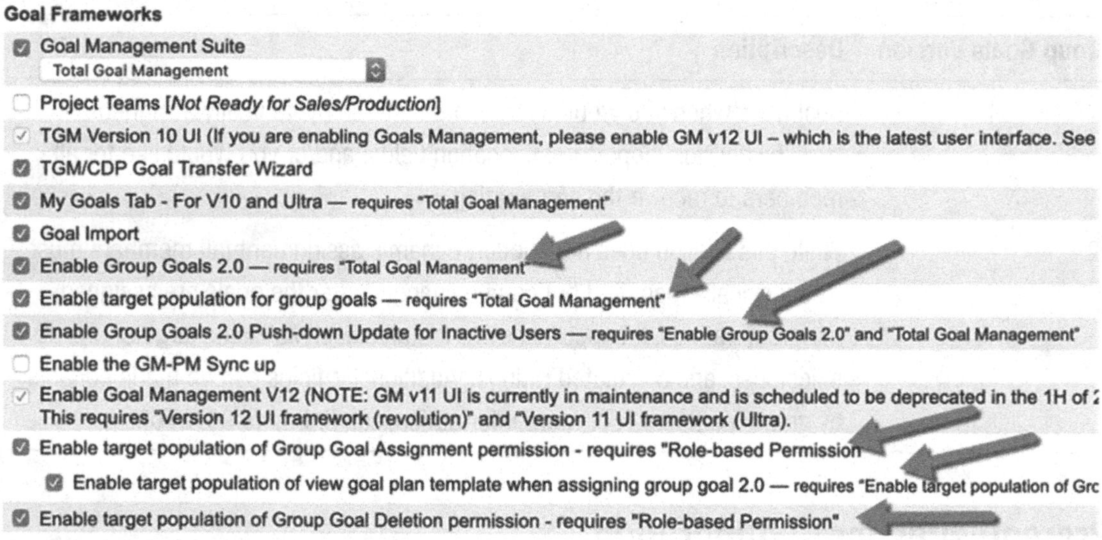

Figure 5-21. Enabling Group Goals v2 and Options

Configuring Group Goals

To allow group goals in your goal plan, simply edit the XML <obj-plan-template> element attribute "allow-group-goal" to be "true."

Sample code is shown in the following:

```
...
<obj-plan-template … allow-group-goal="true" ...>
...
```

Assigning End User Permissions

Once we've completed setup in provisioning and have turned on group goals in our plan, we can make permission role assignments to our end users. Follow these instructions:

1. Type and select "Manage Permission Roles" in the search bar.

2. Click the name of the permission role you wish to edit.

3. Click "Permission...:" and then click "Goals" on the left.

4. Select the "New Group Goal Creation" and "Group Goal Assignment" permissions as shown in Figure 5-22.

Figure 5-22. *Group Goal Permissions*

Note   The "Target Population" permission in the preceding figure would only appear if you chose the "Enable target population for group goals" option in provisioning; you will also need to make sure to define a target population in your role. Similarly, if you chose the "Enable target population of Group Goal Assignment permission" and "Enable target population of Group Goal Deletion permission" in provisioning, then those options would appear as we have shown in Figure 5-22.

---

5. Click "Done."

6. On the main permission role edit screen, be sure to update/add target populations as needed under the "Grant this role to..." section by clicking "Add..." or "Edit granting" and defining the target population as needed.

7. On the main permission role edit screen, click "Save Changes."

Using Group Goals

Now that we've finished configuration and assigned permissions, let's start using our group goals! Follow these instructions:

Note   We will demonstrate group goals v2 here since it supports the features we have configured thus far in our example code.

---

1. Log in as a person to whom you've assigned the group goal permissions (in our example, it is a manager).

2. In the navigation menu, navigate to "Goals."

3. Click "Add Goal" in the upper right-hand corner of the screen and select "Create a New Goal." The "Create a New Goal" screen should appear with an option to create a "Group Goal" as shown in Figure 5-23.

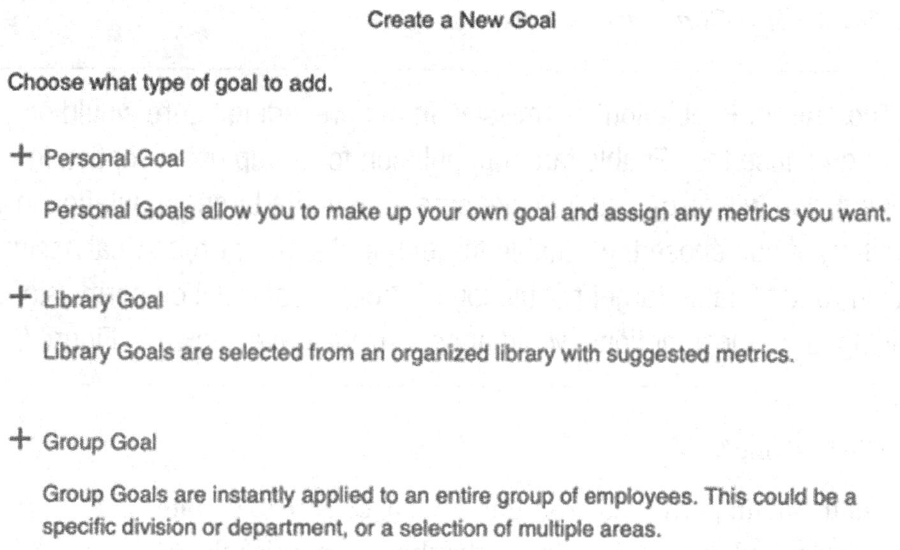

Create a New Goal

Choose what type of goal to add.

+ Personal Goal

Personal Goals allow you to make up your own goal and assign any metrics you want.

+ Library Goal

Library Goals are selected from an organized library with suggested metrics.

+ Group Goal

Group Goals are instantly applied to an entire group of employees. This could be a specific division or department, or a selection of multiple areas.

Figure 5-23. *Creating a Group Goal*

4. Click "Group Goal." The "Create a Group Goal" screen will appear as shown in Figure 5-24. Note that the fields that appear will correspond to the fields configured in your XML; the main difference here is that the "Type" field will show as read-only and display as "Group (Version 2.0)."

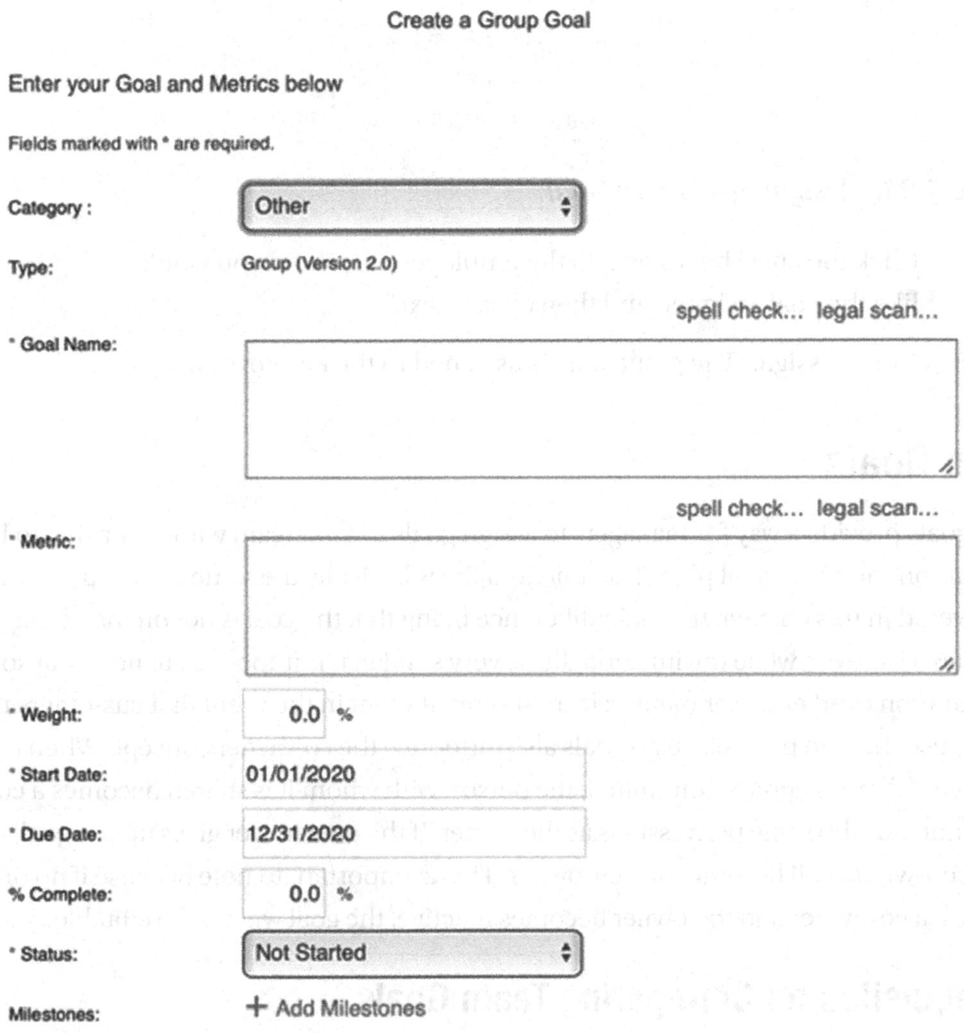

Create a Group Goal

Enter your Goal and Metrics below

Fields marked with * are required.

Category :   Other   ▲▼

Type: Group (Version 2.0)

                                         spell check... legal scan...

* Goal Name:

                                         spell check... legal scan...

* Metric:

* Weight: 0.0 %

* Start Date: 01/01/2020

* Due Date: 12/31/2020

% Complete: 0.0 %

* Status: Not Started   ▲▼

Milestones: + Add Milestones

Figure 5-24. *Adding a Group Goal*

5. Fill in the fields as desired and click "Save Changes." The goal will be added to the goal plan.

6. Click the box next to the goal on the goal plan and then click "Assign" as shown in Figure 5-25.

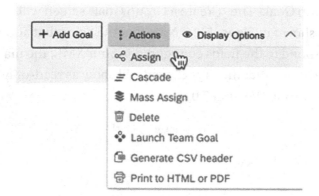

Figure 5-25.   *Assigning a Group Goal*

7.   Click the checkboxes next to the employees to whom you would like the goal assigned and then click "Next."

8.   Click "Assign." The group goal is assigned to the employees.

Team Goals

Team goals provide a way for managers to assign goals to their team without having to have the goals on their own goal plan. The functionality is basically the same as group goals 2.0 just covered in this chapter, the main difference being that the goal is not on the manager's goal plan. However, while the functionality is very similar, it is important to note that some configurations and end user menu selections are different in the event that customers may want to use them in parallel. Team goals also introduce the co-owner concept. When a team goal "share" action is committed, the person with whom it is shared becomes a co-owner and has the same permissions as the owner. If the owner ever gives up the goal, one of the co-owners will become the new owner. This is important to note because if no one becomes a co-owner and the owner becomes inactive, the goal will not be editable.

Prerequisites for Configuring Team Goals

Prior to configuration, be sure to follow these steps to activate team goals in provisioning:

1.   Log in to provisioning for your company and click "Company Settings."

2.   Check the box next to "Enable Team Goals" as shown in Figure 5-26.

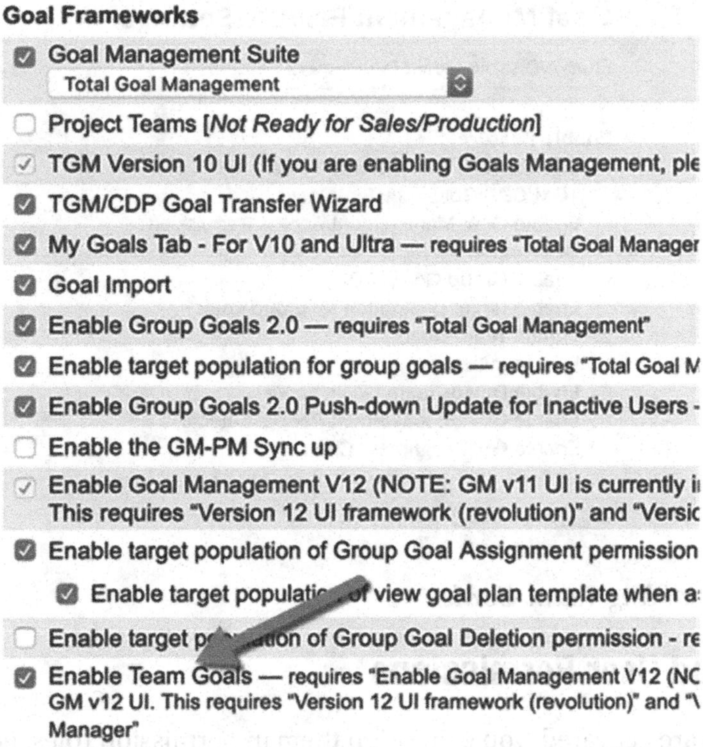

Goal Frameworks

- ☑ Goal Management Suite
  - Total Goal Management
- ☐ Project Teams [*Not Ready for Sales/Production*]
- ☑ TGM Version 10 UI (If you are enabling Goals Management, ple
- ☑ TGM/CDP Goal Transfer Wizard
- ☑ My Goals Tab - For V10 and Ultra — requires "Total Goal Manager
- ☑ Goal Import
- ☑ Enable Group Goals 2.0 — requires "Total Goal Management"
- ☑ Enable target population for group goals — requires "Total Goal M
- ☑ Enable Group Goals 2.0 Push-down Update for Inactive Users -
- ☐ Enable the GM-PM Sync up
- ☑ Enable Goal Management V12 (NOTE: GM v11 UI is currently i
  This requires "Version 12 UI framework (revolution)" and "Versic
- ☑ Enable target population of Group Goal Assignment permission
  - ☑ Enable target populati... of view goal plan template when a:
- ☐ Enable target p... ...on of Group Goal Deletion permission - re
- ☑ Enable Team Goals — requires "Enable Goal Management V12 (NC
  GM v12 UI. This requires "Version 12 UI framework (revolution)" and "\
  Manager"

Figure 5-26. *Enabling Team Goals*

3. Click "Save."

Configuring Team Goals

As we covered in group goals, you will need to add the same XML code to set the "allow-group-goal" attribute to "true."

In addition, you will need to follow these steps:

1. Type and select "Goal Management Feature Settings" in the search bar.

2. Check the boxes for "Enable Team Goals" and "Enable Delete Team Goals Share" options as shown in Figure 5-27.

3. Click "Save."

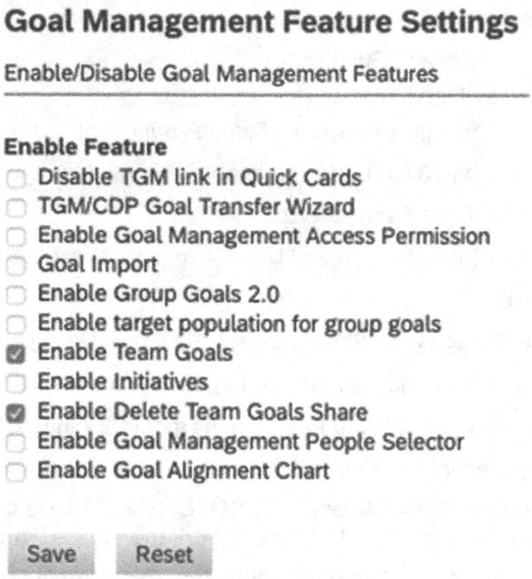

Goal Management Feature Settings

Enable/Disable Goal Management Features

Enable Feature

☐ Disable TGM link in Quick Cards
☐ TGM/CDP Goal Transfer Wizard
☐ Enable Goal Management Access Permission
☐ Goal Import
☐ Enable Group Goals 2.0
☐ Enable target population for group goals
☑ Enable Team Goals
☐ Enable Initiatives
☑ Enable Delete Team Goals Share
☐ Enable Goal Management People Selector
☐ Enable Goal Alignment Chart

[Save]   [Reset]

Figure 5-27. *Enabling Team Goals*

Assigning End User Permissions

Once team goals are activated, you can assign them in permission roles. Follow these steps:

1. Type and select "Manage Permission Roles" in the search bar.

2. Click the name of the permission role you would like to edit (we recommend using a manager role).

3. Click "Permission...:"

4. On the left side of the popup, click "Goals" and then click the checkboxes next to "Manage Team Goals," "Assign Team Goals," and "Share Team Goals" as desired.

Note   Take note on this screen that "Manage Team Goals" and "Assign Team Goals" require permission targets while "Share Team Goals" does not!

---

5. Click "Done."

6. On the main permission role edit screen, be sure to update/add target populations as needed under the "Grant this role to…" section by clicking "Add…" or "Edit granting" and defining the target population as needed.

7. On the main permission role edit screen, click "Save Changes."

Using Team Goals as an End User

Now that we've configured and assigned team goal permissions, let's try it out! Follow these steps:

1. Log in as a user to whom you assigned the permissions (e.g., a manager).

2. In the navigation menu, choose "Goals."

3. Click "Actions" in the upper right-hand corner of the screen and choose "Launch Team Goal" as shown in Figure 5-28.

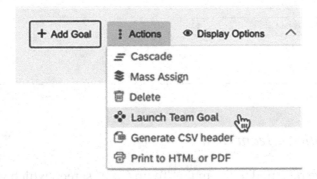

Figure 5-28. *Launch Team Goal*

4. In the new screen that appears, click "Create Team Goal" in the upper right-hand corner.

5. You will see the "Create a Team Goal" screen as shown in Figure 5-29. The screen will appear with fields as you have configured them in your primary XML configurations. The "Type" field will show the value "Team." Fill out the fields as desired and click "Save Changes."

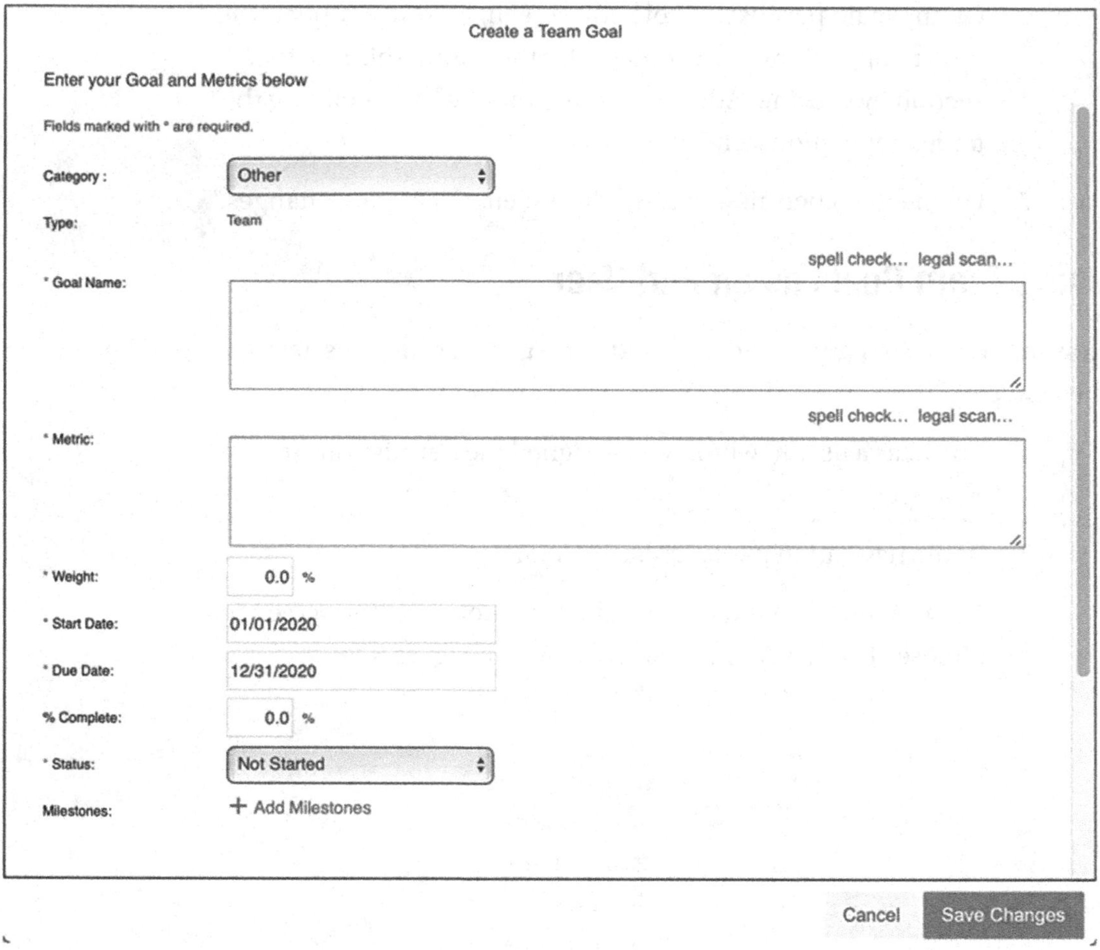

Figure 5-29. *Creating a Team Goal*

6. You will be returned to the main "Team Goal" screen which will now display the team goal you just created (along with any others for which you are the owner). Click the icon under the "Actions" column for your goal and choose "Assign." An example is shown in Figure 5-30.

Team Goal
Search Team Goal
Create Team Goal
Team Goal Name
Created On
Modified On
Created By
Assigned To
Actions
Sample Team Goal
7/13/20
7/13/20
Reilly Francis
0
Edit
Delete
Share
Assign
Unassign
Assign

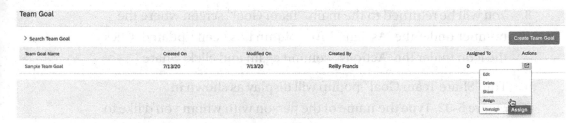

***Figure 5-30.** Team Goal Screen Showing the Actions Menu*

7. The popup will automatically show the members of your team as seen in Figure 5-31. Click the checkboxes next to their names and click "Next." Then click "Assign."

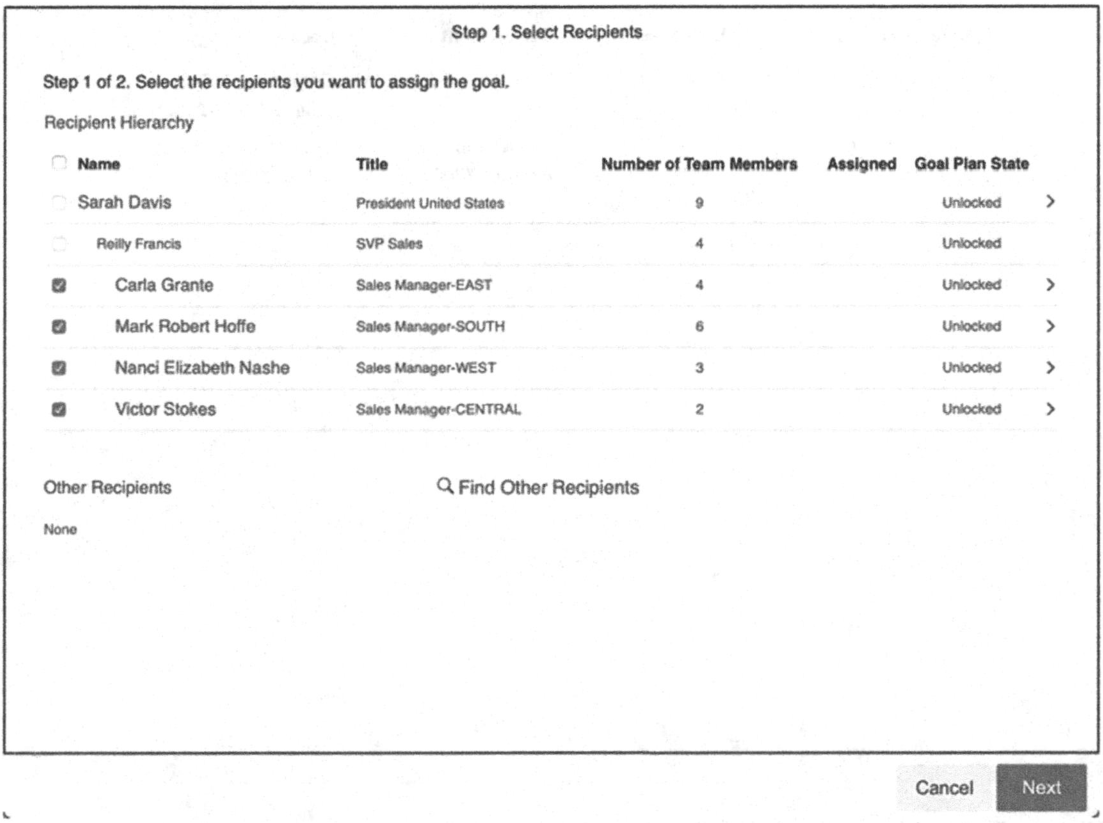

Step 1. Select Recipients
Step 1 of 2. Select the recipients you want to assign the goal.
Recipient Hierarchy
Name
Title
Number of Team Members
Assigned
Goal Plan State
Sarah Davis
President United States
9
Unlocked
Reilly Francis
SVP Sales
4
Unlocked
Carla Grante
Sales Manager-EAST
4
Unlocked
Mark Robert Hoffe
Sales Manager-SOUTH
6
Unlocked
Nanci Elizabeth Nashe
Sales Manager-WEST
3
Unlocked
Victor Stokes
Sales Manager-CENTRAL
2
Unlocked
Other Recipients
Find Other Recipients
None
Cancel
Next

***Figure 5-31.** Selecting Employees to Receive Team Goals*

8. You will be returned to the main "Team Goal" screen where the number under the "Assigned To" column has been updated. Click the icon under the "Actions" column again and click "Share."

9. The "Share Team Goal" popup will display as shown in Figure 5-32. Type the name of the person with whom you'd like to share the goal (e.g., the manager's manager) and click "Add." Then click "Done."

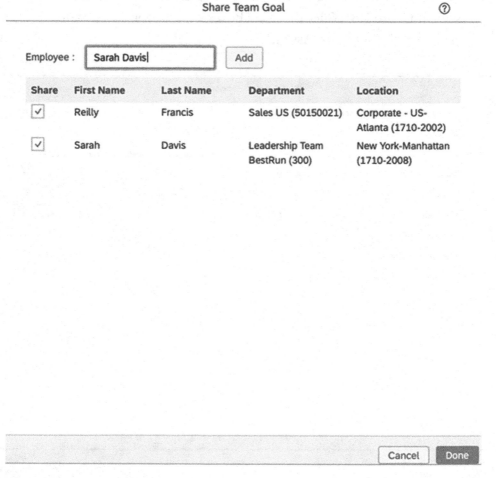

Figure 5-32. *Share Team Goal*

10. Click "Goal Panel" to return to the goal plan. You will notice the goal does not show on your goal plan as the manager. You can look at the team member goal plans and notice the goal is on their

plans. You can also try logging in as the manager's manager to see that the goal is not on their plan either, but they can see the goal in the "Team Goal" screen since it has been shared.

You're all done! You have now created, aligned, and shared a team goal!

Initiatives

Initiatives provide a way for organizations to set up high-level objectives across a corporate, division, or department level to which employees may align their individual goals. Initiatives can also be grouped together into an initiative group. Initiatives can be assigned and also shared in the same way that team goals are shared (making someone else a co-owner of the initiative).

Note   In our experience, initiatives are easy to configure and can provide focus for high-level objectives.

Prerequisites for Configuring Initiatives

Prior to configuration, be sure to follow these steps to activate initiatives in provisioning:

1. Log in to provisioning for your company and click "Company Settings."

2. Check the box next to "Enable Initiatives" as shown in Figure 5-33.

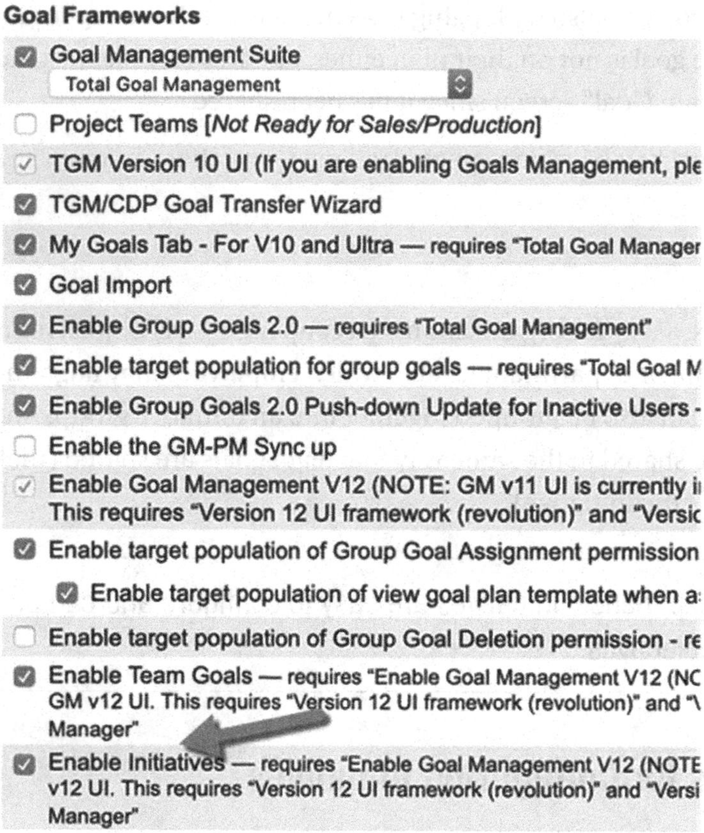

Goal Frameworks

☑ Goal Management Suite
   Total Goal Management

☐ Project Teams [*Not Ready for Sales/Production*]

☑ TGM Version 10 UI (If you are enabling Goals Management, ple

☑ TGM/CDP Goal Transfer Wizard

☑ My Goals Tab - For V10 and Ultra — requires "Total Goal Manager

☑ Goal Import

☑ Enable Group Goals 2.0 — requires "Total Goal Management"

☑ Enable target population for group goals — requires "Total Goal M

☑ Enable Group Goals 2.0 Push-down Update for Inactive Users -

☐ Enable the GM-PM Sync up

☑ Enable Goal Management V12 (NOTE: GM v11 UI is currently ii
   This requires "Version 12 UI framework (revolution)" and "Versic

☑ Enable target population of Group Goal Assignment permission

   ☑ Enable target population of view goal plan template when a:

☐ Enable target population of Group Goal Deletion permission - re

☑ Enable Team Goals — requires "Enable Goal Management V12 (NC
   GM v12 UI. This requires "Version 12 UI framework (revolution)" and "\
   Manager"

☑ Enable Initiatives — requires "Enable Goal Management V12 (NOTE
   v12 UI. This requires "Version 12 UI framework (revolution)" and "Versi
   Manager"

Figure 5-33. *Enable Initiatives*

3. Click "Save."

Configuring Initiatives

Once activated in the system, configuring initiatives is a simple process. Follow these steps:

1. Type and select "Goal Management Feature Settings" in the search bar. The screen will appear as shown in Figure 5-34.

2. Check the box next to "Enable Initiatives."

3. Click "Save."

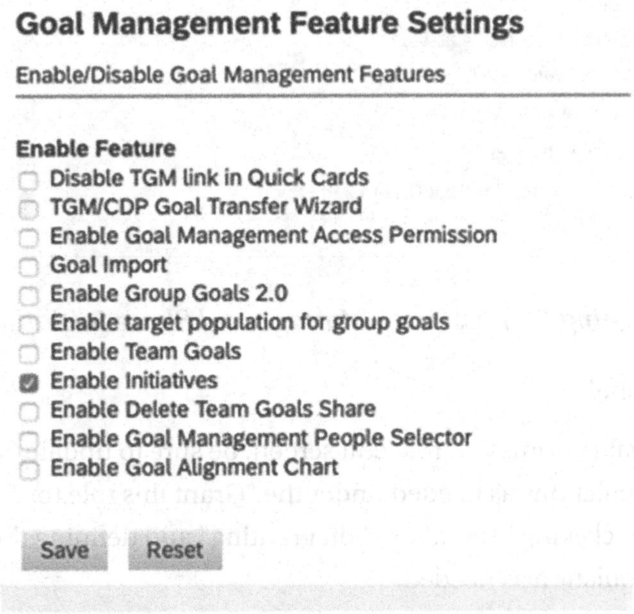

Goal Management Feature Settings

Enable/Disable Goal Management Features

Enable Feature
- Disable TGM link in Quick Cards
- TGM/CDP Goal Transfer Wizard
- Enable Goal Management Access Permission
- Goal Import
- Enable Group Goals 2.0
- Enable target population for group goals
- Enable Team Goals
- ☑ Enable Initiatives
- Enable Delete Team Goals Share
- Enable Goal Management People Selector
- Enable Goal Alignment Chart

Save   Reset

Figure 5-34. *Configuring Initiatives*

Assigning End User Permissions for Initiatives

Now that initiatives are activated in the system and configured, we can assign them to end users. Follow these steps to assign permissions to manage and share initiatives:

1. Type and select "Manage Permission Roles" in the search bar.

2. Click the name of the permission role you would like to edit (we recommend using a manager role or HR admin role).

3. Click "Permission…:"

4. On the left side of the popup, click "Goals" and then click the checkboxes next to "Manage Initiatives" and "Share Initiatives" as desired. An example is shown in Figure 5-35.

Figure 5-35. *Assigning Permission to Manage and Share Initiatives*

5. Click "Done."

6. On the main permission role edit screen, be sure to update/add target populations as needed under the "Grant this role to..." section by clicking "Add..." or "Edit granting" and defining the target population as needed.

7. On the main permission role edit screen, click "Save Changes."

Using Initiatives as an End User

Now that our configuration is complete and our roles are assigned, we can start using initiatives! Follow these steps to manage, share, and align goals to initiatives:

1. Log in to your company instance as the user to whom you assigned permissions.

2. Type and select "Manage Initiatives" in the search bar. The "Manage Initiatives" screen will appear as shown in Figure 5-36.

Figure 5-36. *The Manage Initiatives Screen*

3. Click the "Create Initiative Group" button in the upper right-hand corner. Enter an initiative group name and description and mark the initiative as active. Add individual initiatives to the group by

clicking the "Add Initiative" button as needed and entering an initiative name and description as desired. When you are finished, click "Save." An example is shown in Figure 5-37.

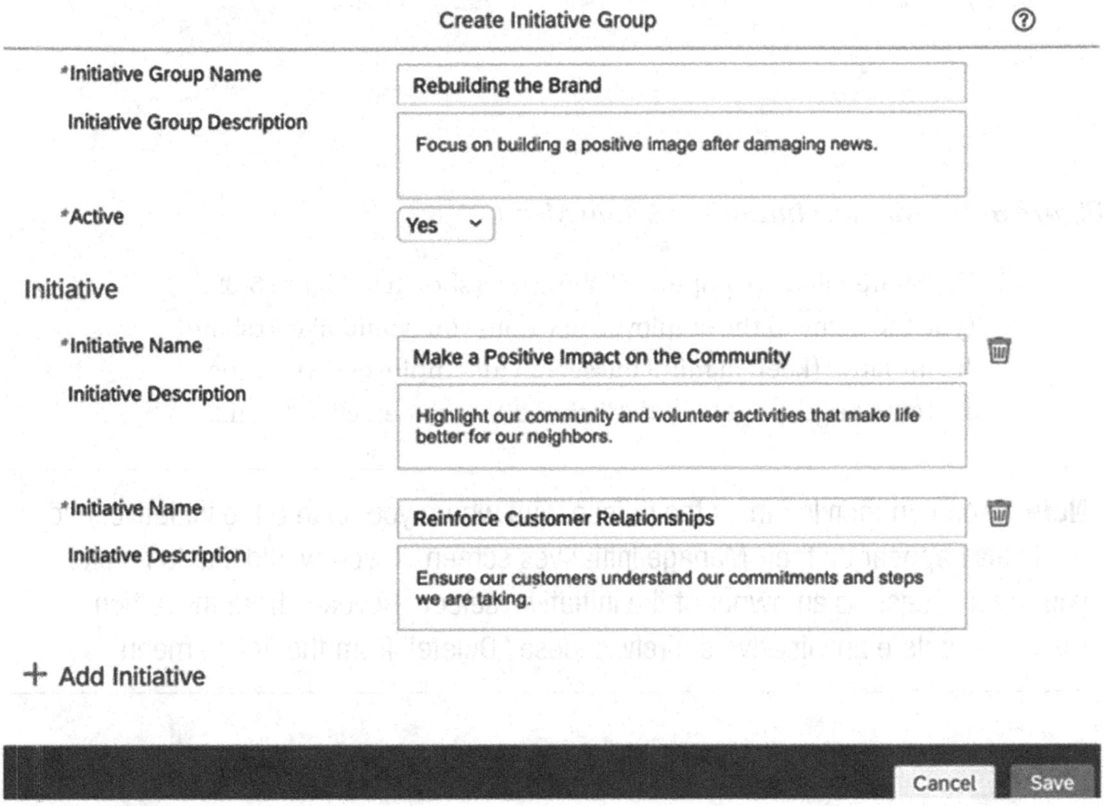

Create Initiative Group   ⑦

*Initiative Group Name	Rebuilding the Brand
Initiative Group Description	Focus on building a positive image after damaging news.
*Active	Yes ⌄

Initiative

*Initiative Name	Make a Positive Impact on the Community	🗑
Initiative Description	Highlight our community and volunteer activities that make life better for our neighbors.	
*Initiative Name	Reinforce Customer Relationships	🗑
Initiative Description	Ensure our customers understand our commitments and steps we are taking.	

＋ Add Initiative

Cancel   Save

Figure 5-37. *Creating an Initiative Group and Initiatives*

4.   You will be returned to the main "Manage Initiatives" screen where your initiative group will be shown in the list as seen in Figure 5-38. Click the icon under the "Action" column and select "Share" to share the initiative.

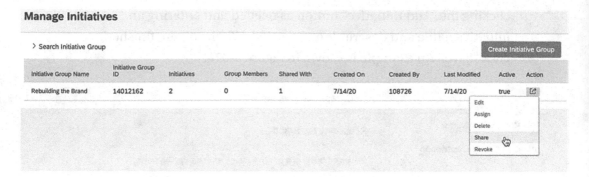

Figure 5-38. *Manage Initiatives Action Menu*

5. The Share Initiative popup will appear as shown in Figure 5-39. Type the name of the employee to whom you would like to share the initiative (keep in mind the search for employees will respect the role's target population). Click "Add" and then click "Done."

Note You can then log in as the person with whom you shared the initiative, and it will also appear on their Manage Initiatives screen. If you would like to revoke your own access as an owner of the initiative, select "Revoke" from the Action menu. To delete an initiative entirely, choose "Delete" from the Action menu.

Share Initiative   ⑦

Employee : | Carla Grante | | Add |

Share	First Name	Last Name	Department	Location
☑	Reilly	Francis	Sales US (50150021)	Corporate - US-Atlanta (1710-2002)
☑	Carla	Grante	Sales US (50150021)	Boston (1710-2017)

Figure 5-39. *The Share Initiative Screen*

6. You will be returned to the Manage Initiatives main screen. Click the icon under the "Action" column and click "Assign." The Initiative group Assignment popup will appear as shown in the

following figure. Here, you can create groups dynamically using the fields in the user data file (UDF). An example is shown in Figure 5-40.

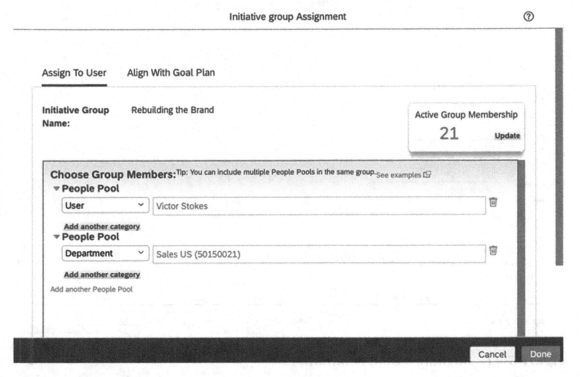

Figure 5-40. *Example Initiative Group Assignment*

7. Once you have completed creating your group of assignees, click the "Align With Goal Plan" tab. Check the box next to the goal plan(s) to which you would like to add the initiative. Then click "Done."

8. Navigate to "Goals" from the main navigation menu and select the goal plan of one of your assignees. Click "Edit" next to the goal. The initiative group that was assigned will appear at the bottom of the Edit Goal screen with available initiatives you can choose to align with the goal as shown in Figure 5-41.

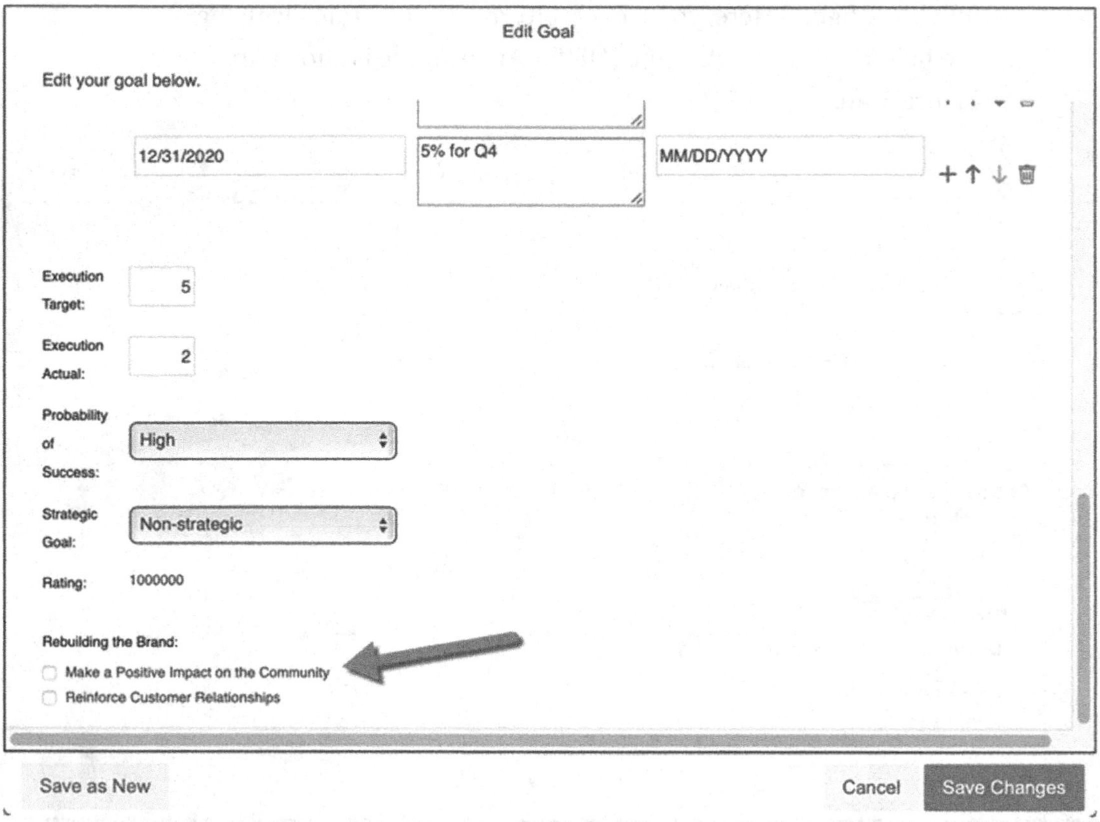

Figure 5-41. *Aligning a Goal to Initiatives*

Congratulations! You have now created, shared, assigned, and aligned goals to initiatives!

Conclusion

In this chapter, we have covered alternate functionalities and management techniques for goal plans. While in our experience the basic goal plan meets most organizations' needs, it is not uncommon to see organizations use one or more functionalities covered in this chapter.

We started the chapter showing you how to manage goals outside of directly editing the goal plans of individual users by using the mass import and goal transfer functions. We then began covering alternate concepts beginning with Goal Execution which showed us how to track progress of goals across the organization. We then talked about the goal plan state feature which can allow alternate permission schemas based on the state which is often used for "locking" goal plans. Next, we explored how to automatically calculate ratings for individual goals. We also covered group goals v1 and v2 which allow you to automatically push goal changes to all participants as well as team goals which are used similar to group goals but when the manager does not want to be assigned to the goal. You should now have a solid understanding of how these three functionalities are closely related but used for different scenarios when collaborating on goals across the organization. Finally, we covered initiatives which can be used to align goals to key business initiatives driven by specific groups of employees you define within the organization.

It is important to note that while all of these features could technically be run in parallel, we have never seen this as a real-world scenario. The range of concepts to be communicated to employees would be confusing in a scenario where group goals, team goals, and initiatives were all used together, for example. In this case, you would likely lose the point of driving the business goals in the noise of trying to get employees to understand how the goal plans work. In most cases, we find customers use a basic goal plan and maybe one or two of the features in this chapter at a time. The key takeaway here is knowing that these functionalities exist so that the vast majority of customer special requirements can be met on an exceptional basis and system implementers should not feel compelled to use all of them.

CHAPTER 6

Introduction to Performance Management

Performance Management helps develop talent, measure individuals' goals that are aligned to corporate objectives, identify training needs, and reward performance. The performance review process is used to evaluate an employee's effectiveness in achieving goals and competencies and is a vehicle to identify development needs for the next year. Once performance has been rated and discussed, the result may be used in Calibration, Succession Planning, and Compensation decisions.

SAP SuccessFactors Performance Management simplifies the annual review process by automating it with highly configurable templates and route maps. For example, a typical performance form incorporates an employee's goals and competencies and moves from person to person throughout the course of the year. Progress on achieving goals may be noted and comments added. At year-end, the employee can rate how well they think they achieved their goals. The manager will make the final rating decisions. The manager and employee will then sit down to discuss the performance for the year and plan for the following year.

This automated process is managed by an HR administrator and allows forms to be generated for specific groups of employees on a specific day. The admin can intervene during the process if forms need to be moved backward or forward, if due dates need to be revised, or if forms need to be deleted or restored.

Note To complete configuration steps in this chapter, we assume you have completed the configurations for Goal Management as outlined in Chapter 4. Additionally, we assume you have either associated competencies to job roles as outlined in Chapter 3 or marked competencies as "core" so they can be pulled into forms.

© Susan Traynor, Michael A. Wellens and Venki Krishnamoorthy 2021
S. Traynor et al., *SAP SuccessFactors Talent: Volume 1*, https://doi.org/10.1007/978-1-4842-6600-7_6

We are going to discuss Performance Management in the next several chapters. Here, we will cover the initial steps to get Performance Management configured which includes:

1. Enabling settings in Provisioning

2. Creating role-based permissions

3. Configuring a route map

4. Configuring rating scales

5. Configuring a performance form template

In Chapter 7, we will dig deeper into the performance form template to gain a better understanding of the template sections. We will learn the purpose, configuration, and permissions for each template section.

Once we have completed the setup of the performance form template in Chapter 7, we will move on to administering performance forms in Chapter 8. Chapter 9 will provide a walk-through of the performance process from a user's perspective. Chapter 10 will cover the performance form template XML and translations. And finally, in Chapter 11, we will learn more about Ask for Feedback, Get Feedback, and Add Modifier functionality.

Decisions to Make When Configuring the Performance Form Template

As part of the implementation process, you will be tasked with reviewing the functionality available for Performance Management and making decisions on which features and functions to enable. You will also make decisions on the layout, permissions, and content of the performance form that you are going to create.

The types of decisions that you will need to make include the following:

-   What are the steps in the performance review process?

-   Which roles are involved in each step?

-   What are the labels and text used in the route map?

-   Will the goal plan be integrated into the performance form?

-   Will development goals be used on the form?

- Which roles can see and do what in each step?

- Can goals be added to or deleted from the form?

- Will competencies be included? If so, core, role specific, or custom?

- What sections will appear on the form?

- What are the required fields on the form?

- What type of overall ratings will be used?

- Will the ratings be text, circles, or stars?

- Will the form include Get Feedback and Ask for Feedback attachments and CPM achievements tied to goals?

- Will a manual overall rating be used?

- What are the goals and competency weights used in the overall form rating?

The result of this exercise will be a completed configuration workbook. The decisions made in the workbook will drive the configuration of Performance Management in your instance.

Use the following link to access the Performance Management configuration workbook:

```
https://partneredge.sap.com/en/products/successfactors-hcmsuite.html
```

Provisioning

Let's start in Provisioning. We will be setting up SAP SuccessFactors Performance Management v12 Acceleration which is the latest version and will continue to be updated and enhanced in subsequent releases.

Go to "Company Settings" and enable the following:

- Performance Management

- Performance Management Access Permission – requires "Version 11 UI framework (ULTRA)"

- Workflow

- GM-PM Sync up

These are optional but recommended Performance Management–related features to enable:

- Team Overview Access Permission

- Team Rater for Performance Management

- Team Rater for Performance Management – Enable display of all forms but self

- Relative Dates for Form Routing

- Collapsible Route Map

There are optional features that may already be enabled. If not, they are recommended:

- Legal Scan

- Enable full form Legal Scan

- Spell Check

- Enable full form Spell Check

- Language Packs (if you wish to customize phrases and labels)

- Show ToDo Portlet

- Show the home page after login

- Dynamic Groups V2

If you are using competencies, these features should be enabled as well:

- Competency Library Management Suite

- Writing Assistant (if using SuccessFactors 2.1 Competency Library)

As mentioned earlier, as an optional setting, "GM-PM Sync up" allows goals to sync up to the performance form with some additional configuration. This feature enables any goal updates made on a performance form to update the goal plan as well. It works in the opposite direction too; if a user adds a goal to their goal plan, their active performance form will be updated as well.

For ad hoc Performance Management reporting, make sure Ad Hoc Builder is enabled. Then enable the following:

- "Performance Management" under Additional Adhoc Sub domain Schemas Configuration

- "Performance Management" under Enable INCLUDE STARTING FROM USER in people pill

Save the updates that have been made. Remember that some sections of "Company Settings" need to be saved individually.

Now that we have enabled Performance Management, we will go into the instance to create role-based permissions.

Role-Based Permissions for Performance Management Admin

We will create the permissions needed for an administrator to create and manage performance-related tasks. You may decide a user within HR will handle the administrative tasks rather than having the system administrator manage the performance cycle.

Either create a permission group that contains the user/users that should have the Performance Management admin role or identify an existing role to add the performance-related access to.

Type and select "Manage Permission Roles" in the search bar. Then select and open an existing role to update. Instead, you may create a new permission role.

Once you have opened the role, go to the permission settings portion of the Permission Role Detail page, click the "Permission" button, and a popup will display the permission settings as seen in Figure 6-1.

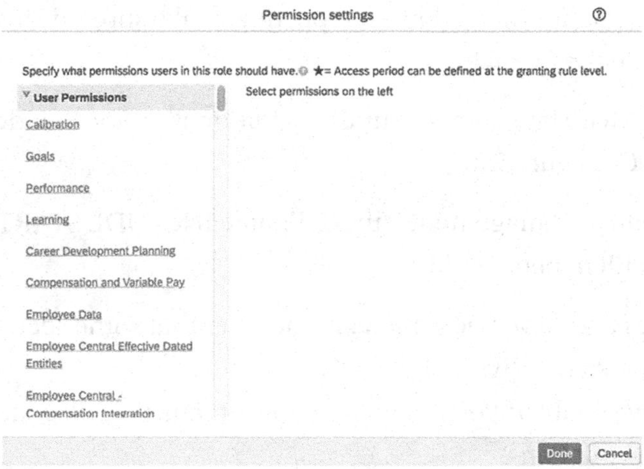

Figure 6-1. *Overview of Permission Settings*

Under the User Permissions section of the page seen on the left side of the screen, find and select "Performance". Performance-related permissions will display to the right of this section.

Select "Performance Management Access" as seen in Figure 6-2.

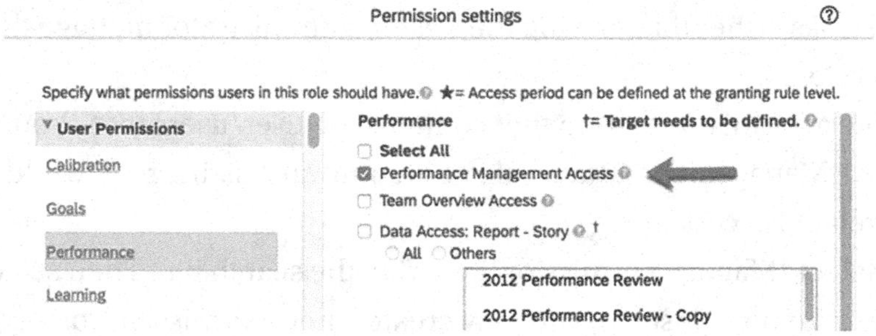

Figure 6-2. *Performance Management Access Permission*

Continue scrolling down on the left side of the page to find and then select "General User Permission". See the options here and select "Permission to Create Forms (all)."

Back on the left side of the page, scroll down to the "Administrator Permissions" section of the role permissions.

Look for each of the subsections listed in the following to add the following permissions:

- Manage Documents: Enable all permissions except for any 360 related.

- Manage Form Templates: Enable all except Corporate Goals (which is now obsolete).

- Manage System Properties: Enable "Performance Management Feature Settings" and "E-Mail Notification Templates Settings."

- Manage User: "Documents Transfer," "Manage Users," Employee Export," "Proxy Management," "Import Employee Data," and "Manage Employee Dynamic Groups."

Additionally, in User Permissions ➤ Reports Permission, you may include

- Ad Hoc Report Builder Standard Reports Bin (if using EC)

- Report Center

- Classic Reports

- Detail Report

- List View

- Analytics Tiles and Dashboards

  - Select any performance-related tiles and dashboards.

- Create Report

  - Performance Management

- Run Report

  - Select any performance-related tiles and dashboards.

Optional more advanced permissions may be added:

- Manage User: "To-Do Admin," "Manage Home Page," "Include Inactive Employees in the search," "Employee Export," "Export Extended User Information," "Import Extended User Information," "Import Employee Data," "Proxy Management," and "Manage Dynamic Employee Groups"

- Manage System Properties: "Manage Employee Files"

- Manage Dashboards/Reports ➤ Select All

- Manage Job Profile Builder: Select All (only if using Job Profile Builder)

Once the permissions are selected, click "Done," and you will now be able to assign a permission group or standard role to the permission role. For the admin role, you could assign users to an admin permission group and then select this group for the role. Next, select the target population the permission group will have access to. For the admin role, the target population may be "Everyone" as seen in Figure 6-3. If your admin is also a regular user, you may click "Exclude Granted User from having the permission to access him/herself."

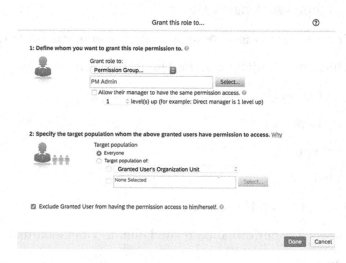

Figure 6-3. *Role and Target Population*

It is also possible that you have Performance Management admins in different regions of the country or of the world. You may wish to limit their target population to a specific geographic location or other criteria. In this situation, you would create permission groups to use as the target population. This may also require additional admin permission groups that are specific to a region, country, or other criteria.

Click "Done" after the desired options have been chosen. Click "Save Changes," and your admin role will now be able to configure a performance form template.

We have now enabled Performance Management v12 Acceleration and created performance permissions for the Performance Management (PM) admin role. You may have to log out and log back in to have the permissions applied.

Performance Management Feature Settings

We will now enable features that will be used in Performance Management. Type and select "Performance Management Feature Settings" in the search bar. The settings screen is seen in Figure 6-4.

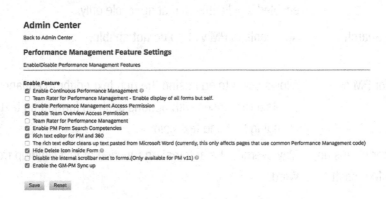

Figure 6-4. *Performance Management Feature Settings*

A description of each feature is contained in Table 6-1.

Table 6-1. *Performance Management Features*

Feature	Description
Enable Continuous Performance Management	Applicable only if you are using Continuous Performance Management (CPM) with goals linked to achievements. Within goal or development goal sections, will display a goal column to indicate a CPM achievement attached to a goal.
Team Rater for Performance Management – Enable display of all forms but self	Controls if *Team Rater* can be used for raters other than the direct manager (e.g., EMM, EX). Must have also Team Overview *Access Permission* enabled. Applicable to manager role only.
Enable Performance Management Access Permission	**Required.** Used within RBP to identify roles that will be able to access the Performance tab from the main menu.
Enable Team Overview Access Permission	**Recommended.** Used within RBP to identify roles that will be able to access the Team Overview sub-tab in Performance. Applicable to manager role only.

(continued)

Table 6-1. (*continued*)

Feature	Description
Team Rater for Performance Management	Used within Team Overview to compare subjects side by side to rate competencies. Must have Team Overview Access Permission enabled. Applicable to manager role only.
Enable PM Form Search Competencies	Applicable to PM v11 so do not enable.
Rich text editor for PM and 360	Allows users to edit using the rich text editor to enhance comments and text responses with options such as formatting text and changing font and text color.
The rich text editor cleans up text pasted from Microsoft (MS) Word	May override the automating function of text cleanup from MS Word.
Hide Delete Icon within Form	Will not see the delete button inside a form.
Disable the internal scrollbar next to forms	Applicable to PM v11 only.
Enable the PM-GM Sync up	**Highly Recommended**. To sync goals on the goal plan to goals on the performance form.

The required and recommended features are noted. Save the updates and we will move on!

There are two features that are very useful in the performance form: Spell Check and Legal Scan. We will look at both.

Spell Check

Most performance forms have sections where users may add comments. We have enabled Spell Check so that users may verify there are no spelling errors. When enabled, there is nothing else the admin needs to do unless they wish to add additional words to the company dictionary. This may be especially helpful for users if they want to include company vernacular in their comments.

In order to manage the company dictionary, role-based permissions need to be added to the admin role. Within the role permissions, use the following path:

Administrator Permissions ➤ Manage System Properties ➤ Company Dictionary

Type and select "Manage Dictionary" in the search bar. A sample of the dictionary screen is seen in Figure 6-5.

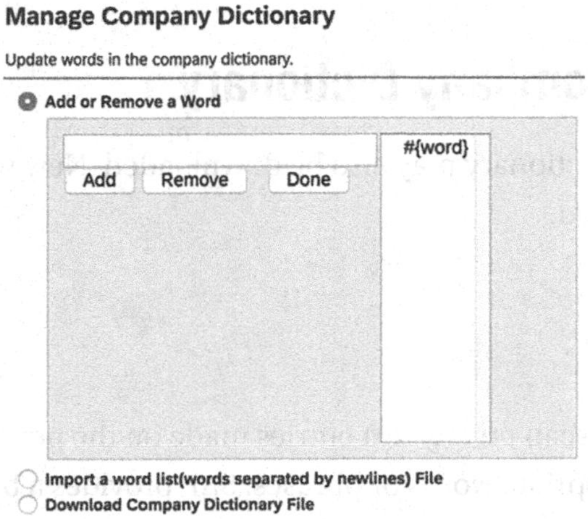

Manage Company Dictionary

Update words in the company dictionary.

⊙ Add or Remove a Word

| | | | | #{word} |
| Add | Remove | Done | | |

○ Import a word list(words separated by newlines) File
○ Download Company Dictionary File

Figure 6-5. *Add/Remove Words to/from the Company Dictionary*

Here, there will be three options to add words:

1. Add or remove a word.

2. Import words via a CSV file.

3. Download the Company Dictionary File

Add or Remove a Word

Click the "Add or Remove a Word" button, and you will be able to add a word or remove a word to or from the company dictionary directly on this screen. To add a word, type the word in the text box and click the "Add" button. Any existing words may be deleted in the same manner. After all updates are complete, click "Done," and the dictionary will be saved with the modifications.

Import Words

Click the "Import a word list" button to add words to the company dictionary via a CSV file.

There is no sample template to download in order to build a file. Instead, create a simple file with each word on a separate line, save the file in the CSV format, and import the file.

Download the Company Dictionary

The existing company dictionary may also be downloaded. New words may be added to the file and then imported.

Legal Scan

The user may do a legal scan on any text entries made on the performance form to find any offensive or inappropriate words or phrases. SAP provides a basic legal scan library which contains controversial terms with suggested replacements.

Manage Legal Scan Library

In order to manage the Legal Scan Library, there are role-based permissions to be added to the admin role. Within the role permissions, use the following path:

Administrator Permissions ➤ Manage Competencies and Skills ➤ Legal Scan Library

Administrator Permissions ➤ Manage Competencies and Skills ➤ Legal Scan Library Import

Words or phrases may be added to the library via "Legal Scan Library" seen in Figure 6-6.

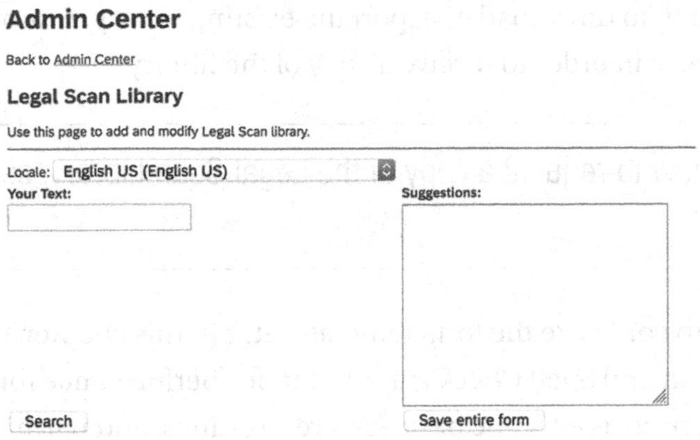

Admin Center

Back to Admin Center

Legal Scan Library

Use this page to add and modify Legal Scan library.

Locale: English US (English US)

Your Text: Suggestions:

Search   Save entire form

Figure 6-6. *Add to the Legal Scan Library*

The admin would enter a word or phrase in the "Your Text" box and then enter suggested alternatives in the "Suggestions" box. Be sure to create entries for multiple variations of a word or phrase since the scan uses an exact match.

Legal Scan Library Import

A legal scan library may be imported. Type and select "Legal Scan Library Import" in the search bar. An example of the import screen is seen in Figure 6-7.

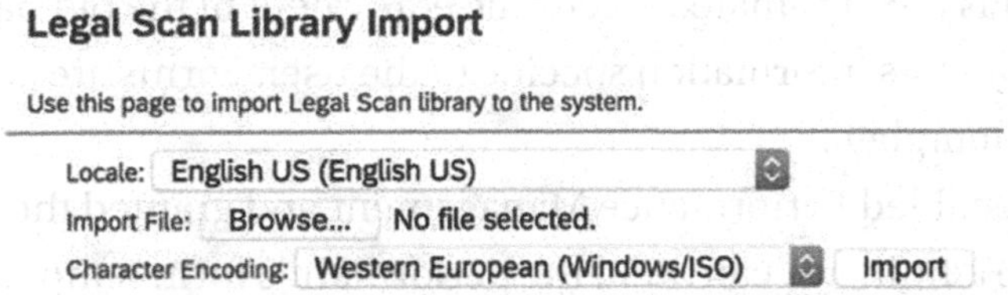

Legal Scan Library Import

Use this page to import Legal Scan library to the system.

Locale: English US (English US)

Import File: Browse...   No file selected.

Character Encoding: Western European (Windows/ISO)   Import

Figure 6-7. *Legal Scan Library Import*

Here, the admin would import a file which contains the word/phrase to replace and the suggested alternative.

There is no template available to download to see the file layout. However, the file layout is straightforward. The import file contains two columns with no header.

Column A contains the keyword that you are looking to replace. It must be in lowercase.

Column B contains the suggested replacement word or phrase.Then save the file using the CSV format.

There is no option to download or export the existing library. A support ticket needs to be opened with SAP in order to receive a copy of the library.

Note   To learn how to request a copy of the Legal Scan Library, see SAP note #2219367.

When we start to configure the form template later in this chapter, we will see how to enable the Legal Scan and Spell Check features for our performance forms.

Now that we have covered some basic features, settings, and permissions, let's dig into the Performance Management template.

Form or Template?

First, let's clarify the difference between the terms *performance form* and *performance form template*. Some mistakenly use these terms interchangeably, but they are not the same. A form template is a like a blueprint that defines the layout of the performance form and the sections within the form, along with the workflow, rating scale, and roles and permissions. Performance forms are generated for employees based on the form template settings and options. The performance form is the actual performance review for an individual. It is the automated electronic equivalent of the old paper performance form. Each form contains information specific to the user. Forms are generated from a performance form template.

Once we have enabled Performance Management and granted the role-based permissions for the admin, we can build the performance form template. The form template is comprised of:

- Route map

- Rating scale

- Sections

Before we can create a form template, there are some perquisite steps to complete. We will look at route maps and rating scales, and then we may finally begin creating a performance form template.

Route Maps

You can think of a route map as the road map for the performance form template. The route map defines the flow (steps) of the form. It identifies who will have possession of the form at each step and what the user may do. In more formal terms, the route map defines the movement of the form through the performance review process; it identifies the sequence of steps and defines the roles assigned to each step. The route map may also define start and end dates for each step of the process. Route map–related text, labels, and buttons seen on the form are identified here as well.

The roles assigned to the route map steps are based on relationships relative to the user that the form is generated for. The employee role (E) is assigned to this user. The EM role is the user's manager, the EH role is the employee's HR manager, and so forth.

Here is an example:

1. The employee receives their performance form in their Performance Inbox and does self-assessment. Goals and competencies are rated and comments are added.

2. The form routes to the manager. The manager will see all of the ratings and comments made by the employee. The manager completes the evaluation of the employee. Ratings and comments are added for the goals and competencies. Overall form rating is calculated based on the goal and competency ratings done by the manager.

3. The form goes to the second-level manager for review. The second-level manager may add optional comments.

4. The form moves to the next where the manager has a year-end performance discussion with the employee. Here, feedback is given and ratings are reviewed.

5. The form goes to the employee for signature. This is to acknowledge that the year-end evaluation meeting has been conducted.

6. The form goes to the manager for signature. This is to
    acknowledge that the year-end evaluation meeting has been
    conducted with the employee.

7. After the manager signs the form, it is completed. A copy of the
    review will appear in all of these users' Performance Completed
    folder.

We will be building a step in the route map for each of these form movements.

During our setup of Performance Management in Provisioning, some optional
route map–related features were mentioned. "Enable Relative Dates for Form Routing"
controls the option to use relative dates for steps in your route map. If you don't know
what this means, we will get to the explanation shortly. If it is enabled but you decide
later not to use it, having it enabled won't impact your route map. If you decide to use it
in a future route map, the option will be already available for use.

"Enable Collapsible Route Map" is another option you may have enabled. This
feature can be handy if your performance form is lengthy. The user may collapse the
route map on their form to free up some space if there is a lot of scrolling to do. The route
map may be expanded at any time.

The admin role–based permission that we set up included permission to create
and edit route maps. The permission is found in the following path: Administrator
Permissions ➤ Manage Form Templates ➤ Routing Maps. This permission grants access
to create and edit route maps.

The route map must be created prior to configuring the performance form template.
The route steps along with the associated roles are used to build permissions for buttons,
sections, and fields in the template.

A route map may be used by multiple performance form templates, while a performance
form template may only have one route map. This will make more sense as we go along.

The route map will display on the performance form which is helpful to users to
track what step of the process the form is in and to see step due dates and descriptions of
the steps and which user/role is assigned to each step. A sample is shown in Figure 6-8.

Figure 6-8. *Route Map on the PM Form*

As mentioned earlier, route maps are based on steps and roles. Let's look at roles first so you can see how they work in a route map.

Earlier chapters talked about roles. For performance forms, we will work primarily with the employee role (E), employee's manager role (EM), HR rep role (EH), and maybe the second-level manager role (EMM). For each step, we will need to identify which role will have the form in their inbox.

Manage Route Maps

Now let's learn more about route maps. Type and select "Manage Route Maps" in the search bar. *The Route Map List* will display as seen in Figure 6-9. Until you have created a route map, this list will be blank. In order to explain the columns on this page, we will look at a list that contains existing route maps.

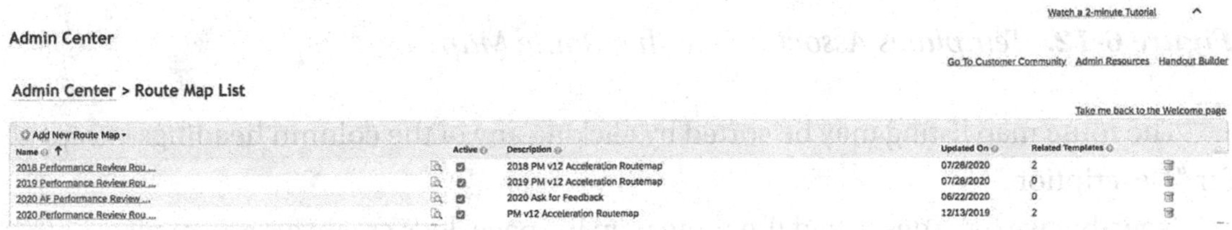

Figure 6-9. *Route Map List*

Once you have created a route map, it will display on this overview page. The route map name will be listed in the first column. Following the name column, you will see a display icon. Click this icon to see the route steps as shown in Figure 6-10.

Figure 6-10. *Route Map Steps Preview*

Next, there is an "Active" column. If the checkbox is empty, the route map is inactive and cannot be used in a template.

The "Description" column follows and is used to contain a brief description of the route map. The description will not appear anywhere but on this route map overview page. If the description is too long, the column will contain "..."; and by hovering, the description may be viewed as seen in Figure 6-11.

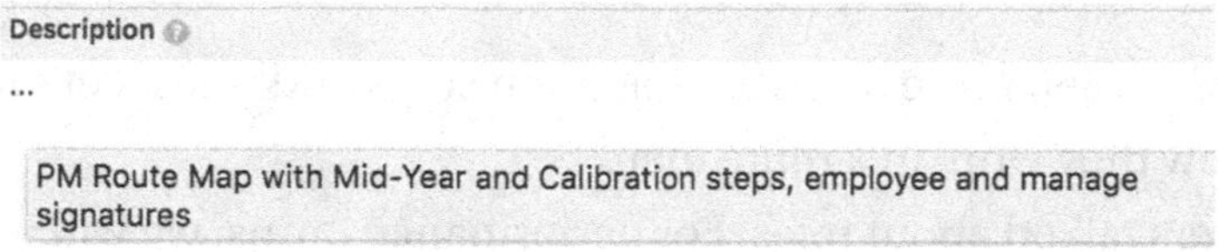

Figure 6-11. *Route Map Description*

The "Updated On" column contains the date when the route map was last modified.

The "Related Templates" column displays the number of performance templates that use the route map. Click the number, and you will see the names of templates that use the route map as seen in Figure 6-12.

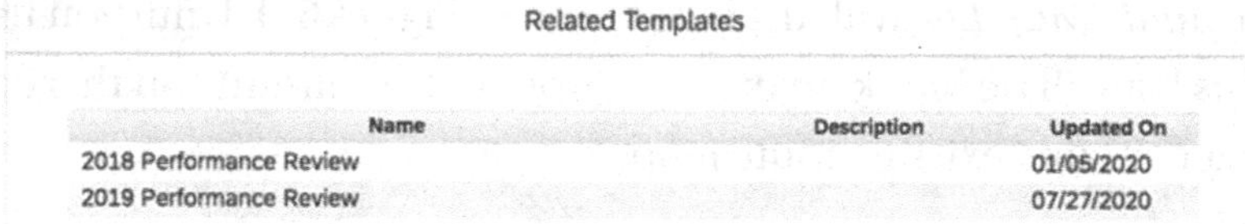

Figure 6-12. *Templates Associated with a Route Map*

The route map listing may be sorted by clicking any of the column headings except for "Description."

Now that we have described the route map list page, let's create a route map!

Route Map Creation

Click "Add New Route Map," and you will have the option to build your own route map or choose from the library. We will look at both options starting with "Choose from Library." As seen in Figure 6-13, a popup will display with all of the route maps available in SuccessStore.

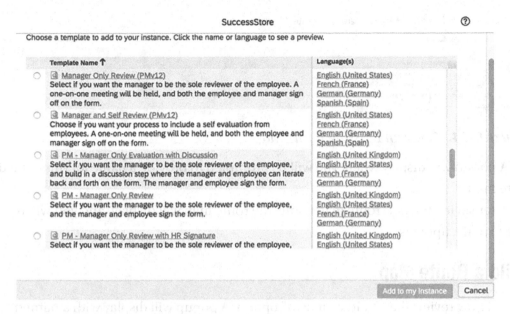

Figure 6-13.   *Route Maps Available in SuccessStore*

SuccessStore Route Maps

Here, you will see predefined route maps for 360, compensation, and performance templates. You can scroll through the list, read the descriptions, and see the languages available for each. You may select one of the Performance route maps and use it as a starting point in creating a route map that meets your needs.

Once selected, the "Add to my Instance" button will become active. You will be prompted to name your route map, and it will open on your screen. You may find it easier to start out by using a SuccessStore route map since it provides a shell that contains some steps with associated roles. You can add or delete steps, modify the existing steps, or reorder the steps. There will still be a lot of text and label decisions to make since these fields are not populated.

Copy a Route Map

You may also copy a current route map to edit and use to associate with the form template we will build shortly. You would open an existing route map and click "Save As..." as seen in Figure 6-14.

241

Admin Center > Route Map List > 2019 Performance Review Routemap

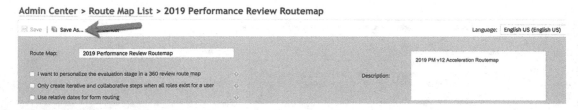

Figure 6-14. *Copy an Existing Route Map*

A popup will display where you will be prompted to provide a name for this copied route map.

After saving the new route map name, the route map will display, and you will be able to make updates.

Build a Route Map

We will now review the "Build your own" option. A popup will display with a named route map that contains no steps as seen in Figure 6-15.

Figure 6-15. *Blank Route Map*

Give the route map a meaningful name. If you plan on using this route map for one specific performance form template, you can use a name similar to the performance form template name. If you plan on using this route map for several performance form templates, you can use a name that is general enough for them all. You will need to identify the route map name when you create your performance form template from a list of all of your route maps, so make the name meaningful and easy to find. You will not be able to save your route map until you add a step, so let's move on to learn about the components of the route map.

There is a question mark icon available for almost every field on the route map page. This is a great resource that provides a description of what the field is used for. An example is shown in Figure 6-16.

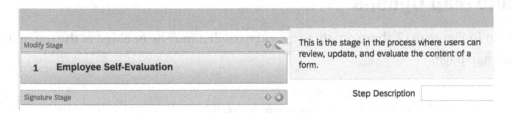

Figure 6-16. Information Icon

Route Map Stages

On the left side of the route map screen, you will see three stages: Modify, Signature, and Completion. Within the stages, steps are built. The steps identify the flow of the form and the roles involved with each step:

1. *Modify Stage* is where most of the action takes place. Steps in this stage allow users to review and update form content.

2. *Signature Stage* is used to sign or acknowledge the form contents. This step is used by an employee and/or manager to acknowledge that the year-end performance discussion and rating has taken place. Electronically signing the form does not signify agreement with the final rating but rather acknowledgment that the discussion took place. At most, the user may provide comments in this stage, and the rest of the form is not editable. Upon submission, the form will contain the user's name in the signature line along with the date the form was signed.

3. *Completion Stage* occurs after the final signature step has been submitted. No steps may be created for this stage, and within the form, the user may take no action. At this stage, the form has been routed to the user's Performance Completed folder. All users that had a role on the route map will receive a copy of the form in their Completed folder.

Now that we have seen the three route map stages, let's explore some optional features. Typically, these are left unchecked, but we will review the purpose of each.

Route Map Options

As seen in Figure 6-17, there are three checkboxes that may be enabled at the top of the route map page.

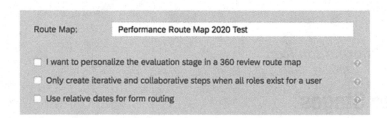

Route Map: Performance Route Map 2020 Test

☐ I want to personalize the evaluation stage in a 360 review route map

☐ Only create iterative and collaborative steps when all roles exist for a user

☐ Use relative dates for form routing

Figure 6-17. *Route Map Options*

1. I want to personalize the evaluation stage in a 360 review route map: Leave this unchecked. This is applicable to 360 review templates only. 360 forms will be covered in Chapter 12.

2. Only create iterative and collaborative steps when all roles exist for a user: Using an example may be the best way to describe this option. Let's say your performance form has a step that starts with the employee (E) and then goes to a manager step (EM) followed by a step that is shared by the manager (EM) and the HR manager (EH). If the employee does not have an HR manager in the EH role (the HR field in the user data file contains no HR user ID), this manager/HR manager step will be bypassed and the form will route to the next step.

3. Use relative dates for form routing: You will only see this option if "Enable Relative Dates for Form Routing" is enabled in Provisioning ➤ Company Settings. When enabled, step start, exit, and due dates are based on the number of days before or after a form activity rather than using set calendar days. You will see an example in Figure 6-18.

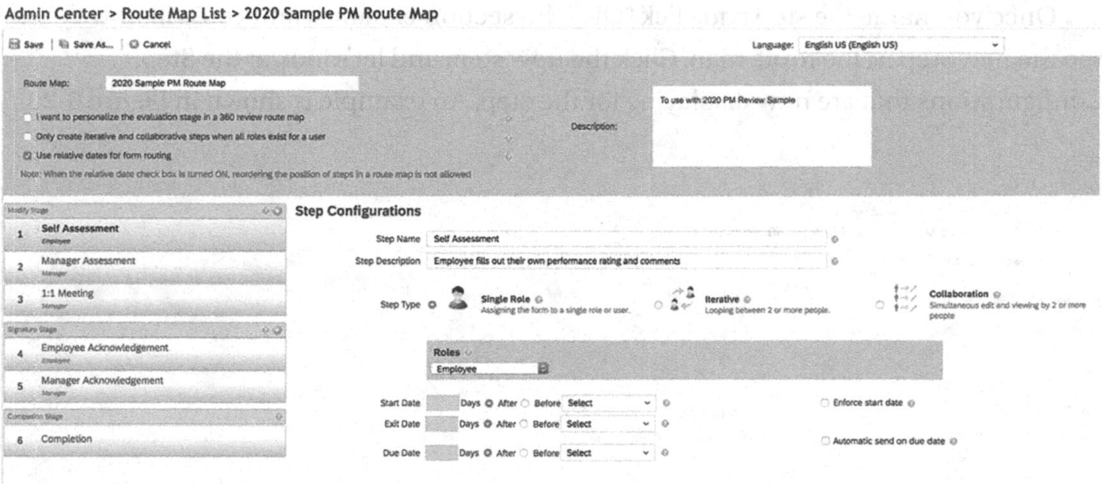

Figure 6-18. *Relative Dates in a Route Map*

Depending on the step and if "Before" or "After" is selected, the number of days will be relative to form creation date, same step due date, same step exit date, or form due date. For example, selecting "Before" for the start date in the first step of the route map, the three date field options will be "X" number of days before the form due date, same step due date, or same step exit date. If the "After" radio button was selected, the number of days will be relative to the form creation date. Once enabled, when editing a route map, the steps cannot be reordered.

Modify Stage Steps

Now we will build the steps for our route map by using the workflow designer. Within the Modify Stage section, click the "Add Step" icon. You will be prompted to name your step as seen in Figure 6-19.

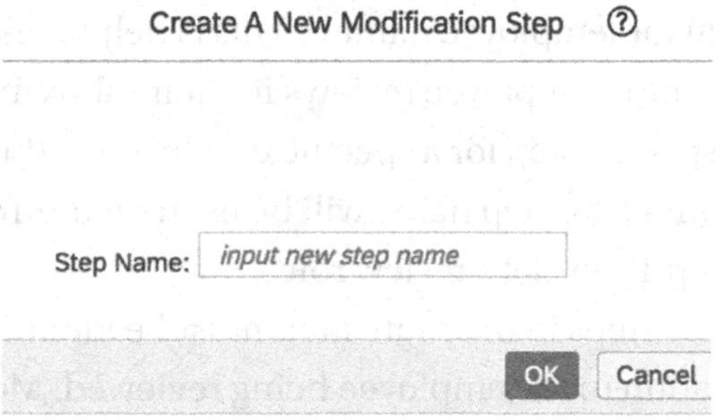

Figure 6-19. *Create a Modify Step*

Once you name the step and click "OK," the section expands, and you will now see the new step in the route map. Click the new step, and let's look at the Step Configurations that are now displaying for the step. An example is shown in Figure 6-20.

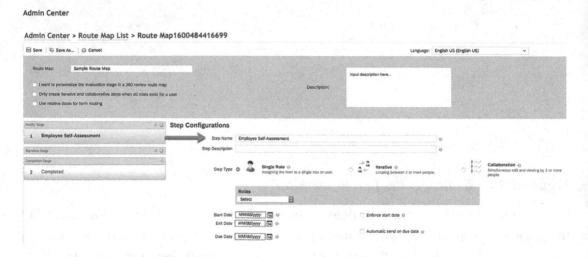

Figure 6-20. *Step Configurations*

We will now walk through these fields.

Step Name was created when you added the step to the route map. As you can see from the preceding figure, the step name is shown in the Step Name field in Step Configurations. You may change the step name in either spot. The name should be a short descriptor of what happens in the step. For example, "Employee Self-Assessment" is the step name and will display in the route map on the performance form.

Step Description will appear in the Performance To-Do tile on the user's home page. This tile contains all pending performance-related tasks for a user. For example, if you describe the step as "Self-Assessment for 2020," the To-Do item in the tile will show as "Self-Assessment for 2020 for [employee name]." This is helpful especially in later stages when a manager has dozens of employee reviews in their inbox and they are trying to find a specific form in a specific step for a specific employee. If this field is left blank when creating the route map, the step name will be used on the To-Do list.

Before we look at "Step Type," let's review roles.

The role for each of the steps in the route map must be identified. This is the role that the user holds in relation to the employee being reviewed. Most common roles are employee (E), manager (EM), HR rep (EH), and second-level manager (EMM). It is recommended to avoid using the custom role since this role is not available for use in the performance form.

Underneath the "Step Type" section, there is a box to select roles. Click the downward arrow to see the list of standard roles available as seen in Figure 6-21.

Figure 6-21. *Roles for a Step*

We will select roles for each step of the route map. Now we will look at "Step Type."

Step Type identifies the roles used in a step and how the step will act. The Step Type options will be available for Modify and Signature Stage steps only. There are three types to choose from as shown in Table 6-2.

Table 6-2. *Step Types*

Step Type	Description
Single	There is only one role in this step. For example, you want the form to go to the user in the employee role.
Iterative	Multiple roles will have access to the form in this step. However, the form is only with the user in one role at a time. The form will remain in the step but will be passed back and forth between them. You will need to identity the role that must be the first in the step (entry user) and the role that will be able to route the form to the next step (exit user). Each role will have a button to send the form to the other role in the step. Only the exit user will have a button to route the form to the next step.

(*continued*)

Table 6-2. (*continued*)

Step Type	Description
Collaborative	Multiple roles share the step. Based on permissions in the performance form template, all of the roles may edit or view the form. However, each role in the step cannot be in the form at the same time. The form does not get passed back and forth within the step. All roles that are in this step have the form in their inbox, but if one role is editing, the other role may only view the form which is locked from edits. At the top of the form, it will say "Form currently with [employee name]." That is the clue that the other collaborator is editing the form. Once the role that is editing the form saves and closes the form, it will be available to edit by the other role. Only the role designated as the exit role will have the button to route the form to the next step. The entry user may only save/close or cancel.

An example of a collaborative step is seen in Figure 6-22. The step is shared by the employee and manager. The manager is identified as the exit user which means only the manager will see the submit button in this step. The employee will not be able to route the form.

Figure 6-22. *Collaborative Route Map Step*

When the form is in an iterative step, the employee may edit the form but may not submit it to the next step as seen in Figure 6-23. The only options available are "Cancel" and "Save and Close."

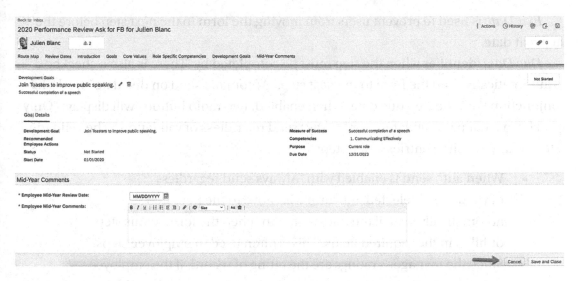

Figure 6-23. *Role in an Iterative Step That Is Not the Exit User*

We are going to backtrack now and return to the route map. Once the step has been named and its type and the roles that are a part of the step identified, we will look at step dates.

Step Dates

Step dates are optional entries, available for Modify and Signature Stage steps. Dates are mostly used when you are concerned with forms being in a certain step on a specific date during the performance cycle.

We will explain what these dates are and how they are used.

Start Date is the date the step starts. If the form lands in a user's inbox before the step start date, the user can work on the form in this step, and the form is not locked. There is also a checkbox to enforce the start date. Enforcing the start date makes the form in the user's inbox read-only until the day the step begins. The user will see the form in their inbox, but it will not be editable until the step start date. Enforcing the step start date may be helpful for the first step if forms are generated before the form cycle begins.

The user will see the message in Figure 6-24 when trying to edit the form prior to the step start date.

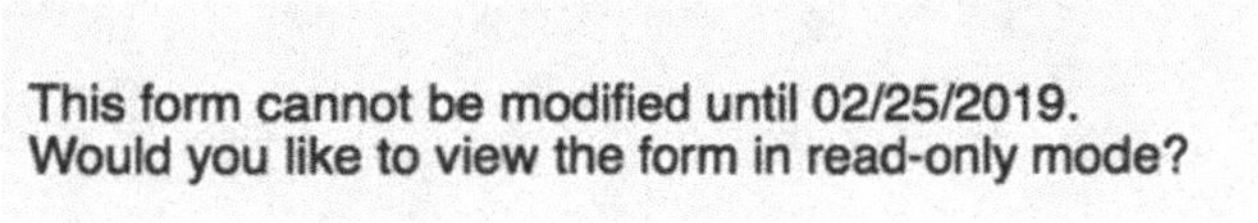

> This form cannot be modified until 02/25/2019.
> Would you like to view the form in read-only mode?

Figure 6-24. *Popup for the Step Not Started Yet*

Exit Date is used to prevent users from moving the form to the next step before the step exit date.

Due Date identifies when the step must be completed by. There is also a checkbox to automatically send the form to the next step. "Automatic send on due date" works in conjunction with the step due date. When enabled, two radio buttons will display: "Only send forms that pass validation" or "Always send regardless of validation." The validation refers to any required entries in the step:

- When auto send is enabled with "Always send regardless of validation" selected, the form will move to the next step automatically even if the role has not touched the form in this step or filled in the required fields. This is often used in employee steps. Since the manager's ratings are the rating of record, if the employee did not enter their self-assessment, the form is moved on to the next step for the manager to rate. Not entering the required employee ratings doesn't impact the overall form rating, so it is probably safe to move the form forward. The auto send option moves the form the day after the step due date. If using this option and there is also a step exit date, it has to be earlier than the due date.

- When auto send is enabled with "Only send forms that pass validation" selected, the form will not move to the next step automatically after the step due date has passed if the user for this step did not fill in all the required fields on the form. Using this option is recommended if the step contains fields necessary for the review process. An example would be a manager assessment step. The manager must enter individual goal ratings, comments, and an overall rating. If the manager hadn't opened the form or saved the form without completing all the required fields, when the step due date arrives, the form will stay in the current step.

For the route map you are building from scratch, you are able to save the route map once you have named a step and identified the step type and role.

Route Map Advanced Options

Within Step Configurations for a step, click "Show advanced options," and you will see an additional series of fields to complete. Advanced options are available for Modify, Signature, and Completion Stages. However, the fields for each stage will differ. The advanced options for a Modify Stage step are shown in Figure 6-25.

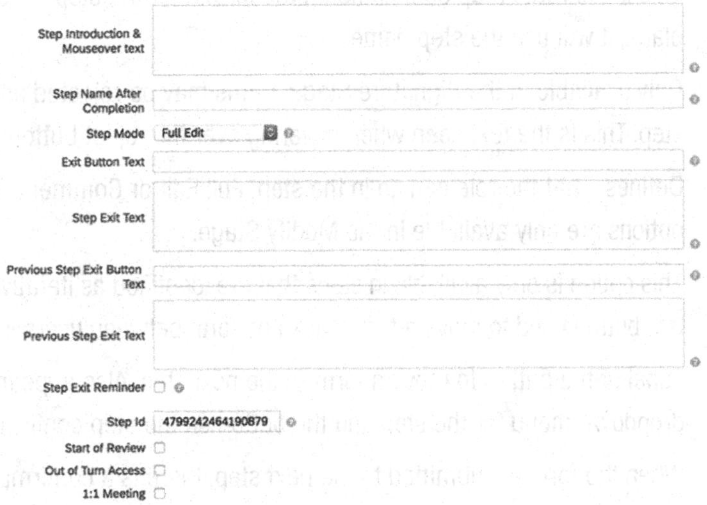

Figure 6-25. *Advanced Options*

Refer to Table 6-3 to learn what these fields represent and their purpose on the PM form.

Table 6-3. *Advanced Step Options*

Advanced Option	Description
Step Introduction & Mouseover	The route map appears on the top of the performance form, and when hovering over the current step, this text provides information on what the step is used for.
Step Name After Completion	This is the route map step name on the form after the step is completed. If left blank, it will use the step name.
Reject Button Mouseover Text	Only available in the Signature Stage, forms may be rejected and moved back a step. This is the text seen when hovering over the reject button.
Step Mode	Defines what the role can do in the step: Full Edit or Comment Only. These options are only available in the Modify Stage.
Iterative Step Button Text	This option is only available in steps that are identified as iterative. You may lavel this button used to move a form back and forth between users in the same step.
Exit Button Text	Label of the button to move a form to the next step. Also appears on the dropdown menu for the step and the button on the step confirmation page.
Step Exit Text	When the form is submitted to the next step, there is a confirmation page, so you may define the text that will appear there, for example, what their action means or what they need to do.
Previous Step Exit Button Text	If the user is sending the form back a step, this is the label on the button on the form.
Previous Step Exit Text	When the form is sent back a step, there is a confirmation page, and you may define the text that will appear there.
Step Exit Reminder	When enabled, the route map page expands so you can create reminder text that will display when submitting the form to the next step. This message will appear as a popup when submitting the form. Does not apply to iterative steps.
Step Id	Auto generated, system identifier when using a SuccessStore route map, for example, "5139493800574679." It will be blank when creating a route map from scratch. It is recommended to relabel the system-generated IDs to use a short name so it is easier to reference in the template XML, for example, "ESign" for the employee signature step. Create short easily recognized step ids when creating a route map from scratch.

(continued)

Table 6-3. (*continued*)

Advanced Option	Description
Start of Review	Only one step may have this enabled. Identifies that this is the start of the review and that a Team Overview page is created for the manager. All steps will appear on Team Overview including the "Start of Review" step.
Out of Turn Access	Allows reviewers to access the form on Team Overview to provide their ratings before the form is in their inbox. Requires "Start of Review" enabled to use this option but cannot assign to the first step. Not supported for iterative or collaborative steps.
1:1 Meeting	May be enabled for a step in the Modify Stage. This will give the manager a "Confirm 1:1 Meeting" button on Team Overview. This will route the form to the signature step without opening the form. Recommended for a single role (EM) and should be the last of the modify steps.

After creating the initial step, add another step completing the same fields as applicable. Create all of the steps in the order in which they should occur in the process. As a reminder, once the form hits the Signature Stage, the form is not editable beyond adding comments in the Signature section of the performance form.

Signature Stage Steps

Once all of your steps within the Modify Stage have been added, click the add icon within the Signature Stage to a create signature step. An example of a route map in this stage is displayed in Figure 6-26.

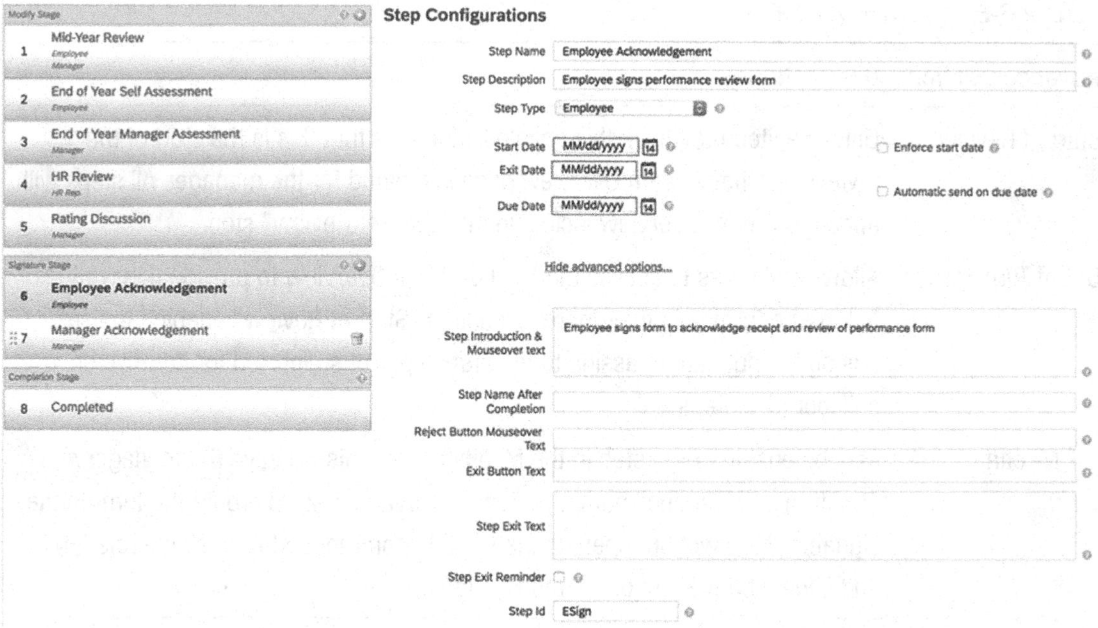

Figure 6-26. *Signature Step*

In this stage, the "Step Type" options are not "Single Role," "Iterative," or "Collaboration" as in the Modify Stage. Instead, there is a dropdown listing which permits a single role to be selected.

You may create multiple steps in this stage, one for each role that should sign the form. After you name the step, you will see the same Step Configurations section as the Modify Stage. However, when you expand the advanced options, you will see fewer fields that you will need to complete. You cannot move forms back to the Modify Stage, so you will not see the "Previous Step Exit Text" and "Previous Step Exit Button Text" options. There are no "Start of Review," "Out of Turn Access," and "1:1 Meeting" options either. However, there is an option to define the reject button mouseover text. If the form template is configured to reject a form at the signature step, here you may identify the mouseover text that would appear on hovering over the reject button.

Table 6-3 also mentioned renaming the step ids for system-generated route maps since they use long number strings. Replacing with descriptive names is helpful if the form template XML needs to be updated and you need to reference the step id. You will learn about the performance form template XML in Chapter 10.

Completion Stage Step

Once you have identified the signature steps, the last stage of the route map is "Completion" as seen in Figure 6-27.

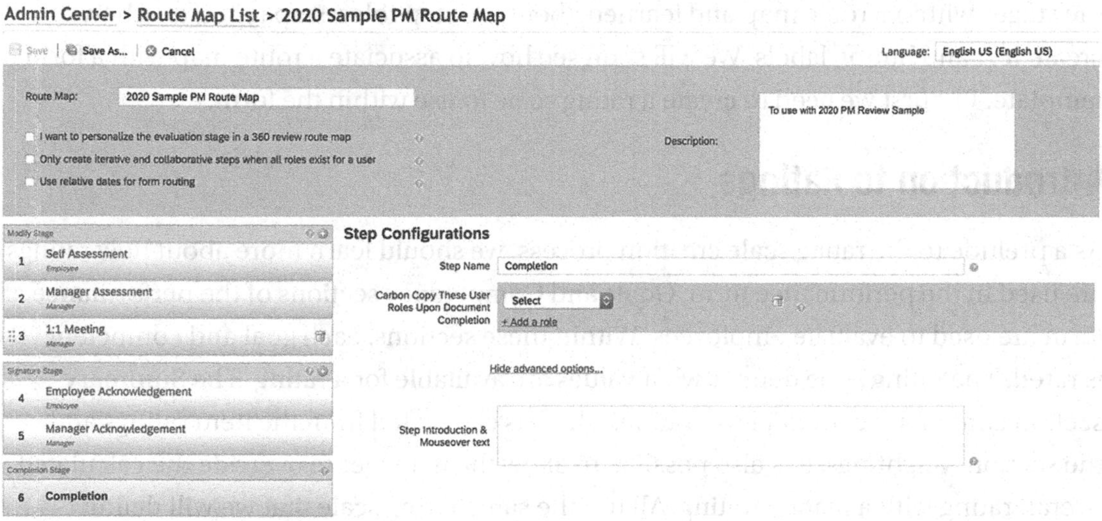

Admin Center > Route Map List > 2020 Sample PM Route Map

Figure 6-27. Completion Stage of the Route Map

There are no actions in this stage. Once the final signature is submitted from the Signature Stage, the form goes directly into the Performance Completed folder for users in each role of the route map.

There is very little that is configured for the Completion Stage. You may enter step introductory text and step introduction mouseover text. There is an additional option to select additional roles that should receive a copy of the completed performance form.

Save your route map after you have completed its build. You have now learned how to create a route map.

As mentioned earlier, existing route maps may be deleted, copied, or edited. A route map from SuccessStore or a copied route map may be used as a starting point to create a new route map to use with a new form template. It is best to avoid deleting any route maps unless they are not used in any performance form templates. It is advised to only make text or label changes for existing route maps already associated with a performance form template. It is not recommended to add or delete steps of an existing route map if it is already associated with a performance form template as it will corrupt the permissions within the form.

Any changes you make via "Manage Route Maps" will not impact live forms. To make changes to live forms, you will need to use the option "Modify Form Route Map." You will learn more about this feature in Chapter 8.

We have now learned how to download a route map from SuccessStore. We have copied an existing route map and have created a brand-new route map. We have seen the stages within a route map and learned about the step roles, step types, and how to create text and button labels. We will soon see how to associate a route map with a form template. But first we need to create a rating scale to use within the form.

Introduction to Ratings

As a prelude to the rating scale creation process, we should learn more about how ratings are used in the performance form. Goals and Competency sections of the performance form are used to evaluate employees. Within these sections, each goal and competency is rated. The rating scale defines what values are available for a rating. The Summary section contains the overall form rating, which is calculated from the item ratings and the section weightings. It is also possible to allow the manager to override the calculated overall rating with a manual rating. All use the same rating scale that we will define shortly.

Since the regular Summary section does not calculate an overall objective and an overall competency score, there is an optional Objective Competency Summary section for this purpose. There is another optional summary section which is used by a manager to enter a manual overall performance rating and a potential rating. These summary sections are used for Succession and use Succession matrix rating scales. Since these summary sections do not use a performance rating scale, the rating for these sections will be addressed separately. For now, we will look at the rating scale used in the Goals, Competency, and Summary sections of the form template.

Note   For more about ratings, such as how calculations occur in specific scenarios, see SAP note #2078768.

Rating Scale

The purpose of the performance review is to give an employee an overall rating for the year. Therefore, before we can create the performance form, we need to set up the rating scale to define what each possible rating value will be.

The rating scale defines a numerical set of values complete with score labels and descriptions. An interesting thing about this numerical rating scale is that its default appearance on the form is a set of stars. There are options that permit circles to appear in place of stars, or you may opt to use text for the rating scales instead. Once we start to configure the performance form template, we will talk more about these options.

The scale will be used in the Objective Competency Summary and Summary sections. It is possible to use different rating scales for different form sections, but it is not advisable because this may cause inaccuracies in the overall rating and in reporting and dashboards.

There is a role-based permission needed in order to create a rating scale. Type and select "Manage Permission Roles" in the search bar. Select and open the admin role to add the permission. Use the path Administrator Permissions ➤ Manage Form Templates ➤ Rating Scales to add this permission to the role.

Once your role has access to create/edit rating scales, type and select "Rating Scales" in the search bar. The *Rating Scale Overview* page will display as seen in Figure 6-28.

Figure 6-28. *Rating Scale Designer Overview Page*

Similar to the route map overview page, there are columns Name, Description, and "Active." Rating scales can be deactivated or deleted although it is not recommended to delete a rating scale that has been used in prior year forms. Only active rating scales may be used in a performance form template. There are columns for the scale creation date, the date the scale was last updated, and the user who made the last update as well.

We will be able to use one of three prebuilt rating scales, create a brand-new rating scale, or copy an existing rating scale. We will explore all of these options.

For more information on customizing rating scales, see SAP note #2078766.

For best practices, see SAP note #2078781.

Create a New Rating Scale

We will be defining how many scores are in the rating scale and will then create associated text labels and descriptions for each score. The rating labels will appear on the performance form if you are using text for ratings. The rating description will display on the form if you mouse over the rating scale. This is helpful for users so they will see the ratings with their descriptions before providing a rating.

Click "Create New Rating Scale," and the Rating Scale Designer will display as shown in Figure 6-29.

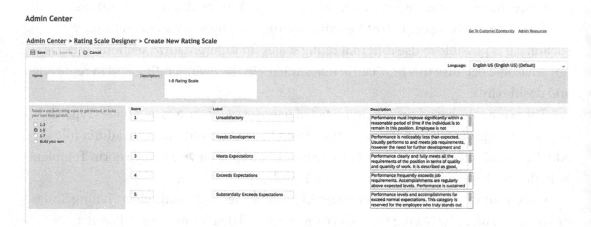

Figure 6-29. *Create a Rating Scale*

Rating Scale Options

Here, you will have the option to select from three prebuilt scales or to create your own scale. The default five-point scale will display with labels and descriptions. You may use this five-point scale and make any revisions to the labels or descriptions.

You could delete scores or add more scores for this scale. There are also options to create a three- or seven-point scale. The other option is to build your own scale.

It is recommended to use a five-point scale. This scale size provides a midpoint score and enough differentiation between ratings. The lowest rating is "1," with "5" being the highest.

It is possible to use a reverse scale where "5" is the lowest rating. To enable this, the scale setting needs to be reversed in Provisioning. Within "Company Settings", enable "Rating Scale Order: lower values are considered MORE favorable (e.g. "1" is better than "5") (Used for Dashboards & Reports only)." A reverse scale is not recommended.

Beware that once this setting is enabled, the reverse scaling will apply to all rating scales in all performance templates and reports that include performance ratings. If you are using circles or stars for ratings with a reverse scale, the rating scale will appear as a dropdown list instead. If you plan on implementing Career Worksheet within the Career Development Planning module, a reverse scale is not supported.

Build Your Own Scale

As soon as you click the "Build your own" button, the Rating Scale Designer page changes, and you will see a blank scale. An example is seen in Figure 6-30.

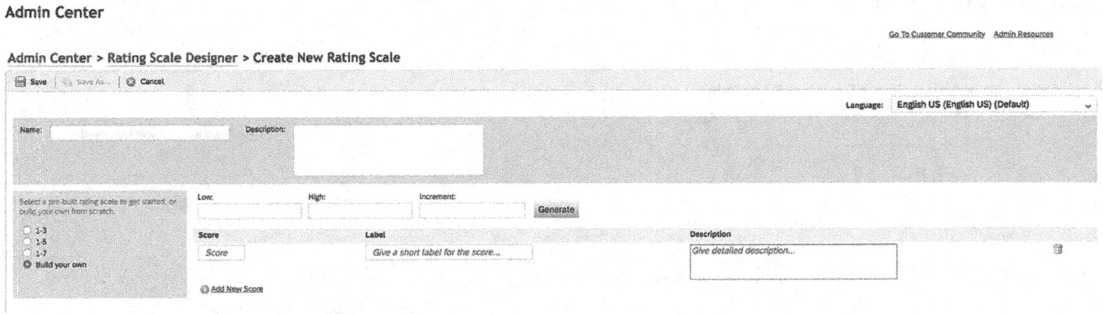

Figure 6-30. *Build Your Own Rating Scale*

You may start to build the scale by entering a score with a label and description and then clicking "Add New Score" in order to add a new blank score row.

To avoid having to add one line at a time using the "Add New Score" option, you may enter values in the *Low*, *High*, and *Increment* boxes above the score rows. This method will generate a rating scale based on the minimum and maximum scores you select and the increment between each score.

In the example seen in Figure 6-31, the low score is 1, the high score is "7", and the scores are incremented by 1.

Figure 6-31. *Generate a Rating Scale*

After clicking the "Generate" button, the rating scale is created with seven ratings as seen in Figure 6-32.

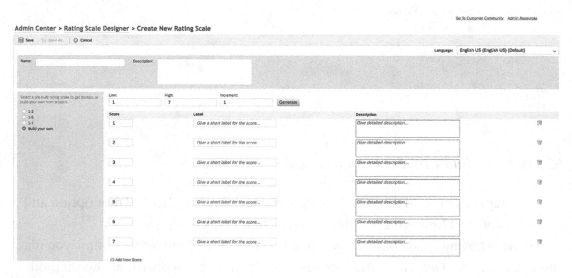

Figure 6-32. *Generated Rating Scale*

Using this method eliminates the need to add a new score one at a time. However, the label and description for each score still need to be entered. Although not recommended, it is possible to create a rating scale with up to 40 scores.

Copy a Rating Scale

You may open an existing rating scale, click "Save As..." as seen in Figure 6-33, and provide a new scale name; and you will have created a copy of an existing rating scale.

Figure 6-33. *Copy an Existing Rating Scale*

You may then edit the new rating scale, change labels and descriptions, or modify the number of scores.

The route map and rating scale are now configured, so let's move on to the performance form template.

Manage Templates

We are going to begin to configure our Performance Management form template. The template defines the components and structure of the performance form. It will identify the route map, rating scale, and goal plan, as well as the competencies and optional development plan to use. The appearance and behavior of a performance form that is launched are based on these configuration decisions.

Type and select "Manage Templates" in the search bar. This will look similar to creating a goal plan template. You will now see an additional tab, "Performance Review" which will appear before the "Goal Plan" tab as seen in Figure 6-34.

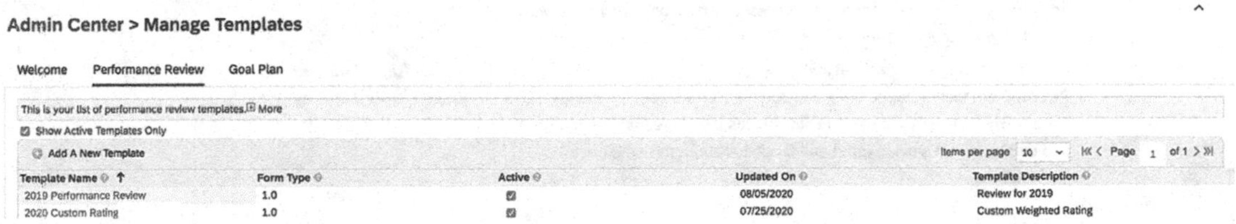

Admin Center > Manage Templates

| Welcome | Performance Review | Goal Plan | | | |

This is your list of performance review templates. ⊞ More

☑ Show Active Templates Only

⊕ Add A New Template

Items per page 10 ▾   ⧏⧏ ⟨ Page 1 of 1 ⟩ ⧐⧐

Template Name ⬦ ↑	Form Type ⬦	Active ⬦	Updated On ⬦	Template Description ⬦
2019 Performance Review	1.0	☑	08/05/2020	Review for 2019
2020 Custom Rating	1.0	☑	07/25/2020	Custom Weighted Rating

Figure 6-34. *Performance Review Tab of Manage Templates*

We will not see any templates listed until we have downloaded a prebuilt SuccessStore performance form template. Once we have a form template, we can copy it to make a new version, perhaps for a new plan year. It is recommended to have a separate template for each performance review cycle.

Applicable when we have multiple form templates, click the "Template Name," "Updated On," or "Template Description" column heading to change the template sort order. The Form Type field identifies the version. Only templates that are active may be used.

Similar to goal plan templates, when "Show Active Templates Only" is enabled, only active templates will display. Inactive plans cannot be used or launched. Since templates cannot be deleted, you can hide inactive templates to make the overview list more manageable.

Template descriptions fewer than 50 characters will display, and like the goal plan and route map descriptions, mouse over "..." to view longer template descriptions.

Add a Template from SuccessStore

Similar to creating a goal plan and a route map, we can add a new template from SuccessStore. Click "Add a New Template," and the prebuilt best practice templates will display as seen in Figure 6-35.

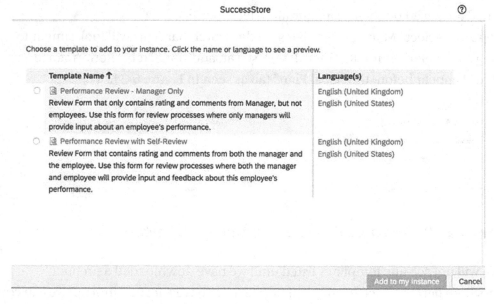

Figure 6-35. *SuccessStore Performance Form Templates*

Select a template to add to your instance. You will be prompted to name your template as seen in Figure 6-36.

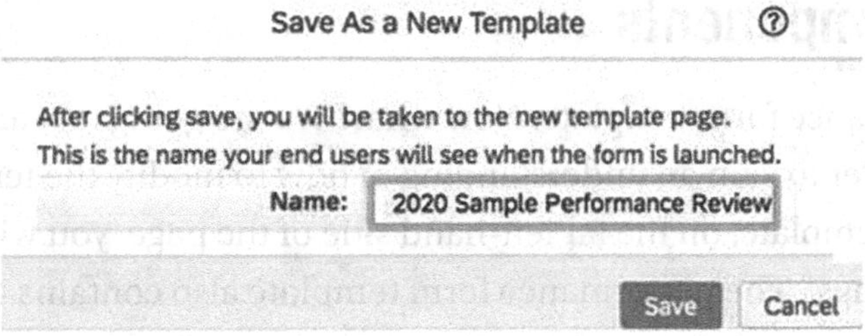

Save As a New Template   ⑦

After clicking save, you will be taken to the new template page.
This is the name your end users will see when the form is launched.

Name: 2020 Sample Performance Review

Save   Cancel

Figure 6-36. *Naming a Performance Form Template*

It is recommended to include the year or cycle in the template name. This name will display on the performance form, so be sure to make it meaningful. An example is shown in Figure 6-37.

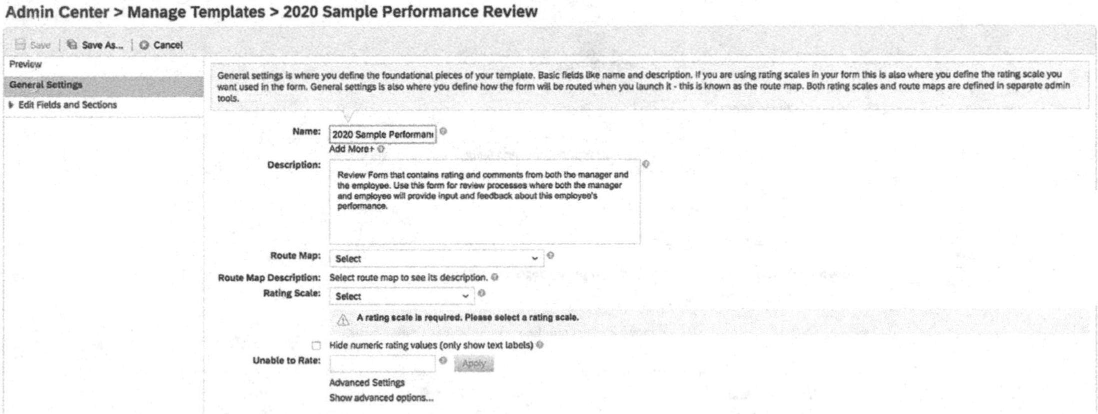

Admin Center > Manage Templates > 2020 Sample Performance Review

💾 Save | 📋 Save As... | ⊘ Cancel

Preview
General Settings
▶ Edit Fields and Sections

General settings is where you define the foundational pieces of your template. Basic fields like name and description. If you are using rating scales in your form this is also where you define the rating scale you want used in the form. General settings is also where you define how the form will be routed when you launch it - this is known as the route map. Both rating scales and route maps are defined in separate admin tools.

Name: [2020 Sample Performanc] ⊘
          Add More+ ⊘

Description: [Review Form that contains rating and comments from both the manager and
              the employee. Use this form for review processes where both the manager
              and employee will provide input and feedback about this employee's
              performance.] ⊘

Route Map: [Select   ▾] ⊘
Route Map Description: Select route map to see its description. ⊘
Rating Scale: [Select   ▾] ⊘
              ⚠ A rating scale is required. Please select a rating scale.

              ☐ Hide numeric rating values (only show text labels) ⊘
Unable to Rate: [   ] ⊘ [Apply]
              Advanced Settings
              Show advanced options...

Figure 6-37. *Starter Performance Form Template*

Copy a Form Template

The other way to create a template is to copy any existing template. It is not possible to create a template from scratch. Similar to copying a goal plan template, open an existing performance form template and click "Save As...." When prompted, provide a new name, and save the template. You will now have a copy of the form template to edit. However, some of the advanced form template settings will not be copied over. We will talk more about this later.

Template Components

We have a performance form template. Now what? We are going to learn about its components in order to gain an understanding of how to modify the template. Just like the goal plan template, on the far left-hand side of the page, you will see "Preview" and "General Settings." The performance form template also contains "Edit Fields and Sections."

We will cover "General Settings" in this chapter, and we will continue with "Edit Fields and Sections" in the next chapter.

General Settings Overview

A sample of the "General Settings" for the form template may be seen in Figure 6-38.

Figure 6-38. *General Settings of a Form Template*

You will find the template name and description within "General Settings," and here you will identify the route map and rating scale to use. "Hide numeric rating values," "Unable to Rate," "Advanced Settings," and "Show advanced options..." are additional options that we will need to decide upon.

If you get stuck along the way, you will see the question mark icons for many fields in all of the template sections. Mouse over the icon to get helpful information about the field.

Section Overview

Click "Edit Fields and Sections" to see the layout and content of the form template, which is listed below "General Settings" as seen in Figure 6-39.

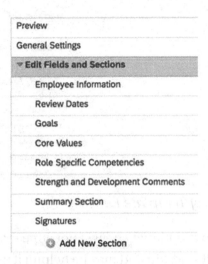

Figure 6-39. *Form Template Sections*

The expanded view will list the sections that will appear in the template.

Now, let's go back to "General Settings" to learn more.

General Settings

Here we will define the template name and identify the route map and rating scale to associate with the form template. These fields are required. Upon selecting the route map and rating scale, their descriptions will populate based on the descriptions you assigned to the route map and rating scale when they were created.

The template name may be localized by clicking "Add More+." As seen in Figure 6-40, a popup will display, and you may add labels for selected languages.

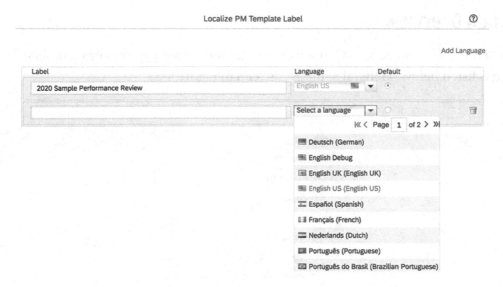

Figure 6-40. *Localization of Template Labels*

The template description is optional and will not appear anywhere in the form. It is more informational for the admin and may be helpful if it contains a summary of the flow of the form, the roles used, and what is being rated. Like the goal plan and route map, if the description contains more than 50 characters, it will not display in the Template Description column on the template overview page. Instead, you will need to mouse over "..." to see the description.

A route map must be attached to the form template to identify the workflow for the form. If you try to select the route map here, you will see a warning popup similar to what is seen in Figure 6-41.

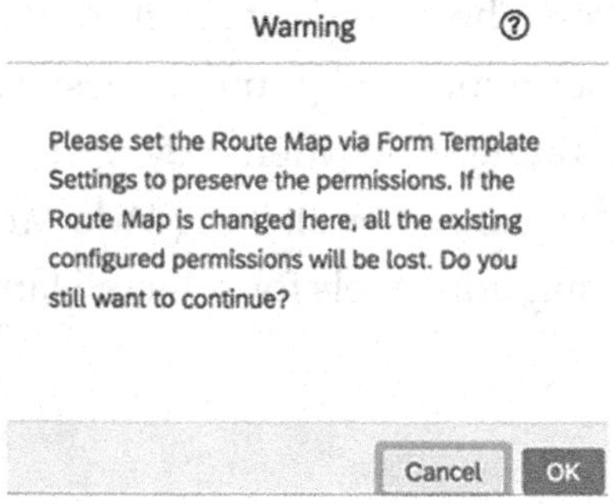

Figure 6-41. *Route Map Selection Warning*

A form template downloaded from SuccessStore has no route map attached, so it is safe to choose your route map here.

In situations where you have copied a form template, the route map and performance scale from the original form template show in "General Settings." If you then create a new route map to use with the copied template and select it here, the existing permissions get broken. To avoid this, you need to choose the new route map in "Advanced Settings."

It is recommended to always select the route map in "Advanced Settings" so you will get in the habit of using this method and you won't have to worry about causing any route map/role permission issues.

Now we will need to identify the rating scale that will be used in the form. Click the dropdown arrow in the Rating Scale field to display all active scales. An example is shown in Figure 6-42.

```
Select
✓ Performance Rating Scale
PIP Rating Scale
Readiness
Default Scale
IntScale
Likert
OCOC
Potential Rating
```

Figure 6-42. *Rating Scale Selection*

Select our newly created rating scale. The rating scale selected will apply to all sections of the template that have ratings.

There is a checkbox to enable for "Hide numeric rating values (only show text labels)." This option will cause the rating scale to display as a dropdown listing with the score labels. This option may be used if your organization is used to having text ratings. If not enabled, the default rating scale uses stars.

"Unable to Rate" is used to define a label for a neutral rating and is applicable to all form sections that use ratings. For example, it may be used to denote "Not Applicable" or "Too New to Rate." This neutral value will be part of the scale but will not be used in calculating overall rating. After entering a label, click "Apply" as seen in Figure 6-43.

267

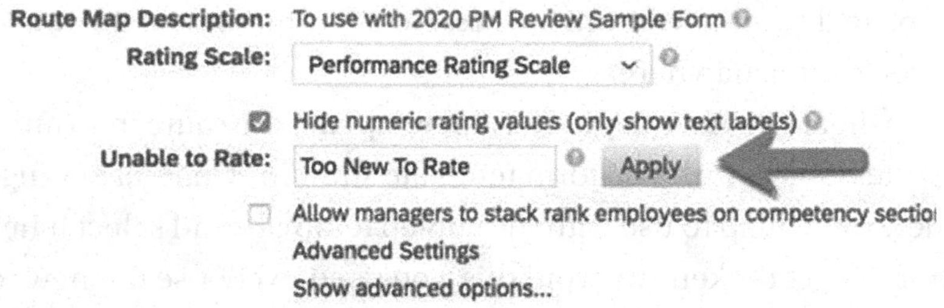

Route Map Description: To use with 2020 PM Review Sample Form ⓘ

Rating Scale: Performance Rating Scale ⌄ ⓘ

☑ Hide numeric rating values (only show text labels) ⓘ

Unable to Rate: Too New To Rate   ⓘ   [Apply] ⟵

☐ Allow managers to stack rank employees on competency section

Advanced Settings

Show advanced options...

Figure 6-43. *Applying Neutral Rating to a Rating Scale*

This will cause the "Unable to Rate" value to apply to all sections of the form that have ratings.

You will be unable to save your updated form template at this point. The goal plan must be identified in the Goals section in order to save. But we will continue discussing the settings and options until we arrive at the Goals section.

Now we will move on to the advanced settings within "General Settings."

Advanced Settings

Click "Advanced Settings" and a popup will display, also referred to as *form template settings.* A subset of these settings is shown in Figure 6-44.

Managing Form Templates

Use this page to manage existing form templates.   Note: any in-progress forms using this template will be immediately updated with the settings below.

Template Name: | 2019 Performance Review
English US (English US)
Template Type: | PM Review
Last Modified: | 2020-08-05 23:07:09.0
Routing Map: | 2018 Performance Review Routemap
Default Dates for Form Creation:
Warning - Mixing Fixed and Relative to Form Creation Date can result in invalid dates set.
Default Start Date: ◉ Fixed ○ Relative | 01/01/2019
Default End Date: ◉ Fixed ○ Relative | 12/31/2019
Default Due Date: ◉ Fixed ○ Relative | 02/28/2021
☐ Disable Ask For Feedback functionality
☑ Enable Ask for Feedback Responses in Supporting Pod permissions. If this switch is not enabled, the Ask for Feedback responses will use the original permission model which is to only be displayed to the user who requested the feedback
  ☐ Disable the external email address feedback option
  Date range for collecting feedback from employees:
    Start Date: ○ Fixed ◉ Relative to: Form Creation Date | 0 | Days after(+) or before(-)
    End Date: ○ Fixed ◉ Relative to: Default Due Date | -7 | Days after(+) or before(-)
☑ Display circle icon as rating
☑ Display check mark instead of rating in Team Overview

Display Last Competency Ratings:
◉ From a Form Template ○ From Rating Sources
None
Default Due Notification Date (in days): | 3
Default Late Notification Date (in days): | 1
Template Status: | Enable
Template Flag: | Public
○ Do Not Transfer Documents
◉ Automatic Manager Transfer.
  ☑ Automatic insertion of new manager as next document recipient if not already.
    ☑ Manager
  ☑ Automatic Inbox Document Transfer To New Manager
    ☑ Manager
  ☑ Automatic En Route Document Transfer To New Manager
    ☑ Manager
  ☑ Automatic Completed Document Copy to New Manager
    ☑ Manager
  ☐ Hide Visibility After Document Transfer
When the system is configured to remove documents for inactive employees, apply these overrides so that the system does not remove documents for this form template
  ☐ Do Not Remove Inactive Employee's In-Progress Documents.
  ☐ Do Not Remove Inactive Employee's Completed Documents.
Default Targets: | Self and Direct Reports
☐ Hide Route Map on the Form
☐ Keep last touched version upon Document completion
☐ Enable Auto Restore Deleted Form When Importing User
☑ Enable Spell Check

Figure 6-44. *Form Template Settings*

Here, you will see a large number of settings which enable some features and define some of the form behaviors. When updating these settings, some will apply immediately to live forms, and some will only be effective in newly launched forms.

Select the route map to be used with the template. Find "Routing Map" on the left side of the page, and you will see that there is not a route map assigned to the template as seen in Figure 6-45.

Managing Form Templates

Use this page to manage existing form templates.   Note: any in-progress forms using this template will be immediately updated with the settings below.

Template Name: | 2020 Test
English US (English US)
Template Type: | PM Review
Last Modified: | 2020-08-07 17:32:32.0
Routing Map: | No route

Figure 6-45. *Selection of a Route Map*

Click the dropdown arrow to select the map that we created. Next, scroll to the very bottom of this settings page, and you will see a button labeled "Update Form Template." Click this button to save the settings.

Now we will highlight some of the common settings that you may enable. We will start with default dates as seen in Figure 6-46.

Figure 6-46. *Select Dates for Form Creation*

Default Dates for Form Creation

These dates will define the performance review evaluation period and the form due date. You may use fixed dates or relative dates. These dates impact any email notifications since they are date driven.

Similar to relative dates on the route map, *relative dates* are based on a number of days before or after the form creation date, default start date, default end date, or default due date. Using a negative number represents days before the selected date.

An example is shown in Figure 6-47.

Figure 6-47. *Relative Form Dates*

For this example, the default start date is 0 day after the form creation date. This means the evaluation start date is the same as the day the forms were generated. The default due date is 100 days after the form creation date. The default end date is 10 days before the default due date.

Selecting "Fixed" default dates will cause a change to the date options. You will now select actual calendar dates as seen in Figure 6-48.

Figure 6-48. *Fixed Default Form Dates*

Most often, fixed dates are used for annual performance forms. You can enter a January 1 start date with a December 31 end date. The due date is often 15–30 days after the evaluation period end date.

Regardless of the default dates' type, these dates will be pulled in when launching forms for this template and will display in the Review Dates section of the form.

If you make no changes to these dates, the default dates will be used.

Next, we will look at the default notification dates. An example is shown in Figure 6-49.

Default Due Notification Date (in days):   3
Default Late Notification Date (in days):   1

Figure 6-49. *Default Notification Dates*

These dates are used to determine when to send a form due date notification and a past due form notification, based on "X" number of days before the form due date:

- Default Due Notification Date (in days)

- Default Late Notification Date (in days)

When we discussed the copying of a form template, we mentioned that some of the advanced settings did not copy over from the original form template. This applies to all of these date fields. They revert to zero, and the default due date is 30 days after creation date.

Refer to Table 6-4 for some of the common settings.

Table 6-4. *Common Form Template Settings*

Setting	Description
Automatic Manager Transfer	Select all of the options under Automatic Manager Transfer. This setting allows forms to reroute based on relationship changes. *To learn more, refer to SAP note #2077194.*
Display circle icon as rating	Stars are the default rating type. You may opt to show circles instead of stars for ratings.
Display checkmark instead of rating in Team Overview	In Team Overview for launched forms, the manager will see a checkmark in the step column to identify step completion rather than showing the numeric rating in the step.
Enable Spell Check	Recommended when using the company dictionary. To use, the company dictionary must first be enabled in Provisioning.
Enable Legal Scan	Recommended when you have a legal library. To use, the legal library must first be enabled in Provisioning.
Enable Writing Assistant	Applicable to forms with competencies only.
Disable Ask For Comment Routing	Have this option checked (to disable) if not using the Get Feedback option.
Disable Ask For Edit Routing	Have this option checked (to disable) if not using the Get Feedback option.
Hide Add/Remove Signer buttons	Have this option checked (to disable).
Disable Send and Open Next Form Button	Have this option checked (to disable).
Disable Delete button	Have this option checked (to disable).
Disable Note button	Have this option checked (to disable).
Disable Form button	Have this option checked (to disable).
Disable 360 button	Have this option checked (to disable).
Show Signoff routing step names in Signoff Stage	Enable. When the form is in the Signature Stage, displays the name of the step in the routing map.
Display Step Start Date	Have this option checked (to disable).

(continued)

Table 6-4. (*continued*)

Setting	Description
Show digital signatures in Document Print Preview	Enable. Specifies that the signer's name is shown on the printed copy of the form as well as their role and the date when the user signed the form.
Disallow users from changing the End Date	Have this option checked (to disable).
Disallow users from changing the Due Date	Have this option checked (to disable).
Enable form routing to previous step	Optional, enable only if you are allowing forms to go back a step.
Display the signature line when a signature step is skipped	Recommended to enable. Used to display an empty signature line in the signature area of the form when the signature step is skipped, rather than displaying no signature information at all.
Enable Attachments	Enable to add attachments to a performance form.

Save any updates and close this popup.

Note   To see the complete list of advanced settings and their purpose, please reference SAP note #2077413.

We will now discuss the advanced options available for the template.

Show Advanced Options

Beneath the Advanced Settings link, click "Show advanced options..." as seen in Figure 6-50.

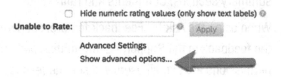

Figure 6-50. *Show Advanced Options*

This section will expand as seen in Figure 6-51.

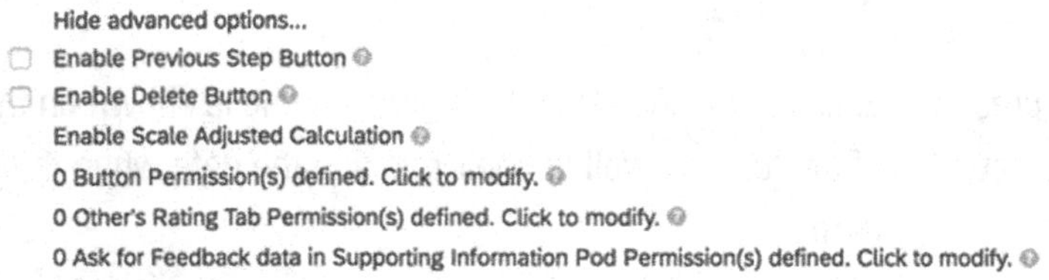

Hide advanced options...
☐ Enable Previous Step Button ❓
☐ Enable Delete Button ❓
Enable Scale Adjusted Calculation ❓
0 Button Permission(s) defined. Click to modify. ❓
0 Other's Rating Tab Permission(s) defined. Click to modify. ❓
0 Ask for Feedback data in Supporting Information Pod Permission(s) defined. Click to modify. ❓

Figure 6-51. *Advanced Options*

When expanded, the "Show advanced options..." changes to "Hide advanced options...". You may click this label to hide these options, and the section collapses.

Refer to Table 6-5 for the option details.

Table 6-5. *Advanced Options*

Option	Description
Enable Previous Step Button	When enabled, there will be a button on the form that will move the form back one step. Must be enabled in the advanced form template settings in order to use this.
Enable Delete Button	Not recommended to enable. When enabled, may define the steps and role when the delete button will be available. Must be enabled in the advanced form template setting in order to use this.
Enable Scale Adjusted Calculation	Used in summary sections, creates an "adjusted calculated score" to use instead of the calculated form rating which is always numeric. Maps scores to labels and may also map scores based on a minimum or maximum value for each score. *We will cover this in greater detail in the Summary section of the next chapter.*
Button Permission(s) defined	Defines button permissions for roles for each step. If not defined, all roles in all steps will have the button permissions.
Other's Rating Tab Permission(s) defined	To allow a role to see the "Other's Rating" tab for goal, competency, and summary sections. Comments and rating options.
Ask for Feedback data in Supporting Information Pod Permission(s) defined	When using the Ask for Feedback feature, set permissions to see the feedback in the Supporting Information pod on the form. If no permissions are set, all users will see the feedback at all steps. *We will learn about* Ask for Feedback *in Chapter 11.*

As you can see from the advanced options, a checkbox is used to enable some options, and some options define permissions. "Enable Scale Adjusted Calculation" will be discussed in the Summary Section of the next chapter.

You will not see the "Ask for Feedback data in Supporting Information Pod Permission(s)" option if Ask for Feedback was not enabled in the advanced form settings. We will learn about this feature in Chapter 11.

Saving the Template

Just a reminder, you will not be able to save your updated template until you have chosen the goal plan that you will be using in the review process. You may use the goal plan that you created in Chapter 4. If you wish to save the template now, expand "Edit Fields and Sections," find the Goals section, and select the goal plan to link to the template. An example is seen in Figure 6-52. Now click "Save" to save the updated form template.

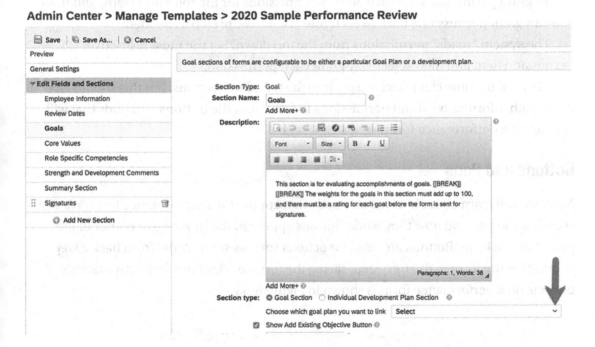

Figure 6-52. *Link a Goal Plan to a Performance Form Template*

Next, we will review how to use permissions in the template.

Advanced Options Permissions

We will dig deeper into the permissions used in a performance form template as we go along, but here are some high-level concepts to keep in mind. In addition to role-based permissions for Performance Management, there are also permissions in the form template specific to the roles in the route map that control what a user can see and do.

Form permissions reflect the viewer of the form in relation to the subject of the form. Here is an example. Joe (employee role) works for Dan (manager role), and Cindy is Joe's HR manager (HR rep role). A performance form was created for Joe. You will need to decide what each of these roles (employee, manager, and HR manager) can see and do during the steps in the process.

The default form permissions are "Enabled" for the form sections and "Write" for the section fields. These permissions grant access for all roles to see and do everything in all steps of the process.

To grant permissions, remove default permissions for the roles and steps, and then you can grant permissions back to each role at each route step as needed.

The system "reads" permissions from the top down. Set the most restrictive permission first, and then selectively grant each permission.

This will become clear once we get into the template sections, but this should give us enough information about permissions to talk about the buttons and pods that will appear on a performance form.

Buttons and Pods

Next, we will learn about buttons and pods that appear on a performance form. We will see what they do and how they work. Buttons appear in the lower-right corner of the performance form. Buttons are used for actions such as sending the form back a step, submitting the form to the next step, saving the form, or signing a form. An example of buttons on a performance form is shown in Figure 6-53.

Figure 6-53. Buttons on a Performance Form

Pods display across the top of the performance form and contain data from the form. Pods may contain the overall form rating and identify the number of required fields to enter for the step or to hold attachments. Here, we will grant permission to buttons and pods for the roles at each step in the route map.

Figure 6-54 is an example performance form header with the five available pods.

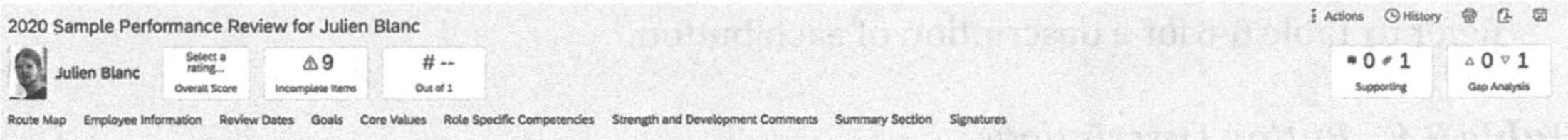

Figure 6-54. *Pods on a Performance Form*

The route map that we linked to the performance form template defined route steps and the roles in each step. Button permissions will be set based on the roles in the route steps. We will define which buttons are visible and hidden for each role in each step in the route map.

For example, for a route map that has the employee role in the Employee Self-assessment step, the buttons the employee will have access to in this step must be defined.

Button permissions are in the advanced options within "General Settings." Click "0 Button Permission(s) defined. Click to modify." A popup to add button permissions will display. Click "+ Add Another" as seen in Figure 6-55.

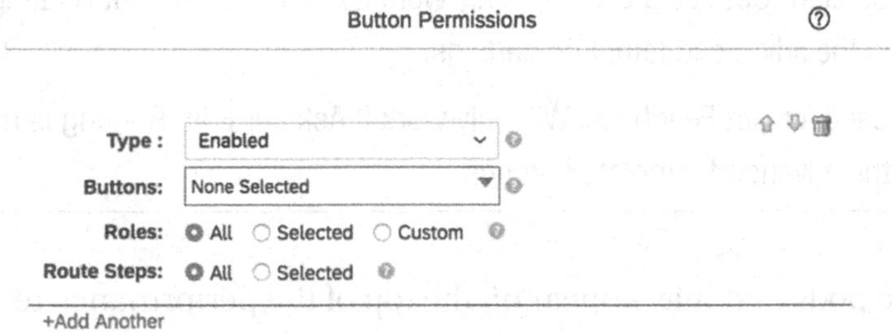

Button Permissions

Type :	Enabled
Buttons:	None Selected
Roles:	◉ All ○ Selected ○ Custom
Route Steps:	◉ All ○ Selected

+Add Another

Figure 6-55. *Add Button Permissions*

You will need to identify the permission type, buttons, roles, and route steps to grant button permissions. The options to complete for the permissions are shown in the following.

Type defines the access:

- *Enabled* makes the button visible and clickable in the step.

- *None* makes the button invisible to the user in the step.

277

Buttons identifies the buttons and pods being permitted for a role in a step.

Roles identifies which role the permission is being set for.

Route Steps identifies at which step the button is permitted for. The route steps are those from the route map linked to the form template.

Refer to Table 6-6 for a description of each button.

Table 6-6. *Button Descriptions*

Button	Description
Reject	Sends the form from a signature step back to the last Modify Stage step.
Finalize Form	Sends the form to the next step. Label for this button configured in the route map.
Sign	Used in the Signature Stage. Clicking the sign button electronically signs the form and adds a date.
Send to Previous Step	Sends the form back one step. Label for this button configured in the route map.
Delete Form	Will only work if the delete button is not disabled in advanced template settings. The delete button appears on the form toolbar.
Get Comments	Used for Get Feedback. Will only work if Ask For Comment Routing is not disabled in the advanced template settings.
Get Edits	Used for Get Feedback. Will only work if Ask For Edit Routing is not disabled in the advanced template settings.

There are five pods that may appear on the top of the performance review form. Refer to Table 6-7 for the pod descriptions.

Table 6-7. *Pod Descriptions*

Button	Description
Overall Score	This button will only display the form rating after the final rating is given and is only visible to users that have permission to rate items in all the sections.
Gap Analysis	Comparison graph of the difference between employee and manager ratings.
Incomplete Items	The pod contains the count of the required fields. The user will not be able to submit their form if all of the required fields are not populated. They can click this pod to see which required fields have not been entered. Very useful for steps that have required entries. Clicking a required field in the pod will move the form to the section where it needs to be entered.
Team Ranker	A manager can see a rating ranking on each of their direct reports' forms for those already rated using the same form template.
Supporting Information	May contain attachments, notes from Employee Profile, and Ask for Feedback comments if settings are configured in advanced template settings.

We need to identify button permissions by role and step. The button permissions are based on the roles in the route map associated with the performance form template. These decisions should have been made in the configuration workbook. But as a refresher, for the role within the route map, we should consider

- Buttons/pods not to be used in the form at all steps

- Buttons/pods needed for all steps

- Buttons/pods needed for certain steps

- Buttons/pods not needed at certain steps

- Pods to display on the completed form

To start, identify all the buttons and pods that you don't want to see on the form at any step.

As an example for a basic template, you would not need

- Get Edits

- Get Comments

- Reject

- Delete Form

You may not need the following pods:

- Gap Analysis

- Team Ranker

Our first button permission would identify the buttons and pods that should never appear on the form. The type would be "None," and we would select which buttons and pods to hide. This means putting a checkmark next to each button that you don't want visible on the form. Next, we would select all roles and all steps. For example, Figure 6-56 has six buttons that will not be visible for all the roles in every step.

Figure 6-56. *Buttons to Hide from the Form*

If you click the downward arrow for Buttons, you will see the buttons that we selected.

Since we have removed permissions for specific buttons and pods for all roles and steps, we may now identify buttons and pods that we want to see in every step and every role.

In light of "no permissions granted means button permission is granted," it still may be useful to create button/pod permissions for each step and role. That does not mean a separate permission for each button and pod for each step and for each role. Instead, you would identify all the buttons and pods needed and hidden for each role at each step.

First, you could create the "Enabled" permissions. Identify the buttons and pods to be available for the step and the role associated with the step.

For the buttons or pods to hide in the step, you would create a "None" permission and identify the buttons and pods that should not be visible for the role. You would repeat this process for each step in the route map.

Using this method allows you to easily find any permission issues because you can see what was permitted for each step. For example, during testing, you are expecting the manager to be able to send the form back to the employee during the manager assessment step. However, the button is not found on the bottom of the form. So as the admin you would be able to go back into the template, open the button permissions, locate the manager assessment step button permissions, and find that this button was not enabled for the manager role. You could correct the permission by adding the "Send to Previous Step" button to this step for the manager role. This will not correct the live form. You would need to relaunch the form to test that it is now working correctly. With that said, having defined "None" and "Enabled" permissions for each step would make it simpler to find any issues.

Thinking back on our route map, there is a button that we only need to use for one step. The manager assessment step allows the form to go back to the employee. To be able to use this button, we had to first enable "form routing to previous step" in the advanced template settings. With this enabled, we can permit the "Send to Previous Step" button for the manager in the manager assessment step as seen in Figure 6-57.

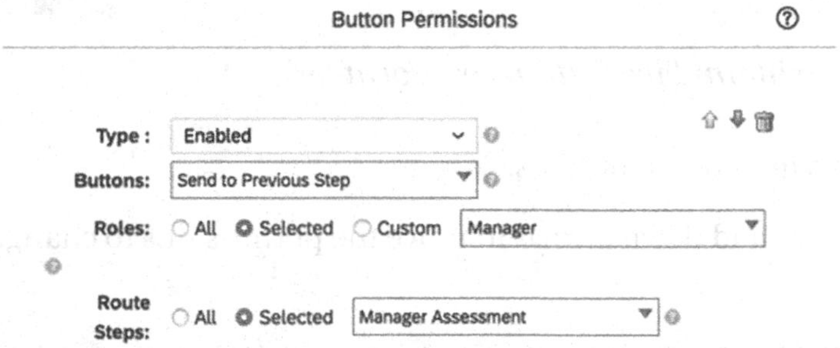

Figure 6-57. *Permission to Send a Form Back One Step*

Each step in the Modify Stage of the route map needs the "Finalize Form" button. This is the button that is used to move the form to the next step. You should identify the route map steps in the Modify Stage and make sure the "Finalize Form" button is enabled for each of those steps.

For signature steps, the "Sign" button should be enabled. This is necessary to have the signature and date electronically added to the form.

Only five buttons may appear at the bottom of a form. Of the five, "Save and Close" and "Cancel" will always appear. If you have permitted more than five buttons for a step, some will be grouped within the "More Actions" based on the button priority.

The button priority is:

1. Finalize Form or Sign or Confirm 1:1 (one of these)

2. Reject

3. Send

4. Get Feedback/Recall Feedback

5. Send to Previous Step

6. Add Modifier

7. Add Signer

An example of a performance form with more than five buttons is seen in Figure 6-58.

Figure 6-58. *Maximum Five Buttons on Form*

Things to keep in mind for buttons:

- Use the up and down arrows to move the permissions to change their order.

- For collaborative and iterative route steps, only the exit user for the step will see the "Finalize Form" button. This is true even if you grant button access to both roles in the step.

- If you create button permissions for Get Comments, Get Edits, and Delete Form, if the settings are not enabled in the advanced template settings, these buttons will not display on the form. The same is true for routing the form back a step.

- If forms have been launched and you later update the button permissions in the form template, these changes will not impact live forms. You will need to relaunch the forms to have the permission updates applied.

- If a button is disabled in the form template advanced settings but permitted in the template's advanced options, the form template advanced settings permission is used.

Based on button permissions, you may define which pods will display on completed forms by role. For example, you may decide to allow an employee to view their overall rating pod on their completed form, while the manager can see the Overall Score pod, the Gap Analysis pod, and the Team Ranker pod. We will learn how to set up the permissions in Chapter 7.

Other's Rating Tab Permissions

The final permission to define in this section is for the Other's Rating tab as seen in Figure 6-59. This permission grants access to view the goal and competency ratings and comments entered by other users on the form.

Figure 6-59. *Other's Rating Tab on Performance Form*

Figure 6-60 shows the form template section where the other's rating permission is found.

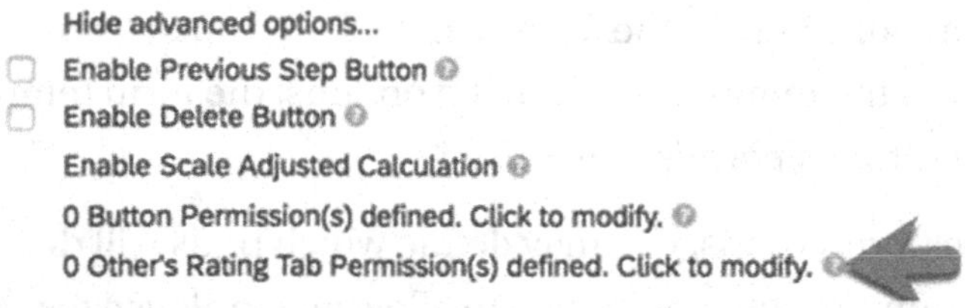

Hide advanced options...
☐ Enable Previous Step Button ⊙
☐ Enable Delete Button ⊙
    Enable Scale Adjusted Calculation ⊙
    0 Button Permission(s) defined. Click to modify. ⊙
    0 Other's Rating Tab Permission(s) defined. Click to modify. ⊙ ⬅

Figure 6-60. *Other's Rating Tab Permissions to Be Defined*

This permission is used to grant access to a role in a route step to see the comments and ratings made by others. An example is in Figure 6-61.

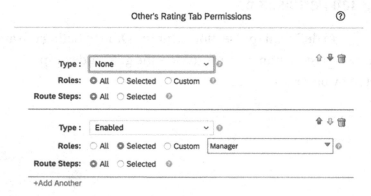

Figure 6-61. *Other's Rating Tab Permissions*

For example, during self-assessment, the employee enters a rating and comment for each goal on their form. When the form moves to the manager assessment step, with this permission, the manager will be able to see the ratings and comments made by the employee.

To do this, identify if the tab is visible ("Enabled") or hidden ("None") for each step and each role in the step. This is done through "Type." It is best to start with "None" and then add any steps where you would like to have the tab visible. This ensures that the Other's Rating tab is not visible for any role at any step. Then you can gradually add in permission based on role and step. An example of the permissions is seen in Figure 6-62.

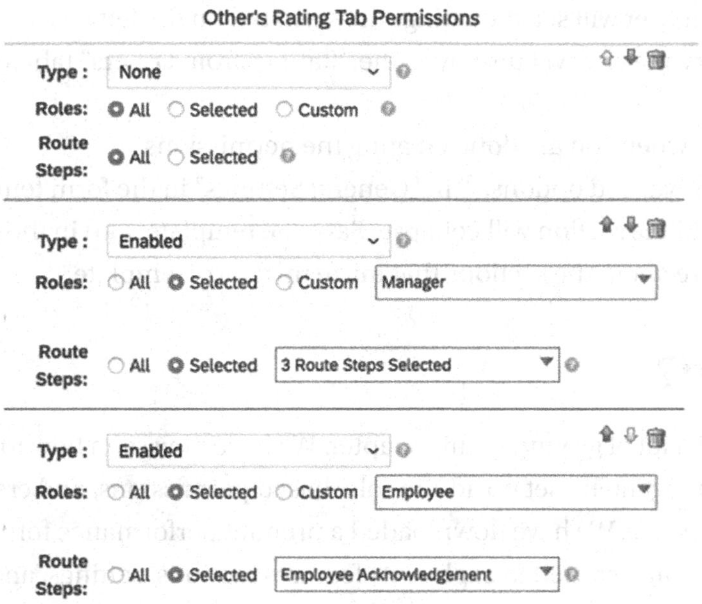

Other's Rating Tab Permissions

Type :	None ▾ ⓘ	⇧ ⇩ 🗑
Roles:	● All ○ Selected ○ Custom ⓘ	
Route Steps:	● All ○ Selected ⓘ	

Type :	Enabled ▾ ⓘ	⇧ ⇩ 🗑
Roles:	○ All ● Selected ○ Custom	Manager ▾
Route Steps:	○ All ● Selected	3 Route Steps Selected ▾ ⓘ

Type :	Enabled ▾ ⓘ	⇧ ⇩ 🗑
Roles:	○ All ● Selected ○ Custom	Employee ▾
Route Steps:	○ All ● Selected	Employee Acknowledgement ▾ ⓘ

Figure 6-62. *Other's Rating Tab Permissions Hidden for the First Step*

See Figure 6-63 for an example where the form is in the first step and the Ratings from Others tab displays with "There are no Ratings from Others." This occurred because there was not a "None" permission set for the role and the step.

Figure 6-63. *Other's Rating Tab with No Ratings*

The "Other's Rating Tab Permissions" define the tab permissions for all form sections that have ratings.

The logged-in user will see the ratings they entered on the left side of the screen; the ratings from everyone else will display in the "Ratings from Others" tab on the right side of the screen.

Click "Done" when you are done creating the permissions.

Click "Hide advanced options..." in "General Settings" in the form template to hide these options, and the section will collapse. Save the template, and in the next chapter, we will learn more about the sections that make up a form template.

What's Next?

We have covered a lot of ground in this chapter. We have now seen how to enable Performance Management, set up admin role–based permissions, and create a route map and a rating scale. We have downloaded a prebuilt performance form template from SuccessStore and started to explore its features, options, settings, and permissions.

In the next chapter, we will dig deeper into the performance form template and learn about how to configure and grant permissions to the form sections.

CHAPTER 7

Performance Form Template Settings

In the previous chapter, we enabled Performance Management, set up permissions, and started to look at the components of the performance form template. We will continue our discussion here by exploring the form template sections that define the layout and content that the user will see in their performance form. We will also learn about permissions that may be configured for sections and fields.

We will go back into our form template to set up the sections and permissions. Type and select "Manage Templates" in the search bar. Go to the Performance Review tab and select the performance form template to update.

Template Sections

When the template displays, expand the "Edit Fields and Sections" section. An example is shown in Figure 7-1.

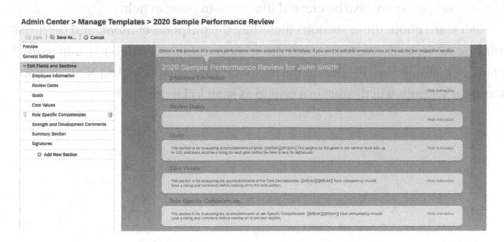

Figure 7-1. *Edit Fields and Sections View of the Template*

© Susan Traynor, Michael A. Wellens and Venki Krishnamoorthy 2021
S. Traynor et al., *SAP SuccessFactors Talent: Volume 1*, https://doi.org/10.1007/978-1-4842-6600-7_7

In this chapter, we will focus our attention on this section. Based on the prebuilt form template downloaded from SuccessStore or a copied form template, the sections that you see on your template may differ. However, any of the standard sections may be added, and it is also possible to create custom sections.

Listed in the following are the standard sections that may be used in the template:

- Introduction

- Employee Information

- Review Dates

- Mid-Year

- Additional Comments

- Goals/Objectives (and Development Objectives)

- Competency (role, core, and custom)

- Summary

- Performance Potential Summary

- Objective Competency Summary

- Customized Weighted Rating

- Signature

Custom sections may also be created that contain custom fields.

We will learn about these sections including the purpose, content, and permissions that may be set for each. We will look at the sections that are available to add to the form template. Beneath the last section in the template, find and click "Add New Section," and the standard sections will display in a popup as seen in Figure 7-2.

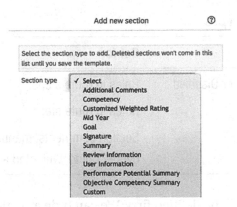

Figure 7-2. *New Section Options*

If any of these sections are already in your template, they may not appear in the listing. Some sections may only be used once per template, such as Employee Information, Review Dates, Summary, and Signature. Sections that do not display in the "Section type" dropdown listing are already in the template so they cannot be added again. Goals, Competency, and custom sections may appear more than once in your form template. Select a section name, click "Add," and the section will be added to the template. It will display as the last section of the form template.

Each section will appear on your performance form in the order listed in the form template. The section order may be rearranged by clicking a section and dragging to a new spot. Save the template as you make updates.

Section, Action, and Field Permissions

In Chapter 6, we reviewed button permissions and the "Other's Rating Tab Permissions" found in the advanced options section of "General Settings" in the form template. Within this portion of the form template, there are section, action, and field permissions to configure. There will be different features and permissions to configure based on the section type.

Table 7-1 lists the permission types along with permission options.

Table 7-1. *Permission Types*

Type	Permission	Set for
Section	Enabled, Hidden, or Disabled	Roles in route steps
Action	Enabled, None	Roles in route steps
Field	None, Read, Write	Section comments, manual overall rating, calculated overall rating, weighted average

Section permissions will be defined first. We can hide a section, view a section ("Disabled"), or edit a section ("Enabled"). The section must be enabled for any step where the user may edit an action or field. For example, if you did not enable a section for the step where a user will add a goal rating, a "Write" permission for fields within the section would not be honored.

The order of permissions matters. The system reads them from top to bottom. Each new permission overrides any previous permissions that it may conflict with.

Some basic rules to keep in mind are the following:

- When permissions are not set, the system grants all permissions to all users.

- Use "Disabled" for all roles for all steps for sections that are "Read" only.

- To grant permission to some and not all roles, define the "None" permissions for all roles in all steps. Then you can gradually add permissions for roles and steps that will need to see the section.

- If a section is enabled, field permissions within the section can be used to hide fields for certain roles.

- If a section is editable but field permissions are "None," the user will only see the section title and header.

- Hide Summary and Signature sections until the step in the route map where they are needed.

- To see fields on the completed form, start with "Read" permission for all roles, and then set "Write" permission to edit, "Read" permission to view, or "None" permission to hide fields in certain steps.

Now we will look at each section of the form template and how to set it up.

As we have just seen, there are standard performance form template sections. Each section has different features, options, and permissions. It is also possible to create custom sections. Custom sections may contain a description, section comments, and custom fields.

If you click a section, you may update section labels, add labels for additional languages, and set permissions. Now we will walk through the section types. We will see the section in the template and how it looks on the performance form, and we will learn how to configure the section and field permissions.

Introduction Section

This section may be configured to display some information about the performance review process and instructions on how to complete the form or may include a link or an image. A sample of this section is seen in Figure 7-3.

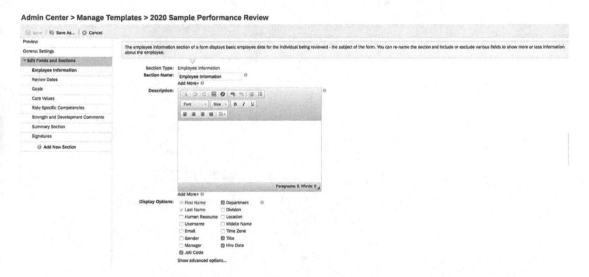

Figure 7-3. Introduction Section

The only options available for this section are Section Name and Description, and both may have local labels. There are no fields in this section, so there are no field permissions to set. Only a section permission can be set, either "Hidden" or "Disabled." Since there are no fields in this section, even if you chose "Enabled" or did not set permissions for the section, the section would still be read-only.

Figure 7-4 is an example Introduction section with an embedded image.

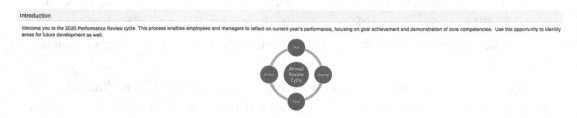

Figure 7-4. *Introduction Section with Image*

Employee Information Section

The Employee Information section may be configured to display some basic information about the employee. A sample of this section is seen in Figure 7-5.

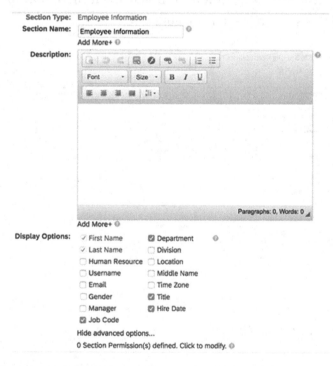

Figure 7-5. *Employee Information Section*

You may change the section name and add local section labels. You may also add a description with local labels. The contents of the Description field will display in the section on the form and may be text, an image, a link, or a combination of each. The description will display above the fields that are selected for "Display Options."

The fields that may appear in the section on the form are listed in "Display Options." Click the checkbox next to a field so it will display in this section.

A sample of the Employee Information section is shown in Figure 7-6.

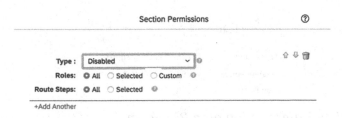

Employee Information

This section contains information about the employee.

Last Name	Blanc		First Name	Julien
Title	European Labor Law		Department	Employee Relations (50007728)
Manager	Marcus Wright		Location	Corporate - US-Philadelphia (1710-2001)

Figure 7-6. *Employee Information Section on a PM Form*

There are additional fields that you may include in this section, but they must be added in the form template XML which we will cover in Chapter 10. The additional fields include:

- Emp ID

- Business Phone Number

- Fax Number

- Home Address

- Review Frequency

- Last Review Date

- Any of the custom 01-15 fields in the user data file

It is possible to reorder the field display in the XML as well.

This section is read-only, and the permission type should be "Disabled" for all roles and route steps as seen in Figure 7-7. If no section permissions are granted, the section will still display.

Section Permissions   ⑦

Type : [Disabled   ⌄] ⓘ   ⇧ ⇩ 🗑
Roles: ● All   ○ Selected   ○ Custom ⓘ
Route Steps: ● All   ○ Selected ⓘ
+Add Another

Figure 7-7. *Permissions for a Read-Only Section*

Review Dates Section

There are three standard fields that display in the Review Dates section.

You may add a description that will display above the standard fields. You may also add local labels for the section name and description.

The section displays the name of the user who launched the form (the originator). This section also pulls in the default start date and default end date from the advanced settings on the form template. These dates are used for the performance evaluation period along with the default due date.

An example of the Review Dates section on the template is shown in Figure 7-8.

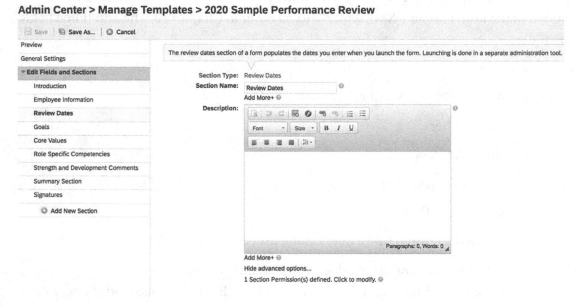

Figure 7-8. *Review Dates Section*

No additional fields may be added to the section, and none can be deleted or reordered. An example of the section on a performance form is shown in Figure 7-9.

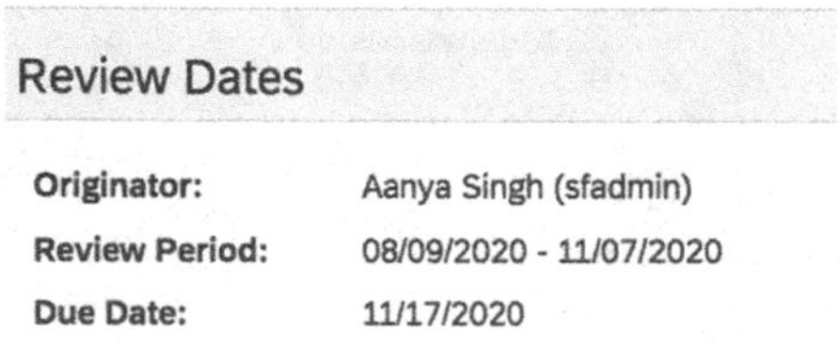

Review Dates

Originator:	Aanya Singh (sfadmin)
Review Period:	08/09/2020 - 11/07/2020
Due Date:	11/17/2020

Figure 7-9. *Review Dates Section on a PM Form*

In the sample shown in the preceding figure, the originator is the user that launched the form. Seeing this field may be confusing to users, but it cannot be removed. Since this is an optional section, many organizations choose not to use it. You may delete the section by clicking the trash can icon; the other option is to hide the section. To use this section in your form template, it should be disabled for all roles and all steps.

Mid-Year Section

The Mid-Year section can be used to track any discussions at midyear. The employee and manager may sit down midyear to review progress made toward achieving their goals. There would be no rating done at this time but would be a *course correction* opportunity to address any issues that may have arisen. Development goals may be created to address any areas of weakness that can be worked on before year-end. Additional goals may be added or removed based on the discussion.

An example of the section as seen in the template is shown in Figure 7-10.

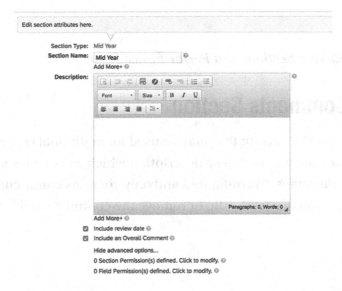

Figure 7-10. *Mid-Year Section*

This section may include a date field to identify the date of mid-year conversation. An overall section comment may be enabled as well.

This section maybe hidden, enabled, or disabled. The only field permissions available for this section are section comments.

Here is an example of how to permit this section. Your performance review process contains an initial step where employees set goals for the year. The form then goes to the manager to edit the goals. The Mid-Year and Assessment sections would be hidden during these steps. The Mid-Year section displays and is editable during the midyear step with the assessment steps hidden that occur after the midyear review. Once the assessment steps occur, the Mid-Year section would be read-only.

A sample Mid-Year section is shown in Figure 7-11.

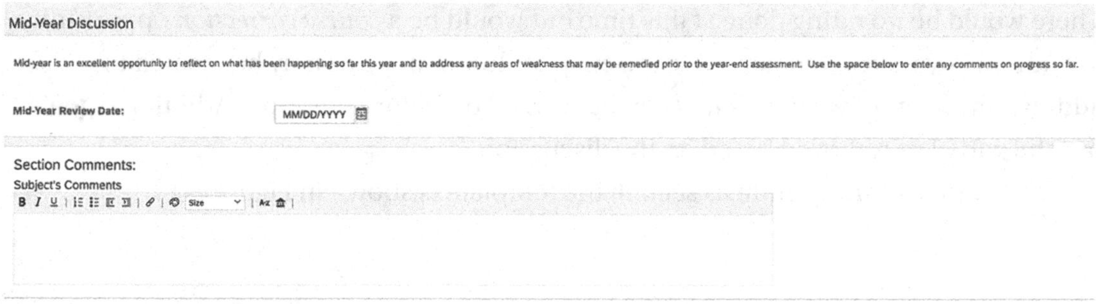

Figure 7-11. *Mid-Year Section on a Performance Form*

Additional Comments Section

There is another optional section that may be used for additional comments. You may rename this section and include a description which will display at the top of the section. This section comes preconfigured and only contains comment text boxes as seen in Figure 7-12. You may add, edit, or remove the comments fields and localize the labels.

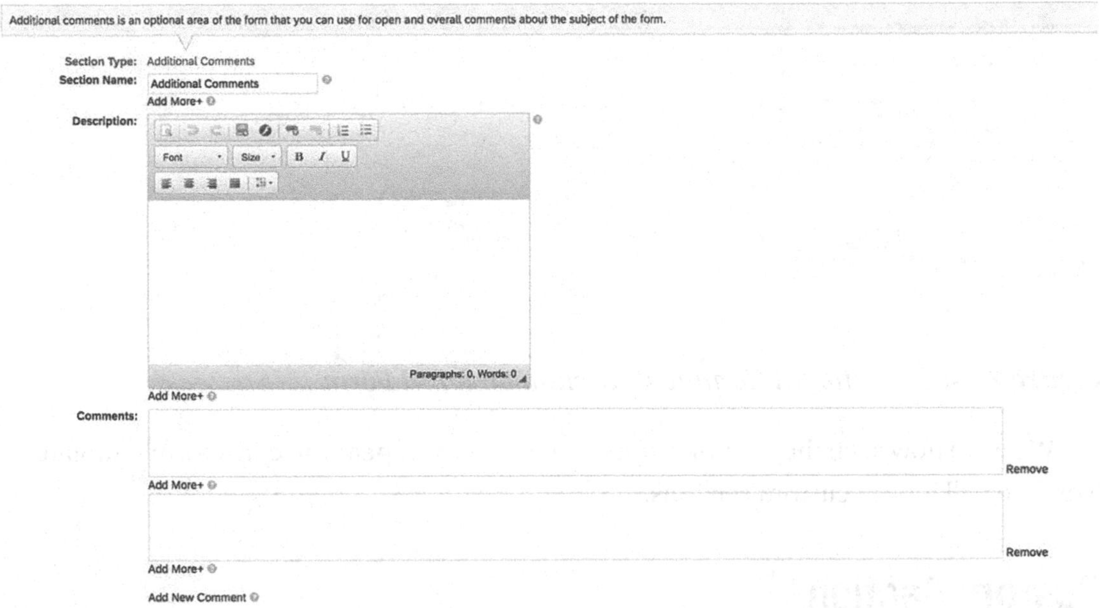

Additional comments is an optional area of the form that you can use for open and overall comments about the subject of the form.

Section Type: Additional Comments

Section Name: Additional Comments

Add More+

Description:

Font ·   Size ·   B *I* U

Paragraphs: 0, Words: 0

Add More+

Comments:

Remove

Add More+

Remove

Add More+

Add New Comment

Figure 7-12. *Additional Comments Section*

This section can be helpful if you wish to have a comments section that is separate from Goals or Competency section comments. You are able to create a long text string that acts as the label for your textarea response. Figure 7-13 shows an example.

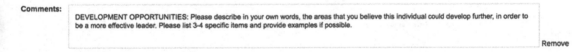

Comments:

DEVELOPMENT OPPORTUNITIES: Please describe in your own words, the areas that you believe this individual could develop further, in order to be a more effective leader. Please list 3-4 specific items and provide examples if possible.

Remove

Figure 7-13. *Adding Text as a Comments Field Label*

This section has no permissions which means in any Modify Stage steps, any role may add comments. This also means any role may overlay or delete comments from previous steps. You may add permissions within the form template XML to remedy this, but it may be easier to create a custom section because it gives you more field types and permission options.

A sample comments section as seen in a performance form is displayed in Figure 7-14. You can see that the section has been renamed, and there the Description field populates above the comments.

Figure 7-14. *Additional Comments Section on a PM Form*

We have now seen the basic sections that may only appear once in a form template. Next, we will look at custom sections.

Custom Section

In addition to the standard sections, it is possible to create custom sections. You may have multiple custom sections in a form template. Custom sections may contain a section comment and description like most of the standard sections. Unique to custom sections, it is possible to edit the description when doing a mass launch of forms. The custom section of the template is seen in Figure 7-15.

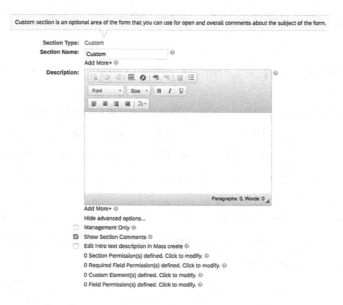

Figure 7-15. *Custom Section*

There are several types of custom elements as shown in Figure 7-16.

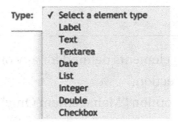

Figure 7-16. *Custom Element Types*

Custom fields may be created for Goals, Competency, and custom sections. Custom fields are also permissible in the Summary section but must be added via the form template XML.

In a section, custom fields will display vertically, not side by side, so you will not be able to set the layout of the fields in the section beyond the field order. In the Goals and Competency sections, the custom fields will display above the rating fields.

There are eight custom element types that may be used as shown in Table 7-2.

Table 7-2. *Custom Element Types*

Element	Description
Label	Will display as bolded text label with no data field to enter.
Text	Label field and open box for one line of text.
Textarea	Multiline text box.
Date	Date entry.
List	Dropdown list.
Integer	Text box for a whole number.
Double	Text box for a number with decimals.
Checkbox	Checkbox with label. Specify "evalue"; otherwise, nothing is stored when checked.

With the exception of the "Label" element type, each custom element may have a label defined which will precede the entry field. You may decide to add a custom field or fields within the section. Permissions will need to be defined for which roles in each step can see the section, view the section, or edit the section.

> **Note**   For more details on how to configure custom fields, please reference SAP note #2888737.

Please note that the custom elements defined for any of the sections would have to be recreated to use in another section.

The custom section has the option "Management Only" as seen in Figure 7-17.

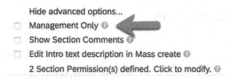

Figure 7-17. *Management Only Option in a Custom Section*

When checked, this option acts as a section permission, and only manager and HR roles will see the section on the performance form.

An example of a custom section using several of the custom elements is shown in Figure 7-18.

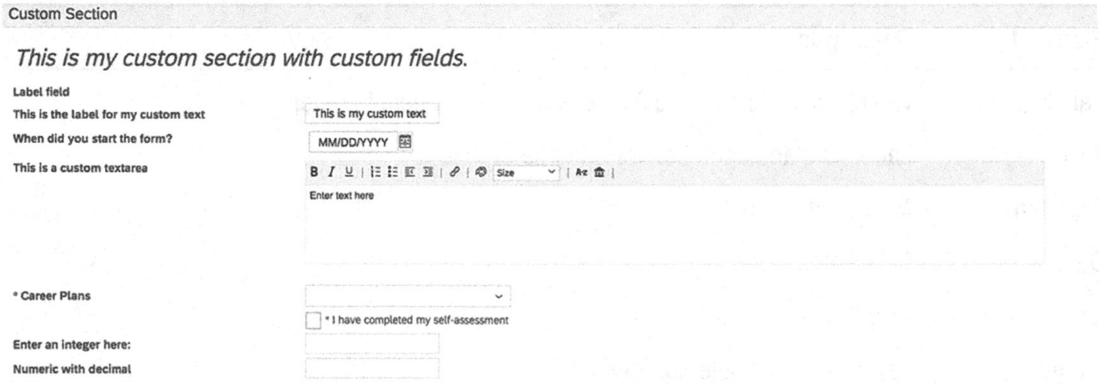

Custom Section

This is my custom section with custom fields.

Label field
This is the label for my custom text   This is my custom text
When did you start the form?   MM/DD/YYYY
This is a custom textarea   B I U | ⅛ ⅛ ⅛ ⅛ | ∅ | ⊘ Size   ∨ | A‌z 🛒 |
                                                 Enter text here

* Career Plans   ∨
                                                 ☐ * I have completed my self-assessment
Enter an integer here:
Numeric with decimal

Figure 7-18. *Custom Section in a Performance Form*

The next several sections that we will look at are used for assessment. We can rate goals from the goal plan and competencies that are job specific, core, or custom. These ratings will be used to calculate an overall performance rating. Before we look at the Goals and Competency sections, let's look at weights and their impact on these sections.

Weights

Weights are optional and may be used for sections or for items within sections or both. Goals and Competency section weights are used in the overall form rating calculation. Within a section, you may define the target total weight for the items in the section.

Things to know about weights are as follows:

- Weights can be set as editable or read-only.

- Typically, item competencies are not weighted.

- If weighting is not used, item and section weights are treated equally.

- Weight can be a number or percentage.

- Set a section weight to 0 to exclude the section from being used in the calculation of the overall score.

Now that we have some background on weights and we know about ratings, we can move on to the Goals and Competency sections.

Goals Section

Most often, achievement of yearly goals is the measure of performance. The template should include the goal plan that is being used by your organization. An example of the Goals section on the form template is shown in Figure 7-19.

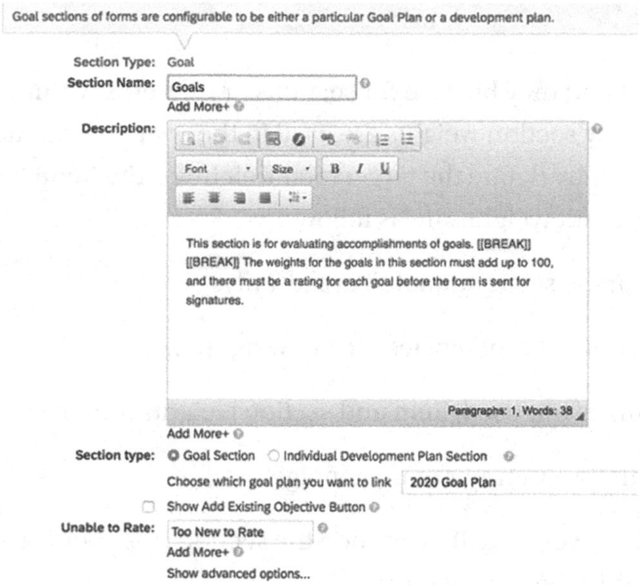

Figure 7-19. *Goals Section on a Form Template*

In the preceding figure, there is a section name and description to be filled in. You will also need to identify the goal plan used in the section. The Goals section may appear multiple times in a form template, ideally once for the goal plan and once for the development goal plan. It is possible to have additional goal plan sections, but it is not recommended; the form should just use one goal plan to rate. The section type is identified by a radio button for Goal Section or Individual Development Plan Section. The dropdown listing for the plan to link to the template will be based on the section type radio button selected.

There are two ways to populate the goals to a performance form: auto-populate and auto-sync.

Auto-populate pulls in the goals from the goal plan during the form creation. A drawback of this method occurs if any goals are added to the goal plan after the performance form has been launched. These goals will not appear on the form unless you configure and use the "Add Existing Goal" button. This would require the user to manually add the goal in their performance form.

Auto-sync synchronizes goals between the goal plan and the performance form. The performance form will contain the goals from a user's goal plan. Any changes to the goal plan will reflect in the performance form; and any goal updates, deletions, or additions made in the performance form will reflect back in the goal plan.

Tip   You can enable auto-sync in Advanced Options by checking the "Synchronize goals from a goal plan and a review form" option.

If enabled, goals may be added or deleted by a user on the performance form. Additionally, comments may be added to each goal, added as an overall goal section comment, or both. A rating for each goal may be entered by the employee and manager.

Other features of the Goals section include:

- Spell Check

- Legal Scan

- Rating Scale Descriptions

A sample Goals section of a performance form is seen in Figure 7-20.

Figure 7-20. *Sample Goals Section on a Performance Form*

The options and features for the Goals section are based on what is enabled within the form template and the form template XML in Provisioning. Here, we will focus on the features that may be updated in the form template via "Manage Templates." Chapter 10 will walk through the XML updates that can be made.

Before we discuss the form template options, let's look at the sample Goals section shown in the preceding figure. You see that there is an initial Goals section that acts as the header. The description of the section here would be the Goals section header. The Goals section header is followed by each goal from the user's goal plan, separated into its own goal subsection.

For each goal, you see its name and description. The rating scale that we created and identified in the form template will be used to rate each goal. The default view of the rating scores is represented by stars. The user may enter comments and ratings for each goal. It is also possible to have an overall goal comments section that follows the last goal on the form. Any of the goal changes in the form would be reflected in the goal plan.

When going through the configuration workbook, decisions should be made regarding:

- Which roles at which steps can add, edit, or delete goals?

- Which roles at which steps can enter ratings?

- Will there be comments for each goal? If so, at which step, for which role, and are they optional?

- Which role at which step can see the Other's Rating tab?

- Will a goal summary section be included? If so, which role at which step can add or view comments? Are comments optional or required?

- The goal is what percentage of the overall rating?

- What goal section data is viewable by other users in other steps?

These decisions drive how to configure the section. For our purposes, we are going to allow the employee and manager to add goal item comments and provide a rating for each goal.

Please reference SAP note #2077252 for an explanation of the field and section permissions.

There are a lot of options in addition to the settings, so let's start at the top. We will first look at the options that follow after "Description." Click "Show advanced options..." to expand the section as seen in Figure 7-21.

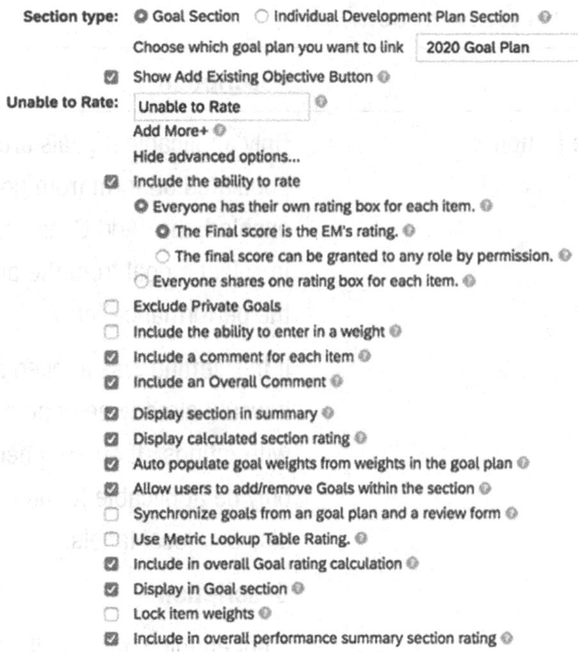

Section type: ⦿ Goal Section   ○ Individual Development Plan Section   ❓

Choose which goal plan you want to link | 2020 Goal Plan

☑ Show Add Existing Objective Button ❓

Unable to Rate: | Unable to Rate   ❓

Add More+ ❓

Hide advanced options...

☑ Include the ability to rate

⦿ Everyone has their own rating box for each item. ❓

⦿ The Final score is the EM's rating. ❓

○ The final score can be granted to any role by permission. ❓

○ Everyone shares one rating box for each item. ❓

☐ Exclude Private Goals

☐ Include the ability to enter in a weight ❓

☑ Include a comment for each item ❓

☑ Include an Overall Comment ❓

☑ Display section in summary ❓

☑ Display calculated section rating ❓

☑ Auto populate goal weights from weights in the goal plan ❓

☑ Allow users to add/remove Goals within the section ❓

☐ Synchronize goals from an goal plan and a review form ❓

☐ Use Metric Lookup Table Rating. ❓

☑ Include in overall Goal rating calculation ❓

☑ Display in Goal section ❓

☐ Lock item weights ❓

☑ Include in overall performance summary section rating ❓

Figure 7-21. *Goals Section of a Form*

Select a radio button to identify if you are using a goal or development plan in this section. Use the dropdown listing to select the goal plan to use in the performance template. This will pull the goals into the performance form from the goal plan selected.

Note   Development goals are not typically rated. However, if you would like to include a development plan to appear on the performance form, you may add an additional Goals section. You may configure that section to be able to add or delete development goals but not to rate.

Refer to Table 7-3 to learn what each of the settings is.

Table 7-3. *Goal Section Advanced Settings*

Setting	Description
Show Add Existing Objective Button	Only applicable if goals are not auto-populated on form from goal plan. When enabled, the "Add Goal" button allows user to select a goal from the goal plan to add to the performance form.
Unable to Rate	If this setting was applied in General Settings, it would already be populated for all sections with ratings. If entered here, the label would only be applicable to the goal section. May also add local labels.

Advanced Options	Description

Include the ability to rate
Used to identify if the section will be rated. If so, each goal will be rated. For each assessment step, the role will have their own rating box for each goal. The manager's rating becomes the final rating, or you may opt to set another role's rating to be the final rating.
Or for each assessment step, there will be a rating box for each goal, and each step's rating overlays the rating entered in the prior step.
	If not enabled, there will be no option to rate goals.
	When enabled:
	
	• Everyone has their own rating box for each goal item.
	
	  o The final score is the manager's rating (RECOMMENDED).
	
	  o May identify any role's rating as the final rating.
	
	• Everyone shares one rating box for each goal. The last rating entered will be the final rating.

(continued)

Table 7-3. (*continued*)

Setting	Description
Exclude Private Goals	When enabled: • If your goal plan has private goals and auto-sync is on, the private goals will not appear in the Goals section of the performance form. • If your goal plan has private goals, auto-sync is not on, and "Add Existing Goal" is enabled, the private goals may not be selected. • When adding a goal within the performance form is enabled, you will not be able to create a private goal.
Include the ability to enter in a weight	Allows a user to update goal weights. Weights are used in the goal rating calculation.
Include a comment for each item	A comment box will display for each goal. May permit which roles in which step can add or view the comments.
Include an Overall Comment	After each individual goal, may include a goal summary section and allow users to add or view goal section comments.
Display section in summary	Goal item weights and ratings to display in the form summary section.
Display calculated section rating	Overall calculated goal rating to display in the form summary section.
Auto populate goal weights from weights in the goal plan	When auto-synced with the goal plan, weights from each goal on the goal plan will populate goals on the performance form.

(*continued*)

Table 7-3. (*continued*)

Setting	Description
Allow users to add/remove Goals within the section	Enables users to add or delete goals to or from the performance form. Use in conjunction with action permissions.
Synchronize goals from a goal plan and a review form	Changes made to the goal plan auto-sync to the Goals section of the performance form. Change made to goals within the performance form flow to the goal plan.
Use Metric Lookup Table Rating	Enables metric lookup table rating if the goal plan has a metric lookup table.
Include in overall Goal rating calculation	To indicate that the goals in this section will be used to calculate the overall goal rating.
Display in Goal section	When using the Objective Competency Summary section, goals from this section will appear here.
Lock item weights	Prevents a user from changing goal weights.
Include in overall performance summary section rating	To include a Goals section in the overall performance summary section.
Minimum Goals Required	Minimum number of goals on the performance form.
Maximum Goals Allowed	Maximum number of goals on the performance form.
Section Weight of Objective Competency Summary	Applicable only if using the Objective Competency Summary section. Identifies objective rating weight to use for the objective competency rating calculation.
Total Weight	Total weight for all goals in the section.

(*continued*)

Table 7-3. (*continued*)

Setting	Description
Rating Scale	If selected in General Settings of the template, all sections with ratings will use this scale. May select a different scale within the section but is not recommended.
Hide numeric rating values	Ratings are selected from a dropdown list using the rating labels rather than stars or circles.
Default Rating	May define the default rating that displays when opening a form.
Choose an alternate label for the rating field	Define another label for the rating field such as "Select a rating."

Before we began our discussion of rating scales, we touched briefly on the format of the rating scale.

Rating Scale Appearance

The default rating scale displays as stars as seen in Figure 7-22.

Figure 7-22. Default Star Rating

The "Too New to Rate" value appears at the far left of the scale as the "no circle" icon.

In the form template's advanced settings, you may opt to display the rating scale using circles. An example of the circle rating scale is shown in Figure 7-23.

Figure 7-23. Circle Rating

The "Too New to Rate" value appears at the far left of the scale as the "no circle" icon. The final rating scale display is text in a dropdown listing as seen in Figure 7-24.

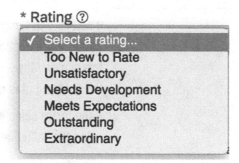

Figure 7-24. *Text Rating*

The text used in the dropdown listing uses the rating scale text labels.

Regardless of the rating scale type, all three show the rating descriptions in the question mark icon as seen in Figure 7-25.

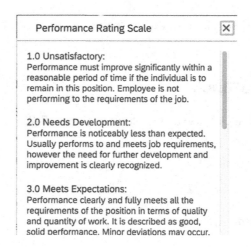

Figure 7-25. *Rating Descriptions*

The "Too New to Rate" value is the first rating in the dropdown listing.

In each of these rating scales, "Too New to Rate" has no numerical value and is not used in the overall form calculation.

The scale type selected will apply to the goal and competency item ratings as well as the manual overall rating in the Summary section. The calculated overall form rating will use the numeric scale. We will talk more about the overall form rating in our discussion of the template Summary section.

Permissions for a Section

Five types of permissions may be set for a section:

1. Section

2. Action (only applicable to Goals and Competency sections)

3. Field

4. Required Field

5. Custom Element (applicable to Goals and Competency sections only and the Summary section using XML)

Not all of these permissions are applicable to every section. For example, actions, fields, and required fields are not options for Employee Information, Introduction, Review Dates, and Additional Comments sections, to name a few.

Figure 7-26 is a sample of the permission types available for a Goals section of the template.

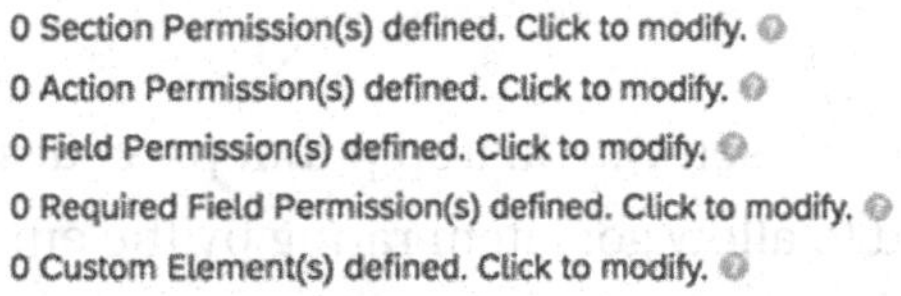

0 Section Permission(s) defined. Click to modify. ❼
0 Action Permission(s) defined. Click to modify. ❼
0 Field Permission(s) defined. Click to modify. ❼
0 Required Field Permission(s) defined. Click to modify. ❼
0 Custom Element(s) defined. Click to modify. ❼

Figure 7-26. *Section Permission Types*

We will look at each permission type.

Section Permissions

We start with the section permissions. Sections can be hidden, editable, or read-only. Permission types are "Hidden," "Enabled," or "Disabled." For each template section, identify if the section is invisible, editable, or viewable by role and step.

Action Permissions

Action permissions are used in the Goals and Competency sections to add or remove goals or competencies. Action types are "None" or "Enabled." The action options are "Add item" or "Remove item." These permissions will only work if "Allow users to add/remove Goals within the section" is enabled for the section. These permissions should be set by role and step.

Field Permissions

Field permissions define which fields are hidden, viewable, or editable by role in each step. For example, you may have a section visible; but based on role and step, certain fields may be hidden.

Options are "None," "Read," and "Write."

Goal and competency fields include:

- Item Rating (manager's rating)

- Unofficial User Rating

- Item Weight

- Section Weight

- Item Comments

- Subject Rating (employee's self-rating)

- Section Comments

- Custom fields

Typically, the employee will self-rate in a step that precedes the manager assessment. The rating field to allow goal item rating by the employee is "Subject Rating." Use "Item Rating" for the manager's rating. Any other roles that are defined in a route map step would use the "Unofficial User Rating."

Required Field Permissions (Optional)

We can identify which fields (if any) must be filled in before the form may be sent to the next step. Define the role and step for each required field. The required field permissions in the form template are shown in Figure 7-27.

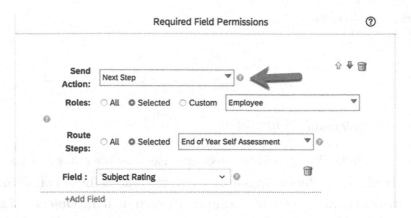

Figure 7-27. Send Action for Required Fields

Unique to the required field permissions is the "Send Action." You must identify if the send action is "Next Step" or "Signature." For "Next Step," the field is a required entry before sending the form to the next step. The "Signature" action is used if the field is required before moving to the signature step.

For example, if a user must enter goal ratings, make this a required field for the step where it should be entered. The user will be unable to submit their performance form to the next step unless the required fields are entered. If permitted, the Incomplete Items pod will show the number of required fields for the step.

It is recommended to make ratings required in order to submit the form to the next step.

Custom Element Permissions (Optional)

We discussed custom sections earlier in this chapter and learned about custom fields. Custom fields may be added to Goals and Competency sections. After creating any custom fields, you would need to define the permissions by step and role. It is also possible to make a custom field required.

If "Include an Overall Comment" is enabled in the section, you will see a comments section that comes after the final goal. You may set permissions to view or create a comment by step and role. An example of a section comment is displayed in Figure 7-28.

Overall Comments on Goal Achievement
Subject's Comments

Figure 7-28. *Overall Goal Comment*

As you can see, individual goals are rated, and users cannot enter an overall goal rating. The individual goal item ratings are used in calculating the overall form rating. The overall form rating will appear in the Summary section. If the Objective Competency Summary section is used, the calculated overall goal rating can be displayed.

Development Goals Section

Including a development plan in the form template is an optional section. To add the section, choose the "Goal" section type as seen in Figure 7-29.

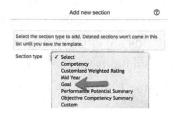

Figure 7-29. *Add a Development Goals Section*

This is the same section used for goals, so the options and settings are the same. Just be sure to select the radio button for "Individual Development Plan Section" and then select the development plan to link to the form template. Name the section, add a description, and you may allow users to add or remove development goals. Although it is possible to rate development goals, it is discouraged. Development goals identify areas to work on which does not seem appropriate to rate. Oftentimes, the inclusion of this section on the form is more for informational purposes or to allow a user to add development goals based on how well they are achieving their goals. Development goals are future facing, while rating goals is for past behavior.

If included, you make this section read-only but allow the employee to add a development goal or possibly add a comment to an existing development goal. An example is shown in Figure 7-30.

314

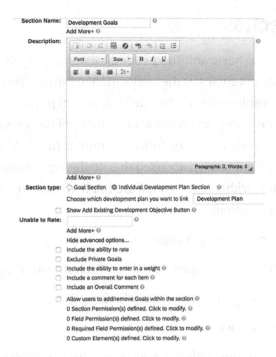

Figure 7-30. *Development Goals Section Advanced Options*

A sample development goal within the Development Goals section of the form is displayed in Figure 7-31.

Figure 7-31. *Development Goal on a Performance Form*

Based on the permissions set for this example, the development goal may be edited or deleted, and additional development goals may be added. There is no rating on the development goals.

Competency Section

Competencies describe the basic abilities needed for an employee to perform their job. The inclusion of competencies in the performance form makes sense because competencies are observable and measurable and impact performance.

In addition to rating employees on the achievement of their goals, it is also possible to rate competencies. Like the Goals section, each item is rated. Along with the goal item ratings, the competency item ratings are used in calculating the overall form rating.

In the configuration workbook, decisions are made to determine how to set up the form template section including:

- Use of role, core, or custom competences

- Use of comments on competencies, by which role and which step

- Who can rate competencies and at which step

- Use of overall competency comments

If you are using a competency library, preferably the SuccessFactors 2.1 Competency Library with competencies linked to job codes, you would be able to pull an employee's role-specific competencies into the form to rate. If you also have identified "core" competencies, you may have a separate core competency section on the form as well.

It is also possible to permit users to add additional competencies to the performance form. You may wish to proceed with caution since that could dilute the importance of weighting role and core competency ratings.

Other optional features of the Competency section include:

- Spell Check

- Legal Scan

- Writing Assistant

These options would have been enabled in Provisioning as well as in the form template advanced settings.

A sample Competency section for a performance form is seen in Figure 7-32.

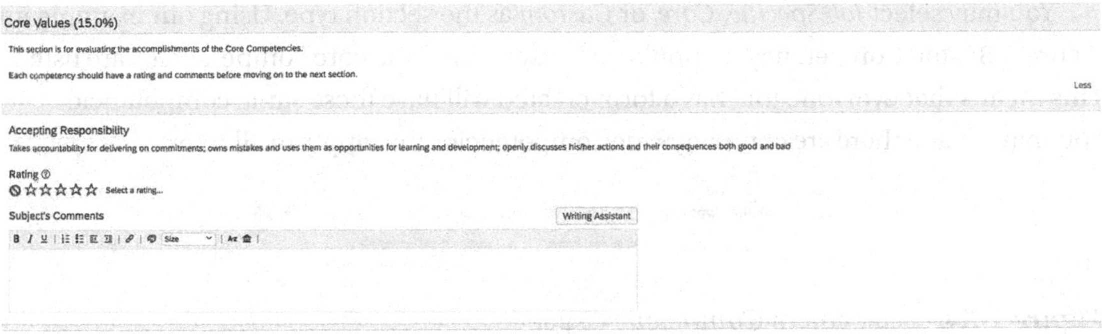

Figure 7-32. *Core Competency Section on a Performance Form*

Most of the goal features and options to configure are identical for the Competency section. We will point out notable differences. A sample of a Competency section in the form template is shown in Figure 7-33.

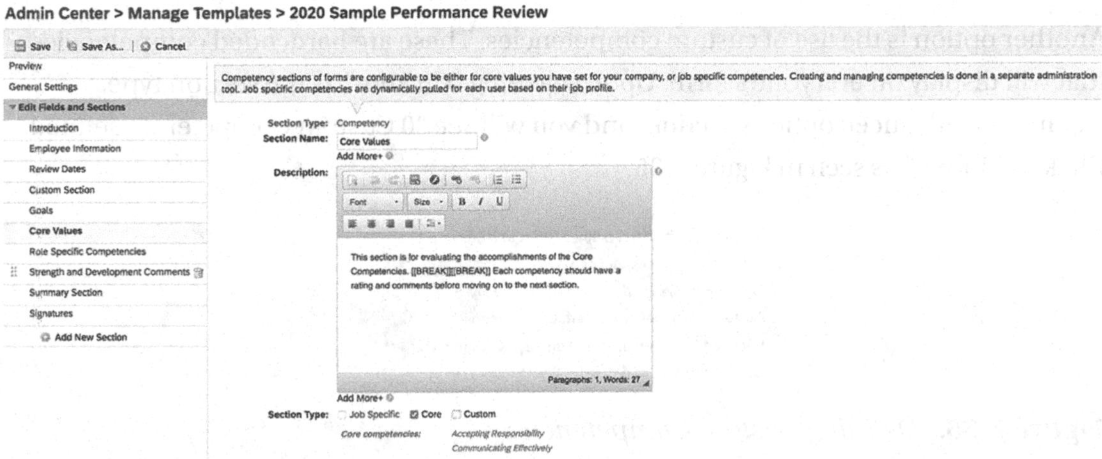

Figure 7-33. *Competency Section*

Competency Section Types

You may have multiple Competency sections on your form. Ideally, you would create a separate Competency section for each competency type. However, it is possible to include custom competencies with job-specific competencies in the same section or custom competencies with core competencies. Job-specific and core competencies cannot appear in the same section.

You may select *Job Specific, Core,* or *Custom* as the section type. Using our example in Figure 7-34, the Competency section type is "Core," and the core competencies are listed. This means that everyone that has a form created will have these same competencies. You may decide there are companywide competencies that apply to all roles.

Figure 7-34. *Selection of Competency Type*

These competencies were identified as "core" using Job Profile Builder. If you had selected "Job Specific," all of the competencies linked to the user's job role would populate the Competency section.

Custom Competencies

Another option is the use of custom competencies. These are hardcoded competencies that will display on everyone's form. Upon selecting "Custom" as the section type, expand the advanced options section, and you will see "0 Custom Competency defined. Click to Modify" as seen in Figure 7-35.

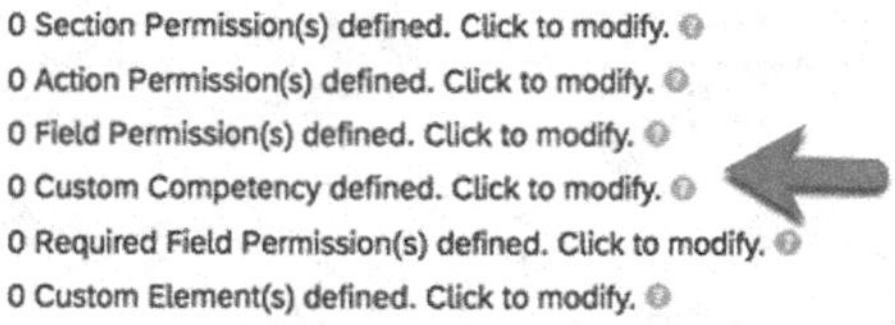

0 Section Permission(s) defined. Click to modify. ⊙
0 Action Permission(s) defined. Click to modify. ⊙
0 Field Permission(s) defined. Click to modify. ⊙
0 Custom Competency defined. Click to modify. ⊙
0 Required Field Permission(s) defined. Click to modify. ⊙
0 Custom Element(s) defined. Click to modify. ⊙

Figure 7-35. *Defining Custom Competencies*

You would define the custom competencies within the template. You may select the competencies that should be hardcoded on the form from any existing competencies. You may create new competencies that are not tied to a job code or are not core and then select these in the template.

An example of creating a custom competency is seen in Figure 7-36. The competency is created using Job Profile Builder. Refer to Chapter 3 to learn more about Job Profile Builder.

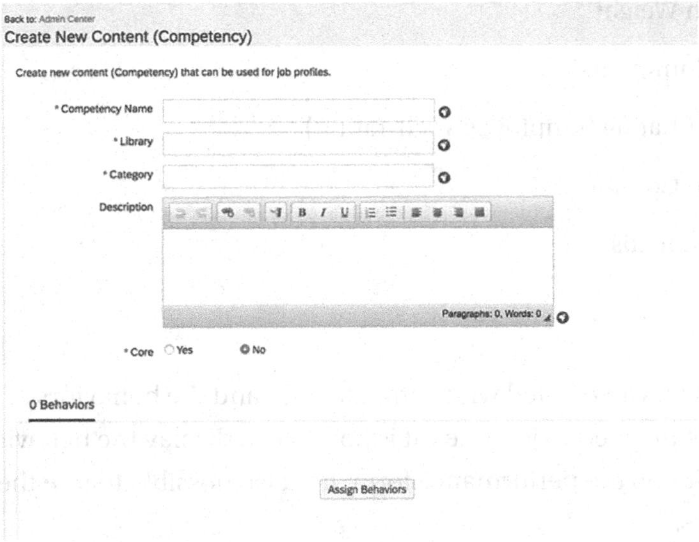

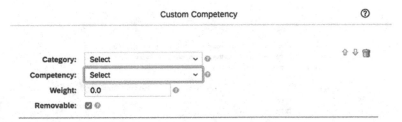

Figure 7-36. *Create a New Competency*

Once a new competency has been created, it may be selected as a hardcoded competency to appear on all users' performance forms. An example is shown in Figure 7-37.

Figure 7-37. *Selecting Hardcoded Competencies*

Competency Permissions

Similar to the Goals section, you would need to set the section, field, required field, and custom field permissions. The same fields are available as the Goals section fields as seen in the following:

- Item Rating (manager's rating)

- Unofficial User Rating

- Item Weight

- Section Weight

- Item Comments

- Subject Rating (employee's self-rating)

- Section Comments

- Custom fields

Behaviors

If you have behaviors associated with competencies and the behaviors of the competencies are mapped to job roles, it is possible to display the behaviors associated with competencies on the performance form. It is also possible to rate the competencies by their behaviors.

Figure 7-38 is an example of a competency with associated behaviors.

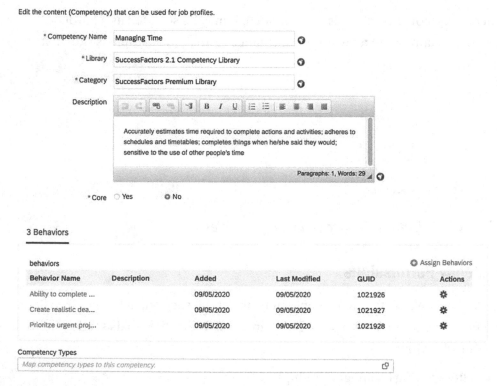

Figure 7-38. *Competency with Associated Behaviors*

The competency is linked to a job role as seen in Figure 7-39.

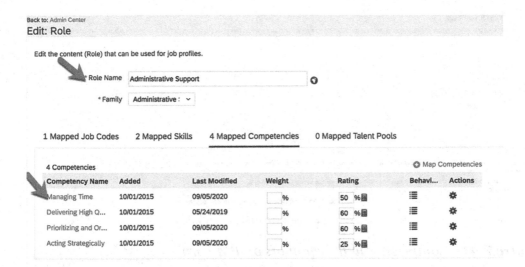

Figure 7-39. *Competency Associated with a Job Role*

By electing "Show Behaviors," the behaviors with each competency will display. You may also select the display mode so the behaviors can appear above or below the competency rating in the performance form.

An example is shown in Figure 7-40.

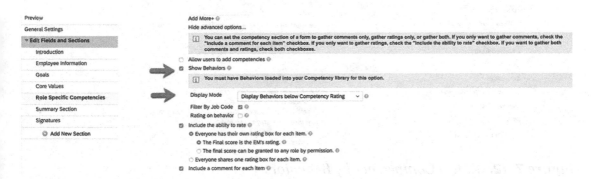

Figure 7-40. *Show Behaviors for Each Competency*

Figure 7-41 displays an example of how the behaviors appear below the competency in a performance form.

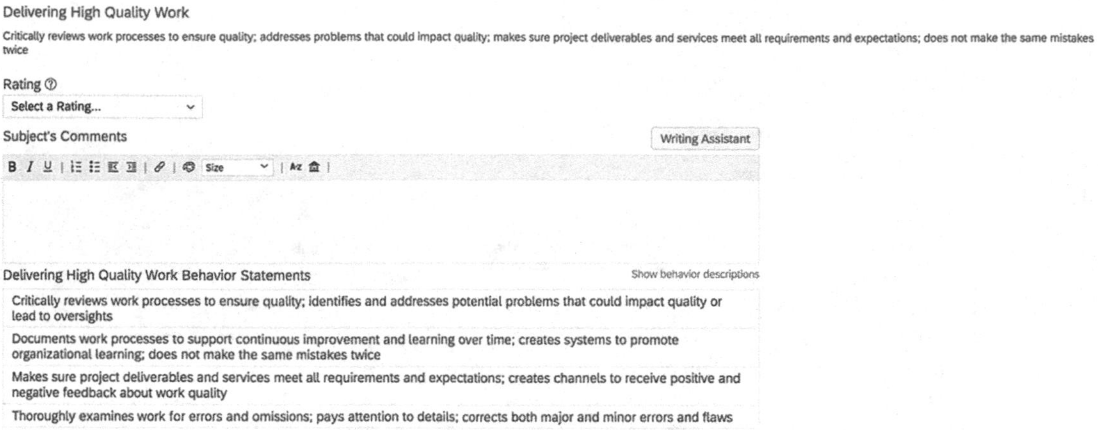

Delivering High Quality Work

Critically reviews work processes to ensure quality; addresses problems that could impact quality; makes sure project deliverables and services meet all requirements and expectations; does not make the same mistakes twice

Rating ⓘ

Select a Rating...   ⌄

Subject's Comments   Writing Assistant

B *I* U̲ | ≔ ⋮≡ ⎌ ⎯ | 𝒫 | ⊕ Size   ⌄ | A𝓏 🏛 |

Delivering High Quality Work Behavior Statements   Show behavior descriptions

Critically reviews work processes to ensure quality; identifies and addresses potential problems that could impact quality or lead to oversights

Documents work processes to support continuous improvement and learning over time; creates systems to promote organizational learning; does not make the same mistakes twice

Makes sure project deliverables and services meet all requirements and expectations; creates channels to receive positive and negative feedback about work quality

Thoroughly examines work for errors and omissions; pays attention to details; corrects both major and minor errors and flaws

Figure 7-41. *Competency with Behaviors on PM Form*

In this example, the user rates and comments on the competency and sees the associated behaviors.

It is also possible to rate on behaviors instead of the competencies. If a competency has multiple behaviors, each behavior is rated, and the system will then calculate the overall behavior rating for each competency. An example is seen in Figure 7-42.

Figure 7-42. *Rate a Competency by Behaviors*

For example, if a competency has five associated behaviors, each behavior is rated, and then there will be a calculated overall behavior rating for each competency.

The example shown in Figure 7-43 has two behaviors to rate to create a calculated rating for the competency.

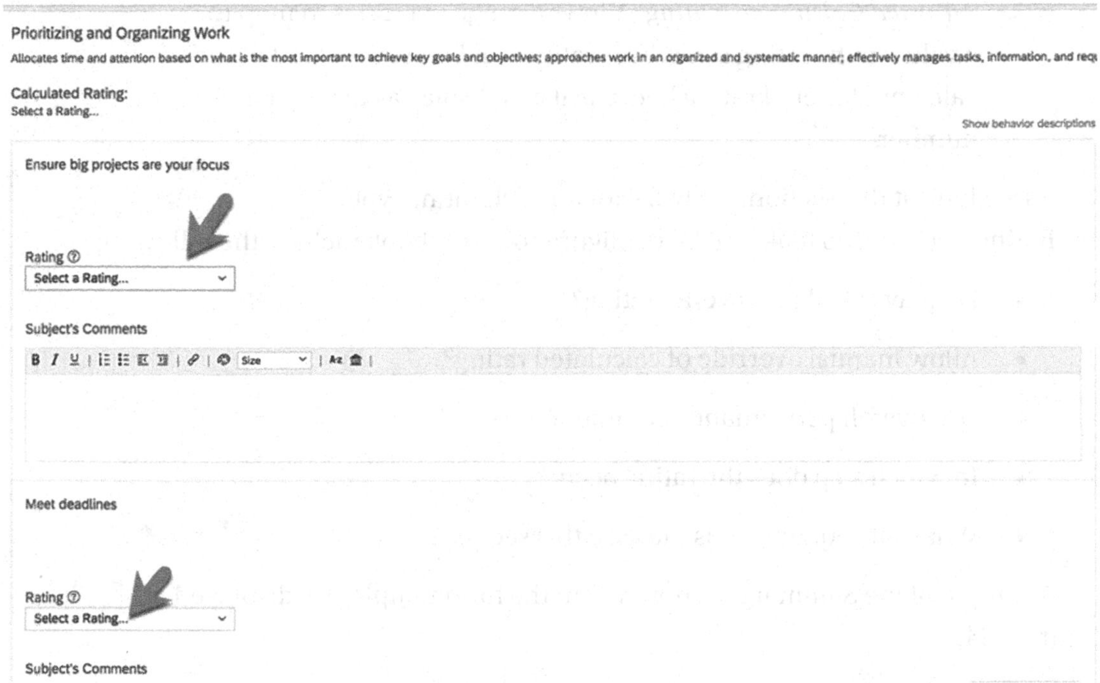

Prioritizing and Organizing Work

Allocates time and attention based on what is the most important to achieve key goals and objectives; approaches work in an organized and systematic manner; effectively manages tasks, information, and requ

Calculated Rating:
Select a Rating...

Show behavior descriptions

Ensure big projects are your focus

Rating ⑦
Select a Rating...   ∨

Subject's Comments

B *I* U | ⁝⁝ ⁝⁝ ⬚ ⬚ | 🔗 | ⊘ | Size   ∨ | A⋅z 🏠 |

Meet deadlines

Rating ⑦
Select a Rating...   ∨

Subject's Comments

Figure 7-43. *Competency with Behaviors to Rate on a PM Form*

Summary Section

The overall performance summary section includes summarized rating information from all of the evaluation sections (Goals and Competencies).

There are three types of overall form ratings that may be used in the Summary section:

1. *Calculated Overall Rating:* This is the default rating and is based on the item ratings from the Goals and Competency sections and the section weights. The rating will be numeric even if you are using stars, circles, or text for your item rating and manual overall rating.

2. *Manual Overall Rating:* Allows the manager to create an overall form rating that is used instead of the calculated overall form rating. If using stars or circles, the manual overall rating displays as stars or circles in the Summary section.

3. *Adjusted Calculated Rating:* Allows a range of ratings to map to
    a value in the rating scale. This rating can be used instead of the
    calculated overall rating because it can display as text, not as a
    number.

As we look at this section, we will explain each rating type.

Rating decisions to make in the configuration workbook include the following:

- Display calculated overall rating?

- Allow manual override of calculated rating?

- Use overall performance comments?

- In which step does the rating occur?

- What subsequent steps may see this section?

A sample of the Summary section within the form template is displayed in
Figure 7-44.

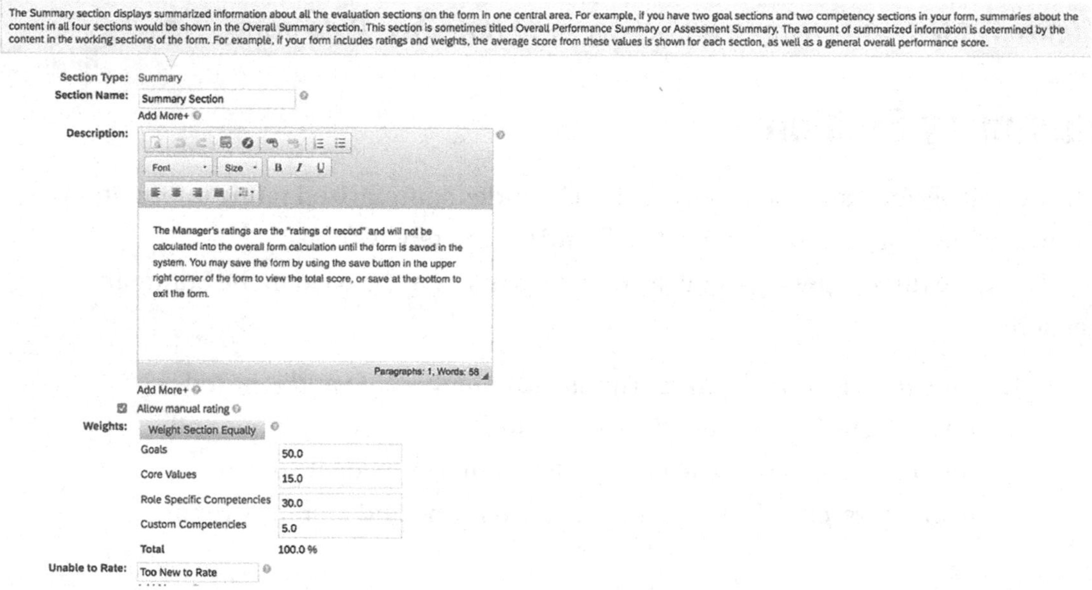

The Summary section displays summarized information about all the evaluation sections on the form in one central area. For example, if you have two goal sections and two competency sections in your form, summaries about the content in all four sections would be shown in the Overall Summary section. This section is sometimes titled Overall Performance Summary or Assessment Summary. The amount of summarized information is determined by the content in the working sections of the form. For example, if your form includes ratings and weights, the average score from these values is shown for each section, as well as a general overall performance score.

Figure 7-44. Performance Summary Section

Options

- *Allow manual rating* would create a rating entry in the Summary section that can be used in lieu of the calculated rating. The manual score will override the calculated score and become the rating of record.

- *Weights* is used to define the weight of each section that is used in the overall rating calculation. You may weigh sections equally or define the percentage for each rating section. These weights must total 100% and will be used in calculating the overall rating. The weighting percentages will display in the section labels.

- If you have a rating section that you wish to exclude from the overall rating, set the weight to 0 but make sure the remaining section weights add up to 100%.

- *Unable to Rate*, also called the "unrated rating," provides a label here to represent a non-score that does not impact the rating calculation, such as "Too New to Rate" or "Not Applicable." If this had been set in "General Settings," it would already be populated.

This section uses the rating scale identified in "General Settings." The average score from these ratings and weights of each section will appear in the Summary section, as well as a calculated overall performance score. You can also allow managers to manually enter an employee's overall performance rating in this section.

Let's look at the advanced options as seen in Figure 7-45.

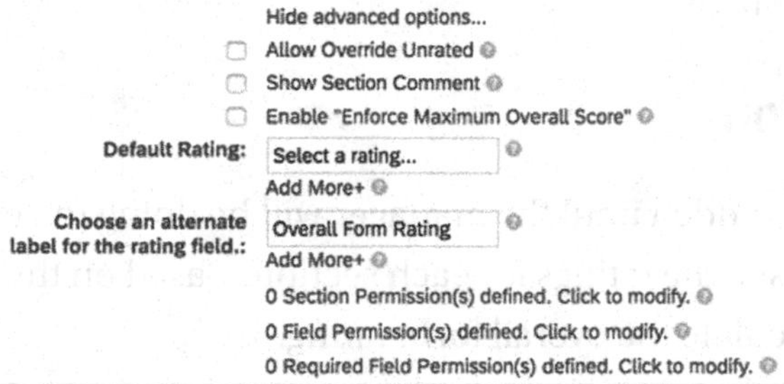

Hide advanced options...
☐ Allow Override Unrated ⊙
☐ Show Section Comment ⊙
☐ Enable "Enforce Maximum Overall Score" ⊙
Default Rating: Select a rating...   ⊙
Add More+ ⊙
Choose an alternate label for the rating field.:   Overall Form Rating   ⊙
Add More+ ⊙
0 Section Permission(s) defined. Click to modify. ⊙
0 Field Permission(s) defined. Click to modify. ⊙
0 Required Field Permission(s) defined. Click to modify. ⊙

Figure 7-45. *Summary Section Advanced Options*

A description of the options is displayed in Table 7-4.

Table 7-4. *Advanced Options*

Option	Description
Allow Override Unrated	Works with "manual rating" and allows the calculated rating to overwrite the unrated manual rating when sending the form to the next step.
Show Section Comment	Creates a summary comments section.
Enable "Enforce Maximum Overall Score"	Set maximum possible overall score to be selected by the rater, based on minimum scores at the goal or competency level. Prevents the rater from giving a higher score than what is permitted. *For more information, see SAP note #2077218.*
Default Rating	Rating value when no selection is made. Could use to display "Select a rating" so the user knows to enter a rating. This default rating also displays in the overall score pod until rating is saved.
Choose an alternate label for the rating field	This allows you to change the Overall Form Rating label in the Summary section. However, this is not working in the form template, so the label must be updated in the form template XML.

The Summary section needs to have section, field, and required field permissions set. The fields to permit include:

- Section Comments
- Calculated Overall Rating
- Manual Overall Rating
- Weighted Average

Section Permission

This section should be hidden until the manager will be doing the evaluation. In this step, the manager will see the ratings for each section. Based on the weights, the section ratings display and calculate the overall form rating.

An example of a performance form summary section is shown in Figure 7-46.

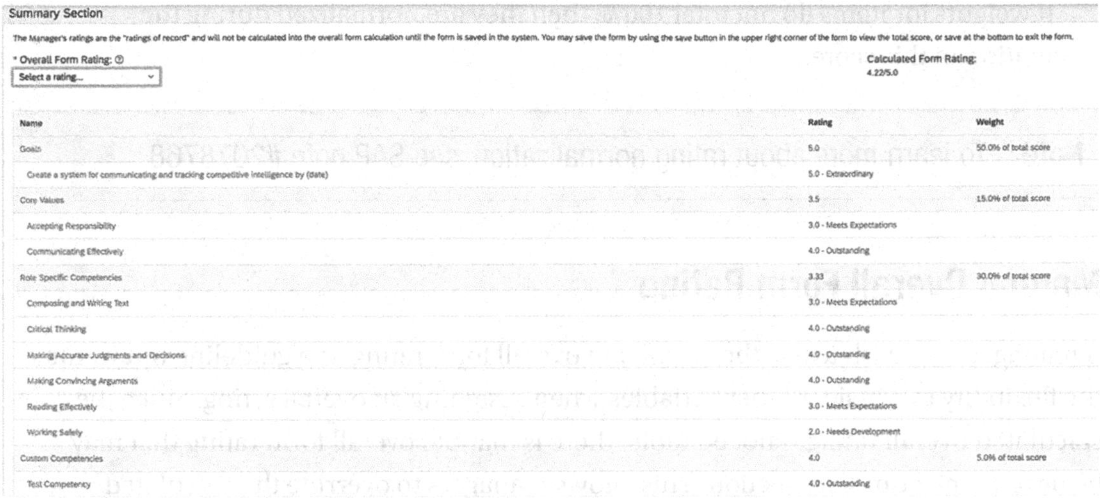

Figure 7-46. *Summary Section on a PM Form*

In the example shown in the preceding figure, "Display in summary section" is set in the Goals and Competency sections, so the Summary section will contain a line for each goal and competency with their rating. Additionally, the section rating will display.

Section Rating Calculation

The section rating that appears is calculated as

$$\sum(\text{item rating} * \text{item weight}) / \sum(\text{item weight})$$

Now, we are ready to walk through the form ratings that you may use.

Calculated Overall Form Rating

The section contains a calculated overall form rating based on the goal and competency item ratings and section weights.

The calculated overall form rating formula is

$$\sum(\text{section rating} * \text{section weight}) / \sum(\text{section weight})$$

To see this rating in the section, the "Calculated Overall Rating" field should have "Read" for any roles and steps that should see this rating. Typically, if you are also allowing a manual overall rating and it will override the calculated rating, the manager will see the calculated rating as well but the employee would not in any subsequent steps.

If weights for items do not total 100%, then they are normalized during the calculation of this score.

Note   To learn more about rating normalization, see SAP note #2078768.

Manual Overall Form Rating

A manager may wish to use the calculated overall form rating as a guideline but wants the flexibility to consider other variables when assigning an overall rating. Since the calculated overall rating is not editable, there is manual overall form rating that may be used in the Summary section. This allows managers to override the calculated form rating. Make sure that "Allow manual rating" is enabled in this section as seen in Figure 7-47.

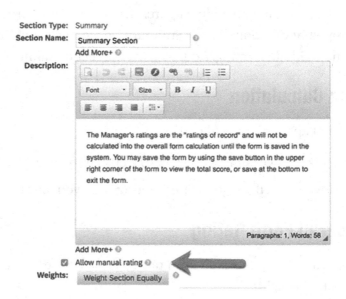

Figure 7-47.   *Enable Manual Overall Rating*

When a manual overall rating is used, the manual overall form rating will be the overall form rating and the rating of record.

"Manual Overall Rating" should have "Write" permission for the manager in order to enter a manual rating. When enabled, the default is the manager's rating, and it will be the rating of record. Since this becomes the overall form rating, it is highly recommended to hide the calculated form rating from the employee in all subsequent steps.

Adjusted Calculated Rating

Within the Summary section, it is possible to use an adjusted rating scale which maps to the overall rating score. A calculated overall rating is numeric, so the use of an adjusted rating scale enables you to map rating text labels to the numeric scores. In addition, you may map a range of ratings to a specific score. This forces the calculated rating to a specific rating.

This does not work when ratings appear as stars or circles. The adjusted calculated rating will appear as text. To use this, you will need to permit the overall rating because it populates this field and is read-only.

Go back to "General Settings," and click "Enable Scale Adjusted Calculation" as seen in Figure 7-48.

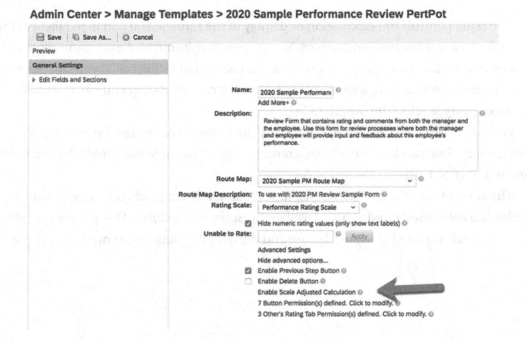

Figure 7-48. *Enable Scale Adjusted Calculation*

You will see a checkbox to enable as seen in Figure 7-49.

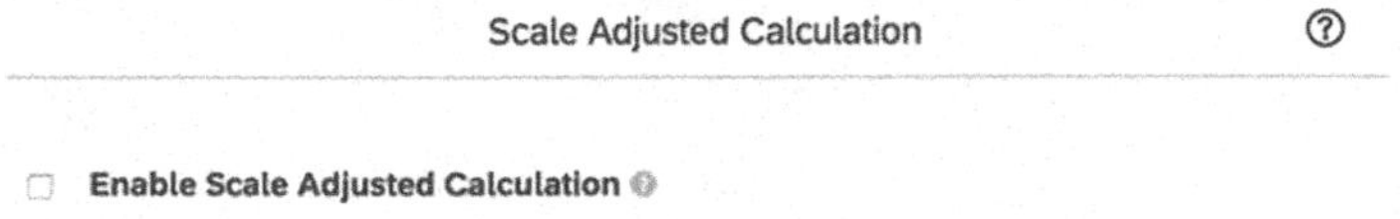

Scale Adjusted Calculation   ⑦

_____

☐ **Enable Scale Adjusted Calculation** ⊙

Figure 7-49. *Enable Scale Adjusted Calculation Checkbox*

When enabled, there are options to set the values for each rating in your scale as seen in Figure 7-50.

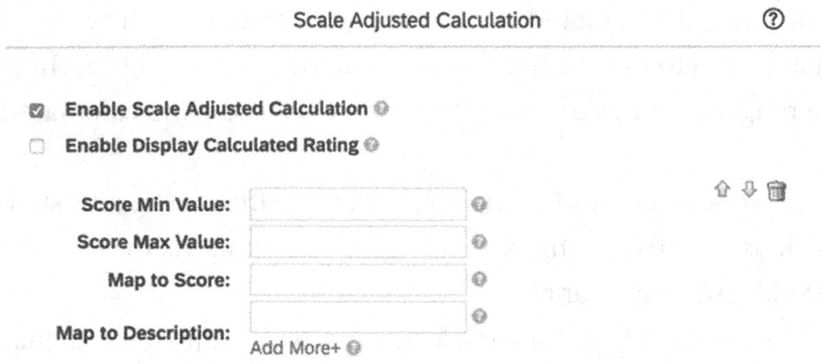

Figure 7-50. *Set Values for Scale Adjusted Calculation*

The scale controls the calculation or display of the ratings. You can map labels to the scores if you are using numeric ratings. You may set minimum and maximum scores to map to a rating from the scale. For instance, if a calculated rating is 3.7, you can decide that any rating from 3.51 to 4 should map to a rating of 4. And then you can display the adjusted rating label as the overall rating.

With this option enabled, you can display the adjusted rating label (the "Map to Description" field) and/or the adjusted rating value ("Map to Score" field). An example is shown in Figure 7-51.

The second checkbox, "Enable Display Calculated Rating," when enabled, will display the calculated rated value as well in the Summary section. This means you will see the overall adjusted calculated score and the overall calculated score in this section.

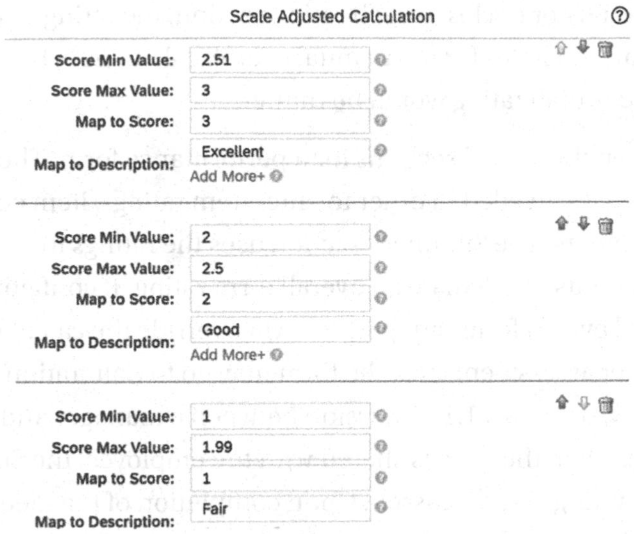

Figure 7-51. *Setting the Values for the Scale Adjusted Calculation*

When the adjusted scale is configured in "General Settings," it may be used in the Summary section.

When the manual rating is not enabled, the overall rating is the adjusted calculated rating. There is no separate adjusted calculated rating to permit, so if you enabled the scale adjusted calculation, the field to read is "Calculated Overall Rating".

The rating of record is determined based on the following order:

- Default overall rating is the calculated overall form rating.

- If used, the adjusted calculated rating is the overall form rating.

- Manual overall rating supersedes all other ratings.

- Manager's rating is the rating of record.

Rating Scale Appearance

- The default rating scale is stars.

- If your rating scale using stars has more than seven scores, the scale becomes a dropdown list.

- You may change from stars to circles in the template's advanced settings.

- You may display the rating scale using the score labels. This is set in each section.

- If you use stars or circles in each rating section, the rating scale will be stars or circles for the manual overall calculation, but the calculated overall rating would be numeric.

We have now seen the typical sections for a performance form. The Goals and Competency sections are needed in order to enter item ratings, item comments, and overall section comments. The Summary section uses the ratings from these sections with their section weights to calculate an overall form rating. If configured, the manager may create a manual overall form rating which will override the calculated rating.

After the manager assessment step, the form may go to Calibration, go to a second-level manager review, or go to a 1:1 discussion between a manager and an employee. During the meeting, when the form is shared with the employee, the Summary section will display and the ratings are discussed. Upon completion of the meeting, the form typically gets routed to the employee so that they may acknowledge that the discussion meeting took place. This is the Signature section that we will review next.

Signature Section

The final section of the form is for signatures as seen in Figure 7-52.

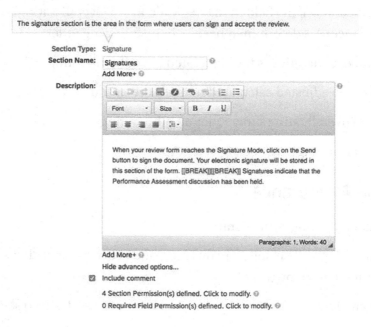

Figure 7-52. *Signature Section of a Form Template*

This section is used for electronic signatures and displays the date the form was signed. Once the form moves from the Modify Stage to the Signature Stage, the only entries allowed on the form are signature comments.

You may use the Description field to create text or add images or a URL that will appear before the signatures. Comments are the only field that can be added to this section. Custom fields are not an option. There are section and required field permissions to set for this section. Required field permissions can only be set for section comments if "Include comment" is enabled.

For section permissions, the Signature section should be hidden for all steps until you are ready for signatures. The section should be "Enabled" for the signature step(s) if signature comments can be made and you may make the comments required.

If you are not using comments, the section should be disabled for the steps where the Signature section should be visible. You are able to sign the form without having the section permission enabled.

Upon submission, the form is electronically dated and signed. You may have multiple steps in this stage in order to get multiple signatures such as employee, manager, and HR manager signatures. After the final signature has been submitted, the form will go to the Performance Completed folder for all users that were part of the route map.

An example of a form's Signature section is shown in Figure 7-53.

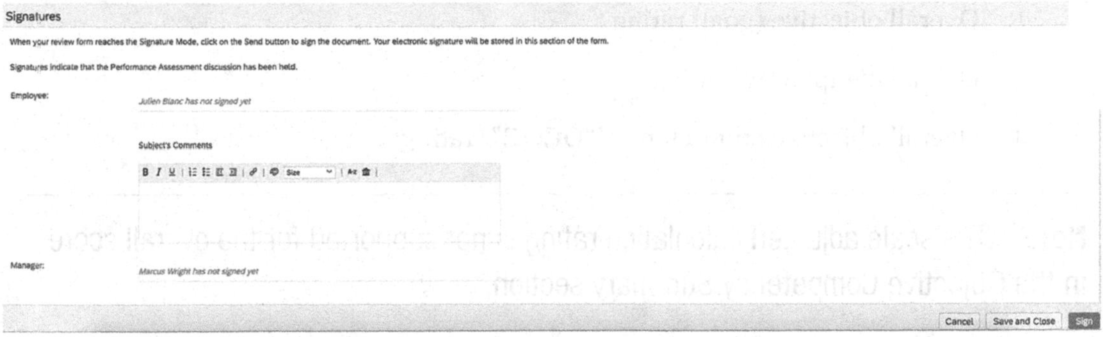

Figure 7-53. *Signature Section of a Performance Form*

As you can see from the example, there are some text lines before the signature lines. This is from the Description field in the form template. When there are multiple signature steps, "[employee name] has not signed yet" will display until the form is submitted by the user in the subsequent signature steps. You may permit entry of comments at any or all signature steps.

Now that we have seen the most commonly used sections of the performance form template, we will review the additional summary sections that may be used: Performance Potential Summary and Objective Competency Summary. There is an additional Customized Weighted Rating section as well.

Objective Competency Summary Section

The Objective Competency Summary section provides some different overall ratings as well as an overall form rating.

Note   The terms "objective" and "goal" are used interchangeably. Throughout this chapter, we have been referring to objectives as goals, but understand that the standard Objective Competency Summary section may be relabeled to "Goal Competency Summary."

The Objective Competency Summary section may be used with or instead of the Summary section that we have just learned about. There is a caveat worth mentioning. If you do not have a Succession license, you will be unable to use this summary section type because it relies on Succession matrix ratings.

The Objective Competency Summary section generates three ratings:

1.   Overall objective (goal) rating

2.   Overall competency rating

3.   Overall objective competency ("OCOC") rating

Note   The scale adjusted calculation rating is not supported for the overall score in the Objective Competency Summary section.

While the standard Summary section uses the goal item and competency item ratings to calculate an overall form rating, this section aggregates the competency item ratings to calculate an overall competency rating and aggregates the goal item ratings to calculate an overall goal rating.

This section also can create an overall objective competency ("OCOC") rating which is calculated based on these overall scores and the weights configured for the Goals and Competency sections. This rating is based on the rating scale identified in "General Settings" of the form template. If both summary sections are on the form template, the overall score from the Summary section would be the rating of record. If you want the "OCOC" rating as the rating of record, you should omit the standard Summary section.

As mentioned, this section uses matrix rating scales for the overall goal and competency ratings rather than using the regular performance rating scale that the other sections use. The intersection of these two scores can be plotted on a "How vs. What" matrix grid. These rating scales typically contain three ratings which allow for a 9-box rating.

The benefit of using this summary section in your form template is to create the overall competency and overall objective ratings to be used throughout the Succession module. The scores may be used in matrix grid reporting, Talent Profile, and dashboard portlets.

There is an important consideration if you are going to use this summary section along with the standard Summary section. We had just mentioned that the matrix grid rating scales typically contain three ratings in order to build a 9-box matrix. If you have a three-point matrix rating scale that is used for the overall competency and goal scores and a five-point scale in the rest of the form, this will cause inconsistences for reporting and in the Talent Profile portlets. This will cause the scores to be "normalized."

It is recommended to use the same number of scores in your form rating scale and your matrix rating scales for consistency. If you use a five-point rating scale, your matrix scales should have five scores as well. The labels do not have to be the same for the two rating scales.

You will learn much more about the matrix grid rating scales and how to configure the 9-box matrix in Volume 2, Chapter 5. We will look at these features briefly in order to see how the scales are used in the Objective Competency Summary section of the performance form.

You will need "Succession Management" configured in Provisioning; you will need "Matrix Grid Reports (9-Box)" and "Matrix Grid How Vs. What Report (9-Box)" enabled as well.

Please refer to Volume 2, Chapter 5 to learn how to configure the rating scales and matrix grids.

Now that we have introduced the concept of the matrix rating scales and grids, let's go back to our template to configure the Objective Competency Summary section:

- Add the "Objective Competency Summary" section to the form template. You may move it so that is appears before the Signature section.

- We can use this section in place of the Summary section and use the "OCOC" calculated score as the overall rating. If this is the case, delete the Summary section; otherwise, the regular Summary section overall rating takes precedence.

- This section can be in addition to the Summary section, and the Summary section rating will be the rating of record.

- Make sure the Goals and Competency sections that will be part of the overall scores have enabled the setting to include in the overall goal or competency rating calculation.

- Configure the matrix grid rating scales for goals and competencies if not done already for Succession setup. It is preferable to use the same number of ratings in the scale as the performance rating scale.

- Configure the "How vs. What" matrix grid report if you are going to display the chart in the Objective Competency Summary section of the performance form.

A few things to keep in mind while setting up this section are as follows:

- Make sure your form template does not use stars or circles for ratings.

- In "General Settings", enable "Hide numeric rating values (only show text labels)."

- Matrix grid rating scales can only be displayed as a dropdown list.

- Although you may use manual overall objective and competency ratings, it is not recommended.

The Objective Competency Summary section of the form template is shown in Figure 7-54.

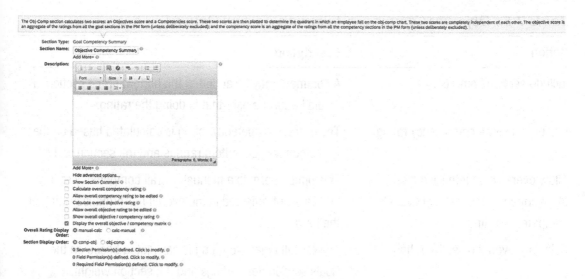

Figure 7-54. Objective Competency Summary Section

Here are some basic guidelines about which rating will become the rating of record:

1. If you are using the "OCOC" score and also have an overall Summary section, the Summary section rating will be the rating of record.

2. If you are using the "OCOC" score and do not have an overall Summary section, the "OCOC" rating will be the overall form rating and will be the rating of record.

3. If you do not identify the Goals and Competency section weights for the Objective Competency Summary section or the ratings, the "OCOC" rating will be "unrated."

4. If you are using the "OCOC" score and also have a Performance Potential Summary section, the Performance Potential Summary section rating will be the rating of record.

There are some settings for this section that need to be configured in the form template XML, and we will cover that in Chapter 10.

Table 7-5 identifies the options that may be selected for this section.

Table 7-5. *Objective Competency Summary Section Options*

Option	Description
Include section comments	A comment may be added at the bottom of the section; it would be for the user that is doing the rating.
Calculate overall competency rating	The overall competency rating is calculated based on the Competency section item ratings and the section weight.
Allow overall competency rating to be edited: allow manual overall competency rating	This option permits a manual overall competency rating. Edits are not reflected in the overall performance rating of the form.
Calculate overall objective rating	The overall objective rating is calculated based on the Goals section item ratings and the section weight.
Allow overall objective rating to be edited: allow manual overall objective rating	This option permits a manual overall goal rating. Edits are not reflected in the overall performance rating of the form.
Show overall objective competency rating	Referred to as the "OCOC" rating, this is the calculated overall rating based on the overall competency and overall goal ratings.
Display overall objective competency rating matrix	The matrix grid will display on the form; it will identify the quadrant that the employee's overall competency rating and overall goal rating intersect in.
Overall Rating Display Order	This option is not supported. If you are allowing manual and calculated overall ratings, the manual rating always displays before the calculated rating regardless of the order you select.
Section Display Order: show competencies than objectives or objectives followed by competencies.	Determines if the competencies or the goals will display first in this section.

The Objective Competency Summary section needs to have section, field, and required field permissions set.

The fields to permit include:

- Section Comments

- Competency Manual Overall Rating

- Objective Manual Overall Rating

If these fields have "None" permissions, there will be no comments for the section, and only the calculated overall competency and overall objective ratings will be used.

Figure 7-55 is a sample of an Objective Competency Summary section in a PM form. You can see that the overall competency rating is comprised of two competency sections (role specific and core), each weighted differently. The rating scale is the three-point matrix rating. The overall competency rating is comprised of two competency section ratings.

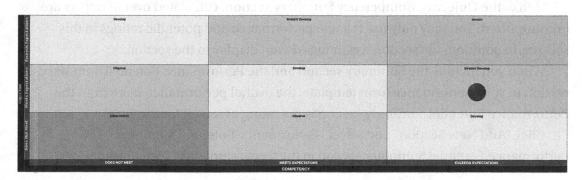

Objective Competency Summary

OCOC Rating: 2.2 / 3.0

Calculated Form Rating: 2.4 / 3.0

Core Values	2.6	20.0% of total score
Accepting Responsibility	Excellent	
Communicating Effectively	Good	
Job Competencies	2.33	30.0% of total score
Composing and Writing Text	Good	
Critical Thinking	Good	
Making Accurate Judgments and Decisions	Excellent	
Making Convincing Arguments	Excellent	
Reading Effectively	Good	
Working Safely	Good	

Calculated Form Rating: 2.0 / 3.0

Goals	2.0	50.0% of total score
Create a system for communicating and tracking competitive intelligence by year-end.	Fair	
Get PMP Certification	Excellent	

Figure 7-55. *Objective Competency Summary Section in a PM Form*

The overall rating ("OCOC") is comprised of the three section ratings multiplied by their % of the total score and then summed.

Figure 7-56 is the matrix grid that shows the intersection of the objective and competency overall ratings.

Figure 7-56. *Matrix Grid of the Objective Competency Summary Section*

Unless you plan on using Succession, this section may not be helpful to include.

Performance Potential Summary Section

We will now discuss the Performance Potential Summary section. This section is used to create a manual overall performance rating and a manual overall potential rating. These scores populate a Succession matrix grid. This is often used to identify high-potential talent.

This section behaves like the Objective Competency Summary section but uses different rating scales. Like the Objective Competency Summary section, Succession matrix grid ratings are used. In this case, the matrix rating scales are "Performance" and "Potential." The two scores are used on a matrix grid to show the intersection between the two ratings. Like the Objective Competency Summary section, it is recommended that the matrix rating scales and the form rating scale have the same number of scores in their scales.

The Performance Potential Summary section is used to enter manual ratings:

1. Overall performance rating

2. Overall potential rating

In addition to creating the potential matrix rating scale and the performance rating scale, the "Performance-Potential" matrix grid report would need to be configured. For more information on this configuration, see Volume 2, Chapter 5.

This section is used primarily for Succession purposes, specifically the nomination process. If you decide to allow a manual performance rating in this section, it will become the overall form rating and the rating of record. If you enabled the customized rating calculation in the form template settings, this rating will be the rating of record.

Unlike the Objective Competency Summary section, calculated overall ratings are not supported. You may only use manual performance and potential ratings in this section. In addition, the section weightings do not display in the section.

When you include the Summary section and the Performance Potential Summary section in your performance form template, the overall performance score from the Performance Potential Summary section is the rating of record for the form.

Click "Add New Section" and select "Performance Potential Summary." The Performance Potential Summary section in the form template is seen in Figure 7-57.

The Performance-Potential summary section supports two overall scores: an overall Performance score and an overall Potential score. These two scores can then be plotted to determine the quadrant in which an employee fall on the performance-potential chart. These two scores are completely independent of each other. The section currently only supports manual ratings for both Performance and Potential scores.

Section Type: Performance Potential Summary

Section Name: Performance Potential Summary
                 Add More+

Description:

Paragraphs: 0, Words: 0

Add More+

Hide advanced options...

☐ Show Section Comment
☐ Allow overall performance rating to be edited.
☐ Allow overall potential rating to be edited.
☐ Display the overall performance - potential matrix

Section Display Order: ⦿ Performance section/Potential section   ◯ Potential section/Performance section

0 Section Permission(s) defined. Click to modify.
0 Field Permission(s) defined. Click to modify.
0 Required Field Permission(s) defined. Click to modify.

Figure 7-57. *Performance Potential Summary Section*

Because there are no calculated ratings in this section, there are fewer options than the Objective Competency Summary section.

Listed in the following are the options available:

- Include section comments

- Allow overall performance rating to be edited

- Allow overall potential rating to be edited

- Display overall performance–potential matrix.

- Section Display Order: performance/potential or potential/performance

The Performance Potential Summary section needs to have section, field, and required field permissions set.

The fields to permit include

- Section Comments

- Performance Manual Overall Rating

- Potential Manual Overall Rating

If the manual ratings are not permitted, there will be no values in this section.

Figure 7-58 is a sample of a Performance Potential Summary section in a PM form.

Here, the manager selects performance and potential ratings which come from the matrix grid rating scales.

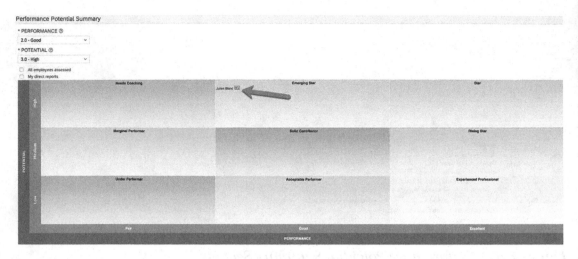

Figure 7-58. *Performance-Potential Matrix Grid on a Performance Form*

The intersection of the two data points displays in the matrix grid. This information is also available to include on Employee Profile and in Succession reporting.

There is one final overall rating section that is available.

Customized Weighted Rating Section

The final summary section calculates an overall customized weighted rating. The customized weighted rating is calculated based on different roles in different steps giving a manual overall rating (from the official rating field). The ratings and weights from the steps and roles are defined in a business rule. Another rule defines the trigger step used to calculate the overall weighted rating.

The section shows the ratings by users and steps that are used in the calculated form rating. A manual override rating may be configured as well.

The calculated form rating is calculated based on the ratings and weights from the steps and roles that were designated in business rules. You would configure which step in the route map triggers the calculation.

Note   The admin role would need permission to create business rules.

Click "Add New Section" and select "Customized Weighted Rating" to add the section to the form template.

The Customized Weighted Rating section of the form template is displayed in Figure 7-59.

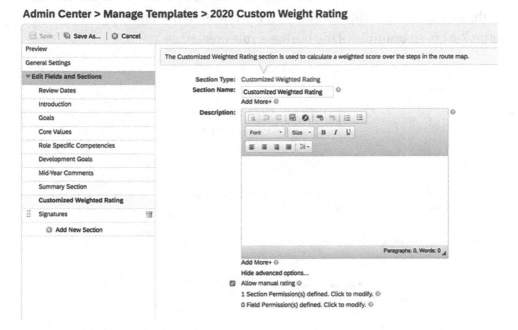

Figure 7-59. *Customized Weighted Rating Section in a Form Template*

There is an option to allow a manual rating to override the calculated rating. The field permissions are for the manual rating and the calculated rating. There is no section comment, and there are not any custom or required fields.

An example of the Customized Weighted Rating section in a performance form is shown in Figure 7-60.

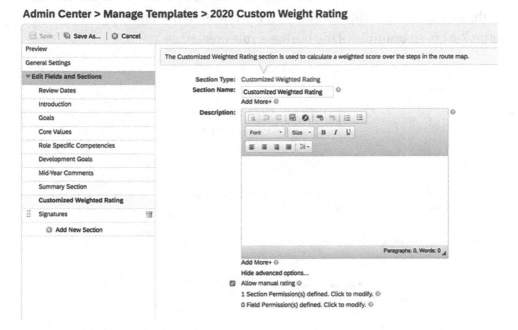

Figure 7-60. *Customized Weight Rating Section of a PM Form*

This example shows the overall rating given in each step by which user/role. A business rule was created to determine the weighting of these scores based on role and step. A trigger rule was also created which determines which step the final rating should be calculated at.

A business rule identifies the steps where the rating will be used in the calculation. It defines the weight of these ratings based on the role and the step.

Figure 7-61 is an example of the business rule created.

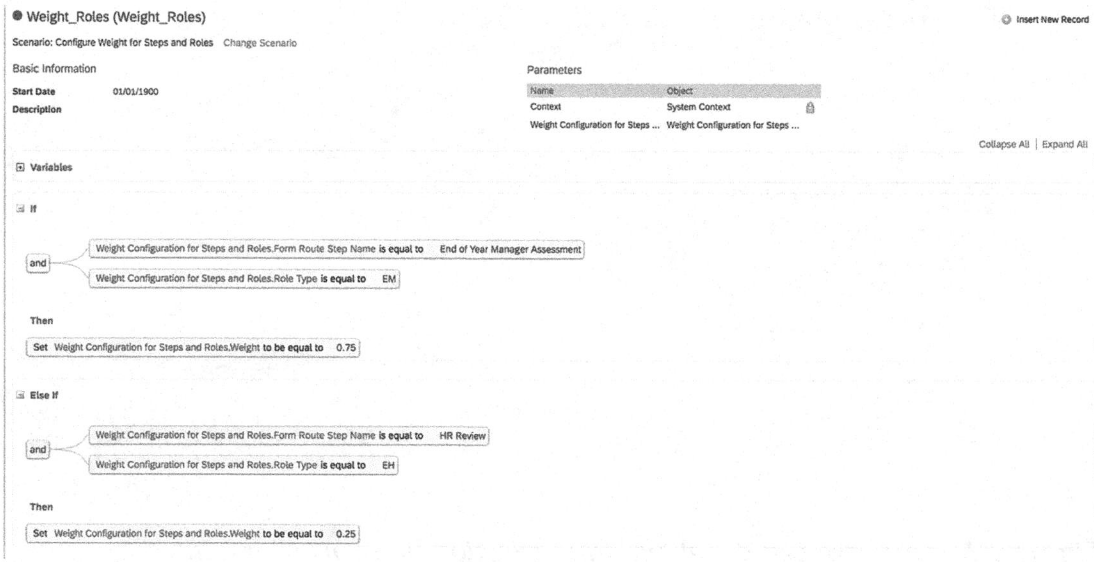

Figure 7-61. Business Rule for Weighted Rating

In this example, the rating from the manager role in the assessment step will be 75% of the calculated rating. The rating from the HR manager role in the HR review step will be 25% of the overall calculated rating.

A trigger is created to use these weightings in the form calculation. An example of a trigger rule is seen in Figure 7-62.

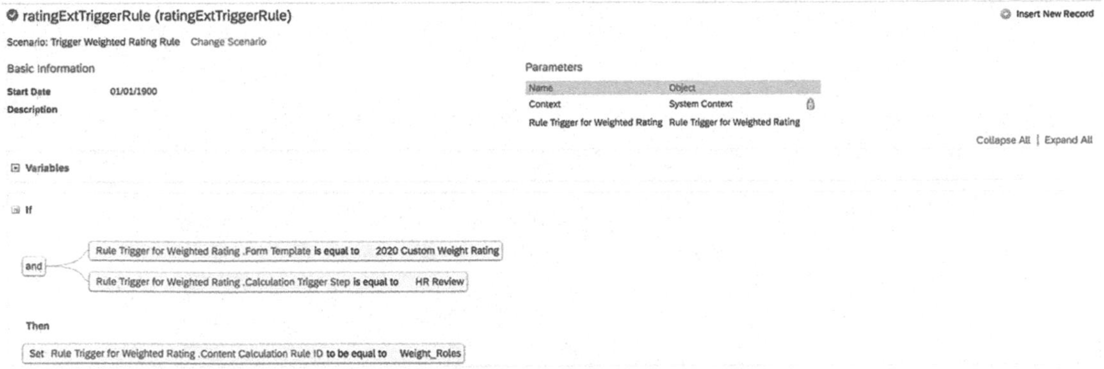

ratingExtTriggerRule (ratingExtTriggerRule)   Insert New Record

Scenario: Trigger Weighted Rating Rule   Change Scenario

Basic Information   Parameters

Start Date   01/01/1900   Name   Object
Description   Context   System Context
                                                         Rule Trigger for Weighted Rating   Rule Trigger for Weighted Rating

                                                                                          Collapse All | Expand All

⊟ Variables

⊟ If

┌─────┐   ┌─ Rule Trigger for Weighted Rating .Form Template **is equal to**   2020 Custom Weight Rating ─┐
│ and │───┤
└─────┘   └─ Rule Trigger for Weighted Rating .Calculation Trigger Step **is equal to**   HR Review ─┘

Then

┌─ Set Rule Trigger for Weighted Rating .Content Calculation Rule ID **to be equal to**   Weight_Roles ─┐

Figure 7-62. *Trigger Rule to Calculate Overall Rating*

The trigger rule identifies the form template to use, the step on which the calculation should be applied, and the calculation rule to use. In our example, the overall form rating calculation will use the "Weight_Roles" calculation rule in the HR review step of a form launched using the "2020 Custom Weight Rating" form template.

This summary section uses the calculated overall rating and the manual overall rating. The calculated overall rating is triggered at the step based on the business rule. The manual overall rating can be modified by the role at the step set in the form template permissions.

New with the H1 2020 release, this summary section may now be used in Calibration.

We have now seen the sections that may be used in a performance form. We have learned the purpose of each section and gained an understanding on how to set up permissions for each section and field by role and step.

Conclusion

In the next chapter, we will set up employee role–based permissions, enable email notifications, and launch a performance form. We will also cover some functions that an admin may do during the performance review process.

CHAPTER 8

Administering Performance Management Forms

Now that we have enabled Performance Management and created our form template, we have a few more steps before we can launch performance forms. We will start by setting up the email notifications that will be sent to employees during various steps in the review process. We will also set up the employee, manager, and HR manager role-based permissions to allow these roles to access Performance Management. We will decide on any route map step start and due dates and will learn how to launch forms now or schedule a form launch for a later date. We will cover such topics as deleting and restoring forms, making forms invisible to certain users, routing forms, and importing overall scores.

Email Notifications

There are a series of email notifications specific to performance forms that may be enabled. The notification is sent to the user associated with the task or action required. The emails are triggered based on movement of a performance form or an action required by a user. Performance form–related email notifications include:

- Creating, routing, and completion of a performance form
- Step due and step overdue notifications
- Ask for Feedback notifications

© Susan Traynor, Michael A. Wellens and Venki Krishnamoorthy 2021
S. Traynor et al., *SAP SuccessFactors Talent: Volume 1*, https://doi.org/10.1007/978-1-4842-6600-7_8

The most commonly used notifications are routing and step due notifications. The routing notification tells a user that a form is in their Performance Inbox and ready for their action. A step due notification reminds a user that the form is still in their inbox and requires action by the step due date.

In Chapter 6, the admin role had permission set for "E-Mail Notification Templates Settings" found under "Manage System Properties" in the Administrator Permissions section of the role.

To see all of the notifications that may be enabled, type and select "E-Mail Notification Templates Settings" in the search bar. An example of the screen is shown in Figure 8-1.

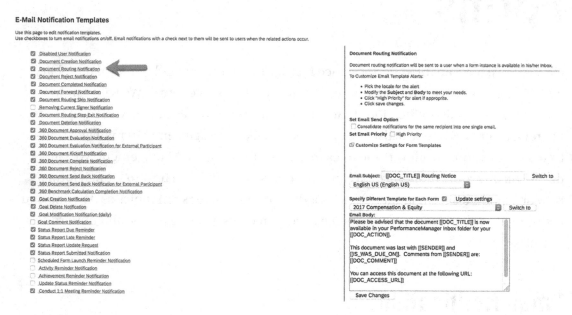

Figure 8-1. *Email Notifications*

Refer to Table 8-1 for the performance-related notifications that can be enabled.

Table 8-1. *Email Notifications for Performance Forms*

Email	Description	Recipient
Document Creation	Created when the form is launched to notify the user that the form is in their Performance Inbox.	First step owner.
Document Routing	Sent when the form has been routed and is in the user's inbox.	Step owners for the "routed to" step.
Document Reject	Form rejected at Signature Stage.	Step owner of the prior step.
Document Completed	Form has been completed and user is notified that the form is in their Performance Completed folder.	All roles in the route map but if enabled may select additional recipients.
Document Forward	Sent to a user when a completed form has been forwarded to their Performance Completed folder.	User who is getting the forwarded completed form.
Removing Current Signer	Sent to the current signer of a form when the signer is removed from the form.	Current signer.
Document Routing Step Exit	Sent when a step has completed.	Step owners for the step.
Document Deletion	Sent when a document has been deleted.	May select from manager, manager and employee, manager, employee and HR, and the entire routing chain.
Mass Create Form Instances	Sent when a group of forms were launched.	Sent to the user that launched the forms.
Document Due	Reminder notification sent that the form is due soon. Dependent on the default due date from form template advanced settings along with the default # of days prior to due date.	Step owner.

(*continued*)

Table 8-1. (*continued*)

Email	Description	Recipient
Document Late	Uses the default due date from form template advanced settings along with the default # of days late from due date.	Step owner.
Step Due	Sent based on the due date in the route map step and default # of days due set in form template advanced settings.	To the owner of the step that is approaching step due date.
Step Overdue	Sent once the step is overdue, based on the due date in the route map step and default # of days late set in form template advanced settings.	To the owner of the step that is past the step due date.
Request Feedback	Sent by the manager in Team Overview to request feedback for their direct report.	Sent to feedback requestee and cc'd to feedback requestor.
Performance Evaluation Kickoff Manager Notification	Manager receives notification of employees with forms generated including form due date. All steps of the form are listed with their start and due dates.	No longer supported.
Performance Review Process Update for Manager Notification	Manager receives updates on self-review and feedback request status. If the current step of a form has no specified due date, the form due date will be used for this email notification.	No longer supported.

Click the checkbox next to an email template name to enable the notification. Click a notification name on the left side of the page to see the notification default details on the right. You may set the notification priority to high and update the email subject and body for each notification type. Making these modifications will cause all forms associated with the email template to use the updated version.

Custom Notification by Template

The email subject and body for some notification types may be customized so that different verbiage may be used for each performance form template. The notifications listed in the following may be customized:

- Document Creation

- Document Routing

- Document Completed

- Document Due

- Document Late

- Step Due

- Step Overdue

Here is an example using the step due notification. You may wish to have specific text in the step due notification for your 2020 performance form. The other forms associated with this email notification type should all use the default text.

This is accomplished through a few steps:

1. Click the checkbox to the right of "Specify Different Template for Each Form" as seen in Figure 8-2. This checkbox will not be active for any of the notifications not mentioned in the preceding list.

Figure 8-2. *Update Email per Form Template*

2. A popup will display warning the user that each form template associated with the notification may be manually updated. Click "OK" to continue as seen in Figure 8-3.

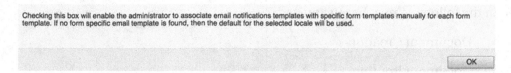

Figure 8-3. *Warning When Customizing Notification*

3. Beneath "Specify Different Template for Each Form," click the dropdown listing and choose the PM form template that you wish to have a custom notification created for. Next, click the "Update settings" button as seen in Figure 8-4.

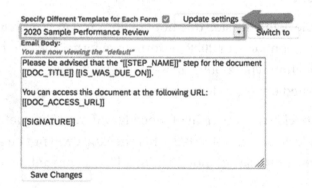

Figure 8-4. *Select the Form Template to Customize*

4. The screen will refresh, and you will see a warning message that there is no template for the language and form template combination as seen in Figure 8-5.

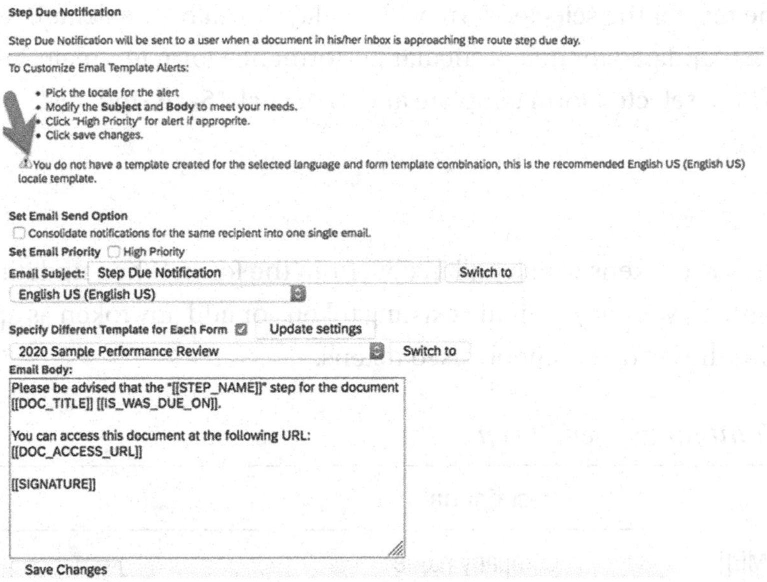

Step Due Notification

Step Due Notification will be sent to a user when a document in his/her inbox is approaching the route step due day.

To Customize Email Template Alerts:

- Pick the locale for the alert
- Modify the **Subject** and **Body** to meet your needs.
- Click "High Priority" for alert if appropriate.
- Click save changes.

⚠ You do not have a template created for the selected language and form template combination, this is the recommended English US (English US) locale template.

Set Email Send Option
☐ Consolidate notifications for the same recipient into one single email.
Set Email Priority ☐ High Priority
Email Subject: Step Due Notification   Switch to
English US (English US)

Specify Different Template for Each Form ☑   Update settings
2020 Sample Performance Review   Switch to
Email Body:

Please be advised that the "[[STEP_NAME]]" step for the document
[[DOC_TITLE]] [[IS_WAS_DUE_ON]].

You can access this document at the following URL:
[[DOC_ACCESS_URL]]

[[SIGNATURE]]

Save Changes

Figure 8-5. *Warning When Creating Custom Notification Text*

5. Make any modifications to the email subject and body and text to use for this form template and click "Save Changes" as seen in Figure 8-6.

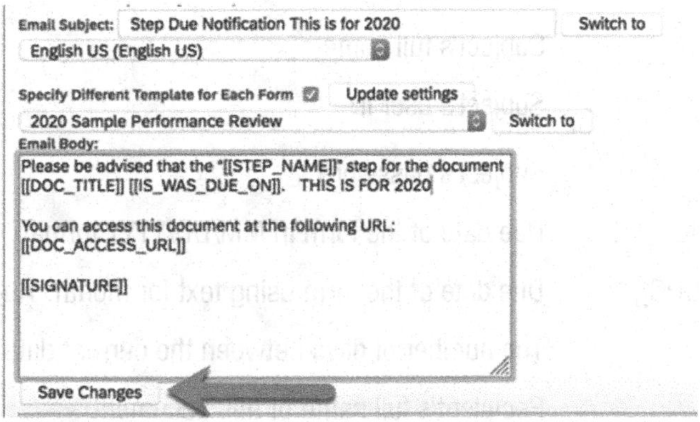

Email Subject: Step Due Notification This is for 2020   Switch to
English US (English US)

Specify Different Template for Each Form ☑   Update settings
2020 Sample Performance Review   Switch to
Email Body:

Please be advised that the "[[STEP_NAME]]" step for the document
[[DOC_TITLE]] [[IS_WAS_DUE_ON]].   THIS IS FOR 2020

You can access this document at the following URL:
[[DOC_ACCESS_URL]]

[[SIGNATURE]]

Save Changes

Figure 8-6. *Customization for Notifications*

You have now created a custom notification for the 2020 Sample Performance Review form template step due notification.

To see the notification for any of the other form templates for this notification, select another form template from the dropdown listing and click "Switch to." The page will refresh, and the text for the selected form will display; it will be the default text unless it had already been updated for that particular performance form template. You may make modifications for a selected form template and then click "Save Updates."

Tokens

The notifications use tokens which pull in data from the form. When updating the email notification content, you may omit the existing tokens or add any token as appropriate. See Table 8-2 for the list of commonly used tokens.

Table 8-2. *Commonly Used Tokens*

Token	Description
[[COMPANY_NAME]]	Company name
[[DOC_COMMENT]]	Comment from the sender to be included in the email
[[DOC_COMPLETION_DATE]]	Date of form completion
[[DOC_DUE_DATE]]	Due date of the form
[[DOC_LAST_MODIFIED]]	Date the form was last modified
[[DOC_TITLE]]	Form name
[[EMP_NAME]]	Subject's full name
[[EMP_USER_ID]]	Subject's user ID
[[EMP_PASSWORD]]	Subject's password
[[IS_WAS_DUE_ON]]	Due date of the form in MM/DD/YYYY format
[[IS_WAS_DUE_ON_LONG]]	Due date of the form using text for month: August 12, 2020
[[NO_OF_DAYS]]	The number of days between the current date and form due date
[[RECIPIENT_NAME]]	Recipient's full name of this document
[[RECIPIENT_USERNAME]]	Recipient's username of this document
[[REVIEW_END_ON]]	End date of the review
[[SENDER]]	Name of the form sender
[SIGNATURE]]	Signature

To prevent users from adding comments when a form is being routed, remove "[DOC_COMMENT]" from the email body.

Customize Notification Settings

Some of the email notifications have customizable settings. For each form template associated with a notification, there are settings to turn off notifications, set the consolidation interval, and select additional recipients to receive the notification.

Notifications that allow customization of settings include:

- Document Creation

- Document Routing

- Document Reject

- Document Forward

- Document Completion

- Document Deletion

These notifications will have "Customize Settings for Form Templates" displayed as seen in Figure 8-7.

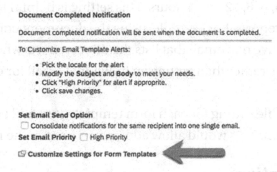

Figure 8-7. *Customize Settings for Form Templates*

After clicking this link, a popup will display with all active form templates associated with the notification as seen in Figure 8-8. This listing will include any recruiting and compensation form templates as well.

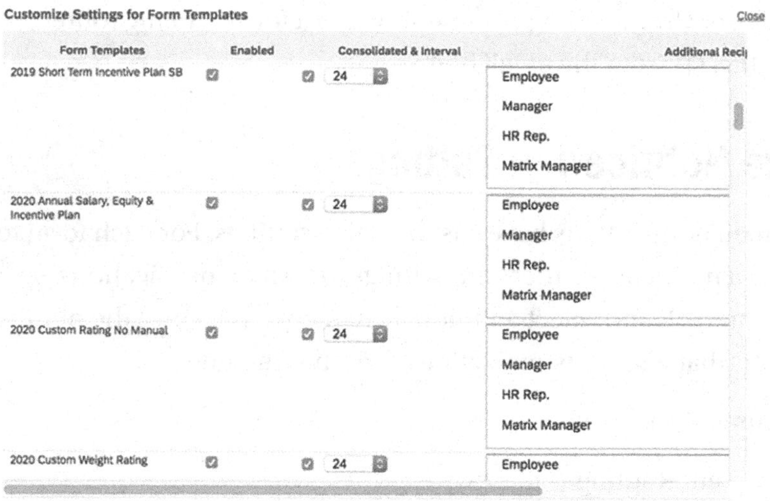

Customize Settings for Form Templates   Close

Form Templates	Enabled	Consolidated & Interval	Additional Reci
2019 Short Term Incentive Plan SB	☑	☑ 24 ⬍	Employee Manager HR Rep. Matrix Manager
2020 Annual Salary, Equity & Incentive Plan	☑	☑ 24 ⬍	Employee Manager HR Rep. Matrix Manager
2020 Custom Rating No Manual	☑	☑ 24 ⬍	Employee Manager HR Rep. Matrix Manager
2020 Custom Weight Rating	☑	☑ 24 ⬍	Employee

Figure 8-8. *Customize Settings*

The settings that may be customized are found under three columns: "Enabled," "Consolidated & Interval," and "Additional Recipients."

To turn off any form templates from having the notification sent, deselect the checkbox in the "Enabled" column.

When "Consolidated & Interval" is enabled, all notifications of this type will be sent in a single email to a recipient. You also select how often the consolidated email is sent. Options are every 1, 2, 4, 6, 8, 12, or 24 hours. This setting is helpful for a manager with a large number of direct reports. For example, using the document completed notification, the manager would receive one email that lists the direct reports who have completed their performance forms rather than getting an individual email for each completed form.

The final customizable setting for each form template is to add additional recipients to receive the notification. This would allow adding users not in the route map.

Set Email Send Option

For some notifications that do not have the option to set up a customized interval, there is an option called "Set Email Send Option" as seen in Figure 8-9.

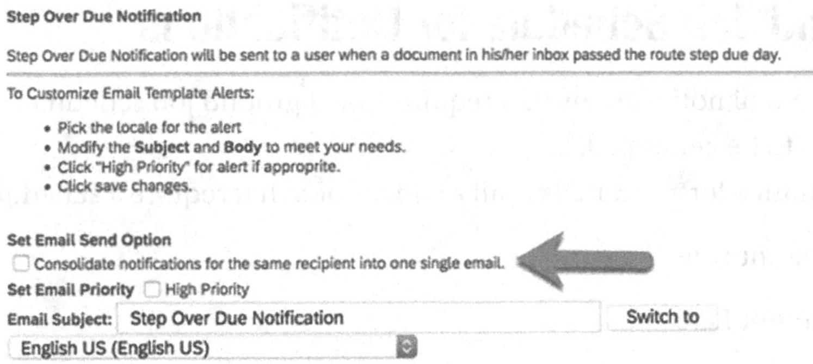

Step Over Due Notification

Step Over Due Notification will be sent to a user when a document in his/her inbox passed the route step due day.

To Customize Email Template Alerts:

- Pick the locale for the alert
- Modify the **Subject** and **Body** to meet your needs.
- Click "High Priority" for alert if appropirte.
- Click save changes.

Set Email Send Option
☐ Consolidate notifications for the same recipient into one single email.
Set Email Priority ☐ High Priority
Email Subject: Step Over Due Notification   Switch to
English US (English US)

Figure 8-9. *Email Consolidation Option*

When enabled, this option works with "Interval For Consolidated Emails (In Hours Starting From 12:00am)" found at the bottom of the *E-Mail Notification Templates* page. Here you can select the default interval to send a consolidated email with options of 1, 2, 4, 6, 8, 12, or 24 hours as seen in Figure 8-10.

Interval For Consolidated Emails (In Hours Starting From 12:00am): 24
Save Notification Settings

Figure 8-10. *Set Interval to Send Consolidated Email*

The notifications that allow customized settings also have this option:

- Document Create
- Document Routing
- Document Reject
- Document Completed
- Document Forward
- Document Deletion

These notifications can set a consolidated interval for specific form templates. The notifications listed in the following set a consolidated interval for all form templates associated with the notification.

The two notifications that cannot be customized but may have consolidated mails sent are:

- Step Due
- Step Overdue

Background Job Schedule for Notifications

There are a few email notifications that require a background job scheduled in order for the notifications to be generated.

The performance form–related email notifications that require a scheduled job are:

- Document Due

- Document Late

- Step Due

- Step Late

The background jobs to schedule are:

- Send Form Due Notification

- Send Form Late Notification

- Send 360 Step Due Notification

- Send 360 Step Late Notification

The 360 step due and 360 step late notification jobs work for PM and 360 forms.

To set these up, in Provisioning, go to "Manage Scheduled Jobs" as seen in Figure 8-11.

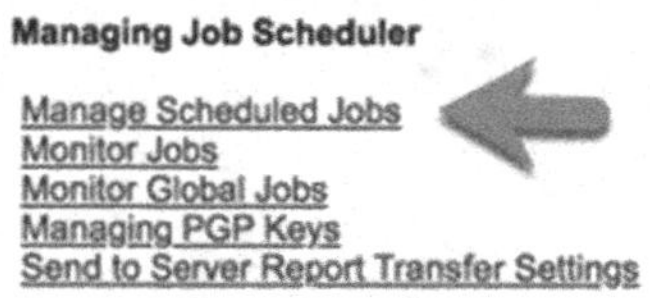

Figure 8-11. *Manage Scheduled Jobs*

Next, go to "Create New Job" as seen in Figure 8-12. Here we will set up daily jobs to run for these four notifications.

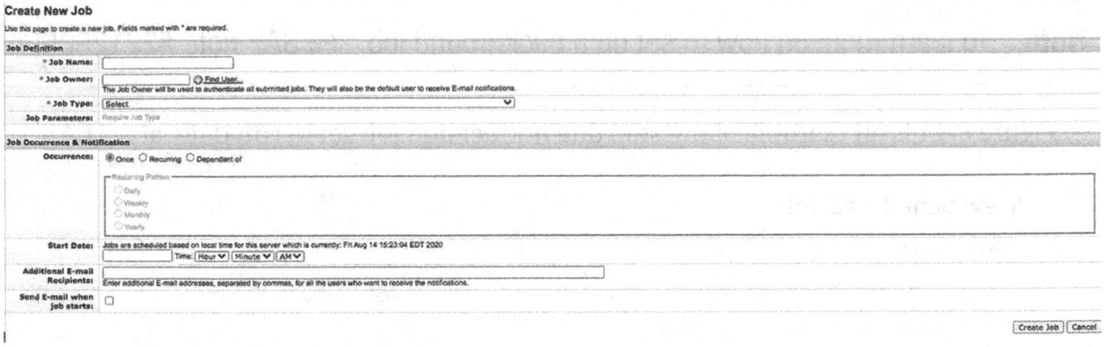

Create New Job

Use this page to create a new job. Fields marked with * are required.

Job Definition	
* Job Name:	
* Job Owner:	⊕ Find User...
	The Job Owner will be used to authenticate all submitted jobs. They will also be the default user to receive E-mail notifications.
* Job Type:	Select
Job Parameters:	Require Job Type

Job Occurrence & Notification	
Occurrence:	◉ Once ○ Recurring ○ Dependant of
	┌ Recurring Pattern ────────────────────────
	○ Daily
	○ Weekly
	○ Monthly
	○ Yearly
Start Date:	Jobs are scheduled based on local time for this server which is currently: Fri Aug 14 15:23:04 EDT 2020
	Time: [Hour ▼] [Minute ▼] [AM ▼]
Additional E-mail Recipients:	
	Enter additional E-mail addresses, separated by commas, for all the users who want to receive the notifications.
Send E-mail when job starts:	☐

[Create Job] [Cancel]

Figure 8-12. *Create New Job*

Click the "Job Type" dropdown listing to find the job name from the preceding list. An example is shown in Figure 8-13.

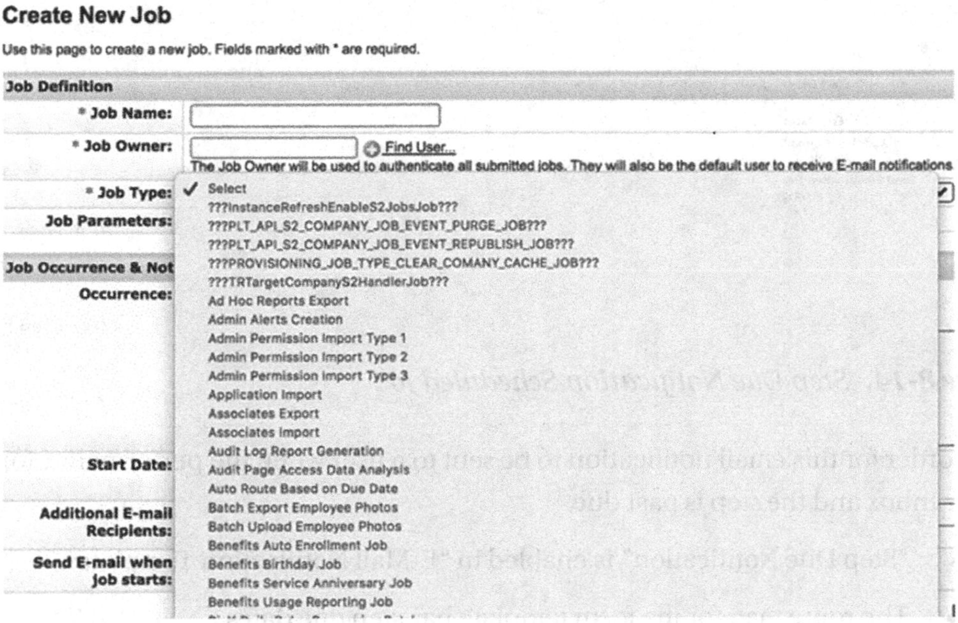

Create New Job

Use this page to create a new job. Fields marked with * are required.

Job Definition	
* Job Name:	
* Job Owner:	⊕ Find User...
	The Job Owner will be used to authenticate all submitted jobs. They will also be the default user to receive E-mail notifications
* Job Type:	✓ Select
Job Parameters:	???InstanceRefreshEnableS2JobsJob???
	???PLT_API_S2_COMPANY_JOB_EVENT_PURGE_JOB???
	???PLT_API_S2_COMPANY_JOB_EVENT_REPUBLISH_JOB???
Job Occurrence & Not	???PROVISIONING_JOB_TYPE_CLEAR_COMANY_CACHE_JOB???
Occurrence:	???TRTargetCompanyS2HandlerJob???
	Ad Hoc Reports Export
	Admin Alerts Creation
	Admin Permission Import Type 1
	Admin Permission Import Type 2
	Admin Permission Import Type 3
	Application Import
	Associates Export
	Associates Import
	Audit Log Report Generation
Start Date:	Audit Page Access Data Analysis
	Auto Route Based on Due Date
Additional E-mail	Batch Export Employee Photos
Recipients:	Batch Upload Employee Photos
	Benefits Auto Enrollment Job
Send E-mail when	Benefits Birthday Job
job starts:	Benefits Service Anniversary Job
	Benefits Usage Reporting Job

Figure 8-13. *Select Job Type*

During the schedule creation, give the job a name and set how often it runs. It should be Recurring for a job to be run daily. You can set an early morning run so that the forms will move early in the morning after the step/form was due. After making the entries, save the job and submit it. This ensures that the job will start running as of the start date that you selected in the job.

Note   To learn more on how to set up a background job, see SAP note #2212605.

Figure 8-14 is an example of the step due notification job set to run daily at 5:51 AM.

View Scheduled Job

View the scheduled job configuration.

* Job Name:	Send_360_Step_Due_Notification_Job
* Job Owner:	v4admin
* Job Type:	Send 360 Step Due Notification
Job Parameters:	

Job Occurrence & Notification

Occurrence: ◯ Once ◉ Recurring ◯ Dependant of

┌─ Recurring Pattern ───┐
│ ◉ Daily   │
│ ◯ Weekly   Hold the **Ctrl** key down to select multiple hours.   │
│ ◯ Monthly   Example: For 5:30AM and 5:30PM, select "5" and "17" in the hours, and "30" in the minute. │
│ ◯ Yearly   │
│   ┌────┐   minutes   │
│   │ 2 │   51 ∨   │
│   │ 3 │   │
│   │ 4 │   │
│   │ 5 │   │
│   │ 6 │   │
│   │ 7 │   │
└───┘

Start Date:	Jobs are scheduled based on local time for this server which is currently: Fri Aug 14 16:48:45 EDT 2020 07/23/2017 2:46 AM
End Date:	: AM
Additional E-mail Recipients:	
Send E-mail when job starts:	☐

[Cancel] [Close]

Figure 8-14.   *Step Due Notification Scheduled Job*

In order for this email notification to be sent to a user when the performance form is in their inbox and the step is past due

- "Step Due Notification" is enabled in "E-Mail Notification Templates."

- The route map for the form template has step due dates.

- The form template has "Default Due Notification Date (in days)" set in advanced settings.

- The form template does not have Step Exit Notification disabled in advanced settings.

- The background job is scheduled to run daily.

Figure 8-15 is a sample email for step due notification.

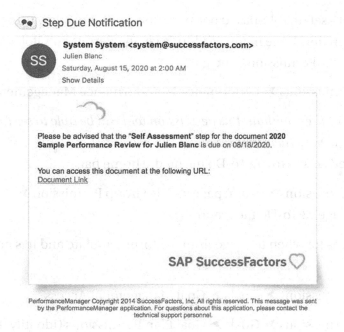

Figure 8-15. *Step Due Notification*

The route map had 8/18/20 as the self-assessment step due date. The advanced settings for the template had three days prior to due date for notification. This email was received by the employee three days before the step was due.

Role-Based Permissions

Let's set up the role-based permissions needed for users to access Performance Management. We will start with the employee role.

Employee Permissions

Users will need access to the following:

- Performance tab in the Home menu

- To-Do tile on the home page

- Goal plan

- Development plan (if displaying in the performance form)

We will need to set up role-based permissions in order to allow users to see the Performance tab in the Home menu. Within "Manage Permission Roles," open the employee role, click "Permission," and go to

- User Permissions ➤ Performance ➤ Performance Management Access

Please note that users without this permission will still be able to see the Performance tab if they have a form in their inbox.

Users will need access to the To-Do tile on the home page:

- User Permissions ➤ Homepage v3 Tile Group Permission ➤ Homepage v3 To-Do tile group

The following is for when using goals in the form template and it is not already enabled:

- User Permissions ➤ Goals ➤ Goal Management Access

- User Permissions ➤ Goals ➤ Goal Plan Permissions (identify the specific plan)

The following is for when using a development plan in your form template and it is not yet enabled:

- User Permissions ➤ Career Development Planning ➤ Career Development Plan (CDP) Access Permission

- User Permissions ➤ Goals ➤ Goal Management Access ➤ Goal Plan Permissions (identify the specific dev plan)

Manager Permissions

In order for the manager to create or run performance-related ad hoc reports, make sure reports permissions are enabled.

Within "Manage Permission Roles," open the manager role, click "Permission," and go to User Permissions ➤ Reports Permission. You may include

- Ad Hoc Report Builder Standard Reports Bin (if using EC)

- Report Center

- Classic Reports

- Detail Report

- List View
- Analytics Tiles and Dashboards
  - Select any performance-related tiles and dashboards.
- Create Report
  - Performance Management
- Run Report
  - Select any performance-related tiles and dashboards.

Also grant Performance Management access and "Team Overview Access" to the manager role:

- User Permissions ➤ Performance ➤ Performance Management Access
- User Permissions ➤ Performance ➤ Team Overview Access

The following is for when using goals in the form template and it is not already enabled:

- User Permissions ➤ Goals ➤ Goal Management Access
- User Permissions ➤ Goals ➤ Goal Plan Permissions (identify the specific plan)

The following is for when using a development plan in your form template and it is not yet enabled:

- User Permissions ➤ Career Development Planning ➤ Career Development Plan (CDP) Access Permission
- User Permissions ➤ Goals ➤ Goal Management Access ➤ Goal Plan Permissions (identify the specific dev plan)

HR Manager Permissions

In addition to the admin generating forms, you may decide that HR managers can create forms as well. For instance, later you may create a hybrid performance form used for performance improvement. In a situation like this, the manager can contact the HR manager who supports the group to have a form generated. Using the HR manager for this task gives more confidentiality to the process rather than involving an admin to launch the form.

You may set the same permissions for the HR manager that you just set for the manager role. Like the manager role, you may grant access for reporting.

Within "Manage Permission Roles," open the HR manager role, click "Permissions," and go to User Permissions ➤ Reports Permission. Within the Reports Permission options, you may include the following:

- Ad Hoc Report Builder Standard Reports Bin (if using EC)

- Report Center

- Classic Reports

- Detail Report

- List View

- Analytics Tiles and Dashboards

  - Select any performance-related tiles and dashboards.

- Create Report

  - Performance Management

- Run Report

  - Select any performance-related tiles and dashboards.

Unlike the manager role, give access to create forms:

- User Permissions ➤ General User Permission ➤ Permission to Create Forms (identify the form to create)

Give access to launch forms:

- Administrator Permissions ➤ Manage Form Templates ➤ Mass Create Form Instances (Launch forms now)

- Administrator Permissions ➤ Manage Form Templates ➤ Schedule Mass Form Creation (Launch forms later)

Save the roles, and we will now talk about the route map.

Set Route Map Dates

Before we launch a performance form, we will need to set any step start or step due dates in our route map. Type and select "Manage Route Maps" in the search bar. Then open the route map that is linked to the performance form template that will be used in the form launch.

Oftentimes, HR will plot the dates for the various steps in the performance review cycle. Based on the review process start and end dates, you will need to find out if they are using specific windows for each step of the process. Some companies have Goal Setting in the early part of the year and keep the initial step of the form open for employees to track progress and add comments. Then they communicate dates for a midyear check-in step. They may wish to stop any forms going to manager review until a certain date. With all of this in mind, you can review the performance cycle dates and see if you need to add step start and due dates to your route map.

Most often, step start and step due dates are used, with step exit dates more unlikely. You will need to find out if step start dates are going to be communicated and if start dates are going to be enforced. For example, the enforcement of a step start date can be used when forms are launched ahead of time and you don't want employees going in and editing their forms yet. They will have read access only until the step start date.

Another important decision pertains to step exit dates. If a user does not complete the form when it is in their inbox by the step due date, do you want the form to automatically route to the next step? If so, you set a step due date and would enable "Automatic send on due date" in the route map step.

As seen in Figure 8-16, the first step of the route map has the step due date defined. When the "Automatic send on due date" option is enabled, two additional options display:

- Only send forms that pass validation: If there are required fields in this step, do not move the form forward. This could be used in a step that has required ratings to enter. Forms that pass validation will move forward; those with errors will not.

- Always send regardless of validation: The form is auto routed to the next step regardless of the step having required fields to enter.

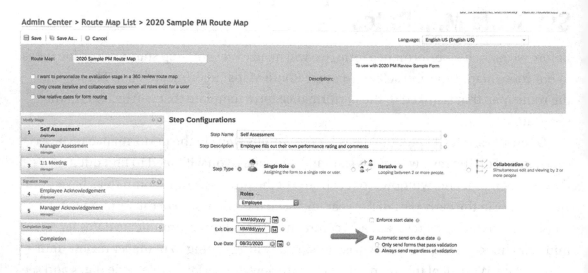

Figure 8-16. *Configure Step Dates*

Using the auto route feature may be helpful when the form is in a step where there are no required fields. Maybe you have a step early in the process where the employee enters comments on the form. Rather than having to run reports to track where employees are in the process, you can have the form auto route on the due date.

If you are going to use step dates, they are not needed for each step. This also applies to *Automatic send on due date* and step start date enforcement. You may have a start date for one step and a step exit date with auto route for another step. Just make sure there are no step date overlaps which could cause forms to get stuck.

Exercise caution when using the auto move option. For example, your route map does not have some early steps with *Automatic send on due date* enabled, but you enable this option on a later step. Forms in earlier steps aren't automatically moving forward. Forms that have not yet reached the auto route step will not get auto routed when the step is due. This means any forms not yet at the auto route step will not get auto routed. The auto route only occurs once for a step, based on the step due date. If a form reaches the auto route step after the step due date, the form will not auto route. Only forms that are in the step with a due date with auto route enabled will be moved to the next step.

If you have set up any auto route steps, you will need to set up a background job that will run daily to handle the routing. We will cover this next.

Schedule Auto Route Step Due Background Job

Earlier in this chapter, we discussed email notifications set up and the background jobs needed for step due and step overdue notifications. If you are using the auto route option, it makes sense to enable the step due date email notification as a reminder to users to complete the step before the form will move.

As we discussed, if you plan on sending step due notifications, the notifications were enabled in the advanced template settings on the form template, the email notifications enabled, and the background job set up.

The auto routing process requires a background job as well. This job will move the form the day after the step due date at the time set in the job.

To set this job up, go into Provisioning, go to Manage Scheduled Jobs ➤ Create New Job as seen in Figure 8-17, and set up the "Auto Route Step Due Doc" scheduled job.

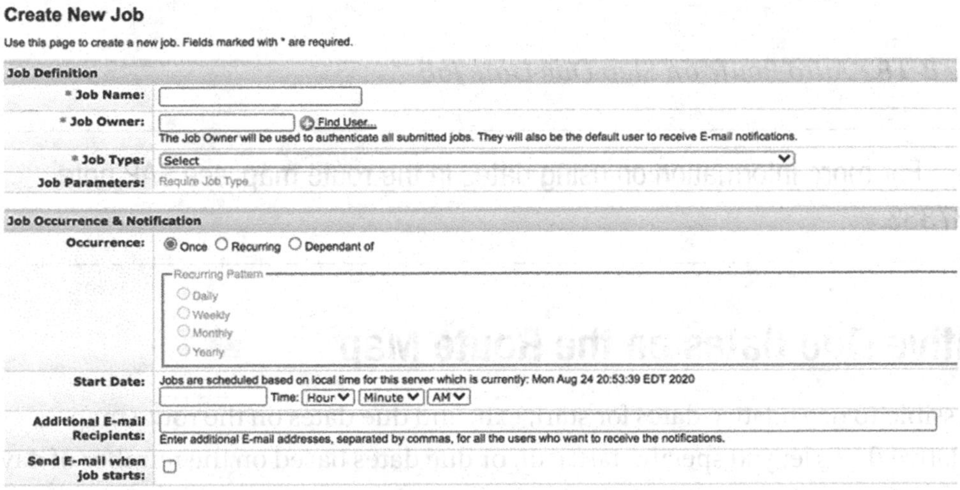

Figure 8-17. *Create a New Background Job*

Click the downward arrow in the "Job Type" field to find "Auto Route Based on Due Date." Give the job a name and set the occurrence. It should be "Recurring" to be run daily. You can set an early morning run so that the forms will move early in the morning after the step was due. Save the job and submit. This ensures that the job will start running as of the start date that you selected in the job.

An example of the created job is seen in Figure 8-18.

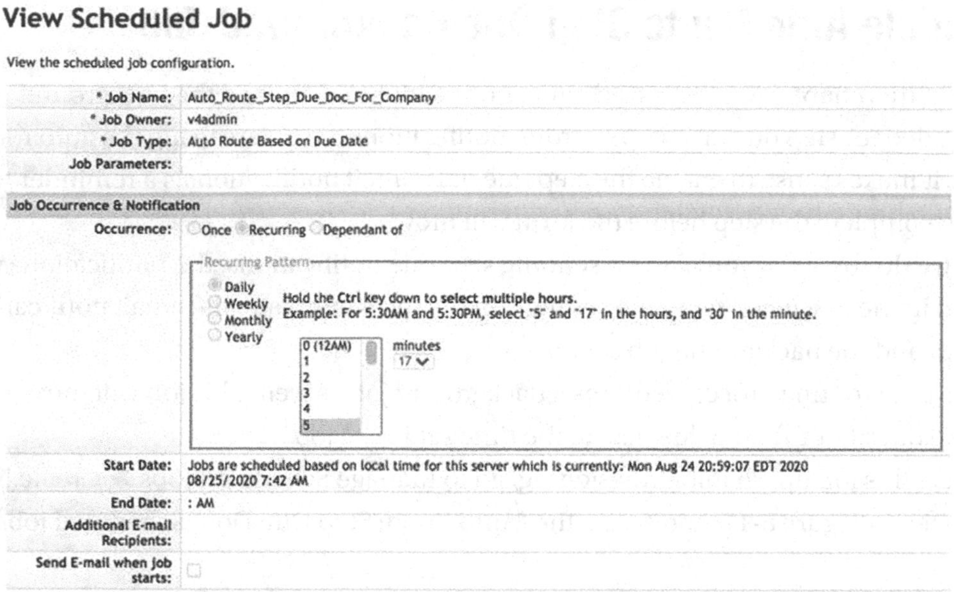

View Scheduled Job

View the scheduled job configuration.

* Job Name:	Auto_Route_Step_Due_Doc_For_Company
* Job Owner:	v4admin
* Job Type:	Auto Route Based on Due Date
Job Parameters:	

Job Occurrence & Notification

Occurrence:	○ Once ● Recurring ○ Dependant of
	┌─Recurring Pattern───┐
	● Daily Hold the Ctrl key down to select multiple hours.
	○ Weekly Example: For 5:30AM and 5:30PM, select "5" and "17" in the hours, and "30" in the minute.
	○ Monthly
	○ Yearly 0 (12AM) minutes
	1 17 ∨
	2
	3
	4
	5
Start Date:	Jobs are scheduled based on local time for this server which is currently: Mon Aug 24 20:59:07 EDT 2020
	08/25/2020 7:42 AM
End Date:	: AM
Additional E-mail Recipients:	
Send E-mail when job starts:	☐

Figure 8-18. *Auto Route on Step Due Date Job*

Note   For more information on using dates in the route map, see SAP note #2087333.

Relative Due Dates on the Route Map

It is possible to use relative dates for start, exit, and due dates on the route map.

Relative dates let you specify start, exit, or due dates based on the number of days before or after another activity.

In order to use relative dates on route maps, it must be set up in Provisioning. To do this, go to "Company Settings" and enable this option: "Enable Relative Dates for Form Routing."

Once enabled, your route maps will now display the option "Use relative dates for form routing" as seen in Figure 8-19.

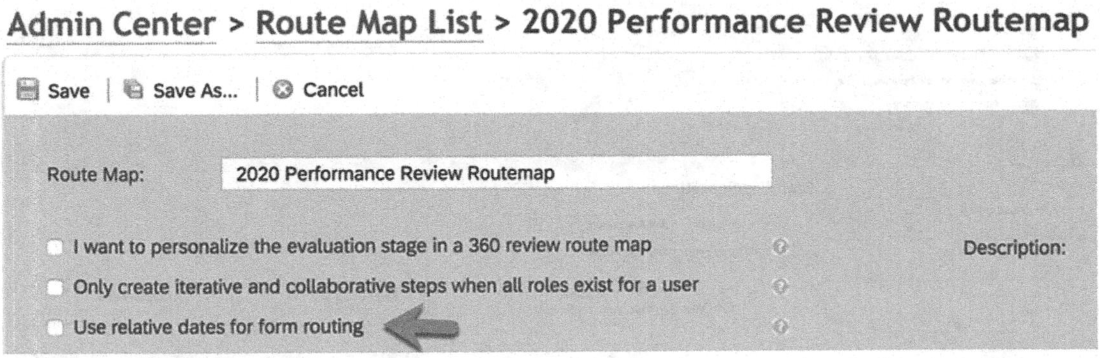

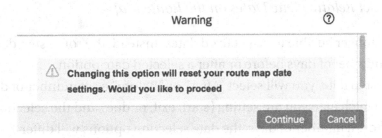

Figure 8-19. *Option to Use Relative Dates*

When selected, you will see a popup warning: "Changing this option will reset your route map date settings. Would you like to proceed." An example is shown in Figure 8-20.

Figure 8-20. *Warning Message When Using Relative Dates*

Select "Continue." A note will appear that explains that when relative dating is turned on, reordering the position of steps in a route map is not allowed.

You will notice that the step start, step exit, and step due date options on the route map have now changed. An example route map is shown in Figure 8-21.

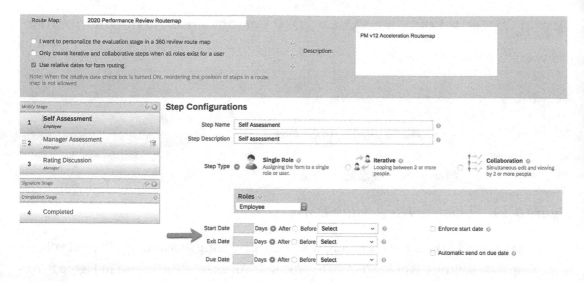

Figure 8-21. *Set Relative Due Dates on the Route Map*

You will no longer be able to select fixed dates. Instead, the route step date will be relative to the number of days before or after a selected date option.

For a route step date, you will select "After" or "Before" a set number of days. Depending on which date you are setting (start, exit, or due) and the selection of "Before" or "After" a number of days, the date selection options will differ. An example is shown in Figure 8-22.

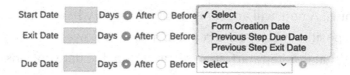

Figure 8-22. *Relative Date Options*

Possible selections that will be displayed in the dropdown listing may include the following:

- Form Creation Date

- Form Due Date

- Same Step Start Date

- Same Step Due Date

- Same Step Exit Date

- Previous Step Exit Date

- Previous Step Due Date

You will never see all of these options when setting a relative date; the options are based on the type of route step date you are setting and if the date will be "Before" or "After" a selected date.

An example of setting a step start and due date is shown in Figure 8-23.

Figure 8-23. *Setting First Step Dates*

For the first step of this route map, an enforced step start date is set for 10 days after the form creation date. The step is due 30 days after the step start date.

To-Do Tile

We have one more setup task before we can launch our form.

On the home page, a Performance Management–related To-Do tile will display within the To-Do panel. Any performance-related actions required of a user will appear in this tile. An example is shown in Figure 8-24.

Home
Ask HR
To-Do
Update Your Status
Last updated: 84 days ago
Review Performance
8
Reviews
1 due in 8 days
Approve Requests
3
Requests
Take Courses
1
Course
Due Anytime
My Info
My Profile
100% Complete
Org Chart
1
Peer
Quick Links
My Specialty
Admin Center
Admin Favorites
Admin Alerts 2.0
66
Admin Alerts

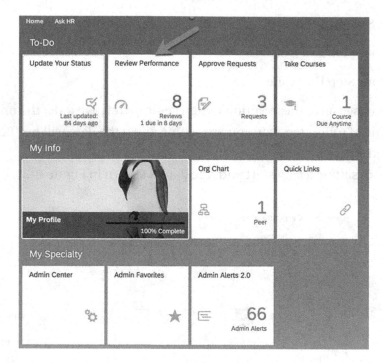

Figure 8-24. *To-Do Panel on the Home Page*

Items on this To-Do tile can come from performance forms routed to the user. An example is shown in Figure 8-25. Items that require an action contain a link that takes the user to the requested action or form to complete the task.

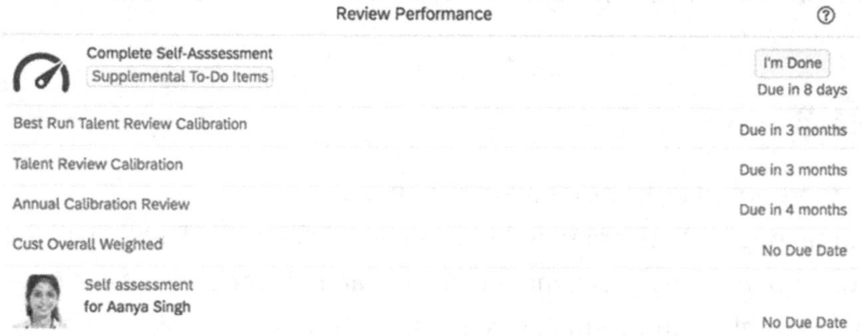

Review Performance
Complete Self-Asssessment
Supplemental To-Do Items
I'm Done
Due in 8 days
Best Run Talent Review Calibration
Due in 3 months
Talent Review Calibration
Due in 3 months
Annual Calibration Review
Due in 4 months
Cust Overall Weighted
No Due Date
Self assessment for Aanya Singh
No Due Date

Figure 8-25. *Performance-Related To-Do Items*

The admin may add supplemental To-Do items to the tile as well.

In Chapter 6, we talked about some optional admin permissions that may be granted. If not done already, the admin role will need access to update the To-Do tile. Type and select "Manage Permission Roles" in the search bar. Open the admin role and add the following permissions. Under the Administrator Permissions section, find "Manage User" and select "To-Do Admin" and "Manage Home Page." Save the role and we may continue.

To set this tile up, type and select "Manage Home Page" in the search bar. Next, click "To-Do Settings" as seen in Figure 8-26. You will see all of the options that may be updated.

Figure 8-26. *To-Do Settings*

General Settings

Click "General Settings" as seen in Figure 8-27. Here we can change the default dates for when To-Do items display.

The settings are

- Pending items

- Hide supplemental items

- Hide overdue items

These settings are used to identify when pending To-Do items will display and if supplemental To-Do items or overdue items may be hidden after a specified number of days. Be mindful that any changes here will impact all To-Do tiles.

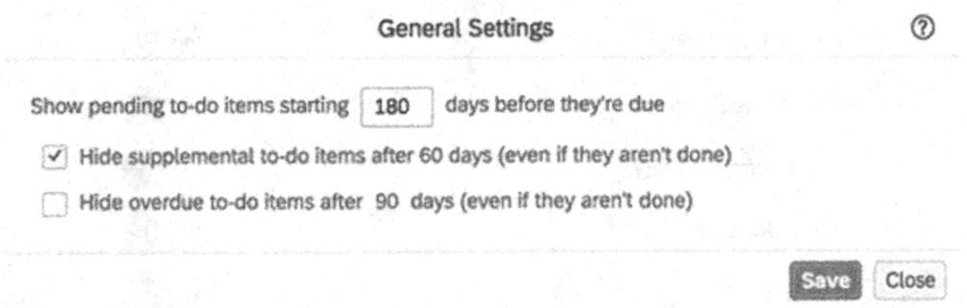

General Settings   ⑦

Show pending to-do items starting [180] days before they're due

☑ Hide supplemental to-do items after 60 days (even if they aren't done)

☐ Hide overdue to-do items after 90 days (even if they aren't done)

Save Close

Figure 8-27. *General Settings*

Rename To-Do Tiles

Also, under "To-Do Settings," you may rename the "Review Performance" To-Do tile as seen in Figure 8-28. Change the label in the "Display Name" column.

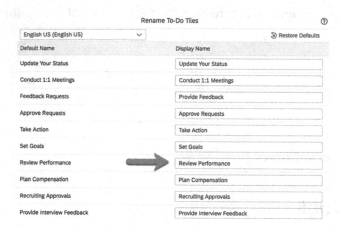

Figure 8-28. *Rename To-Do Tiles*

Show/Hide To-Do Tiles

Next, we need to make sure the To-Do tile for *Performance Management* is enabled. This setting is also within "To-Do Settings." Click "Show/Hide To-Do Tiles," and a popup will display as seen in Figure 8-29. Make sure "Review Performance" is set to show. If it is not, change to "Yes" and save.

Figure 8-29. *Enable "Review Performance" To-Do Tile*

Supplemental To-Do Items

You may also add supplemental To-Do items. For example, if you aren't using step due email notifications, you wish to have a reminder for employees that the self-assessment step of their performance review is due shortly.

Click "Supplemental To-Do Items" within "To-Do Settings," and a popup will display as seen in Figure 8-30. Select the tile where the additional To-Do item will reside, and give the "To-Do" item a name, along with its due date. You also identify which role will see this additional To-Do item. In this example, a To-Do item will reside in the "Review Performance" To-Do tile with a label "Complete Self-Assessment" along with the due date. The employee role will see the item.

Figure 8-30. *Adding a Supplemental Performance-Related To-Do Item*

Figure 8-31 shows an example of a supplemental To-Do item in a user's "Review Performance" To-Do tile.

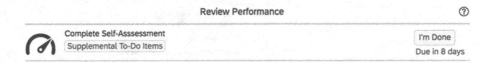

Figure 8-31. *Supplemental To-Do Item*

If the user clicks "I'm Done," the item will be removed from their To-Do list. Things to consider for this section are as follows:

- The To-Do list uses the route map step description not the route map step name.

- To-Do items use the step due date. If there is no step due date, the To-Do item will show "No Due Date" in the tile.

- To-Do items are listed by due date and then alphabetically.

- To-Do items are grouped together in in the To-Do tile if they have the same route map step name and same step due date.

We have now completed all of the setup and configuration needed to launch a form, so let's begin!

Launch Form

We will now launch forms which are based upon the form templates. We will identify which form template is used to create performance forms for which employees and when. The role that will be launching forms will need the role-based permissions "Mass Create Form Instances" and "Schedule Mass Form Creation" within *Manage Form Templates* in the *Administrator Permissions* for the role.

In addition, the role will need permission to create forms. Typically, the admin role will be able to create any form since permission would have been granted for all forms. But if you would like a role to only be able to launch specific forms, within the role's permissions, go to User Permissions ➤ General User Permission ➤ Permission to Create Forms as seen in Figure 8-32.

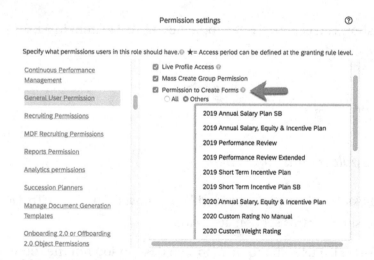

Figure 8-32. *Permission to Create Forms*

You would click the "Others" radio button and select the specific forms that may be created by the role. Save the updates, and we will start the launch process.

Type and select "Launch Forms" in the search bar. The Launch Forms screen is seen in Figure 8-33.

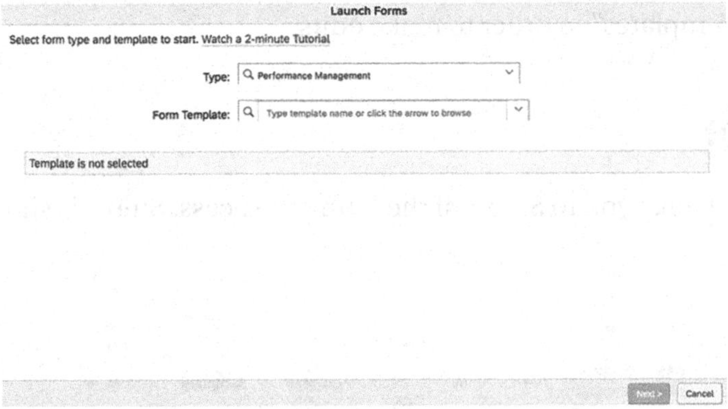

Launch Forms

Select form type and template to start. Watch a 2-minute Tutorial

Type: 🔍 Performance Management ⌄

Form Template: 🔍 Type template name or click the arrow to browse ⌄

Template is not selected

Next >   Cancel

Figure 8-33. *Select a Form Template to Launch*

On the initial Launch Forms screen, select the type of form to generate and then select the form template. The template type dropdown listing will have selections for "All," 360, or Performance Management. Select "Performance Management."

Based on Performance Management selected as the type, the "Form Template" dropdown listing will contain all active performance templates that the user has permission to create.

After selecting the form, information about the form template will display as seen in Figure 8-34 upon selection.

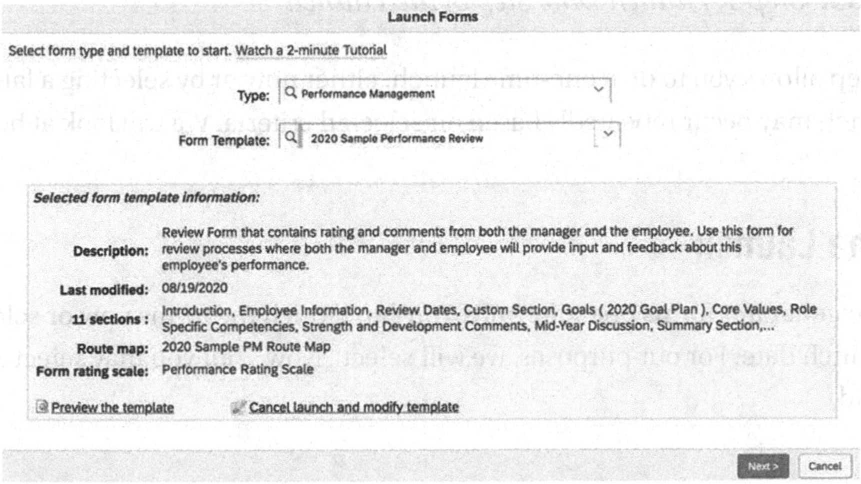

Launch Forms

Select form type and template to start. Watch a 2-minute Tutorial

Type: 🔍 Performance Management ⌄

Form Template: 🔍 2020 Sample Performance Review ⌄

Selected form template information:

Description: Review Form that contains rating and comments from both the manager and the employee. Use this form for review processes where both the manager and employee will provide input and feedback about this employee's performance.

Last modified: 08/19/2020

11 sections : Introduction, Employee Information, Review Dates, Custom Section, Goals (2020 Goal Plan), Core Values, Role Specific Competencies, Strength and Development Comments, Mid-Year Discussion, Summary Section,...

Route map: 2020 Sample PM Route Map

Form rating scale: Performance Rating Scale

📄 Preview the template   ✏️ Cancel launch and modify template

Next >   Cancel

Figure 8-34. *Form Template Information*

The form template description, route map, rating scale, template sections, and last modified date will display. On this step of the launch, you may preview the form template or cancel the launch. If you cancel, you are returned to the form template within "Manage Templates" in order to make edits.

Launch Date

Clicking "Next" will take you to Step 1 of the launch process. Step 1 is shown in Figure 8-35.

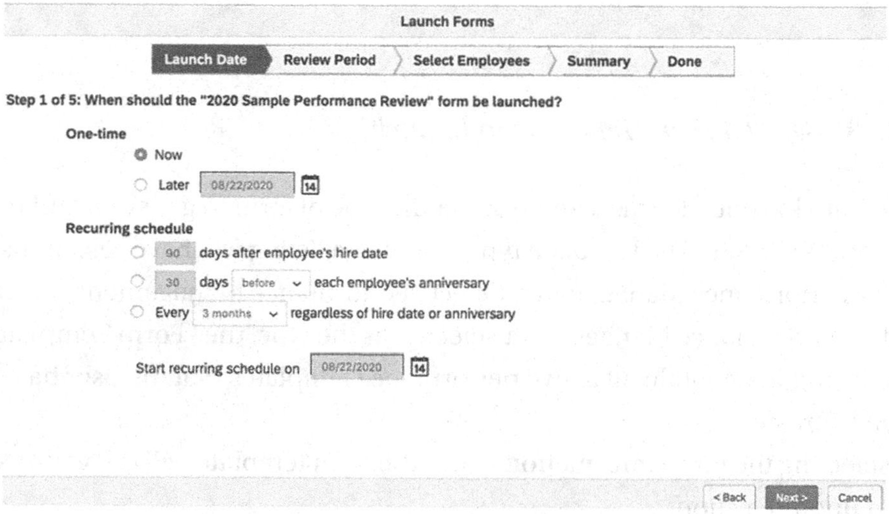

Figure 8-35. *Step 1, Launch Date Step of the Launch*

This step allows you to do a one-time launch, either now or by selecting a later date. Or the launch may occur repeatedly based on selected criteria. We will look at both options.

One-Time Launch

This option generates forms one time only. You can launch the forms now or select a specific launch date. For our purposes, we will select "Now," but you may select a future date instead.

Recurring Schedule

The other option enables a recurring launch. This option is used in situations where you want to mass create forms repeatedly based on specific date-driven criteria. Employees who fit the criteria at the time of the launch will have a form generated.

There are three date-related options to choose from:

1. Hire Date: Select a number of days after the hire date to launch forms. For example, new hires have not been at their job long enough to participate in the annual review process, so you have created a new hire probationary form that is used to comment on progress or used as a framework to set goals. After the selected number of days, the new hire will have their probationary form launched.

2. Anniversary Date: Select a number of days before or after the anniversary date to launch forms. This option can be used if your organization does performance evaluations by employees' anniversary dates rather than all employees having the same review cycle.

3. Launch forms based on a selected number of months (1, 3, 6, or 12) without regard to the hire or anniversary date.

For example, if you opted to launch forms 90 days after the hire date, anyone who had a hire date 90 days ago from today would have a form generated today. Tomorrow, anyone who had a hire date 90 days ago would have a form generated then and so on. The recurring scheduled launch looks at the number of days/months or year selected relative to the current day to determine who gets a form generated today.

To use any of these options, a background job would need to be set up to run daily. The daily job would run, check who meets the criteria today, and generate forms for those users. We will talk about this at the end of our discussion on launching forms.

After selecting one of these options, you would then identify the date the recurring scheduled job should start to run. Click "Next" to move to Step 2.

Review Period

Step 2 of the launch process is used to define the period of time the review is being conducted for. There are four options to select from as seen in Figure 8-36.

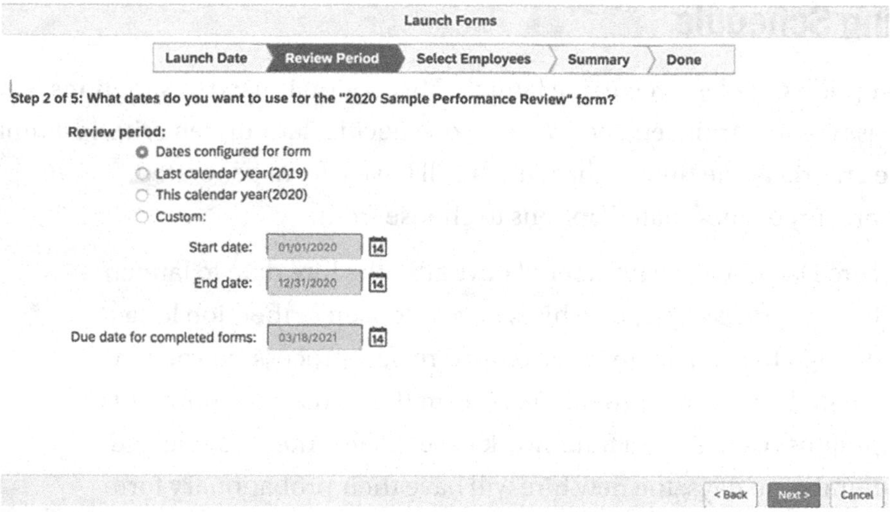

Figure 8-36. *Step 2, Review Period Step of the Launch*

Review Period Options

1. Dates configured for form: The dates come from the default start, end, and due dates from the form template advanced settings.

2. Last calendar year: Uses start date of January 1 and end date of December 31 of the last calendar year.

3. This calendar year.: Uses start date of January 1 and end date of December 31 of the current year.

4. Custom: You select review period start and end dates.

Options 2, 3, and 4 also require a due date for completed forms.
Click "Next" to move to Step 3 of the launch process.

Select Employees

In Step 3 of the launch process, you will select the users to generate forms for. A sample of the screen is shown in Figure 8-37.

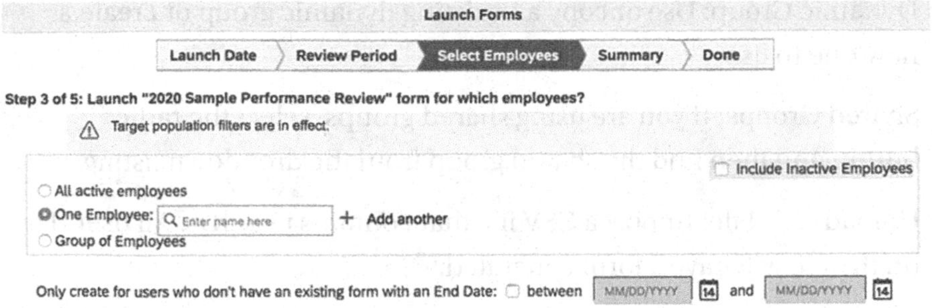

Figure 8-37. *Select Employees Step of the Launch*

There are several options to choose from:

- All active employees as of the launch date

- One Employee – search by name, and you may continue to add users one by one

- Group of Employees

There are two options that may be used with the selected employees:

1. You may opt to include inactive employees. This may be enabled for any of the employee options except for dynamic groups which already exclude inactive employees.

2. Only create forms for users that don't have an existing form within a selected date range.

Selecting "Group of Employess" will expand the section with more group options to choose from as seen in Figure 8-38.

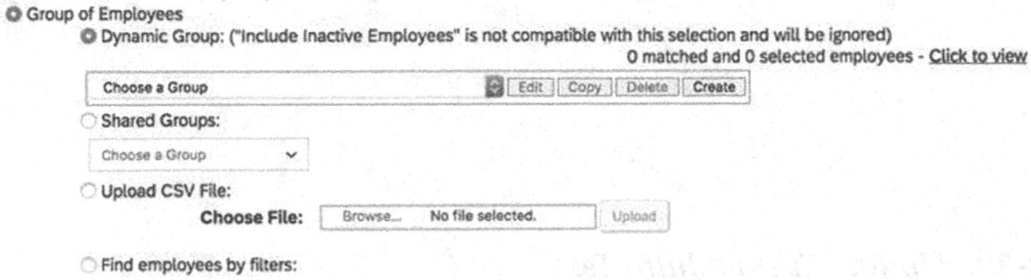

Figure 8-38. *Select Group of Employees for Form Launch*

- Dynamic Group: Use or copy an existing dynamic group or create a new one to use.

- Shared Groups: If you are using shared groups, select the radio button and then find the shared group from the dropdown listing.

- Upload CSV File: Import a CSV file that contains user IDs. All user IDs on the file will have a form generated.

- Find employees by filters: Click this option, and you will see filters to select from.

Keep in mind the employees who will be included in your selection are dependent on your target population and the launch date.

Make your selection, and click "Next" to move on to the next launch step.

For further information about creating groups, see SAP note #2088248.

Edit Introduction Texts

If you had a custom section in the form template and enabled "Edit Intro text description in Mass create," you would see an additional step as seen in Figure 8-39.

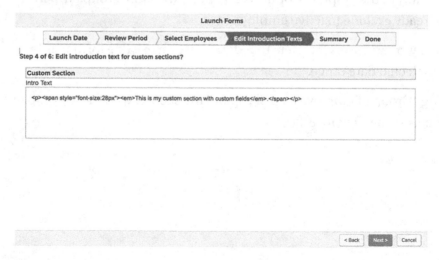

Figure 8-39. *Update Custom Intro Text*

When used, the text entered here will display at the top of the custom section of the form.

Summary

The Summary section of the launch process as seen in Figure 8-40 displays all of the selections from the prior steps.

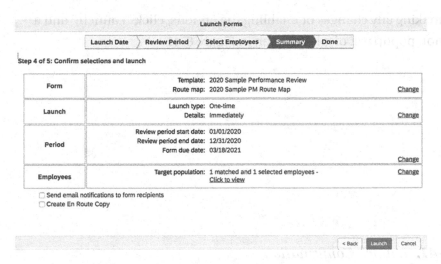

Figure 8-40. *Summary Step of the Launch*

Any or all of the step decisions may be changed. Click "Change" in any section and it will take you back to the associated step, and you may make any edits prior to launch. Then you would step the launch screens until you are back at the *Summary* step again.

There are two checkboxes on the Summary screen as well:

- Send email notifications to form recipients: The first person in the route map process will receive a notification that a form has been created. The form will be in the user's Performance Inbox, and there will be a To-Do item in the Performance tile on their home page. If the Document Creation email notification is enabled but this option is not checked, the email will not be generated.

    It is recommended to enable this option so that at the start of the review process, the first user in the route map will know when the form is in their inbox. For subsequent steps, the routing email would be sent to let users know that the form is in their inbox and ready for their action.

- Create En Route Copy: The user who launched the forms gets copies of the forms sent to their En Route form folder. If the admin who launches the forms checks this option, they will be inundated with forms, so it is not recommended to use.

After making any changes or enabling the options, click "Launch," and a confirmation popup will display as seen in Figure 8-41.

Figure 8-41. *Launch Confirmation*

Upon clicking "OK," you will see the "Done" step as seen in Figure 8-42.

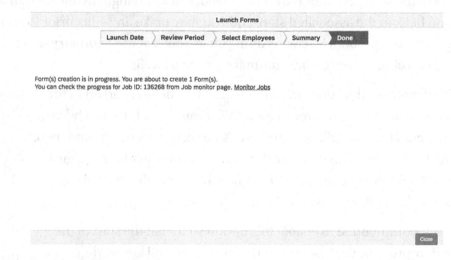

Figure 8-42. *Done Step of the Launch*

If you have not enabled the Mass Create Form Instances notification and you want to make sure the launch has completed, make note of the Job ID listed in the "Done" step and then click "Monitor Jobs."

The "Mass Create Form Jobs Monitor" will display in a popup screen. Click the expand icon next to "Filter" as seen in Figure 8-43.

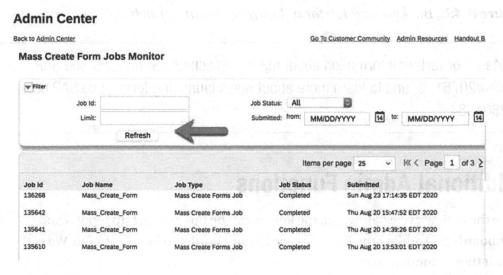

Figure 8-43. *Mass Create Form Jobs Monitor*

Continue to click the "Refresh" button until you see the Job ID for the forms that you have launched as seen in Figure 8-44.

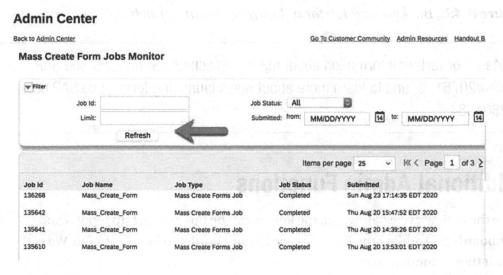

Figure 8-44. *Refresh Until the Job Completes*

Once you see the Job ID and the Job Status is "Completed," you have successfully launched performance forms! Close the popup and then close the launch page.

When we were in the Launch Date step of the launch and we selected a recurring form launch, we spoke briefly about the need for a background job to be set up. Use the same procedure as setting up the job for email notifications to run. Go into Provisioning, go to Manage Scheduled Jobs ➤ Create New Job, and create the "Schedule Form Creation". Schedule the job to run daily. An example is shown in Figure 8-45.

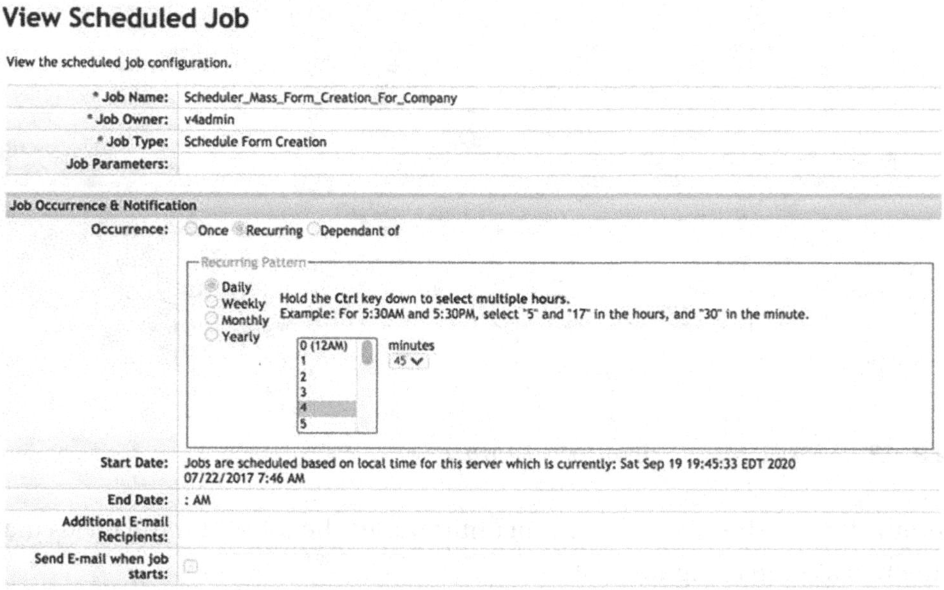

Figure 8-45. *Background Job for a Recurring Form Launch*

Note   For further information about managing scheduled reviews, see SAP note #2076115; and to learn more about mass launching forms, see SAP note #2601584.

Additional Admin Functions

Once the review cycle has begun, the admin can be busy setting up reports and dashboards and adding the Performance History Portlet to People Profile. We will look at these functions next.

Reporting

Here, we will look at some of the Performance Management–related reporting that is available. As part of our manager and HR manager role permission setup, we granted access to standard reports, dashboards, and ad hoc reporting.

Standard Reports

For the reports that we are going to look at here, the manager and HR manager roles will need access to Classic Reports and List View reports. To verify that the roles have these permissions, type and select "Manage Permission Roles" in the search bar. Select the role to check the permissions. Found within the User Permissions section, look for "Reports Permission" and select "Classic Reports" and "List View." Save the role.

Here, we will look at Classic Reports and List View reports. When the user has access to reporting, it will appear in the Home menu as seen in Figure 8-46.

Figure 8-46. *Home Menu*

From the Home menu, select "Reporting". If the Report Center view displays, click "Switch to Classic View" as seen in Figure 8-47.

Figure 8-47. *Report Center*

The standard reports will be listed as shown in Figure 8-48. Please note that based on permissions, you may not see as many reports as shown.

Figure 8-48. *Classic Reports*

On the left-side panel, reports are grouped in categories. Select "All Reports by Type" to see the view as seen in Figure 8-49.

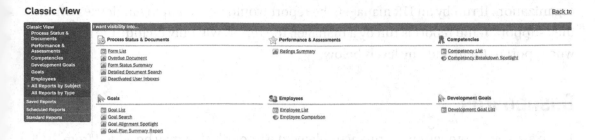

Figure 8-49. *Reports Displayed by Type*

Performance-related reports include:

- Form List

- Overdue Document

- Form Status Summary

- Ratings Summary

Figure 8-50 is a sample of the Form List.

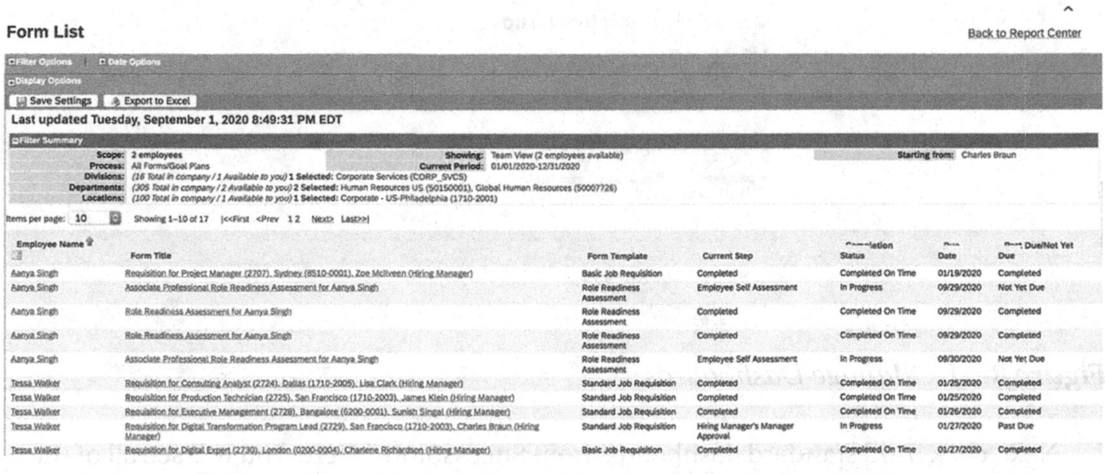

Figure 8-50. *Form List Report*

This report lists the current forms for users. Each row also shows the form template associated with the performance form, the status of the form, the current step, the due date, and if the form is completed. The admin can run this report to report across the organization. If run by an HR manager, the report would only contain employees whom they support. If the report is run by a manager, the report will only include the employees who report to them and any levels below.

Dashboards

There are some standard performance-related dashboards that may be added from SuccessStore. We will briefly walk through the process to do this.

Type and select "Manage Dashboards" in the search bar. As seen in Figure 8-51, click "Manage Standard Dashboards" and "YouCalc Files".

Figure 8-51. *Manage Dashboards*

Next, click "Add standard dashboards from SucessStore". Here, you will see all of the dashboards and tiles that are available from SuccessStore. As seen in Figure 8-52, there are performance-related tiles and dashboards.

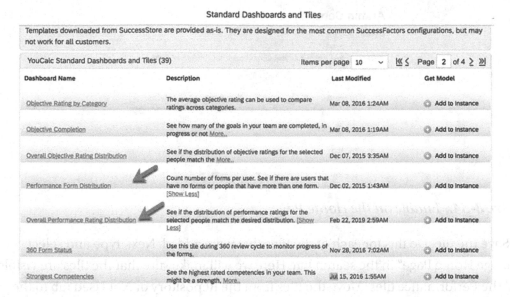

Standard Dashboards and Tiles

Figure 8-52. *Performance-Related Dashboards and Tiles*

The standard performance-related tiles are:

- Performance Form Distribution

- Performance Form Status

- Performance Forms Overdue

- Overall Performance Rating Distribution

Once added, go to the Action column and click "Edit" as shown in Figure 8-53.

Figure 8-53. *Edit Tile*

To make the tile available on the home page, go to the Availability tab and select "Homepage" as seen in Figure 8-54.

Figure 8-54. *Enable on the Home Page*

Save the tile. Do this for each of the tiles that were added. Next, type and select "Manage Home Page" in the search bar. Here we will make sure that the tiles are visible. Find the Performance tiles. Move the tiles from the Repository or Not Used tab to the Default tab as seen in Figure 8-55.

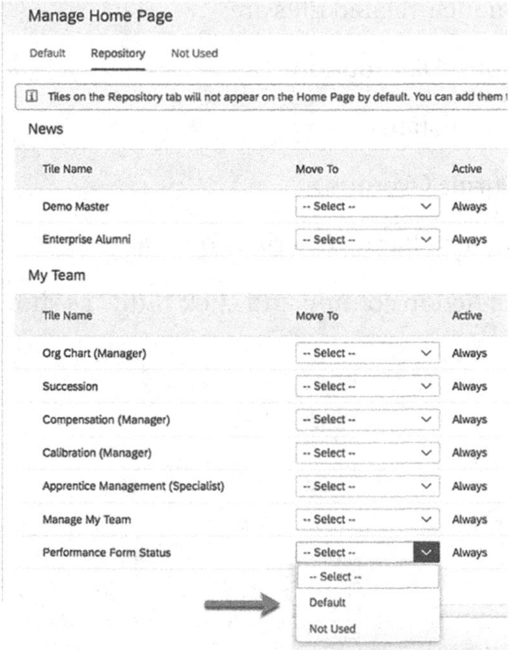

Figure 8-55. *Move Tiles to the Default Tab*

Put them in the My Team block with the other manager-related tiles. An example is seen in Figure 8-56.

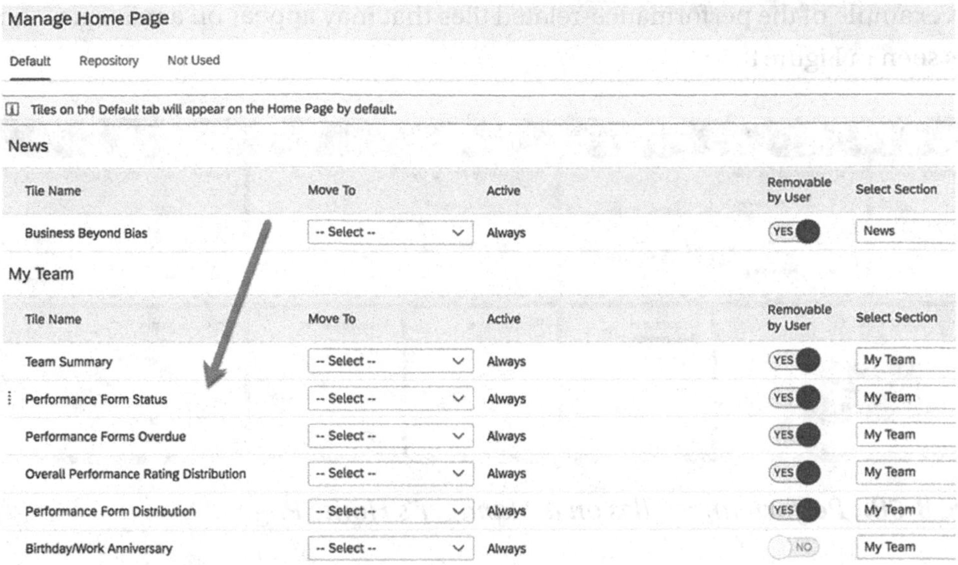

Manage Home Page

Default   Repository   Not Used

ⓘ Tiles on the Default tab will appear on the Home Page by default.

News

Tile Name	Move To	Active	Removable by User	Select Section
Business Beyond Bias	-- Select -- ⌄	Always	YES	News

My Team

Tile Name	Move To	Active	Removable by User	Select Section
Team Summary	-- Select -- ⌄	Always	YES	My Team
Performance Form Status	-- Select -- ⌄	Always	YES	My Team
Performance Forms Overdue	-- Select -- ⌄	Always	YES	My Team
Overall Performance Rating Distribution	-- Select -- ⌄	Always	YES	My Team
Performance Form Distribution	-- Select -- ⌄	Always	YES	My Team
Birthday/Work Anniversary	-- Select -- ⌄	Always	NO	My Team

Figure 8-56. *Tiles Added to My Team*

Save the updates. As long as the manager role has Analytics Tiles and Dashboards enabled, they will see them on their home page. The permissions needed are shown in Figure 8-57.

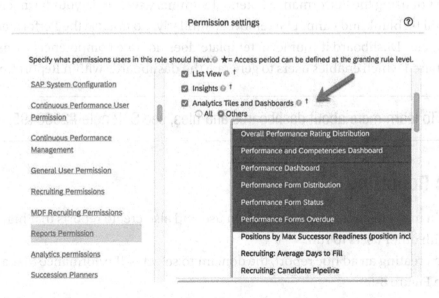

Figure 8-57. *Manager Permissions for Tiles and Dashboards*

An example of the performance-related tiles that may appear on a manager's home page is seen in Figure 8-58.

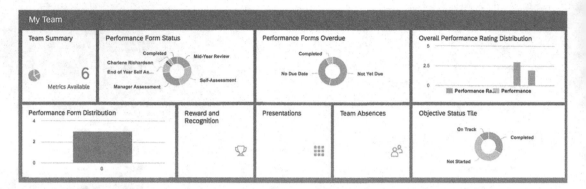

Figure 8-58. *Performance Tiles on a Manager's Home Page*

There are also standard performance dashboards available:

- Performance Dashboard

- Performance and Competencies Dashboard

Please note the Performance Dashboard contains a tile for Performance vs. Potential. If you are not using the Performance Potential Summary section in your form template, this tile will be blank and cannot be removed. Similarly, do not use the Performance and Competencies Dashboard if your form template does not rate competencies. Dashboards may be shared which enables users to generate the dashboards within Report Center.

Note   To learn more about dashboards and tiles, see SAP note #2536495.

Ad Hoc Reporting

The admin may create reports for their own use and also create reports that may be shared with other users to run.

When creating an ad hoc report, the domain to select is "Performance Management" as seen in Figure 8-59.

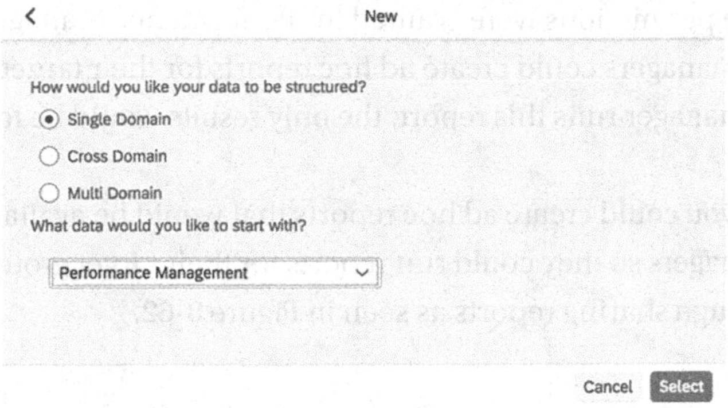

Figure 8-59. *Domain for Performance Management Reporting*

A wizard walks you through a series of steps to build your report. An example is seen in Figure 8-60.

Figure 8-60. *Steps to Create an Ad Hoc Report*

When walking through the wizard to create an ad hoc report, on the People tab, select "Logged In User" and the number of levels that the manager should have access to. An example is shown in Figure 8-61.

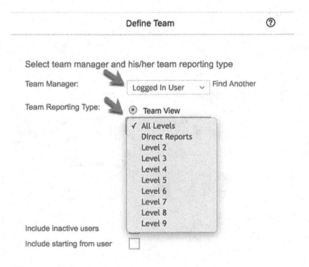

Figure 8-61. *Select Reporting Type*

If ad hoc create permissions were granted for Performance Management data, HR managers and/or managers could create ad hoc reports for their target groups. For example, when a manager runs this report, the only results would be for the employees in their team.

As the admin, you could create ad hoc reports that would be available to HR managers and managers so they could run reports for their target groups. This is accomplished through sharing reports as seen in Figure 8-62.

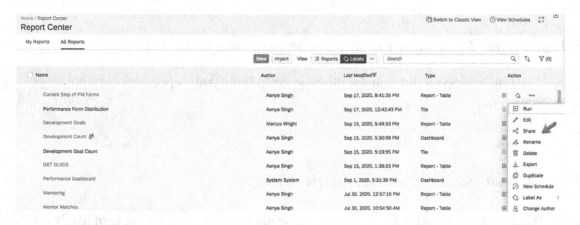

Figure 8-62.   *Sharing Ad Hoc Reports*

Then you may select whom to share the report with. The report may be shared by role as seen in Figure 8-63.

Figure 8-63.   *Sharing Reports by Role*

There are many fields that may be reported on as seen in Figure 8-64.

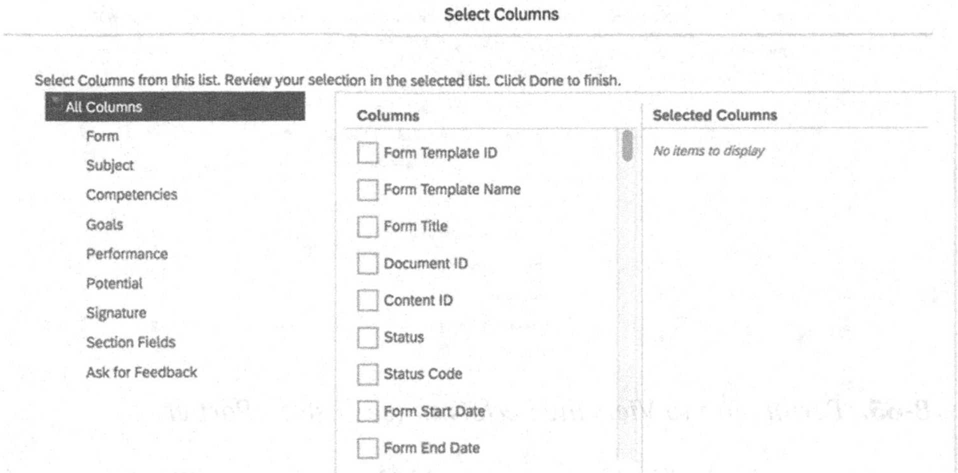

Figure 8-64. *Performance Form Fields*

Note   To learn more about ad hoc reporting, see SAP note #2536445.

Performance-Related Blocks on People Profile

If performance rating background elements were configured and permitted in the data model, they may be displayed in People Profile. Typically, these appear in a Talent Profile section of the profile that has visibility to only the employee and manager. Some of these blocks may be permitted for only the manager to see.

For any rating background elements from the data model, make sure the appropriate roles have permission to view them. Within a role, in User Permissions ➤ Employee Data, go to the Background Elements section. In Figure 8-65, permission to the Performance History Portlet is being granted to the manager role.

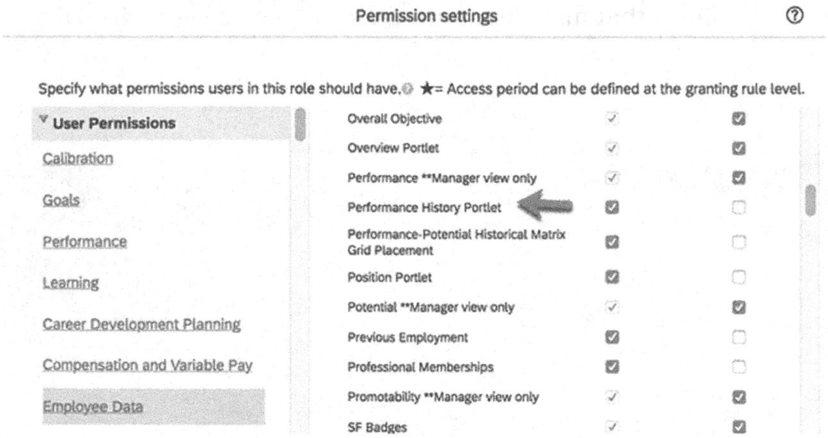

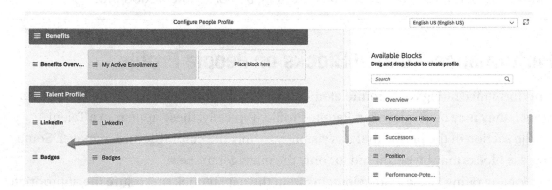

Figure 8-65. *Permission to View the Performance History Portlet*

After saving the role, the block needs to be added to People Profile.

Type and select "Configure People Profile" in the search bar. Find the Performance History Portlet from the Available Blocks section of the screen and drag and drop to the Talent Profile section on the left side of the screen as seen in Figure 8-66.

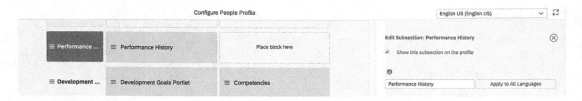

Figure 8-66. *Add the Performance History Portlet to People Profile*

Name the subsection created for the block as seen in Figure 8-67.

Figure 8-67. *Name the Subsection of the Talent Profile Section*

You may relabel the block as well as seen in Figure 8-68.

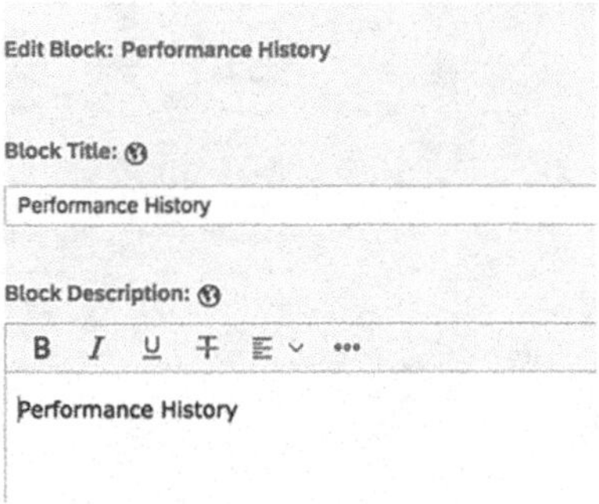

Figure 8-68. *Rename the Performance History Block*

If your template included the Performance Potential Summary section or the Objective Competency Summary section, these blocks may be permitted and configured to appear in People Profile as well. In the next chapter, you will see the blocks in a user's profile.

Now that we have seen how to report on performance data, we will look at some of the administrative functions that an admin may need to perform during the review cycle.

Delete a Form

There may be a situation where a form needs to be deleted. Perhaps a new form needs to be launched so the original form will be deleted. Type and select "Delete Form" in the search bar. There you will see the multiple ways to delete a form. A sample is shown in Figure 8-69.

Delete Document

Step 1: Search for Documents

○ Employee Document Folder   ◉ Advanced Search

This is used to view the contents of a specific user's inbox, En   'Advanced Search' is used to find documents based on one or more of the criteria below. Document retrieved will meet all criteria specified.
Route folder, or Completed folder.

Employee Name: 🔍   Find User...   ▼ Based on User attributes:
     Look in: All   First Name: Department: Select...
                                                       Last Name: Division: Select...
                                                       Username: Location: Select...
                                                          Title: Job Code:
                                                 Organization Unit: Select...   Location ID: Select...
                                                       Position ID: Select...   Employee Group: Select...
                                               Employee Sub Group: Select...   Veteran Status: Select...
                                                          Union: Select...   Leadership Tier: Select...
                                                      Pay Grade: Select...   Rehire Date: Select...
                                       Last Position Change Date: Select...   Suffix: Select...
                                               Total Service Date: Select...   Job Function: Select...
                                                     Job Family: Select...
                                                  Choose a Group: Select...

                                                       ▼ Based on form attributes:
                                                       Start Date: from: mm/dd/yyyy to: mm/dd/yyyy   Create Date: from: mm/dd/yyyy to: mm/dd/yyyy
                                                         End Date: from: mm/dd/yyyy to: mm/dd/yyyy   Due Date: from: mm/dd/yyyy to: mm/dd/yyyy
                                                    Form Template: Select...   Form ID:
                                                       Created By: 🔍   Find User...

                                                       ▼ Based on CSV Upload
                                                       Choose File: Browse... No file selected.   Upload Download Template

                                                       Search

Figure 8-69. Delete a Form

An advanced search may be done based on user or form attributes. Additionally, a file that contains the document ids may be uploaded. All forms that meet the criteria will display; and you may select one, many, or all to delete. An example is shown in Figure 8-70.

Admin Center

Back to Admin Center   Go To Customer Community   Admin Resources   Handout Build

Delete Document

Step 2: Search for Documents

⊞ Search Criteria

↵ Delete	☐ Select all 17 documents in search results	Selected documents: 0					Items per page 10 ▼	｜K < Page 1 of 2 > >｜
☐ **Form ID**	**Title**	**Start Date**	**End Date**	**Due Date**	**Current Step Name**	**Owned By**	**Subject User**	
☐ 33420	2020 Sample Performance Review for William Zamchelli	01/01/2020	12/31/2020	03/18/2021	Self-Assessment	William Zamchelli	William Zamchelli	
☐ 33419	2020 Sample Performance Review for Tessa Walker	01/01/2020	12/31/2020	03/18/2021	Self-Assessment	Tessa Walker	Tessa Walker	
☐ 33417	2020 Sample Performance Review for Sarah O' Carroll	01/01/2020	12/31/2020	03/18/2021	Self-Assessment	Sarah O' Carroll	Sarah O' Carroll	
☐ 33416	2020 Sample Performance Review for Robert Mancini	01/01/2020	12/31/2020	03/18/2021	Self-Assessment	Robert Mancini	Robert Mancini	
☐ 33415	2020 Sample Performance Review for Marcus Wright	01/01/2020	12/31/2020	03/18/2021	Self-Assessment	Marcus Wright	Marcus Wright	
☐ 33414	2020 Sample Performance Review for Lisa Clark	01/01/2020	12/31/2020	03/18/2021	Self-Assessment	Lisa Clark	Lisa Clark	
☐ 33413	2020 Sample Performance Review for Lauren Robbins	01/01/2020	12/31/2020	03/18/2021	Self-Assessment	Lauren Robbins	Lauren Robbins	
☐ 33411	2020 Sample Performance Review for Jordan Robinson	01/01/2020	12/31/2020	03/18/2021	Self-Assessment	Jordan Robinson	Jordan Robinson	
☐ 33410	2020 Sample Performance Review for Jacob Curran	01/01/2020	12/31/2020	03/18/2021	Self-Assessment	Jacob Curran	Jacob Curran	
☐ 33409	2020 Sample Performance Review for Elizabeth Wall	01/01/2020	12/31/2020	03/18/2021	Self-Assessment	Elizabeth Wall	Elizabeth Wall	

Figure 8-70. Form Selection for Deletion

Restore a Form

There may be a situation where a form was deleted for an inactive user that has now returned to work or a form was accidently deleted. Similar to the *delete a form* action, forms may be restored as well. Type and select "Restore Form" in the search bar. An example is seen in Figure 8-71.

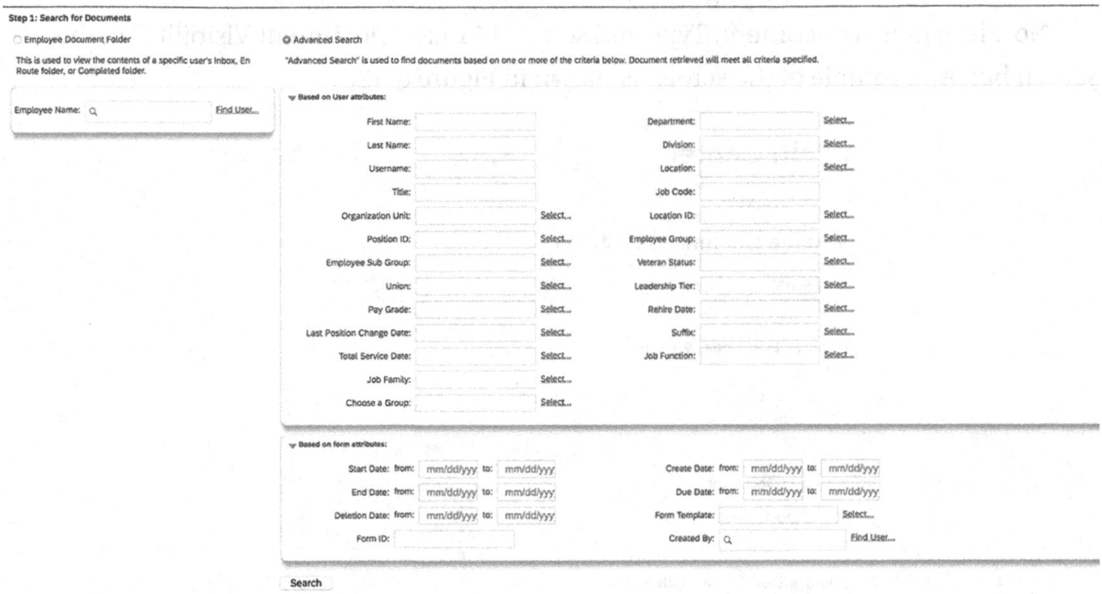

Figure 8-71. *Restore a Form*

Advanced search options are based on user attributes or form attributes. The forms that meet the search criteria will display, and you may select which forms to restore. The form is restored to the step it was deleted in.

Hide Document Visibility

It is possible to hide forms from a user. For example, a manager has copies of performance forms from 2016 to 2019 for their direct reports. The forms are in their Performance Completed folder. The manager moves into an individual contributor role and should no longer have access to these forms. We want these forms to no longer appear in this user's Performance Completed folder. This can be accomplished by hiding the document visibility from a user. This action will not delete the form, and other users that have copies of the form will not be impacted. This feature works for forms in a user's Performance En Route or Completed folder. It will not hide forms from a user's inbox.

The admin role will need permission to perform this action if not granted already. Type and select "Manage Permission Roles" in the search bar. Select the role to add the permission. Found within the *Administrator Permissions* section, look for "Manage Documents" and select "Manage Document Visibility." Save the role.

Now let's hide a document. Type and select "Manage Document Visibility" in the search bar. An example of the screen is shown in Figure 8-72.

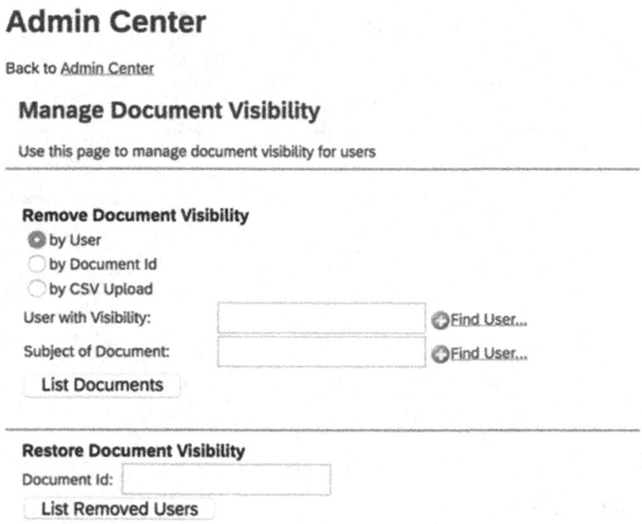

Admin Center

Back to Admin Center

Manage Document Visibility

Use this page to manage document visibility for users

Remove Document Visibility
- by User
- by Document Id
- by CSV Upload

User with Visibility: ⊕Find User...

Subject of Document: ⊕Find User...

List Documents

Restore Document Visibility

Document Id:

List Removed Users

Figure 8-72. *Manage Document Visibility*

To locate the specific form to hide, there are three options:

- by User

- Bb Document Id

- by CSV Upload

Based on the radio button selected, the required entries will vary. We will look at each option.

By User

- To hide one user's forms from another user

- To remove document visibility, the user with visibility and the subject of the document are needed. An example is shown in Figure 8-73.

Manage Document Visibility

Use this page to manage document visibility for users

Remove Document Visibility
- ⦿ by User
- ⦾ by Document Id
- ⦾ by CSV Upload

User with Visibility: ghill   ⊕Find User...

Subject of Document: jbaker   ⊕Find User...

List Documents

Documents
☐ 869 - 2012 Performance Review for Jada Baker
☐ 2012 - 2013 Performance Review for Jada Baker
☐ 2182 - 2014 Performance Review for Jada Baker
☐ 9908 - 2015 Annual Salary, Equity, & Incentive Plan Jada Baker (jbaker)
☐ 4653 - 2015 Performance Review for Jada Baker
☐ 9804 - 2015 Short Term Incentive Plan Jada Baker (jbaker)
☐ 12001 - 2016 Performance Review for Jada Baker
☐ 23490 - 2017 Performance Review for Jada Baker
☐ 30343 - 2018 Performance Review for Jada Baker
☐ 33435 - 2020 Sample Performance Review for Jada Baker
☐ 15402 - 90 Day Performance Review for Jada Baker
☐ 4705 - Performance Review Extended for Jada Baker
☐ 11910 - Performance Review Extended for Jada Baker
☐ 32779 - Talent Review for Jada Baker

Remove Visibility

Figure 8-73. *Remove Documents by User*

In the example, all of the forms for Jada Baker that manager George Hill has copies of are listed. The admin may select any or all forms to remove from George's visibility. Upon selection, click "Remove Visibility." A confirmation popup will display as seen in Figure 8-74.

Manage Document Visibility   ⑦

Are you sure you want to remove document visibility for Geoff Hill from document: 23490 - 2017 Performance Review for Jada Baker 30343 - 2018 Performance Review for Jada Baker ?

Cancel   OK

Figure 8-74. *Confirm Document Visibility*

By clicking "OK," the form name and the user that lost visibility display. An example is shown in Figure 8-75.

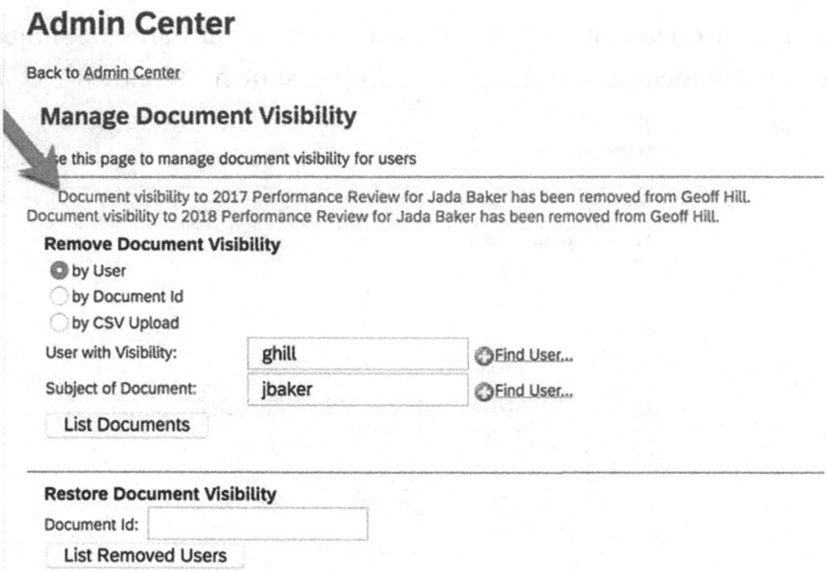

Admin Center

Back to Admin Center

Manage Document Visibility

~~se~~ this page to manage document visibility for users

Document visibility to 2017 Performance Review for Jada Baker has been removed from Geoff Hill.
Document visibility to 2018 Performance Review for Jada Baker has been removed from Geoff Hill.

Remove Document Visibility
- ● by User
- ○ by Document Id
- ○ by CSV Upload

User with Visibility: ghill   ⊕Find User...

Subject of Document: jbaker   ⊕Find User...

List Documents

Restore Document Visibility
Document Id: [   ]
List Removed Users

Figure 8-75. *Forms Have Been Hidden*

By Doc ID

Forms may be hidden based on the document id.

- To hide one user's forms from another user

- To remove document visibility, the document id and the user with the form visibility are needed. An example is shown in Figure 8-76.

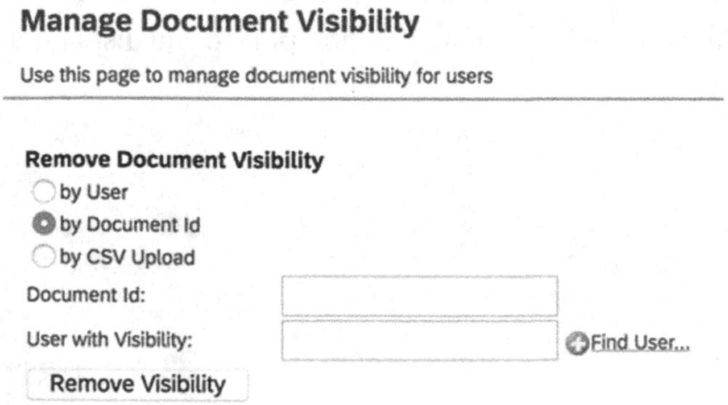

Manage Document Visibility

Use this page to manage document visibility for users

Remove Document Visibility
- ○ by User
- ● by Document Id
- ○ by CSV Upload

Document Id: [   ]

User with Visibility: [   ]   ⊕Find User...

Remove Visibility

Figure 8-76. *Remove Visibility by Doc ID*

This option works the same way as the removal of forms by user. Select the document id and the user with visibility. Once the search results display, select the form and remove visibility. When the confirmation popup displays, click "OK" to hide the document. The form will no longer be visible to the selected user.

By CSV Upload

A file upload may be used to remove document visibility in the following ways:

- To do a mass removal of form visibility.

- To hide multiple forms for multiple users.

- Two file templates are available: by role or by user ID.

Click the "by CSV Upload" button, and you will be able to download one of the file templates to use for the upload. An example is shown in Figure 8-77.

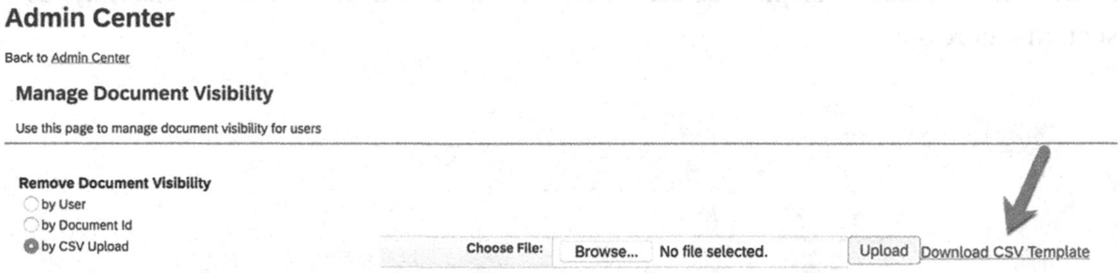

Admin Center

Back to Admin Center

Manage Document Visibility

Use this page to manage document visibility for users

Remove Document Visibility
- by User
- by Document Id
- by CSV Upload

Choose File: Browse... No file selected. Upload Download CSV Template

Figure 8-77. *Download Template for Document Removal Upload*

You may download the By Roles template or the "By User ID" template.

The "By Roles" template uses a form ID and user role. An example with entries is shown in Figure 8-78

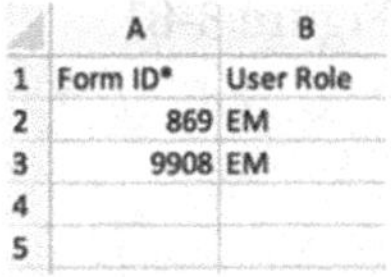

	A	B
1	Form ID*	User Role
2	869	EM
3	9908	EM
4		
5		

Figure 8-78. *"By Roles" Template*

The "By Roles" template uses the form ID and the role of the user in the route map. This is based on the role of the user in the route map of the form.

The "By User ID" template uses the form ID and the user ID. The user ID is for the employee that you wish to hide the form from.

The method for the two uploads is identical. We will do an upload by user ID.

An example of the "By User ID" template is shown in Figure 8-79.

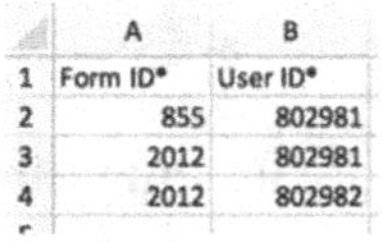

	A	B
1	Form ID*	User ID*
2	855	802981
3	2012	802981
4	2012	802982

Figure 8-79. *User ID File to Hide Form Visibility*

On the file, you may enter multiple form IDs with user IDs. You may opt to hide the same form from multiple users.

After saving the CSV file, choose the file and upload the file.

The screen will refresh. If there are no file issues, you will see "Success," and the list of forms from the file will display. Select the forms to hide and click "Remove Visibility" as seen in Figure 8-80.

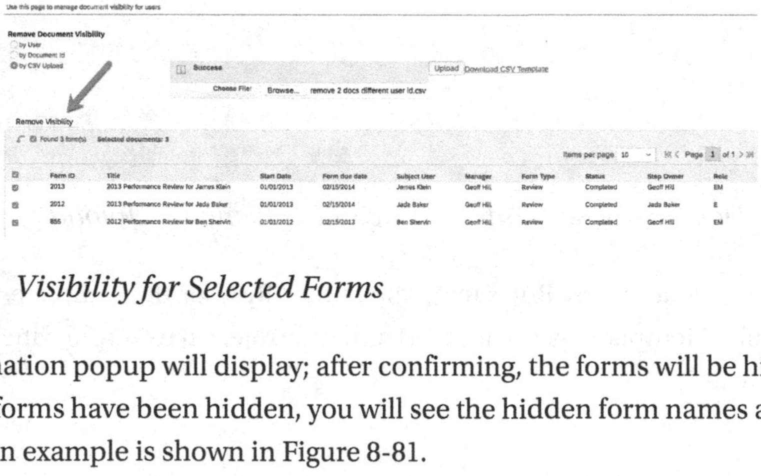

Figure 8-80. *Visibility for Selected Forms*

A confirmation popup will display; after confirming, the forms will be hidden.

After the forms have been hidden, you will see the hidden form names and usernames. An example is shown in Figure 8-81.

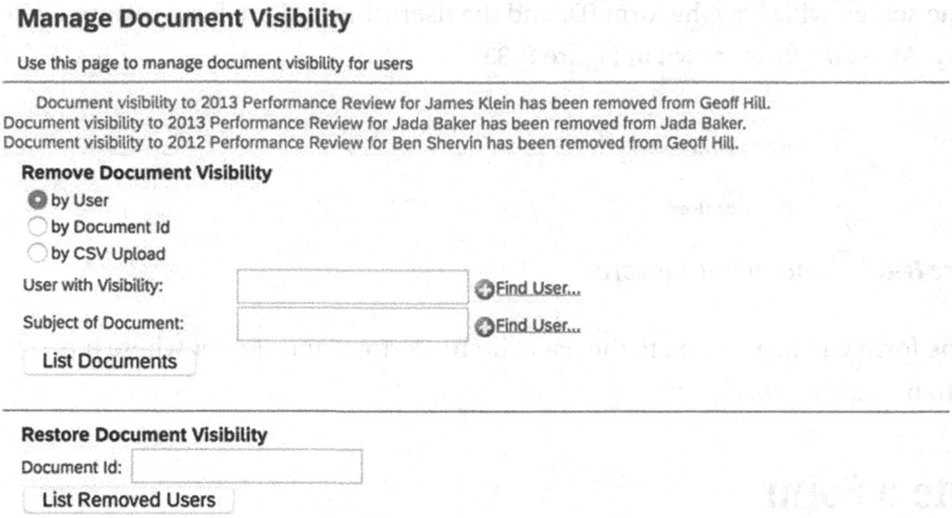

Manage Document Visibility

Use this page to manage document visibility for users

Document visibility to 2013 Performance Review for James Klein has been removed from Geoff Hill.
Document visibility to 2013 Performance Review for Jada Baker has been removed from Jada Baker.
Document visibility to 2012 Performance Review for Ben Shervin has been removed from Geoff Hill.

Remove Document Visibility

- by User
- by Document Id
- by CSV Upload

User with Visibility: _____ ⊕Find User...

Subject of Document: _____ ⊕Find User...

List Documents

Restore Document Visibility

Document Id: _____

List Removed Users

Figure 8-81. Forms Have Been Made Invisible

Keep in mind, if you remove document visibility for all users that have access to the form, the system deletes the document.

Now that we have seen how to hide forms, let's learn how to restore hidden forms.

Restore Document Visibility

It is possible to restore the visibility of any hidden document. This action is found at the bottom of the Manage Document Visibility screen. Documents may be restored one at a time by entering the document id. Click "List Removed Users," and all users that lost visibility of the document will display. An example is shown in Figure 8-82.

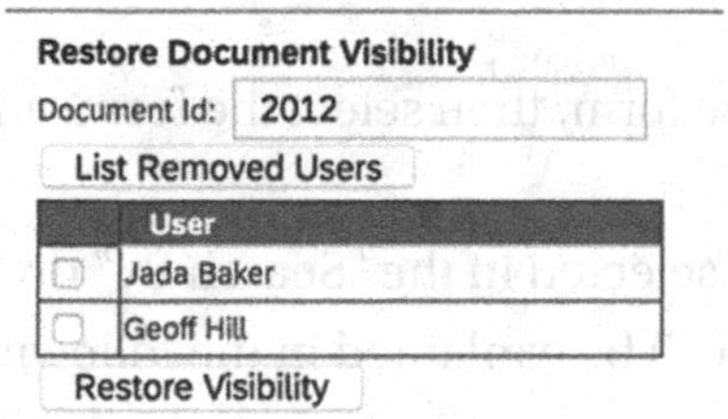

Restore Document Visibility

Document Id: 2012

List Removed Users

User
☐ Jada Baker
☐ Geoff Hill

Restore Visibility

Figure 8-82. Restore Document Visibility

Select the users, and a confirmation popup will display. After confirming, the form is restored.

The screen will show the form ID, and the users that had the form restored will display. An example is shown in Figure 8-83

Figure 8-83. Document Restored

The form will be restored to the users in the Performance folder where it had resided prior to being hidden.

Route a Form

As an admin, you may need to move forms to a prior step or move a form forward. This may be done for one form or several. There are a series of screens to walk through in order to route a form. Type and select "Route Document" in the search bar. Here we will start the process. An example of the screen is shown in Figure 8-84.

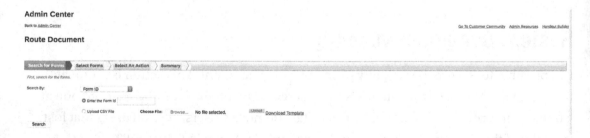

Figure 8-84. Route a Form

You will first search for the form, then select the form, and then decide how to route the form.

Based on the search type selected in the "Search By" dropdown listing, you will have different search options that will be explained in the following.

Search by Form ID

When selected, search options include entering the document number of one form or uploading a CSV file containing multiple form IDs. This method allows you to move forms for multiple users as well as a single form.

Search by Form Template

When selected, you can search through all of form templates including inactive ones. Once selected, you further define the search with user or form attributes. There are additional search options as seen in Figure 8-85.

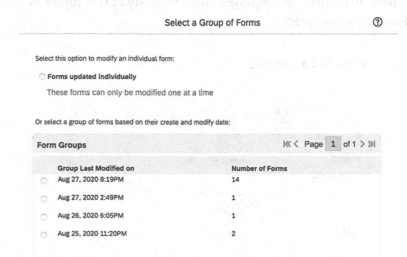

Figure 8-85. *Select a Group of Forms for a Specific Template*

This option is useful when you need to move a large group of forms that were launched at the same time. Maybe you decide to skip a mid-year step and move forms right to the year-end assessment. This method will take care of the move. Select the group of forms, and the forms will display by step as seen in Figure 8-86.

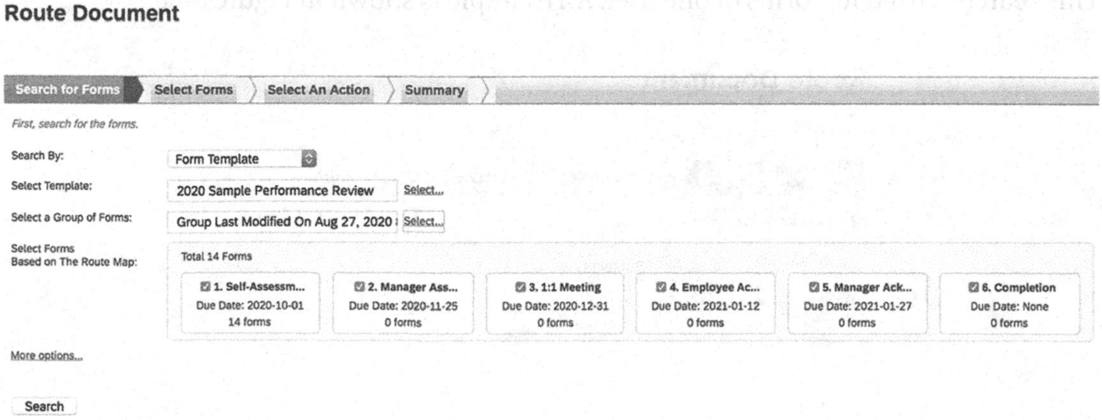

Route Document

Figure 8-86. *Select Forms by Step*

You may deselect forms from any step to just target on forms in a specific step or steps. Then, you will be able to select which forms in the selected step to move.

Search by Employee's Folder

This search is used to identify an employee and which My Forms folder to search in. An example is shown in Figure 8-87.

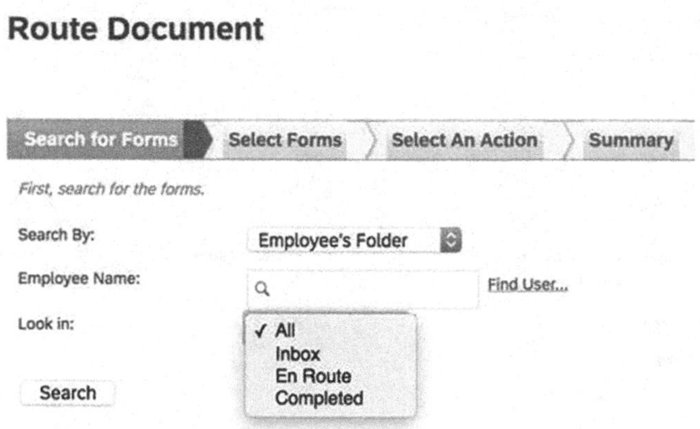

Route Document

Search for Forms	Select Forms	Select An Action	Summary

First, search for the forms.

Search By: Employee's Folder

Employee Name: 🔍   Find User...

Look in: ✓ All
                    Inbox
                    En Route
                    Completed

        Search

Figure 8-87. *Search by Employee's Folder*

This search is used for forms of one user.

Search by Subject User

The final search type is by username. You may also search by user or form attributes. This search is used for forms of one user. An example is shown in Figure 8-88.

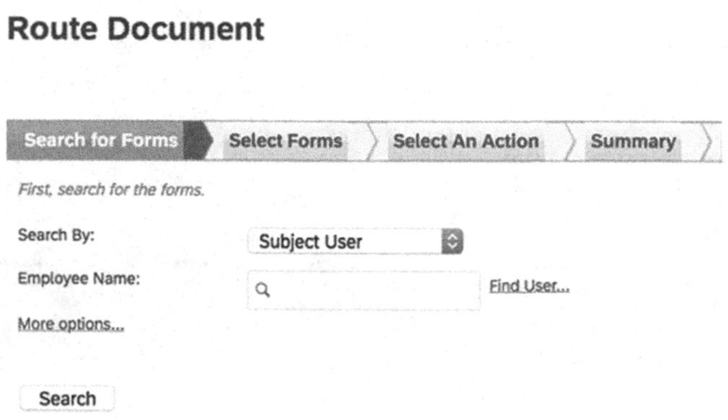

Route Document

Search for Forms	Select Forms	Select An Action	Summary

First, search for the forms.

Search By: Subject User

Employee Name: 🔍   Find User...

More options...

        Search

Figure 8-88. *Search by Subject*

410

This search is used to route forms for one user.

Once the forms have been selected, the routing option must be selected. An example is shown in Figure 8-89.

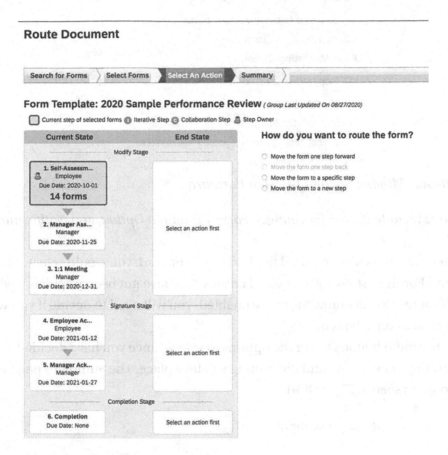

Figure 8-89. *Routing Options*

Based on the current step, you may move forms one step forward or one step backward, move to a specific step, or move to a new step. The radio button selected will provide different options.

An example of moving the forms forward one step is shown in Figure 8-90.

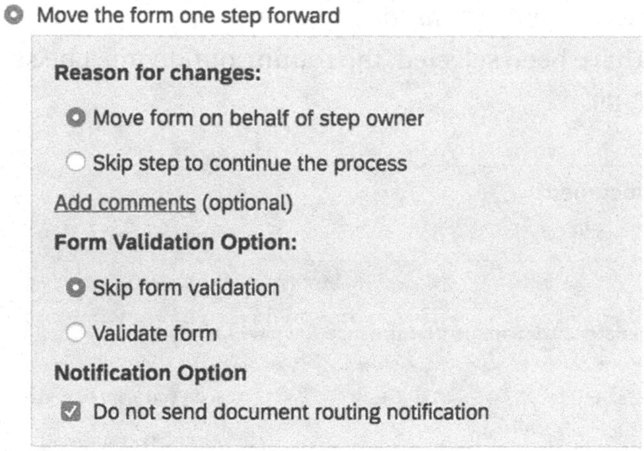

○ Move the form one step forward

Reason for changes:

◉ Move form on behalf of step owner

○ Skip step to continue the process

Add comments (optional)

Form Validation Option:

◉ Skip form validation

○ Validate form

Notification Option

☑ Do not send document routing notification

Figure 8-90. *Moving Forms One Step Forward*

Options include *Reason for changes*, *Form Validation Option*, and *Notification Option*.

If you want forms with required fields to move forward, you would select "Skip form validation." Forms in steps with required entries that have not been populated will be routed. If routing email notifications are enabled, you will need to decide if you want the routing notification to be sent.

Click the radio buttons to see the options to select. Once you have decided on the routing option, click "Next," and the routing will take place. The Summary page will show the outcome as seen in Figure 8-91.

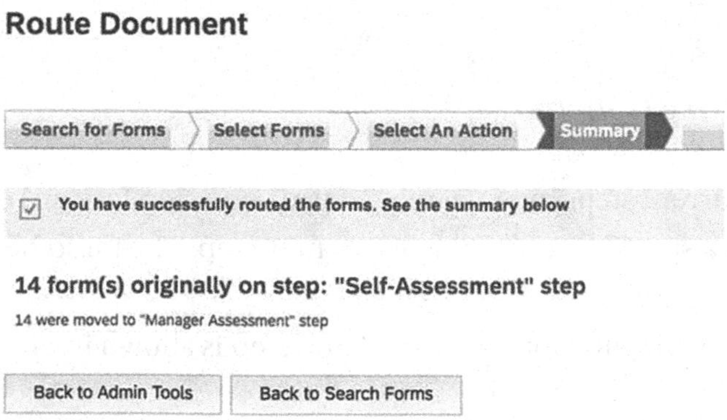

Route Document

Search for Forms ⟩ Select Forms ⟩ Select An Action ⟩ **Summary**

☑ You have successfully routed the forms. See the summary below

14 form(s) originally on step: "Self-Assessment" step

14 were moved to "Manager Assessment" step

| Back to Admin Tools | Back to Search Forms |

Figure 8-91. *Form Routing Confirmation*

You have now successfully moved performance forms.

Modify a Route Map

We have seen how to route forms to another step. Now we will see how to change the route map for launched forms.

Let's say you are in the midst of the performance review cycle and you are using step due dates in your route map. A decision has been made to extend the period for entering ratings. This would require a change to a step due date for the launched forms. Rather than deleting forms and starting over, it is possible to change the step due date for any steps on the route map.

The four options for route map modification are:

1. Modify common options.

   Change text for route map labels; change step dates.

2. Change step types and permissions.

   For a specific step, change its type and permissions.

3. Add a step.

   Add a step to the route map for selected forms.

4. Remove a step.

   Remove a step from the route map for selected forms.

To begin, type and select "Modify Form Route Map" in the search bar. An example of the screen is displayed in Figure 8-92.

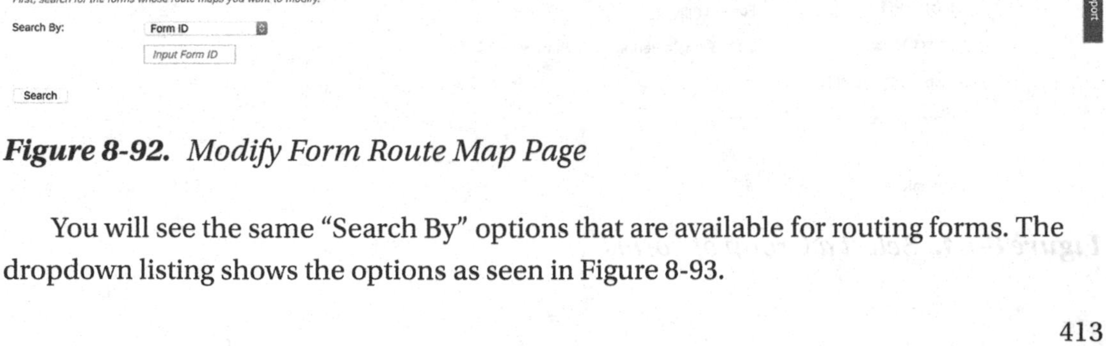

Admin Center

Back to Admin Center

Modify Form Route Map

Warning: If using PM v12 Acceleration and the Out of Turn Access feature together, routing forms to steps out of sequence can delete the draft ratings and comments entered (form must be in the inbox of the out of turn user to be recorded). It is recommended to only route forms one step at a time when Out of Turn Access applies to a step. For additional information, please contact Customer Success as needed.

| Search for Forms | Select Forms | Select An Action | Modify Form Route Map | Summary |

First, search for the forms whose route maps you want to modify.

Search By: Form ID

            Input Form ID

Search

Figure 8-92. *Modify Form Route Map Page*

You will see the same "Search By" options that are available for routing forms. The dropdown listing shows the options as seen in Figure 8-93.

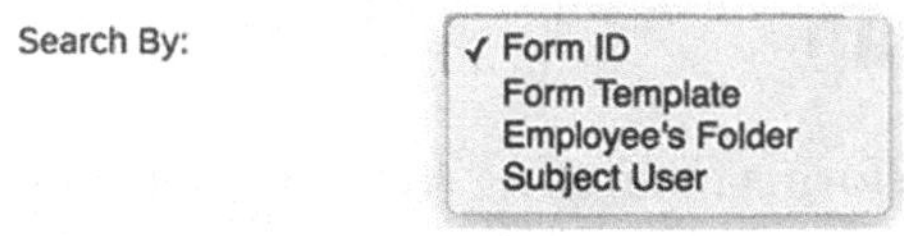

Search By:

✓ Form ID
Form Template
Employee's Folder
Subject User

Figure 8-93. *Search Options*

Dependent on the search type, there are different search criteria:

- *Form ID:* Select the form ID.

- *Form Template:* Select the template, and you may also add a search by user and template attributes.

- *Employee's Folder:* Select the employee's name and folder (*All, Inbox, En route, or Completed*).

- *Subject User:* Select the employee's name, and you may also add a search by user and template attributes.

Based on the search, you may select one form or multiple forms. For our example, we are going to modify a step due date for a group of forms. We will search by template name.

Changing route map step dates is the most common use for this tool. We go into detail on this type of change and briefly touch upon the other options.

Change Step Due Date

Select the template and select the group of forms for that template as seen in Figure 8-94.

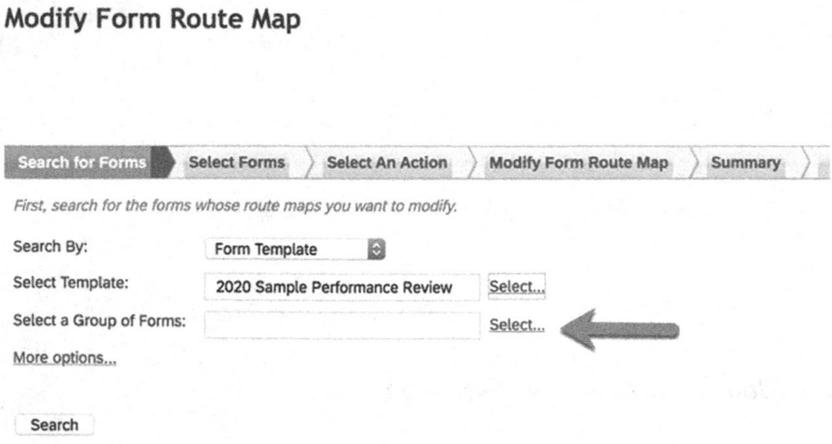

Modify Form Route Map

| Search for Forms | Select Forms | Select An Action | Modify Form Route Map | Summary |

First, search for the forms whose route maps you want to modify.

Search By: Form Template
Select Template: 2020 Sample Performance Review   Select...
Select a Group of Forms: Select...
More options...

Search

Figure 8-94. *Select a Group of Forms*

Click "Select" to view the groups of launched forms for the selected template as shown in Figure 8-95. Groups are forms that were created during a single launch.

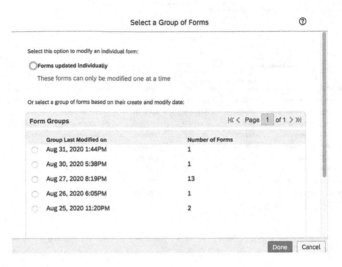

Figure 8-95. *Select Forms*

After selecting a group, click "Done," the popup will close, and the group will be populated as seen in Figure 8-96. Click "Search."

Admin Center

Back to Admin Center

Modify Form Route Map

Warning: If using PM v12 Acceleration and the Out of Turn Access feature together, routing forms to steps out of sequence can delete the draft ratings and comments entered (form must be in the inbox of the out of turn user to be recorded). It is recommended to only route forms one step at a time when Out of Turn Access applies to a step. For additional information, please contact Customer Success as needed.

Search for Forms	Select Forms	Select An Action	Modify Form Route Map	Summary

First, search for the forms whose route maps you want to modify.

Search By: Form Template

Select Template: 2020 Sample Performance Review   Select...

Select a Group of Forms: Group Last Modified On Aug 31, 2020   Select...

Select Forms
Based on The Route Map: Total 13 Forms

☑ 1. Self-Assessm...	☑ 2. Manager Ass...	☑ 3. 1:1 Meeting	☑ 4. Employee Ac...	☑ 5. Manager Ack...	☑ 6. Completion
Due Date: 2020-10-01	Due Date: 2020-11-30	Due Date: 2020-12-31	Due Date: 2021-01-12	Due Date: 2021-01-27	Due Date: None
0 forms	13 forms	0 forms	0 forms	0 forms	0 forms

More options...

Search ⬅

Figure 8-96. *Search for Forms*

Select all forms and click "Next" as seen in Figure 8-97. This will change the step due date for all forms in this group.

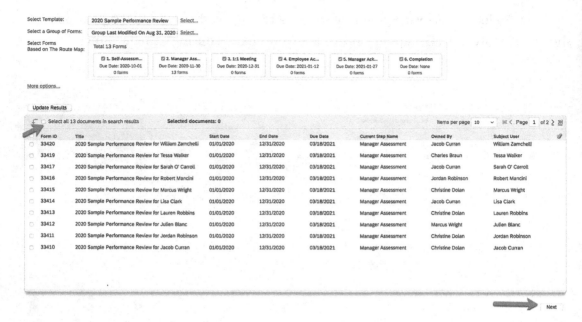

Figure 8-97. *Select All Forms*

Upon selection, the options are shown in Figure 8-98. Select "Modify common options" and click "Next." This will enable us to change a step due date.

Figure 8-98. *Select an Action*

The route map associated with the selected form template will display as seen in Figure 8-99.

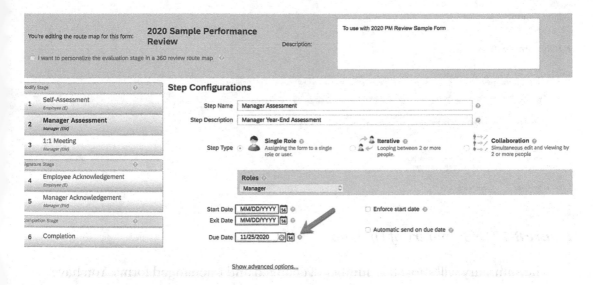

Figure 8-99. *Update the Route Map*

Here, we will change the step due date as seen in Figure 8-100.

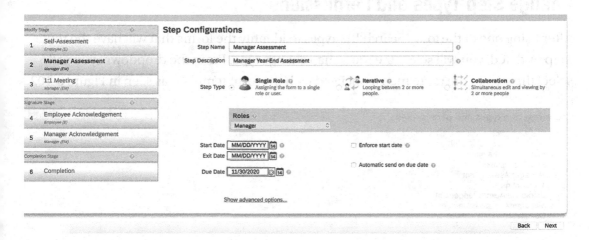

Figure 8-100. *Updating Step Due Date*

Click "Next," and the summary screen will display as seen in Figure 8-101.

Admin Center

Back to Admin Center

Modify Form Route Map

Warning: If using PM v12 Acceleration and the Out of Turn Access feature together, routing forms to steps out of sequence can delete the draft ratings and comments entered (form must be in the Inbox of the out of turn user to be recorded). It is recommended to only route forms one step at a time when Out of Turn Access applies to a step. For additional information, please contact Customer Success as needed.

| Search for Forms | Select Forms | Select An Action | Modify Form Route Map | **Summary** |

☑ You have successfully modified options for the forms. See the summary below:

Number of Changed Forms: 13
Number of Unchanged Forms:0
Form Template: 2020 Sample Performance Review
Route Map: 2020 Sample PM Route Map

| Back to Admin Tools | Back to Search Forms |

Figure 8-101. *Summary of Updates*

The summary will show the number of changed and unchanged forms. You have successfully updated the step due date on a group of launched forms.

We will briefly look at the other three options.

Change Step Types and Permissions

After using one of the four "Search By" types to identify the forms that will have the route map updated, you will select the route map change type. From the dropdown, you will select the step in the route map associated with the form template as seen in Figure 8-102.

Figure 8-102. *Select a Step*

Once selected, the screen will show the number of forms that will be modified. An example is shown in Figure 8-103. Please note that the changes are applicable only to forms not yet in the selected step.

Back to Admin Center

Modify Form Route Map

Warning: If using PM v12 Acceleration and the Out of Turn Access feature together, routing forms to steps out of sequence can delete the draft ratings and comments entered (form must be in the inbox of the out of turn user to be recorded). It is recommended to only route forms one step at a time when Out of Turn Access applies to a step. For additional information, please contact Customer Success as needed.

Search for Forms 〉 Select Forms 〉 Select An Action 〉 Modify Form Route Map 〉 Summary 〉

Select an action you want to do for the route map:

○ **Modify common options**

Common values include step name, step name after completion, step introduction, exit button text, step exit text, step date, due date, exit date and auto route options.

◉ **Change step types and permissions**

You can change the step type and associated permission for a specific step. These changes will only be applied to documents that have not reached the selected step.

| Manager Assessment   ∨ | 1 forms will be modified.

○ **Add a step**

Add a new modification, evaluation or signature step.

○ **Remove a step**

Remove a modification, evaluation or signature step. The step will only be removed for documents that have not reached the selected step.

Back   Next

Figure 8-103. Forms to Be Updated

After clicking "Next," the route map will display, and the step to update will be highlighted. You will be able to make your changes to the route map as seen in Figure 8-104. Click "Next" when finished.

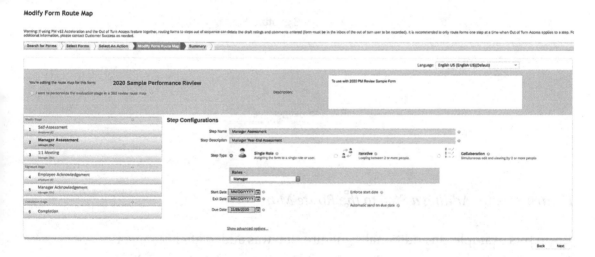

Figure 8-104. Update the Route Map Step

A summary screen will display with the number of changed and unchanged forms.

Add a Step

After selecting the forms to update, in the "Select An Action" step of the wizard, you will select "Add a step." The route map opens, and you may add a step as seen in Figure 8-105.

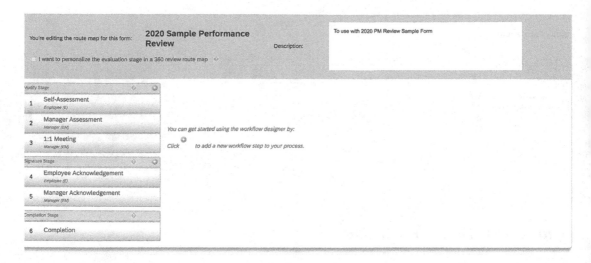

Figure 8-105. *Route Map to Add a Step*

A popup will display where you will name the step as seen in Figure 8-106.

Figure 8-106. *Adding a Step to the Route Map*

In this example, an additional signature step was added after Manager Acknowledgement. As seen in Figure 8-107, the summary of changes displays.

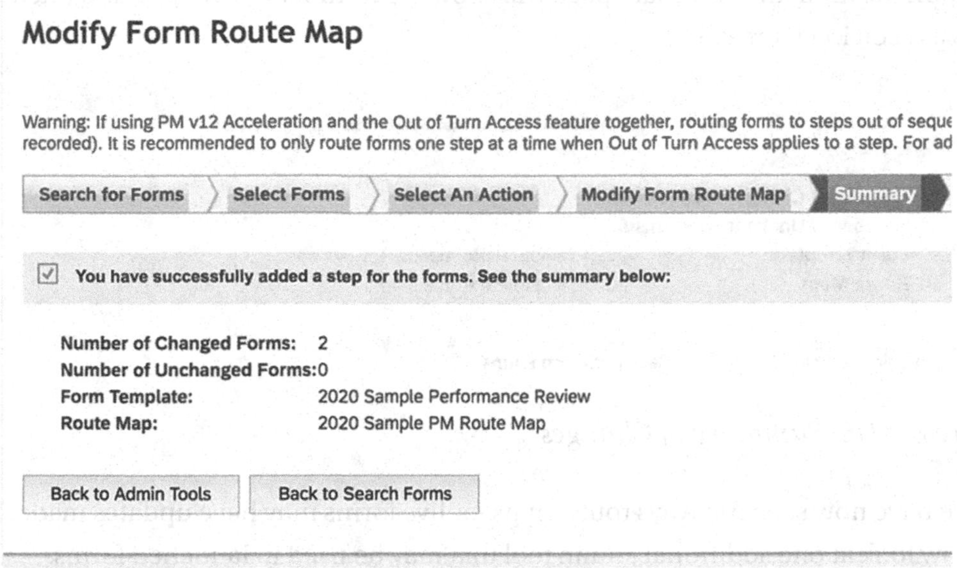

Modify Form Route Map

Warning: If using PM v12 Acceleration and the Out of Turn Access feature together, routing forms to steps out of seque
recorded). It is recommended to only route forms one step at a time when Out of Turn Access applies to a step. For ad

> Search for Forms > Select Forms > Select An Action > Modify Form Route Map > **Summary**

☑ **You have successfully added a step for the forms. See the summary below:**

Number of Changed Forms: 2
Number of Unchanged Forms: 0
Form Template: 2020 Sample Performance Review
Route Map: 2020 Sample PM Route Map

[Back to Admin Tools]   [Back to Search Forms]

Figure 8-107. *Summary of Changes*

You have now added a step to the route map for the selected forms.

Remove a Step

The final option for updating a route map for live forms is to delete a step.

After searching and finding the forms to modify, select "Remove a step" as seen in Figure 8-108.

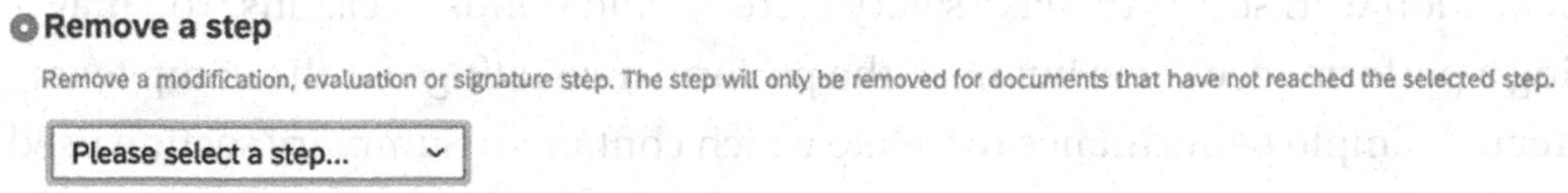

◉ **Remove a step**
Remove a modification, evaluation or signature step. The step will only be removed for documents that have not reached the selected step.

[Please select a step... ⌄]

Figure 8-108. *Select Route Map Change Type*

From the dropdown, you will select the step to remove. After selecting the step, the number of forms that will be modified displays as seen in Figure 8-109.

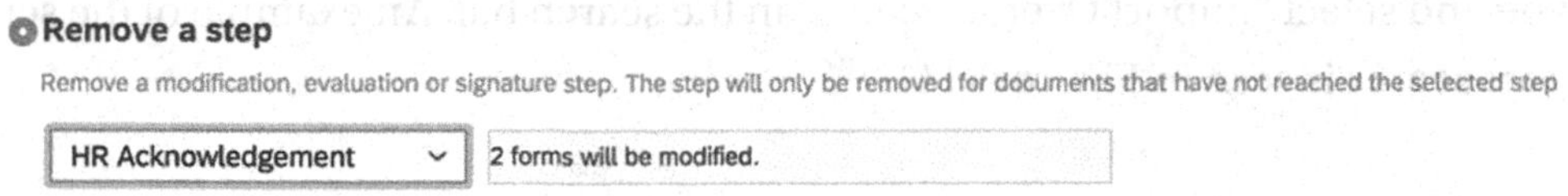

◉ **Remove a step**
Remove a modification, evaluation or signature step. The step will only be removed for documents that have not reached the selected step

[HR Acknowledgement ⌄] [2 forms will be modified.]

Figure 8-109. *Forms to Be Modified*

Upon deletion, the Summary page will show the number of changed and unchanged forms as seen in Figure 8-110.

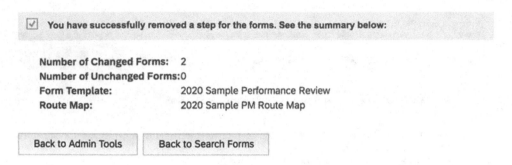

Figure 8-110. *Summary of Changes*

We have now seen the ways route maps for live forms may have updates made. We will now look at one additional admin tool that may be used in launched forms.

Import Overall Scores

There are situations where you may need to load overall performance ratings into performance forms. For example, you have already started the review process in your old legacy system and are converting to the SAP SuccessFactors Performance Management module. Some employees have been rated, and you are looking to load these ratings into a new SAP SuccessFactors performance form. Another example involves the SAP SuccessFactors Compensation module. Ratings from performance forms are loaded into compensation worksheets to make salary increase and bonus decisions. You may not be running a performance cycle but need the performance ratings for the comp team. You can create a simple performance template which contains a Summary section used to enter a manual overall rating. The import file could load the ratings into these forms, and then the Compensation module can use the ratings in the worksheets.

The admin role needs permission to import scores. The role-based permission to import scores can be added to the admin role's permissions. Found under Administrator Permissions, the access is granted through Manage Documents ➤ Import Overall Scores.

Type and select "Import Overall Scores" in the search bar. An example of the screen to import scores is seen in Figure 8-111.

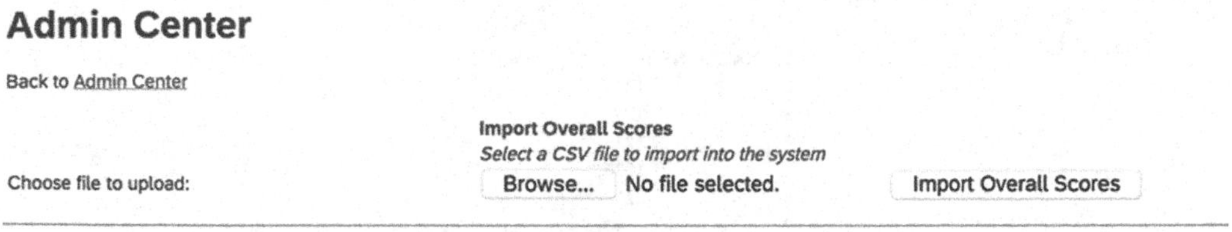

Admin Center

Back to Admin Center

Import Overall Scores
Select a CSV file to import into the system

Choose file to upload: Browse... No file selected.   Import Overall Scores

---

Figure 8-111. *Import Overall Scores*

A very simple import file is used. Here are some things to keep in mind:

- It should be a CSV file.

- The file must contain a header record.

- The first column heading must be "DOCUMENT_ID." This is the unique identifier of a user's performance form. You may easily find this number by looking at the "info" icon on an individual form. However, to do a mass upload of scores, you may run an ad hoc query to get the document ids for a specific template.

- The performance template must contain a Summary section with a manual overall rating field.

- Use the same rating scale in the ratings load as what is used in the template.

- Ratings may contain decimals.

Manual overall performance rating scores may be imported for the Performance, Performance Potential, and Objective Competency Summary sections.

Prior to importing the ratings, all of the forms that will have ratings loaded will need to be moved to the step where the manual rating would be entered. Refer back to the Route a Form section earlier in this chapter.

The column headings for the manual overall rating scores are:

- PERFORMANCE

- POTENTIAL

- COMPETENCY

- OBJECTIVE

A sample file is shown in Figure 8-112.

	A	B
1	DOCUMENT_ID	PERFORMANCE
2	1234	2
3	1235	3
4	1235	4
5	1236	3
6	1237	3
7	1238	3
8	1239	2
9	1240	1
10		

Figure 8-112. *Sample Import Performance Ratings File*

In the example, performance ratings are being loaded for the document ids listed. The numeric rating is used.

Only include columns for the rating types being loaded. After the import, a system email will be generated with the import results. An example is shown in Figure 8-113.

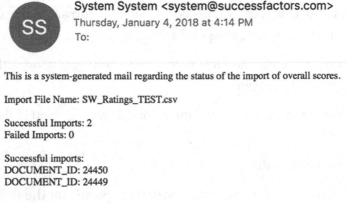

Figure 8-113. *Sample Import Email*

Once a successful load is completed, go into any of the forms listed in the file, and you will see the overall rating in the Summary section.

Conclusion

We have taken what we have learned in the basic principles for Performance Management and put them into practice. We have set up email notifications, identified the role-based permissions needed for the user roles, configured step dates in our route map, and set up some background jobs. We wrapped up with some simple administrative actions that the PM admin may have to do during the review process.

We have gained a better understanding of how configuration decisions, permissions, and enabled features impact how the form works. In the next chapter, we will walk through the performance review form from a user's perspective.

CHAPTER 9

Using Performance Management Forms

In the previous three chapters, we configured Performance Management, granted role-based permissions, and created a rating scale, route map, and performance form template. We have learned about the sections of a form template and have seen the types of tasks a PM admin can perform. Finally, we launched a performance form. In this chapter, we will walk through the performance review process from a user's perspective.

Performance Form Walk-Through

After the form launch, if the "Document Creation" email notification is enabled, the user in the first step of the review process will be notified that the performance form is in their Performance Inbox.

A sample notification is shown in Figure 9-1.

Figure 9-1. *Email Notification for a Form in the Inbox*

© Susan Traynor, Michael A. Wellens and Venki Krishnamoorthy 2021
S. Traynor et al., *SAP SuccessFactors Talent: Volume 1*, https://doi.org/10.1007/978-1-4842-6600-7_9

The user may click the link in the email to access the form or go to the SuccessFactors home page. In the To-Do panel on the home page, there will be a Performance tile that will display when a user has a performance-related action to take. An example is shown in Figure 9-2.

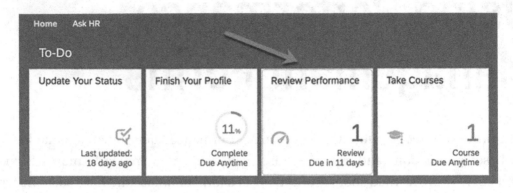

Figure 9-2. *Performance To-Do Tile*

The tile will show a count of items pending and the due date for the item. If there is more than one action pending, the number of days until the first item is due will display. Clicking the Performance To-Do tile will display a popup of pending To-Do Performance items as seen in Figure 9-3. In the case of a manager, the list may be quite long when the forms reach the manager review step.

Figure 9-3. *Performance To-Do Item*

Notice that the route map step description is shown followed by the name of the employee being evaluated. If this step of the form has a due date, the number of days until it is due will display as well. Clicking the link will open the form.

The other way to access the performance form is through the Home menu which we will discuss next.

Performance Inbox

As we have seen, the user may access the form through the notification email or through the Performance To-Do tile on the home page. The Performance Inbox may also be accessed through the Home menu. Click the Home dropdown arrow and select "Performance" as shown in Figure 9-4.

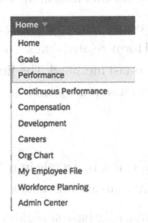

Figure 9-4. Access to Performance Through the Home Menu

Clicking the link will take the user to My Forms, the performance inbox as seen in Figure 9-5.

Figure 9-5. Performance My Forms

On the left side of the screen, the My Forms folders are listed: *All Forms*, *In Progress*, and *Completed*. Each folder will have different display options. The display options cannot be reordered or deleted. However, the user may hide a column by deselecting it. We will look at each folder.

In Progress

Forms will be in the user's Inbox or En Route folder.

- Forms that are currently in the user's step will appear in the Inbox. These forms require action.

- En Route forms are with another user in the route map.

The overview of forms in the user's Inbox shows the name of the employee the form is for, the current step name, and form-related dates. You can also see whom the form came from and when the form was last modified. The En Route folder is helpful to see who currently has the form and what step the form is in.

Completed

Any completed documents that the user had a role in will display here. In addition, if configured, a completed form sent from another user would appear here as well:

- This is the only folder that may have subfolders added.

- Expanding this folder, you will see "Create New Folder" and "Un-filed."

- Completed forms reside in the "Un-filed" folder until the user moves them to a created and named Completed folder.

For any of the categories, there is an Action column. As long as the "Disable Info" button is not checked in the form template advanced settings, the user will see an information icon in the Action column. Clicking the icon will open a view of the form that is shown in Figure 9-6.

Figure 9-6. *Informational View of the Performance Form*

This view contains the form properties along with the approval chain. Based on the route map, the steps are displayed along with the user for each step and the form status. There is also an audit trail that shows any comments made when moving the form to the next step.

You may click the "Close" button in the Properties section or click the "Back to:" link at the top of this page to close this view.

For more information on these settings and how to limit the access to this, see SAP note #2075925.

Using the link from the email, the link from the item in the Performance To-Do tile, or the link from the Performance *My Forms* Inbox will open the performance form.

View of the Performance Form

We will take a look at some of the features seen on the form. An example is shown in Figure 9-7.

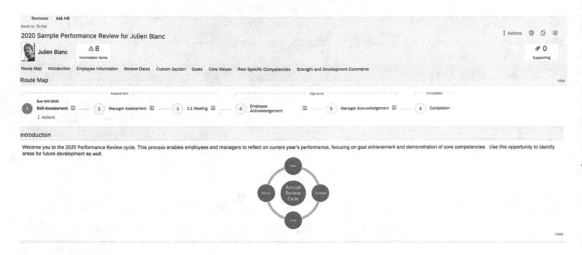

Figure 9-7. *View of the Performance Form*

We will see the performance form title across the top of the form and some form actions.

Above the form title, there is also a link back to the Performance Inbox.

On the top-right side of the form, there are a series of icons that may differ based on the settings in the form template. An example is shown in Figure 9-8. The Actions options may include Spell Check and Legal Scan for the entire form, a link to see the form's properties, and a link to add to Outlook.

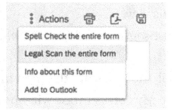

Figure 9-8. *Form Options*

An Outlook meeting request is created with a form link and form due date. The user can send themself the meeting request in order to get a calendar reminder.

To learn how to set this up, see SAP note #2089432.

There may be icons for print, save as PDF, and save.

The form template sections are listed across the top of the form as seen in Figure 9-9.

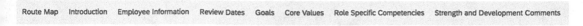

Figure 9-9. *Links to Sections of the Form*

Clicking one of the sections will move the user to that section of the form.

Route Map on the Form

Next, we will look at the route map that displays at the top of the form. A sample is shown in Figure 9-10.

Figure 9-10. *Route Map on the Form*

The route map associated with the form template displays across the top of the performance form. The steps are shown in the Assessment, Signature, and Completed stages of the route map. The current step number is highlighted. If the step has a due date set in the route map, it will appear above the current step name. You will not see the due dates for other steps, just for the current step.

An information icon displays to the right of each step name. Clicking the icon will display the route map step due date, the name of the user and their role, and the step description. An example is shown in Figure 9-11.

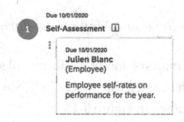

Figure 9-11. *Step Name Information*

You may click any of the step information icons to see this information. Here is where you can see future step due dates.

For the current step, you will also see "Actions" underneath the step name as seen in Figure 9-12.

Figure 9-12. *Actions for a Route Step*

Clicking "Actions," you will see all of the actions available for the step. The actions that display are the button names that move the form for the step. If you go to the bottom of the form, you will see that the button name is the same as the action in the current step. An example is shown in Figure 9-13.

Figure 9-13. *Buttons on the Bottom of the Form*

Buttons that do not move the form will not display under "Actions." This means "Cancel" and "Save and Close" will not be listed under the "Actions" option in the route map step.

In "Company Settings" in Provisioning, the "Enable Collapsible Route Map" option allows the route map to be collapsed. Click "Hide" in the Route Map section of the form as shown in Figure 9-14. This frees up some space if the user needs to scroll down through many sections of the form.

Figure 9-14. *Option to Hide the Route Map on the Form*

When collapsed, the route map section of the form will show the name of the user that the form is with along with the step due date. Click "Show" to have the route map on display again. An example is shown in Figure 9-15.

Figure 9-15. *Collapsed Route Map*

Pods on the Form

The pods that display across the top of the form are based on the permissions set in the form template. Pod permission is based on role and route step.

In our example, there are two pods visible for the employee assessment step – Incomplete Items and Supporting Information – as seen in Figure 9-16.

Figure 9-16. *Pods on the Performance From*

The placement of the pods cannot be changed; each pod has a set location on the form.

Required Fields

In our example, the Incomplete Items pod is enabled, and the form has required entries. This pod shows the number of items that need to be filled in before the form may move to the next step. If you click the pod, the list of incomplete items will display as seen in Figure 9-17.

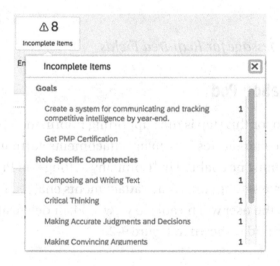

Figure 9-17. *Incomplete Items*

Click any of the listed items in the pod to go directly to the required entry on the form. Required entries are marked with a red asterisk. An example is shown in Figure 9-18.

Figure 9-18. *Required Rating*

If the pod is enabled but the step has no required entries, the count in the pod will be zero.

If you save the form while you are entering required fields, the number of incomplete items will be reduced.

If the required fields are not entered, when submitting the form to the next step, an error message will display and the form will not move until all the required fields have been entered. A popup will display as seen in Figure 9-19.

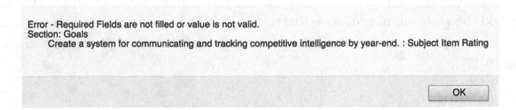

Figure 9-19. *Error Message for Required Fields*

Supporting Information Pod

The other pod enabled for this step is the Supporting Information pod. The number next to the paperclip icon indicates how many attachments currently exist for the form. Attachment Manager must be enabled in "Company Settings" in Provisioning, and the advanced form template settings must have attachments enabled for this to work.

Click the pod; and the user will be able to view, add, or delete attachments based on their permissions. The pod is shown in Figure 9-20.

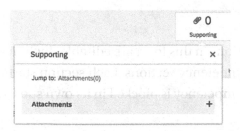

Figure 9-20. *Add Attachments in the Supporting Information Pod*

File types that may be attached are bmp, doc, docm, docx, gif, htm, html, jpg, jpeg, msg, pdf, png, ppt, pptx, rtf, tif, txt, xls, and xlsx.

Typically, the user that added the attachment is the only user that may delete the attachment. Most often, any user in the route map may view the attachments added by others from prior steps. However, the form template XML controls the attachment permissions. You will know more about how to configure this in Chapter 10.

View-Only Sections

In the form template that we configured, we used several read-only sections: Introduction, Employee Information, and Review Dates. These are informational in nature. An example of these sections is shown in Figure 9-21.

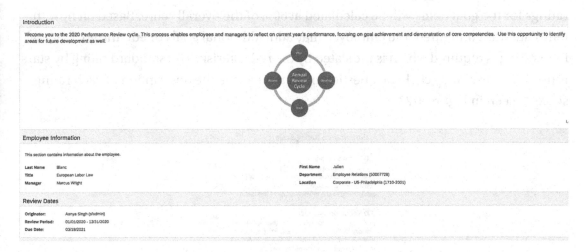

Figure 9-21. *View-Only Sections of the Performance Form*

Editable Sections

The remainder of the sections in this form are editable. Included is a custom section, a goals section, and two competency sections. Each section starts with a description, and each individual goal or competency is blocked in its own subsection. We will look briefly at each section.

Goals Section

A sample of a Goals section is shown in Figure 9-22.

Goals (60.0%)			+ Add Goal
This section is for evaluating accomplishments of goals.			
The weights for the goals in this section must add up to 100, and there must be a rating for each goal before the form is sent for signatures.			Less
Goals			
Create a system for communicating and tracking competitive intelligence by year-end. 🖉			Completed
CI tracking system created			
* Rating ⑦			
⊘ ☆ ☆ ☆ ☆ ☆ Select a rating...			
Goal Details Other Details			
Goal Name	Create a system for communicating and tracking competitive intelligence by year-end.	**Metric** CI tracking system created	

Figure 9-22. *Goals Section*

The section name shows the percentage of the overall score. In this example, the ratings for the goal items will be calculated at 60% of the overall score. Based on how the template was configured, the employee may add additional goals or edit the goal. A goal item rating is required which is indicated by the red asterisk. The standard rating by stars is used. The user may click the question mark icon to see the description of each rating score as seen in Figure 9-23.

Performance Rating Scale   ☒

1.0 Unsatisfactory:
Performance must improve significantly within a reasonable period of time if the individual is to remain in this position. Employee is not performing to the requirements of the job.

2.0 Needs Development:
Performance is noticeably less than expected. Usually performs to and meets job requirements, however the need for further development and improvement is clearly recognized.

3.0 Meets Expectations:
Performance clearly and fully meets all the requirements of the position in terms of quality and quantity of work. It is described as good.

Figure 9-23. *Description of Ratings*

There are no goal item comments in our example, but there is an overall goal section comment as seen in Figure 9-24.

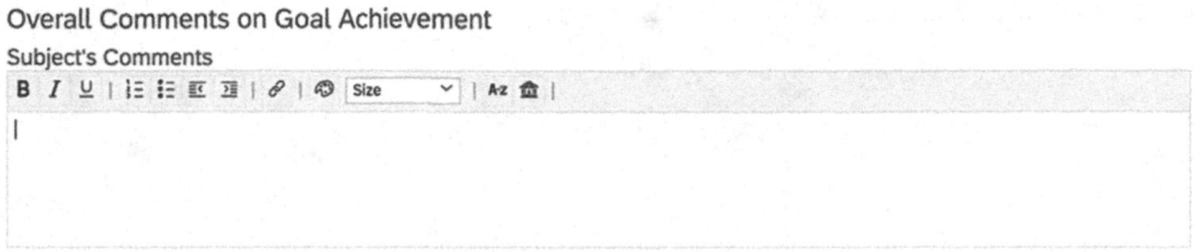

Figure 9-24. *Goal Section Comment*

Rather than having the user comment on each goal which may become cumbersome if there are a large number of goals, an overall section comment has been configured. This enables the user to highlight key points about goal achievement in one spot. In our example, the overall comment is optional.

Competency Sections

In Chapter 7, when we reviewed the form template settings, we learned that there can be multiple competency sections: core, job specific, and custom. Each section can be assigned a different weighting, and not all competency sections need to be included in the overall form rating calculation. For illustration purposes, we will assume we have two competency sections: core and job specific. Both sections will have comments on each competency but no overall section comments.

Writing Assistant

If you are using competencies with item comments and have enabled Writing Assistant, the "Writing Assistant" button will appear above each competency item comment box as shown in Figure 9-25.

Core Values (15.0%)

This section is for evaluating the accomplishments of the Core Competencies.

Each competency should have a rating and comments before moving on to the next section.

Less

Accepting Responsibility

Takes accountability for delivering on commitments; owns mistakes and uses them as opportunities for learning and development; openly discusses his/her actions and their consequences both good and bad

Rating ⓘ
◎ ☆ ☆ ☆ ☆ ☆ Select a rating...

Subject's Comments   Writing Assistant

B I U | ≔ ≔ ≝ ≊ | ✐ | ⟲ Size   ∨ | At 🖼 |

Figure 9-25. *Writing Assistant on Competency Comments*

Clicking the "Writing Assistant" button will cause a popup to display. Suggested comments specific to the competency are listed. These may be used as a starting point when adding comments to a competency or used as is. An example is shown in Figure 9-26.

Find a quote about Julien's competency   ⓘ

Reading Effectively

Accurately interprets written information associated with his/her job; able to follow logic and arguments contained in written materials; able to process large amounts of written information in a relatively short amount of time

Select topics below

Improve	Meets	Exceeds
▪ cannot articulate and synthesize written documents	▪ able to follow logic and arguments contained in written materials	▪ able to read quickly and articulate what was read to others
▪ does not retain written information	▪ able to interpret documents that are lengthy, confusing or use highly technical language	▪ able to synthesize large amounts of written material
▪ misinterprets written materials		▪ accurately interprets complex
▪ reads slowly		

Describe Behavior   Give Advice

Select a Narrative:

◉ I ◯ Julien

Preview Quote Below

Close   Place Quote

Figure 9-26. *Composing Comments for a Competency*

These *teaser* phrases are attached to competencies in the standard competency library. If you are using a custom library, they may be added. The phrases are grouped in varying degrees like *Improve, Meets*, or *Exceeds*. The user chooses first ("I") or third person (employee name) for the voice of how the comment will appear. Click a phrase, and then click "Place Quote." Do this for each quote to add; click "Close" when done.

The comments will then appear in the competency item comments as seen in Figure 9-27. These comments may be edited.

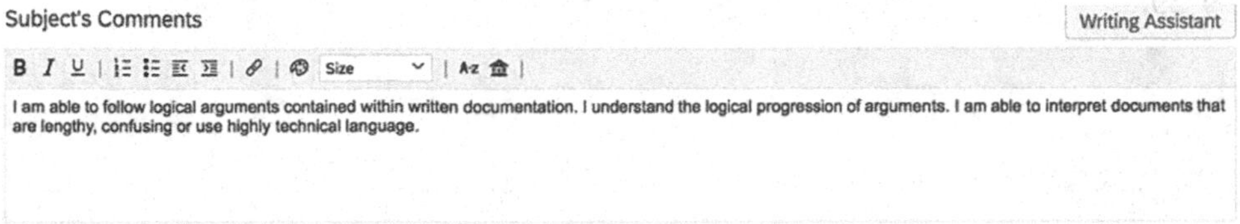

Figure 9-27. Comments Added from Writing Assistant

When a manager uses Writing Assistant, "You" or the employee name are the narrative options.

Note   For more information on how the Writing Assistant works and how to configure it, see SAP note #2086614.

The role-specific competencies will be in a separate section. A sample role-specific competency section is shown in Figure 9-28.

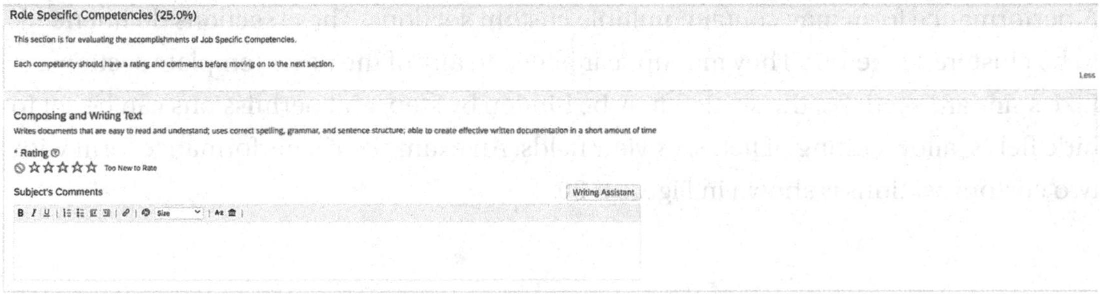

Figure 9-28. Role-Specific Competencies

In the example shown, there is a rating and comment for each competency. You may opt to have no item comments for this competency section. You may also include an overall competency comment or make any of these fields required or hidden. When you have multiple competency sections, they may use different fields and permissions.

Additional Comments Section

Another standard section is the Additional Comments section. An example is shown in Figure 9-29.

Figure 9-29. *Additional Comments Section*

This section cannot be permitted in the form template which means any role in any step may add or edit the comments unless the section is hidden or disabled. In Chapter 10, we will learn how to edit the performance form template XML to add these permissions.

Custom Section

A performance form may contain multiple custom sections. These sections do not need to be clustered together. They may appear between any of the other template sections. Like standard sections, the section may be hidden by step, and permissions can be set to hide fields, allow editing of fields, or view fields. An example of a performance form with two custom sections is shown in Figure 9-30.

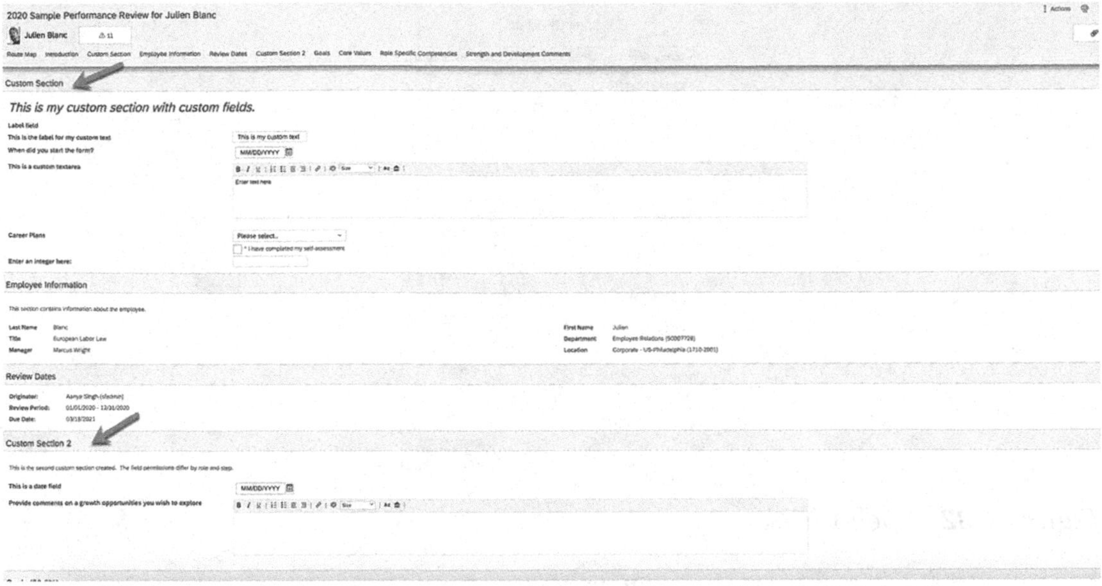

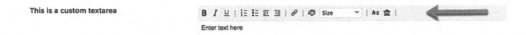

Figure 9-30. *Custom Sections with Custom Fields*

This example shows the various types of fields that may be used: *text, textarea, date, number, checkbox, or dropdown list.* Any textarea fields have multiple options available as seen in Figure 9-31.

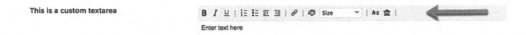

Figure 9-31. *Textarea Options*

In addition to text formatting options, the user may add a URL, perform spell-check, or do a legal scan. Spell Check and Legal Scan are explained next.

Spell Check

As part of our setup of Performance Management in Provisioning, we enabled Spell Check and Legal Scan.

When enabled, we also added the following in the advanced settings of the form template: "Enable Spell Check" and "Enable Legal Scan."

This gives the user three options for spell-check on the form:

1. Spell-check a textarea field by clicking the "A–Z" spell-check icon.
   A popup displays as seen in Figure 9-32.

443

Figure 9-32. *Spell-Check*

Suggested word changes will display.

2. Go to "Actions" at the top of the form and select "Spell Check the entire form" as seen in Figure 9-33.

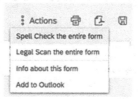

Figure 9-33. *Actions on the Form*

This option will do a spell-check on all text entries in the form.

3. Click the submit button to move the form to the next step, and a popup will display as seen in Figure 9-34.

Scan the Form   ✕

Please choose which action you would like to perform on the form before submitting

☑ Perform Spell Check
☑ Perform Legal Scan

Cancel and Return to Form   Next

Figure 9-34. *Start of Form Scan*

There will be a series of screens that will check the form text entries, and if any errors are found, the user will be prompted to make a change. In this example, both spell-check and legal scan are performed. Once the scans are complete and there are no required entry errors, close the scan popup, and the user will be at the confirmation screen to go to the next step.

Legal Scan

When Legal Scan is enabled, the user will have the same three options as Spell Check. The popup for Legal Scan will find any inappropriate words or phrases and make alterative suggestions as seen in Figure 9-35.

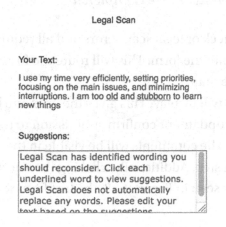

Legal Scan

Your Text:

I use my time very efficiently, setting priorities,
focusing on the main issues, and minimizing
interruptions. I am too old and stubborn to learn
new things

Suggestions:

Legal Scan has identified wording you
should reconsider. Click each
underlined word to view suggestions.
Legal Scan does not automatically
replace any words. Please edit your
text based on the suggestions.

Figure 9-35. *Legal Scan*

If you wish to avoid seeing the popup to scan the form each time you submit a form to the next step, in the advanced form template settings, click the "Disable Spell Check On Route" and "Disable Legal Scan on Route" options as seen in Figure 9-36.

Figure 9-36. *Options to Turn Off Form Scans*

The user will still be able to do full form scan by using the "Actions" option or by each textarea separately.

Submitting a Form to the Next Step

After the employee has entered all the required fields and provided any comments, the form may be sent to the next step. For a form with a large number of required fields, it is helpful for the user to click the save icon on the top-right side of the form occasionally during the process. Doing this will update the count for the Incomplete Items pod. This is an easy way to ensure you can submit the form without getting any errors. The Incomplete Items pod when all required fields are entered is seen in Figure 9-37.

Figure 9-37. *All Required Items Are Completed*

If there are no spell-check or legal scan errors and all required fields have been entered, the user may submit the form. This will route the form to the next step in the process based on the route map.

A confirmation screen will display. This gives the user one last chance to go back into the form to make any updates or confirm submission to the next step. The user will be able to add comments. The comments will be visible in the document routing email sent to the user in the next step. Additionally, clicking the question mark next to the comments section label as seen in Figure 9-38, the text from the route map displays.

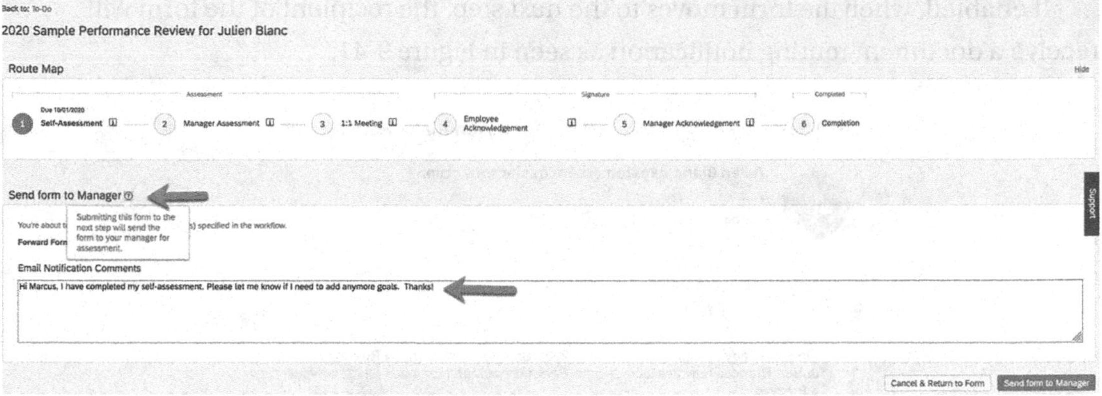

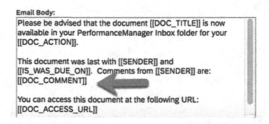

Figure 9-38. *Confirmation Page*

In the routing email notification, the "DOC_COMMENT" token controls if a comment may be entered. An example is shown in Figure 9-39.

```
Email Body:
Please be advised that the document [[DOC_TITLE]] is now
available in your PerformanceManager Inbox folder for your
[[DOC_ACTION]].

This document was last with [[SENDER]] and
[[IS_WAS_DUE_ON]].  Comments from [[SENDER]] are:
[[DOC_COMMENT]]

You can access this document at the following URL:
[[DOC_ACCESS_URL]]
```

Figure 9-39. *Email for Routing Document*

If the token is removed, the user will not have the option to add comments to the email notification when submitting the form.

After submission, the My Forms page displays. The form is no longer seen in the user's Inbox folder. Click "En Route" and you will see that the form is now with the user's manager. An example is shown in Figure 9-40.

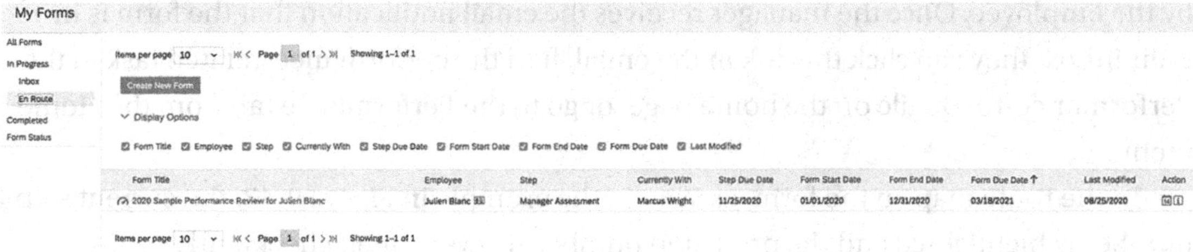

Form Title	Employee	Step	Currently With	Step Due Date	Form Start Date	Form End Date	Form Due Date ↑	Last Modified	Action
2020 Sample Performance Review for Julien Blanc	Julien Blanc	Manager Assessment	Marcus Wright	11/25/2020	01/01/2020	12/31/2020	03/18/2021	08/25/2020	

Figure 9-40. *Form in the En Route Folder*

If enabled, when the form moves to the next step, the recipient of the form will receive a document routing notification as seen in Figure 9-41.

Figure 9-41. *Routing Notification*

The email notification shows the employee's name as the sender. The notification also contains comments added by the user on the submission confirmation page along with the step due date. The form is now in the manager's Performance Inbox.

Manager View of the Form

Now we will look at the launched form from the manager's perspective after it was sent by the employee. Once the manager receives the email notification that the form is in their inbox, they can click the link in the email, find the performance-related task in the Performance To-Do tile on the home page, or go to the Performance tab from the Home menu.

In the route map on the form, as seen in the example in Figure 9-42, the current step number is highlighted and the prior step number shows a green checkmark.

Figure 9-42. *Form in the Manager Assessment Step*

The previous step name has been updated in the displayed route map shown in the preceding figure. The label to show after the step was completed was set when creating the route map. It is the text for "Step Name After Completion" in first route map step.

Similar to what you saw in the prior step, the current step shows the step due date along with the actions applicable to the step. As mentioned earlier, the step due date only displays for the current step.

In our example, for the Manager Assessment step, all of the pods have been included. Since this is the step where the overall rating is given, we have included the Overall Score pod as well. The pod will show the overall score once the manager enters the final rating. We will now look at each pod.

Team Ranker Pod

The Team Ranker pod shows the ranking of the manager's direct reports by their overall rating. This is different from the Team Rater option that appears in Team Overview. Team Rater is used to enter scores on competencies; Team Ranker shows the ranking of each direct report by overall form score. The employees who have not been rated yet will have no ranking as shown in Figure 9-43. This pod is for managers only. If the employee role is granted permission for this pod, it will not be visible to them.

--
Out of 3
Julien is #-- in the team of 3
1
Scott Leiter
4.0 - Outstanding
--
Bettina Grosser
Select a rating...
--
Julien Blanc
Select a rating...

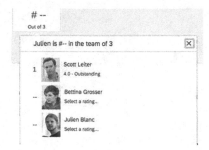

Figure 9-43. *Team Ranker Pod*

Gap Analysis Pod

The Gap Analysis pod will display the number of manager's ratings that are higher or lower than the employee's self-ratings. These numbers will change as the manager enters ratings and saves the form. An example is shown in Figure 9-44.

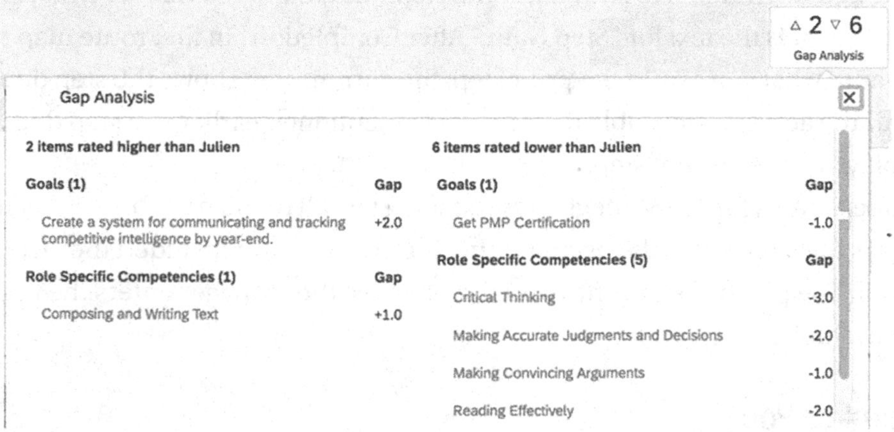

△ 2 ▽ 6
Gap Analysis
Gap Analysis
2 items rated higher than Julien
Goals (1)
Gap
Create a system for communicating and tracking competitive intelligence by year-end.
+2.0
Role Specific Competencies (1)
Gap
Composing and Writing Text
+1.0
6 items rated lower than Julien
Goals (1)
Gap
Get PMP Certification
-1.0
Role Specific Competencies (5)
Gap
Critical Thinking
-3.0
Making Accurate Judgments and Decisions
-2.0
Making Convincing Arguments
-1.0
Reading Effectively
-2.0

Figure 9-44. *Gap Analysis Pod Detail*

When you click the pod, the details show which manager item ratings are higher and lower than the employee's self-ratings. The degree of difference between the manager and employee item ratings is expressed as "+" or "-". For example, if an employee gave a self-rating on an item as *Extraordinary*, the numeric score for this label is "5." If the manager gave a rating of *Meets Expectations* which is a numeric score of "3," then the gap between the two ratings is "-2". This means the manager's rating was two scores lower than the employee's rating. If the manager and employee gave the same rating for an item, there is no gap.

Supporting Information Pod

The Supporting Information pod is shown in Figure 9-45. The number count shows how many attachments are in the pod. Based on the configuration in this example, the manager may view the attachment added by the employee, add another attachment, or delete an attachment they had added. You may decide to allow the manager to delete attachments added by the employee or hide the pod in certain steps.

Figure 9-45. *Supporting Information Pod*

You will also notice that this pod has a comment bubble icon with a count in addition to the paperclip icon and count for attachments. This pod may also contain Ask for Feedback comments as well as notes. Even though our form is not configured to use Ask for Feedback, the manager will see the comment icon and count. We will learn about the Ask for Feedback feature in Chapter 11.

Now that we have covered the pods that are available at the top of the form, we will look at some additional section features.

EZ-Rater

There is a feature that may be enabled in the form template XML called "EZ-Rater." This appears in the Goals and Competency sections of the form. For each goal and competency rating, the manager will be able to see the gaps between the employee self-rating and the manager rating. This can be useful information for the year-end discussion with the employee.

An example is seen in Figure 9-46.

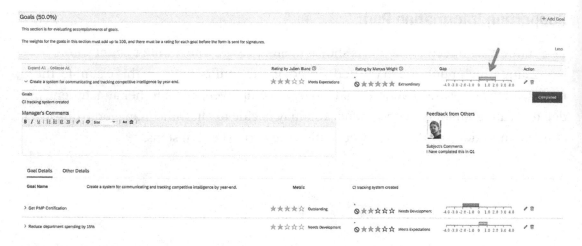

Figure 9-46. *EZ-Rater*

The gap graph will be visible for all subsequent steps and roles after the manager enters and submits the form to the next step.

Other's Rating Tab

When configuring the form template, we set the permissions for the manager to be able to see the ratings and comments from the other rater in all steps. This means the item ratings and item comments made by the employee in the prior step will be visible to the manager. An example is seen in Figure 9-47.

Figure 9-47. *Other's Rating Tab*

In all of the steps prior to signature, the user will see their ratings and comments on the left side of the section. For all steps, if the user has permission, the ratings and comments in the Other's Rating tab will appear on the right side of the section.

We also discussed accessing forms through My Forms within the Performance tab. If enabled and permitted, managers will also have access to the Team Overview tab as seen in the example in Figure 9-48.

Figure 9-48. *Access to Team Overview*

Click "Team Overview," and you will see a screen similar to Figure 9-49.

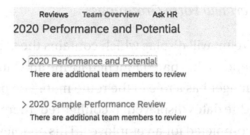

Figure 9-49. *Team Overview*

This page provides the manager with an *at a glance* view of which forms are launched, which employees have forms launched, and what step each form is in. If there are forms generated from multiple templates, each form template with associated forms will be grouped by day. Expand any form group to see the details. An example is shown in Figure 9-50.

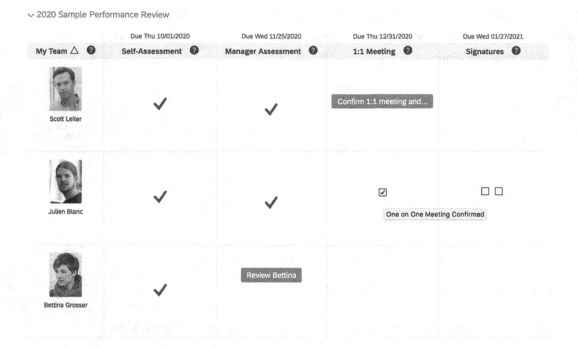

Figure 9-50. *Team Overview Form Groupings*

Once expanded, My Team will display which contains the list of forms to review. This list includes direct reports that have launched forms and launched forms for other employees where the manager has a role in the route map. The page will have the route map steps with any step due dates displayed. If configured, there will be a checkmark in each step that has been completed for an employee. This enables the manager to easily see where each form is in the process. Completed one-on-one steps will show a different icon. Hover over the icon to see that the step is confirmed as seen in the example shown in the preceding figure.

Based on the step and the role of the manager, there may be buttons that will take the manager directly into a form. A form may be in a manager assessment step, for example. A button with a link will display "Review {employee name}". If the manager clicks the button, the form will open, and they can complete the manager assessment step for the employee. Any form that is currently in a manager step will have a button to go into the form to complete the action.

There may also be an Ask for Feedback button which would appear which enables a manager to request comments from another user. The comments will appear in the Supporting Information pod seen on the form. You will learn how to configure Ask for Feedback in Chapter 11. There will also be a discussion on how this feature works and how it differs from another feedback-gathering option called Get Feedback.

Forms in the Signature Stage show the number of signatures needed and who needs to sign the form first. There is a step here that enables the manager to recall the form. An example is shown in Figure 9-51.

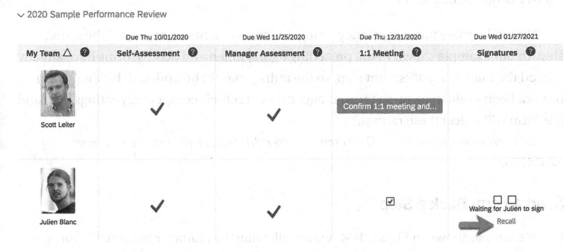

Figure 9-51. *Signature Step in Team Overview*

Clicking the "Recall" link will move the form back a step. This is helpful if the form does not have the option to move it back a step.

There is also Team Rater which allows the manager to rate the competencies for the direct reports that have a form launched. The option is shown in Figure 9-52.

Figure 9-52. *Team Rater Option*

In the example seen in Figure 9-53, there is a dropdown listing to select the competency type. Our form has core and job-specific competencies, so each section would be rated separately.

Figure 9-53. *Team Rater*

This will update the competency ratings in forms that have not passed the rating step. In our example shown in the preceding figure, Julien and Scott's forms have already passed the manager assessment step, so the ratings cannot be updated. Bettina's form has not been evaluated yet, so the manager may enter their competency ratings here and her form will reflect these ratings.

To learn more about Team Overview and its additional features, see SAP note #2078755.

Send a Form Back a Step

In the example shown in Figure 9-54, we are allowing the manager to route the form back to the employee in the prior step.

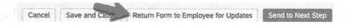

Figure 9-54. *Send a Form Back One Step*

In the example, the manager decides to send the form back to the prior step for the employee to make an update. If the manager had already started to enter some ratings on the form and saved the form before sending it back, the employee would not see any of the entries made by the manager. The form will look exactly as it was when it was with the employee provided permissions were set to "None" for any fields that the manager would populate in their step. This means the employee step should have "None" permissions for the manager rating and manager comments fields. All of the editable fields from the employee step will be editable when the form is returned to this step. Once the employee makes revisions, they will submit the form, and it will go to the manager step again. Any entries that the manager had made in this step will have been retained.

Summary Section

The Summary section used by the manager will contain ratings from all of the Goals and Competency sections of the form provided they had weights identified in the Summary section of the form template. An example is shown in Figure 9-55.

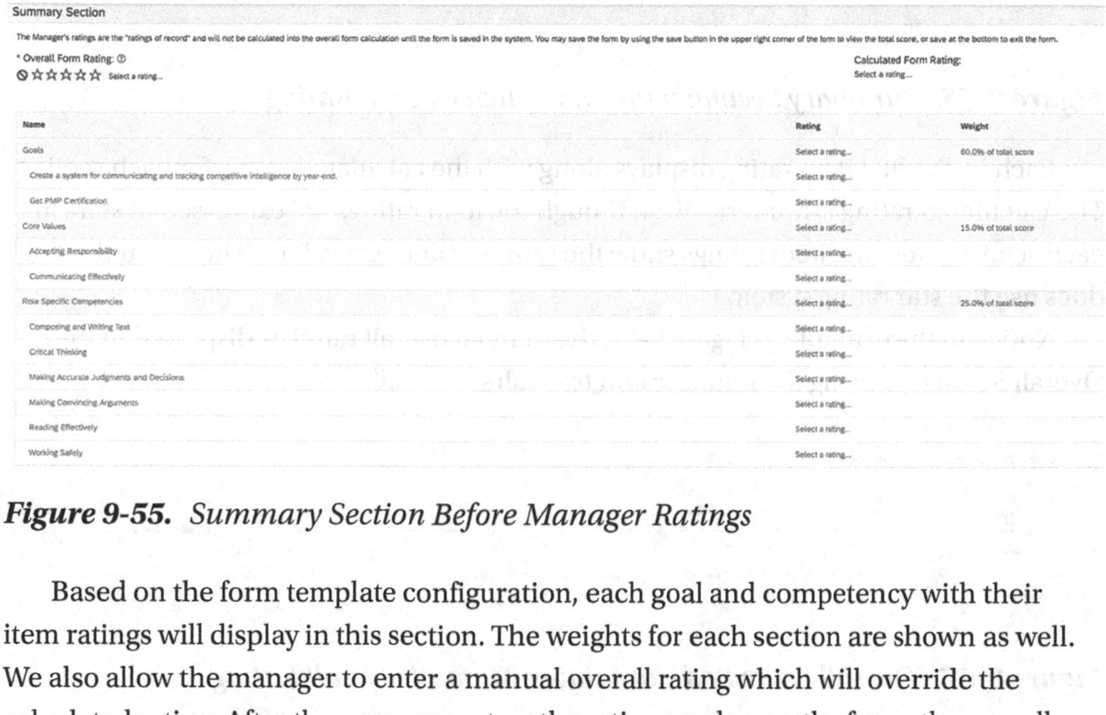

Figure 9-55. *Summary Section Before Manager Ratings*

Based on the form template configuration, each goal and competency with their item ratings will display in this section. The weights for each section are shown as well. We also allow the manager to enter a manual overall rating which will override the calculated rating. After the manager enters the ratings and saves the form, the overall form rating will be calculated. In this example, the manual overall form rating is a required entry. Once this rating is entered, the Overall Score pod will be updated with this rating and will be the rating of record. An example of the Summary section with all the ratings populated is seen in Figure 9-56.

Summary Section

The Manager's ratings are the "ratings of record" and will not be calculated into the overall form calculation until the form is saved in the system. You may save the form by using the save button in the upper right corner of the form to view the total score, or save at the bottom to exit the form.

Overall Form Rating: ⑦

★ ★ ★ ☆ ☆ Meets Expectations

Calculated Form Rating:

2.78/5.0

Name	Rating	Weight
Goals	2.5	60.0% of total score
Create a system for communicating and tracking competitive intelligence by year-end.	3.0 - Meets Expectations	
Get PMP Certification	2.0 - Needs Development	
Core Values	3.0	15.0% of total score
Accepting Responsibility	3.0 - Meets Expectations	
Communicating Effectively	3.0 - Meets Expectations	
Role Specific Competencies	3.33	25.0% of total score
Composing and Writing Text	4.0 - Outstanding	
Critical Thinking	3.0 - Meets Expectations	
Making Accurate Judgments and Decisions	4.0 - Outstanding	
Making Convincing Arguments	4.0 - Outstanding	
Reading Effectively	2.0 - Needs Development	
Working Safely	3.0 - Meets Expectations	

Figure 9-56. *Summary Section with Calculated Overall Rating*

Each individual item rating displays along with the calculated rating for each section. The calculated rating is numeric. Even though the item ratings are expressed in stars in each section, here the item ratings show the numeric and text values. The manual rating does use the star rating system.

Notice in the example in Figure 9-57, the manual overall rating is displayed in the Overall Score pod using the numeric and text values as well.

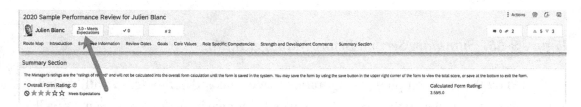

Figure 9-57. *Overall Score Pod Containing Manual Overall Rating*

Team Ranker Pod

After the overall score is set for the employee, you can see that the Team Ranker pod has been updated to include the ranking for this form based on the overall score. An example is shown in Figure 9-58.

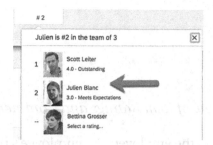

Figure 9-58. *Updated Team Ranking*

Confirmation Screen with No Comment Option

Using our sample template, the step after the manager completes the performance rating is the year-end discussion with the employee. The manager is the role owner in this step, so when the confirmation page displays, there is no option for comments as seen in Figure 9-59.

Figure 9-59. *Confirmation Screen Without Comment Option*

This occurs because the form is going to the same user in the next step, so an email notification is not necessary.

View of Ratings on the Form

Based on who is looking at the form, the ratings and comments are situated differently. The user who enters the ratings and comments will see these fields on the left side of each goal and competency item. In our example in Figure 9-60, the manager's ratings and comments are on the left side under the goal. The employee's ratings and comments for the item are found on the right side under Rating from Others.

Accepting Responsibility

Takes accountability for delivering on commitments; owns mistakes and uses them as opportunities for learning and development; openly discusses his/her actions and their consequences both good and bad

* Rating ⓘ
★★★★☆ Outstanding

Manager's Comments
Julien can process and manage a large volume of work without getting overwhelmed. Julien is well-organized and highly efficient at managing multiple tasks at once.

Ratings from Others
Rating ⓘ
★★★☆☆ 3.0 - Meets Expectations

Subject's Comments
I develop realistic long-range plans. I break large projects down into short-term activities and for the most part stay focused on the big picture.

Figure 9-60. *Manager View of Item Ratings and Comments*

When viewing the form as the employee, the employee's ratings and comments are on the left, and the manager's ratings and comments are found on the right side under Ratings from Others as seen in Figure 9-61.

Accepting Responsibility

Takes accountability for delivering on commitments; owns mistakes and uses them as opportunities for learning and development; openly discusses his/her actions and their consequences both good and bad

Rating ⓘ
★★★☆☆ Meets Expectations

Subject's Comments
I develop realistic long-range plans. I break large projects down into short-term activities and for the most part stay focused on the big picture.

Ratings from Others
Rating ⓘ
★★★★☆ 4.0 - Outstanding

Manager's Comments
Julien can process and manage a large volume of work without getting overwhelmed. Julien is well-organized and highly efficient at managing multiple tasks at once.

Figure 9-61. *Employee View of Item Ratings and Comments*

Calculated Overall Rating

If you are using the calculated overall rating in the Summary section and also allowing for a manual overall rating, the manual rating will be the rating of record. It is highly recommended to hide the calculated rating for any subsequent steps. The section with the calculated score is shown in Figure 9-62.

Summary Section

The Manager's ratings are the "ratings of record" and will not be calculated into the overall form calculation until the form is saved in the system. You may save the form by using the save button in the upper right corner of the form to view the total score, or save at the bottom to exit the form.

Overall Form Rating: ⓘ
★★★☆☆ Meets Expectations

Name	Rating	Weight
Goals	3.5	60.0% of total score
Create a system for communicating and tracking competitive intelligence by year-end.	3.0 - Meets Expectations	
Get PMP Certification	4.0 - Outstanding	
Core Values	4.0	15.0% of total score
Accepting Responsibility	4.0 - Outstanding	
Communicating Effectively	4.0 - Outstanding	
Role Specific Competencies	3.5	25.0% of total score
Composing and Writing Text	3.0 - Meets Expectations	
Critical Thinking	4.0 - Outstanding	
Making Accurate Judgments and Decisions	3.0 - Meets Expectations	
Making Convincing Arguments	3.0 - Meets Expectations	
Reading Effectively	4.0 - Outstanding	
Working Safely	4.0 - Outstanding	

Section Comments:
Manager's Comments
Great year!

Figure 9-62. *No Calculated Rating Visible*

Signature Step

Once all of the modify steps have been completed, ratings have been given, and year-end discussions have taken place, the form will go to the Signature Stage.

The form at this stage is read-only. The only editable section is the Signature section where comments may be added. The names of the users that need to sign the form can be displayed if configured in the advanced form template settings. An example is shown in Figure 9-63.

Figure 9-63. *Signature Section Before Signing*

Once the user submits the form, the sign date and an electronic signature are added to the form. An example of the Signature section after the employee signs is shown in Figure 9-64.

Figure 9-64. *Signature Section with One Signature*

If you decide not to use the Signature section, just hide the section in the form template, and then the forms will go to the completed step following the last modify step.

Completed Step

Once the final signature has been added and the form submitted, the form goes to the Completed folder of My Forms as seen in Figure 9-65. Any user that had a role in the process will receive a copy of the form in their Performance Completed folder as well.

Figure 9-65. Forms in the Completed Folder

Reporting

If the manager has been given reporting access, they may be able to run standard reports, run ad hoc reports created for them, create their own ad hoc reports, view tiles, and generate dashboards.

Dashboards/Tiles

There are standard performance form–related tiles that the admin may add from SuccessStore and then place on the home page for managers. An example is shown in Figure 9-66.

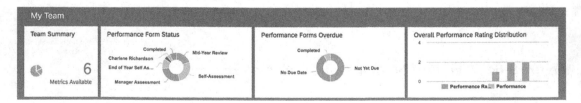

Figure 9-66. Performance Tile on the Home Page

Drill Down

Within a tile, the manager may drill down to see details. An example is shown in Figure 9-67.

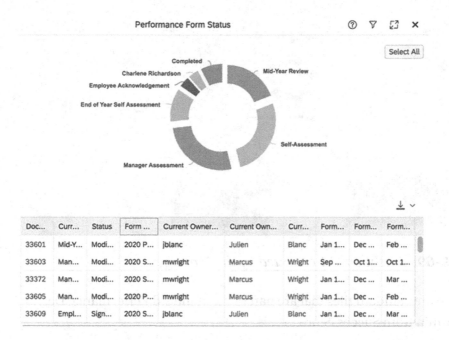

Figure 9-67. *Drill down into a Tile*

Results may be downloaded as an Excel or CSV file.

Report Center

Within Report Center, dashboards that managers are given access to can be generated. The Type column will show "Dashboard" as seen in Figure 9-68.

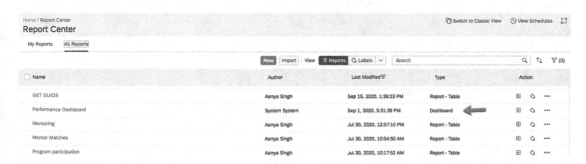

Figure 9-68. *Report Center Reports*

The manager may run this report, and the data generated appears in tiles. An example is shown in Figure 9-69.

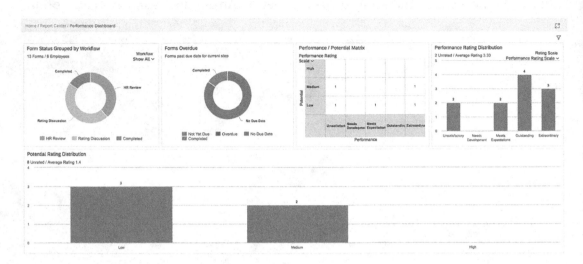

Figure 9-69. *Dashboard Generated by the Manager*

These are standard tiles that are part of the standard Performance Dashboard added by the admin from SuccessStore.

Ad Hoc Reports

When permission is granted, managers may run reports created for them. The admin would create and then share the report. A shared report will show an icon to identify it as shared. The manager will only see results for their direct reports and any levels down based on the levels set on the manager role permissions. An example is show in Figure 9-70.

Figure 9-70. *Running Shared Ad Hoc Report*

Managers may create their own reports if their role has permission granted to create them. There is a wizard to walk through the steps to create a report. Typically the report type selected is "Table" with the domain being "Performance Management" as seen in Figure 9-71.

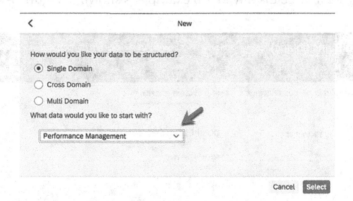

Figure 9-71. *Create Ad Hoc Report*

Like the shared reports and the tiles, the manager will only see results for their direct reports and any levels down based on the levels set on the manager role permissions.

The HR manager role may also be given reporting permissions, and the results would include the employees they support.

Another way to see performance-related information is through *People Profile*. We will now look at some portlets and blocks available.

Performance History Portlet

There are performance-related portlets and blocks which may appear in the user's People Profile. Typically, these appear in a Talent Profile section of the profile that has visibility to only the employee and manager. An example of the Performance History Portlet is shown in Figure 6-72.

Figure 9-72. *Performance History Portlet on People Profile*

If the Objective Competency Summary section is in the form template, the Objective Competency Portlet may be displayed. An example is shown in Figure 9-73.

Figure 9-73. *Objective Competency Matrix Grid on the Profile*

In addition, if rating background elements are configured and permitted in the data model, blocks may be set up in People Profile. An example of the overall potential rating block and latest performance ratings is shown in Figure 9-74.

Figure 9-74. *Overall Potential and Performance Rating Blocks*

We have now walked through the performance process from the user's perspective.

Conclusion

In the last three chapters, we have enabled Performance Management, set permissions, and created a form template. In this chapter, we walked through the performance review process through the eyes of an employee and their manager.

In the next chapter, we will dig into the details of some of the configuration that must be done in the backend in the form template XML. We will also learn about some advanced features that you may use.

CHAPTER 10

Performance Management XML and Translations

As we have seen with goal plan templates, not all configuration can be made in the UI. There are some actions, permissions, and formatting that must be done in the form template XML found in Provisioning. In this chapter, we will look at the general structure and way of modifying the performance form template XML. We will then identify XML-only configurations needed in relevant sections and learn about the types of modifications that can be made only in the XML (you won't see all section types covered here unless there's a specific need for XML-only configuration).

We take a section-by-section approach to examining the XML to avoid confusion (even when an end-to-end solution for a feature may cross sections). We first look how to access the XML. Then we look at the meta section in detail. Then we look at the structure of a performance section in general and what is configurable. We then move to specific sections including the Introduction section, Employee Information section, Review Dates section, Goals section, Competency section, Summary Section, custom section, and Signature section. Finally, we will take a look at how translations are updated via a special "message key" methodology.

Note   This is probably the most challenging chapter in the book. We assume you have followed the steps in all the earlier Performance Management chapters prior to attempting to edit the XML directly as shown in this chapter. In our experience, most customer needs are met by configuring the performance form exclusively in the online tool; however, it is good to be aware of those features that are still available when customers ask! It is also important to understand how the XML

© Susan Traynor, Michael A. Wellens and Venki Krishnamoorthy 2021
S. Traynor et al., *SAP SuccessFactors Talent: Volume 1*, https://doi.org/10.1007/978-1-4842-6600-7_10

works so that technical issues that can be difficult to understand become clear. For example, issues with permissions on specific route map steps or translations not appearing correctly can often only be figured out by examining the XML directly.

While we've covered many scenarios requested by customers in this section that require direct XML edit, this does not represent all XML edits that are possible. When in doubt, download and examine the sf-form.dtd from SAP note 229273 to fully understand the structure and capabilities of the XML in full detail.

Accessing the XML

We will use the form template that we downloaded from SuccessStore and have updated in the UI. To access the form template XML, within Provisioning, go to "Form Template Administration" as seen in Figure 10-1.

Figure 10-1. *Access the Form Template XML*

All templates for the instance will display. The list will include existing performance, 360, compensation, role readiness, and recruiting templates. The template name, type, and system-generated ID are shown as seen in Figure 10-2.

All Form Templates
Select a template to edit:

Template Name	Type	ID
2011 Compensation & Equity	Compensation	13
2012 Performance Review	Form	102
2012 Performance Review - Copy	Form	241
2013 Performance Review	Form	103
2014 Annual Salary & Incentive Plan	Compensation	16
2014 Business + Individual Incentive Plan	Compensation	121
2014 Performance Review	Form	104
2014 Short Term Incentive Plan	Compensation	17
2015 Annual Salary, Equity & Incentive Plan	Compensation	402
2015 Performance Review	Form	105
2015 Short Term Incentive Plan	Compensation	401
2016 Compensation & Equity	Compensation	14
2016 Performance Review	Form	441
2017 Annual Salary, Equity & Incentive Plan	Compensation	761
2017 Compensation & Equity	Compensation	15
2017 Global Salary, Equity & Incentive Plan	Compensation	841
2017 Performance Review	Form	741
2017 Short Term Incentive Plan	Compensation	762
2018 Annual Salary, Equity & Incentive Plan	Compensation	923
2018 Performance Review	Form	801
2018 Short Term Incentive Plan	Compensation	922
2019 Annual Salary Plan SB	Compensation	1144
2019 Annual Salary, Equity & Incentive Plan	Compensation	1141
2019 Performance Review	Form	1145
2019 Performance Review Extended	Form	742
2019 Short Term Incentive Plan	Compensation	1142
2019 Short Term Incentive Plan SB	Compensation	1143
2020 Annual Salary, Equity & Incentive Plan	Compensation	181
2020 Custom Rating No Manual	Form	1201
2020 Custom Weight Rating	Form	1200

Figure 10-2. *Form Template Listing*

As we have seen in the UI, inactive form templates may be hidden but not deleted. In Provisioning, active and inactive templates are shown, and there is no way to differentiate between them. This means your list can get very long and unwieldy. One way to handle this is to rename the inactive form templates in the UI. You can add "ZZZ" preceding the form template name. Then in Provisioning, all the renamed inactive templates are easily identifiable and are moved to the end of the listing as seen in Figure 10-3.

Total Rewards Plan	Compensation	501
US Job Requisition	Job Req	281
ZZZ 2020 Performance Review with Ask for FB	Form	1199
ZZZ 2020 Sample Obj Comp	Form	1211
ZZZ Defunct 2012 Performance Review	Form	1
ZZZ Defunct 2013 Performance Review	Form	2
ZZZ Defunct 2014 Performance Review	Form	3
ZZZ Defunct 2015 Performance Review	Form	4
ZZZ Defunct Development Plan Review	Form	6
ZZZ Defunct Role Readiness Assessment	Form	7
ZZZ Defunct Talent Review	Form	8
ZZZ Old 2016Review	Form	81
ZZZ OLD2016 Performance Review	Form	421

Figure 10-3. *Inactive Form Templates*

We will open the form template that we downloaded and modified from SuccessStore. An example is shown in Figure 10-4.

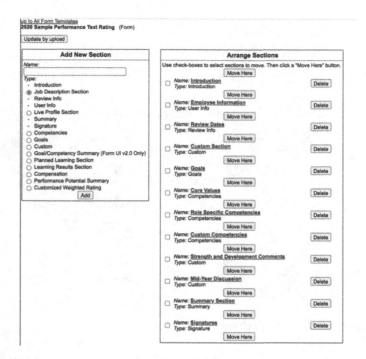

Figure 10-4. *Add and Rearrange XML Sections*

Sections

The XML sections are the backend view of the form template sections configured in the instance. However, the XML sections have additional functionality to set attributes, labeling, and permissions.

At the top of the XML, there are options to add a new section and also to rearrange sections. These options are also available in the form template in the UI, and it is often easier to add or reorder sections there. However, if you wish to add additional Goals and Competency sections to your form template, it may be easier done in the XML.

Adding a Section in the XML

From "Add New Section," select the section type and click "Add" as seen in Figure 10-5.

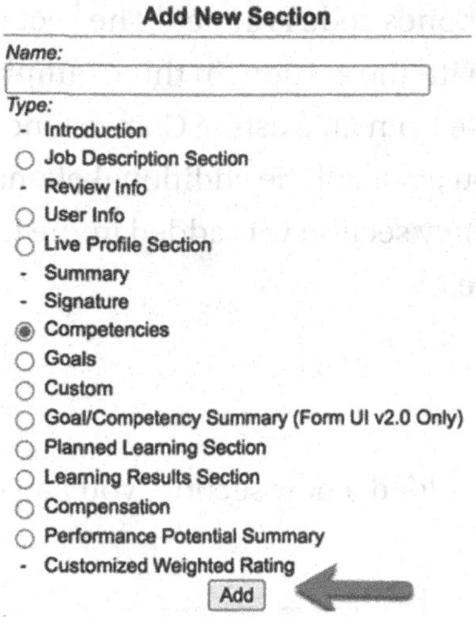

Add New Section

Name:

Type:
- Introduction
- ○ Job Description Section
- Review Info
- ○ User Info
- ○ Live Profile Section
- Summary
- Signature
- ◉ Competencies
- ○ Goals
- ○ Custom
- ○ Goal/Competency Summary (Form UI v2.0 Only)
- ○ Planned Learning Section
- ○ Learning Results Section
- ○ Compensation
- ○ Performance Potential Summary
- Customized Weighted Rating

[Add] ⬅

Figure 10-5. *Add New Section*

The section will be added at the bottom of the form template. An example of a new Competency section is shown in Figure 10-6.

```
Save Form
<?xml version="1.0" encoding="UTF-8"?>
<!DOCTYPE competency-sect SYSTEM "sf-form.dtd">
<competency-sect index="10" configurable="true" mgt-
only="false" use-jobcode="false" use-core-comp="false"
category-filter-opt="no-filter" no-rate="false" no-
weight="false" summ-opt="0" split-cmt="false" rating-opt="0"
cmt-opt="0" suppress-item-comments="0" behavior-rating-
opt="0" behavior-cmt-opt="1" behavior-mode-opt="0" in-summ-
display="true" in-overall-rating="true" no-group="true" use-
behavior="false" if-no-ratings-then-ignore-section="true"
lock-item-weights="false" in-objcomp-summ-display="false" in-
objcomp-summ-overall-rating="false" show-comp-expected-
rating="false" show-comp-proficiency-level="false" comp-
expected-rating-format="0" show-behavior-expected-
rating="false" behavior-expected-rating-format="0" behavior-
weighted="false" min-competencies-required="-2147483648" max-
competencies-allowed="2147483647" sect-mode="normal" ez-
rater-expand-all="false" show-calculated-section-
rating="true" lock-behavior-content="false" hide-
waca="false">
  <comp-sect-name><![CDATA[*****]]></comp-sect-name>
  <fm-sect-config>
    <rating-label><![CDATA[Rating]]></rating-label>
    <rating-label-others><![CDATA[Rating]]></rating-label-
others>
    <default-rating><![CDATA[unrated]]></default-rating>
    <hidden-strength-threshold>0.0</hidden-strength-
threshold>
    <blind-spot-threshold>0.0</blind-spot-threshold>
    <num-decimal-places>2</num-decimal-places>
    <publish-button-label><![CDATA[Publish Content]]>
</publish-button-label>
  </fm-sect-config>
  <sect-weight>0.0</sect-weight>
  <meta-grp-label><![CDATA[Group]]></meta-grp-label>
</competency-sect>
```

Figure 10-6. *Adding a Competency Section*

As you can see, very barebones code is added. The section is not named, and there is no rating scale associated with the section. In this example using a new Competency section, you can copy the code from an existing Competency section and paste it over in the new section. This way, you get all of the additional elements and attributes that you would not get if the Competency section was added in the UI. Then you may tweak any permissions or attributes here.

Move Sections

In a case where you have just added a new section, you can use the "Arrange Sections" option as seen in Figure 10-7.

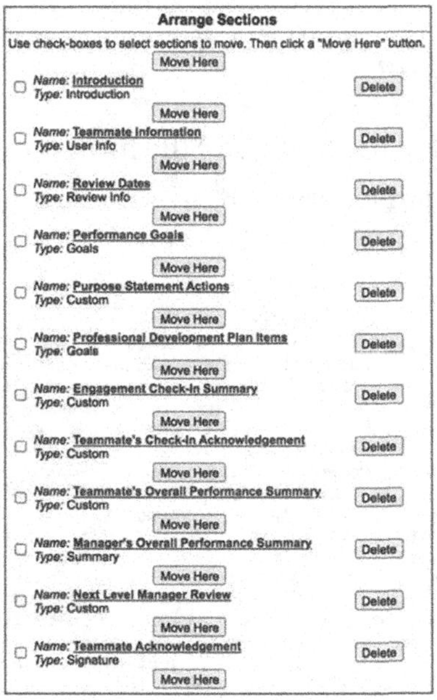

Figure 10-7. Move Sections

Click the checkbox next to the section name you wish to move. Click the "Move Here" button to identify where to place the section.

Scrolling down the XML, there is a section where the form attributes can be edited. An example is shown in Figure 10-8.

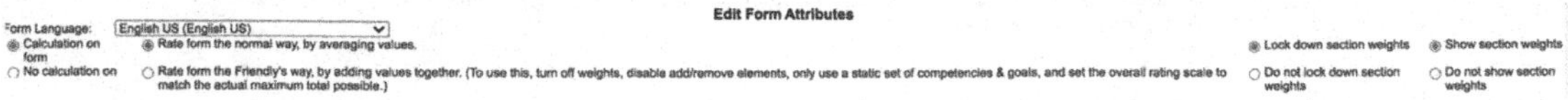

Figure 10-8. Edit Form Attributes

These attributes are also configurable in the form template.

Route Step IDs

Throughout the XML sections, you will see permissions based on roles and route map steps. The route map step references use step id names from the route map. An example is in Figure 10-9.

Previous Step Exit Text	
Step Exit Reminder	☐ ⊙
Step Id	EMP
Start of Review	☑
Out of Turn Access	☐
1:1 Meeting	◯

Figure 10-9. *Step ID in a Route Map Step*

In Chapter 6, we talked about the system-generated route map ids for templates downloaded from SuccessStore. There, we recommended updating the step ids to a short meaningful name. This was suggested to avoid seeing step ids as shown in Figure 10-10.

```
<section-permission type="hidden">
    <role-name>*</role-name>
    <route-step stepid="10363296119954507"/>
    <route-step stepid="10363296120179310"/>
    <route-step stepid="10362654251537189"/>
    <route-step stepid="10451036062641794"/>
    <route-step stepid="10363296120868334"/>
</section-permission>
<section-permission type="enabled">
    <role-name>E</role-name>
    <route-step stepid="10363296119954507"/>
</section-permission>
<section-permission type="enabled">
    <role-name>EM</role-name>
    <route-step stepid="10363296119954507"/>
    <route-step stepid="10363296120179310"/>
</section-permission>
<section-permission type="enabled">
    <role-name>E</role-name>
    <route-step stepid="10451036062641794"/>
    <route-step stepid="10363296120868334"/>
</section-permission>
```

Figure 10-10. *System-Generated Route Map Step IDs*

If you need to add permissions by step, it will be much easier using easily identifiable step names as seen in Figure 10-11.

```
<section-permission type="disabled">
   <role-name>*</role-name>
   <route-step stepid="*"/>
</section-permission>
<section-permission type="hidden">
   <role-name>*</role-name>
   <route-step stepid="mgr_check1"/>
   <route-step stepid="emp_chk2"/>
   <route-step stepid="chk1_discuss"/>
   <route-step stepid="emp_ack1"/>
   <route-step stepid="chk2_discuss"/>
   <route-step stepid="mgr_chk2"/>
</section-permission>
<section-permission type="enabled">
   <role-name>E</role-name>
   <route-step stepid="self"/>
</section-permission>
<section-permission type="disabled">
   <role-name>EM</role-name>
   <route-step stepid="mgr_review"/>
   <route-step stepid="meet"/>
</section-permission>
<section-permission type="disabled">
   <role-name>EMM</role-name>
   <route-step stepid="emm_review"/>
```

Figure 10-11. *Route Map Step IDs Easily Identifiable*

This is helpful when you need to manually add route step permissions to the XML referencing step ids.

Meta Section

The meta section of the XML contains permissions and settings that are applicable to the entire form. The form template "General Settings" that were configured are housed here, including button and pod permissions and Ask for Feedback permissions.

Rating Scale

The rating scale is set here for the form template. A code segment sample is shown in the following:

```
<fm-sect-scale show-value="true">
    <scale-source>1</scale-source>
    <scale-id><![CDATA[Performance Rating Scale]]></scale-id>
    <scale-type><![CDATA[null]]></scale-type>
    <scale-adjusted-calculation enable="false" display-calculated-
    rating="false">
    </scale-adjusted-calculation>
  </fm-sect-scale>
```

The *<scale-source>* tag identifies the rating scale. Normally, the source is "1." The default rating scale used for the form template is identified here using the *<scale-id>* tag. If you wish to use a different scale by section, the alternate scale-id would need to be identified in those Goals or Competency sections.

To see a dropdown list for the rating scale, <scale-type> must be "DROPDOWN."

Ratings to Display as Text

Use "show-value" in <fm-sect-scale> to show the numerical value of ratings and for the overall score to be numeric. When this attribute is set to "false," the text value of the ratings will display.

This can be used in the meta section for the calculated overall rating or individually by Goals and Competency sections.

To see the text name for the ratings instead of numeric and text, the sect-scale show-value should be equal to "false."

A sample of the meta data section is shown in Figure 10-12.

```
<?xml version="1.0" encoding="UTF-8"?>
<!DOCTYPE fm-meta SYSTEM "sf-form.dtd">
<fm-meta>
   <meta-form-id>-1</meta-form-id>
   <meta-rated>true</meta-rated>
   <meta-rating>0.0</meta-rating>
   <meta-scale>0.0</meta-scale>
   <meta-grp-label><![CDATA[Group]]></meta-grp-label>
   <fm-sect-scale show-value="false">
      <scale-source>1</scale-source>
      <scale-id><![CDATA[Performance Rating Scale]]></scale-id>
      <scale-type><![CDATA[null]]></scale-type>
```

Figure 10-12. *Text for the Rating Option*

Note We have noticed that when you choose the "Hide numeric rating values" option from the General Settings screen in the online editor, a popup appears asking you if you want to change other sections. However, it does not identify and change all sections! Thus, it is important to review each section for this setting in the XML if you would like this to show consistently throughout the form.

Button Permissions

Most buttons may be configured in the front-end configuration tool. However, all buttons may be updated in the XML. Specifically, the "add-modifier" and "add-signer" can only be added via the XML and are associated with the "Add Modifier" and "Add Signer" functionality we will cover later in this chapter.

Button and pod permissions may be set by role and step of the route map. Within the button-permission tag, the permission type is defined ("None" or "Enabled"), the roles are identified, the buttons are identified (using reference IDs), and the route map step is defined. A code segment sample is shown in the following:

```
<button-permission type="none">
    <role-name>*</role-name>
    <button refid="reject"/>
    <button refid="gap-analysis-pod"/>
    <button refid="team-rank-pod"/>
    <button refid="delete"/>
    <button refid="get-comments"/>
    <button refid="get-edits"/>
    <button refid="add-modifier"/>
    <button refid="add-signer"/>
    <route-step stepid="*"/>
 </button-permission>
```

Note   We have set roles and steps to "*" here so that all roles have access to the buttons at all steps. Normally you would choose specific steps and roles. We have outlined best practices on identifying steps in the prior section. For a complete list of roles available in Performance Management, reference SAP note 2087940.

Attachments

In earlier chapters, we learned about attachments that may be added to a performance form. The attachments are found in the "Supporting Information" pod on the form. To use attachments, multiple steps must be performed, the last of which can only be performed in the XML. First, "Enable attachments" must be checked in the advanced form template settings. An example is shown in Figure 10-13.

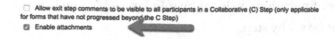

Figure 10-13. *Enable attachments in Advanced Template Settings*

In the form template's "General Settings," permissions to access the Supporting Information pod are needed as well. An example is shown in Figure 10-14.

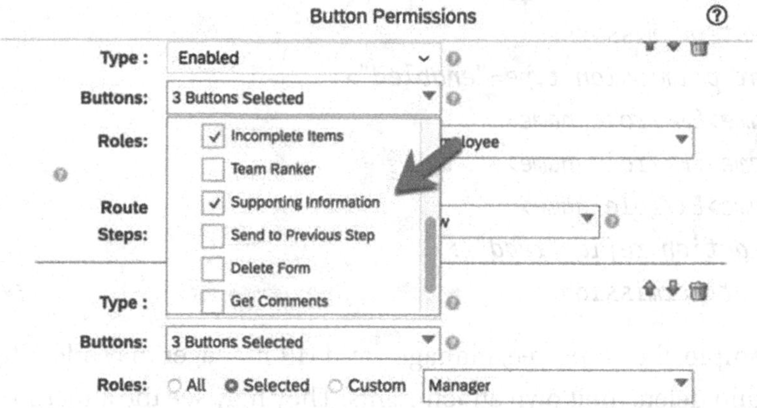

Figure 10-14. *Button Permission for the Supporting Information Pod*

To allow users to add, view, or remove attachments within the "Supporting Information" pod, attachment permissions must be added in the meta section of the form template XML.

There are attachment permissions and attachment action permissions. Attachment permissions are set for read and edit actions by role. These permissions can only be set in the XML.

Attachment permissions are "None" or "Enabled."

Attach-action permissions are "Read" or "Edit":

- "Read" permission for attach-actions allows a user to view all attachments and add, rename/edit, or delete their own attachments.

- "Edit" permission for attach-actions allows all read permissions, and users may also delete and rename/edit attachments for all other users.

The <attachment-permission> is set by role for each <attach-action>. Attachment permission cannot be set by step.

A code segment sample is shown in the following:

```
<attachment-permission type="none">
    <role-name>*</role-name>
    <attach-action refid="read"/>
    <attach-action refid="edit"/>
  </attachment-permission>
  <attachment-permission type="enabled">
    <role-name>EM</role-name>
    <role-name>EH</role-name>
    <role-name>E</role-name>
    <attach-action refid="read"/>
  </attachment-permission>
```

In this example, the employee, manager, and HR manager may add attachments and edit/rename and delete their own attachments. They may see the attachments added by others but cannot edit/rename or delete these attachments.

The *<attachment-permission>* is placed before *<askforfeedback-permission>* if used; otherwise, it appears before <tab-permission>.

Ask for Feedback Permissions

If your form template is configured to use the Ask for Feedback functionality, you will see the *<askforfeedback-permission>*. It will come after <attachment-permission> and before *<tab-permission>*:

```
<askforfeedback-permission type="none">
    <role-name>*</role-name>
    <route-step stepid="ESign"/>
    <route-step stepid="M1"/>
    <route-step stepid="Calibration"/>
    <route-step stepid="MY"/>
    <route-step stepid="E1"/>
    <route-step stepid="Discussion"/>
    <route-step stepid="MSign"/>
```

```
</askforfeedback-permission>
<askforfeedback-permission type="none">
  <role-name>E</role-name>
  <route-step stepid="*"/>
</askforfeedback-permission>
<askforfeedback-permission type="read">
  <role-name>EM</role-name>
  <role-name>EH</role-name>
  <route-step stepid="ESign"/>
  <route-step stepid="M1"/>
  <route-step stepid="Calibration"/>
  <route-step stepid="MY"/>
  <route-step stepid="E1"/>
  <route-step stepid="MSign"/>
</askforfeedback-permission>
```

Goal Tab Permissions

Goal tab permissions set in the meta section apply to all goal (objectives), development, and competency items in their corresponding sections. The permissions are set by role and step. They may only be configured in the XML.

The goal tabs that may be permitted are:

- Learning Activities

- Other Ratings

- Last Review Rating

- Goal Details

- Other Details

- Achievements

See Table 10-1 for an explanation of each tab.

Table 10-1. *Goal Tab Permissions*

Tab refid	Description	Section Used In
learning-activities	Tab will display learning activities associated with a development goal.	Development Goals section
others-rating		Performance goal, Development Goals, and Competency sections
last-review-rating	Last competency rating.	Competency section
goal-details	Displays non-table goal plan fields identified in the <form-layout> section of the goal plan XML.	Performance goal and Development Goals sections
other-details	Contains goal table fields such as milestones, tasks, and sub-goals.	Performance goal and Development Goals sections
achievements	CPM achievement associated with a goal or development goal.	Performance goal and Development Goals sections if CPM is used

We will look at some of the tabs that may display for goals.

The most important tab is the "Other's Rating" tab. The standard label for this tab is "Ratings from Others." The tab contains the goal or competency rating and comments given by another user. For example, the employee self-rates each goal and competency. If configured, the employee may also include a comment for each goal or competency. When the form goes to the manager for review, the employee's rating and comments will display in the "Ratings from Others" tab.

An example is shown in Figure 10-15.

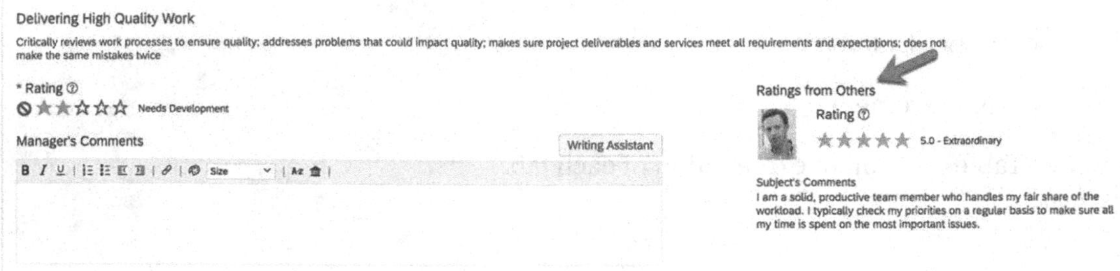

Figure 10-15. *Other's Rating Tab*

In the example, the manager is able to see the competency rating and comments made by the employee. We will learn about granting access to the contents of this tab later when we cover the Goals section of the XML in more detail (if you would like, see section "Other's Rating Tab Field Permissions Within a Section").

The "Achievements" tab for a goal item is shown in Figure 10-16. The tab shows the achievement name and date. A trophy icon displays as well. This tab is only available for plan goals and development goals when Continuous Performance Management is used.

Figure 10-16. Achievements Tab for a Goal Item

Goals without an associated achievement will show in the "Achievements" tab, and a statement "There are no Achievements" will display. It is not possible to hide the tab for goals without achievements. If permitted, the "Achievements" tab is always the first tab displayed.

An example of the "Goal Details" tab is shown in Figure 10-17. All goal plan fields that were permitted in the goal plan XML will display except for goal plan table fields.

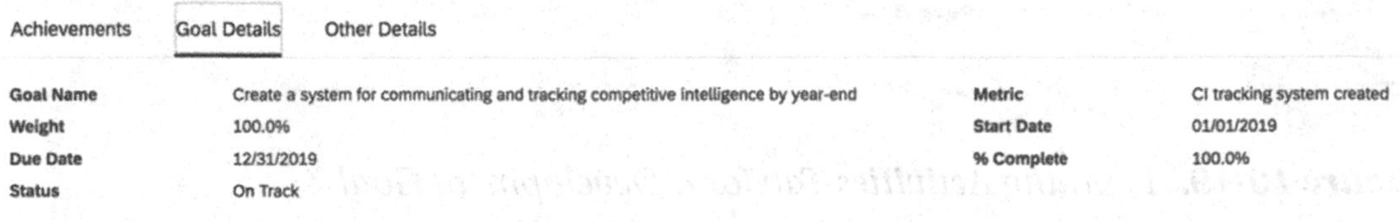

Figure 10-17. Goal Details Tab for a Goal Item

The "Other Details" tab as seen in Figure 10-18 displays goal plan table fields. This includes tasks, subtasks, and milestones.

Financial
Create a system for communicating and tracking competitive intelligence by year-end ✎
CI tracking system created

* Rating ⑦

Select a Rating... ⌄

Achievements	Goal Details	Other Details

Deliverable:

Deliverable	Requirements document created
% Complete	25.0%

Deliverable	System configured
% Complete	15.0%

Deliverable	Test plan created
% Complete	0.0%

Milestones:

Target Date	05/31/2019
Milestone	Tracking system requirements finalized
Actual Date	

Target Date	08/31/2019
Milestone	Tracking system configured
Actual Date	

Figure 10-18. *Other Details Tab for a Goal Item*

Milestones will display as a list instead of a table.

The "Learning Activities" tab may be permitted to display for development goals. An example is shown in Figure 10-19.

Development Goals
Become a better written and spoken communicator
--Completion of online coursework to improve communication skills.
--Submit white paper for peer review
--Speak at conference

Achievements	Learning Activities	Goal Details	Other Details

Status	Planned		Product Type	Test
Start Date	09/02/2020		Completed Date	

Figure 10-19. *Learning Activities Tab for a Development Goal*

If permitted, this tab will display for all development goals, even those without learning activities. The tab will contain the message "You have no Learning Activities for development goal" if there are no learning activities associated with a development goal. The tab order cannot be changed. If the "Achievements" tab is also enabled, it will be the first tab listed.

Now that we have seen the goal tabs that may be used, let's learn how to grant access to them. If enabled, these tabs are view-only.

The tab permissions will appear after the Ask for Feedback permissions in the meta section of the XML. Permission types are "None" or "Enabled" which means the tabs will be visible or hidden. Permissions for each tab type may be set separately by role and step.

A code segment sample that contains tab permissions is shown in the following:

```
<tab-permission type="enabled">
    <role-name>EM</role-name>
    <tab refid="goal-details"/>
    <tab refid="other-details"/>
    <tab refid="achievements"/>
    <tab refid="others-rating"/>
    <route-step stepid="*"/>
</tab-permission>
```

In this example, the manager role may see the Goal Details, Other Details, Achievements, and Other's Rating Tabs for all applicable sections.

It is possible to set separate tab permissions for specific roles and steps.

It is also possible to set these goal tab permissions at the section level. In the "Goals Section" of this chapter, we will learn how to hide the tab in a specific section in the form.

Next, we will look at the sections that users will see on the performance form.

Sections

Each section has its own settings, labels, fields, and permissions. Sections do have some common elements. Elements used in sections are

- fm-sect-name
- fm-sect-intro
- fm-sect-config
- fm-element

The order of the sections is based on the fm-sect index found in each section.

Each section contains the index with the first section index number starting with "0." A code segment sample is shown in the following:

```
<?xml version="1.0" encoding="UTF-8"?>
<!DOCTYPE fm-sect SYSTEM "sf-form.dtd">
<fm-sect index="0" mgt-only="false" split-cmt="false" cmt-opt="1">
```

Section Name Tag

The Introduction, Employee Information, Review Dates, and custom sections have their name defined in the <fm-sect-name> tag.

A code segment sample for a <fm-sect-name> tag is shown in the following:

```
<fm-sect-name><![CDATA[Introduction]]></fm-sect-name>
```

The section name tag differs for the Goals (objective), Competency, Objective Competency Summary, and Performance Potential Summary sections as seen in the following:

- *<obj-sect-name>*

- *<comp-sect-name>*

- *<summary-sect-name>*

- *<pp-sect-name>*

- *<oc-sect-name>*

Section Introduction Tag

The Introduction, Employee Information, Review Dates, and custom sections will use the <fm-sect-intro> tag. This corresponds to the introduction text that may be added in the form template in the instance. A code segment sample for a *<fm-sect-name>* tag is shown in the following:

```
<fm-sect-name><![CDATA[Employee Information]]></fm-sect-name>
```

The section intro tag differs for the Goals (objective), Competency, Objective Competency Summary, and Performance Potential Summary sections as seen in the following:

- *<obj-sect-intro>*
- *<comp-sect-intro>*
- *<summary-sect-intro>*
- *<pp-sect-intro>*
- *<oc-sect-intro>*

Rating Options

In our review of the performance form thus far, we've shown where different ratings can be provided by different raters. Rating options determine which rating provided in the form will act as the rating of record. The rating of record is important because it is the final output of the performance form that is used in other modules and for reporting.

The rating option attribute, "rating-opt," is how the rating option is set. It can have the values described in Table 10-2.

Note   These options will change in the XML automatically based on your selections in the online form editor, so it is not necessary to edit them in the XML; however, it is important to understand how they affect permissions and ratings of record as you test your form and make adjustments!

Table 10-2. *Rating Option Values*

Value	Description
0	This is the default value and the simplest. All users share one rating box for each item. In the XML, this item rating is shown as "item-rating." The system will use your permission settings to determine which users can view and edit this field. In effect, users with Write permission can override one another's ratings so that ultimately the last user in the route map with Write permission has the final say. When viewing comments as an end user, no ratings are displayed next to a user's comments.

(continued)

Table 10-2. (*continued*)

Value	Description
1	This option is typically used when you want employees to provide their own rating that does not count as official and can be compared with a manager rating. With this setting, by default all users can edit the item-rating field which is the rating of record. You can override this by setting different permissions. Similar to value "0," the last person to edit the rating gets the final say as to what the rating of record will be. The other key difference besides default permission is that the employee will also have their own separate rating where they can rate themself. This extra rating is shown as "item-cmt-rating" in the XML. This rating does not count as rating of record. Because of this, you would want to set "item-rating" permission to "Read" or "None" for the employee so they do not mistakenly set the rating of record. When viewing comments as an end user, the rating scale is displayed next to the subject's comment. *Note: item-cmt-rating cannot be set to required.*
2	This option is typically used when you want more than just the employee to have access to view or edit the unofficial rating. This is the most dynamic option in that any combination of roles could read or edit the official and/or unofficial ratings. By default, everyone is given access to the "item-cmt-rating" and the "item-rating." You simply set "Read" or "None" permission for those roles you do not want to edit one or the other or both. When viewing comments as an end user, the rating scale is displayed next to all evaluators' comments. *Note: When using Get Feedback and allowing edits, the rating is the unofficial user rating which is identified by <item-cmt-rating>. In order for this to work properly, do not use rating-opt "2." By granting Read permission to the manger for this field, the manager would see an additional blank item-cmt-rating under the manager's item-rating. It would be impossible to hide this additional field for the manager without hiding the item-cmt-ratings from the Other's Rating tab as well. Use Read permission for this field in order to see the ratings given by the feedback provider.*
3	This option is used when you want only the manager to edit the official rating, but you want the employee to still get a popup warning that their own self-rating is required. The nonofficial employee ratings appear in the XML as "subject-item-rating" and the manager's as "item-rating." When viewing comments as an end user, each user sees their rating scale side by side with the employee's rating.

Note   For more information, see SAP note 2185897.

EZ-Rater Graph Visibility

When using EZ-Rater in a Goals or Competency section (*sect-mode="EZ-Rater"*), each goal or competency will have the *Gap Analysis* graph which shows the difference between a subject and manager's rating.

To remove the *Gap Analysis* graph visibility in any of the Goals or Competency sections, add <ez-rater show-gap="false"/> as the last line </fm-sect-config>.

This cannot be updated in the UI using "Manage Templates."

Section Config Tag

Within each section, the *<fm-sect-config>* tag contains some basic settings for the section. Section permissions, required fields, and default rating labels may all be defined within this tag.

For Goals and Competency sections, the tag will also contain

- Configuration for a rating scale if it differs from the default rating scale in the meta section

- "Unable to Rate" text

- Item weights

A code segment sample for a Goals section is shown in the following:

```
<fm-sect-config>
  <rating-label><![CDATA[Manager's Rating]]></rating-label>
  <rating-label-others><![CDATA[Teammate's Rating]]></rating-label-others>
  <default-rating><![CDATA[Select a Rating...]]></default-rating>
  <weight-total><![CDATA[100.0]]></weight-total>
  <hidden-strength-threshold>0.0</hidden-strength-threshold>
  <blind-spot-threshold>0.0</blind-spot-threshold>
  <section-comments-label><![CDATA[Overall Comments on Goal
  Achievement]]></section-comments-label>
  <section-manager-comments-label><![CDATA[Manager's Comments]]>
  </section-manager-comments-label>
  <section-subject-comments-label><![CDATA[Teammate's  Comments]]>
  </section-subject-comments-label>
```

```
<manager-comments-label><![CDATA[Manager's Comments:]]>
</manager-comments-label>
<subject-comments-label><![CDATA[Teammate's Comments:]]>
</subject-comments-label>
<section-permission type="disabled">
  <role-name>*</role-name>
  <route-step stepid="*"/>
</section-permission>
<section-permission type="enabled">
  <role-name>EM</role-name>
  <route-step stepid="mgr_check1"/>
  <route-step stepid="chk1_discuss"/>
  <route-step stepid="chk2_discuss"/>
  <route-step stepid="mgr_chk2"/>
</section-permission>
<section-permission type="enabled">
  <role-name>E</role-name>
  <route-step stepid="self"/>
</section-permission>
<section-permission type="enabled">
  <role-name>EM</role-name>
  <route-step stepid="mgr_review"/>
</section-permission>
<section-permission type="disabled">
  <role-name>EMM</role-name>
  <route-step stepid="emm_review"/>
</section-permission>
<section-permission type="disabled">
  <role-name>E</role-name>
  <route-step stepid="emp_sign"/>
</section-permission>
```

```
<required-fields>
  <role-name>E</role-name>
  <field refid="subject-item-rating" min-value="-1.0" max-value="-1.0"/>
  <route-step stepid="self"/>
  <send-action sendid="next_step"/>
</required-fields>
<required-fields>
  <role-name>EM</role-name>
  <field refid="item-rating" min-value="-1.0" max-value="-1.0"/>
  <field refid="item-comments" min-value="1.0" max-value="4000.0"/>
  <route-step stepid="mgr_review"/>
  <send-action sendid="next_step"/>
</required-fields>
<weight-total-option><![CDATA[enforce]]></weight-total-option>
<num-decimal-places>2</num-decimal-places>
<publish-button-label><![CDATA[Publish Content]]></publish-button-label>
</fm-sect-config>
```

Section Element Tag

The <fm-element> tag is used to define custom fields. This tag may be in any section that supports custom fields. It is also used in the Employee Information section to identify the employee-related fields that will display in the section.

A code segment sample is shown in the following:

```
<fm-element index="0" type="3">
  <ekey><![CDATA[LASTNAME]]></ekey>
  <ename><![CDATA[]]></ename>
  <evalue><![CDATA[]]></evalue>
</fm-element>
<fm-element index="1" type="3">
  <ekey><![CDATA[FIRSTNAME]]></ekey>
  <ename><![CDATA[]]></ename>
  <evalue><![CDATA[]]></evalue>
</fm-element>
```

The index is defined for the field order, and for each element, the key, name, type of value, and value are populated. If evalue is left blank, the field is not prepopulated.

Table 10-3 contains the custom element types that can be used.

Table 10-3. *Custom Element Types*

Element	Description	Element Type
Label	Will display as bolded text label with no data field to enter.	2
Text	Label field and open box for one line of text.	3
Textarea	Multiline text box.	4
Date	Date box.	5
List	Dropdown list.	6
Integer	Text box for a whole number.	7
Double	Text box for a number with decimals.	8
Checkbox	Checkbox with label. Specify "evalue"; otherwise, nothing is store when checked.	9

In the code sample shown in the following, the fm-element index identifies the field as being the first displayed; the type "3" indicates a text field:

```
<fm-element index="0" type="3">
```

Introduction Section

The Introduction section is read-only and contains an introductory text. There are no fields to permit, just the section permission that can be set in the form template.

Note   In the introductory text, it is possible to link directly to the employee profile. For more information, see SAP note 2384502.

Employee Information Section

This section displays read-only information about the user being reviewed.

This section only permits certain fields to display along with any of the 15 custom fields configured in the Succession Data Model.

A code sample of the section is shown in the following:

```
<fm-sect
index="1"
mgt-only="false"
split-cmt="false"
cmt-opt="1">
 <fm-sect-name><![CDATA[User Information]]></fm-sect-name>
  <fm-sect-intro><![CDATA[]]></fm-sect-intro>
  <fm-sect-config>
    <rating-label><![CDATA[Rating]]></rating-label>
    <rating-label-others><![CDATA[Rating]]></rating-label-others>
    <default-rating><![CDATA[unrated]]></default-rating>
    <hidden-strength-threshold>0.0</hidden-strength-threshold>
    <blind-spot-threshold>0.0</blind-spot-threshold>
    <num-decimal-places>2</num-decimal-places>
    <publish-button-label><![CDATA[Publish Content]]></publish-button-label>
  </fm-sect-config>
  <fm-element index="0" type="3">
    <ekey><![CDATA[FIRSTNAME]]></ekey>
    <ename><![CDATA[]]></ename>
    <evalue><![CDATA[]]></evalue>
  </fm-element>
  <fm-element index="1" type="3">
    <ekey><![CDATA[LASTNAME]]></ekey>
    <ename><![CDATA[]]></ename>
    <evalue><![CDATA[]]></evalue>
  </fm-element>
```

```
<fm-element index="2" type="3">
  <ekey><![CDATA[HR]]></ekey>
  <ename><![CDATA[]]></ename>
  <evalue><![CDATA[]]></evalue>
</fm-element>
<fm-element index="3" type="3">
  <ekey><![CDATA[USERNAME]]></ekey>
  <ename><![CDATA[]]></ename>
  <evalue><![CDATA[]]></evalue>
</fm-element>
 </fm-sect>
</userinfo-sect>
```

The updates to this section that may only be made in the form template XML include the following:

- Change the display field order.

- Rename a field.

- Add one of the 15 custom fields.

- Change Display Now vs. Time of Launch.

The <fm-elements> are found after the <fm-sect-config> tag.

Change the Display Field Order

With the Employee Information section, the field order may be changed. **However, this is not possible to do through "Manage Templates" in the UI.** The field order display is based on the order of the fields in the XML. The fm-element index number controls the display field order.

Looking at an element, the index identifies the order number. The first field to display is 0.

Type ="3" means the field displays on one line. An example is shown in Figure 10-20.

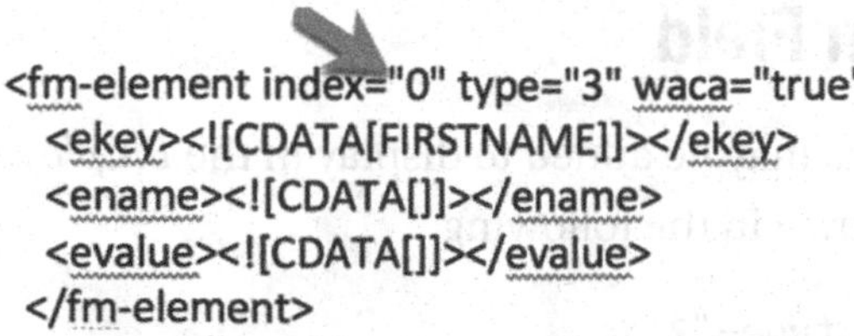

```
<fm-element index="0" type="3" waca="true">
  <ekey><![CDATA[FIRSTNAME]]></ekey>
  <ename><![CDATA[]]></ename>
  <evalue><![CDATA[]]></evalue>
</fm-element>
```

Figure 10-20. *Field Element in the Employee Information Section*

To reorder, manually rearrange the <fm-elements> and then update the index to match.

Rename a Field

Any of the labels that accompany a field in the *Employee Information* section may be renamed. This is done in the *<ename>* tag for a field. The label must use all capital letters; otherwise, it will not be used in the form. The label will not display in all capital letters in the form. An example is shown in Figure 10-21.

```
<?xml version="1.0" encoding="UTF-8"?>
<!DOCTYPE fm-sect SYSTEM "sf-form.dtd">
<fm-sect index="1" mgt-only="false" split-cmt="true" cmt-
opt="1">
 <fm-sect-name><![CDATA[Employee Information]]></fm-sect-name>
  <fm-sect-intro><![CDATA[<p>This section contains information
about the employee.</p>
]]></fm-sect-intro>
  <fm-sect-config>
    <rating-label><![CDATA[Rating]]></rating-label>
    <rating-label-others><![CDATA[Rating]]></rating-label-
others>
    <default-rating><![CDATA[unrated]]></default-rating>
    <hidden-strength-threshold>0.0</hidden-strength-threshold>
    <blind-spot-threshold>0.0</blind-spot-threshold>
    <section-permission type="disabled">
      <role-name>*</role-name>
      <route-step stepid="*"/>
    </section-permission>
    <num-decimal-places>2</num-decimal-places>
    <publish-button-label><![CDATA[Publish Content]]>
</publish-button-label>
  </fm-sect-config>
  <fm-element index="0" type="3">
    <ekey><![CDATA[LASTNAME]]></ekey>
    <ename><![CDATA[]]></ename>
    <evalue><![CDATA[]]></evalue>
  </fm-element>
  <fm-element index="1" type="3">
    <ekey><![CDATA[FIRSTNAME]]></ekey>
    <ename><![CDATA[]]></ename>
    <evalue><![CDATA[]]></evalue>
  </fm-element>
  <fm-element index="2" type="3">
    <ekey><![CDATA[LOCATION]]></ekey>
    <ename><![CDATA[GEOGRAPHIC AREA]]></ename>
    <evalue><![CDATA[]]></evalue>
  </fm-element>
  <fm-element index="3" type="3">
    <ekey><![CDATA[CUSTOM05]]></ekey>
```

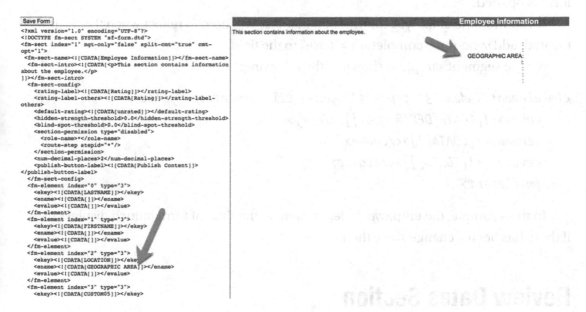

Figure 10-21. *Renaming a Field*

You will also notice that in the preview section of the sample, the field is relabeled.

Include a Custom Field

Any of the 15 custom fields may be added to display in the *Employee Information* section.

A code segment is shown in the following:

```
<fm-element index="4" type="3">
    <ekey><![CDATA[CUSTOM05]]></ekey>
    <ename><![CDATA[DIVISION]]></ename>
    <evalue><![CDATA[]]></evalue>
 </fm-element>
```

Enter the system key for the field in the <ekey> tag.

Enter a label name for the field in the <ename> tag, using all capital letters.

Update View of Data

The data that displays in this section reflects the employee data effective at the time the form is opened.

If you want the employee information that displays here to reflect when the form was created, add sync-until-completion ="false" to the field.

A code segment sample is shown in the following:

```
<fm-element index="3" type="3" sync-until-completion="false">
    <ekey><![CDATA[DEPARTMENT]]></ekey>
    <ename><![CDATA[]]></ename>
    <evalue><![CDATA[]]></evalue>
  </fm-element>
```

In this example, the employee's department at the time of form launch displays even if there has been a change since then.

Review Dates Section

The *Review Dates* section is read-only and may contain an introductory text. There are no fields to permit, just the section permission that can be set in the form template. Fields cannot be omitted, reordered, or relabeled. Standard or custom fields may not be added to this section. Figure 10-22 shows an example of the section.

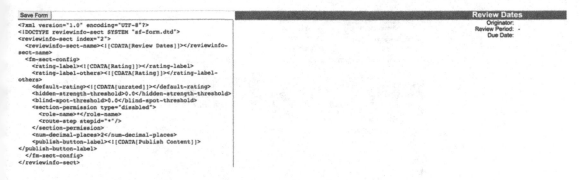

Figure 10-22. *Review Dates Section*

Now that we have covered the non-editable sections of the form template, we will move on to the Goals and Competency sections.

Goals Section

The Goals section identifies the source of the goal plan and how the goals are being evaluated.

The Goals section pulls in goal items from a user's goal plan. The source of the goal plan is set in the Goals section of the form template within <obj-sect-plan-id>. An example is seen in Figure 10-23.

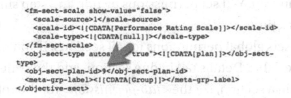

Figure 10-23. *Goal Plan ID in the Goals Section*

The plan id corresponds to the plan id found in the goal plan XML and in *Managing Plan Template* for the goal plan template as seen in Figure 10-24.

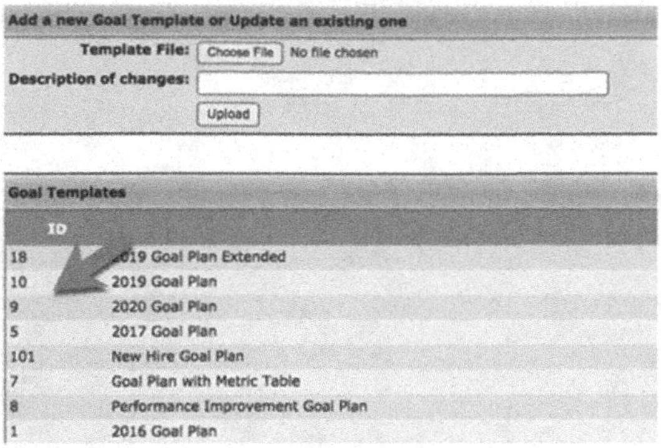

Figure 10-24. *Goal Plan ID*

We will look at some of the attributes that may be configured in this section.

Hide Goal Tabs by Section

If you wish to hide the Goal Details or Other Details tab for the Goals or Development Goals section, at the section level, add the desired permissions to each Goals section in the form instead of in the meta section.

In a situation where you have Goals sections and Development Goals sections on your form template, you may wish to see the Goal Details tab on goals but not on development goals. You may wish to hide the Other Details or Goal Details tab for a certain role in a certain step. You set permissions by role and step similar to how it is handled in the meta section.

The meta section sets global permissions for all sections. If you just need to remove the Goal Details or the Other Details tab in one section, add the code at the section level.

To hide a tab within a section, set the *<tab-permission>* for the role, tab, and step.

For example, if you want to hide the Other Details tab in the Goals section only for all roles at all steps, you can add the following code to restrict visibility:

```
<tab-permission type="none">
<role-name>*</role-name>
<tab refid="other-details"/>
<route-step stepid="*"/>
</tab-permission>
```

Another example is shown in the following code segment. In this example, the employee cannot see the other-details tab of the Goals section in the employee assessment step.

```
<tab-permission type="none">
  <role-name>E</role-name>
  <tab refid="other-details"/>
  <route-step stepid="EMP"/>
</tab-permission>
```

Other's Rating Tab Field Permissions Within a Section

The "Other's Rating" tab contains the rating and comments for a goal or competency given by another role. The rating and comments fields may be made visible or hidden for each role and step.

The *other-rating-tab-item-permission* defines field-level access within the "Other's Rating" tab. This permission may be defined for Goals, Development Goals, and Competency sections.

An example of the code segment is shown in the following:

```
<others-ratingtab-item-permission type="enabled">
  <role-name>EM</role-name>
  <tab-item refid="item-rating"/>
  <route-step stepid="MGR"/>
</others-ratingtab-item-permission>
```

For the code shown, in the Other's Rating tab in the manager assessment step, the manager may see the item ratings given by the employee.

Rating and Comments Visibility in the Other's Rating Tab

As we just learned, it is possible to set the "Other's Rating" tab permissions by section. We also saw how to grant access to view item ratings and comments in this tab by role and step in a section. We may combine the two to allow the "Other's Rating" tab to be visible and control the Other's Rating tab field visibility in a step.

The *other-rating-tab-item-permission* defines field-level access within the "Other's Rating" tab.

Do not define the "Other's Rating" tab permission in the meta section. Use the Other's Rating tab permission in the Goals or Competency section and also use *<others-rating-tab-item-permission>* to identify the goal fields, roles, and steps.

Insert after *<field-permission>* and before *<sect-weight>*.

A code segment is shown in the following:

```
<others-ratingtab-item-permission type="enabled">
  <role-name>EM</role-name>
  <tab-item refid="item-rating"/>
  <route-step stepid="MGR"/>
</others-ratingtab-item-permission>
<tab-permission type="enabled">
  <role-name>EM</role-name>
  <tab refid="others-rating"/>
  <route-step stepid="MGR"/>
</tab-permission>
```

In this example, the manager may see the Other's Rating tab with the item rating in the manager assessment step. This means the manager can see the goal item ratings given by the employee. The ratings will display in the Other's Rating tab. The goal item comments in this example were not permitted.

These permissions may be defined in each Goals, Development Goals, or Competency section.

Item Comments by Role

In a form template, it is possible to identify the role that is writing goal or competency section comments. An example of the field permission is shown in Figure 10-25.

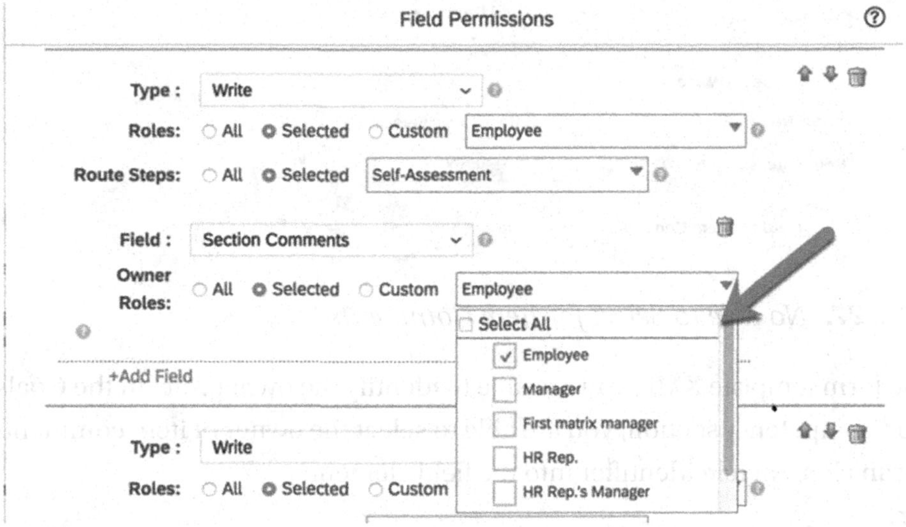

Figure 10-25. *Goal Section Comments by Role*

To see item comments, it must be enabled as seen in Figure 10-26.

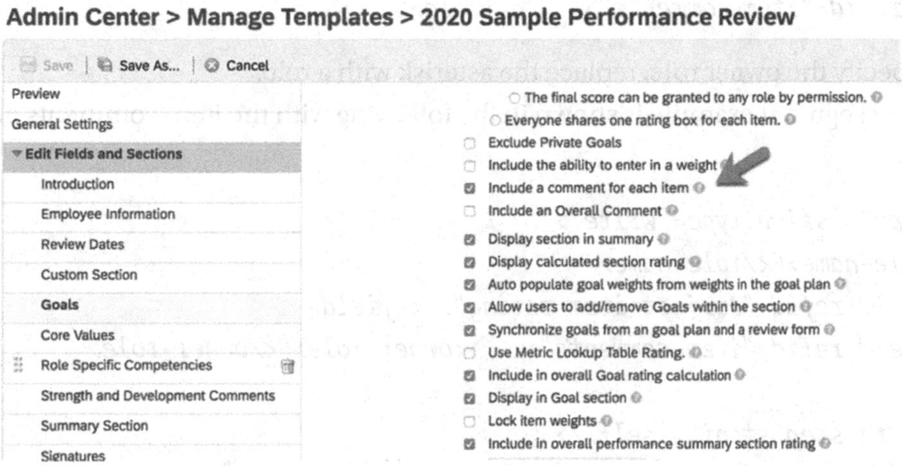

Figure 10-26. *Item Comments in the Goals Section*

When setting up the field permissions for the item comments, this option is not available. You may select the role for the permission (*Read, Write, None*) and the "item comments" field, but there is no option to select the owner of the item comments. An example of the field permission is shown in Figure 10-27.

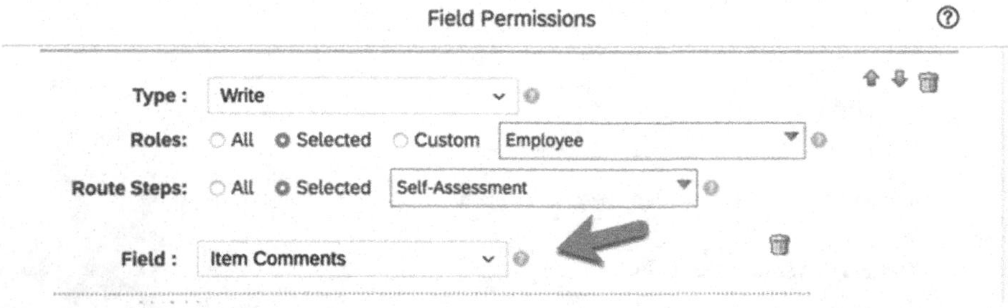

Figure 10-27. *No Role to Select for Item Comments*

In the form template XML, you are able to identify the owner role. In the Goals section or Competency section, you are able to select the owner of item comments by inserting an element role identifier into the field element.

Insert

```
<owner-role>*</owner-role>
```

into

```
<field refid="item-comments">    </field>
```

To specify the owner role, replace the asterisk with a role.

A code segment example is shown in the following with the item comments defined by role:

```
<field-permission type="write">
    <role-name>E</role-name>
    <field refid="subject-item-rating"> </field>
    <field refid="item-comments">    <owner-role>E</owner-role>
</field>
    <route-step stepid="self"/>
  </field-permission>
```

In this example, the employee is writing item comments in the self-assessment step. The employee may enter item comments as seen in Figure 10-28.

Figure 10-28. *Employee Adds Item Comments*

The manager can view the comments of the employee and enter item comments as well. An example is shown in Figure 10-29.

Figure 10-29. *Manager Adds Item Comments*

Goal Plan Fields That Display in the Goals Section

The plan fields that display for each goal on the form are based on the goal fields in the <form-layout> section of the goal plan XML. This is covered in detail in Chapter 4.

Make Goal Plan Fields Read-Only

When an employee opens their form, they may see the pencil (edit) icon for each goal. If the section is enabled for a user, this icon will appear, but in certain goal plan configuration scenarios, the goal will still be read-only. Clicking the icon, the user will see the goal fields but will not be able to edit the goal. The use of the pencil icon is misleading because the user cannot edit the goal in this situation. An example of a goal with the pencil icon is shown in Figure 10-30.

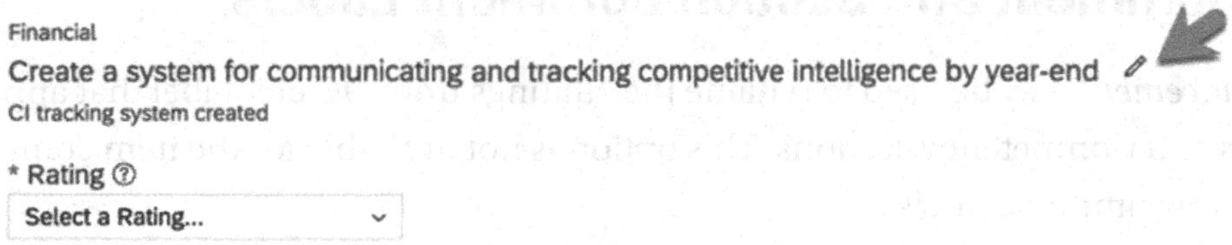

> Financial
> Create a system for communicating and tracking competitive intelligence by year-end 🖉
> CI tracking system created
>
> * Rating ⑦
> [Select a Rating...   ⌄]

Figure 10-30. *Edit a Goal in the Performance Form*

There is an option to make all goal fields read-only in the Goals section of a form. This option is independent of the goal details read-write settings on the goal plan.

This means within the performance plan, when opening a goal, it is all read-only, and the user cannot edit any of the goal plan fields.

This is done through the use of "tgm-fields."

A code segment sample is shown in the following:

```
<field-permission type="read">
    <role-name>*</role-name>
    <field refid="tgm-fields"></field>
    <route-step stepid="*"/>
 </field-permission>
```

In the example, all roles may read only and not edit the goal fields in any step. You may add this as the first field permission in the section.

After this permission is added to the Goals section, XML goals no longer display the pencil icon as seen in Figure 10-31.

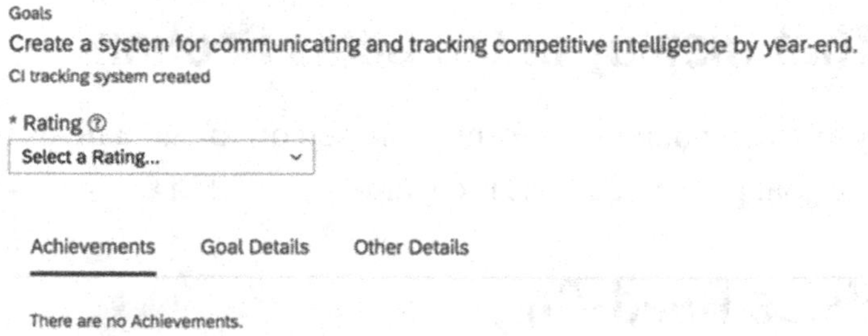

Figure 10-31. *Goal No Longer Editable*

The Goal Details tab may be viewed, but no changes may be made to the goal. If the user wishes to update the goal, it may be done in the goal plan. Once the user reopens the form, the updated goal would display.

Item Comment and Section Comment Labels

Text Replacement may be used to rename the "Ratings from Others" label that appears for Goals and Competency sections. This option is not available for the item comment and section comment labels.

The item comment and section comment labels in the Goals, Competency, and Summary sections are very generic and refer to employees as "subjects." These comment labels may be modified in the XML. The section summary comment section may be relabeled as well.

If comments are used for goals and/or competencies, the employee and manager item comment labels may be customized. The label to use for custom item comments are

```
<manager-comments-label>
<subject-comments-label>
```

If the section allows for section comments, there will be a comment summary section following the section. An example of a goal comments section of a form is shown in Figure 10-32.

Figure 10-32. *Standard Comment Labels for the Goals Section*

In the example shown in the preceding figure, the form is currently with the manager. The manager and subject (employee) comment labels are shown.

The labels for section comments are shown in the following:

```
<manager-comments-label>
<subject-comments-label>
```

Insert after the <blind-spot-threshold> tag.

A code segment sample is shown in the following:

```
<blind-spot-threshold>0.0</blind-spot-threshold>
  <section-comments-label><![CDATA[Overall Goal Comments Section]]>
  </section-comments-label>
    <section-manager-comments-label><![CDATA[These are the Manager Overall
    Goal Section Comments]]></section-manager-comments-label>
    <section-subject-comments-label><![CDATA[These are the Employee Overall
    Goal Section Comments]]></section-subject-comments-label>
```

After these tags are added to the Goals section XML, the goal comments section reflects the new labels as seen in Figure 10-33.

Figure 10-33. *Custom Section and Section Comment Labels*

The goal summary section was relabeled in addition to the manager and employee goal section comment labels.

Item Comment Labels

Now that we have seen how to update the section comment labels, we will see how to update the item comment labels. This will be for the comment on each goal or competency. The labels for item comments are *<manager-comments-label> and <subject-comments-label>*. The standard item comments are shown in Figure 10-34.

Figure 10-34. *Standard Item Comments*

A code segment sample for customized item and section comments is shown in the following:

```
<blind-spot-threshold>0.0</blind-spot-threshold>
<section-comments-label><![CDATA[Overall Goal Comments Section]]>
</section-comments-label>
 <section-manager-comments-label><![CDATA[These are the Manager Overall
 Goal Section Comments]]></section-manager-comments-label>
 <section-subject-comments-label><![CDATA[These are the Employee Overall
 Goal Section Comments]]></section-subject-comments-label>
```

```
<manager-comments-label><![CDATA[These are the Manager Goal Item
Comments]]></manager-comments-label>
<subject-comments-label><![CDATA[These are the Employee Goal Item
Comments]]></subject-comments-label>
```

A sample of the updated goal item comments is shown in Figure 10-35.

Figure 10-35. Updated Goal Item Comment Labels

Item Rating Labels

It is also possible to rename the existing manager goal and competency item rating labels. The standard rating labels are shown in Figure 10-36.

Figure 10-36. Standard Item Rating Labels

The standard rating labels are shown in the following:

```
<rating-label><![CDATA[Rating]]></rating-label>
 <rating-label-others><![CDATA[Rating]]></rating-label-others>
```

<rating-label> normally is the manager's rating; simply replace [Rating]] with your updated verbiage.

Do the same for the <rating-label-others> tag to represent the employee rating.

A code segment sample is shown in the following:

```
<fm-sect-config>
    <rating-label><![CDATA[This is the Manager Goal Rating]]></rating-label>
    <rating-label-others><![CDATA[This is Employee Goal Rating]]></rating-
    label-others>
```

See Figure 10-37 for the updated goal item rating and comment labels.

Figure 10-37. *Custom Item Rating and Item Comment Labels*

Filter Goal Categories to Be Included in the Performance Form

If your goal plan has multiple goal categories, it is possible to limit which goal categories will appear on the performance form. The goal categories to be included must be added to the Goals section XML.

Normally goals in all categories will appear in the Goals section of the PM form as shown in the following code segment sample:

```
<obj-sect-type><![CDATA[plan]]></obj-sect-type>
<obj-sect-plan-id>3</obj-sect-plan-id>
```

This code is at the bottom of the Goals section XML.

To limit the goals that auto-populate from the goal plan to specific categories, you use the *<obj-category>* tag to identify the categories.

Note   You will need to download the goal plan XML to find the goal category IDs.

A code segment sample from the goal plan XML is shown in the following:

```
<category id="Financial">
    <category-name>Financial</category-name>
</category>
<category id="Customer">
    <category-name>Customer</category-name>
</category>
```

```
<category id="Internal Business Processes">
    <category-name>Internal Business Processes</category-name>
</category>
<category id="Learning and Growth">
    <category-name>Learning and Growth</category-name>
</category>
```

Use the category IDs for the categories you wish to see on the PM form.

A code segment sample to use in the Goals section of the performance form template is shown in the following. The *<obj-category>* tag is added for each category of the goal plan to display:

```
obj-sect-type><![CDATA[plan]]></obj-sect-type>
<obj-sect-plan-id>3</obj-sect-plan-id>
<obj-category><![CDATA[Customer]]></obj-category>
<obj-category><![CDATA[Financial]]></obj-category>
```

In this example, the auto-populated goals will come from the *Customer* and *Financial* categories of the goal plan.

To hide numeric item ratings for the goal and competency sections, set the show-value to "false". An example is shown in Figure 10-38.

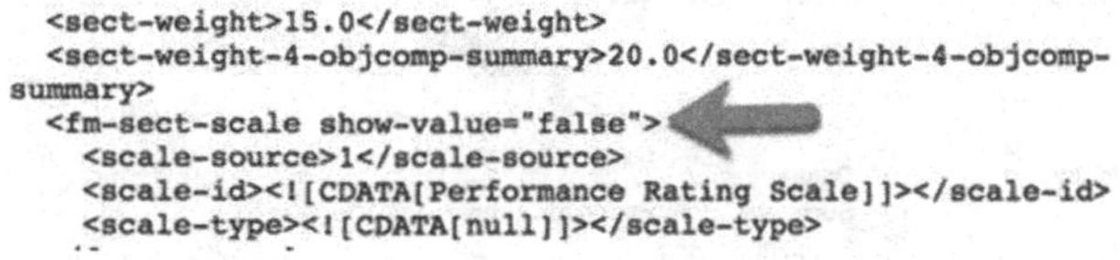

```
<sect-weight>15.0</sect-weight>
<sect-weight-4-objcomp-summary>20.0</sect-weight-4-objcomp-
summary>
    <fm-sect-scale show-value="false">
        <scale-source>1</scale-source>
        <scale-id><![CDATA[Performance Rating Scale]]></scale-id>
        <scale-type><![CDATA[null]]></scale-type>
```

Figure 10-38. *Numeric Ratings in Sections*

Competency Section

Competency Categories on the PM Form

Like the Goals section, the comment and rating labels are configurable.

Competency Match in the Core Competency Section

For the core Competency section, it is possible to limit the core competency categories that appear on a user's form. This is done through a competency match. Based on the specified category, the form will only pull in core competencies in that category:

```
<include type="category" match="[insert category name here]"/> <!-- include
competencies in specified category -->
```

Restrict a Job-Specific Competency Category

For the job-specific Competency section, it is possible to restrict competencies to one category.

This is accomplished by identifying the category for *category-filter-opt*. The categories may be found in the competency library.

You can get the categories in the instance. Type and select "Manage Job Profile Content" in the search bar. Select "Competency," and you can find the categories as shown in Figure 10-39.

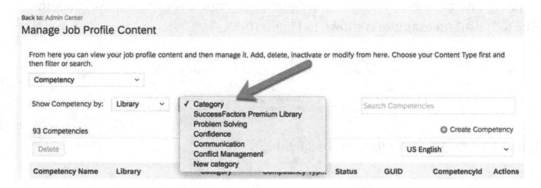

Figure 10-39. *Competency Categories*

Use category-filter-opt to show "specified-category." A snippet from the job-specific Competency section is shown in Figure 10-40.

```
Save Form
<?xml version="1.0" encoding="UTF-8"?>
<!DOCTYPE competency-sect SYSTEM "sf-form.dtd">
<competency-sect index="6" configurable="false" mgt-
only="false" use-jobcode="true" use-core-comp="false"
category-filter-opt="specified-category" no-rate="false" no-
weight="true" sum        pt="999" split-cmt="true" rating-opt="3"
cmt-opt="2" su         s-item-comments="0" behavior-rating-
opt="0" beh       or-cmt-opt="1" behavior-mode-opt="0" in-summ-
display=       se" in-overall-rating="true" no-group="true" use-
behavior="false" if-no-ratings-then-ignore-section="true"
```

Figure 10-40. *Set category-filter-opt*

Then scroll to the bottom of this Competency section. Here is where we will identify the competency category by inserting the following:

<comp-category><![CDATA[insert category here]]></comp-category>

A code segment sample is shown in the following:

```
<fm-sect-scale show-value="false">
    <scale-source>1</scale-source>
    <scale-id><![CDATA[Performance Rating Scale]]></scale-id>
    <scale-type><![CDATA[null]]></scale-type>
</fm-sect-scale>
<comp-category><![CDATA[Problem Solving]]></comp-category>
    <meta-grp-label><![CDATA[Group]]></meta-grp-label>
</competency-sect>
```

In the preceding example, only "Problem Solving" job-specific competencies will auto-populate the form.

Summary Section

Within the Summary section, the manual overall rating and overall calculated rating labels may be changed using the following labels:

<overall-rating-label>
<calc-rating-label>

The labels are added after the field permissions and directly before *</summary-sect>*.

To rename the manual overall rating, insert the following code making sure to give the label a name:

```
<overall-rating-label><![CDATA[insert manual overall rating label here]]>
</overall-rating-label>
```

```
<overall-rating-label><![CDATA[insert manual overall rating label here]]>
</overall-rating-label>
```

To rename the overall calculated rating, use <calc-rating-label>. A code segment sample for the two labels is shown in the following:

```
<overall-rating-label><![CDATA[insert manual overall rating label here]]>
</overall-rating-label>
<calc-rating-label><![CDATA[insert name for calculated rating here]]>
</calc-rating-label>
```

Note   Rating labels can be changed in the Performance Potential Summary section and the Objective Competency Summary section by finding the XML code containing "rating-label" and following the same process. We do not cover those sections in detail since we have already covered relevant XML-only changes that would apply to them already in this chapter.

Custom Section

If your custom section has section comments and you wish to use custom labels, the "split-cmt" attribute controls how the subject and manager comments display. Left unchanged, the standard comment labels will display.

In the <fm-sect> tag, change split-cmt to "true" as shown in the following code segment:

```
<fm-sect index="3" mgt-only="false" split-cmt="true" cmt-opt="0">
```

To update the section comment labels, within the <fm-sect-config> tag, add the label tags:

```
<section-comments-label>
<section-manager-comments-label>
<section-subject-comments-label>
```

Insert these after *<blind-spot-threshold>* and before *<section-permissions>* as seen in the following code segment sample:

```
<blind-spot-threshold>0.0</blind-spot-threshold>
    <section-comments-label><![CDATA[This is the Custom Section Comments
Section]]></section-comments-label>
    <section-manager-comments-label><![CDATA[These are the Manager Section
Comments]]></section-manager-comments-label>
    <section-subject-comments-label><![CDATA[These are the Employee Section
Comments]]></section-subject-comments-label>
```

Based on these custom labels added to the custom section in the XML, the custom comment labels are as seen in Figure 10-41.

Figure 10-41. *Custom Comment Labels Example*

Signature Section

A custom comment label may be added which appears after

```
<blind-spot-threshold>0.0</blind-spot-threshold>
```

The code segment sample is shown in the following:

```
<subject-comments-label><![CDATA[insert comment text here]]></subject-
comments-label>
```

Congratulations! You should now be familiar with how to edit the performance form XML and be aware of some configuration items that can only be edited there. Now let's take a look at how translations work within the Performance Management module.

Translation with the Performance Management Module

There are a few areas within the Performance Management module where translations are configured. Specifically, these need to be configured within route maps and rating scales in addition to within the performance form itself.

Note   If your form uses competencies, be sure to translate these in the Job Profile Content. Refer to Chapter 3 for more information.

Translations within route maps and rating scales are accomplished in the UI by simply selecting the desired language in the Language dropdown on the config screen as seen in Figure 10-42. The screen refreshes for all of the open text fields that can be translated for the language selected. After the screen refreshes, just type in the translation for each label you wish to translate and click "Save." All finished!

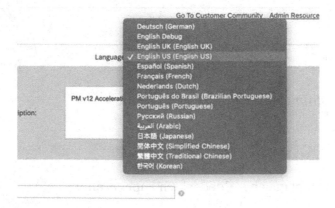

Figure 10-42. *Language Translation Dropdown as Seen in Route Map and Rating Scale Screens*

For the PM form itself, the process requires the use of message keys in the XML which are used for each label you want to translate.

Note   Per SAP note 2087186, there is a process to translate Performance Management forms without direct XML edit. However, in our experience, we find this process does not work and it is better to edit the XML directly to ensure message key IDs make sense and follow a convention for more straightforward maintenance.

First, you should add which languages you wish to translate in the online editor. Type and select "Manage Templates" in the search bar. Then click the form you wish to edit and click General Settings. Under the name of the form, you will see an "Add More" link as shown in Figure 10-43.

Note   Be sure you have already turned on the languages you need in "Company Settings" within Provisioning.

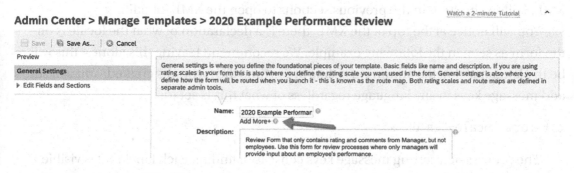

Figure 10-43. *Add More Link*

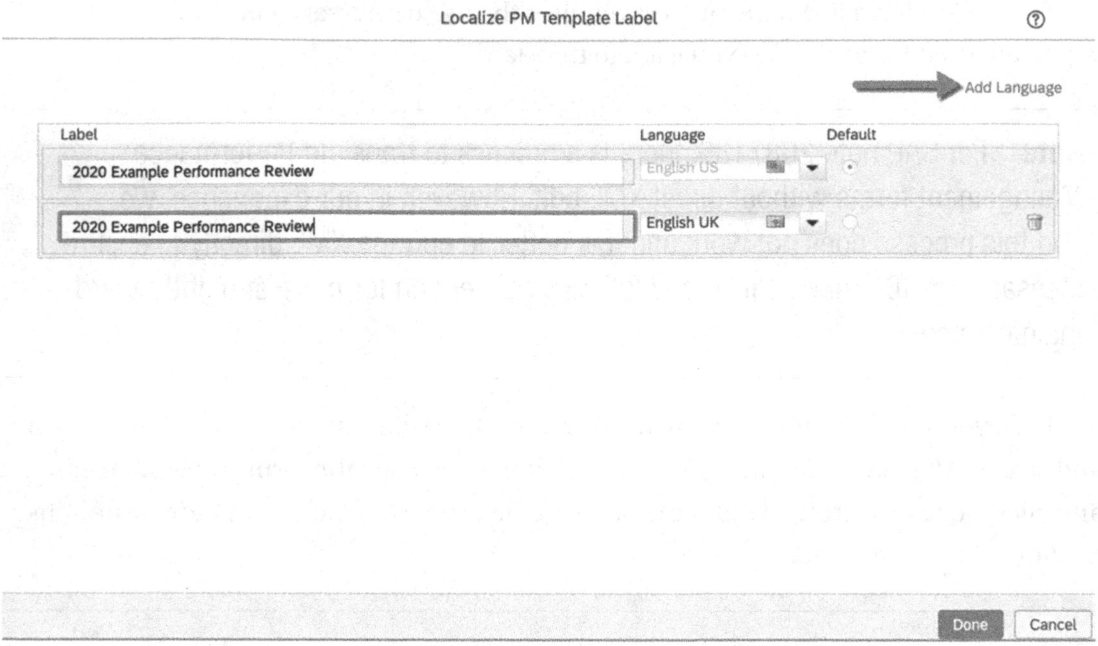

Figure 10-44. *Adding Translations to the Template Name*

Click Done and then click Save. You will now need to add message keys to the XML. Follow the steps in the previous sections to open the XML for editing.

You will notice at the top of the XML, there is a declaration of what the locale is on the form as seen in the following example. We recommend leaving this alone – this will be the language that the admin was using at the time the form was created. You can still add message keys in any language regardless of what this is set to:

```
<sf-form locale="en_US">
```

The process of inserting message keys consists of finding each label that is visible to the end user and adding the attribute msgKey="MESSAGEKEYID" to each labeled element where MESSAGEKEYID is the unique ID for each label. See the following example:

```
<fm-sect-name msgKey="PM_SectionNameEmployeeInfo"><![CDATA[Employee
Information]]></fm-sect-name>
```

The following elements with labels should be considered for message key insertion within each section:

- *-sect-name
- *-sect-intro
- rating-label
- rating-label-others
- unrated-rating
- default-rating
- *-comments-label
- *-button-label

When this code is inserted, the system will attempt to find uploaded translations associated with these message keys for the language of the end user. If the language is not found, it will use the default language set for the label in the message key. If that is not found, the system will default to showing the CDATA entry, in this case "Review Dates."

Note   Keys can be used across multiple forms, so it is important to come up with a msgKey ID that will make sense across forms. For example, if you copy a form, all the message keys will still work unless you add a field or section that has no message key yet. If you decide to change what the label says, you can then edit the one key, and it will change across all the forms that use it.

Once you have inserted message keys into the XML code, you will need to upload the translations associated with each key. This is accomplished in the "Manage Form Label Translations" screen. Type and select ""Manage Form Label Translations" in the search bar to navigate to the screen. Click "Export Form Label Translations." Click the radio button for "Export label keys by form template" and click the "Select" button to choose your form template. Then click Export. An example is shown in Figure 10-45. If you have not uploaded any keys yet, this will export just the headers of the template so you can add keys as needed. Otherwise, it will export all keys used on that template so you can make updates and add keys as needed.

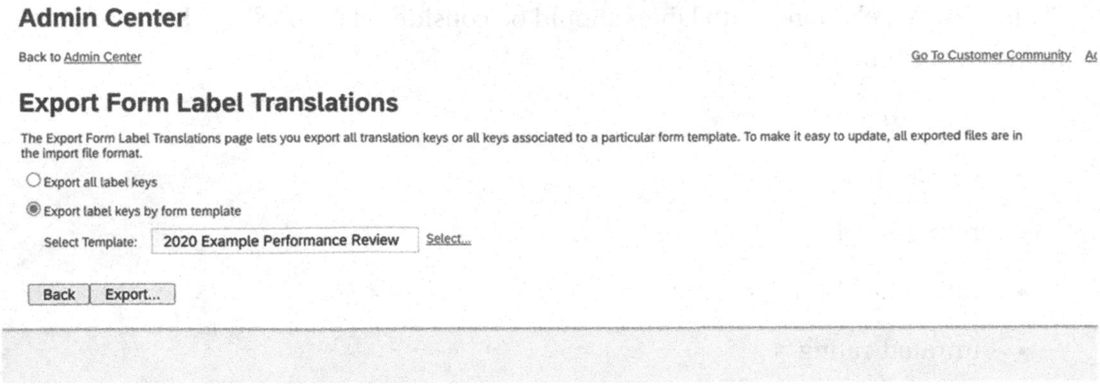

Admin Center

Back to Admin Center

Go To Customer Community   Ac

Export Form Label Translations

The Export Form Label Translations page lets you export all translation keys or all keys associated to a particular form template. To make it easy to update, all exported files are in the import file format.

○ Export all label keys

◉ Export label keys by form template

Select Template: | 2020 Example Performance Review | Select...

[Back]   [Export...]

Figure 10-45. Exporting Form Label Translations Prior to Upload

Edit the .csv field and add/update labels as needed for each message key you added to the XML. The message keys will not show up automatically after you updated your XML; you will need to add each if this is your first time adding translations on this screen. Be sure the values you insert for the label_key match exactly (including case) with each msgKey value in your XML. Provide the default locale code to use in column B. Then provide the translation for each locale in the subsequent columns.

A	B	C	D	E	F	G	H
label_key	default	ar_SA	de_DE	en_DEBUG	en_GB	en_US	es_ES
PM_SectionNameEmployeeInfo	en_US	Employee Information	Employee Information	Employee Information	Employee Information	Employee Information	Employee Information

Figure 10-46. Example msgKey Translations Entered into .csv Template

When you are finished making your edits, click "Back" and then click "Import Form Label Translation File." Choose the file and click "Upload". If your file is formatted properly, you will receive a success message as shown in Figure 10-47.

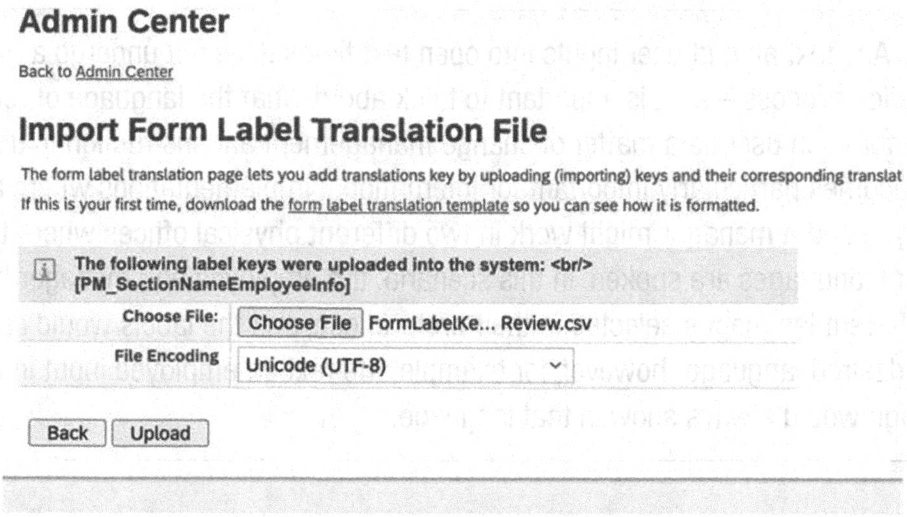

Admin Center

Back to Admin Center

Import Form Label Translation File

The form label translation page lets you add translations key by uploading (importing) keys and their corresponding translat

If this is your first time, download the form label translation template so you can see how it is formatted.

> **ⓘ** **The following label keys were uploaded into the system:
**
> **[PM_SectionNameEmployeeInfo]**

Choose File: [Choose File] FormLabelKe... Review.csv

File Encoding   [Unicode (UTF-8)   ∨]

[Back] [Upload]

Figure 10-47. *Successful Import of msgKey Translations*

Now you can return to the main screen by clicking "Back." You will be able to search for the labels you uploaded on this screen or search by the specific form template. In this manner, if you use the same keys on multiple templates, you can also see all the templates that use the same key by clicking the link with the number of templates on the right. An example is shown in Figure 10-48.

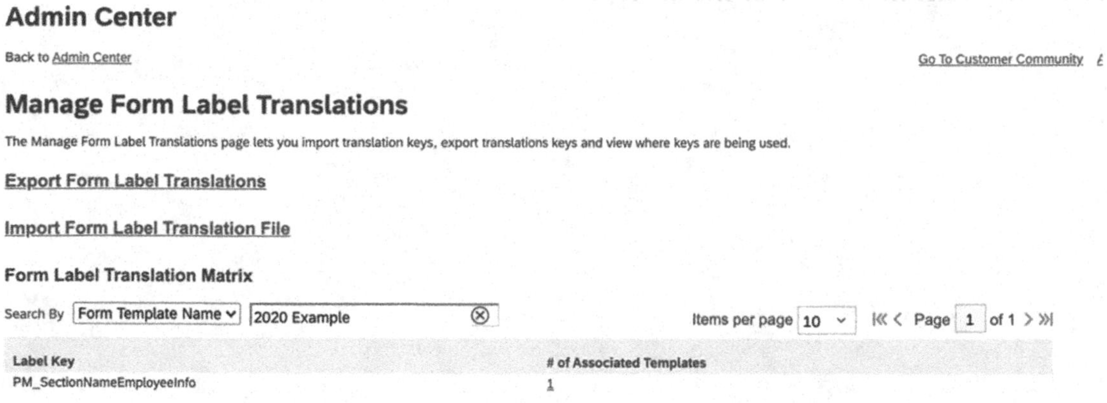

Admin Center

Back to Admin Center   Go To Customer Community £

Manage Form Label Translations

The Manage Form Label Translations page lets you import translation keys, export translations keys and view where keys are being used.

Export Form Label Translations

Import Form Label Translation File

Form Label Translation Matrix

Search By [Form Template Name ∨] [2020 Example   ⊗]   Items per page [10 ∨] |≪ < Page [1] of 1 > ≫|

Label Key	# of Associated Templates
PM_SectionNameEmployeeInfo	1

Figure 10-48. *Search msgKey Labels by Template Name*

Congratulations! You now know how to add translations to the performance form template! Now when a user views the performance form when they have chosen a different language in their user settings, they will see the translations for the labels.

Note   Any text an end user inputs into open text fields does not undergo a translation process – so it is important to think about what the language of record will be for each user as a matter of change management and instruction to users. This becomes particularly important for international implementations where an employee and a manager might work in two different physical offices where two different languages are spoken. In this scenario, the employee and manager have two different languages selected in their preferences, and the labels would change to the desired language; however, for example, the text an employee input in their language would always show in that language.

Conclusion

We hope you have enjoyed your tour through the XML and advanced options available in Performance Management configuration! At this point, you should be familiar with how to make updates directly in the performance template XML, including those options that are only available for edit in the XML. Additionally, we showed you how to manage translations within the performance template. We hope you found this chapter useful as a reference for these trickier topics!

CHAPTER 11

Ask for Feedback, Get Feedback, Add Modifier, and Add Signer

Now that we've covered Performance Management from end to end, let's take a look at a few unique Performance Management features that can provide value but are little known and/or confusing to many SuccessFactors consultants and users. These are the Ask for Feedback, Get Feedback, Add Signer, and Add Modifier functionalities. In this chapter, we cover considerations when using each feature before diving into configuration. We wrap up each section with a walk-through of how to use each as an end user. We feel these features are important to cover because they can sometimes resolve "dealbreaker" situations where a complex business requirement does not fit into the typical Performance Management route map.

Ask for Feedback

Ask for Feedback enables the manager to send an email to solicit feedback from an internal user or external user. This can be helpful if feedback is required from someone who does not have a SuccessFactors user within your instance such as a sister company, an external vendor, or a customer. The performance form is not sent to the feedback provider; instead, they reply to the email with their comments. Consider the following when using Ask for Feedback:

- It is typically used when information is needed from individuals who cannot be identified through the standard relationships supported in a route map.

© Susan Traynor, Michael A. Wellens and Venki Krishnamoorthy 2021
S. Traynor et al., *SAP SuccessFactors Talent: Volume 1*, https://doi.org/10.1007/978-1-4842-6600-7_11

- It is only as secure as the email system of the recipient (Get Feedback is more secure since it does not rely on email but is restricted to users within your SuccessFactors instance).

- Once the feedback email request is sent, *it cannot be recalled.*

- The feedback provider has no visibility on what the employee is being evaluated, so the comments may or may not necessarily be relevant.

- Once comments are provided, they cannot be deleted.

- The comments will appear in the Supporting Information pod as well as in Team Overview.

Configuring Ask for Feedback

The form template must have Ask for Feedback enabled. Within the form template advanced settings, there are two Ask for Feedback checkboxes and two date-related fields to set. An example is shown in Figure 11-1.

Managing Form Templates

Use this page to manage existing form templates.   Note: any in-progress forms using this template will be immediately updated with the settings below.

Template Name:	2020 Performance Review Ask for FB
	English US (English US)
Template Type:	PM Review
Last Modified:	2020-08-07 15:46:35.0
Routing Map:	Performance Review Routemap

Default Dates for Form Creation:
Warning - Mixing Fixed and Relative to Form Creation Date can result in invalid dates set.

Default Start Date:	◉ Fixed ○ Relative	01/01/2020
Default End Date:	◉ Fixed ○ Relative	12/31/2020
Default Due Date:	◉ Fixed ○ Relative	02/15/2021

☐ Disable Ask For Feedback functionality

☑ Enable Ask for Feedback Responses in Supporting Pod permissions. If this switch is not enabled, the Ask for Feedback responses will use the original permission model which is to only be displayed to the user who requested the feedback

☑ Disable the external email address feedback option

Date range for collecting feedback from employees:

Start Date:	○ Fixed ◉ Relative to:	Form Creation Date	0	Days after(+) or before(-)
End Date:	○ Fixed ◉ Relative to:	Form Creation Date	30	Days after(+) or before(-)

Figure 11-1. *Advanced Template Settings for Ask for Feedback*

To use Ask for Feedback in the form, select "Enable Ask for Feedback Responses in Supporting Pod permissions." If this option is not visible, deselect "Disable Ask for

Feedback functionality," and it should now be visible. The other checkbox for Ask for Feedback, "Disable the external email address feedback option," determines if feedback may be requested within the organization only or externally as well.

The date range for collecting feedback must be defined. The start and end dates may be fixed or relative. Relative dates are based on the number of days before or after any of the following dates:

- Form Creation Date

- Default Start Date

- Default End Date

- Default Due Date

Ask for Feedback dates are independent of any route map dates.

When using "Before," be sure to use a negative number to denote the number of days prior to the relative date.

General Settings

After "Ask for Feedback" is enabled and the advanced settings are saved, close the advanced settings popup window. Save and close the template. When you go back into the form template, return to "General Settings," click "Show advanced options...," and you will now be able to create permissions for Ask for Feedback as seen in Figure 11-2.

Figure 11-2. *Ask for Feedback Permissions*

The manager will be able to see the Ask for Feedback responses in Team Overview. The comments are also found in the Supporting Information pod on the performance form. Within *Button Permissions*, access to the Supporting Information pod needs to be granted for each role in each step that should have access to the comments. An example is shown in Figure 11-3.

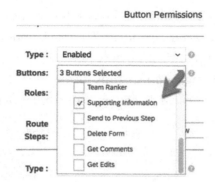

Figure 11-3. *Supporting Information Pod Permission*

Granting the pod access does not grant permission to see the feedback comments; it only provides visibility of the pod on the form.

Based on an organization's transparency, some hide the feedback comments from the employee. In those situations, the feedback is used solely for the manager to help in making rating decisions. In addition, feedback responders may feel less inclined to give honest feedback knowing that it will be visible to the employee.

Access to the feedback responses is set in "Ask for Feedback data in Supporting Information Pod Permissions." An example is shown in Figure 11-4.

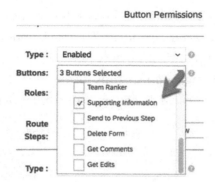

Figure 11-4. *Ask for Feedback Permissions*

Permission types are "None" or "Read." With "None" permission, a user will not see the comments in the Supporting Information pod. "Read" permission grants a user the visibility of the feedback comments in the Supporting Information pod. In the example shown in the preceding figure, "None" permission was granted for the employee for "All" steps. This ensures the employee will not see the comments in any modify and signature step in addition to the completed form. To allow users access to the comments, a "Read" permission is granted to a role for certain steps. If permissions are not set, all users will see the feedback in all steps. If no feedback is given, the comment icon will appear with a zero count in the Supporting Information pod.

Route Map Setting

In addition to the settings and permissions in the form template, there is a setting to enable in the first step of the route map associated with the form template. Type and select "Manage Route Maps" in the search bar.

Open the route map associated with the form template. Go to the first step and click "Show advanced options." Scroll to the very bottom of the screen, and beneath "Step Id," you will see three checkboxes as seen in Figure 11-5. Enable "Start of Review" and save the route map.

Figure 11-5. *Start of Review Enabled for the First Step*

This setting identifies the start of the step as the start of the review process. It also ensures that the Ask for Feedback button is available in Team Overview.

Email Notification

Ask for Feedback is based on email notifications that are sent to feedback providers who in turn respond directly within the email. There is an email notification to enable for the email request functionality to work. Type and select "E-Mail Notification Templates Settings" in the search bar. Enable "Request Feedback Notification" as seen in Figure 11-6. You can also modify the content of the email template here.

Figure 11-6. *Enable Request Feedback Notification*

Note   "Feedback Request Reminder Notification" is no longer supported, so do not enable it.

Using Ask for Feedback

Within Team Overview, a manager can ask for feedback by sending an email to one or more individuals (please ensure your managers have the Team Overview Access Permission). Feedback may come from many different sources. The request may go to anyone within the organization that has a valid email address. It is also possible to allow external responses. The individuals provide feedback by replying to the email. The response is stored in a pod on the performance form. The response is text only with no attachments. In our experience, we find Ask for Feedback is typically used in the following scenarios:

- When feedback is required from several individuals (up to 30 requests are permitted)

- When you would like the manager to be able to edit the form while the feedback responses are pending

- When you do not want the feedback providers to have any visibility of the performance form

- When you would like to have feedback on the employee that may not be specific to the goals and competencies found on the performance form

- When you would like to have the option for external feedback

- When you would like to allow feedback over a specific period of time which may span several steps of the review process

Team Overview

Any live forms for the manager's direct reports will display on the Team Overview screen; and it is here where the Ask for Feedback feature is used to request feedback, track if feedback has been given, and view feedback. Type and select Team Overview in the search bar to access it. Team Overview will display launched forms grouped by form template. An example is shown in Figure 11-7.

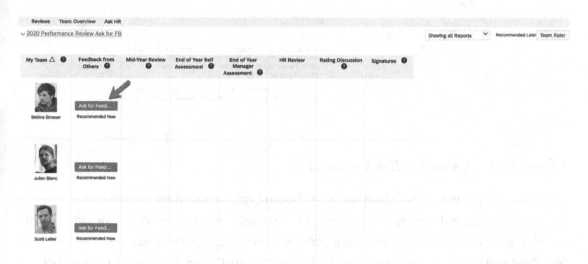

Figure 11-7. *Ask for Feedback*

You see that there is an Ask for Feedback button for each employee. The "Feedback from Others" column displays prior to the route map step columns.

Note   The manager can track the step for each form and, depending on the feedback date range, continue to ask for feedback until the maximum of 30 requests is met or the end date for giving feedback has passed.

Click the "Ask for Feedback" button, and a popup will display as seen in Figure 11-8.

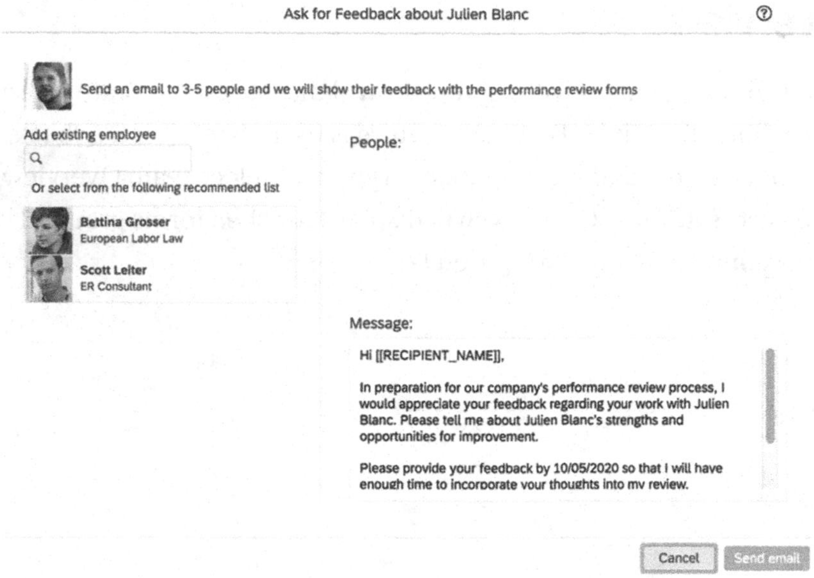

Figure 11-8. *Ask for Feedback Request*

The manager may search for a name or choose from the recommended list of employees who are the peers of the employee. A predefined message will be included in the email request although it may be customized by the manager prior to sending. As names are searched and selected, they appear under People as *New Requests* as seen in Figure 11-9.

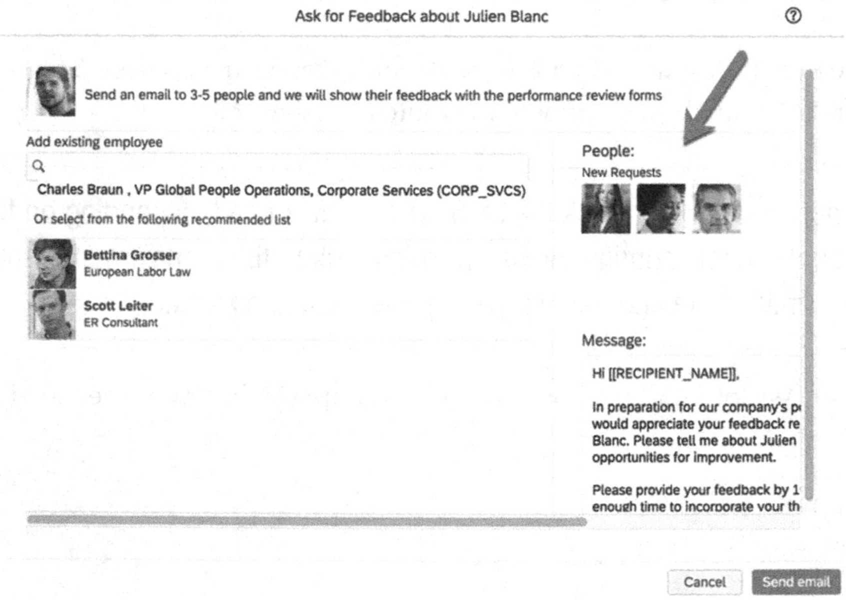

Figure 11-9. *Selected Recipients*

If external user feedback is enabled, there will also be an option to select an external email address as seen in Figure 11-10.

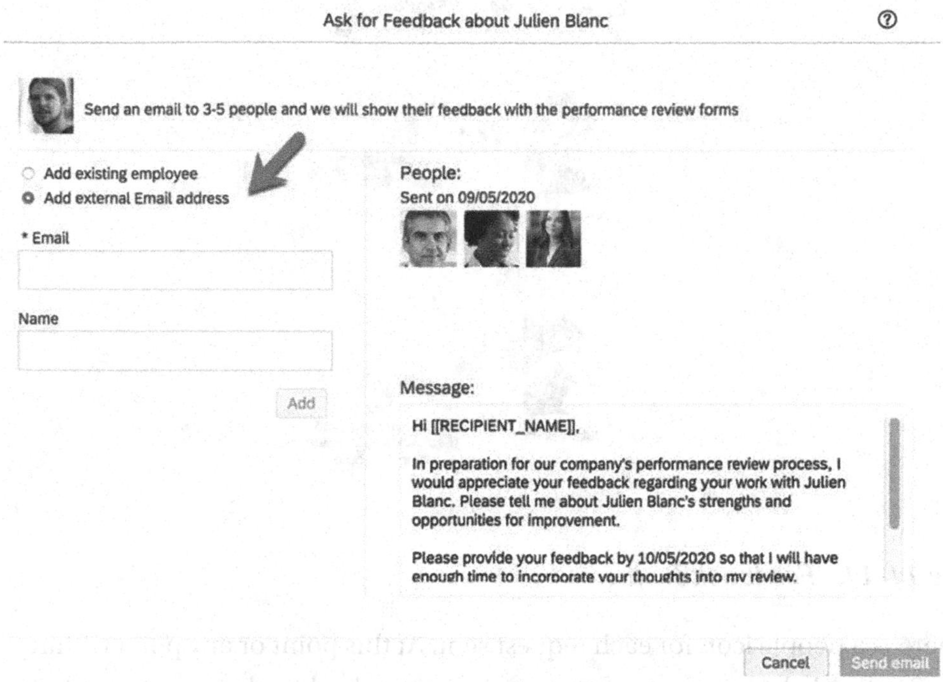

Figure 11-10. *Feedback from an External Person*

Once the email is sent, the Team Overview page shows that feedback has been requested by displaying a people icon. An example is shown in Figure 11-11.

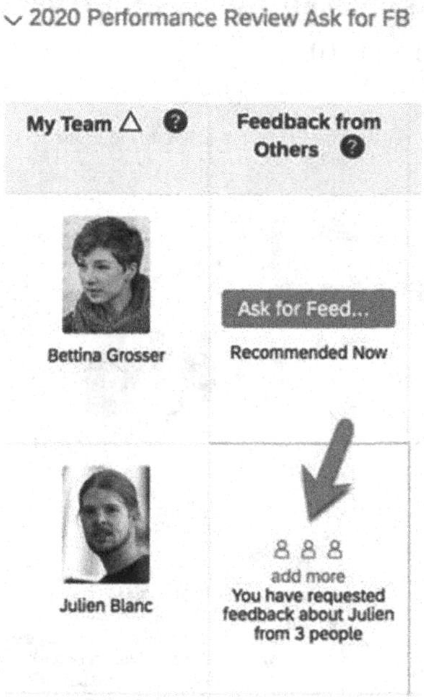

Figure 11-11. *Feedback Requested*

There is a people icon for each request sent. At this point or any point within the Ask for Feedback date range, the manager may come back and request more feedback up until 30 requests have been made. The email request is received by each feedback provider as seen in Figure 11-12.

Performance Feedback request for Julien Blanc

SYSTEM <system@successfactors.com>
Charles Braun; Marcus Wright
Saturday, September 5, 2020 at 12:41 PM
Show Details

~~~~~Click on reply and enter your text to add feedback~~~~~

Hi Charles Braun,

In preparation for our company's performance review process, I would appreciate your feedback regarding your work with Julien Blanc. Please tell me about Julien Blanc's strengths and opportunities for improvement.

Please provide your feedback by 10/05/2020 so that I will have enough time to incorporate your thoughts into my review.

Thank you,
Marcus Wright

Request Feedback #b11bc483991a290e205519f1a53bcdc6$

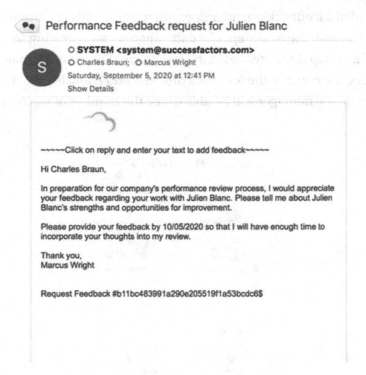

Figure 11-12. *Ask for Feedback Email*

The recipient of the feedback request replies to the email with comments as seen in Figure 11-13.

To: feedbackSFPART050144@mail-sd4.successfactors.com
Cc:
Subject: Re: Performance Feedback request for Julien Blanc

Julien worked with me on a six month project that required a lot of his time, patience and expertise. His efforts were resulted in a well-executed project under budget and on time.

From: SYSTEM <system@successfactors.com>
Reply-To: <feedbackSFPART050144@mail-sd4.successfactors.com>
Date: Saturday, September 5, 2020 at 12:41 PM
To: Charles Braun <catgleek@gmail.com>
Cc: Marcus Wright <straynor@worklogix.com>
Subject: Performance Feedback request for Julien Blanc

~~~~~Click on reply and enter your text to add feedback~~~~~

Hi Charles Braun,

In preparation for our company's performance review process, I would appreciate your feedback regarding your work with Julien Blanc. Please tell me about Julien Blanc's strengths and opportunities for improvement.

Please provide your feedback by 10/05/2020 so that I will have enough time to incorporate your thoughts into my review.

Thank you,
Marcus Wright

Request Feedback #b11bc483991a290e205519f1a53bcdc6$

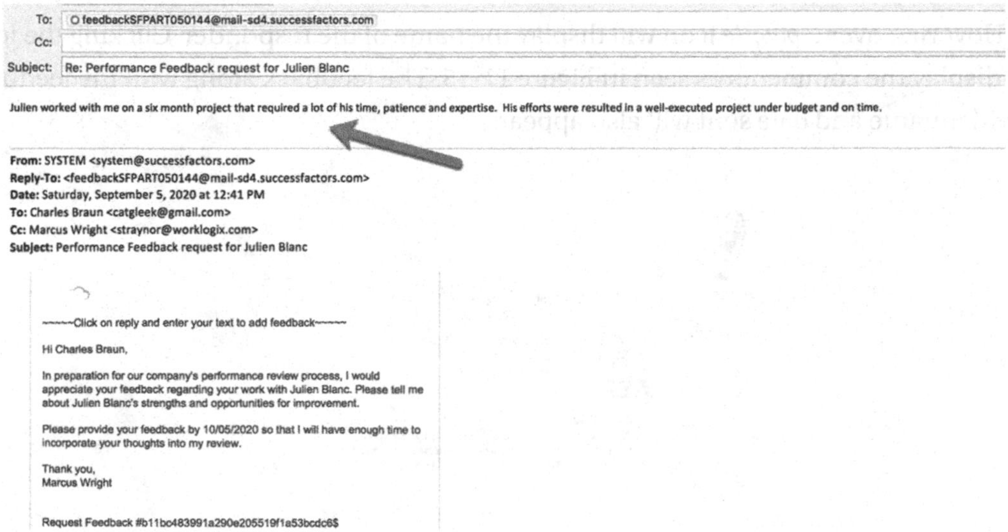

Figure 11-13. *Feedback Reply*

Keep in mind, if a feedback provider does not respond, this will not prevent the form from moving on to the next step. The date range set for receiving feedback is independent of any step due dates set in the route map. The manager may hover over the people icon to see the name of the feedback provider and if any feedback was received. As feedback is sent, the manager will be able to see the number of replies as seen in Figure 11-14.

Figure 11-14.   *Count of Responses Received*

Hovering over a *people* icon will display the name of the responder. Clicking the icon will display the comments as seen in Figure 11-15. The feedback along with the feedback provider name and date sent will also appear.

Figure 11-15.   *View of Feedback*

When the manager goes into the employee's form, the Supporting Information pod shows the comments as well. As seen in Figure 11-16, the comment icon in the pod shows that there are two comments. The pod also shows attachments. In the example, there is an attachment as well. Attachments are separate from feedback and may be permitted differently.

Figure 11-16. *Feedback in the Supporting Information Pod*

Clicking the pod will display its contents as shown in Figure 11-17.

Figure 11-17. *View of Feedback from the Supporting Information Pod*

The count of feedback received will display along a count of attachments. There is a jump to either section. The comments, the feedback provider, and the date sent will display for each feedback received. If the Supporting Information pod was configured for attachments, the manager may add or view any attachments.

In the example seen in Figure 11-18, when the form moves to the employee self-assessment step, there is no visibility of the feedback in the Supporting

Information pod. The employee may only add or view attachments. This example is based on the permissions set in the form template and the form template XML. The employee may view the attachment added by the manager or add additional comments.

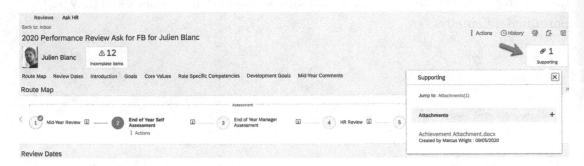

Figure 11-18. *Employee View of the Supporting Information Pod*

We have now completed our tour of the Ask for Feedback functionality. You've seen some scenarios when this should be used as well as considerations to take when deciding to use it. We then walked through detailed configuration steps and have seen the Ask for Feedback functionality in use. Now let's take a look at Get Feedback.

Note   If you are having trouble receiving feedback, there might be an issue with the mail system blocking the emails. In this event, you may have to work with the mail system technical resources to ensure the emails are added to a whitelist. We also recommend not using large graphics that an email system may reject. For more troubleshooting tips, please refer to SAP note 2078040.

Get Feedback

Get Feedback enables the user to send the performance form to a user outside the route map to get edits and/or comments directly on the form. Unlike Ask for Feedback, this is limited to only users within your SuccessFactors instance. This can be useful when a person who is not easily identified within one of the standard SuccessFactors roles may have beneficial input into the subject employee's review. After the feedback is completed, the form is then sent back in the same step to the original user. Take the following into consideration when using Get Feedback:

- When a form is sent for feedback, it is removed from the user's inbox and is not available for edit. The user would have to recall the form or wait for the feedback provider to complete the form.

- The use of Get Feedback does not create a new step. It acts somewhat like an iterative step in that one user can edit while the other user in the step may view the form.

- The form can only be sent to one feedback provider at a time. Once it is out for feedback, it cannot be sent to another feedback provider until they complete the review or the manager recalls the form.

- Get Feedback cannot be used in a collaborative step.

- The feedback provider would get an email notification if the document routing notification is turned on; otherwise, they would only see a To-Do item on their home page.

- When the feedback provider submits the form, it goes back to the step where the request was made. The form cannot be routed to the next step.

- The name of the feedback provider is associated with any comments made.

- The form cannot be routed to the next step until the feedback has been added or the manager has recalled the form.

Configuration of Get Feedback

To use Get Feedback, there are two checkboxes to deselect in the advanced form template settings. When deselected, ratings and comments can be requested. There are also button permissions to enable in the form template which will allow the use of the Get Feedback button. In addition, there are comments and rating field permissions to be granted in the Goals, Competency, and Summary sections. The template can be configured to allow comments and ratings.

Asking for comments without "Ask for Edit Routing" enabled and permitted will allow only comments, not ratings.

Form Template Advanced Settings

In the advanced settings of the form template, ensure that "Disable Ask For Comment Routing" is not checked. If you are allowing the feedback providers to rate as well, make sure "Disable Ask For Edit Routing" is not checked. See Figure 11-19 for an example of the settings.

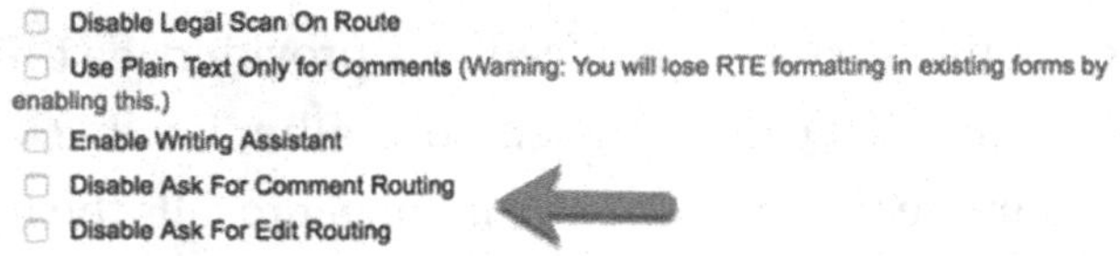

Figure 11-19. *Settings for Get Feedback*

These options control the visibility of the Get Feedback button on the performance form. When both routing types are disabled, the Get Feedback button will not be visible. And users will have the option to ask for either comments or edits in the Get Feedback confirmation page after selecting the user they want to send the form to.

Note   It is important to note that private goals will be visible to the recipient of the form through Get Feedback. This can come as a surprise to many customers and is important to cover during the testing process. For more information, see SAP note 2072246.

When both options are deselected, the Get Comments and Get Edits buttons may be permitted to allow comments and ratings when using Get Feedback. If you have only deselected "Disable Ask For Comment Routing," you may only grant permission for the Get Comments button. Similarly, when only "Disable Ask For Edit Routing" is deselected, you may only grant permission for the Get Edits button. The Get Feedback button will appear on the form if either the Get Comments or Get Edits button has been permitted. The difference lies in which option the feedback provider may do.

Button Permissions

The button permissions for Get Comments and Get Edits allow comments or ratings to be added by the feedback provider on the form. Depending on which feedback type you wish to allow, set these button permissions by roles and steps. Set permission to "None" or "Enabled" for these buttons in the step where feedback may be provided. The buttons should only be "Enabled" in steps where you want to see the Get Feedback button on the performance form.

An example is shown in Figure 11-20.

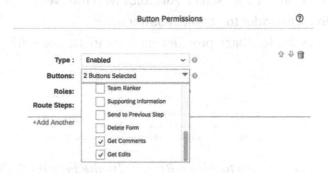

Figure 11-20. *Get Feedback Button Permissions*

Section and Field Permissions

If a section or field is hidden or disabled for all roles in all steps, it must be enabled for all roles in the step where Get Feedback is enabled. An example is shown in Figure 11-21.

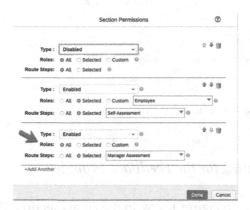

Figure 11-21. *Permission for the Feedback Provider to Edit the Section*

Based on your requirements, set the comments and rating field permissions in the Goals, Competency, or Summary section. You will use "All" roles for enabling the permissions for the step where Get Feedback is used. You don't have to allow comments or ratings in all sections. For example, you may decide to allow the feedback provider to enter comments for goals and ratings for competencies along with a Summary section comment.

In another example, to enable item comments by the feedback provider at the manager step in the Goals section, select "All" roles with the "Write" permission. This will allow the feedback provider to provide comments.

To allow ratings by the feedback provider, it is best to use the settings shown in Figure 11-22.

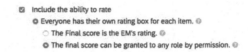

Figure 11-22. *Rating Options to Allow Ratings by the Feedback Provider*

This option will give every role a rating box, and the final score is granted to a specific role using the rating field permission in a step.

When allowing the feedback provider to rate goals or competencies, the field to permit is "Unofficial User Rating" as seen in Figure 11-23.

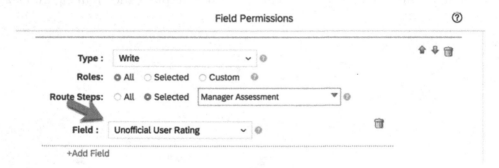

Figure 11-23. *Item Rating for the Feedback Provider*

In the example shown in Figure 11-24, in the Goals section, the "The Final score is the EM's rating" option only allows a subject's rating and manager rating. This means an "other's rating" is not possible. Do not use this option if you want the feedback provider to do item ratings in a section.

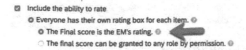

Figure 11-24. *Rating Option That Does Not Allow Ratings by Others*

Once you have set your permissions, save and close the form template. We will now look at the email notification for Get Feedback.

Email Notification

Type and select "E-Mail Notification Templates Settings" in the search bar. Verify that "Document Routing Notification" is enabled if you wish to notify the user providing the feedback.

Using Get Feedback

The manager can send the Get Feedback request from two locations on the performance form. In the route map shown across the top of the form, the current step has a dropdown list for the actions available. As seen in Figure 11-25, Get Feedback is available.

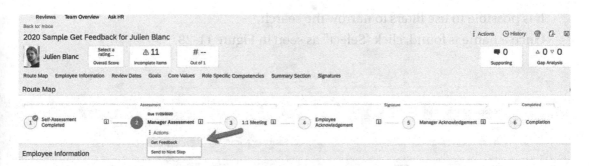

Figure 11-25. *Get Feedback Through Route Step Action*

Scrolling down the form to the buttons section, the Get Feedback button will appear as seen in Figure 11-26.

Figure 11-26. *Get Feedback Button*

Using either option, a series of screens will display starting with a name search. An example is shown in Figure 11-27.

Figure 11-27. *Search for Feedback Providers*

It is possible to use filters to narrow the search.

Once a name is found, click "Select" as seen in Figure 11-28.

Figure 11-28. *Select a User for Feedback*

The "Confirm" step displays. Here, you select if comments or edits are being requested. You may add a comment that will display in the email. If you select "Edits," if ratings and comments are permitted for sections, the user will be able to do both. An example is shown in Figure 11-29.

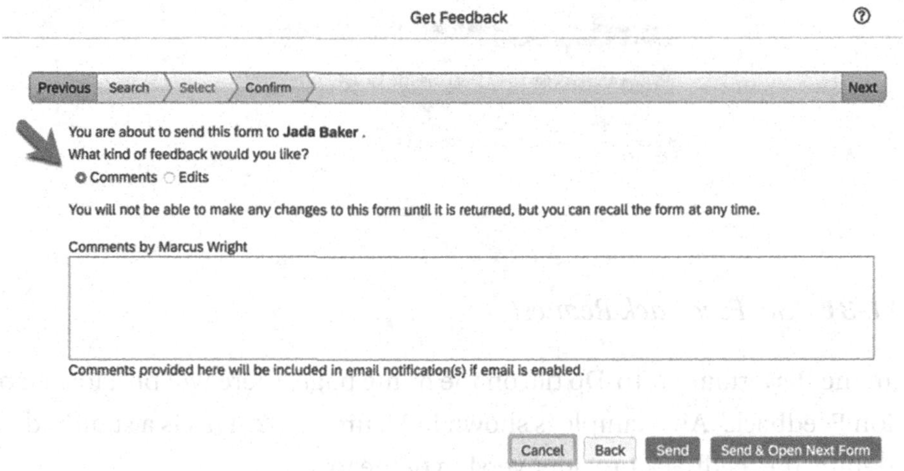

Figure 11-29. *Selecting Feedback Type*

Once the form is sent, the manager's inbox displays. The form will not be seen here. Instead, the form is in the manager's En Route folder as seen in Figure 11-30. This means the form is read-only for the manager.

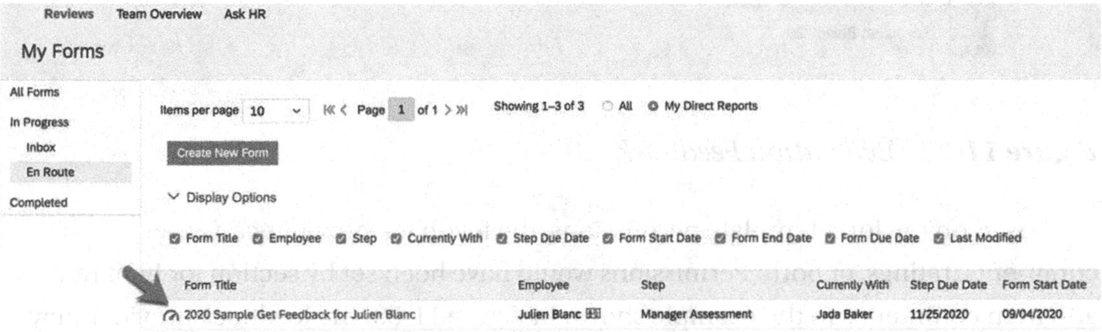

Figure 11-30. *Form in the Manager's En Route Folder*

When the manager requests feedback, an email is sent. An example is shown in Figure 11-31.

Figure 11-31. *Get Feedback Request*

Within the Performance To-Do tile on the home page, there will be a form labeled "Evaluation Feedback." An example is shown in Figure 11-32. This is a standard phrase used to identify the feedback provider version of the form.

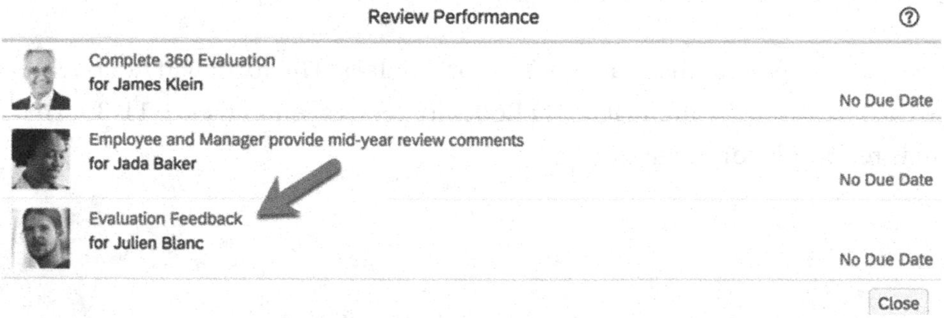

Figure 11-32. *Evaluation Feedback*

Based on the form template permissions, the feedback provider can enter comments, ratings, or both. Permissions would have been set by section for item ratings and item comments. In the example shown in Figure 11-33, the feedback provider may add goal item ratings and comments.

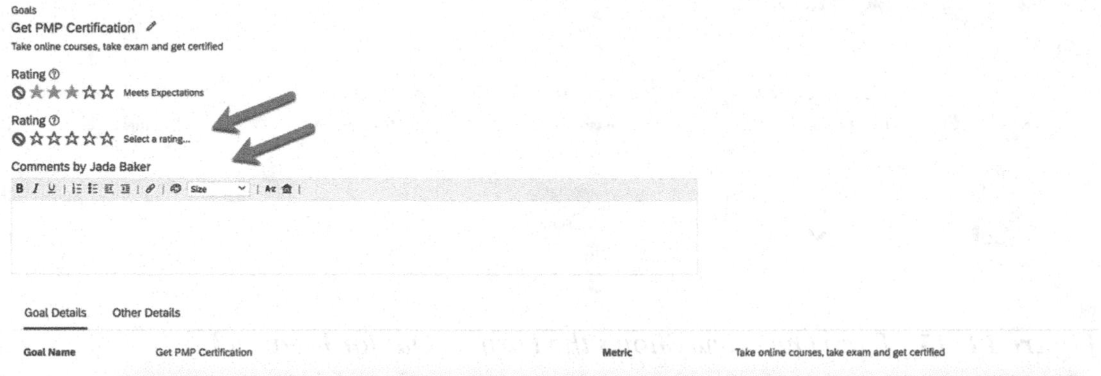

Goals

Get PMP Certification 🖉

Take online courses, take exam and get certified

Rating ⓘ
🚫 ★ ★ ★ ☆ ☆   Meets Expectations

Rating ⓘ
🚫 ☆ ☆ ☆ ☆ ☆   Select a rating...

Comments by Jada Baker

| B *I* U | ≔ ≔ ≖ ⊞ | 𝒫 | ⊕ Size ⌄ | A̲ 🏠 |

Goal Details   Other Details

Goal Name   Get PMP Certification   **Metric**   Take online courses, take exam and get certified

Figure 11-33. *Feedback Provider Adds Goal Item Rating and Comments*

In the example, the manager had entered goal item ratings, saved the form, and then sent for feedback. The feedback provider is then able to see the manager rating and enter their own rating. When the form is sent back to the manager, the manager will have read access to the feedback provider's comments and ratings, and their own rating may be edited. While with the feedback provider, the form is read-only for the manager who knows who has the form. The manager may recall the form by the route step action or the "Recall Feedback" button at the bottom of screen. An example is shown in Figure 11-34.

Figure 11-34. *Recall a Form via the Step Action*

When the form has been sent for feedback, the only button available is "Recall Feedback." If the form is recalled, it is removed from the inbox of the feedback provider and returns to the manager's inbox. You can also see if a form is out for feedback in Team Overview as seen in Figure 11-35.

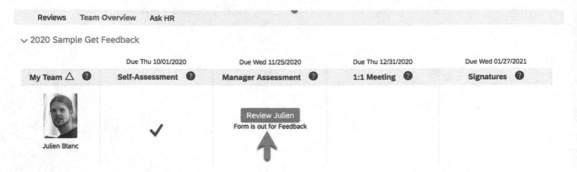

Figure 11-35. *Team Overview Shows the Form Is Out for Feedback*

You now know how to configure and use Get Feedback! Now let's take a look at Add Modifier and Add Signer.

Add/Remove Modifier or Signer

The Add Modifier option allows a user to send the form to someone outside the route map to get ratings and comments or to add a signer. Unlike Get Feedback, the form gets routed to a new step and then moves on to the next step from there. This can be useful when a person who is not easily identified within one of the standard SuccessFactors roles may have critical input into the subject employee's review and you may want them to participate in the rating or signing process.

It is important to take the following considerations when using Add Modifier:

- There is not a way to limit the number of modifiers that a user may add.

- This feature creates a new user-defined step.

- The form does not go back to the user who sent the form. The form will move on to the next step.

- Adding additional steps may interfere with route map steps with enforced exit dates. If the additional steps are not completed prior to the due date of a later step, the form would not auto route for the later step.

- The new step and associated username become part of the route map seen at the top of the form.

Configuration

In the advanced settings of the form template, there is an option which allows a user to add or remove a signer to the form. The setting is shown in Figure 11-36.

Figure 11-36. *Deselect Hide Add/Remove Signer buttons*

To allow adding a signer, this option must not be checked.

There is also an option to identify when a modifier may be added as seen in Figure 11-37.

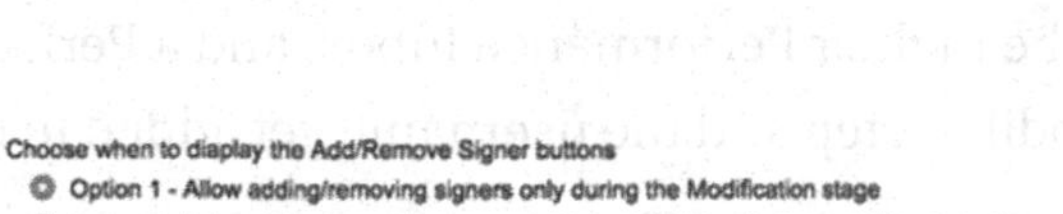

Choose when to display the Add/Remove Signer buttons
- Option 1 - Allow adding/removing signers only during the Modification stage
- Option 2 - Allow adding/removing signers during both the Modification and Signature stages

Figure 11-37. *Select Stages for the Button*

With the option to add a signer at the Modification stage only, the new signer is inserted before the existing signers. If the current signer of the form adds an additional signer, the form will be routed to the new signer next.

Note   Remember that for both the Add Modifier and Add/Remove Signer features, the button permissions are set in the form template XML as we saw in the Button Permissions section. Also, Goals, Competency, and Summary sections would need to be enabled for all roles so that the additional users may edit. Last, the Add Modifier step will use the same document routing notification as a regular step.

Using Add Modifier or Add Signer

The user will have access to the Add Modifier or Add Signer feature through a button at the bottom of the form as well as an action in the current route step seen in the route map at the top of the performance form based on button permissions. This action may only be added before the form has gone to the signature step.

An example is shown in Figure 11-38.

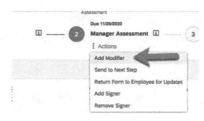

Figure 11-38. *Actions to Add a Modifier*

Once the user selects a modifier, upon submission of the form, a new step is created for them. If the document routing email notification is enabled, the *modifier* will be notified. The form will be in their Performance Inbox, and a Performance To-Do item will be created. The modifier step and the username get added to the route map on the form.

Once the modifier has completed their feedback, the form will go on to the next step in the route map.

After clicking Add Modifier or Add Signer, a wizard will pop up that walks the user through the steps to select a modifier or signer. The process begins with a name search as seen in the example in Figure 11-39.

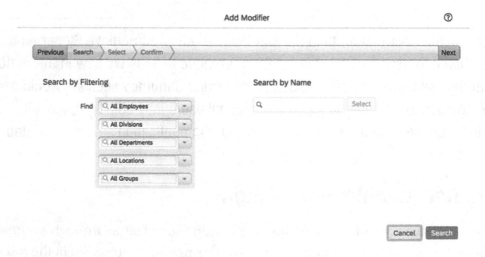

Figure 11-39. *Search for a Modifier or Signer*

After the name selection, in the confirmation step of the sign wizard, you may cancel, save, or add more modifiers or signers as seen in Figure 11-40.

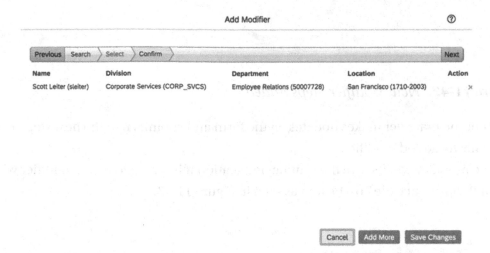

Figure 11-40. *Confirm a Signer*

In the Action column, you can delete the selected modifier as well.

Click "Add More" to select additional modifiers or signers. The Search and Select steps will repeat. In the Confirm step, the modifiers or signers may be deleted or reordered. Reordering impacts which modifier will precede the other. An example is shown in Figure 11-41.

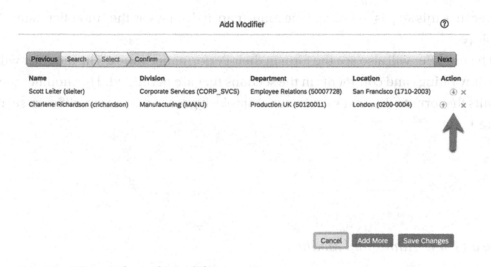

Figure 11-41. *View Selected Modifiers or Signers*

When finished adding or editing modifiers or signers, click "Save Changes." The route map at the top of the form will reflect the additional modifiers or signers as new steps as seen in Figure 11-42 (shown as "added signer" for signers).

Figure 11-42. *New Modifier Steps Added*

After the manager makes updates on the form and submits it to the next step, it will go the newly added modifier.

The modifier will receive the routing notification if it is enabled. The modifier will have a Performance tile To-Do item as seen in Figure 11-43.

Figure 11-43. *To-Do Item for the Modifier*

Because this step is not part of the route map, it displays as the "modifier' name" for [employee].

The modifier will also see the form in their Performance Inbox. The modifier will make any ratings and comments in the sections that are permitted. The modifier then submits the form to the next step. In our example, it goes to another modifier as seen in Figure 11-44.

Figure 11-44. *Additional Modifier*

Once this modifier completes the evaluation, the form will continue on to the next step from the existing route map. When the form has gone through all the steps to completion, the modifier will also get a copy of the form in their Completed folder.

Any managers who were added as signers may also access the form through Team Overview as seen in Figure 11-45.

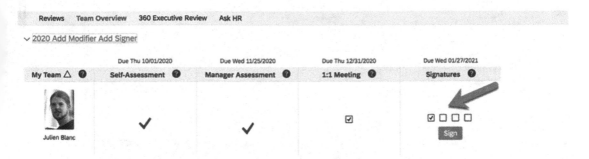

Figure 11-45. Sign Form Through Team Overview

When the user clicks the "Sign" button, a popup displays, and the user may add comments prior to signing as seen in Figure 11-46.

Figure 11-46. Sign from Team Overview

When the user clicks "Sign," the signature and any comments are added, and the form routes to the next signer.

As seen in the example in Figure 11-47, the form shows the signatures of the additional signers.

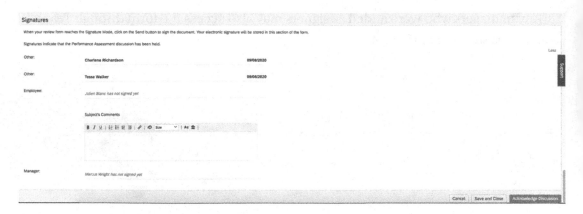

Figure 11-47. *Form with Signatures of Additional Signers*

Once all the signature steps are finished, the form will appear in the *Completed* folder for all those in the route map and the added signers as well.

Note   The user that added signers is the only user that may remove those signers. When new signers receive the form in their inbox but are later removed as signers, an email notification may be sent. For this to happen, the "Removing Current Signer Notification" must be enabled in "E-Mail Notification Templates Settings."

Conclusion

We hope you enjoyed this chapter! We covered a few fun topics that many consultants and users of SuccessFactors are not familiar with: Ask for Feedback, Get Feedback, Add Modifier, and Add Signer. You should now understand the differences between these functionalities and when they might be used. You should also be able to configure each and have an understanding of how they work for end users. In our experience, these features can be used as a creative way to adjust the system to complex requirements.

CHAPTER 12

360 Review

The 360 Review module in SuccessFactors enables the manager and the employee to solicit feedback from other stakeholders (both internal and external) during the performance review process. A typical performance review conducted using SuccessFactors Performance & Goals Management includes the assessment and scoring of objectives and goals by the line manager and the employee. This does not provide all-encompassing feedback about the employee's performance or development needs that would help the manager to better support the employee during performance calibration or a one-to-one meeting with the employee. To specifically support this scenario, organizations leverage the 360 Review module to get feedback from all stakeholders that the employee has worked with, directly or indirectly.

As you can see in Figure 12-1, an employee or the reporting manager on behalf of the employee can request performance feedback from different stakeholders. Getting feedback from team members and other stakeholders helps the employee and the manager to get a more accurate assessment of the employee's performance. These stakeholders can also provide fair and unprejudiced feedback regarding the success and failure stories and can help managers to better understand the development needs of their employees.

© Susan Traynor, Michael A. Wellens and Venki Krishnamoorthy 2021
S. Traynor et al., *SAP SuccessFactors Talent: Volume 1*, https://doi.org/10.1007/978-1-4842-6600-7_12

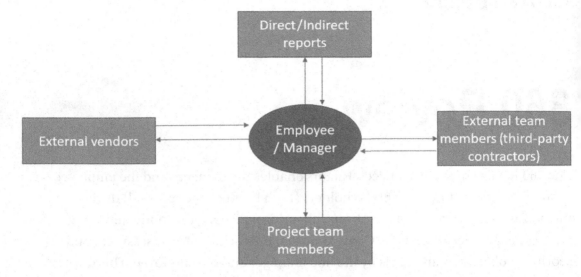

Figure 12-1. *Overview of 360 Review process*

In this chapter, we will review the functionalities of SuccessFactors 360 Review and discuss how to configure a 360 Review feedback form. Also, we will discuss how to integrate with Career Development Planning (CDP) and LMS. We have also provided XML code snippets that can be referred to while configuring the 360 Review feedback template.

Participants in a 360 Review Feedback Process

Before we begin the configuration, let's go over some key concepts about participants. In this section, we will define the different participants in the SuccessFactors 360 Review feedback process. We will refer to the following participants throughout this chapter:

- *Subject*: This is the employee for whom the 360 Review feedback form is launched. There can be only one subject in a form.

- *Originator*: This is the person who will generate the form. This role is automatically assigned by the system to the person who generates the form. Typically, the person in this role will be the 360 Review feedback form administrator or somebody from HR.

- *Process Owner*: This is the person who will distribute the form to the participants and starts the evaluation phase of the process. This role is automatically assigned to the person who clicks the button on the form to distribute the form for evaluation. A form can have one process owner only. Typically, the process owner will be the originator or the subject or the manager of the subject.

- *Approver*: During the approval phase, the approver is the person who review the feedback and choice of participants and approves the process. Typically, this role is assigned to the subject's manager or somebody from HR.

Note   Any role assigned to the process and part of the route map is considered an approver.

Approvers have two subtypes.

- *Privileged approver*: This role is assigned to the person who at the end of the process will manage and work with the feedback data.

- *Participant reviewer*: This role is assigned to the person who during the evaluation phase will receive the form and provide feedback about the subject. The participant reviewer has the option to decline or participate in the review process. Participant reviewers who decline to participate in the feedback process are not included in the feedback results. A subject can also be a participant reviewer; in other words, the subject can do a self-assessment. The process can have multiple participant reviewers.

Now that you understand what part each participant will play in the process, let's start prepping the system by activating the 360 functionality in Provisioning.

Activating 360 Review in Provisioning

In SuccessFactors Provisioning, you are required to activate the following switches. These switches are available in "Company Settings".

Tip   On the displayed page, you can press Ctrl+F and search for these settings. Remember to save your settings.

- 360 Multi-Rater

- Enable 360 Executive Review Page — requires 360 Multi-Rater and Role Based Permission

- Graphical Report (360) — requires 360 Multi-Rater

- Rich text editor for PM and 360

- Team Rater for 360

- Ad Hoc Report Builder: 360 Multi-Rater Subject

Note   For now, we will not activate the switch called "360 Review – SAP Fiori Version [Not Ready for Sales/Production] — requires 360 Multi-Rater." We will discuss SAP Fiori in more detail later in this chapter.

Named and Anonymous 360 Process

You can configure the 360 Review feedback form to be an anonymous or named process. In Provisioning, click the configuration step called Form Template Administration. On the displayed page, click the 360 Review feedback form that you will be using. On the displayed page, in the Edit Form Attributes section, you can choose the option "Anonymous 360 or Participant names on 360."

In the anonymous process, the users of the forms will not see the names of the raters in the form's Evaluation Summary section. However, if you would like the participant's names to be displayed in the Evaluation Summary section of the form, enable the switch called "Show Participants in Status Summary (Applicable to Anonymous 360's only)," available in Form Template Settings section of the specific 360 Review feedback form template. In Form Template Settings, when you enable the switch "Hide the email sender for 360 Document Complete Notification and 360 Document Reject Notification. (Only applicable for Anonymous 360)," the From field is hidden, so the subject's manager cannot see the name of the sender.

In a named process, the participant names are visible in the Evaluation Summary section of the 360 Review feedback form. Later in the chapter, we will discuss how to make the 360 Review feedback form anonymous for some and named for others.

With this background, in the next section, we will review the permissions that need to be configured prior to configuring the 360 Review feedback form template.

Permissions

Before we start discussing the configuration of the 360 Review feedback form, let's review the permissions that are needed to access the Admin Center–related configuration steps (see Table 12-1).

Note   In this section, we will discuss permissions specific to the 360 Review feedback process only. We will not review user-specific permissions, etc.

Table 12-1. *Permissions to Be Assigned for the 360 Review Feedback Process*

User/Administrator Permission	Permission Name	Description
Manage Documents	Change 360 Process Owner	This permission provides access to the admin tool to change the process owner for a completed or in-flight 360 Review feedback form.
	Change Participant Category	This permission provides access to the admin tool to change the participant category for a completed or in-flight 360 Review feedback form.
	Complete/Decline 360 document	This permission provides access to the admin tool to complete or decline a 360 Review feedback form on behalf of a rater.
	Restore Completed 360	This permission provides access to restore a completed a 360 Review feedback form.
	360 Executive Review	This permission provides access to view the 360 Executive Review page.

(continued)

Table 12-1. (*continued*)

User/Administrator Permission	Permission Name	Description
	360 Executive Review : Add Approver	A role with this 360 Executive Review permission can add an approver.
	360 Executive Review : Delete 360 Form	A role with this 360 Executive Review permission can delete a 360 Review form.
	360 Executive Review : Export as XML (For Completed Forms)	A role with this 360 Executive Review permission can export a completed form in XML format.
	360 Executive Review : Get Feedback for Form	A role with this 360 Executive Review permission can send a 360 Review feedback form for the Get Feedback process.
	360 Executive Review : Modify Competency (Add/Remove Competency)	A role with this 360 Executive Review permission can modify competencies in the form.
	360 Executive Review : Modify Participants (Add/Remove Participants)	A role with this 360 Executive Review permission can modify participants list in the form.
	360 Executive Review : Send Back Form	A role with this 360 Executive Review permission can send the form back a step. This is valid in the signature step only.
	360 Executive Review : Send Copy	A role with this 360 Executive Review permission can send a copy of the 360 Review feedback form to another user.
	360 Executive Review : Send Email Reminder	A role with this 360 Executive Review permission can send email reminders to the participants list.
	360 Executive Review : View Detailed 360 Report	A role with this 360 Executive Review permission can view the detailed 360 Review report for a completed form.

(*continued*)

Table 12-1. (*continued*)

User/Administrator Permission	Permission Name	Description
	360 Executive Review : View Participant Ratings (For Completed Forms)	A role with this 360 Executive Review permission can view individual participant ratings for a completed form.
General User Permission	Permission to Create Forms	A role with this permission can create 360 Review feedback forms.
Manage Form Templates	Form Templates	A role with this permission can create and maintain 360 Review feedback form templates.
	Schedule Mass Form Creation (Launch forms later)	A role with this permission role can schedule the mass creation of forms for a later date/time.
	Mass Create Form Instances (Launch forms now)	A role with this permission can mass launch forms.
	Routing Maps	A role with this permission will have access to the config screen Routing Maps to create and maintain routing maps that will be used in 360 Review feedback forms.
	Rating Scales	A role with this permission will have access to the config screen Rating Scales to create and maintain rating scales that will be used in 360 Review feedback forms.

Note   The permissions discussed in this section can be accessed in the Admin Center. Execute Manage Permission Roles to access the permissions. It is strongly suggested the permissions discussed in this section are assigned to the right role, prior to configuring the 360 Review feedback form.

Having discussed the required permissions, remember to assign these permissions to the required group. This will help us to prepare for our review of the different configuration steps available in the Admin Center.

Admin Center–Related Configuration Steps

Now that we have the needed permission to conduct our configurations, let's begin! The configuration screens related to 360 Review can be accessed in the Admin Center in the section Company Processes and Cycles and 360 Review (see Figure 12-2). Table 12-2 describes at a high level the functionality of each config screen.

Table 12-2. *360 Review Feedback Form's Config Screens*

Configuration Screen	Description
Change 360 Process Owner	This config screen is executed to change the owner of the 360 Review feedback form.
Change Participant Category	This config screen is executed to change the participant categories in the 360 Review feedback form.
Complete / Decline 360 Form	This config screen is executed to complete or decline the 360 Review feedback form assigned to that user. **Note:** When you execute this config screen, on the landing page you will see the option Mass Decline/Complete 360 Documents. You can use this config option to import a CSV file containing the document ID of 360 Review feedback forms that you want to complete/decline. This option is typically used when you have multiple 360 Review feedback forms to process.

(continued)

Table 12-2. (*continued*)

Configuration Screen	Description
E-Mail Notification Templates Settings	You execute this config screen to access the email template settings tied to the 360 Review review process. On the displayed page, search for *360* to access all the email templates used by the 360 Review process. On this config screen, you can enable or disable the delivered email templates. Where needed, you can change the content of the email template by configuring the settings in the displayed email section. **Note:** This config screen is used to access all email templates that are used by the different modules and by the platform.
Form Template Settings	Use this config screen to make changes to the 360 Review form settings, as well to download an existing feedback form or import a new form.
Launch 360 Review	On this config screen, you can create and launch 360 Review forms.
Manage Route Maps	Use this config screen to create and maintain route maps used in 360 Review forms.
Manage Scheduled Review	On this config screen, you can modify or cancel the launch of a 360 Review feedback form.
Manage Templates	On this config screen, you can change the configuration of and maintain the 360 Review feedback form.
Rating Scales	The rating scales used in the 360 Review form are created and maintained on this config screen.
Restore Completed 360	On this config screen, we can restore a completed 360 Review feedback form to evaluation for a participant or for the process owner.

Figure 12-2. *Configuration steps for 360 Review available in Admin Center*

With this background of different config screens, in the next section we will discuss how to configure a new 360 Review feedback form.

Configuring a 360 Review Feedback Form

We will start by configuring a new 360 Review feedback form. Prior to configuring a new form, we will configure the route map that will be used in the 360 Review feedback form.

Configuring a Route Map

We can configure the route map by executing the config screen Manage Route Maps. On the displayed page, click Getting Started. On the displayed page, click Add New Route Map. This will display two options (see Figure 12-3). We can manually build a new route map or use one of the predelivered route maps available in the library.

Admin Center > Route Map List

Take me back to the Welcome page

Add New Route Map ▾		Active	Description	Updated On	Related Templates	
Build Your Own		☑	PM v12 Acceleration Routemap	10/31/2018	1	🗑
Choose from Library						

Figure 12-3. *Creating a new route map*

We will discuss both options in this section.

Building a New Route Map Using Predelivered Ones from the Library

As shown in Figure 12-3, click the option Choose from Library. This will display all the route maps that are available in SuccessStore. 360 Review–specific route maps have the prefix "360" (see Figure 12-4).

Tip   In Figure 12-4, when you click a particular route map name, the system will display the route map for you. You can review all the 360 Review–related route maps and select the one that best fits your business needs. If you do not find any route map that meets your needs, you can manually create a new route map.

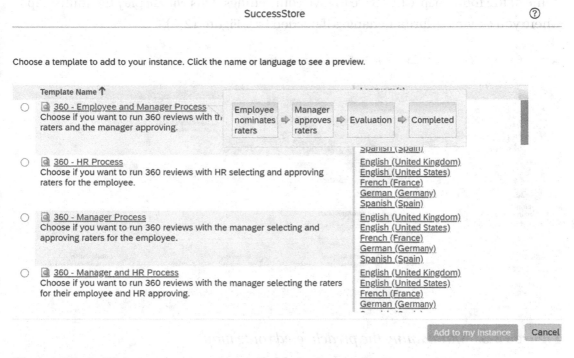

Figure 12-4. Using a route map available in SuccessStore

Note   SuccessFactors offers a number of preconfigured objects available in SuccessStore that can be leveraged by customers and the implementation team during configuration. These preconfigured objects are different from the objects available in Rapid Deployment Solutions (RDS). The objects available in SuccessStore help customers and implementation teams get a head start in configuration. These predelivered objects can be used as a baseline and be configured further to meet the business needs.

For our discussion, we will select the preconfigured route map 360 - Employee and Manager Process. Click the radio button displayed next to that particular route map and click "Add to my instance." This will display a new dialog box, where you can enter the name of the route map. Click Save to save your settings. This will display the route map where you can make further changes if needed (see Figure 12-5).

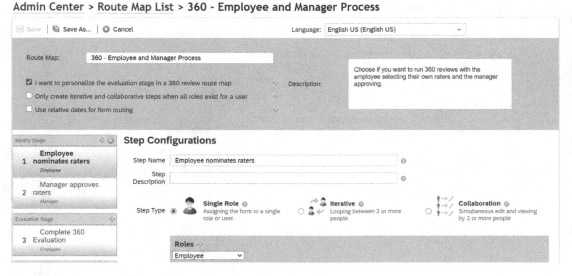

Figure 12-5. *Maintaining the predelivered route map*

Click each process step in the route map; you can add details such as the step name, step description, and what role will own that particular step. When you click Show Advanced Options, you can maintain details such as the step introduction and mouse over text such as Step Name after completion, Step Mode, etc. The step ID will typically be prepopulated, but you can change it (for example, provide a more descriptive one) if needed.

Once you have completed the changes, remember to save them.

With an understanding of how to leverage a preconfigured route map, we will now review how to manually create a new route map for the 360 Review process.

Manually Building a Route Map

We will manually create a new route map where the manager will nominate the rates and send it to HR for approvals before sending the 360 Review form to the employee for evaluation.

As shown in Figure 12-3, click "Build Your Own". The system will create a new route map (see Figure 12-6). On the displayed page, you can enter a new name for the route map and enter a description. (Note that by default the system will display "Route Map" with a number as the name for the new route map.)

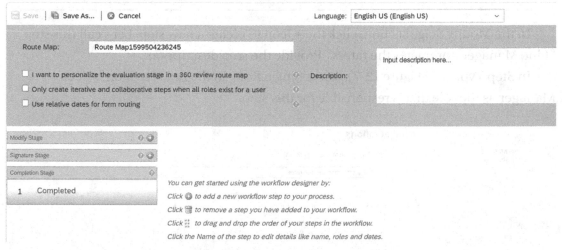

Admin Center > Route Map List > Route Map1599504236245

Figure 12-6. Manually creating a new route map

Under the route name, you will notice there are three options. For our route map, we will select these two options:

- *I want to personalize the evaluation stage in a 360 review route map*:
  Selecting this option will allow you to edit what raters can see in the
  evaluation phase of the process. It is in the evaluation phase that
  raters provide their ratings and feedback on the employee.

- *Use relative dates for form routing*: When you select this option, all route map dates will be relative. By selecting this option, you can define the number of days before/after another step in the process. (Note that you also have the option to enter actual dates for each process step.)

Note   When you select this option, the system will display a warning message: "When the relative date check box is turned ON, reordering the position of steps in a route map is not allowed." This means if you have to re-order the steps, you need to deselect this option to re-order the route map steps and then select this option again if needed.

Tip   You can click the question mark (?) displayed next to each option to learn what it means and where/when it can be used.

In the Modify Stage section, click the + icon to create a new step. Let's call this step "Line Manager nominates the raters." Provide the step description.

In Step Type (see Figure 12-7), select Single Role. In the Roles section, select Manager as the role that is responsible for this step.

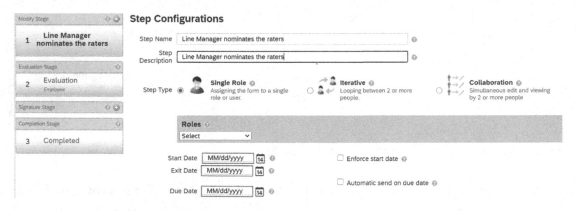

Figure 12-7.   Configuring steps in a route map

Now, click + displayed in Modify Stage to create the second step in the route map. We will call this step "HR Rep approves raters." Enter the step description. In Step Type, select Single Role and select HR Rep as the role that is responsible for this step.

Click Save to save your route map.

In the next step, we will start configuring a new 360 Review feedback form. We will configure the form by executing the config screen Manage Templates.

Managing Templates

On the config screen Manage Templates, we can create a new form, as well as maintain the configured 360 Review feedback review forms. On the displayed page (see Figure 12-8), click the 360 Multi Rater tab. On the displayed page, click Add a New Template to create a new template. This will display preconfigured 360 Review feedback forms that are available in SuccessStore. Click the radio button next to a template to select that particular template. For our discussion, we will select the template called "PE 360 Multi-rater form." Click "Add to my instance" to create the new form. When you click "Add to my instance," the system will display a new dialog box. In that box, you can enter a new name for the template to align with your business needs. Click Save to save your settings. The system will now display the template for you to configure. You can make changes where needed.

On the displayed page, click General Settings. In General Settings, you can provide a name and description of the template. In General Settings, you can configure the Route Map and Rating Scales settings. For our discussion, we will configure the route map 360 - Employee and Manager Process that we discussed earlier. If you want the participants of the 360 Review process to be anonymous, you can select the option "Enabled anonymity in the 360 reporting functions."

Note   Both the Route Map setting and the Rating Scales setting should be preconfigured in General Settings. Route Map is configured by executing the configuration step Manage Route Maps, and Rating Scales is configured on the screen Rating Scales.

When you have completed configuring the section General Settings, click the section Edit Fields and Sections.

Admin Center > Manage Templates

Watch a 2-minute Tutorial

| Welcome | Performance Review | Goal Plan | 360 Multi Rater | Development | Recruiting Management |

This is your list of 360 multi rater templates.⊞ More

☑ Show Active Templates Only

⊙ Add A New Template   Items per page 10 ∨   ⏮ ‹ Page 1 of 1 › ⏭

Template Name ⓘ ↑	Active ⓘ	Updated On ⓘ	Template Description ⓘ
360 Multi-rater form	☑	05/26/2017	

Figure 12-8. *Configuring the 360 Review feedback form*

The first section we will review is Employee Information. In the 360 Review feedback form, the Employee Information section of the form will display employee-related data. In the Manage Templates – Employee Information section, we can name what the section should be called, enter a description of the section, and select what details of the employee data (see Figure 12-9) should be displayed in the 360 Review feedback form.

Click Save to save your changes.

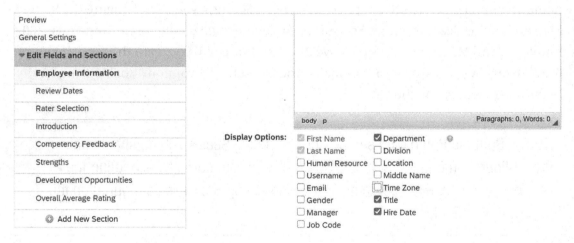

Figure 12-9. *Configuring the Employee Information section*

Note   By default, the first and last names of the employee will be displayed in the 360 Review feedback form. This cannot be changed.

In the 360 Review feedback form, the Review Dates section will display the dates that you entered while launching the form. In the Manage Templates - Review Dates section, you can name the section, as well as enter a description of the section (see Figure 12-10).

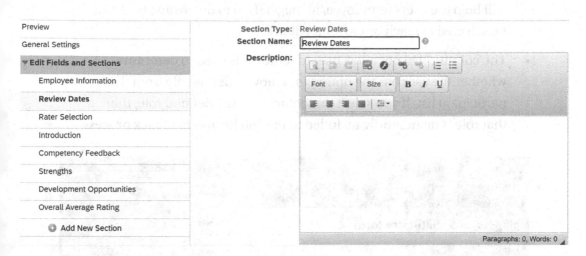

Figure 12-10. *Configuring the Review Dates section*

Under Rater Selection, you can configure the different raters who will be assigned to the form. You can change the default section name and enter a description where needed. The raters configured on this section are assigned to the 360 Review feedback form by default, and the rater labels you configure are displayed next to the role assigned to the raters.

As you can see in Figure 12-11, you can add direct reports, managers, second-level managers, matrix managers, HR staff, and multiple levels of these participants as designated roles to the process.

- In the column Rater Category Name, you enter the label of the role that is assigned to the process. This label is displayed to the users (employee/manager/HR), and they can select the participant list they want to reach out to for feedback.

- When you select Auto Include in Form, the role you have defined is automatically included in the process when the form is launched.

- In the column Role, you define the role that needs to be included in the process. The configured role is automatically assigned to the rater when the form is sent to them for feedback. The role configured here will help the users (employee/manager/HR) to determine who can be selected to reach out to for feedback.

- The column "Do not allow user to remove" is used to determine whether the user has the option to remove a define role from the participant list. If you select this column for the defined role, then that role is mandatorily included in the 360 Review feedback process.

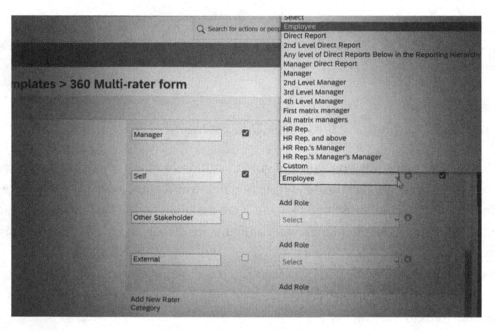

Figure 12-11. *Configuring the Rater Selection section*

In the section Manage Templates – Introduction (see Figure 12-12), you can enter some introduction text about the 360 Review feedback form and what is expected of the participant in the process.

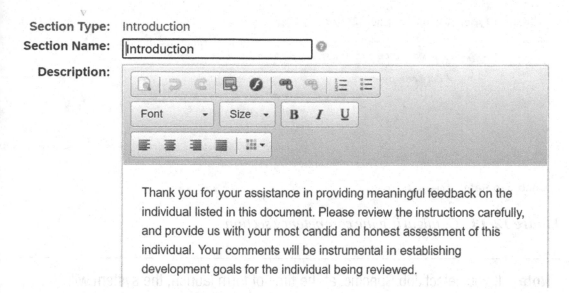

Section Type: Introduction
Section Name: [Introduction]   ?
Description:

Font ▾   Size ▾   **B** *I* U̲

Thank you for your assistance in providing meaningful feedback on the individual listed in this document. Please review the instructions carefully, and provide us with your most candid and honest assessment of this individual. Your comments will be instrumental in establishing development goals for the individual being reviewed.

Figure 12-12. *Introduction section*

Tip   In the Introduction section, customers can provide a link to a document that details what the 360 Review feedback process is about and how the process is leveraged enterprise-wide to support the development aspirations of the employees.

In the section Manage Templates – Competency Feedback, you can configure the competencies to be included in the 360 Review feedback form. The competencies can be set to Core or Job Specific. Similar to the process of configuring the other sections, you can enter the section name and an introduction for the section.

- In Section Type (see Figure 12-13), you can select whether you want to add Job Specific or Core or both types of competencies to the form.

Note   Core and Job Specific competencies should be configured and available in the system for you to use in the template.

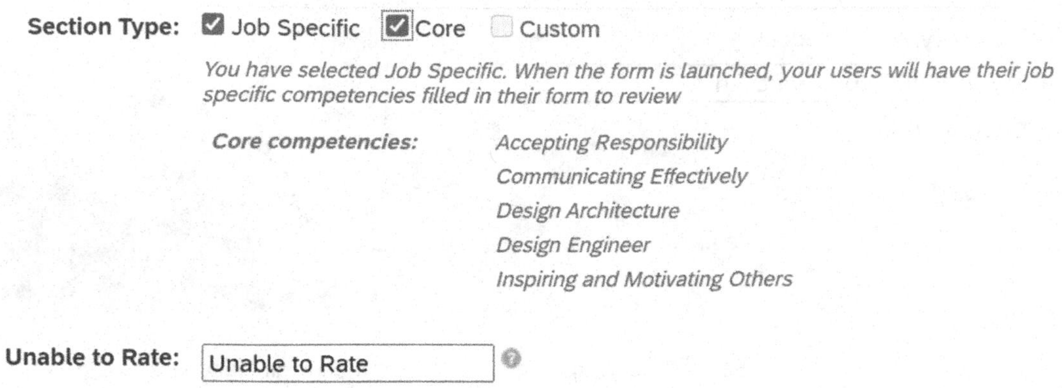

Section Type: ☑ Job Specific ☑ Core ☐ Custom

You have selected Job Specific. When the form is launched, your users will have their job specific competencies filled in their form to review

Core competencies: *Accepting Responsibility*

Communicating Effectively

Design Architecture

Design Engineer

Inspiring and Motivating Others

Unable to Rate: Unable to Rate   ⑦

Figure 12-13. *Configuring the competency section*

Note   If you select Job Specific, at the time of form launch, the system will populate job-specific competencies in the form. Competencies are added as part of the Job Profile Builder configuration. See Chapter 3 for more information.

- The field Unable to Rate is part of the rating scale but is not included in the overall rating. The Unable to Rate is equivalent to N/A. You can either use the system default Unable to Rate or change it to N/A or whatever text you want to be displayed. The rating Unable to Rate means the participant does not have sufficient information or is declining to rate that particular competency.

Click "Show advanced options" displayed below the field Unable to Rate. This will display additional configuration options (see Figure 12-14).

Figure 12-14. *Configuring the advanced options in the competency section*

- *Allow users to add competencies*: If you select this option, it will allow users to be able to add competencies from a list of competencies to the form.

- *Show Behaviors*: If you select this option, if a behavior is attached to the selected competency, the behavior will be displayed in the form.

  If you select this option, the system will display additional options (see Figure 12-15).

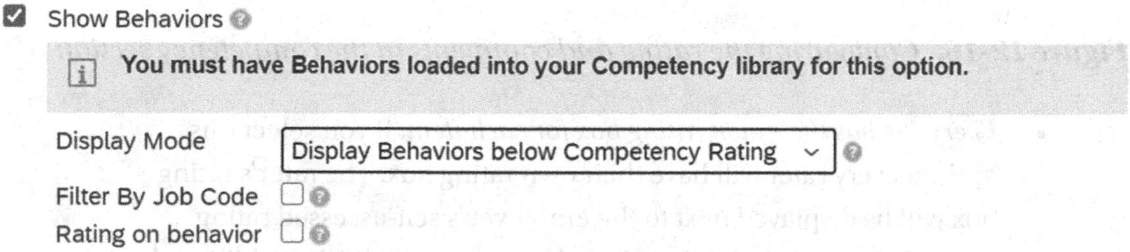

Figure 12-15. *Configuring behaviors in the competency section*

- *Display Mode*: In the display mode, you have the option to display behaviors above or below the competency rating. By default, the behaviors will be displayed below the competency rating.

- *Filter By Job Code*: Select this option if you want only job-specific behaviors to be displayed.

- *Rating on behavior*: Select this option if you want to enable the option to rate behaviors associated with the competency.

- *Include the ability to rate*: Select this option if you want the raters to rate the competency (and behaviors where enabled) using the rating scale configured in the template. If this option is not selected, then the raters will not have the ability to rate the competencies.

When you select the option "Include the ability to rate," the system will display additional options (see Figure 12-16).

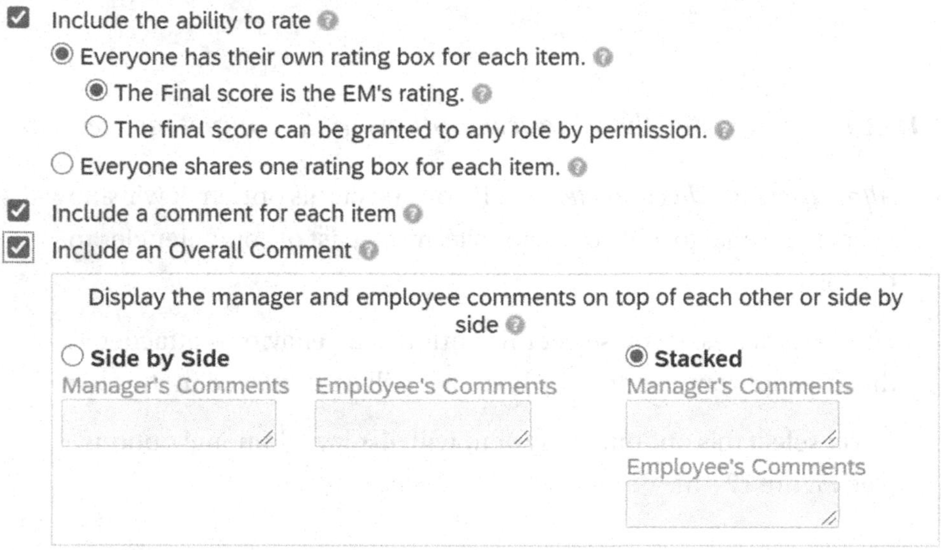

Figure 12-16. *Configuring the rating and comments in the competency section*

- *Everyone has their own rating box for each item*: If you select this option, every rater will have their own rating box. The rater's rating box will be displayed next to the employee's self-assessed rating box. When you select this option, the system will display additional options.

  - *The Final score is the EM's rating*: When you select this option, the form will display the ratings provided by the raters. The system will consider the score provided by the employee's manager (role: EM) as the final score.

  - *The final score can be granted to any role by permission*: When you select this option, you can configure ratings provided by which role should be considered as the final score.

Note   Everyone having their own rating box for every item is the suggested practice in the 360 Review feedback process. This provides the opportunity for the manager and the subject (if permissioned) to review the feedback provided by other raters.

- *Everyone shares one rating box for each item*: If you select this option, only one rating box will be displayed in the form. Which role will have access to the rating box can be permissioned in the template. If the rating box is shared by multiple raters, then the last entered score will be counted as the final score for the competency. When this option is selected, the system will display an additional option (see Figure 12-17).

  - *Except the employee who has a private self-assessment rating box*: If you select this option, the system will display an independent rating box for the employee who can use the rating box for self-assessment.

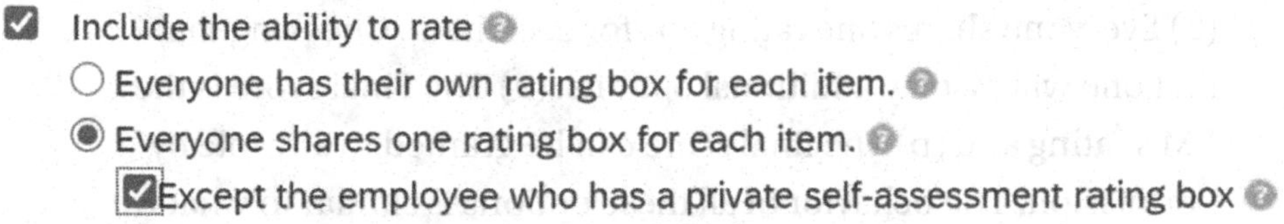

☑ Include the ability to rate 🔘
  ○ Everyone has their own rating box for each item. 🔘
  ◉ Everyone shares one rating box for each item. 🔘
    ☑Except the employee who has a private self-assessment rating box 🔘

Figure 12-17. *Configuring one rating box in the competency section*

- *Include a comment for each item*: If this option is selected, each competency will display a comment box.

- *Include an Overall Comment*: If this option is selected, the form will display a section comment box.

- *Display the manager and employee comments on top of each other or side by*: In this section, you can configure how you want the comments box to be displayed. The two options are side by side or stacked (see Figure 12-16).

The last section we will configure is the Summary section. This section provides a summarized overview of all the assessment sections in the form. The summary section will provide the average score for each assessment section, as well an overall score at the form level.

Similar to the earlier section, in the summary section, you can enter a custom name where needed or you can use the system default. You also have the option to provide a description of the section.

The fields that can be configured in this section are as follows (see Figure 12-18):

- *Allow manual rating*: If you select this option, the form will provide an option to manually enter the overall score. This overall score will override the system-generated overall ratings. However, if you select this option, the system will consider the manually entered ratings as the final score. Hence, even if you determine the system-generated rating to be the final score, you are still expected to manually enter a score that might be the same score as the system-generated overall score.

  When you select this option, the system will display additional options: (1) Everyone has their own rating box for each item and (2) Everyone shares one rating box for each item. Checking the first one will display additional options: (a) The Final score is the EM's rating and (b) The final score can be granted to any role by permission. The behavior of all these options is similar to what we discussed in the competency section.

- *Weights*: If you click the button Weight Section Equally, the system will automatically weigh each assessment section equally to add up to 100%. In our discussion we have only one assessment section: Competency Feedback. Hence, the system has provided 100.0 for that section.

- *Unable to Rate*: This behavior is similar to what we discussed in the competency section.

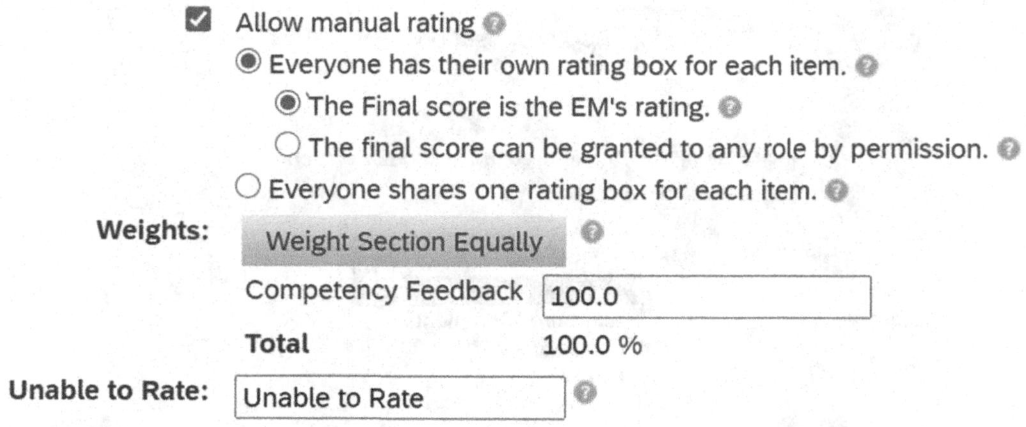

☑ Allow manual rating ❷
   ◉ Everyone has their own rating box for each item. ❷
      ◉ The Final score is the EM's rating. ❷
      ○ The final score can be granted to any role by permission. ❷
   ○ Everyone shares one rating box for each item. ❷

Weights: Weight Section Equally   ❷

            Competency Feedback   100.0

            Total   100.0 %

Unable to Rate: Unable to Rate   ❷

Figure 12-18. *Configuring the summary section*

Tip We can rearrange the order in which different sections in the template are displayed. To move a section to a different order, hover your mouse over the section name. The system will display "3 vertical dots" (see Figure 12-22). If you move your mouse over the 3vertical dots, the cursor will change into a directional cross. Grab that and move it to the place where you want the section to be displayed.

You also have an option Add New Section to the template. This new section needs to belong to one of the following section types: Additional Comments, Competency, Mid-Year, Goal or Signature (see Figure 12-19). Configuration of the new section will be similar to what we discussed in the earlier sections.

Add new section
Select the section type to add. Deleted sections won't come in this list until you save the template.
Section type
Select
Select
Additional Comments
Competency
Mid Year
Goal
Signature
Add
Cancel

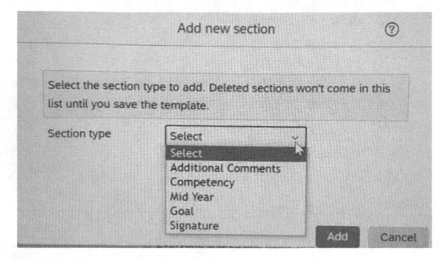

***Figure 12-19.** Available section types*

Note We would typically add a new section to capture comments or ratings that are not captured in the delivered sections. For example, we might want the raters to rate the employee on a competency that are not job specific or a core competency. Or we might add a section to capture the signature of the employee and their manager to finalize the 360 review feedback form.

For our discussion, we will add a section; type **Goal** as a new section. Similar to other sections, we can enter a new section name, as well provide a section description.

In the section type (see Figure 12-20), you can choose between Goals and Individual Development Plans.

Section type:
Goal Section
Individual Development Plan Section
Choose which goal plan you want to link
Select
Show Add Existing Objective Button
Unable to Rate:
Hide advanced options...
Include the ability to rate
Exclude Private Goals
Include the ability to enter in a weight
Include a comment for each item
Include an Overall Comment

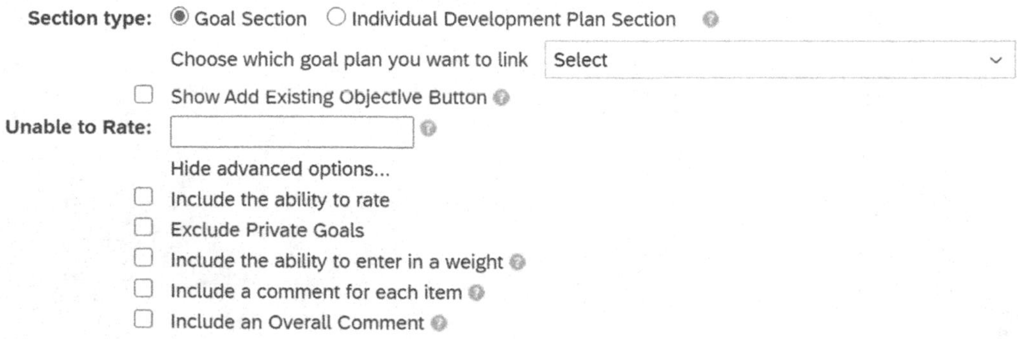

***Figure 12-20.** Add Goal section*

If we select Goal Section, the drop-down "Choose which goal plan you want to link" will display the goal plans that are active in the system.

If we select Individual Development Plan Section (see Figure 12-21), the drop-down will display the active development plans available in the system.

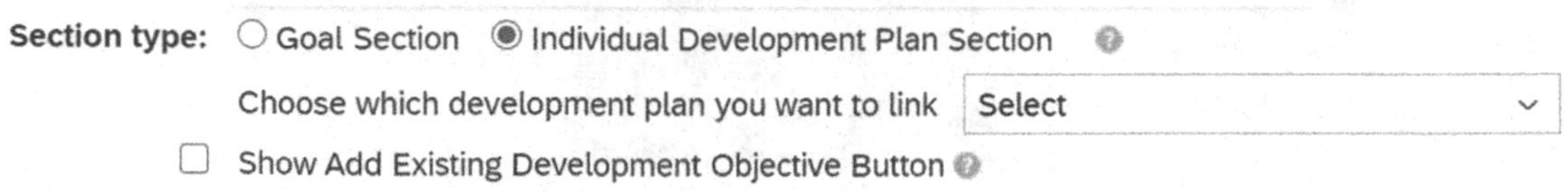

Section type: ○ Goal Section   ◉ Individual Development Plan Section   @

Choose which development plan you want to link | Select   ⌄ |

☐ Show Add Existing Development Objective Button @

Figure 12-21. *Add Development Plan section*

You want the raters to be able to rate the goals, select the option "Include the ability to rate."

If you do not want the private goals to be displayed in 360 review feedback form, then select the option Exclude Private Goals.

If you want goals weights to be factored in scores calculation, select the option "Include the ability to enter in a weight."

If you want raters to include a comment for each item, select the option "Include a comment for each item."

If you want raters to provide an overall comment, select the option Include an Overall Comment. Save your changes.

Tip   If you need raters to rate on both the goals and individual development plans, then create two different sections. One section can be used goals, and the second section for individual development plans.

We can rearrange the order of display of the different sections in the template. To move a section to a different order, hover your mouse in the section name. The system will display a grid of dots. If you move your mouse over the dots, the cursor will change to a directional cross (see Figure 12-22). Grab that and move it to the place where you want the section to be displayed.

Figure 12-22. *Moving the section*

Form Review You can preview the template you have configured by clicking Preview (see Figure 12-23). Previewing the form during configuration or prior to launching the form will help you to understand and visualize the look of the 360 Review feedback form.

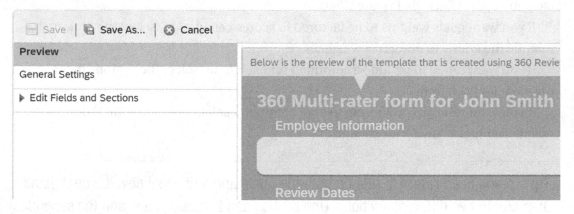

Figure 12-23. *Previewing the configured form*

Form Template Settings

The administration settings of the template can also be configured in the section Form Template Settings. You can access the config screen by executing Form Template Settings. The landing page of the config screen Form Template Settings will display all the forms that are configured and available in the system. From the displayed forms list, select the 360 Review feedback template that you want to configure. The landing page will display the administration settings that are available for configuration (see Figure 12-24).

Managing Form Templates

Use this page to manage existing form templates.

Up to All Forms

360 Multi-rater form

	Download Form Template
Template Name:	360 Multi-rater form
	English US (English US) ⌄
Template Type:	PM 360
Last Modified:	2020-09-18 04:13:35.0
Routing Map:	360 - Employee and Manager Process ⌄

Default Dates for Form Creation:
Warning - Mixing Fixed and Relative to Form Creation Date can result in invalid dates set.

Default Start Date:	○ Fixed	◉ Relative to:	Form Creation Date ⌄	0 — Days after(+) or before(-)
Default End Date:	○ Fixed	◉ Relative to:	Default Due Date ⌄	0 — Days after(+) or before(-)
Default Due Date:	○ Fixed	◉ Relative to:	Form Creation Date ⌄	30 — Days after(+) or before(-)

Default Due Notification Date (in days):	3
Default Late Notification Date (in days):	1
Template Status:	Enable ⌄
Template Flag:	Public ⌄

○ Do Not Transfer Documents
◉ Automatic Manager Transfer.
☑ Automatic insertion of new manager as next document recipient if not already.
☑ Manager

Figure 12-24. *Configuration step: Form Template Settings*

Note   You can access Form Template Settings from within the template in the Manage Templates config screen. In the form template displayed in Manage Templates ➤ Form Template, click General Settings. Scroll to the end of the section. The link Advanced Settings will take you to the config screen Form Template Settings.

In this section (see Table 12-3), we will review the 360 Review feedback form–specific administration settings. (Note: For detailed discussion about the section Form Template Settings, refer to Chapters 6 Introduction to Performance Management and related chapters.)

Table 12-3. *Forms Template Settings Admin Settings*

Administration Settings	Description
Template Name	This is the name that will be displayed in the form when it is launched. You can configure the template name in different languages where needed. **Note:** If the template name changes after the form is launched, the new name will be reflected only on forms launched after the name change. Any in-flight forms will not display the new name.
Template Type	This is a ready-only field. The template type reflects the process for which the template is configured.
Routing Map	The route map that we configured earlier is displayed here. Where needed, you can change the route map. Clicking the drop-down displays all the configured route maps available in the system.
Template Status	This field has two values: Enable and Disable. If the template is active, it will have the status Enable. If you are no longer using the template, then change the status to Disable.
Automatic Process Owner Change To New Manager For In-Progress Documents When Old Manager is Process Owner (Only for 360)	During the 360 Review feedback process, if there is a change in the manager for the employee, selecting this option will automatically transfer the in-flight forms to the new manager. The new manager is also marked as the new process owner of the process. **Note:** You can also change the process owner of the 360 Review feedback forms on the config screen Change 360 Process Owner.
Automatic Process Owner Change To New Manager For Completed Documents When Old Manager is Process Owner (Only for 360)	Selecting this option will automatically transfer the complete documents to the new manager. The new manager is also marked as the new process owner of the process.

(continued)

Table 12-3. (*continued*)

Administration Settings	Description
When transferring 360 documents from old manager's inbox folder to new manager, do not auto decline old manager's participant forms in evaluation.	Selecting this option will enable transfer of the old manager's in-flight participant forms to the new manager. **Note:** When the forms are transferred to the new manager, the new manager can reach out to the old manager (in offline) and gather their input/feedback to do evaluation of the in-flight forms.
When transferring 360 documents which are in evaluation stage, add new manager as a participant. (If a new manager is a removed participant, they will be re-added.)	Selecting this option will add the new manager as a participant in in-flight forms.
Hide dropped users records in 360 Ad Hoc report (Note that report synchronization is required after this configuration to ensure that dropped users in existing forms will not be displayed in a 360 Review ad hoc report. Please go to "Company Settings" and runSync in 360 Multi-Rater Subject.)	Selecting this option will hide the dropped user's records when you generate reports in the Report Center.
Detailed 360 Report Permission Control: Enable 360 Detailed Report Permission for:	Enabling this option will display the 360 Detailed Report link on a 360 Review feedback form. You can enable this option for certain roles only.
Hide the 'decline to participate' button on the 360 form for:	You can enable this option to hide the "decline to participate" button for selected roles only. **Note:** If you select all the roles, then this will not be displayed for all roles in the form.
Enable Add New Participants after 360 Evaluation starts for:	You can enable this option to provide the option to "add new participants" for selected roles.

(*continued*)

Table 12-3. (*continued*)

Administration Settings	Description
Enable Send Back for:	When you enable this option for selected roles, they will see the option Send to Previous Step. When the participant clicks that option, the system will send the form back to the earlier participant in the route map for additional inputs.
Enable Send Reminder Email for:	When this option is enabled, the system will send reminder emails to complete the process. **Note:** To use this option, you should enable the switch Document Due Notification that is available on the config screen E-mail Notification Templates Settings. To send a reminder email to external participants, the switch 360 Document Evaluation Notification for External Participant should be enabled on the same config screen.
Enable Remove Participants after 360 Evaluation starts for:	When this option is enabled for in-flight forms, the selected roles will be able to remove the participants from the 360 Review feedback process.
Enable Gap Analysis View from Detailed 360 Report	When this option is enabled, the system will display the gap analysis view. **Note:** The gap analysis allows you to compare the ratings between two groups of raters and understand the significance in ratings.
Enable Rank View from Detailed 360 Report	When this option is enabled, the system will display the rank view. **Note:** The rank view enables you to view the competencies or behaviors across all categories in a single list. The categories can be sorted highest to lowest or lowest to highest.
Detailed 360 Report Permission Control: Enable 360 Detailed Report Permission for	When this option is checked, the role for whom this is enabled (and permissioned) will see Detailed 360 Report link on the 360 Review feedback form.

(*continued*)

Table 12-3. (*continued*)

Administration Settings	Description
Detailed 360 Report Permission Control: Use Form XML	When this option is enabled, in the template XML, you can grant permission to roles that were not defined in the admin setting Enable 360 Detailed Report Permission for.
Calculate the item ratings by sub-item ratings in Detailed 360 Report	When this option is enabled, all ratings are calculated by averaging all the sections.
Display the ratings in Detailed 360 Report with the decimal places which are set in form template.	The number of decimal places is determined by the configuration setting in the template.
Enable 360 Add External Participants section	When this option is enabled, the external participant section is displayed in the form.

Email Notifications

In this section (see Table 12-5), we will review the 360 Review feedback form–specific email notifications that need to be activated in the system. You can access the configuration by executing the config screen E-Mail Notification Template Settings.

The following notifications are enabled by default and cannot be disabled:

- 360 Executive Review Form Change Notification

- PM 360 Executive Review form(s) mass route notification

Note   In this section, we will review the notifications related to the 360 Review feedback process only. You can refer to Chapters 6 and related chapters to review which notifications are related to PM/GM processes. Like with other notifications, the body of the email (see Figure 12-25) can be customized for your needs.

Table 12-4 describes the common tokens that can be used while configuring the body of the email.

Table 12-4. *Tokens Available for Emails*

Email Tokens	Description
[[DOC_TITLE]]	Displays the title of the document. This is typically used in the subject of the email.
[[EMP_NAME]]	Displays the name of the employee (subject) regarding whose form this notification is generated for.
[[EMP_USER_ID]]	Displays the user ID of the employee (subject). **Note:** Unless the notification is for the employee, this token is typically not used, since the participants may not be familiar with the employee's UID.
[[EMP_PASSWORD]]	Specifies the password of the employee (subject). **Note:** We will not use this token in the 360 Review feedback process.
[[SENDER]]	Specifies the sender of the document.
[[RECIPIENT_USERNAME]]	Specifies the recipient username of this document for whom the notification is generated.
[[RECIPIENT_NAME]]	Specifies the recipient name of this document for whom the notification is generated.
[[COMPANY_NAME]]	Specifies the name of the legal entity.
[[SIGNATURE]]	Contains the signature.
[[DOC_COMPLETION_DATE]]	Specifies the date the document was completed.
[[DOC_LASTMODIFIED_DATE]]	Specifies the date the document was last modified.
[[NO_OF_DAYS]]	This date is autocalculated by the system. This is the number of days between the current date and the due date.
[[DOC_COMMENT]]	Specifies a comment from the sender. If this token is not used in body of the email, the sender will not see the comments box when sending the form to the next step.
[[REVIEW_END_ON]]	Specifies the end date of the review process.
[[IS_WAS_DUE_ON]]	Specifies the due date of the document.
[[IS_WAS_DUE_ON_LONG]]	Specifies the due date of the document in long format. In other words, the date will be displayed as January 01, 1900.

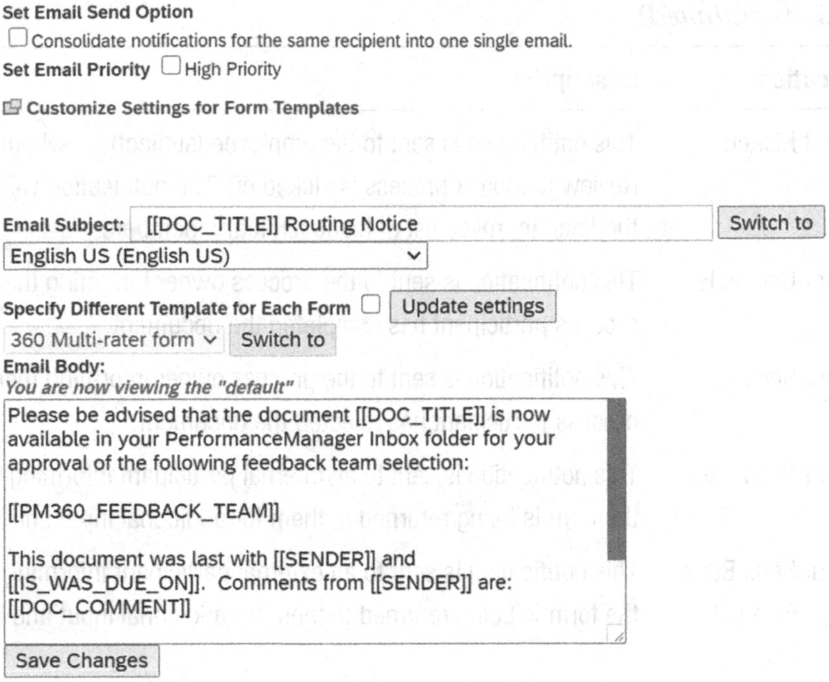

Set Email Send Option

☐ Consolidate notifications for the same recipient into one single email.

Set Email Priority ☐ High Priority

🖳 **Customize Settings for Form Templates**

Email Subject: [[DOC_TITLE]] Routing Notice | Switch to |

English US (English US)   ⌄

Specify Different Template for Each Form ☐ | Update settings |

360 Multi-rater form ⌄ | Switch to |

Email Body:
You are now viewing the "default"

Please be advised that the document [[DOC_TITLE]] is now available in your PerformanceManager Inbox folder for your approval of the following feedback team selection:

[[PM360_FEEDBACK_TEAM]]

This document was last with [[SENDER]] and [[IS_WAS_DUE_ON]]. Comments from [[SENDER]] are: [[DOC_COMMENT]]

| Save Changes |

Figure 12-25. *Configuring the email notifications for the 360 Review feedback review*

Table 12-5. *Enabling Email Notifications for 360 Review Feedback*

Email Notification	Description
360 Document Approval Notification	When feedback team selection requires approval, this notification is generated when the form is available in the user's inbox for approval.
360 Document Evaluation Notification	This notification is generated when the forms are available in the user's inbox for evaluation.
360 Document Evaluation Notification for External Participant	This notification is sent to an external participant to inform them that the form is available for evaluation. The external participant can use the notification to provide their approval to participate (token: [[ACCEPT]]) in the 360 Review feedback process or to decline to participate (token: [[DECLINE]]).

(continued)

Table 12-5. (*continued*)

Email Notification	Description
360 Document Kickoff Notification	This notification is sent to the employee (subject) for whom the 360 Review feedback process is kicked off. The notification will contain the final approved list of feedback team members.
360 Document Complete Notification	This notification is sent to the process owner informing them that a process participant has completed the document.
360 Document Reject Notification	This notification is sent to the process owner informing them that a process participant has rejected the document.
360 Document Send Back Notification	This notification is sent to an internal participant informing them that the form is being returned to them for additional input and feedback.
360 Document Send Back Notification for External Participant	This notification is sent to an external participant informing them that the form is being returned to them for additional input and feedback.
360 Benchmark Calculation Completion Notification	This notification is triggered when the competency job code calculation is completed.

Calibration

In SuccessFactors, the 360 Review feedback forms can be calibrated. The competency section is the only section in the 360 Review feedback form that is available for calibration.

Prerequisites

As a prerequisite, the switch Enable Calibration Mode should be enabled. Execute the config screen Form Template Settings. On the displayed page, select the 360 Review feedback form template that you want to use in calibration. In the displayed admin settings, search for Enable Calibration Mode and activate the switch (see Figure 12-26).

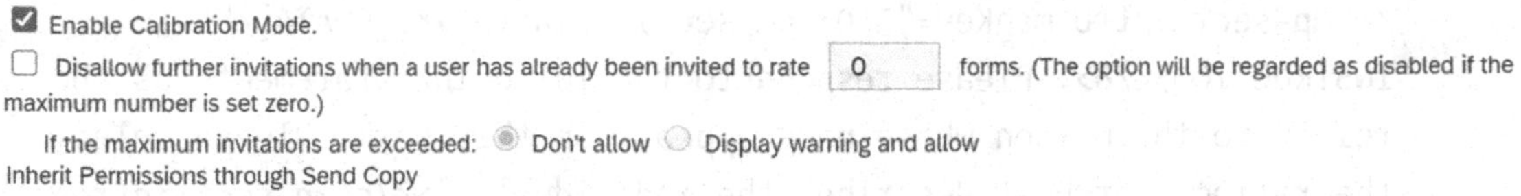

☑ Enable Calibration Mode.

☐ Disallow further invitations when a user has already been invited to rate [0] forms. (The option will be regarded as disabled if the maximum number is set zero.)

If the maximum invitations are exceeded: ● Don't allow ○ Display warning and allow
Inherit Permissions through Send Copy

Figure 12-26. *Enabling calibration mode*

Remember to save your settings.

Note   Calibration is available only if there is at least one competency section available in the form.

In the calibration, you can rate multiple employee forms at the same time. The restriction, though, is that all subjects should be rated on the same competency.

You are required to add the code `<calibration-mode/>` to the competency section of the XML template. In the XML template, you will add this code after `</required-fields>` and before `<default-item-comments-label>`. See the following code that is configured in the XML:

```
<competency-sect index="4" configurable="true" mgt-only="false"
use-jobcode="true" use-core-comp="true" category-filter-opt="no-filter"
no-rate="false" no-weight="true" summ-opt="999" split-cmt="false"
rating-opt="2" cmt-opt="0" suppress-item-comments="0" behavior-rating-opt="0"
behavior-cmt-opt="1" behavior-mode-opt="4" in-summ-display="true"
in-overall-rating="true" no-group="true" use-behavior="false"
if-no-ratings-then-ignore-section="true" lock-item-weights="false"
in-objcomp-summ-display="false" in-objcomp-summ-overall-rating="false"
show-comp-expected-rating="false" show-comp-proficiency-level="false"
comp-expected-rating-format="0" show-behavior-expected-rating="false"
behavior-expected-rating-format="0" behavior-weighted="false"
min-competencies-required="-2147483648" max-competencies-allowed=
"2147483647" sect-mode="normal" ez-rater-expand-all="false"
show-calculated-section-rating="true" lock-behavior-content="false"
hide-waca="false">
        <comp-sect-name msgKey="360_compsection_name"><![CDATA[Competency
        Feedback]]></comp-sect-name>
```

```
<comp-sect-intro msgKey="360_compsection_intro"><![CDATA[<b>
INSTRUCTIONS</b>: Please respond to the following statements as they
relate to the person whose name appears on this form. Please select
the rating that best describes the individual.]]></comp-sect-intro>
<fm-sect-config>
  <section-color><![CDATA[1A4D80]]></section-color>
  <rating-label msgKey="PM_RatingLabel_Rating"><![CDATA[Rating]]>
  </rating-label>
  <rating-label-others msgKey="PM_RatingLabelOthers"><![CDATA[Rating]]>
  </rating-label-others>
  <default-rating><![CDATA[Select one...]]></default-rating>
  <unrated-rating><![CDATA[Unable to Rate]]></unrated-rating>
  <hidden-strength-threshold>1.0</hidden-strength-threshold>
  <blind-spot-threshold>1.5</blind-spot-threshold>
  <required-fields>
    <role-name>*</role-name>
    <field refid="item-rating" min-value="-1.0" max-value="-1.0"/>
    <route-step stepid="*"/>
    <send-action sendid="complete_360"/>
  </required-fields>
  <calibration-mode/>
  <default-item-comments-label><![CDATA[Comments]]></default-item-
  comments-label>
```

Before we end the discussion about calibration, there are a few things that need to be noted.

- Calibration mode does not support open-ended questions.

- Calibration mode supports drop-down rating scales only.

- Item-level comments cannot be edited/changed in calibration mode.

Post-Review Phase

During the 360 Review feedback process, sometimes the subject or the manager will think the feedback received so far is not sufficient, the right type of participants was not involved, or a critical participant was overlooked (not included) or has become available to be included in the process.

After the evaluations are completed but before the start of the completion or signature steps, the process owner can do the following:

- Add more participant reviewers to the form

- Return the form to a participant (or participants)

During the post-review phase, the role with the appropriate permissions can add new participants or remove selected participants. When you click Add New Participant, the system will display a page where you can add new participants. You can add either internal or external participants.

Similarly, clicking Remove Selected Participants will remove the participant from the process.

During the manager evaluation phase, the manager of the subject can return the form to a participant to request a review of the feedback (including comments and/or ratings). When the manager clicks the Recall button (see Figure 12-27), the form is returned to the participant for a re-evaluation. The manager is also provided with an option comments box, where they can enter their comments highlighting their concerns.

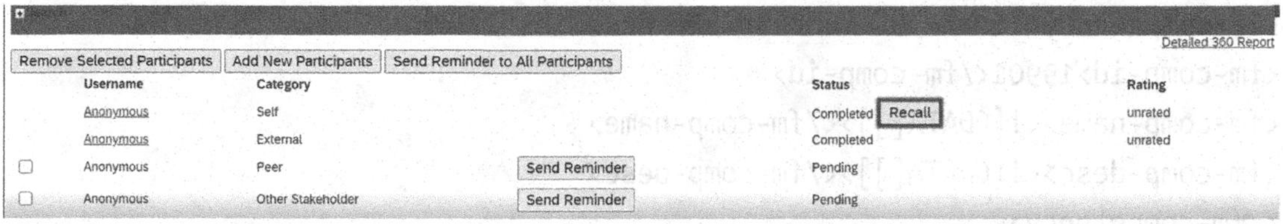

Figure 12-27. *Adding or removing participants and returning the form to the participant*

XML Configuration

In this section, we will review the XML configurations that are specific to the 360 Review feedback process.

> **Note**   We reviewed the XML configuration in detail in the Chapter Performance Management XML and Translations. The XML tags for the 360 Review feedback process are similar to what were used in the performance forms.

Adding a Custom Competency

To be able to add custom competencies to the 360 Review feedback form, the configuration can be done in XML only. If you view the competency section in the template on the config screen Manage Templates, you will notice the custom checkbox is grayed out (see Figure 12-28).

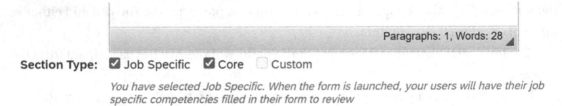

Figure 12-28.   *The ability to add a custom competency is grayed out.*

After you configure the XML, the custom checkbox will be enabled.

To configure the XML, add this piece of code:

```
<fm-competency index="0" removable="false">
<fm-comp-id>19901</fm-comp-id>
<fm-comp-name><![CDATA[]]></fm-comp-name>
<fm-comp-desc><![CDATA[]]></fm-comp-desc>
</fm-competency>
```

This code needs to be added to <competency-sect>. The code needs to be added after </fm-sect-scale> and before <meta-grp-label>. See the following code for the full piece of code that we configured for the template we configured earlier:

```
<competency-sect index="4" configurable="true" mgt-only="false"
use-jobcode="true" use-core-comp="true" category-filter-opt="no-filter"
no-rate="false" no-weight="true" summ-opt="999" split-cmt="false" rating-
opt="2" cmt-opt="0" suppress-item-comments="0" behavior-rating-opt="0"
```

```
behavior-cmt-opt="1" behavior-mode-opt="4" in-summ-display="true"
in-overall-rating="true" no-group="true" use-behavior="false" if-no-
ratings-then-ignore-section="true" lock-item-weights="false" in-objcomp-
summ-display="false" in-objcomp-summ-overall-rating="false" show-comp-
expected-rating="false" show-comp-proficiency-level="false" comp-expected-
rating-format="0" show-behavior-expected-rating="false" behavior-expected-
rating-format="0" behavior-weighted="false" min-competencies-required=
"-2147483648" max-competencies-allowed="2147483647" sect-mode="normal"
ez-rater-expand-all="false" show-calculated-section-rating="true"
lock-behavior-content="false" hide-waca="false">
    <comp-sect-name msgKey="360_compsection_name"><![CDATA[Competency
    Feedback]]></comp-sect-name>
    <comp-sect-intro msgKey="360_compsection_intro"><![CDATA[<b>
    INSTRUCTIONS</b>: Please respond to the following statements as they
    relate to the person whose name appears on this form. Please select
    the rating that best describes the individual.]]></comp-sect-intro>
    <fm-sect-config>
      <section-color><![CDATA[1A4D80]]></section-color>
      <rating-label msgKey="PM_RatingLabel_Rating"><![CDATA[Rating]]>
      </rating-label>
      <rating-label-others msgKey="PM_RatingLabelOthers"><![CDATA[
      Rating]]></rating-label-others>
      <default-rating><![CDATA[Select one...]]></default-rating>
      <unrated-rating><![CDATA[Unable to Rate]]></unrated-rating>
      <hidden-strength-threshold>1.0</hidden-strength-threshold>
      <blind-spot-threshold>1.5</blind-spot-threshold>
      <required-fields>
        <role-name>*</role-name>
        <field refid="item-rating" min-value="-1.0" max-value="-1.0"/>
        <route-step stepid="*"/>
        <send-action sendid="complete_360"/>
      </required-fields>
      <default-item-comments-label><![CDATA[Comments]]></default-item-
      comments-label>
      <num-decimal-places>2</num-decimal-places>
```

```
    <publish-button-label><![CDATA[Publish Content]]></publish-button-
    label>
</fm-sect-config>
<action-permission type="none">
  <role-name>*</role-name>
  <action refid="add-item"/>
  <action refid="remove-item"/>
  <route-step stepid="*"/>
</action-permission>
<action-permission type="enabled">
  <role-name>EM</role-name>
  <action refid="add-item"/>
  <action refid="remove-item"/>
  <route-step stepid="*"/>
</action-permission>
<action-permission type="enabled">
  <role-name>*</role-name>
  <action refid="my-team-rater"/>
  <route-step stepid="*"/>
</action-permission>
<action-permission type="none">
  <role-name>E</role-name>
  <action refid="my-team-rater"/>
  <route-step stepid="*"/>
</action-permission>
<sect-weight>100.0</sect-weight>
<fm-sect-scale show-value="true">
  <scale-source>1</scale-source>
  <scale-id><![CDATA[Performance Rating Scale]]></scale-id>
  <scale-type><![CDATA[null]]></scale-type>
</fm-sect-scale>
<fm-competency index="0" removable="false">
<fm-comp-id>19901</fm-comp-id>
<fm-comp-name><![CDATA[]]></fm-comp-name>
<fm-comp-desc><![CDATA[]]></fm-comp-desc>
```

```
    </fm-competency>
    <meta-grp-label><![CDATA[Group]]></meta-grp-label>
  </competency-sect>
```

Import the configured XML to the system (see Chapter 10 for more information about how to update the performance form's XML). After the XML is imported, view the competency section in the template. You will notice the custom checkbox is now enabled.

Note   Competency ID 19901 (refer to the tag <fm-comp-id>) refers to the ID of the competency that we are using in our instance. This ID should be a valid ID; otherwise, the system will throw the error "Invalid competency ID is found in one of your competency sections. Please open the file and verify the competency exists in the system." If you have the Job Profile Builder in the instance, you can get the competency ID by executing the config screen Manage Job Profile Content. See Chapter 3 for more information.

Making 360 Names for the Manager and Anonymous for All Others

The XML configuration for 360 Review feedback provides flexibility on the level of anonymity that can be maintained in the form. For our discussion, we will make the rating authors visible to the manager and make them anonymous to all other raters including the employee.

Add the following code:

```
<meta-cat hidden-threshold="0" min-count="0" max-count="2147483647">
<![CDATA[Self]]></meta-cat>
<rater-id-permission type="none">
<rater-category>*</rater-category>
<role-name>*</role-name>
<route-step stepid="*"/>
</rater-id-permission>
<rater-id-permission type="enabled">
<rater-category>*</rater-category>
```

```
<role-name>EM</role-name>
<route-step stepid="360EvaluationStage"/>
<route-step stepid="CompletedStage"/>
</rater-id-permission>
```

The code needs to be added to the meta section of the XML and before <meta-360-rollup-category-name>. See the following code to review how we have added the specific code (as discussed earlier):

```
<meta-cat hidden-threshold="1" min-count="1" max-count="20"><![CDATA
[Manager]]></meta-cat>
<meta-cat hidden-threshold="2" min-count="0" max-count="20"><![CDATA
[Other Stakeholder]]></meta-cat>
<meta-cat hidden-threshold="2" min-count="0" max-count="20"><![CDATA
[External]]></meta-cat>
<meta-cat hidden-threshold="0" min-count="0" max-count="2147483647">
<![CDATA[Self]]></meta-cat>
<rater-id-permission type="none">
<rater-category>*</rater-category>
<role-name>*</role-name>
<route-step stepid="*"/>
</rater-id-permission>
<rater-id-permission type="enabled">
<rater-category>*</rater-category>
<role-name>EM</role-name>
<route-step stepid="360EvaluationStage"/>
<route-step stepid="CompletedStage"/>
</rater-id-permission>
  <meta-360-rollup-category-name><![CDATA[Direct Report]]></meta-360-
  rollup-category-name>
  <meta-360-rollup-category-name><![CDATA[Peer]]></meta-360-rollup-
  category-name>
  <meta-360-rollup-category-name><![CDATA[Other Stakeholder]]></meta-360-
  rollup-category-name>
  <meta-360-rollup-category-name><![CDATA[External]]></meta-360-rollup-
  category-name>
```

With this code, during the Evaluation and Completed stage (see the tag route-step, where we have indicated the phases), the manager will see the raters and their ratings, whereas for all other roles, the ratings will be hidden.

Note   In the XML, if the meta-cat tag for Self is already present, delete that code so that you can add the new code to the XML data model. Otherwise, the system will throw an error that the Self meta-cat has a duplicate.

Configuring a Minimum/Maximum Number of Raters

In the XML data model, we can configure the minimum and maximum number of raters. We can also configure a warning or an error message if this setting is not respected in the form.

In the <rater-config> section, we can configure the minimum and maximum as well as the message to be counted.

You can refer to the following code and change it as per your business needs:

```
<rater-config>
    <date-column-format>MM/dd/yyyy</date-column-format>
    <min-rater-count>2</min-rater-count>
    <min-warning-msg><![CDATA[WARNING: Number of Feedback Givers
    selected - [[ACTUAL_COUNT]] - does not meet the minimum number of
    [[EXPECTED_COUNT]]. You must select more Feeback Givers before
    moving to the 360 Evaluation stage.]]></min-warning-msg>
    <max-rater-count>6</max-rater-count>
    <max-error-msg><![CDATA[ERROR: Number of participants selected -
    [[ACTUAL_COUNT]] - exceeds the maximum number of [[EXPECTED_COUNT]].
    Please select no more than 5 participants.]]></max-error-msg>
    <min-rater-complete-count>0</min-rater-complete-count>
    <default-rater category="Direct Report"><![CDATA[ED]]></default-rater>
    <default-rater category="Peer"><![CDATA[EMD]]></default-rater>
    <default-rater category="Manager"><![CDATA[EM]]></default-rater>
    <default-rater removable="false" category="Self"><![CDATA[E]]>
    </default-rater>
</rater-config>
```

In this code, we are saying the minimum number of raters should be 4. If the number is less than 4, then the form will display a warning message. We have configured the maximum number of raters to be 6. For this, we have configured an error message.

We can also configure the number of raters (minimum and maximum) that need to be assigned for each participant category. This configuration is done in the meta section. See the following code for your reference:

```
<meta-grp-label><![CDATA[Group]]></meta-grp-label>
<meta-cat hidden-threshold="2" min-count="0" max-count="20"><![CDATA[
Direct Report]]></meta-cat>
<meta-cat hidden-threshold="2" min-count="0" max-count="20"><![CDATA[
Peer]]></meta-cat>
<meta-cat hidden-threshold="1" min-count="1" max-count="20"><![CDATA[
Manager]]></meta-cat>
<meta-cat hidden-threshold="2" min-count="0" max-count="20"><![CDATA[
Other Stakeholder]]></meta-cat>
<meta-cat hidden-threshold="2" min-count="0" max-count="20"><![CDATA[
External]]></meta-cat>
<meta-cat hidden-threshold="0" min-count="0" max-count="2147483647">
<![CDATA[Self]]></meta-cat>
```

In this code, we have configured that you should have a maximum of 20 raters belonging to the Direct Report category (and other categories such as Peer, Manager, Other Stakeholder, External). We did not configure the minimum number required.

Note   On the config screen Form Template Settings, click the template that you are working with. On the displayed page, there is a config switch called Participants Threshold Control. With this switch, you can control if you want to exclude responses at the participant level or at the item level. When you select the switch Participant Level, you can exclude responses for the entire form. When you select the switch Item Level, you can exclude responses for certain sections of the form. You can refer to KBA 2087236, "Participants Threshold Control - 360 Review," for specific examples of how to add a threshold control in the template settings.

Integration with Career Development Planning

We can configure the integration with Career Development Planning (see Figure 12-29) in the XML data model. In the tag sf-360, set the option embed-cdp-goals to "true". See the provided code for your reference:

```
<sf-360 no-calc="false" anonym="true" overall-rating="true" recall-enabled=
"true" weight-lockdown="true" show-weight="false" embed-cdp-goals="true"
embed-learning="true" unmet-threshold-action="rollup" rating-rollup-type=
"circular">
```

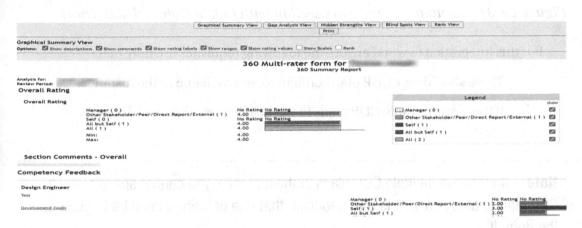

Figure 12-29. *Detailed 360 Review report with link to development goal*

As shown in Figure 12-29, when you click Development Goals, a pop-up will display the Add Development Goal button (see Figure 12-30). When you click this button, the default CDP is displayed, where you can create the development goal for the employee.

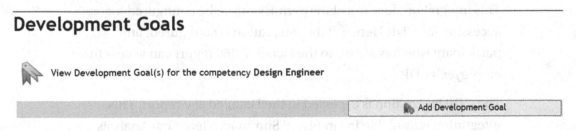

Figure 12-30. *Adding a development goal*

Note   The link to the Detailed 360 report is displayed in the Evaluation Summary section of the form (Figure 12-31).

Figure 12-31. *Evaluation Summary section with link to Detailed 360 report*

For this integration to work, ensure the following requisites are fully met:

- There should be 1 CDP plan configured and available in the instance.

- If there are multiple CDP plans in the instance, ensure one of them is the default plan.

Note   If there are multiple CDP plans in the instance, you cannot specify which CDP plan to use. Hence, it is a prerequisite that one of them should be flagged as the default.

Prior to configuring this integration, consider the following:

- Integrating CDP with a 360 Review feedback review allows the participants to view or add development goals for the employee.

- This integration does not allow permissions to be configured for accessing the CDP. Hence, if the integration is configured, any participant who has access to the Detailed 360 report can access the employee's CDP.

- The CDP integration is accessed in the Detailed 360 report. This integration is available in Graphical Summary View, Gap Analysis View, and Rank View only. This integration is not available in Hidden Strengths View or Blind Spot View.

Integration with Learning

We can integrate SuccessFactors Learning with 360 Review feedback. To make the configuration, you need access to Provisioning.

In Provisioning, click Form Template Administration. On the displayed page, click the 360 Review feedback template that you want to integrate with LMS. On the displayed page, scroll to the section Edit Form Attributes. In that section, click the switch Enable Learning Integration (Figure 12-32). Remember to save your config changes.

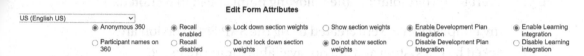

Figure 12-32. *Enable Learning Integration*

This integration will work:

- LMS must be enabled and available in the environment.

- The participant and the subject must be permissioned to access LMS

If this integration is enabled, the Assign Learning link will appear below the individual competency description.

Tip   As an exercise, check whether you can enable/disable this integration in the XML data model. If needed, refer to the code provided in the section "Integration with Career Development Planning" for reference.

SAP Fiori Version

360 Review feedback forms are available in the SAP Fiori version. The version is generally available (GA) with restricted functionality. The Fiori version is supported by SAP UI5 technology and provides an intuitive user experience. You can upgrade to the SAP Fiori version by installing the new UI available in the Upgrade Center. You can access the Upgrade Center by executing the config screen Upgrade Center in the search box. On the displayed page, an option called 360 Review – SAP Fiori Version (Beta) is available in the optional upgrades. Click this option, and on the displayed page (see Figure 12-33), you will see the option to upgrade to the SAP Fiori version.

Note   To upgrade to the SAP Fiori version, it is a prerequisite that 360 Review should be enabled and be available in the system. Any templates that were configured using the old solution need to be updated to the SAP Fiori solution. You can do the update on the config screen Manage Templates. The in-flight forms and completed forms are not affected by the upgrade.

After the upgrade, you have up to 30 days to revert to the old solution. If you revert to the old solution, the following points need to be noted:

- Any templates that were created using the SAP Fiori version are locked by the system and are not available for future usage.

- Any forms that were using the SAP Fiori version can continue to be used. However, these SAP Fiori–based forms cannot be reverted to the old solution.

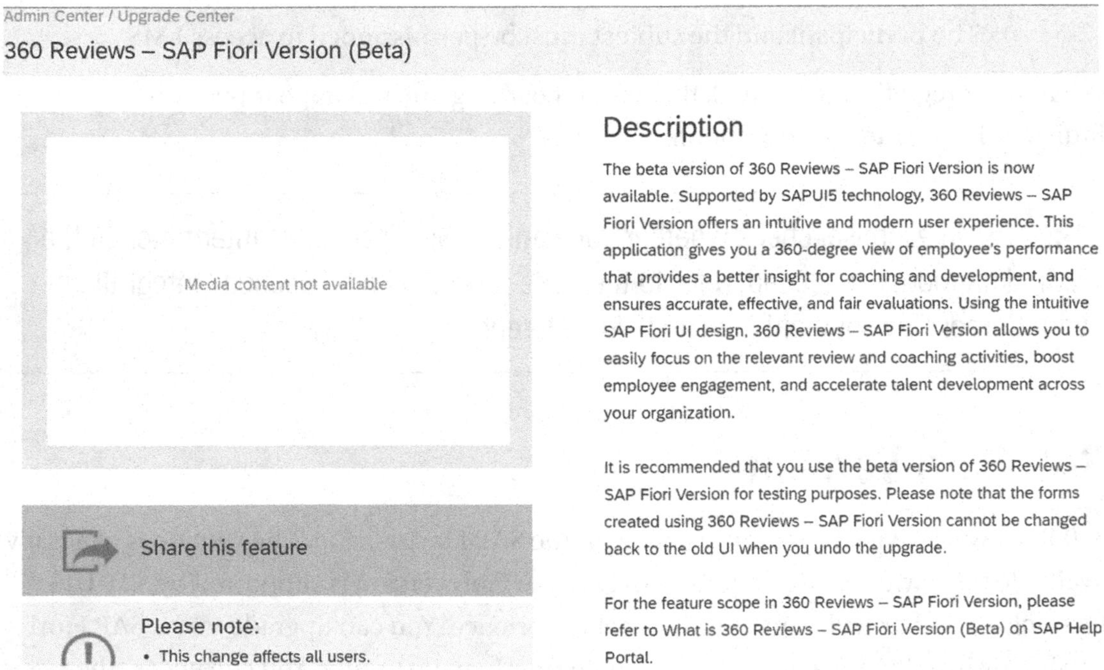

Admin Center / Upgrade Center

360 Reviews – SAP Fiori Version (Beta)

Media content not available

Description

The beta version of 360 Reviews – SAP Fiori Version is now available. Supported by SAPUI5 technology, 360 Reviews – SAP Fiori Version offers an intuitive and modern user experience. This application gives you a 360-degree view of employee's performance that provides a better insight for coaching and development, and ensures accurate, effective, and fair evaluations. Using the intuitive SAP Fiori UI design, 360 Reviews – SAP Fiori Version allows you to easily focus on the relevant review and coaching activities, boost employee engagement, and accelerate talent development across your organization.

It is recommended that you use the beta version of 360 Reviews – SAP Fiori Version for testing purposes. Please note that the forms created using 360 Reviews – SAP Fiori Version cannot be changed back to the old UI when you undo the upgrade.

For the feature scope in 360 Reviews – SAP Fiori Version, please refer to What is 360 Reviews – SAP Fiori Version (Beta) on SAP Help Portal.

Share this feature

Please note:
• This change affects all users.

Figure 12-33. *Upgrading to the SAP Fiori version (beta)*

> **Tip**   After the upgrade, if you notice OData API–related functionalities are not updated, you can refresh the cache. You can access the cache by executing the config screen OData API Metadata Refresh And Export.

Currently, the SAP Fiori version does not support all the functionalities that are available in the old solution. At a high level, the following functionalities are currently (as of the H1'2020 release) not available in SAP Fiori version:

- Development goal section

- Learning activity in development goal section

- The print functionality

- The EZ rater

- The ability to add modifier in the route map

- Performance form history

- 360 Review feedback form history

It is strongly suggested that you review your business needs, understand what functionalities are available, and decide if you want to upgrade.

In the last few sections, we reviewed the configuration of the 360 Review feedback form. With this knowledge, in the next section we will discuss the deployment of 360 Review feedback forms.

Deployment

In this section, we will discuss how to launch forms, how internal users can access the 360 Review feedback form, and how external users can access the form. We will start our review with launching a form.

Launching Forms

The person responsible for launching the form (typically it will be the administrator or the manager or the HR team) can launch the form by executing Launch Forms from the Admin Center or from the search box.

- On the displayed page (see Figure 12-34), for the field Type, select 360. In the field Form Template, select the template you want to use for the form. Click Next.

- On the displayed page, you can select "now" if you plan to launch the form immediately or you can choose Later and schedule for a later date. Click Next.

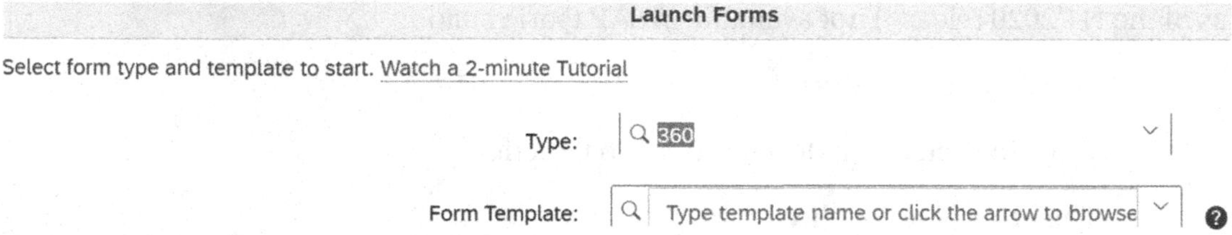

Launch Forms

Select form type and template to start. Watch a 2-minute Tutorial

Type: 🔍 360   ⌄

Form Template: 🔍 Type template name or click the arrow to browse ⌄ ❓

Figure 12-34. *Launching forms*

- On the displayed page, you can enter the review period for which you want to create the form. Click Next.

- On the displayed page, you can select the population for which you want create the form. Click Next.

- The displayed page is the review page where you can review the information that you entered in prior pages. On this page, if you want, you can click the option to send notifications to employees (subject of the form).

Note   The employee (subject of the form) will receive the notification only if you have enabled the notification Document Creation Notification. You can access this notification by executing E-Mail Notifications Template Settings.

- Click Launch to launch the form.

Tip   You can launch the 360 Review feedback form by executing Launch 360 Review. This configuration step will also take you to the same page when executing the configuration step Launch Forms. The landing page of Launch 360 Review will display 360 by default in the field Type (see Figure 12-34).

In the following section, we will review how the employee and the manager can access the form.

Accessing the Form

You (except external raters) can access the form by clicking Performance Management (see Figure 12-35) in the Home drop-down. This will take you to the Performance Management inbox, where you will see the form assigned to you.

Note   The option Performance Management might be labeled differently in your instance. To access the 360 Review feedback form, you are required to go to the inbox of the Performance Management application.

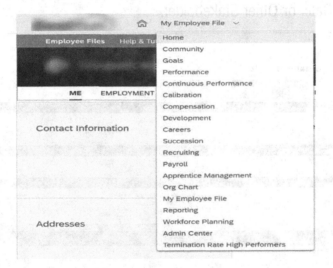

Figure 12-35. Accessing the 360 Review feedback form

Tip   If you received the notification when the form was launched (review the section "Launching Forms"), the notification will contain the URL you can click to access the form.

In the next section, we will review the user experience for how to access the form as the subject and as the manager of the subject.

Reviewing the Form as the Subject

The employee (subject) can access the 360 Review feedback form in the Performance Management inbox. By clicking the link displayed in the inbox, the employee can access the form (see Figure 12-36), and the employee can review the assigned raters, assign competencies, add new goals, and add new raters. If the employee and manager agree, the employee can delete some of the assigned raters.

Note   The employee can add new raters by clicking Modify Participants (see Figure 12-36). When you click Show Assignments, you can get a quick view of the assigned competencies, goals, etc. To add an external rater, you are required to add the rater's email and their first and last names. After adding the external rater, you are required to select the category of the external rater. Typically the category will be External Rater or Other Stakeholder.

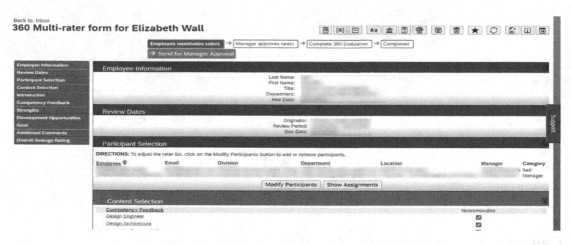

Figure 12-36. *360 Review feedback form as seen by subject*

Remember to save your changes. Depending on the configured route map, you might be required to send it to the manager for approval of the raters prior to completing the evaluation.

Reviewing the Form as the Manager of the Subject

Similar to other internal users, the manager of the subject can access the form from the inbox of Performance Management.

If notifications are configured, the manager will receive a system notification requiring them to approve the raters assigned by the employee. The notification will contain the URL the manager can click to access the form. Clicking the link will take you to the inbox of Performance Management.

Tip The notification that needs to be configured for informing managers (and other roles as defined in the route map) is Document Routing Notification.

The manager will see a tile called Review Performance in the To-Do section of the home page. The manager can click the link "Manager approves raters" (see Figure 12-37), which will take the manager directly to the form. The manager can review and approve the raters to start the evaluation. All the raters will receive a system notification.

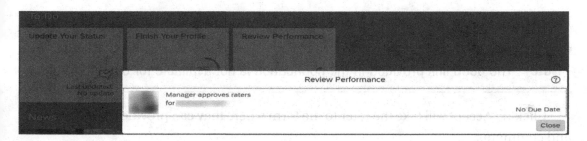

Figure 12-37. To-Do tile to approve raters

Providing Feedback/Ratings as an External Rater

The external rater would have received a system notification (Figure 12-38) requesting them to provide their inputs about the subject.

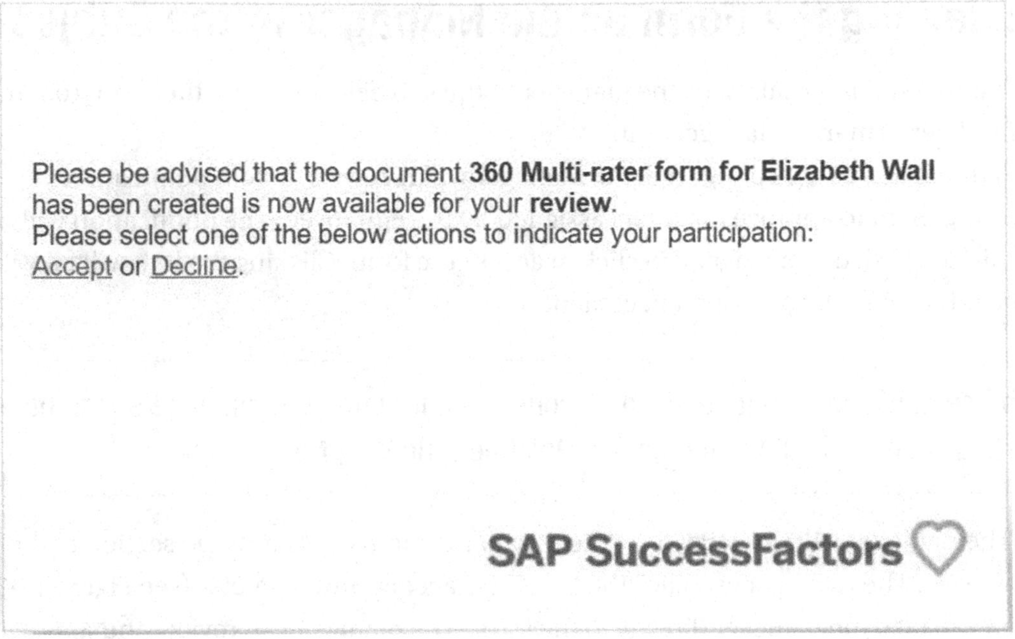

Please be advised that the document **360 Multi-rater form for Elizabeth Wall** has been created is now available for your **review**.
Please select one of the below actions to indicate your participation:
Accept or Decline.

SAP SuccessFactors

Figure 12-38. *Emailing the external rater*

The external rater can accept or decline the request by clicking the respective links.

Note   The deep link provided in the notification is not available for configuration.

Clicking Accept will take the rater to the form where they can provide their ratings and comments.

Note   When an external rater is requested to provide inputs in the 360 Review feedback form, there can be pushback from IT and others that is related to SSO and security. External raters will be able to bypass the configured SSO and have the same user experience as an internal rater. When an external rater is logged into the instance, they will not have access to any other functionality in the system.

Providing Feedback/Ratings as an Internal Rater

All internal raters can access the 360 Review feedback from the inbox of Performance Management. When the internal rater accesses the form, the system will display the option Decline to Participate (Figure 12-39).

Figure 12-39. *360 Review feedback form as seen by an internal rater*

If the internal rater agrees to participate, they can fill out the rater, provide comments, and click Submit Finished Form.

Subject/Manager Rating the Form

The employee and the manager can access the form to provide ratings (an employee to do their self-assessment or a manager to do assessment for the subjects), from the inbox of Performance Management.

Completing the Process

When all the raters have completed providing their ratings, the form is moved to the completion status. On completion of the process, the raters will receive a system-generated notification (see Figure 12-40) informing the raters that the process is completed and that the completed form can be accessed in the completed folder of Performance Management. (Only internal raters will receive the notification.)

Please be advised that the document **360 Multi-rater form for Elizabeth Wall** is completed. If you have participated in the review process, you can view the final version of the document in your PerformanceManager Completed folder.

SAP SuccessFactors ♡

Figure 12-40. *Completion notification sent to raters*

When a rater clicks the form, they can view the ratings provided by the different raters. The names of the raters will be hidden, and the system will display the label "Anonymous" (see Figure 12-41).

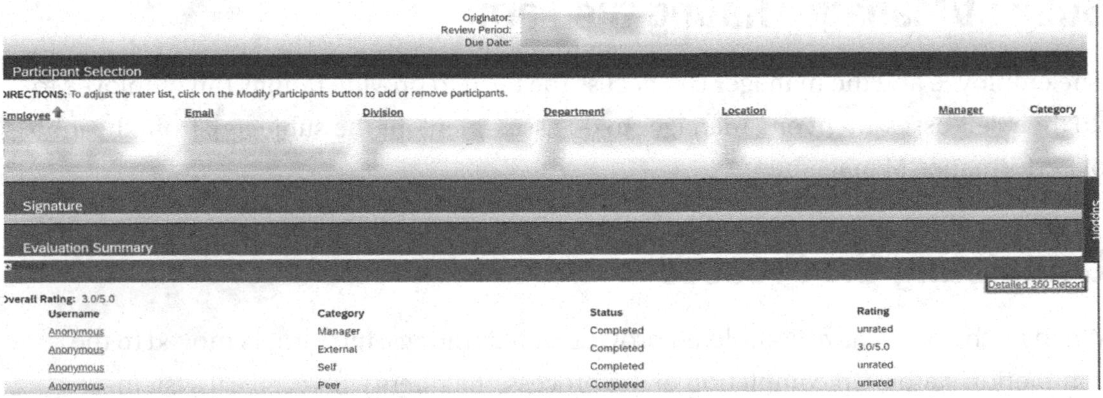

			Originator:				
			Review Period:				
			Due Date:				
Participant Selection							
DIRECTIONS: To adjust the rater list, click on the Modify Participants button to add or remove participants.							
Employee ⬆	Email	Division	Department	Location		Manager	Category
Signature							
Evaluation Summary							

			Detailed 360 Report
Overall Rating: 3.0/5.0			
Username	**Category**	**Status**	**Rating**
Anonymous	Manager	Completed	unrated
Anonymous	External	Completed	3.0/5.0
Anonymous	Self	Completed	unrated
Anonymous	Peer	Completed	unrated

Figure 12-41. *View of completed form*

When you click Detailed 360 Report (see Figure 12-41), the system will display a detailed report highlighting the ratings provided by each rater for the individual competencies, as well the overall section ratings (see Figure 12-42).

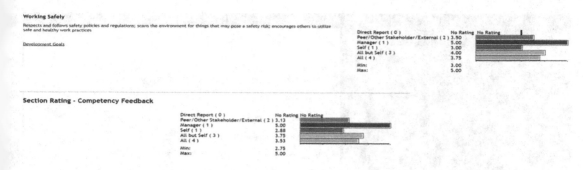

Working Safely

Respects and follows safety policies and regulations; scans the environment for things that may pose a safety risk; encourages others to utilize safe and healthy work practices

Development Goals

Direct Report (0)	No Rating No Rating
Peer/Other Stakeholder/External (2)	3.50
Manager (1)	5.00
Self (1)	3.00
All but Self (3)	4.00
All (4)	3.75
Min:	3.00
Max:	5.00

Section Rating - Competency Feedback

Direct Report (0)	No Rating No Rating
Peer/Other Stakeholder/External (2)	3.13
Manager (1)	5.00
Self (1)	2.88
All but Self (3)	3.75
All (4)	3.53
Min:	2.75
Max:	5.00

Figure 12-42. *Detailed report with ratings*

You can click Graphical Summary View, Gap Analysis View, Hidden Strengths View, Blind Spots View, and Rank View to view the report in different styles highlighting specific data points. Figure 12-43 shows the view of the ratings provided by Self (the subject/employee) and the ratings of all others (this is average rating of all other raters for each competency). The gap displayed in green shows that the raters gave the employee a higher rating than the ratings provided in the self-assessment.

360 Multi-rater form for
360 Hidden Strengths Report

Analysis for:
Review Period:

Competency Feedback	Self	All Others	Gap
Design Engineer	3.00	2.33	0.33
Driving Continuous Improvement	3.00	3.33	0.33
Design Architecture	3.00	3.67	0.67
Communicating Effectively	3.00	4.00	1.00
Working Safely	3.00	4.00	1.00
Delivering High Quality Work	3.00	4.33	1.33
Inspiring and Motivating Others	2.00	4.33	2.33

Figure 12-43. *Hidden strengths report*

Case Study

In a project, the customer wanted to understand the reporting capabilities for 360 Review feedback process. In this case study, we will create a test report to understand what can be reported in the SuccessFactors 360 review feedback process.

In the Report Center, click New, Report-Table, and Single Domain. In the "What data would you like to start with?" field, select 360 Multi-Rater Subject (see Figure 12-44).

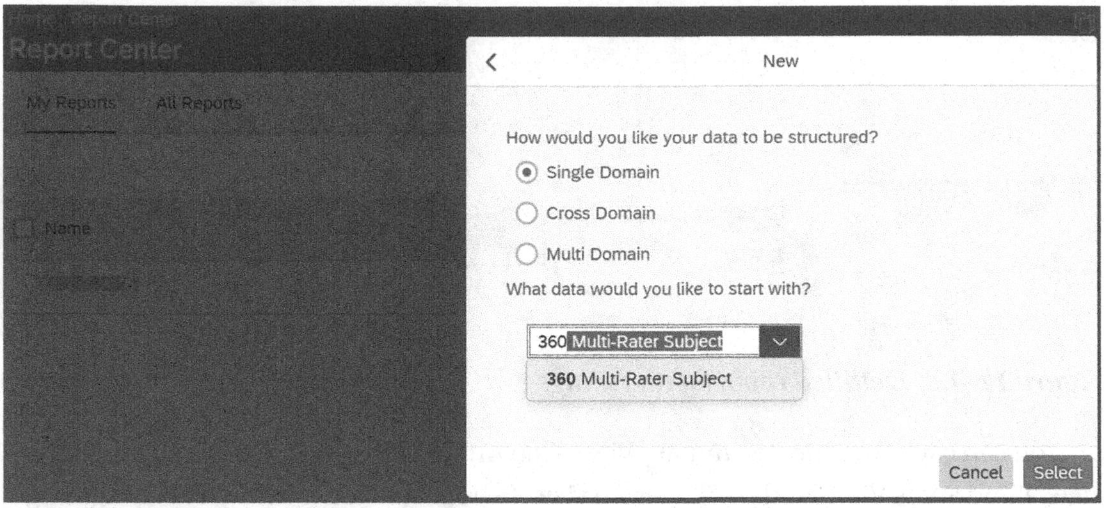

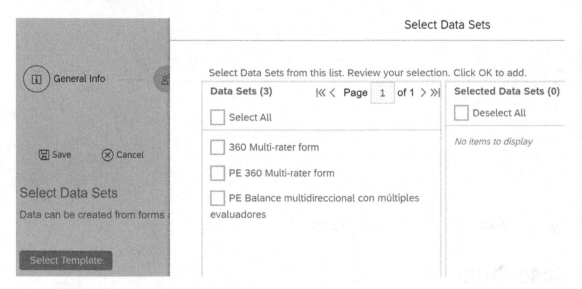

Figure 12-44. *Creating a report*

In the report, in the option Data Sets, click Select Template, and select the template
(s) you want to report on (Figure 12-45).

Figure 12-45. *Selecting the template you want to report on*

In the columns options, select the columns you want to display in the report. You can
also add filters to the report. Click Save and generate the report.

Conclusion

In this chapter, we discussed the functionality of the 360 Review feedback process. We discussed how to activate the functionality in Provisioning. Then we reviewed what permissions need to be assigned to be able to access the different 360 Review feedback configuration steps that are available in AdminCenter. Later we reviewed the different configurations that are required to be completed. While configuring the template, we saw how to add sections to the template. Using XML, we saw how to add custom competencies, as well integrate with CDP and LMS. Toward the end we looked at upgrading to the SAP Fiori version and what functionalities are currently missing in the SAP Fiori version. In the next chapter, we will discuss continuous performance management (CPM) and how to leverage CPM in your performance process.

CHAPTER 13

Continuous Performance Management

Continuous performance management (CPM) is a set of performance feedback processes taking place on a regular basis. In a traditional annual performance management process, for example, the feedback happens once in the middle of the year and once at the end of the year. The drawback with the annual appraisal process is that it is ineffective in today's changing business environments. Managers and employees find the annual process to be dogmatic, providing little or no positive outcomes. Employees feel there is a need to have regular communication with their managers to get feedback on the defined goals and objectives. Managers feel there is a need to have an appraisal process that is agile, where the defined goals and objectives can be calibrated based on changing business needs. That's why more companies are turning toward CPM, which is agile and provides an opportunity for managers and employees to meet and communicate on a regular basis.

As shown in Figure 13-1, in CPM the employee works with their manager to identify and define objectives (and goals). Short-term milestones can be decided on, and the employee will work toward them. Depending on their agreement, the manager and the employee can meet for regular check-ins. Typically these check-ins are every one to three months but can also be ad hoc and even more frequent. Prior to the check-in, the employee can draft an agenda on what they want to accomplish in the check-in and share it with their manager. During the check-in, the manager and the employee should be encouraged to stick to the agenda and try not to include the regular business activities in conversations during the check-in.

© Susan Traynor, Michael A. Wellens and Venki Krishnamoorthy 2021
S. Traynor et al., *SAP SuccessFactors Talent: Volume 1*, https://doi.org/10.1007/978-1-4842-6600-7_13

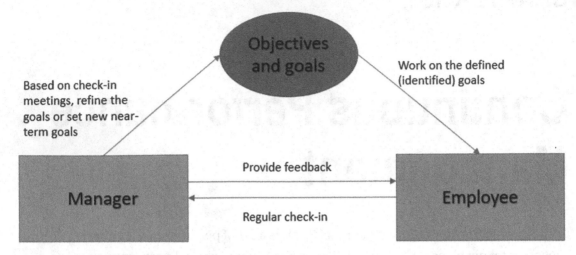

Figure 13-1. *Continuous performance management*

Note   In Figure 13-1, the objectives and goal can include both business objectives and development objectives.

A typical agenda of the check-in meet will include the following:

– Review the defined objectives and goals.

– Identify if there is a need to calibrate the identified objectives and goals; this could include a review if the defined objectives are still a priority. The employee and manager should be open to adding/removing the objectives as needed.

– Track the employee's progress against the objectives and list specific achievements.

– Discuss whether the employee needs any support. The support could include mentoring or learning opportunities, or possibly more regular check-ins.

– During the check-in, the manager and employee should be communicative and transparent.

– The employee should the opportunity to discuss any concerns or priorities they might have.

- The manager and employee should be encouraged to devote some time to the employee's personal development. This discussion will help the manager to assess whether the defined objectives are still relevant or whether any changes are required.

- The outcome of the check-in meet should be tangible action items that the employee and manager will act upon until the next agreed upon meet.

As the workforce continues to evolve, trends in human experience management have demonstrated employees prefer to receive regular feedback on their performance, and CPM neatly fits into this need, compared to the traditional annual performance appraisal process where an opportunity to provide regular feedback is difficult.

In this chapter, we will discuss how SuccessFactors supports the continuous performance management process, including how to activate CPM in the system and integrate CPM with the SuccessFactors Goals, Performance Management, Calibration and Development applications.

Activating Continuous Performance Management

Prior to activating CPM in the Admin Center, you are required to complete the following prerequisites:

- In Provisioning, you are required to enable the switch Enable Continuous Performance Management, which requires Enable Generic Objects, Role-based Permission (this will disable administrative domains), and Enable the Attachment Manager.

Note   Prior to activating this switch, you are required to activate the switches Enable Generic Objects and Enable the Attachment Manager in Provisioning.

- The employee and manager should have permissions to access the FirstName, MiddleName, LastName, Title, and Manager data fields of their reporting manager or the employee.

You can activate CPM in the Admin Center by executing the config called Performance Management Feature Settings (see Figure 13-2).

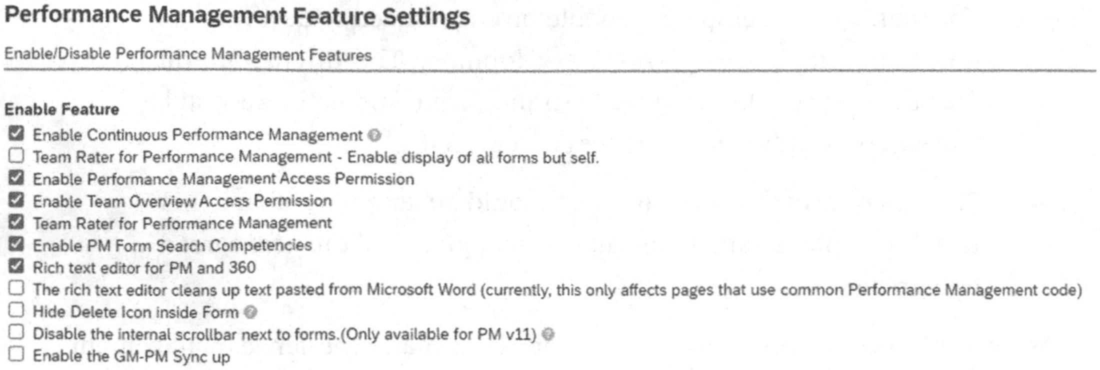

Performance Management Feature Settings

Enable/Disable Performance Management Features

Enable Feature

☑ Enable Continuous Performance Management ⓘ
☐ Team Rater for Performance Management - Enable display of all forms but self.
☑ Enable Performance Management Access Permission
☑ Enable Team Overview Access Permission
☑ Team Rater for Performance Management
☑ Enable PM Form Search Competencies
☑ Rich text editor for PM and 360
☐ The rich text editor cleans up text pasted from Microsoft Word (currently, this only affects pages that use common Performance Management code)
☐ Hide Delete Icon inside Form ⓘ
☐ Disable the internal scrollbar next to forms.(Only available for PM v11) ⓘ
☐ Enable the GM-PM Sync up

Figure 13-2. *Activating CPM*

On the displayed page, select the config switch Enable Continuous Performance Management.

Note that if you do not have access to the config step Performance Management Feature Settings, you can assign the required permissions in Permission Settings ➤ Administrator Permissions ➤ Manage System Properties ➤ Performance Management Feature Settings.

Permission Settings

Depending on the roles, you need to assign the appropriate permissions to the manager, employee, and CPM administrator. The permissions that need to be configured can be accessed at Permission Settings ➤ User Permissions, as well as at Permission Settings ➤ Administrator Permissions

---

Note   In this section, we are reviewing the permissions related to CPM only. We will not review other permissions such as Employee Data, Company System, Logo Settings, etc.

The permissions that need to be assigned are covered in the following sections.

Continuous Performance User Permission

The following are the permission settings available in this category:

- *Access to Continuous Performance Management*: This permission setting will grant access to CPM.

Note   The access to CPM is driven by the assigned target population. Hence, the target population for an employee should include Self, and for Managers it should be Self and Direct Reports.

- *Access Continuous Feedback*: This permission will grant access to the continuous feedback of all employees in the organization.

Note   This permission should be granted to people who need to have access to continuous feedback data of all employees. Line managers and employees should not be granted this permission.

- *Give Continuous Feedback*: This permission will grant access to provide continuous feedback to your direct reports and others who are assigned to receive continuous feedback.
- *Request feedback from others*: This permission will grant access to request permission from others.

Note   The person from whom you are requesting feedback should be in the target population. If the person from whom you are seeking feedback is not available in your target population, then you will not be able to reach out to that person through CPM and request feedback.

This permission should be granted along with the setting "Limit about whom feedback can be requested."

- *Limit about whom feedback can be requested*: This permission will limit who can be reached out to for feedback.

Note   This permission should be granted along with the permission "Request feedback from others."

Continuous Performance Management

The following are the permission settings available in this category (see Figure 13-3):

- *Achievement*: This permission enables you to create, view, and edit achievements.

- *Activity*: This permission enables you to create, view, and edit activities.

- *Discussion Topics*: This permission enables you to create, view, and edit discussion topics.

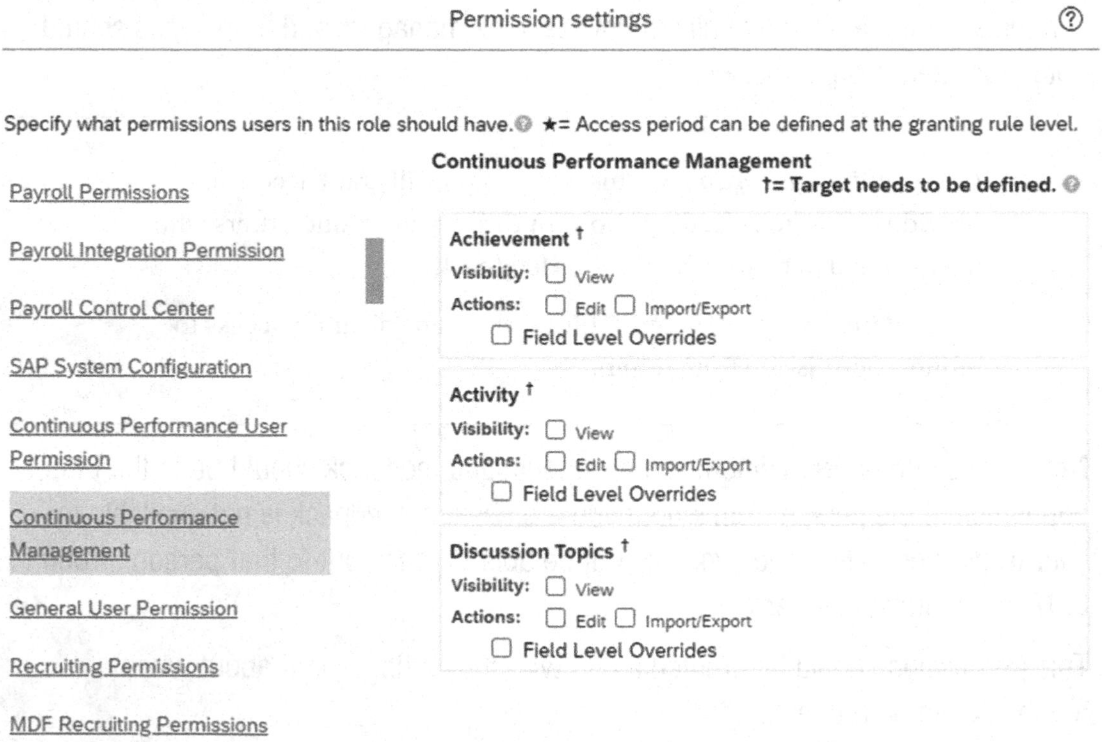

Permission settings   ⑦

Specify what permissions users in this role should have.⊘ ★= Access period can be defined at the granting rule level.

Continuous Performance Management
†= Target needs to be defined. ⊘

Payroll Permissions

Payroll Integration Permission

Payroll Control Center

SAP System Configuration

Continuous Performance User
Permission

Continuous Performance
Management

General User Permission

Recruiting Permissions

MDF Recruiting Permissions

Achievement †
Visibility: ☐ View
Actions: ☐ Edit ☐ Import/Export
          ☐ Field Level Overrides

Activity †
Visibility: ☐ View
Actions: ☐ Edit ☐ Import/Export
          ☐ Field Level Overrides

Discussion Topics †
Visibility: ☐ View
Actions: ☐ Edit ☐ Import/Export
          ☐ Field Level Overrides

Figure 13-3. *CPM-related permission category*

Managing Continuous Performance

The permission category Manage Continuous Performance can be accessed via Permission Settings ➤ Administrator Permissions. The following are the permission settings available in this category:

- *Access to Administrative Configuration page*: This permission should be assigned to the CPM admin only. This permission grants access to the CPM configuration page.

- *Admin Access Permission to all Continuous Performance Management Data*: This permission enables you to link the achievements added in CPM to the goals in Performance Management.

Note   You can access CPM by clicking the option Continuous Performance displayed in the Home drop-down.

Mobile App

If Mobility is enabled in your instance, you can access CPM on your mobile devices. You can enable CPM for access on your mobile devices by executing Enable Mobile Features. On the displayed config page, in Modules, in the section Talent, select the options Goal Management, Performance Review, and Continuous Performance.

The following CPM functionalities are supported on mobile devices:

- Activities

- Achievements

- Feedback process

- Coaching

- Capturing a one-on-one meeting

- Viewing meeting history

- Other topics

> **Note**   The SuccessFactors mobile app can be accessed on iOS (version 8 and newer) or Android (version 4 and newer).

In the next section, we will discuss how to configure CPM.

Continuous Performance Management Configuration

You can access the CPM configuration page by executing the config step Continuous Performance Management in the search bar. The displayed page (see Figure 13-4) has different sections. We will review each section.

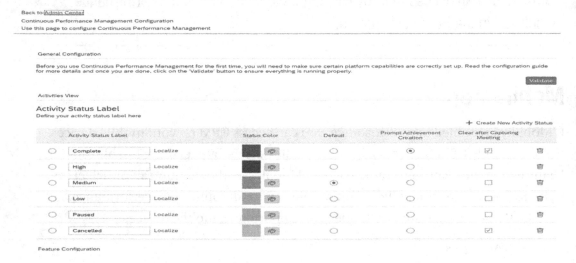

Figure 13-4. *CPM configuration*

- *General Configuration*: The Validate button displayed in this section does configuration and permission checks to ensure the required configurations are completed and are valid.

The check tool does the following:

(i)   Validates the different switches in Provisioning that need to be activated are completed. As shown in Figure 13-5, it validates that the prerequisites (primarily activating the switches in Provisioning) are completed.

(ii) Checks whether the OData APIs required for CPM are available in the instance.

Note   You can view the listing of all OData APIs available in the instance by executing the config step OData API Data Dictionary.

(iii) Verifies whether the Metadata Framework (MDF) entities required for CPM are available in the instance.

(iv) Verifies whether required permissions are assigned in the instance. Specifically, it verifies the following permission settings:

   ✓ Access to Continuous Performance Management

   ✓ Access to Administrative Configuration page

   ✓ Company Info Access

   ✓ User Search

   ✓ Admin access to OData API

   ✓ Read/Write Permission on Metadata Framework

(v)   Verifies whether the following entities required for CPM are available in the instance:

   ✓ ActivityStatus(high)

   ✓ ActivityStatus(medium)

   ✓ ActivityStatus(low)

   ✓ ActivityStatus(paused)

   ✓ ActivityStatus(complete)

   ✓ ActivityStatus(cancelled)

- ✓ OtherTopicStatus(Open)

- ✓ OtherTopicStatus(Closed)

- ✓ FeedbackFlag(Red)

- ✓ CPMNotificationConfig(CPM_1ON1_EMP_TODO_
  NOTIFICATION)

- ✓ CPMNotificationConfig(CPM_1ON1_MANAGER_TODO_
  NOTIFICATION)

- ✓ CPMNotificationConfig(CPM_ACTIVITY_REMINDER_
  NOTIFICATION)

- ✓ CPMNotificationConfig(CPM_ACHIEVEMENT_REMINDER_
  NOTIFICATION

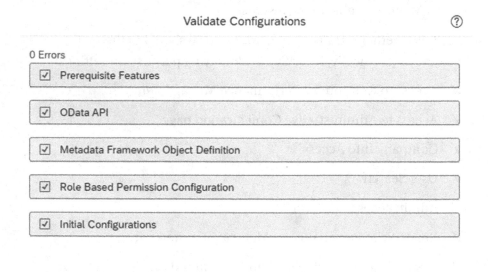

Figure 13-5. *CPM config checks*

- *Activities View*: In this section, we will create the different activities that we will use in CPM. We can define which status will be a default status when an activity is created. We can also define the status, which will trigger creation of an achievement. As shown in Figure 13-4, we have defined that once the activity is marked complete, it will create an achievement in CPM.

- *Feature Configuration*: In this section (see Figure 13-6), we can select/deselect the different options that are available in CPM. For example, if you do not want the ability to delete feedback to be available in the system, you can deselect the option Disable Deleting Feedback.

Feature Configuration

ℹ️ Please be advised, once you enable or disable the feature and receive a confirmation that it was successful, the system performs one additional action (metadata refresh) before your selected configuration can be reflected in the solution.

☑ Enable "Discussion Topics" ⑦

☑ Enable "Coaching" ⑦

☑ Enable Achievement Goal Linking ⑦

☑ Enable Achievement Development Goal Linking ⑦

☑ Enable Continuous Feedback ⑦

   ☑ Enable Activity Feedback ⑦

   ☑ Enable Achievement Feedback ⑦

   ☐ Disable Deleting Feedback ⑦

Cancel   Save Configuration

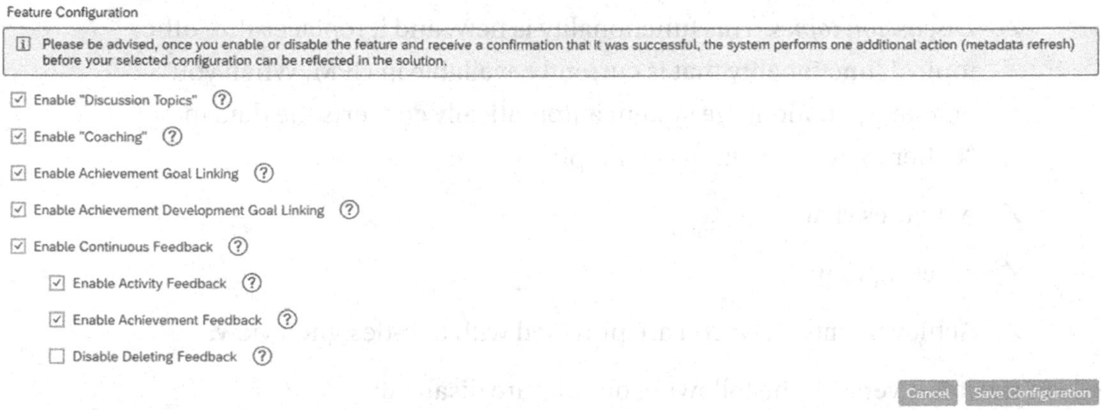

Figure 13-6. *Configuring features in CPM*

Tip   1) If you hover the mouse over the question mark icon, you will get a description of that particular option.

2) After selecting/deselecting an option, if the change is not reflected in the system, do the following: execute the config OData API Metadata Refresh and Export. On the displayed page, click Refresh. This will refresh the cache and update the instance with the changes.

- *Latest Version of Continuous Performance Management*: If you are interested in upgrading to the latest version of CPM, you can enable this option (see Figure 13-7). The latest version is not in General Availability yet, but it has been available since June 2020.

Latest Version of Continuous Performance Management
_____

☐ Enable Latest Continuous Performance Management [Restricted Availability]   ⑦

Cancel   Save Configuration

Figure 13-7. *Enabling the latest version of CPM*

When this option is enabled, the following options are made available:

✓ *Meeting notes*: This is a new functionality.

✓ *Discussion topics*: This functionality is new, and it replaces the "other topics" functionality that is currently available in CPM. When you enable this option, the system automatically converts the data in "Other topics" to "Discussion topics."

✓ Activities view.

✓ Meeting view.

✓ Achievements view: You are provided with a re-designed view.

In the latest version, the following options are disabled:

✓ Activity Feedback

✓ Coaching

✓ Achievement Goal Linking

✓ Achievement Development Goal Linking

✓ Continuous Feedback

✓ Achievement Feedback

Note   If you are enabling the latest version of CPM, SuccessFactors recommends that you enable the Fiori 3 theme and header as well.

- *Notifications*: Here (see Figure 13-8) you can select/deselect the different notifications and reminder options that are available in the instance for the employee and the manager. The values of the number of days should be equal to or greater than 1. Negative or decimals are not accepted. The reminders will be displayed in the ToDo tile on the home page.

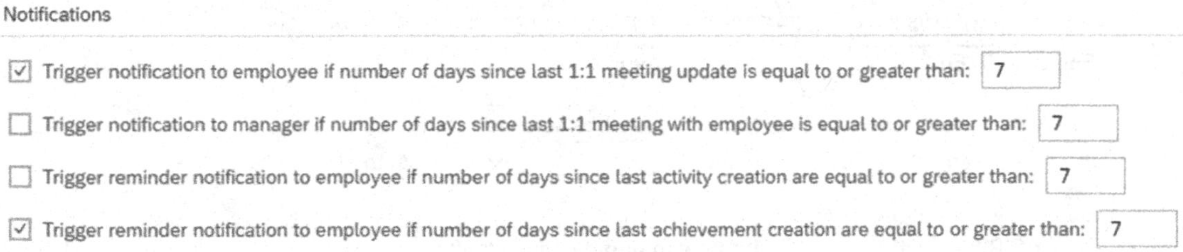

Notifications

☑ Trigger notification to employee if number of days since last 1:1 meeting update is equal to or greater than: 7

☐ Trigger notification to manager if number of days since last 1:1 meeting with employee is equal to or greater than: 7

☐ Trigger reminder notification to employee if number of days since last activity creation are equal to or greater than: 7

☑ Trigger reminder notification to employee if number of days since last achievement creation are equal to or greater than: 7

Figure 13-8. *Enabling notifications in CPM*

Note   If you activate any of these jobs, you are required to configure a scheduled job in Provisioning. The job type will be CPM Notification Job.

You can configure the reminders to be sent as an email as well. If you want to configure reminder notification for Updating Activities, Achievements, or Other Topics, you can do so in the config step E-Mail Notification Templates Settings. (Note: You can access the config screen to configure emails by entering *E-Mail Notification Templates Settings* in the search bar.) This will ensure that the employee or manager gets a reminder email. After executing the config step Email Template Notification, on the displayed page, search for the notification *Update Status Reminder Notification*.

Select the notification and click Save Notification Settings to save your changes. The employee will receive a notification in their email, as well in the ToDo tile on the SuccessFactors home page. The system will generate a reminder every four days, until an activity is updated in CPM.

Tip   You can update delivered text in the notification (Figure 13-9) to suit your business requirements.

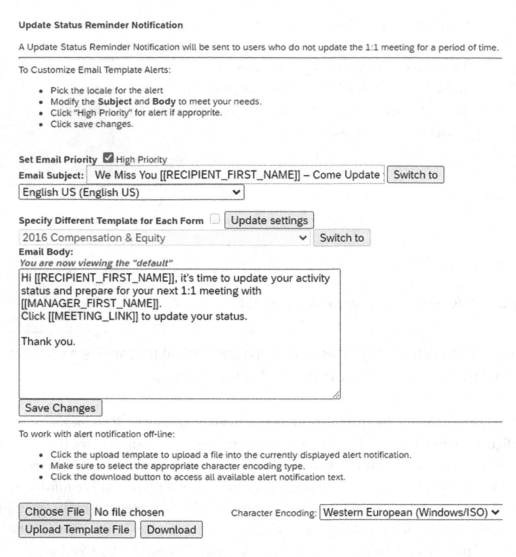

Update Status Reminder Notification

A Update Status Reminder Notification will be sent to users who do not update the 1:1 meeting for a period of time.

To Customize Email Template Alerts:

- Pick the locale for the alert
- Modify the **Subject** and **Body** to meet your needs.
- Click "High Priority" for alert if approprite.
- Click save changes.

Set Email Priority ☑ High Priority
Email Subject: | We Miss You [[RECIPIENT_FIRST_NAME]] – Come Update | Switch to
English US (English US) ⌄

Specify Different Template for Each Form ☐ | Update settings
2016 Compensation & Equity ⌄ | Switch to
Email Body:
You are now viewing the "default"

Hi [[RECIPIENT_FIRST_NAME]], it's time to update your activity status and prepare for your next 1:1 meeting with [[MANAGER_FIRST_NAME]].
Click [[MEETING_LINK]] to update your status.

Thank you.

Save Changes

To work with alert notification off-line:

- Click the upload template to upload a file into the currently displayed alert notification.
- Make sure to select the appropriate character encoding type.
- Click the download button to access all available alert notification text.

Choose File | No file chosen   Character Encoding: | Western European (Windows/ISO) ⌄
Upload Template File | Download

Figure 13-9. *Update Status Reminder Notification page*

If you want to configure a reminder notification to the manager if they don't conduct one-on-one meetings with their direct reports within the configured number of days, you can do so in the config step E-Mail Notification Templates Settings. After executing the config step E-Mail Template Notification, on the displayed page, search for the notification *Conduct 1:1 Meeting Reminder Notification*. Select the notification and remember to save your settings. You can also update the default text in the notification to suit your needs.

We can create an email notification to employees, notifying them when they receive feedback or when they receive a response for their request to feedback. Similar to other notifications, execute the config step E-Mail Notification Templates Settings. On the displayed page, search for the notification *Continuous Feedback Received Notification*. Select the notification and remember to save your settings. You can also update the default text in the notification to suit your needs.

Note   A prerequisite for this notification is that Intelligent Services (IS) should be enabled in the instance.

We can create an email notification to employees to provide feedback when they receive a request from another employee. Similar to other notifications, execute the config step E-Mail Notification Templates Settings. On the displayed page, search for the notification *Continuous Feedback Request Notification*. Select the notification and remember to save your settings. You can also update the default text in the notification to suit your needs.

Note   A prerequisite for this notification is that Intelligent Services (IS) should be enabled in the instance.

We can create an email notification to employees when their reporting manager makes an update or provides a comment in CPM. Similar to other notifications, execute the config step E-Mail Notification Templates Settings. On the displayed page, search for the notification *Activity Update Creation Notification*. Select the notification and remember to save your settings. You can also update the default text in the notification to suit your needs.

Note   Similar to the notifications we have seen before, this notification is triggered by Intelligent Services. To configure the activity, execute the config step Intelligent Services Center. Note that you can access the config screen by executing Intelligent Services Center (ISC) in the search bar. On the displayed page, click Continuous Performance Management Activity.

On the displayed page (see Figure 13-10), select the activity "Notify employee about activity update," and make changes where required. (By default, this flow is sufficient to trigger the email notification.) Click Actions and then Save Flow to save the flow rule.

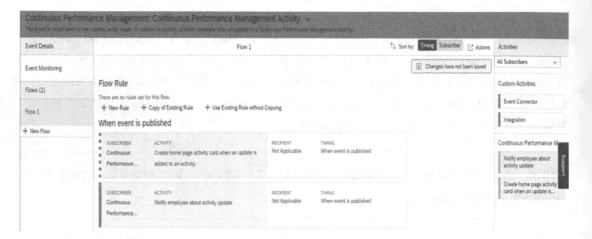

Figure 13-10. *Configuring Intelligent Services for Activity Update Creation Notification*

Whenever the manage makes an update or provides a comment in CPM, the employee will receive an email notification. The changes made by the manager will be visible to the employee directly in CPM as well.

Activities

The tasks that an employee is working on can be tracked as an activity in CPM. Activities may or may not be related to the objectives or goals assigned to the employee. You can request feedback on an activity. All activities in CPM will have a status associated to it. (Note: Refer to the section "Continuous Performance Management Configuration," where we discuss statuses in activities). When an activity is moved to the Completed status, you can create an achievement for that particular activity.

Note   An activity can be linked to a goal only if you are using the default goal plan or default development goal plan.

As shown in Figure 13-11, you can create an activity by clicking Add Activity. On the displayed screen, enter the activity name. By default, the status is set to Medium. You can change the status by clicking the drop-down and selecting the appropriate status. Whenever you have an update to the activity, you can enter the field and click OK to save your entries.

Figure 13-11. *Activity in CPM*

As shown in Figure 13-11, you can request feedback on the activity by clicking Request Feedback. On the displayed screen (see Figure 13-12), you can enter the name of the employee from whom you want to gather feedback.

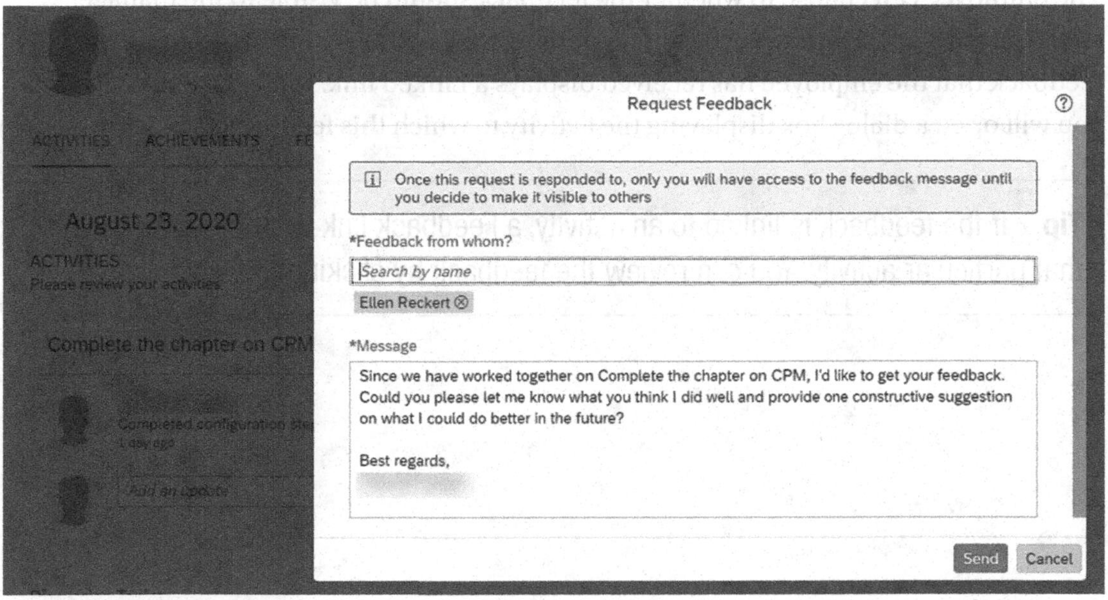

Figure 13-12. *Request for feedback*

> **Note**   If the employee does not receive an email notification requesting feedback, check whether the email notifications are activated and if the email address is correct in the employee file.

The employee who received the request for feedback will see the request in their ToDo section, in the Request Feedback tile. Click the tile, and click Provide Feedback to provide feedback to the employee who requested feedback. The feedback you provide will be visible to the employee.

> **Note**   The employee who receives the request to provide feedback can decline to provide feedback by clicking Decline. The employee who requested feedback can click View Feedback Requests on the Feedback tab and see that the requested person has declined to provide feedback.

The employee can view the feedback by clicking the Feedback tab (see Figure 13-11). The employee can choose to whether the feedback should be visible to the manager (see Figure 13-13). The employee has an option to delete the feedback. Notice that every feedback that the employee has received displays a Linked link. When you click this link, you will open a dialog box displaying the activity to which this feedback is linked.

> **Tip**   If the feedback is linked to an activity, a Feedback link will be displayed in that particular activity. You can review the feedback by clicking the link.

ACTIVITIES   ACHIEVEMENTS   FEEDBACK

                                             ⬚ Request Feedback   ⬚ View Feedback Requests   ⬚ Give Feedback

August 2020

Ellen Reckert
I have reviewed the chapter and I like what I saw.
August 23, 2020
⬚ Linked   ☐ Visible to my manager   🗑 Delete

Figure 13-13. *Feedback received by the employee*

Note   You can request feedback directly on the Feedback tab. When you request feedback directly from the Feedback tab, the feedback will not be linked to any activity. You can click Linked and link the feedback to an activity or to an achievement.

On the Feedback tab, clicking View Feedback Requests displays all the feedback requests the employee has made. The Give Feedback option can be used by the employee to provide feedback to another employee. The other employee can view the feedback on their CPM/Feedback tab and can elect to link the feedback to an activity or to an accomplishment.

Note   As a prerequisite, the ToDo tile on the home page should be enabled for the person who will receive the request for feedback.

Also, the employee requesting feedback should have RBP enabled to request feedback.

In the section Discussion Topics (see Figure 13-11), you can add topics that you want to review with your manager in your next one-on-one meeting.

Note   A manager's view of CPM (see Figure 13-14) will be similar to the employee's (Individual Contributor) view. In a manager's view, the manager will see their direct reports on the same screen. They can click each employee to view the CPM details of that particular person. To view their individual CPM, the manager will need to click their name to view.

Figure 13-14. *A manager's view of CPM*

The manager can create activities and discussion topics and can request feedback for their employees. The manager does not have the ability to hide the feedback received for their employees.

The employee (for whom the manager requested the feedback) can view the feedback in their CPM and can link the feedback to an activity or to an achievement.

In a manager's view, notice there is an additional Coaching section on the Activities tab. In this section, managers can coach their direct reports on what they are doing well and what can be improved. Note that the coaching section will be displayed only if the Coaching option is enabled in the config step Continuous Performance Management.

Clicking the Capture Meeting button will mark that the employee has completed their one-on-one meeting with their manager.

Note   When CPM is enabled in the instance, by default Topics and Coaching are also enabled. If you do not want to use these functionalities, you can disable them in the instance. Execute the config Continuous Performance Management. On the displayed config page, deselect the options Enable Discussion Topics and Enable Coaching. Both these switches are available in the section Feature Configuration.

Remember, when you disable Topics and Coaching, then Topics and Coaching are hidden in the Activities section. If you disable these switches, after they were enabled, all the current data and captured meetings will display activity data only. If reenable these switches, the captured data will be displayed again in the Activities section.

Achievements

The Achievements tab in CPM (see Figure 13-15) lists the achievements that you have logged in the system. You can tag the achievements either by time or by goal. Activities that are tagged as achievements are listed in this tab. (Typically when an activity is completed, you can flag it as an achievement.)

An employee's manager will have access to this tab and can view all the achievements that are tagged by the employee.

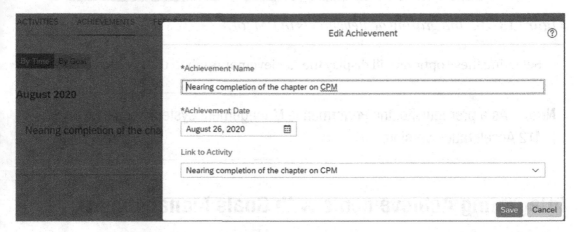

Figure 13-15. Achievements tab in CPM

Note   If you have multiple achievements linked to an activity, you can view all the achievements on the same tab. CPM also displays the achievements in chronological order and offers the functionality to filter achievements by date.

Integrating Achievements with SuccessFactors Performance Management

You can integrate achievements with SuccessFactors Performance Management in the config step Form Template Settings. You can execute the config step in the Admin Center or from the search box. On the displayed page, scroll to the bottom of the page and select the options (see Figure 13-16) on the Enable Achievements tab in the Performance Goal section and on the Enable Achievements tab in the Performance Development

Goal section. If you want the achievements feedback to be displayed in Performance Management, select the options Display Achievement Feedback for Performance Goal Achievements and Display Achievement Feedback for Development Goal Achievements.

☑ Enable Achievements tab in Performance Goal Section

☑ Display Achievement Feedback for Performance Goal Achievements

☑ Enable Achievements tab in Performance Development Goal Section

☑ Display Achievement Feedback for Development Goal Achievements

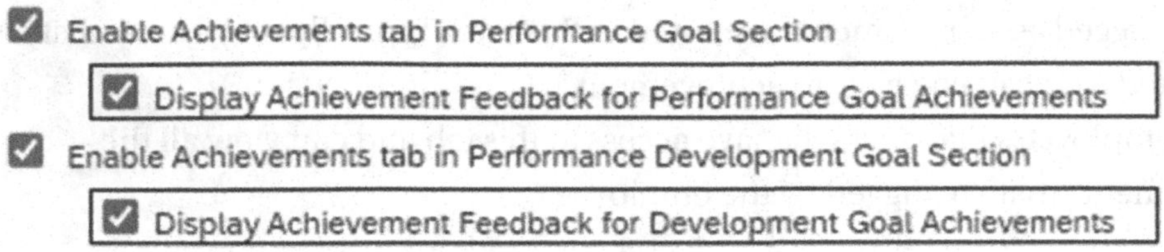

Figure 13-16. *Integrating achievements in PM form*

Selecting these options will display the Achievements tab in the Performance Form.

Note   As a prerequisite, the Performance Management system should be on PM12 Acceleration version.

Integrating Achievements with Goals Management

You can integrate achievements with your SuccessFactors goal plans. By integrating achievements with the goal plan, the employee and their managers can view the achievements and feedback received (if any) that are linked to performance goals directly in the employee's goal plan.

To do the configuration, execute the config step Manage Templates. (Note that you can access the config screen by executing Manage Templates in the search bar.) On the displayed page, click the tab Goal Plan. On the displayed page, select the goal plan you want to integrate with achievements. On the displayed page, select the option General Settings (see Figure 13-17). On the displayed page, select the option "Display Continuous PM Achievements on goal plan." Click Save to save your settings.

Admin Center > Manage Templates >

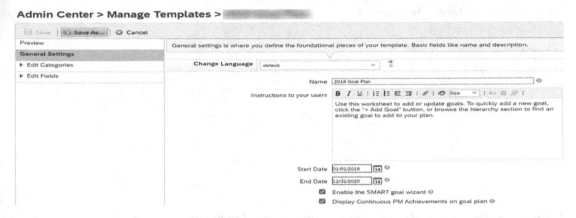

Figure 13-17. *Integrating achievements in a goal plan*

Note   For now, SuccessFactors does not have an option to link multiple goal plans in CPM. This is in the product road map, but when it will be released has not been announced yet by SuccessFactors. The switch Display Continuous PM Achievements on Goal Plan (see Figure 13-17) will allow you to only view the CPM achievements linked to your goals from the goals form. You cannot edit the CPM achievements from goal plans.

Integrating Achievements with Development Goals

You can integrate achievements with your SuccessFactors development goals. By integrating achievements with the development goals, the employee and their managers can view the achievements and feedback received (if any) that are linked to performance goals directly in the employee's development goal plan.

To do the configuration, execute the config step Manage Templates. On the displayed page, click the tab Development. On the displayed page, select the development goal you want to integrate with achievements. On the displayed page, select the option General Settings (see Figure 13-18). On the displayed page, select "Display Continuous PM Achievements on goal plan." Click Save to save your settings.

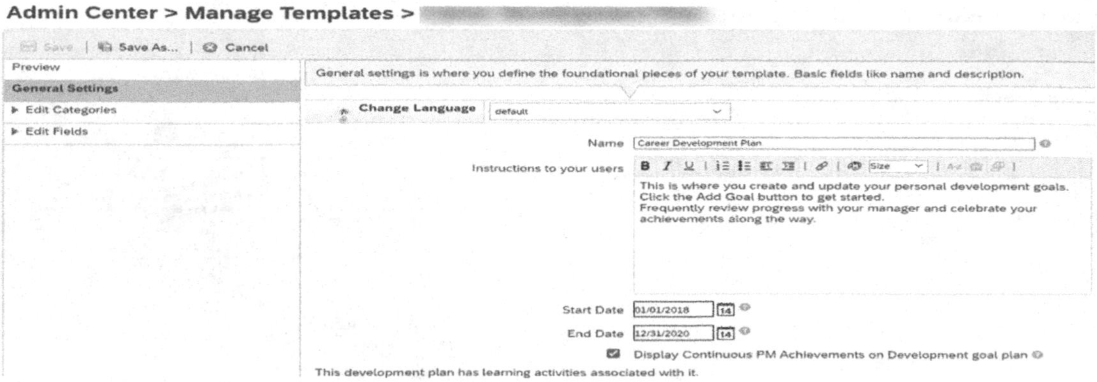

Figure 13-18. Integrating achievements in the development goals plan

Integrate Achievements with Calibrations Templates

You can integrate achievements with the calibration templates. Linking achievements with the calibration template enables managers to view achievements of their direct reports directly in the calibration template.

To do the configuration, execute the config step Manage Calibration Templates. On the displayed page, select the calibration template that needs to be integrated with achievements. On the displayed page, click the tab Data. On the displayed page (see Figure 13-19), scroll to the bottom of the page. Select the option "Allow access to Continuous Performance Management Achievements." Save your settings.

Figure 13-19. Integrating achievements with calibration templates

Reporting

In this case, we will discuss how to create ad hoc reports for CPM. To start with, we will review what permissions are required to access the reporting functionality.

As a prerequisite to creating and running ad hoc reports for CPM, you need to have the appropriate permissions assigned to you. Execute the config step Manage Permission Roles. On the displayed page, click the permission role to which you want to assign permissions to create/execute ad hoc reports for CPM. On the displayed page, click Permission. In the section User Permissions, click Reports Permission (see Figure 13-20). Click the permission Create Report and assign Continuous Performance Management and Continuous Performance Meetings. Scroll down, click the permission Run Report, and assign Continuous Performance Management and Continuous Performance Meetings.

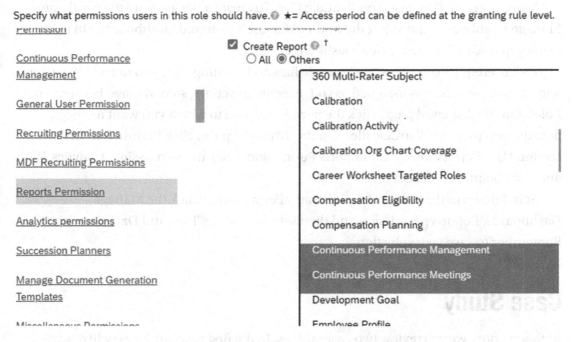

Figure 13-20. Assigning permission to create/execute ad hoc reports for CPM

To create an ad hoc report for CPM, you can select the domain Continuous Performance Management or Continuous Performance Meetings. You can use the domain Continuous Performance Management to create any report using data related to activities, achievements, coaching, and topics.

You can select the domain Continuous Performance Meetings to report on data related to one-on-one meetings.

Note   When you create a Continuous Performance Management report, you can select only one entity at a time; otherwise, you will get erroneous reports. You can use the entity Activity and Achievement to report on activities that are converted to achievements.

Tip   You can create YouCalc files in the system by executing the config step Manage Dashboards and selecting the option Manage Standard Dashboards and YouCalc Files. On the displayed page, select the option Build Tile and select Continuous Performance Management as the domain.

You can create tiles based on YouCalc files. To create a tile, execute the config step Manage Dashboards and select the option Manage Tile-Based Dashboards. On the displayed page, click Create New Dashboard.

As a prerequisite to accessing YouCalc files and creating tiles, you need to have the appropriate permissions assigned to you. Execute the config step Manage Permission Roles. On the displayed page, click the permission role to which you want to assign permissions to access YouCalc files. On the displayed page, click Permission. In the section User Permissions, click Reports Permission. Click the permission Analytics Tiles and Dashboards and select All.

Scroll down to the section Administrator Permissions. Click the Manage Dashboards/Reports permission and then select Analytics Tiles and Dashboards. Remember to save your selections.

Case Study

In this section, we will review two case studies. In the first case study, we will discuss how to integrate achievements with compensation.

Case 1

Customer A has already implemented CPM and other performance applications such as Performance Management, Goals Management, and Development Goals. The customer is currently implementing Compensation and would like to integrate achievements with compensation.

Integrating achievements with compensation will help compensation planners to view an employee's achievements directly in the compensation worksheet.

Solution 1

To integrate achievements with compensation, execute the configuration step Compensation Home. On the displayed page, select the compensation plan you want to integrate with achievements. On the displayed page, click the tab Plan Setup. Click the drop-down in Plan Setup/Settings, and select Advanced Settings. On the displayed page (see Figure 13-21), scroll to the bottom and select the option "Allow access to Continuous Performance Management Achievement view." Click Update Form Template to save your settings.

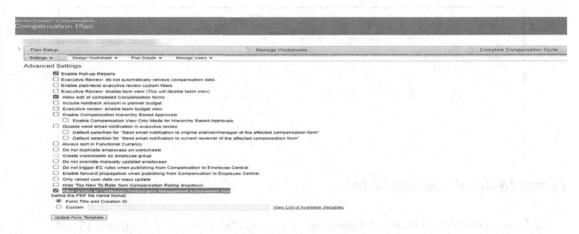

***Figure 13-21.** Integrating achievements with compensation*

In the comp worksheet, the compensation planner can view the achievements by selecting Open Achievements.

Case 2

The customer wants to review a scenario where the employee and the manager request feedback and give feedback.

Solution 2

We will discuss this case study from an employee perspective and a manager perspective.

Request Feedback/Give Feedback as an Employee

When an employee requests feedback, they are requesting feedback for themself (see Figure 13-22). When an employee gives feedback, they are providing feedback for a specific employee (Figure 13-23).

When an employee requests feedback, they can view the status of their feedback requests in View Feedback Requests. When the feedback request is sent out, it will display a status of Pending.

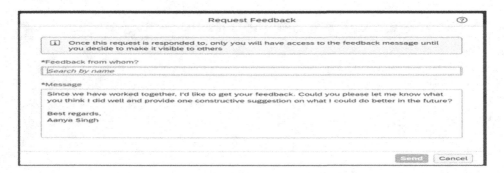

Figure 13-22.   *Requesting feedback*

When an employee receives a feedback request, they can see the request in the To-Do section in the Provide Feedback tile on the home page. When you click the tile, the displayed page will show the Provide Feedback and Decline buttons. The employee can decline to provide feedback by clicking Decline. When the employee declines to provide feedback, the employee who requested for feedback can view the status in View Feedback Requests. It will show Declined.

The employee who received the request for feedback can provide feedback by clicking Provide Feedback. This will display a new dialog box, where the employee (the receiver) can enter their feedback. Remember to click Send. Any feedback that is provided will be visible to the employee who requested the feedback. When the employee provides feedback, the employee who requested for feedback will notice the status has changed to "Responded on <<date>>" when they click View Feedback Requests. The employee can elect to make the feedback visible to their manager by selecting "Visible to my manager." They also can link the feedback to an activity or an achievement.

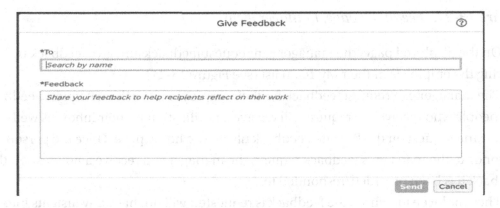

Figure 13-23. *Giving feedback*

When an employee gives feedback to another employee (without it being requested), the employee to whom the feedback was provided will receive a notification that an employee has provided them with feedback. A link to view the feedback is also provided. The feedback will be displayed on the Feedback page, and the employee who received the feedback can elect to make the feedback viewable by their manager as well as link it to an activity or an achievement.

Request Feedback/Give Feedback as a Manager

The manager can request and give feedback to their employees on the Continuous Performance Management/Feedback page (see Figure 13-24).

Figure 13-24. *Feedback page, manager view*

On the displayed page, the manager can request feedback and give feedback by clicking the employee in their My Team list (see Figure 13-24).

The manager can request feedback for their employee by clicking Request Feedback. The people who receive the request will receive a notification in their inbox, as well as view the request on the Provide Feedback tile on the home page. Once the person responds to the manager's feedback request, the manager will receive a notification that feedback has been provided/responded to.

The employee for whom the feedback is requested will not have any insights into the feedback request. They system does not send the employee (for whom the feedback is requested) any notifications, nor does View Feedback Requests display the request made by the manager.

Having said that, the manager can view the request in View Feedback Requests of the employee for whom they have requested feedback.

Once the feedback is provided, the employee for whom the feedback is requested can view the feedback on their Feedback page. They can link the feedback to an achievement or activity, as well as elect to make the feedback visible to their manager.

The manager can view the feedback on the feedback page of that employee.

The manager can provide feedback to their employee by clicking Give Feedback for their employee. Any feedback that is provided will be to the employee on their feedback page. The employee will also receive a notification that their manager has provided feedback.

Conclusion

In this chapter, we reviewed the concept of continuous performance management, the agility it provides, and how it can be integrated into your annual appraisal process. In this chapter, we discussed how achievements in CPM can be integrated with performance management, goals management, development goals, and calibration. As a case study, we saw how achievements can be integrated into compensation worksheets, which helps compensation planners to view achievements directly in the employees' compensation worksheets.

CPM is an exciting HR process, and more organizations are embracing it to provide continual feedback to their employees, as well as have the agility to change activities to align with business and market needs.

CHAPTER 14

Configuring Calibration

Calibration is a process used to appraise employee performance in a fair and consistent manner. Managers meet in calibration sessions to discuss employee performance to achieve agreement on performance ratings. Guidelines may be established so that there is alignment on the definition of each performance rating to enable a common language to use when discussing and evaluating performance. The intent is to help eliminate any potential manager bias when discussing employee performance and finalizing ratings.

SAP SuccessFactors Calibration provides a framework to objectively evaluate employee performance. This tool provides HR and senior managers the means to impartially review and adjust performance ratings across teams, departments, and the organization. The Calibration module provides a visual presentation of employee data that may be viewed in charts, bins, or list formats. The ability to filter and group rating data helps in finding areas of bias. These views are more meaningful than using one-dimensional spreadsheets containing employee names and ratings for managers to evaluate.

Information used within Calibration may be sourced from Performance Management, People Profile, Compensation, or Succession data. Within Performance Management, overall performance, potential, competency, and goal ratings may be calibrated. The Succession-related metrics that may be calibrated are Risk of Loss, Impact of Loss, and Reason for Leaving. Compensation ratios may be evaluated using the salary, bonus, stock, and variable pay components of a compensation template. Overall potential, performance, competency, objective, and two custom ratings may be calibrated from the Talent Profile section of People Profile. Upon completion of a calibration session, ratings are updated in the original source.

Calibration does not support:

- Variable Pay or 360 Reviews data

- Ratings entered directly on compensation forms

- Normalization of data

© Susan Traynor, Michael A. Wellens and Venki Krishnamoorthy 2021
S. Traynor et al., *SAP SuccessFactors Talent: Volume 1*, https://doi.org/10.1007/978-1-4842-6600-7_14

In addition, Calibration should not be used to manage incumbents and succession planning.

In this chapter, we will enable and configure Calibration. We will cover the steps leading to the creation of a calibration session, including the following:

- Enable Calibration in Provisioning.

- Configure the Succession Data Model.

- Set role-based permission for Calibration access.

- Configure the data source template and route map.

- Enable calibration-related email notifications.

- Configure the calibration template.

- Configure calibration settings.

- Configure Calibration Talent Card.

- Assign users to the Executive Reviewer role.

- Enforce comments on rating change.

- Configure the Calibration History Portlet in People Profile.

- Calibration home page tiles.

- Calibration alerts

- Text Replacement

So let's begin!

Enable Calibration in Provisioning

In order to use the SAP SuccessFactors Calibration module, there are a few simple features that must be enabled in Provisioning.

Log in to Provisioning and click the link for "Company Settings".

Search for "Calibration" to find the section called "Enable Calibration." Once found, click the checkbox as seen in Figure 14-1 to enable Calibration in your instance.

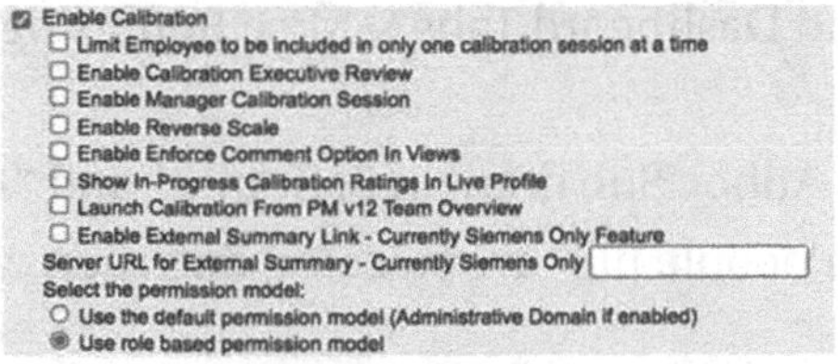

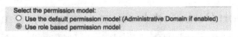

Figure 14-1. *Enable Calibration Within Company Settings*

The additional settings within Enable Calibration may be enabled here or within the instance in Manage Calibration Settings. There are two that are helpful to enable here:

1. Enable Calibration Executive Review

2. Launch Calibration from PM v12 Team Overview

If you plan on using Executive Review, which summarizes calibration activity across sessions for executives and HR, enable it here. This provides access to the Executive Review tab when creating the calibration template.

For managers to be able to create their own calibration sessions in Team Overview in Performance Management, click the checkbox for "Launch Calibration from PM v12 Team Overview." This provides visibility of the Manager Template tab when configuring the calibration settings.

Within Enable Calibration, there is a radio button to identify the permission model used. An example is seen in Figure 14-2. The default permission model is legacy permissions, but you should be using role-based permission (RBPs). Make sure "Use role based permission model" is selected.

Select the permission model:
○ Use the default permission model (Administrative Domain if enabled)
◉ Use role based permission model

Figure 14-2. *Permission Model Selection*

Save this section within "Company Settings" before moving on to the next set of features to enable.

Calibration Reporting Permissions

There are no standard reports or dashboards for Calibration. Any calibration reporting will need to be done using ad hoc reports. There are three Calibration-related domains to enable.

Go to the "Analytics and Dashboard Tabs & Misc Reporting" section of "Company Settings".

Make sure "Additional Adhoc Sub domain Schemas" and "Enable INCLUDE STARTING FROM USER in people pill" are selected and then enable the following:

- Calibration

- Calibration Org Chart Coverage

- Calibration Activity

Save the section and then back out of "Company Settings".

Configuring Calibration in the Succession Data Model

We will need to update the Succession Data Model to incorporate some Calibration-related elements.

Within Succession Management, as seen in Figure 14-3, select "Import/Export Data Model".

Figure 14-3. *Option to Import/Export Data Model*

Once the Import/Export Data Model screen displays, you may select the "Export file" radio button and click the Submit button as shown in Figure 14-4.

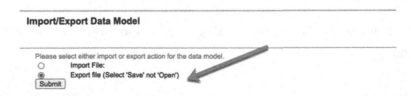

Figure 14-4. *Export of the Data Model*

Now that we have downloaded the data model, open it in an XML editor to make some modifications. There are four elements used for Calibration that we will need to review:

1. Rating Elements
2. Display Options
3. Filter Options
4. Calibration History Portlet

We will look at each element in detail.

Rating Elements

You will need to decide what rating elements to calibrate in your sessions. An existing performance form template can be used if it contains the rating elements you wish to calibrate. You may create a new performance form template to utilize additional rating types such as overall competency, overall goal, and overall potential.

The data model must contain the rating elements that will be calibrated. Most likely you will see all of these in the data model. The rating elements are:

- sysOverallObjective
- sysOverallCompetency
- sysOverallPerformance
- sysOverallPotential
- sysOverallCustom01
- sysOverallCustom02

The following code segment displays an example of the overall performance rating background element:

```
<background-element id="sysOverallPerformance" type-id="31"
scale-id="Performance" feedback-type="8">
    <label>Performance History</label>
    <rating-field rating-name="start-date" required="true" max-length="999"
    display-size="12" max-file-size-KB="1000">
      <label>Start Date</label>
```

```
</rating-field>
<rating-field rating-name="end-date" required="true" max-length="999"
display-size="12" max-file-size-KB="1000">
  <label>End Date</label>
</rating-field>
<rating-field rating-name="name" visibility="none" max-length="2000"
display-size="30" max-file-size-KB="1000">
  <label>name</label>
</rating-field>
<rating-field rating-name="description" visibility="none"
max-length="4000" display-size="30" max-file-size-KB="1000">
  <label>description</label>
</rating-field>
<rating-field rating-name="rating" insert-rating="true"
visibility="none" required="true" max-length="999" display-size="8"
max-file-size-KB="1000">
  <label>Rating</label>
</rating-field>
<rating-field rating-name="label" visibility="edit" max-length="128"
display-size="30" max-file-size-KB="1000">
  <label>Overall Performance Rating</label>
</rating-field>
<rating-field rating-name="min" visibility="none" max-length="999"
display-size="8" max-file-size-KB="1000">
  <label>Minimum Scale Rating</label>
</rating-field>
<rating-field rating-name="max" visibility="none" max-length="999"
display-size="8" max-file-size-KB="1000">
  <label>Maximum Scale Rating</label>
</rating-field>
<rating-field rating-name="source" system-generated="true"
visibility="none" max-length="8" display-size="8" max-file-size-KB="1000">
  <label>source</label>
</rating-field>
```

```
<rating-field rating-name="module" system-generated="true"
visibility="none" max-length="8" display-size="8" max-file-size-KB="1000">
   <label>module</label>
</rating-field>
</background-element>
```

Make sure all of the rating types that you wish to calibrate are included in your data model.

There are three standard elements that may display in some of the views in a calibration session. If you are using SAP SuccessFactors Succession, these are most likely used for talent flags and matrix grid reports:

- riskOfLoss
- impactOfLoss
- reasonForLeaving

A code segment for these elements is seen in the following:

```
<standard-element id="riskOfLoss" required="false" matrix-filter="false">
   <label>Risk of Loss</label>
   <label xml:lang="en-US">Risk of Loss</label>
   <picklist id="riskOfLoss"/>
</standard-element>
<standard-element id="impactOfLoss" required="false" matrix-filter="false">
   <label>Impact of Loss</label>
   <label xml:lang="en-US">Impact of Loss</label>
   <picklist id="impactOfLoss"/>
</standard-element>
<standard-element id="reasonForLeaving" required="false" matrix-filter="false">
   <label>Reason for Leaving</label>
   <label xml:lang="en-US">Reason for Leaving</label>
   <picklist id="reasonForLeaving"/>
</standard-element>
```

Display Options

Because we are talking about the talent flags in the data model, we will jump ahead for a minute so that we can talk about the display options found in a calibration session. Calibration sessions can display data in many views that we will learn about shortly. There is a display option feature that is particularly useful for one of the views. The List View displays data in a table-like format with a row for each employee being calibrated. If there are several columns in this table, there could be a lot of back-and-forth scrolling to see all of the information for an employee. There is a "Display Options" icon that enables users to add or remove certain columns to or from the view. Some are hardcoded and will always show up as display options in a calibration session:

- First Name

- Last Name

- Count

- Quick card

The Quick Card display option may be enabled when configuring the calibration template. More on this later.

When you click the Display Options icon within the calibration session, any of the fields may be deselected, and those columns will no longer display in the view. The Bin View and Matrix View also have the Display Options icon. Deselecting any display option fields will impact these views as well.

There are some icons that may be added as display option fields. Any display option fields defined for Succession in the Matrix Grid Classifier tool in Provisioning or the flags set in Matrix Grid Report Icon Reconfiguration may also be used. In the List View, any of the icons selected would appear in a new column called "Attributes." In Bin and Matrix Views, the icons appear underneath an employee's name. Having these icons readily visible for each employee may be useful when comparing employee ratings.

Refer to Volume 2, Chapter 5 to learn more about configuring these matrix grid icons.

The Display Option feature for a calibration session is shown in Figure 14-5.

Figure 14-5. *Additional Display Options*

Two tabs will display. The Other Options tab contains the four standard fields, and the Employee Attributes tab contains the succession flags.

Filter Options

Filter Options are used in a calibration session to narrow the list of employees that display. If there are a large number of subjects, this is a way to view a smaller group that meets the filter criteria. It may be more manageable to view subsets of employees during the session.

Within a calibration session, the standard fields that are available as filter options are:

- Manager

- Division

- Department

- Location

- Job Code

If Risk of Loss, Impact of Loss, and Reason for Leaving are also in your data model, these fields will also be filter fields.

The 15 custom fields that may be defined in the data model may also be added as filter options.

To set this up, the filter must be defined in the data model.

Located under *<custom-filters>*, add the tag *<filter-module-id="calibration">*.

This should be placed after the default filter as shown in the following code segment sample.

You may add all 15 custom elements or any that you choose, as long they are also identified as default filters.

A code segment sample shown in the following contains the default and calibration filters:

```
<custom-filters>
  <filter-module id="default">
    <standard-element-ref refid="custom01"/>
    <standard-element-ref refid="custom02"/>
    <standard-element-ref refid="custom03"/>
    <standard-element-ref refid="custom04"/>
    <standard-element-ref refid="custom05"/>
    <standard-element-ref refid="custom06"/>
    <standard-element-ref refid="custom07"/>
    <standard-element-ref refid="custom08"/>
    <standard-element-ref refid="custom09"/>
    <standard-element-ref refid="custom10"/>
    <standard-element-ref refid="custom11"/>
    <standard-element-ref refid="custom12"/>
    <standard-element-ref refid="custom13"/>
    <standard-element-ref refid="custom14"/>
    <standard-element-ref refid="custom15"/>
  </filter-module>
  <filter-module id="calibration">
    <standard-element-ref refid="custom01"/>
    <standard-element-ref refid="custom02"/>
    <standard-element-ref refid="custom03"/>
    <standard-element-ref refid="custom04"/>
    <standard-element-ref refid="custom05"/>
    <standard-element-ref refid="custom06"/>
    <standard-element-ref refid="custom07"/>
    <standard-element-ref refid="custom08"/>
    <standard-element-ref refid="custom09"/>
    <standard-element-ref refid="custom10"/>
    <standard-element-ref refid="custom11"/>
    <standard-element-ref refid="custom12"/>
```

```
        <standard-element-ref refid="custom13"/>
        <standard-element-ref refid="custom14"/>
        <standard-element-ref refid="custom15"/>
    </filter-module>
</custom-filters>
```

By importing the updated version of the data model, the filter options in a calibration session will now include the fields identified in the custom calibration filter. The order of the custom fields listed in the filter will be the order in which the fields appear as filter fields in a calibration session.

The following is just to clarify the order of the filter fields:

- The standard fields Manager, Division, Department, and Location are the first filters that display.

- The standard filter fields are followed by the custom fields identified in the custom-filter section of the data model.

- The standard fields Job Code, Risk of Loss, Impact of Loss, and Reason for Leaving are the final filter fields listed.

Adding the custom fields to the calibration filter in the data model will also make these fields available when managing a calibration session. These fields can be used to search for employees when selecting subjects and participants for the session.

The final update to the data model is needed only if you plan on displaying the Calibration History Portlet in People Profile.

Calibration History Portlet

This portlet provides a snapshot of calibration session data along with ratings. In order to use the Calibration History Portlet, the background element must be added to the data model as shown in the following code segment sample.

```
<background-element id="calibrationHistoryPortlet" type-id="138">
    <label>Calibration History Portlet</label>
</background-element>
```

If you also wish to use the portlet in Employee Scorecard, the Calibration History Portlet must be added under the view-template "employeeScoreCard". A code segment sample is shown in the following:

```
<view-template id="employeeScoreCard" visibility="none" pdf-printing-
enabled="true">
    <label>View Template for Employee Scorecard</label>
    <description>This view Template for Employee Scorecard should have only
    1 edit template</description>
    <edit-template id="scorecardEditTemplate">
        <label>Edit Template for Employee Scorecard</label>
        <description>Edit Template for Employee Scorecard</description>
        <background-element-ref refid="sysScoreCardOverviewPortlet"/>
        <background-element-ref refid="sysScoreCardContactPortlet"/>
        <background-element-ref refid="sysScoreCardOrgProfilePortlet"/>
        <background-element-ref refid="sysScoreCardExpSnapshotPortlet"/>
        <background-element-ref refid="sysScoreCardPerfHistoryPortlet"/>
        <background-element-ref refid="sysScoreCardCompetenciesPortlet"/>
        <background-element-ref refid="sysScoreCardCompBehaviorPortlet"/>
        <background-element-ref refid="sysScoreCardObjRatingsPortlet"/>
        <background-element-ref refid="sysScoreCardNominationPortlet"/>
        <background-element-ref refid="sysScoreCardSuccessorPortlet"/>
        <background-element-ref refid="calibrationHistoryPortlet"/>
    </edit-template>
```

Once the modifications have been made, save the file, and then import it via Import/Export Data Model.

Let's review what is done in Provisioning to set up Calibration. Calibration must be enabled in Provisioning along with the reporting components (optional). Rating elements, talent flags for the display options, and filter options need to be configured in the data model. Optionally, the Calibration History Portlet background element needs to be added to the data model.

Instance Setup for Calibration

Next, we will explore the updates needed in the instance. We will start with role-based permissions.

Calibration Role-Based Permissions

Role-based permissions (RBPs) control whom a user can see (target population), what features they have access to, and what actions they may perform.

In order to set up Calibration in your instance, specific action permissions need to be added to some permission roles. There are three types of permissions to set up:

1. Administrative: To configure and administer Calibration

2. End User: To access calibration sessions and the Calibration History Portlet

3. Reporting: To report on calibration-related data

These permissions may be incorporated into existing roles, such as system admin, HR admin, or manager. These roles would work in conjunction with target populations to identify which employees a user can see in a calibration session and which employees the user may perform calibration-related tasks on.

Admin rights are needed to set up Calibration, and end user rights are used to access calibration sessions. At least two roles will need to have calibration-related permission, the administrator role and the manager role. If you are using HR managers as the facilitators of the sessions, an additional role will be needed to manage the calibration sessions.

You will need to decide which roles will perform calibration-related administrative functions. It could be one or more existing roles or a new calibration admin role. The permissions may be split so that your system admin may only set up the role-based permissions and configure the calibration settings. An HR/calibration admin or HR manager may have permission to create and manage sessions, grant user permission to the Executive Summary, and create and run calibration reports. Just remember to consider that the target populations for these roles identify which employees a user can see in a calibration session and which employees the user may perform calibration-related tasks on.

There are a set of roles that are specific to a calibration session and are separate from role-based permissions. They will be discussed in a later section of this chapter.

First, let's look at the calibration-related role-based permissions required. We will start with the admin role and call out any permissions that may also be granted to a manager or HR manager role.

Manage Calibration Permissions

Permissions must be set to manage calibration sessions, settings, and templates. Within Manage Permission Roles, select the admin role to add calibration access to.

Permissions to configure how calibration sessions work within your instance are found within Administrator Permissions, under Manage Calibration as seen in Figure 14-6.

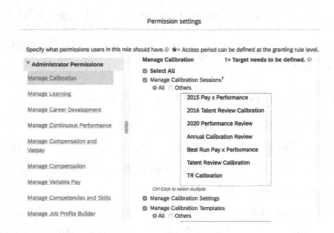

Figure 14-6. *Manage Calibration Permissions*

Click "Select All" in order to allow the role to handle the setup and management of calibration components.

Table 14-1 contains the description of each of the calibration administration features. Review these features if you think you would like to split the calibration administrative tasks across multiple permission roles.

Table 14-1. *Calibration Admin Features*

Feature	Description
Manage Calibration Sessions	Used to set up and manage calibration sessions.
Manage Calibration Settings	To configure what the roles within a calibration session may do and to identify fields that will appear within an employee search when creating a calibration session. Also ,may choose which calibration template a manager may launch from Team Overview in Performance and to set global settings for all calibration sessions.

(*continued*)

Table 14-5. (*continued*)

Feature	Description
Manage Calibration Templates	To create templates used for calibration sessions, to identify the data source for ratings and the views of the data during the sessions.
Mass Create Calibration Sessions	To create multiple calibration sessions via spreadsheet import.
Manage Permissions for Executive Review	To identify the users that may access the Executive Review page for a calibration template.
OData API Calibration Export	To access the Odata API calibration export.

There is a caveat to the calibration permissions. There are permissions to access a calibration session that are not role based. When an admin creates a calibration session, users are identified as facilitators, owners, and participants of the session. This gives the selected users access to the session through the Calibration tab in the Home menu listing. Users identified as facilitators of a session will be able to run the session but not create additional sessions. For any users that need to create sessions, the users should be assigned to a permission group that is tied to a permission role that has permission for Manage Calibration Sessions.

Reporting Permissions

The admin and HR manager roles could be granted permission to create and run ad hoc calibration reports. The permissions are found within User Permissions ➤ Reports Permission. You may enable "Create Report" and "Run Report". The three calibration domains should be selected: Calibration, Calibration Activity, and Calibration Org Chart Coverage. An example is seen in Figure 14-7.

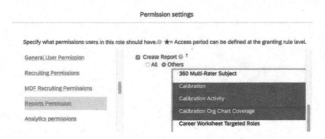

Figure 14-7. Reports Permission Needed for Calibration

You may decide to create the reports as the admin and then share the reports with HR managers to run for the groups that they support. In that case, grant Run Report access to the HR manager role without *Create Report* permission. If the manager role is granted permission to run calibration ad hoc reports, only data for their target population would display.

End User Permission for the Calibration Tab

You may grant the admin, HR manager, and manager roles access to Calibration. After selecting the role to update, click "Permissions." Under User Permissions, you will see Calibration, and select both of the options. The Detailed Calibration Permissions requires a target population and identifies which users may be viewed in a session. The View Calibration tab grants access to the Calibration tab found in the Home menu. The permissions are shown in Figure 14-8.

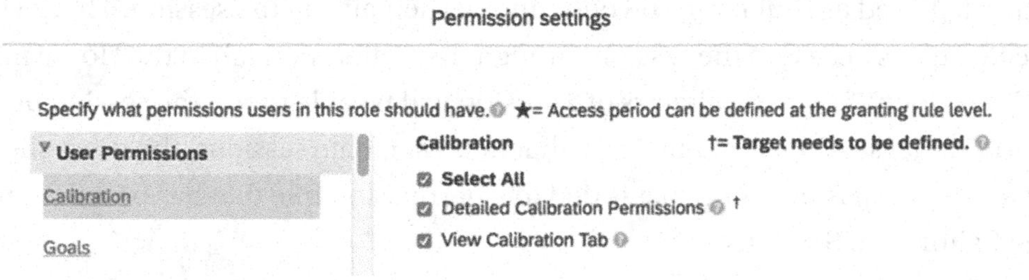

Figure 14-8. *Calibration Permissions for an End User*

Make sure you have a role for all employees that contains General User Permission ➤ Company Info Access ➤ User Search. Without this permission, a user would not be able to open a calibration session and search users as seen in Figure 14-9.

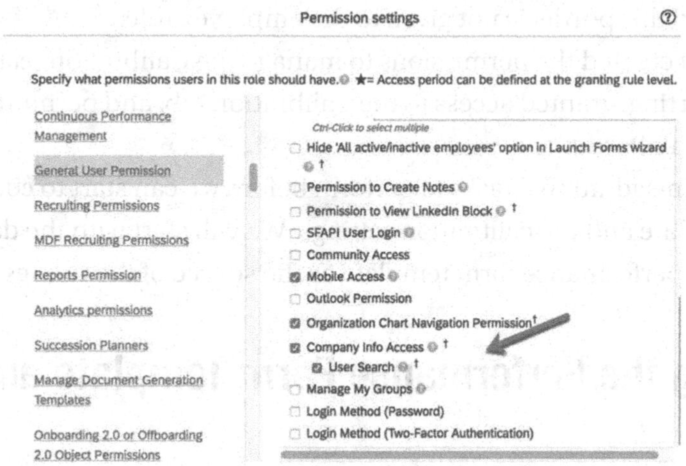

Figure 14-9. General User Permission for Employee Search

Calibration History Portlet Role-Based Permissions

If you plan on using the Calibration History Portlet in People Profile, make sure the admin role can manage employee files in order to configure the portlet. The role-based permission can be found within the role permissions under Administrator Permissions ➤ Manage System Properties.

To include the Calibration History Portlet in People Profile, this background element needs to be permitted. Select the RBP role you'd like to add the permission for. Typically, it would be the admin, HR manager, or manager role.

Found within User Permissions ➤ Employee Data, go to the Background section to find Calibration History Portlet. Enable "View" access as seen in Figure 14-10 and save the role.

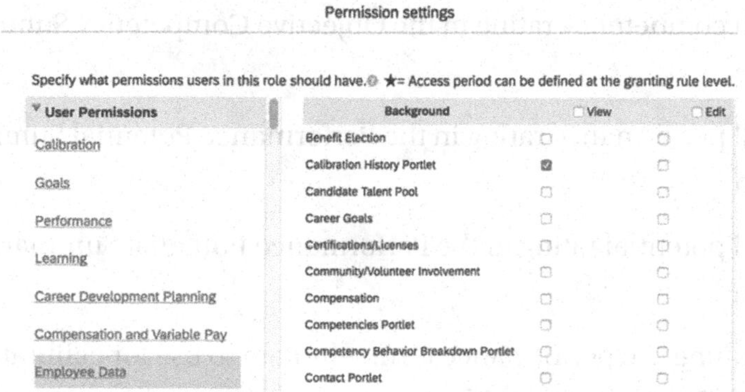

Figure 14-10. Calibration History Portlet Permission

Permission to this portlet is not given to the employee role.

We have now created the permissions to manage the Calibration features, enabled Calibration reporting, granted access to the Calibration tab, and permitted access to the Calibration History Portlet.

There are some additional tasks to perform before we can start to configure the calibration template and the calibration settings. We will start with the data source. We will be using the performance form template as the source of the ratings to be calibrated.

Configuring the Performance Form Template and Route Map

We have to make sure that the performance form template used for calibration has the necessary components. First, a manual rating must be configured in the form template for any of the rating types that you wish to calibrate (overall performance, overall potential, overall objective, or overall competency). Manual ratings are updated in the calibration session and also allow the drag and drop functionality which is an easy method for the facilitator to update ratings.

You may either update your current performance form template or create a new one that contains all of the rating types that you would like to calibrate.

The performance form template must have one of the following ratings enabled:

- Overall performance rating in the Summary, Performance Potential Summary, or Customized Weighted Rating summary section

- Overall objective rating in the Objective Competency Summary section

- Overall competency rating in the Objective Competency Summary section

- Overall performance rating in the Performance Potential Summary section

- Overall potential rating in the Performance Potential Summary section

After determining the performance form template to use for calibration, we need to consider the associated route map. The route map associated with the form template will need to have a dedicated step where calibration will occur. Ideally the step will immediately follow the manager assessment step. It is important to note that when adding this step, the step type cannot be iterative or in the Signature stage. Typically, it is the HR manager role assigned to this step as seen in Figure 14-11.

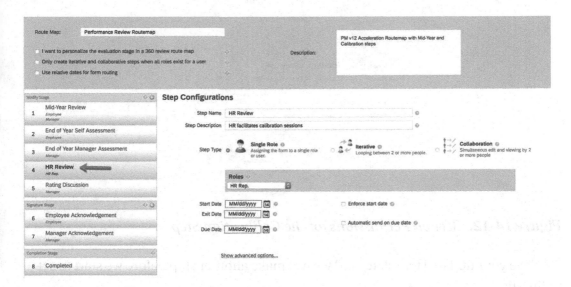

Figure 14-11. *Route Map with a Calibration Step*

If your existing performance form template contains an HR step after the manager assessment step, this can be used as the calibration step, provided it is not an iterative or signature step.

If your performance form template contains a Customized Weighted Rating summary section, make sure the calibration step occurs after the step where the calculation of the weighted rating is triggered.

Once the route map is updated to include the calibration step and saved, the performance form template will need to be updated. If the route map has the new calibration step added, permissions need to be created for this step within sections of the performance form template.

Type and select "Manage Templates" in the search bar. Select your performance form template in order to add permissions for the new step. The HR role will need permission for the form template sections for the calibration step. If the route map already has a step that is going to be used for calibration, the step permissions may not need any updating. Unless you want the role designated for the calibration step to be able to update the form while the form is in the calibration session, you can make all of the fields and sections

663

read-only for the HR role in the calibration step. As seen in Figure 14-12, the Summary section is disabled for the HR review step. This is the calibration step, so the HR manager may not edit the form while it is in a calibration session.

Figure 14-12. *Section Permissions for the Calibration Step*

Save your updated template, and we will make another stop before we start to set up Calibration.

Email Notifications

Type and select "E-Mail Notification Templates Settings" in the search bar. Here, Calibration-specific emails may be enabled. Notifications may be sent at various points in the calibration process. Figure 14-13 shows the email notifications available for Calibration.

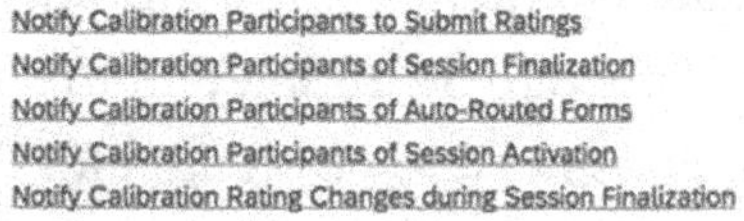

Notify Calibration Participants to Submit Ratings
Notify Calibration Participants of Session Finalization
Notify Calibration Participants of Auto-Routed Forms
Notify Calibration Participants of Session Activation
Notify Calibration Rating Changes during Session Finalization

Figure 14-13. *Calibration Email Notifications*

Four of the Calibration email notifications that may be enabled via E-Mail Notification Templates are shown in Table 14-2.

Table 14-2. *Calibration Email Notification Descriptions*

Email	Description
Notify Calibration Participants to Submit Ratings	Notify the manager of an upcoming calibration session and to submit ratings so that forms can move to the calibration step.
Notify Calibration Participants of Session Finalization	Notify owners and participants that the calibration session has been finalized.
Notify Calibration Participants of Auto-Routed Forms	Notify the manager that a form was auto routed by an admin or facilitator to get the forms to the calibration step.
Notify Calibration Participants of Session Activation	Notification to participants of an upcoming calibration session.

The additional notification, "Notify Calibration Rating Changes during Session Finalization," cannot be enabled here. It is enabled within the Advanced tab of Manage Calibration Templates. You will learn more about this notification in the next section of this chapter.

Calibration Concepts

Before we dig in, it may be helpful to understand some Calibration concepts. Calibration can be thought of in terms of templates, views, roles, and sessions:

- *Calibration Template:* Defines the data source for the ratings, the settings, the views, and the Executive Review graphs. A calibration template is referenced by a calibration session which inherits all of the template settings.

- *Calibration Views:* Identified in the calibration template and define the various ways the subjects and their rating data will display in a calibration session.

- *Calibration Sessions:* Define who is being calibrated (subjects) and by whom (participants). Define the session owners and facilitators, session date, and calibration template used.

- *Calibration Roles:* Set in Manage Calibration Settings to define what each role can do during a session (read, write, delete, finalize, and export).

Calibration Tools

Now that Calibration is enabled and the data model updated in Provisioning, role-based permissions are granted, the route map and performance form template are updated, and Calibration email notifications are turned on, we are ready to start configuring the template, settings, and options for Calibration. The calibration tools will now be available within Admin Center ➤ Tools as shown in Figure 14-14.

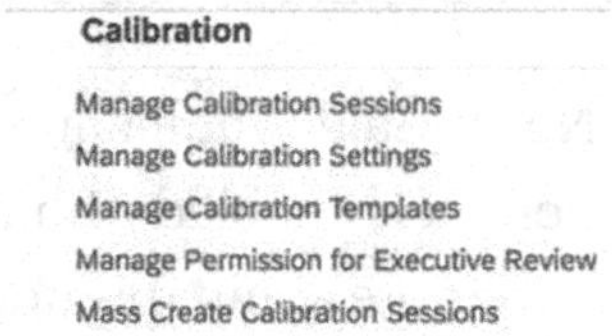

Calibration

Manage Calibration Sessions
Manage Calibration Settings
Manage Calibration Templates
Manage Permission for Executive Review
Mass Create Calibration Sessions

Figure 14-14. *Calibration Tools Within Admin Center*

We will explore how to manage calibration templates and calibration settings as well as how to grant permission for Executive Review access. The remaining features will be discussed in Chapter 15.

Manage Calibration Templates

We will start by looking at calibration templates. The calibration template defines the review period, data sources, and data views for any associated calibration sessions. The template identifies the data to calibrate and how data is presented.

One calibration template may be used for multiple calibration sessions. You may create multiple calibration templates, but only one is linked to a calibration session. Selections in the calibration template apply to all sessions associated with the template. Type and select "Manage Calibration Templates" in the search bar. An overview screen will display; and it is here that calibration templates are created, edited, and deleted. An example is shown in Figure 14-15.

Figure 14-15. *Manage Calibration Templates Overview Page*

The column headings are described in the following:

Template: Name of the calibration template.

Data Source for Calibration History Portlet: For each template, the checkmark will display in this column if the Calibration History Portlet is enabled in the Advanced tab.

Used in Sessions: A count of the number of calibration sessions using the calibration template. An example is shown in Figure 14-16. Clicking the number will display the names of the calibration sessions associated the calibration template.

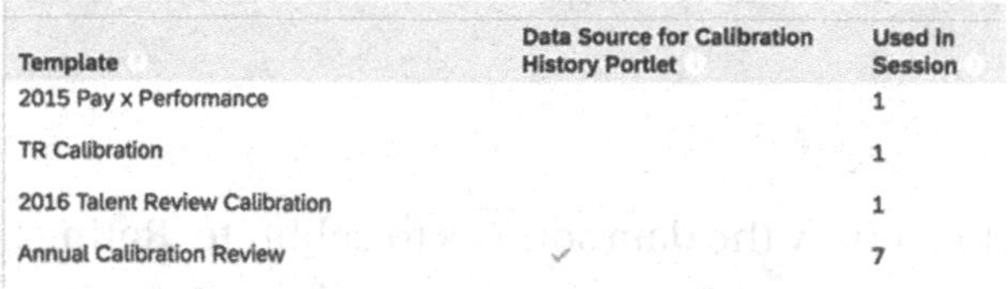

Template	Data Source for Calibration History Portlet	Used in Session
2015 Pay x Performance		1
TR Calibration		1
2016 Talent Review Calibration		1
Annual Calibration Review	✓	7

Figure 14-16. *Count of Calibration Sessions Associated with a Calibration Template*

Date Range: Identifies the review period associated with the template.

Last Modified: Identifies the date that the template was last updated.

Used in Talent Profile: Displays a green checkmark if the template is a data source for Talent Profile. Click the green checkmark to disable this option.

Active: Displays a green checkmark if the template is active. Only active templates can be used to create calibration sessions. Click the green checkmark to disable this option.

Now we will create a calibration template. Click the "Create New" button to set up a new calibration template. As seen in Figure 14-17, there are five tabs that are used to set up the template. Each tab is described in the following.

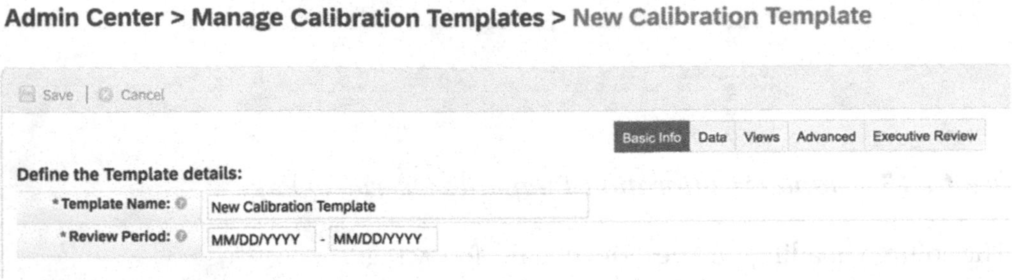

Admin Center > Manage Calibration Templates > New Calibration Template

Figure 14-17. *Tabs Within Manage Calibration Templates*

Basic Info Tab

The first tab, Basic Info, is used to name the calibration template and define its review period. Both entries are required. This review period will also display on the calibration template's overview page as the date range.

Data Tab

The Data tab is used to identify the data sources to calibrate. Ratings to be calibrated may come from many sources. Although we are focusing on performance review ratings as our source, let's look briefly at all the data source options.

Performance

- Overall objective rating

- Overall competency rating

- Overall potential rating

- Overall performance rating

Compensation

- Salary tab: merit, promotion, lumpsum, lumpsum2, extra, and extra2

- Bonus tab: total and target

- Stock tab: stock, options, stockUnits, stockOther1, stockOther2, and stockOther3

- Final compa-ratio

- Final range penetration

Employee Profile

- Potential
- Performance
- Objective
- Custom01
- Custom02

Succession

- Impact of Loss
- Reason for Leaving
- Risk of Loss

Figure 14-18 shows the Data tab and the data sources to select from.

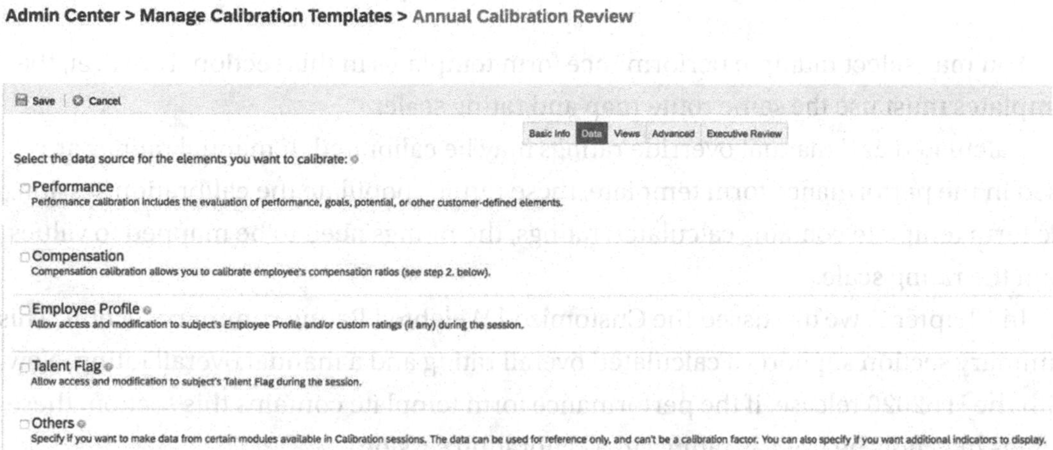

Admin Center > Manage Calibration Templates > Annual Calibration Review

Figure 14-18. *Data Tab*

Once a data source is selected, its section will expand in order to make additional selections. It is possible to select multiple data sources.

Performance

Click the checkbox for "Performance." The section expands to select which performance form template will be used for calibration. Once selected, identify which step in the route map the data should be used. This should be the calibration step. Based on the performance form template selected, the rating types from that template will display. Select which rating(s) should be calibrated. Details are shown in Figure 14-19.

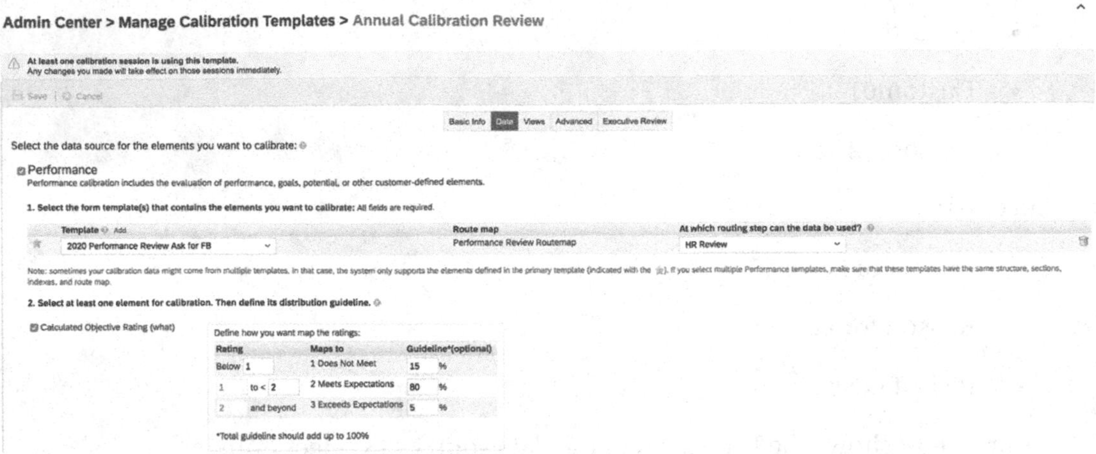

Figure 14-19. *Setting Performance Data Source Options*

You may select multiple performance form templates in this section. However, the templates must use the same route map and rating scale.

Calculated and manual override ratings may be calibrated. If manual ratings are used in the performance form template, these ratings populate the calibration session. If the form template contains calculated ratings, the ratings need to be mapped to values from the rating scale.

In Chapter 7, we discussed the Customized Weighted Rating summary section. This summary section supports a calculated overall rating and a manual overall rating. New with the H1 2020 release, if the performance form template contains this section, these ratings may now be used as ratings in a calibration session.

Guidelines can be applied to a session to encourage users to align to a recommended rating distribution. Based on the performance template rating scale, a percentage is set for each score. Guidelines can be optional or enforced, based on the calibration template's advanced settings. If enforced, the percentages for each rating must be set as shown in Figure 14-20.

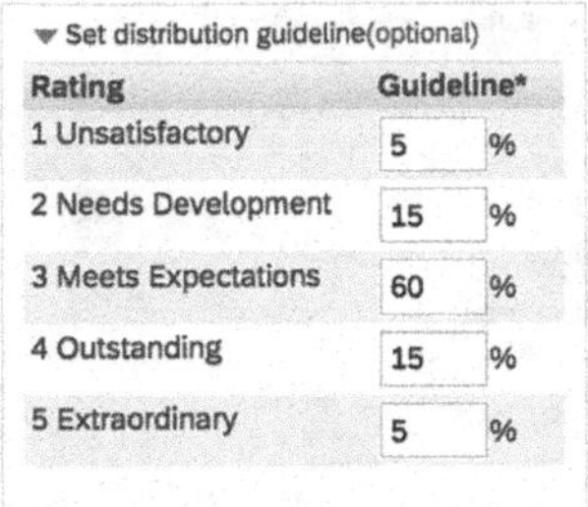

Figure 14-20. *Setting Percentages for Rating Distribution Guidelines*

The percentages must add up to 100%. You can enforce guidelines during the calibration session, or they are merely used as information to aid in evaluating the calibration subjects.

Ratings are pulled into the calibration session based on a series of rules:

- The four ratings that can be read from a performance form template are overall performance, overall potential, overall competency, and overall objective. The ratings are read by section in the following order: Customized Weighted Rating section, Performance Potential Summary section, Objective Competency Summary section, and Summary section.

- Manual ratings in a performance form template take precedence over calculated ratings.

- If you are not showing in-progress ratings from live profiles, those ratings will not be used.

Compensation

Compensation may be calibrated for employee compensation ratios. Any of the standard planning fields can be selected as can either the final range penetration or final compa-ratio benchmark.

Select the compensation template and the route map step where data can be used as seen in Figure 14-21. Like the performance form template, the compensation template must have a single user or collaborative modify step. The template's planning components and range groups display.

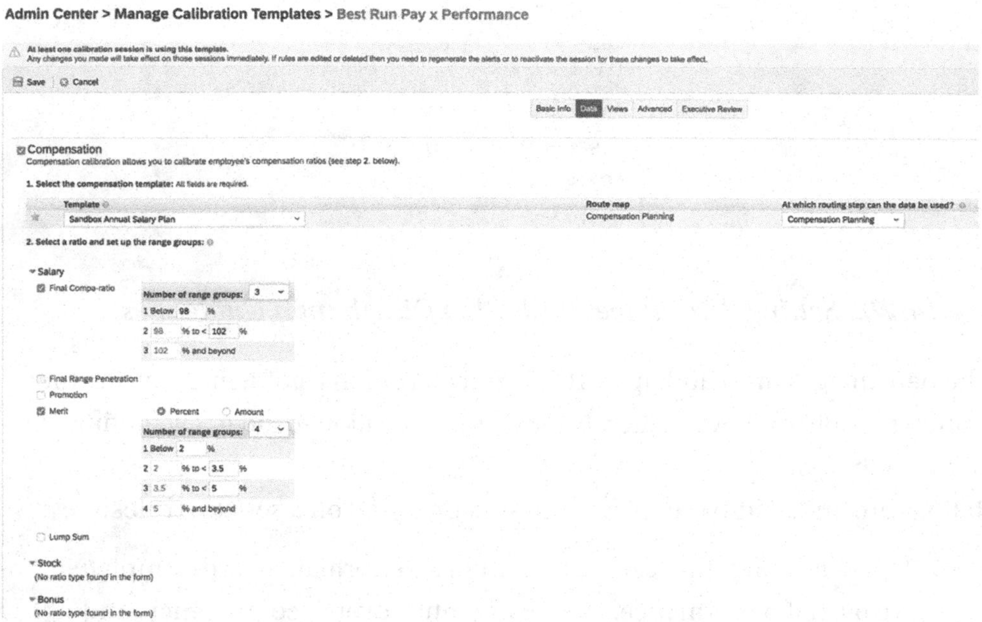

Figure 14-21. *Compensation Data Source*

The available planning components and range groups for selection will vary based on the template. As seen in Figure 14-22, the template only has salary and stock components. Salary, Stock, and Bonus fields may be selected. Notice that Variable Pay cannot be used for calibration.

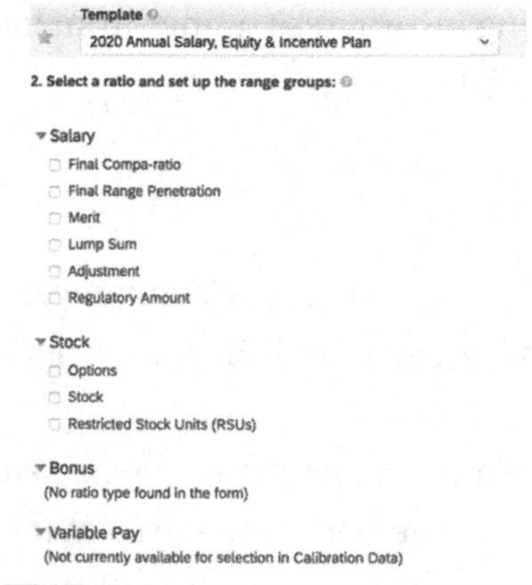

Figure 14-22. *Compensation Planning Fields*

Any standard planning field can be used as the final range penetration or final compa-ratio benchmark. As seen in Figure 14-23, the range grouping must be set.

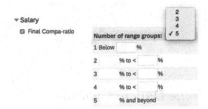

Figure 14-23. *Range Grouping Setup*

Once the elements are selected, the number of range groups (two to five) is set along with the percentages or amounts used for employee placement.

Employee Profile

When this option is enabled, the calibration session will use ratings stored in Employee Profile that are effective during the review period defined in the Basic Info tab. If there are no ratings for the review period, the session creates an unrated rating.

Ratings in Employee Profile are based on the background elements that are configured in your data model. The following are the possible rating types:

- SysOverallPerformance

- SysOverallPotential

- SysOverallCompetency

- SysOverallObjective

- SysOverallCustom01

- SysOverallCustom02

As seen in Figure 14-24, select the rating type to be calibrated. Rating guidelines may be set. Although decimal ratings are supported, they must be mapped to whole numbers.

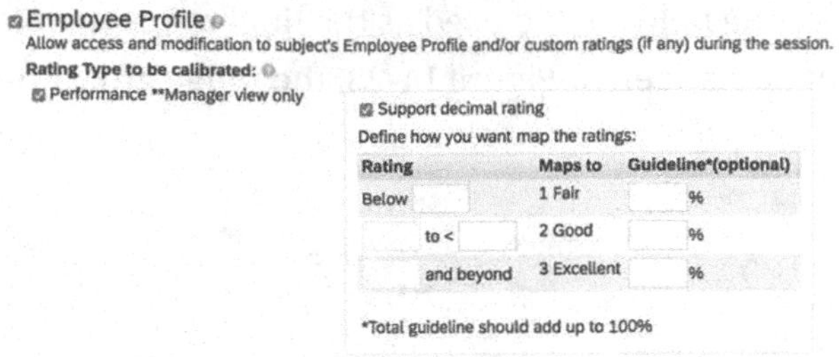

Figure 14-24. Employee Profile Data to Calibrate

To use ratings from Employee Profile, make sure the date range (start and end dates) is within the calibration session date range. The ratings need to be within the minimum and maximum values of the rating scale. Enable the "Support decimal rating" option if your ratings use decimals.

Rating changes made during the calibration session won't display in Employee Profile until the calibration session is finalized unless the template is configured to display in-progress ratings.

Talent Flags

If the standard talent flags, Risk of Loss, Impact of Loss, and Reason for Leaving, are defined in the data model, they may be included in a calibration session. Often these flags are used to plot on a 9-box.

As shown in Figure 14-25, selection of a flag allows distribution guidelines to be set.

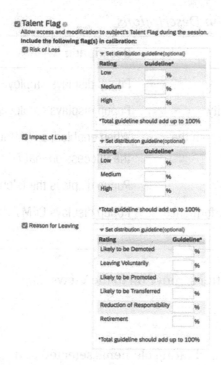

Figure 14-25. *Distribution Guidelines for Talent Flag Data*

Others

The final option in the Data tab is "Others." Additional informational sources can be selected as reference within a calibration session. An example is shown in Figure 14-26. These cannot be calibrated.

Figure 14-26. *Other Options*

Data from these sources can be accessed in a calibration session for a subject using the "More" option. Table 14-3 describes each data source.

Table 14-3. *Others Option Descriptions*

Data Source	Description
Allow access to Development	Popup displays employee's default development plan.
Allow access to Learning Activity	Popup displays employee's learning activities.
Show Succession status icons from the Succession Matrix Report	When enabled, an "Attributes" column will display the Succession matrix grid icons for each employee.
Display QuickCards	Popup displays the talent card.
Allow Access to Continuous Performance Management Achievements	Popup displays CPM Achievements tab.

After saving your selections, move on to the Views tab.

Views Tab

Based on the data sources and rating elements selected in the Data tab, multiple views of the calibration data may be created which allows different ways of looking at the rating data in the session.

The Views tab, as seen in Figure 14-27, defines how the calibration data will be displayed within the calibration session. Multiple views of the data may be configured, and each offers some different features.

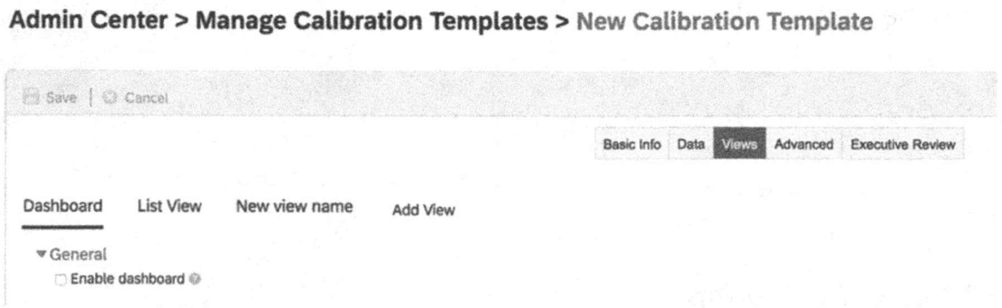

Figure 14-27. *Views Tab Within Manage Calibration Templates*

The view types are Dashboard, List View, Bin View, Matrix Grid, and Executive Review. We will now look at each view type in detail.

Dashboard View

The Dashboard view provides summarized data in a chart format. To use this view, the "Enable dashboard" box should be checked. When enabled, the Dashboard view is the first view that is seen when opening a calibration session.

Any view, except for the List View, may be summarized into a chart. The data may be grouped by gender with an overall gender summary. The charts may be displayed by number of subjects or the distribution percentage.

List View

When the List View is enabled, the calibration data displays in a table-like format. There is a row for each subject being calibrated. Here you may update ratings, see ratings from other views, have access to subject data, make comments, compare subjects, and mark subjects as discussed.

List View selections are shown in Figure 14-28.

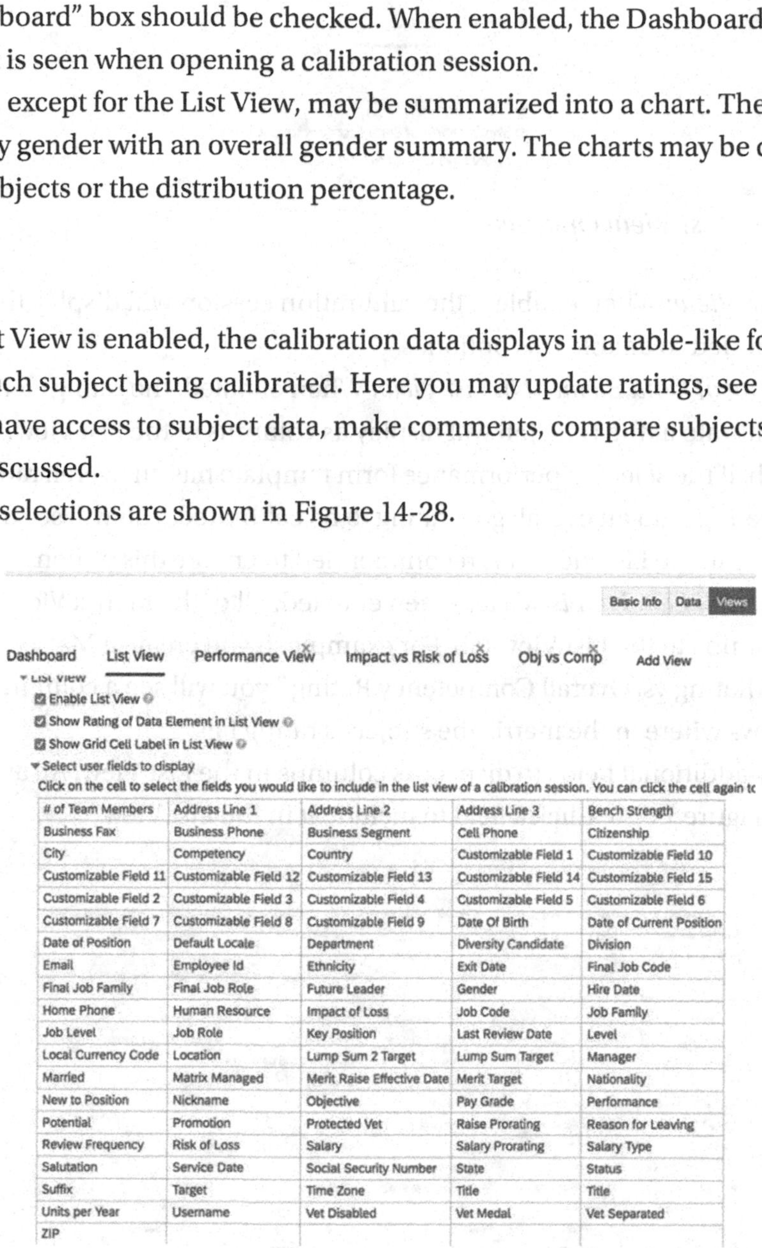

Figure 14-28. List View Setup in the Manage Calibration Templates Views Tab

As seen in Figure 14-29, there are checkboxes to enable in the List View. They are explained in the following.

Figure 14-29. List View Options

Enable List View: When enabled, the calibration session will display the List View. It is recommended to enable this option.

Show Rating of Data Element in List View: When enabled, the rating elements selected to calibrate in the Data tab will display as columns in the List View. For example, in the Data tab, if the selected performance form template has an overall rating, an overall competency rating, and an overall goal rating to be calibrated, you will see a column for each rating type in the List View. It is recommended to enable this option.

Show Grid Cell Label in List View: When enabled, all of the Matrix View ratings will display as columns in the List View tab. For example, if you create a Matrix View for "Overall Goal Rating vs. Overall Competency Rating," you will see a column on the List View that shows where in the matrix the subject's rating lies.

Select any additional fields to display as columns in the List View. All available fields are shown in Figure 14-30. Click a field to include it in the List View.

▼ Select user fields to display
Click on the cell to select the fields you would like to include in the list view of a calibration session. You can click the cell again to de-select it.

# of Team Members	Address Line 1	Address Line 2	Address Line 3	Bench Strength
Business Fax	Business Phone	Business Segment	Cell Phone	Citizenship
City	Competency	Country	Customizable Field 1	Customizable Field 10
Customizable Field 11	Customizable Field 12	Customizable Field 13	Customizable Field 14	Customizable Field 15
Customizable Field 2	Customizable Field 3	Customizable Field 4	Customizable Field 5	Customizable Field 6
Customizable Field 7	Customizable Field 8	Customizable Field 9	Date Of Birth	Date of Current Position
Date of Position	Default Locale	Department	Diversity Candidate	Division
Email	Employee Id	Ethnicity	Exit Date	Final Job Code
Final Job Family	Final Job Role	Future Leader	Gender	Hire Date
Home Phone	Human Resource	Impact of Loss	Job Code	Job Family
Job Level	Job Role	Key Position	Last Review Date	Level
Local Currency Code	Location	Lump Sum 2 Target	Lump Sum Target	Manager
Married	Matrix Managed	Merit Raise Effective Date	Merit Target	Nationality
New to Position	Nickname	Objective	Pay Grade	Performance
Potential	Promotion	Protected Vet	Raise Prorating	Reason for Leaving
Review Frequency	Risk of Loss	Salary	Salary Prorating	Salary Type
Salutation	Service Date	Social Security Number	State	Status
Suffix	Target	Time Zone	Title	Title
Units per Year	Username	Vet Disabled	Vet Medal	Vet Separated
ZIP				

Figure 14-30. Fields to Display as Columns in the List View

Select from the standard user fields configured in the data model.

When users open the List View in a calibration session, they can see the fields that you have chosen to display.

Once selections have been made for the List View, we will move on to the Bin View.

Bin View

The Bin View groups employees in buckets based on one rating element that is being calibrated.

Click the "New view name" tab to create the Bin View as seen in Figure 14-31.

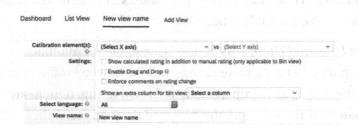

Figure 14-31. *Creation of the Bin View*

Select the rating element to be used in the "X"-axis. The rating elements to choose from are based on the data source(s) selected in the Data tab as seen in Figure 14-32.

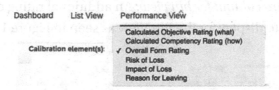

Figure 14-32. *Select a Rating Element for the Bin View*

When the manual rating is enabled in the template Summary section, the calculated rating would not be available in the Bin View of a calibration session.

From the example shown in the preceding figure, the displayed calibration rating elements are based on the performance form template selected. The template has two calculated ratings and a manual overall rating. In addition, the talent flags are enabled to allow access and modification during the session.

When the data source is a performance form template with a Customized Weighted Rating section, either the manual or the calculated rating can be calibrated. However, the calculated rating cannot be displayed in the Bin View.

If you choose an element for the "Y"-axis as well, this is no longer the Bin View; it becomes the Grid (Matrix) View instead.

After providing a name for the view and identifying the calibration rating element to be used, there are some additional settings.

There are three settings that may be enabled:

- *Show calculated rating in addition to manual rating* (only applicable to Bin view): When enabled, the view shows the calculated rating in addition to the manual rating.

- *Enable Drag and Drop:* This option is available for manual performance form template ratings and Employee Profile ratings. You cannot drag and drop a calculated form rating. If there are only calculated ratings selected, the drag and drop option is disabled. Drag and drop is not available for compensation elements either.

- *Enforce comments on rating change:* Whenever a rating is changed in this view, a popup will display, and a comment will need to be written to justify the change.

- *Show an extra column for bin view:* An additional rating column may be selected to display for the Bin View as seen in Figure 14-33.

Figure 14-33. *Select an Additional Rating Column*

Finally, select the language for the view and the view name.

Click the "Add View" tab to create another calibration view. Additional views may be created for any other single rating element. Views may also be created that use any two rating elements that are identified in the Data tab. This is the Matrix View we will learn about next.

Matrix Grid View

The Matrix View plots two different rating sources against one another for a matrix placement of subjects. This is sometimes referred to as a "9-box." Like the Bin View, drag and drop may be enabled, as well as enforcing comments when a rating is changed. You may create multiple views varying the rating sources.

As soon as you select ratings for the "X"- and "Y"-axes, the screen expands, and there are additional selections to make. An example is shown in Figure 14-34.

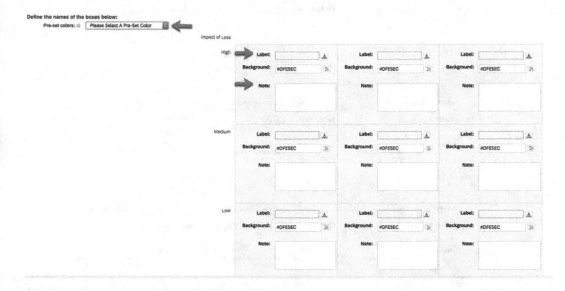

Figure 14-34. *Design the Matrix View*

Define the matrix grid cell labels and choose the preset colors as seen in Figure 14-35. Select one of the default color options. You may choose the preset color based on the default colors set in your Succession settings.

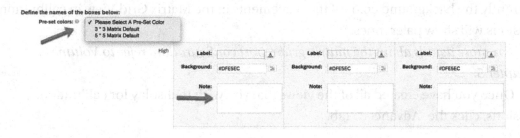

Figure 14-35. *Define the Preset Color*

New with the H1 2020 release, there is also an option to add notes for each cell. These *inline* notes are helpful for the calibration participants to get a better understanding of what each cell represents. The intent is to help avoid unintentional bias.

Figure 14-36 is an example of applying one of the Succession grid settings along with the use of notes.

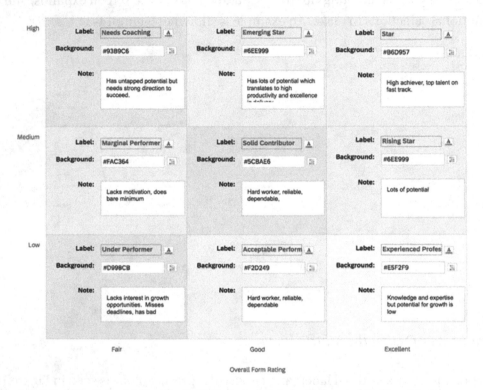

Figure 14-36. *Updated Matrix Cell Colors with Labels and Inline Notes*

If you are going to use the same color codes as the matrix grid report in Succession, currently the background color of the placements in the Matrix Grid View in calibration sessions will show paler tones.

For more details about the matrix grid report configuration, refer to Volume 2, Chapter 5.

Once you have created all of the views that you wish to display for calibration sessions, click the "Advanced" tab.

Advanced Tab

The Advanced tab is used to enable some features that will apply to all calibration sessions associated with the calibration template. The Advanced tab is shown in Figure 14-37.

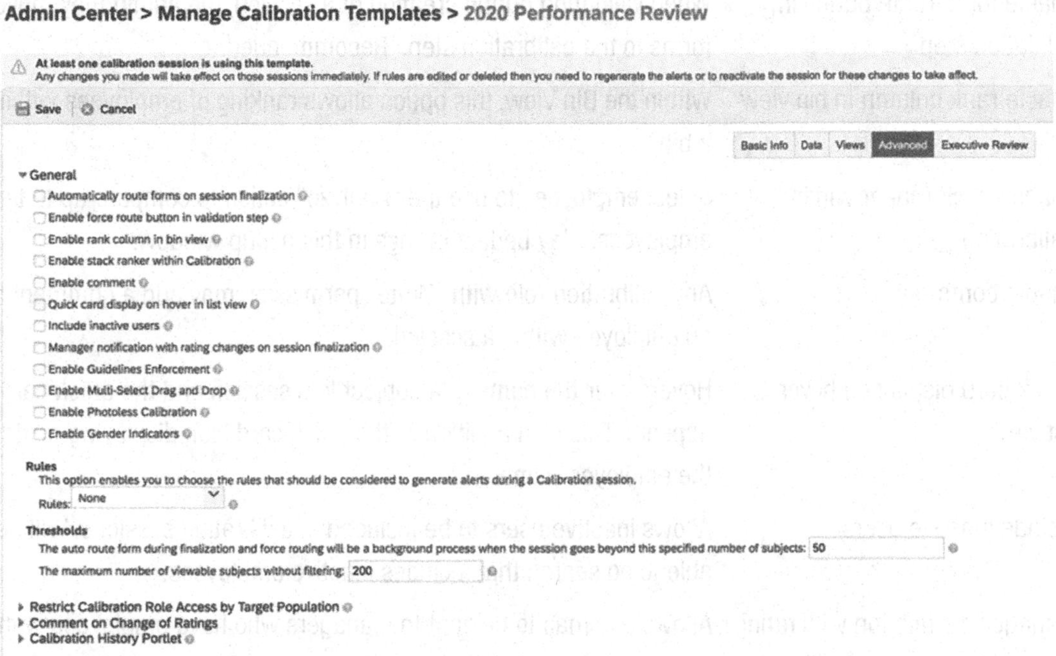

Figure 14-37. *Advanced Options for a Calibration Template*

There are four sections in this tab where you will make selections to enable for the template. We will review each section and what features they enable.

General Options

Table 14-4 details the General options available for a calibration template along with the descriptions. Please review these features and enable those that you wish to use for all of the calibration sessions associated with the template.

Table 14-4. *Description of General Options*

Option	Description
Automatically route forms on session finalization	When a session is finalized, the forms will automatically route to the next route map step. Recommended.
Enable force route button in validation step	When validating during creation of a session, the admin may move forms to the calibration step. Recommended.
Enable rank column in bin view	Within the Bin View, this option allows ranking of employees within a bin.
Enable stack ranker within Calibration	Select employees to use the "Analyze" action to compare up to ten employees. May update ratings in this popup window.
Enable comment	Any calibration role with "Write" permission may add a comment to an employee within a session.
Quick card display on hover in list view	Hovers over the name of a subject in a session and the quick card appears. This is in addition to the quick card icon displaying next to the employee name.
Include inactive users	Allows inactive users to be included in calibration sessions. Will be able to do search that includes inactive employees.
Manager notification with rating changes on session finalization	Allows an email to be sent to managers who have employees with rating changes during a calibration session. The email includes the old and the new calibrated ratings. Sent when the session is finalized. Recommended.
Enable Guidelines Enforcement	Rating changes may only be finalized if they fall within distribution guidelines that are set in the calibration template.
Enable Multi-Select Drag and Drop	Within the Bin View, may select multiple subjects and move them to a new rating bin.
Enable Photoless Calibration	Hide photos in List, Bin, and Matrix Views. Helpful to eliminate bias.
Enable Gender Indicators	To display the gender ratios in List, Bin, and Matrix Views. The Matrix View also displays gender segregation in each of the cells.

A challenge when conducting calibration sessions is to be fair, consistent, and objective. Bias may sneak in unknowingly, and the calibration participant may have blind spots that influence how they evaluate employees. To help avoid bias, the calibration sessions can be made photoless. All of the calibration session views would have the subjects display without a photograph. Calibration sessions without photos can be used in conjunction with enabling the gender indicators. The indicators will simply show gender ratios in the List, Bin, and Matrix Views of a calibration session. The Matrix View will also display the male/female ratio for each cell. These settings are noted in the preceding table.

There are two additional General options, Rules and Thresholds.

Rules

The Rules option will not appear unless business rules have been created to trigger calibration alerts. An example of the Rules section is shown in Figure 14-38.

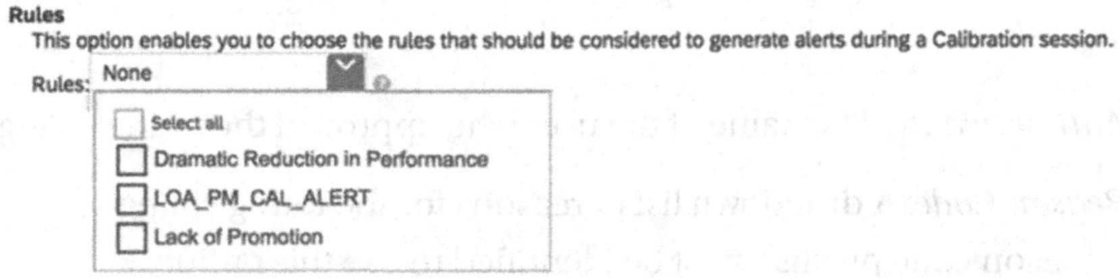

Rules
This option enables you to choose the rules that should be considered to generate alerts during a Calibration session.

Rules: None

- Select all
- Dramatic Reduction in Performance
- LOA_PM_CAL_ALERT
- Lack of Promotion

Figure 14-38. *Select Rules for Calibration Alerts*

Here, any calibration-related business rules may be applied to the template.

We will talk briefly about how to create calibration alerts at the end of this chapter and again in Chapter 15. Business rules define scenarios that may cause bias.

Thresholds

A threshold may be set to identify the number of subjects' forms that will cause a background process when force routing and auto routing during finalization occurs. It is recommended to specify a number no larger than 50. A threshold may also be set for the number of subjects that appear per page of a session. Filters must be used to view subjects above the maximum set.

Restrict Calibration Role Access by Target Population

Calibration sessions allow facilitators, owners, participants, and executive reviewers access to view information for all subjects being calibrated. Access for any selected calibration role may be limited to only subjects in their target population. Figure 14-39 contains the option to restrict calibration role access by target population.

Figure 14-39. *Restrict Role Access*

Comment on Change of Ratings

This option is used to identify the field required to enter when changing a rating. During a calibration session, a popup will display, and the user will be required to enter any of these options:

- *Authorized By:* The name of the user who approved the rating change.

- *Reason Code:* A dropdown list of reasons for the rating change. A reason code picklist must be identified to use this option.

- *Comment:* When a rating is changed within a calibration session, a comment must be entered. The character limit for the comments field is 4000 characters.

An example is shown in Figure 14-40.

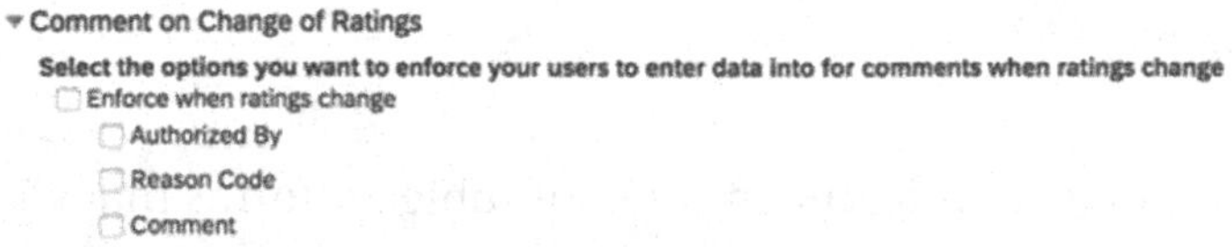

▼ Comment on Change of Ratings

    Select the options you want to enforce your users to enter data into for comments when ratings change
    ☐ Enforce when ratings change
        ☐ Authorized By
        ☐ Reason Code
        ☐ Comment

Figure 14-40. *Rating Change Comment Enforcement*

When "Authorized By" and "Reason Code" are selected, these options are required entries with the comments field optional.

Calibration History Portlet

If you have added the Calibration History Portlet background element to the data model and granted permission to view this portlet, here you will select the rating types to display along with any matrix views. An example is shown in Figure 14-41.

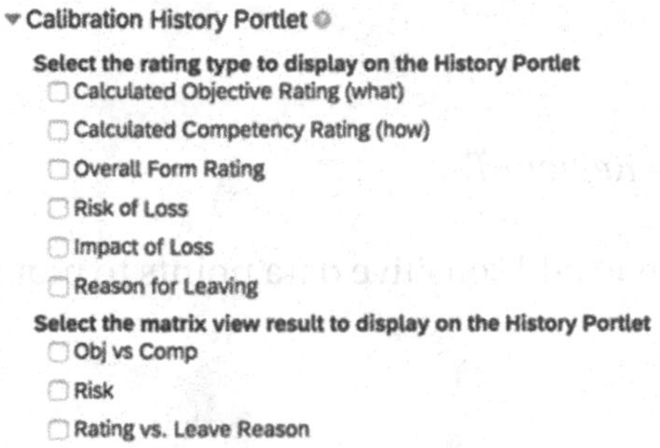

▼ Calibration History Portlet ○

Select the rating type to display on the History Portlet
☐ Calculated Objective Rating (what)
☐ Calculated Competency Rating (how)
☐ Overall Form Rating
☐ Risk of Loss
☐ Impact of Loss
☐ Reason for Leaving

Select the matrix view result to display on the History Portlet
○ Obj vs Comp
○ Risk
☐ Rating vs. Leave Reason

Figure 14-41. *Options When Displaying the Calibration History Portlet*

The options listed are based on the performance form template that is the data source for the ratings.

After all the selections are made in the Advanced tab, click the Executive Review tab.

Executive Review Tab

This tab will only be visible if Executive Review is enabled. It can be enabled in Provisioning to make it available when creating the calibration template. It may also be enabled in "Manage Calibration Settings."

Executive Review provides aggregated graphs and session details across all calibration sessions associated with the template.

The Executive Review tab, as seen in Figure 14-42, identifies the graphs and data that will appear on the Executive Review page for a calibration session. All of the graphs or charts created from views of the calibration template can be aggregated.

687

Figure 14-42. *Executive Review Tab*

There is also the option to add sensitive data points to plot against ratings that have views created:

- Gender

- Risk of Loss

- Impact of Loss

- Reason for Leaving

Save your template. If you make any calibration template changes once calibration sessions are created, the changes will take effect in the sessions using the template.

We have now configured our calibration template. Next, we will manage the calibration settings. To begin, type and select "Manage Calibration Settings" in the action search.

Manage Calibration Settings

Calibration settings apply to all calibration sessions regardless of the calibration template used. The settings are used by the admin to perform several functions:

- Select action permissions for session reviewers.

- Select the calibration template for managers to launch from Team Overview in Performance.

- Select the fields to display after a search while creating a session.

- Select the calibration tools.

There are four tabs of settings:

1. Permissions

2. Manager Template (optional)

3. Search Results Fields

4. Global Settings

We will now look at each tab in more depth.

Permissions Tab

The Permissions tab identifies the actions (Read, Write, Finalize, Export, and Delete) that the various calibration roles may perform for both active and approved sessions.

As seen in Figure 14-43, the calibration roles need to be assigned actions for In Progress and Approved calibration sessions.

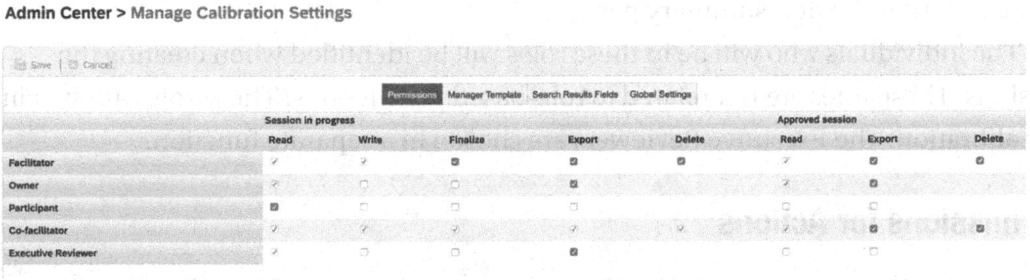

Admin Center > Manage Calibration Settings

	Session in progress					Approved session		
	Read	Write	Finalize	Export	Delete	Read	Export	Delete
Facilitator	✓	✓	☑	☑	☑	✓	☑	☑
Owner	✓	☐	☐	☑		✓	☑	
Participant	☑	☐	☐	☐		☐	☐	
Co-facilitator	✓	✓	✓	✓	✓	✓	☑	☑
Executive Reviewer	✓	☐	☐	☑		☐	☐	

Figure 14-43. Calibration Role Permissions

Active sessions are those currently in progress, while approved sessions have been finalized. The permissions granted for these roles are only applicable to Calibration.

Let's look at the calibration roles that are used within a session:

- Facilitator

- Co-facilitator

- Subject

- Participant

- Owner

- Executive Reviewer

The *Facilitator* is usually someone from HR who can be impartial. The facilitator conducts the calibration session and leads the discussion. The facilitator typically does the updating of the ratings and finalizes the session. The facilitator may also create sessions if the RBP role for an HR manager has *Manage Calibration Sessions* permissions.

A *Co-facilitator* acts as a backup to the facilitator. This role will have the same permissions that the facilitator role has been assigned. Any permissions added or removed for the facilitator role will automatically be updated for the co-facilitator role. The role is optional, and no users need to be identified for this role.

A *Subject* is an employee who is being calibrated in the session.

A *Participant* is involved in the calibration session to make the rating decisions. The role is usually assigned to managers of those being calibrated.

A *Owner* is a high-level manager whose direct reports are participants in the calibration session. The participants' direct reports are being calibrated.

An *Executive Reviewer* is a business or HR executive who needs summarized data across sessions. Users who are assigned this role get direct access to the sessions as well as the Executive Review summary page.

The individuals who will be in these roles will be identified when creating the sessions. These roles are not related to role-based permissions. These roles are specific to Calibration. The Executive Reviewers are chosen in a separate function.

Permissions for Actions

Read, Write, Finalize, Export, and Delete actions need to be set for each calibration role. The permissions can differ for active sessions and finalized sessions, and you must explicitly assign the actions to the roles. The absence of a permission prevents the role from performing the action.

Anyone assigned to a calibration role with "Read" permission will have access to the calibration session. This means that a user without role-based permission for access to Calibration within the Home menu will be able to access the calibration session.

Here are some more details on the calibration session permissions:

- "Read" permission allows the role to see the calibration session but not make any updates to the ratings.

- "Write" permission allows ratings to be updated within the session. This permission is also needed for a role to create comments on an employee in a calibration session.

- *Export* permission allows a role to download the session from any of the session views. The session will download as an Excel file containing a separate tab for each view.

- *Delete* permission allows a role to delete a calibration session. Only the facilitator and co-facilitator roles have the option to delete sessions.

Any action permission that is granted automatically creates a "Read" permission. If you enable "Finalize" permission, the Read and Write actions are automatically granted.

Once you have made the calibration session role permission selections, click "Save" and move on to the Manager Template tab.

The Manager Template tab will not be visible if it is not enabled in "Company Settings" in Provisioning. To allow managers to launch a calibration session for their direct reports without going back into Provisioning, you can go to the Global Settings tab and enable the setting there. You need to save the screen and back out to the home page. When you go back into Manage Calibration Settings, the Manager Template tab will be visible.

Manager Template Tab

The Manager Template tab is used to identify which calibration template should launch for a manager in Team Overview as shown in Figure 14-44.

Admin Center > Manage Calibration Settings

💾 Save	⊗ Cancel

| | Permissions | Manager Template | Search Results Fields | Global Settings |

Please choose a calibration template to use in PMv12 Team overview page to launch calibration session.

| Please select a template... ⌄ |

Figure 14-44. Manager Template Tab

Click the dropdown arrow to select the calibration template that will be used on the Team Overview page. Remember the calibration template is linked to the performance form template that you selected in the Data tab of Manage Calibration Templates. Therefore, when you launch the calibration session, the system will know which performance form template to access.

If a calibration template is not selected, the Calibration button will not be enabled in Team Overview.

In order for this to work, Team Overview must also be permitted for the manager role.

Once your selection is made, click "Save" and move on to the Search Results Fields tab.

Search Results Fields Tab

The settings selected in the Search Results Fields tab are used in the People tab of Managing Calibration Sessions which will be discussed in the next chapter. This tab is used to identify the fields to display after an employee search. The fields selected also identify which additional fields may be added to the view after a search. Figure 14-45 displays the tab.

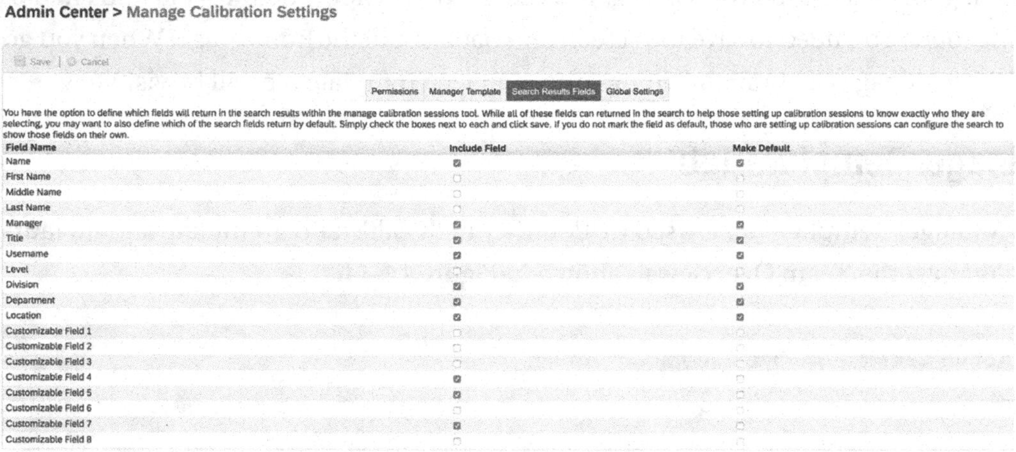

Admin Center > Manage Calibration Settings

Figure 14-45. Search Results Fields Tab

The column on the far right, "Make Default", is used to select fields that display for each employee in the search results when creating a session as seen in Figure 14-46.

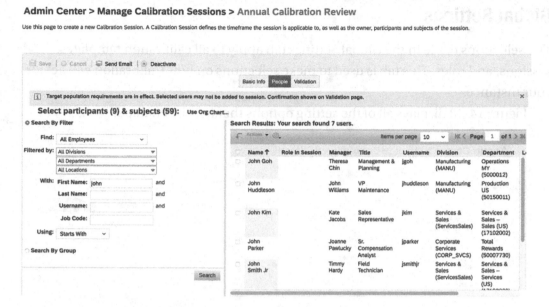

Figure 14-46. *Search Results Table with Selected Display Fields*

In the example shown in the preceding figure, the fields listed in the search results are those selected from the "Make Default" column.

The "Include Field" column in the Search Results Fields tab enables you to choose which additional fields you may add to the view after the search. The selections under the Option icon display all of the default fields used and the additional *include* fields. An example is shown in Figure 14-47.

Figure 14-47. *Display Options Within Search Results*

You may deselect any of the default fields and select any of the others. Click "Done," and the search results table will contain the fields that you selected.

Click "Save" and move on to the Global Settings tab.

Global Settings

The selections made in the Global Settings tab apply to all calibration templates, sessions, and roles. This tab is used to make selections on how Calibration will act for your instance.

Figure 14-48 displays all of the setting options that may be enabled.

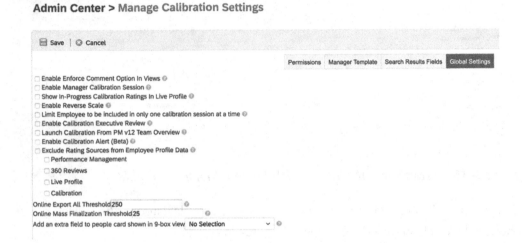

Figure 14-48. *Global Settings*

The first seven features may also be enabled in "Company Settings" in Provisioning.

If some of these features are already enabled, that means that they were already enabled in Provisioning.

Shown in Table 14-5 are the descriptions of each of the global settings.

Table 14-5. *Global Settings' Descriptions*

Permission	Description
Enable Enforce Comment Option in Views	When a rating is changed within a calibration session, a comment is required before saving. This setting can be overridden at the calibration template level.
Enable Manager Calibration Session	Allows a manager to create sessions within Calibration. Gives managers the "Create New" button when accessing Calibration.

(continued)

Table 14-5. (*continued*)

Permission	Description
Show in-Progress Calibration Ratings in Live Profile	Ratings in a calibration session that haven't yet been finalized appear in Employee Profile.
Enable Reverse Scale	If you are using a rating scale where 1 is the highest, this setting should be enabled. It's not recommended to use a reverse scale for any rating scales system-wide.
Limit Employee to be included in only one calibration session at a time	Prevents employees from being subjects in multiple sessions that are in-progress, approving, or approved using the same date range and data source.
Enable Calibration Executive Review	Creates an Executive Review tab in a calibration session. Once a user is identified as an executive reviewer, they will see aggregate session data without being involved directly in each session.
Launch Calibration from PM v12 Team Overview	Enables managers to create sessions directly from the Team Overview tab for PM v12 forms. Manager permission role must have access to Team Overview. Only managers who have direct reports can use the feature on the Team Overview page. If not enabled, the Manager Template tab is not visible within Manage Calibration Settings.
Enable Calibration V12 Org Chart	Replaces the old Org Chart with the v12 Org Chart that supports the display of matrix reports and selection of users by organizational hierarchy levels.
Enable Calibration Alert (Beta)	Allows alerts to appear when bias exists. Alerts are created in Configure Business Rules. Currently showing as a beta feature. Fiori UI for Calibration must be enabled.
Exclude Rating Sources from Employee Profile Data	If the rating source for the calibration session is Employee Profile, may identify any rating types to omit.
Online Export All Threshold	System default is 250. Recommended not to exceed 1000; otherwise, export is done as an offline job.

(*continued*)

Table 14-5. (*continued*)

Permission	Description
Online Mass Finalization Threshold	Represents the number of sessions that may be finalized in mass. Exceeding the threshold will cause finalization to be done as offline job.
Add an extra field to people card shown in 9-box view	Selection of an additional field to appear on the 9-box view. Field can be Manager, Division, Department, Location, Job Code, and the custom01 to custom15 elements defined in the Succession Data Model.

After saving your selections, these settings will be applied to current and new calibration sessions and calibration templates. We have now configured our calibration settings.

There is some additional configuration that we will review next.

Configuring the Calibration Talent Card

The Calibration Talent Card may be opened for a subject in any view of a calibration session. The role-based permission needed for the admin role to configure the talent card is found under Administrator Permissions ➤ Manage Talent Card. The permission is "Manage Talent Card Configuration."

To configure the Calibration Talent Card, type and select "Manage Talent Cards" in the search bar. The screen is shown in Figure 14-49. Click the link "Calibration Talent Card" if you wish to make customizations.

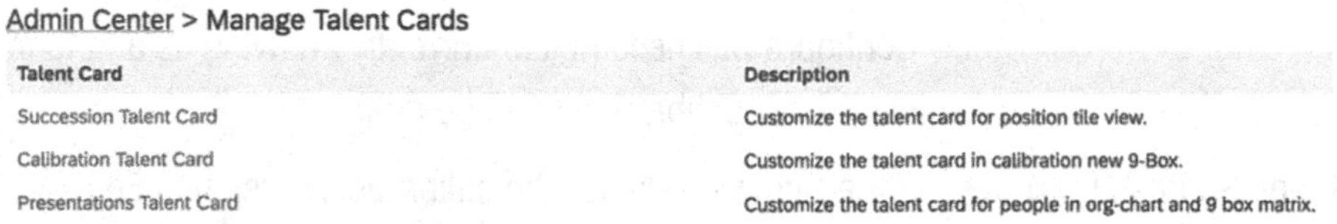

Admin Center > Manage Talent Cards

Talent Card	Description
Succession Talent Card	Customize the talent card for position tile view.
Calibration Talent Card	Customize the talent card in calibration new 9-Box.
Presentations Talent Card	Customize the talent card for people in org-chart and 9 box matrix.

Figure 14-49. *View of Manage Talent Cards*

You can edit sections of the Calibration Talent Card. You may add standard sections or create custom sections as seen in Figure 14-50.

Admin Center > Manage Talent Cards > Calibration Talent Card

Figure 14-50. *Calibration Quick Card*

Any new sections will be visible in the talent card in a calibration session. Make any updates and save the card.

Manage Permissions for Executive Review

After creating a calibration session, you may determine which users should have access to the Executive Review page. Permission is applicable to all calibration sessions that use a specific calibration template.

Type and select "Manage Permissions for Executive Review" in the search bar. Here, we will assign users to the Executive Reviewer role. See Figure 14-51.

Admin Center > Manage Permissions for Executive Review

The Manage Permissions for Executive Review page lets you assign users who will be allowed to access the Executive Review page for a given Calibration template. When access is granted to those users, they will see an extra link in Calibration to "Executive Review". This is where they will see a full aggregation of all data, for all sessions that are in progress or finalized for the named template. Follow the steps below to assign these permissions. If you want to set the permissions for the Executive Review role, this is a separate task and can be done by navigating to Admin Center > Manage Calibration Settings.

Create New Permission

Step 1: Select Template
Select the template you wish to grant access to:

Please select a template...   ⌄

Step 2: Select User
Select the user you wish to grant access to the Executive Review page for the above named template.

🔍

Step 3: Assign the Permission
Click Assign Permission to grant the user access to the Executive Review page for the selected template. This will take effect immediately.

Assign Permission

Reviewing Permissions Already Configured

In this list, you can review which users have been assigned access to see the Executive Review page for each template.

Template Name	Reviewer
2020 Performance Review	○ Aanya Singh
Annual Calibration Review	○ Charles Braun
Talent Review Calibration	○ Aanya Singh

Revoke Permission

Figure 14-51. *Manage Permissions for Executive Review*

Any user selected will have access to data from all sessions tied to a calibration template. They will get access to all of the sessions in addition to seeing the Executive Review page. They will see aggregated data and details done in the subject level.

This screen is used to create new user permissions for the Executive Reviewer role, to review and revoke any existing permissions.

The Create New Permissions section of the screen is shown in Figure 14-52.

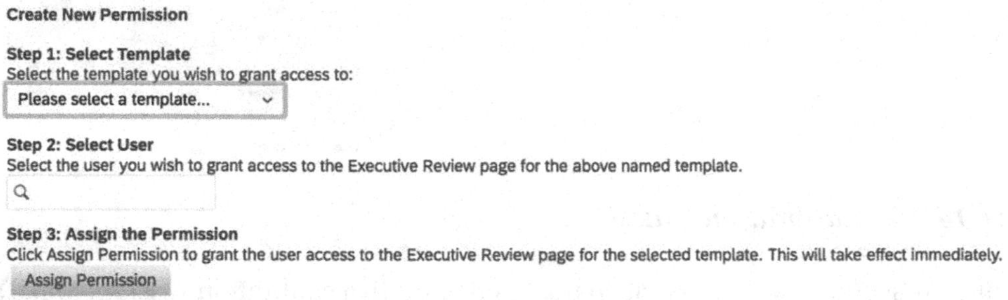

Figure 14-52. *Create Executive Review User Permission*

To create a new permission, identify the calibration template from the dropdown listing of active calibration templates as seen in Figure 14-53.

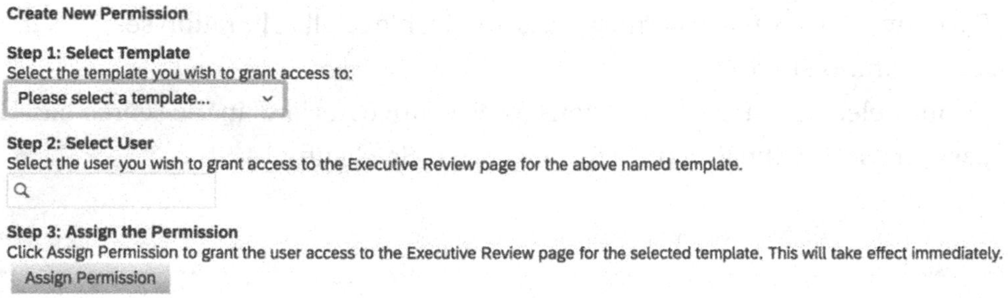

Figure 14-53. *Select a Template for Executive Permission*

Do a name search to find an individual for whom you wish to grant Executive Review privileges. Only one name may be selected at a time. After selecting a name, click "Assign Permission." The user will now have access, and you may add assign additional users.

Once assigned, the names will display in the Reviewing Permissions Already Configured section as seen in Figure 14-54.

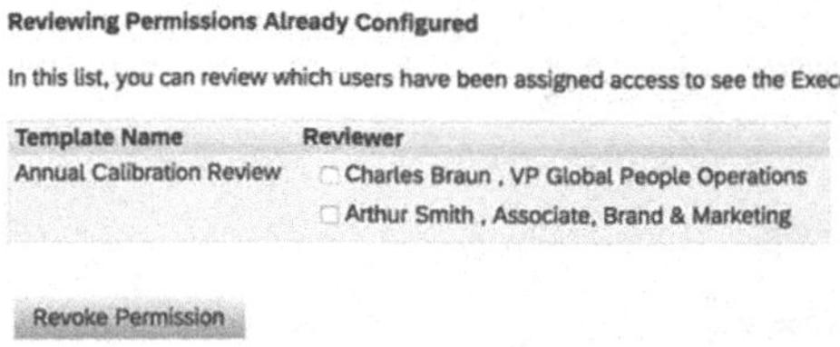

Reviewing Permissions Already Configured

In this list, you can review which users have been assigned access to see the Executive Review page for each template.

Template Name	Reviewer
Annual Calibration Review	☐ Charles Braun , VP Global People Operations
	☐ Arthur Smith , Associate, Brand & Marketing

Revoke Permission

Figure 14-54. *Users with Executive Review Access*

To remove access for any existing Executive Reviewers, click the checkbox next to their name and click "Revoke Permission."

Enforce Comments on Rating Change

In order to require a comment to be added for a subject when a rating is changed, there are three steps that need to be done. The option to enforce a comment on a rating change is set in the calibration template in the Views tab. This option is only available to enable in Bin views. There are two other components that need to be enabled. The paths to the settings needed are shown in the following:

1. Manage Calibration Settings ➤ Global Settings ➤ Enable Enforce Comment Option in Views

2. Manage Calibration Template ➤ [select template] ➤ Views button ➤ select a view tab other than Dashboard or List View ➤ select "Enable comments on rating change"

3. Manage Calibration Template ➤ [select template] ➤ Advanced tab ➤ Comment on Change of Rating (select at least one):

   a. Authorized By

   b. Reason Code

   c. Comment

In the example shown in Figure 14-55, if a reason code must be entered on a rating change, a picklist ID must be identified.

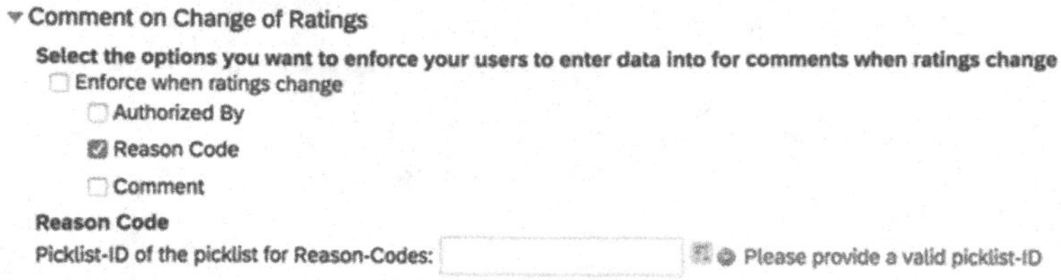

▼ Comment on Change of Ratings
Select the options you want to enforce your users to enter data into for comments when ratings change
☐ Enforce when ratings change
☐ Authorized By
☑ Reason Code
☐ Comment
Reason Code
Picklist-ID of the picklist for Reason-Codes: [_____] ▦ ⊕ Please provide a valid picklist-ID

Figure 14-55. *Enforced Comment Options*

Adding the Calibration History Portlet to Employee Profile

We have added the Calibration History Portlet background element to the data model and granted permission to this data for the admin, manager, and HR manager roles. Next, we need to add the portlet to People Profile. Type and select "Configure People Profile" in the search bar. As seen in Figure 15-56, we will add the Calibration History block.

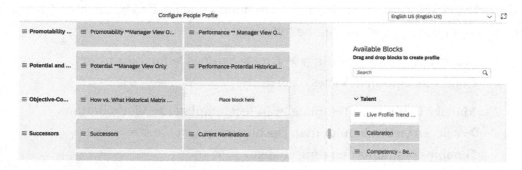

Figure 14-56. *Adding the Calibration History Portlet*

On the right side of the screen, you will see the available blocks. Find the Calibration block, and then drag and drop it to an existing section that has similar blocks. Typically, this would be a section unseen by the employee. It may be in a section with Succession or promotability-related data that only a manager or HR manager would have access to.

You may label the new subsection and the block. The portlet contains four user fields: session name, session review period start and end dates, and any comments made during the session. These fields cannot be removed. You may also add two additional fields to the standard Calibration History fields: Facilitators and Discussed. An example is shown in Figure 14-57.

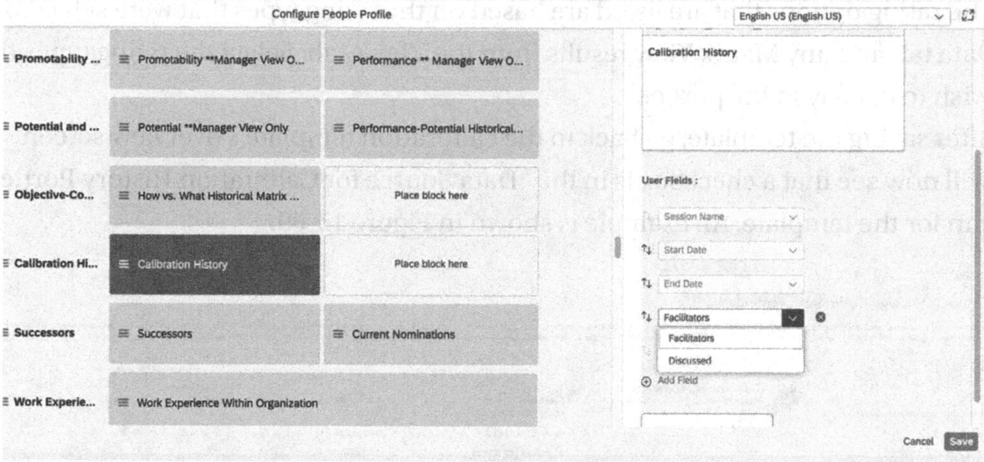

Figure 14-57. *Labels and Additional Fields for the Calibration History Portlet*

The Facilitators field would contain the name of the session facilitator and any co-facilitators. The Discussed field would contain "Yes" or "No" to identify employees who were discussed during the calibration session. Save after making the updates.

We have now added the Calibration History Portlet background element to the data model, granted role permissions to view it, and configured the portlet to appear in People Profile.

Next, we have to select the calibration template ratings to include in the portlet.

We need to go back into the calibration template to select the ratings to appear in the portlet. Type and select "Manage Calibration Templates" in the search bar. Click the template that you are going to reference in the portlet. Go to the Data tab as seen in Figure 14-58. Scroll to the bottom of the screen to find the Calibration History Portlet section.

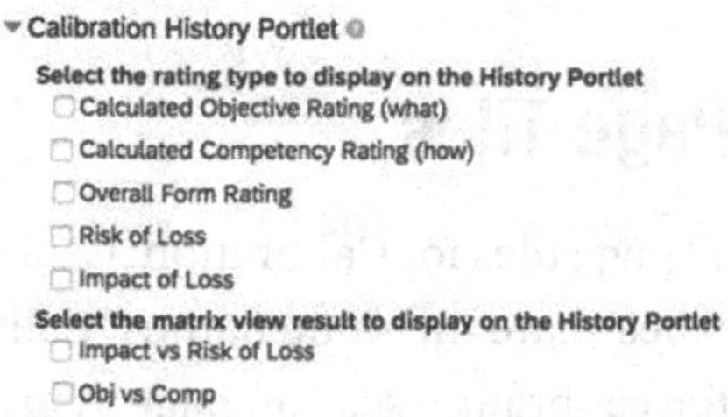

Figure 14-58. *Calibration History Portlet Options*

The rating options that are listed are based on the rating types that were selected in the Data tab and any Matrix View results from the Views tab. Select the rating types that you wish to display in the portlet.

After saving the template, go back to the calibration template's overview screen. You will now see that a checkbox is in the "Data Source for Calibration History Portlet" column for the template. An example is shown in Figure 15-59.

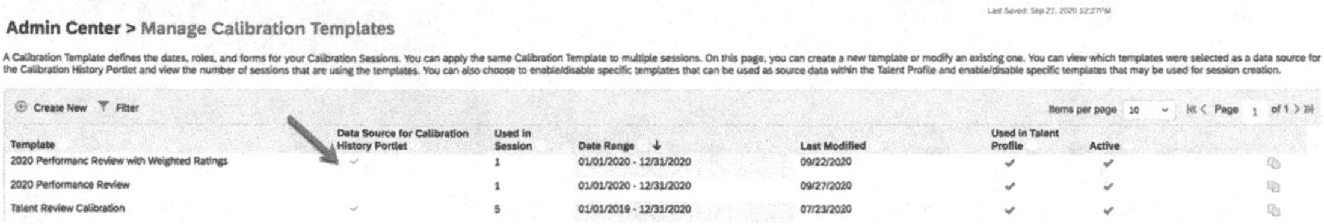

Figure 14-59. *Calibration Template as the Data Source for the Calibration History Portlet*

The portlet is now ready for use. Once the calibration session is finalized, the portlet will be populated.

An example of the portlet is displayed in Figure 14-60.

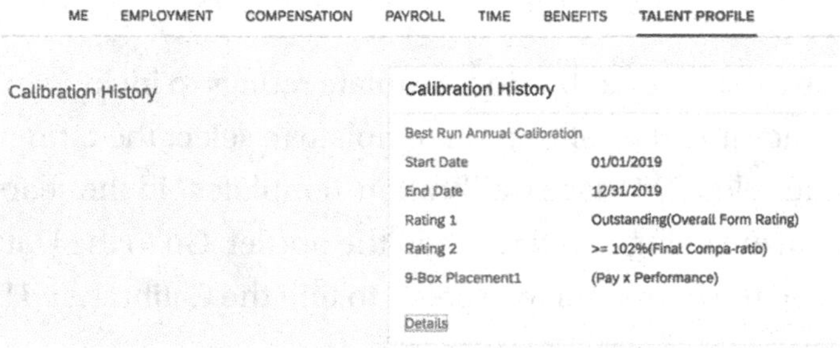

Figure 14-60. *Calibration History Portlet in Employee Profile*

Calibration Home Page Tiles

There are two standard home page tiles for Calibration: Calibration (Manager) and Calibration (Specialist). The tiles share the same name ("Calibration"), act identically, and provide a direct link to the calibration session page. A user would never have both tiles. When enabled, managers will have access to the Calibration (Manager) tile, and non-managers will have access to the Calibration (Specialist) tile.

A manager will see the calibration tile in the My Team section of their home page. Non-managers will see the calibration tile in the My Specialty section of their home page.

To see the tile, Calibration tab and Homepage v3 Tile Group permissions are granted through role-based permissions. For non-managers without access to the Calibration tab, they would only be able to see the calibration tile if they are identified as a participant in a calibration session.

To verify that the tiles are enabled, type and select "Manage Home Page" in the search bar. If the Calibration (Manager) tile is in the Repository or Not Used tab, click the dropdown arrow in the "Move To" column, select "Default," and save the settings. An example is shown in Figure 14-61.

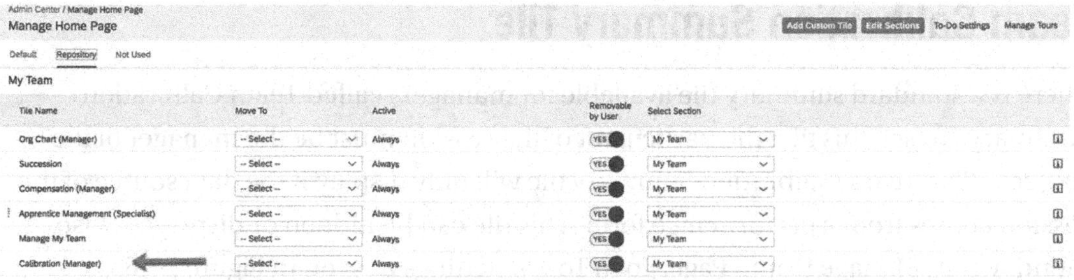

Figure 14-61. *Calibration Tile*

Moving the tile to the Default tab will place it in the My Team section. Next, find the "Calibration (Specialist)" tile. If the tile is in the Repository or Not Used tab, click the dropdown arrow in the "Move To" column, select "Default," and save the settings. The tile will appear in the Default tab in the My Specialty section. The tiles can also be moved to different sections of the home page from any of the tabs by using the dropdown listing for "Select Section." An example is shown in Figure 14-62.

Figure 14-62. *Move a Tile to Another Section*

Team Calibration Summary Tile

There is a standard summary tile available for managers called Team Calibration Summary. To see this tile, the participant of the session must be the manager of the subjects. The Team Calibration Summary tile will only display if the data source of the session comes from a performance form. This tile can be hidden or displayed. Also found within Manage Home Page, go to To-Do Settings as seen in Figure 14-63.

Figure 14-63. *To-Do Settings*

The list of the standard tiles will display as seen in Figure 14-64. The Team Calibration Summary tile may be hidden by moving the toggle to "No" and then saving the settings.

Figure 14-64. *Enable To-Do Tile*

When creating a calibration session, in the Basic Info tab, a session date may be included. This date is used to show how many days until the calibration session begins. If the calibration session does not have a session date, the tile will show the due date of the session 30 days after the session activation date.

Calibration Alerts

If Employee Central, Metadata Framework, and Intelligent Services are enabled, calibration alerts may be set up. Calibration alerts are used to point out situations where bias could impact the evaluation of some subjects or highlight scenarios where evaluators may have blind spots. The alert messages identify the problem and offer possible solutions. Calibration-type business rules are created to define the potential biased scenarios that would trigger a calibration alert. Then the calibration alert business rules are linked to a calibration template.

The standard calibration alerts are as follows:

- Subject had a leave of absence which may have impacted their performance rating since they did not have a full 12 months of work to evaluate.

- Subject had a noticeable reduction in their current year performance rating compared to the prior year rating.

- Subject received very favorable ratings for prior years and has not been promoted.

The alert messages need to be created via Manage Data ➤ Create New ➤ Alert Message. An example is shown in Figure 14-65.

Figure 14-65. *Create Alert Message*

External code, effective status localized header, and localized description are required. The message should identify the issue and offer solutions (localized description).

Next, the business rules for the alerts must be configured and the triggers identified. Type and select "Configure Business Rules" in the search bar and click "Create New Rule." As example is shown in Figure 14-66. Up to three performance form templates can be referenced when creating a business rule.

Figure 14-66. *Create a Calibration Alert Business Rule*

Create an alert scenario using *If/Then* logic or *True/False*. An example is shown in Figure 14-67.

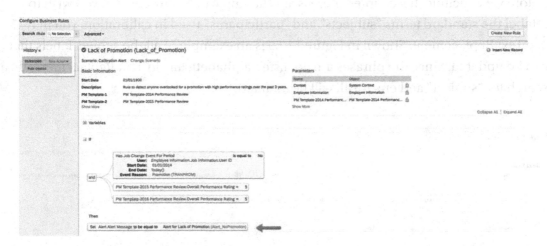

Figure 14-67. *Reference Alert Message in Rules*

Define how the system would respond if the "THEN" or "ELSE" option is met. The calibration alert message created in the prior step must be referenced here.

Once the rule is created, it must be linked to a calibration template. Type and select "Manage Calibration Templates" in the search bar. In the Advanced tab, select the alert rules from the Rules dropdown list. An example is shown in Figure 14-68.

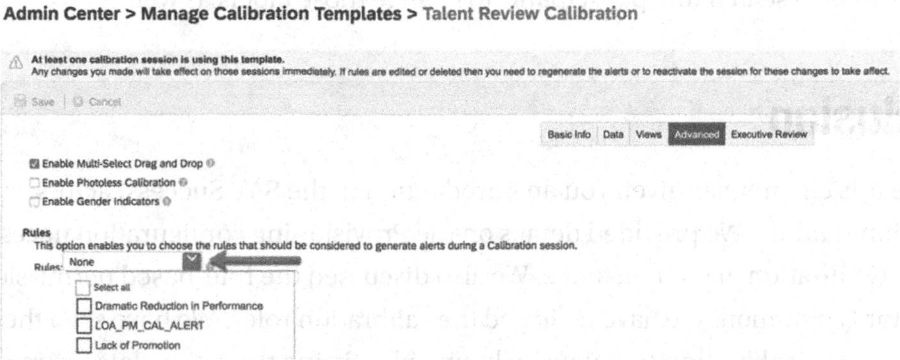

Admin Center > Manage Calibration Templates > Talent Review Calibration

⚠ **At least one calibration session is using this template.**
Any changes you made will take effect on those sessions immediately. If rules are edited or deleted then you need to regenerate the alerts or to reactivate the session for these changes to take affect.

💾 Save | ⊘ Cancel

Basic Info | Data | Views | **Advanced** | Executive Review

☑ Enable Multi-Select Drag and Drop ⓘ
☐ Enable Photoless Calibration ⓘ
☐ Enable Gender Indicators ⓘ

Rules
This option enables you to choose the rules that should be considered to generate alerts during a Calibration session.

Rules: | None ▾

☐ Select all
☐ Dramatic Reduction in Performance
☐ LOA_PM_CAL_ALERT
☐ Lack of Promotion

Figure 14-68. *Tie Business Rules to a Calibration Template*

All sessions linked to the calibration template will use the alerts.

To learn more about configuring the calibration alert rules, see the latest SAP SuccessFactors Calibration Implementation Guide.

Text Replacement

Before we conclude this chapter, there is another topic to briefly cover. If you wish to relabel the standard terms "subjects" and "participants" used in calibration, you may use Text Replacement. Shown in Figure 14-69 is an example of all the subject labels that can be updated. Since the phrases are not listed alphabetically in Text Replacement, do a search for "subject" and ensure all will be updated.

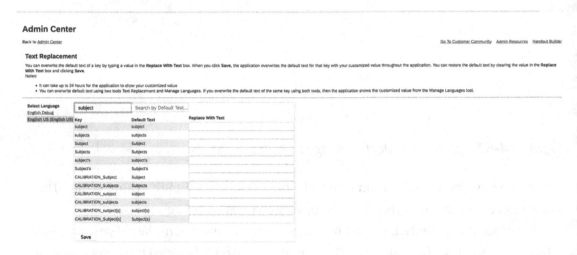

Figure 14-69. *Text Replacement*

You can do a search for "participant" to change those labels as well.

Conclusion

We hope this chapter has given you an introduction to the SAP SuccessFactors Calibration module. We provided details on the Provisioning configuration necessary to set up Calibration in your instance. We also discussed the role-based permissions needed for Calibration. We have reviewed the calibration roles. We have seen the steps to set up a calibration template including identifying the rating data sources and configuring the views of how the data will be displayed. We have seen the settings used to enable various features of Calibration, configured the Calibration Talent Card, and learned how to assign users to the Executive Reviewer role. We have learned how to configure the Calibration History Portlet for Employee Profile. We saw the calibration tiles available on the home page. We learned how calibration alerts can be used to point out bias. We saw how to use Text Replacement to update subject and participant labels to use within calibration sessions. In the next chapter, we will demonstrate how a calibration session is created and conducted.

CHAPTER 15

Calibration Sessions

In the previous chapter, we learned how to enable Calibration in Provisioning. Next, we went into the instance, set up role-based permissions, and reviewed the steps to configure a calibration template. We discussed the calibration settings and saw several additional Calibration-related features. Now we are ready to create a calibration session.

Before we begin, let's review what we have learned to make sure we understand what a calibration session is.

A calibration session is a forum where managers convene to discuss the performance of their employees to achieve agreement on fair, objective performance ratings. The session is used to compare performance ratings for those being calibrated, make changes to ratings, add comments, and review the outcomes of a given calibration cycle.

In the previous chapter on Calibration, we created the calibration template. The template identified the data source of the ratings to be calibrated, identified the data views used for the calibration sessions, and enabled some general features. Next, we configured the calibration settings. The settings defined what each calibration participant role could do, identified search results fields, and enabled global settings. If managers will be able to launch their own calibration sessions in Team Overview in Performance, we identified the calibration template to be used. The features and settings are applicable to each calibration template and each calibration session.

In this chapter, we will explore the various ways to create a calibration session. We will see how an admin may create one or more calibration sessions using the Manage Calibration Sessions tool. We will also learn how an admin may create multiple sessions using the Mass Create Calibration Sessions tool. We will also gain an understanding of how to mass create, approve, and delete calibration sessions.

We will walk through the steps taken by a manager to create sessions via the Calibration tab or the Team Overview tab within Performance. Once we have reviewed these methods and the calibration sessions have been set up, we will walk through a calibration session. We will conclude with a review of the calibration reporting that is available.

© Susan Traynor, Michael A. Wellens and Venki Krishnamoorthy 2021
S. Traynor et al., *SAP SuccessFactors Talent: Volume 1*, https://doi.org/10.1007/978-1-4842-6600-7_15

Manage Calibration Sessions

We will begin by looking at how an admin can manage calibration sessions. This role-based permission is granted to the admin role and to any role that will be responsible for creating or editing calibration sessions. Type and select "Manage Calibration Sessions" in the search bar. A sessions overview screen will display. Here, new calibration sessions may be created; and existing sessions may be edited, cloned, deleted, or exported. An example is seen in Figure 15-1.

Admin Center > Manage Calibration Sessions

Use this page to configure your Calibration Session. You can create a new session, clone(copy) or modify an existing one and delete a session that is not required. A Calibration Session defines the timeframe the session is applicable to, as well as the owner, participants and subjects of the session. You can have multiple active sessions.

Tip! Each Calibration Session generally groups employees with a similar background, allowing for a meaningful comparison.

Session	Template Name	Status ↑	# of Subjects	# of Participants	Facilitator	Attachment
Annual Calibration for Thompson	Annual Calibration Review	Approved	3	1	Aanya Singh, William Muller	
Test Mass1	Annual Calibration Review	Approved	5	2	Aanya Singh, Eric Schwab	
Best Run Annual Calibration	Best Run Pay x Performance	Approved	32	9	Aanya Singh, Angela Rice, Chung Tai, Dana Fiona Curtis, Eric Schwab, Grace Olivo Segura, Linda R. Simpson, Terry Vincent Taylor	
Talent Potentialeinschätzung	Talent Review Calibration	Deactivated	12	4	Aanya Singh, Brigitte Kaiser, Fritz Winter, Heike Hartmann, Tanja Grupp	
Jährliches Kalibrierungsmeeting	Best Run Pay x Performance	Deactivated	12	4	Aanya Singh, Brigitte Kaiser, Fritz Winter, Heike Hartmann, Tanja Grupp	
Cust Overall Weighted	weighted 2020	In Progress	1	3	Aanya Singh	
test	Annual Calibration Review	In Progress	3	2	Aanya Singh	
Best Run Talent Review Calibration	Talent Review Calibration	In Progress	30	6	Aanya Singh, Angela Rice, Chung Tai, Dana Fiona Curtis, Eric Schwab, Grace Olivo Segura, Linda R. Simpson, Terry Vincent Taylor	
Talent Review Calibration	Talent Review Calibration	In Progress	60	9	Aanya Singh, Christine Dolan, Tessa Walker	
Annual Calibration Review	Annual Calibration Review	In Progress	7	9	Aanya Singh, Christine Dolan, Tessa Walker	

Figure 15-1. *Manage Calibration Sessions Overview*

Calibration Sessions Overview Screen

Let's now look at what is displayed on this overview page for each session. Existing calibration sessions of all statuses will appear. The column headings are shown in Figure 15-2.

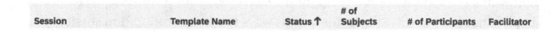

Session	Template Name	Status ↑	# of Subjects	# of Participants	Facilitator

Figure 15-2. *Calibration Session Columns*

The name of each session displays with its associated calibration template, the session status, the number of subjects and participants, and the name of the facilitator.

The statuses associated with phases of the calibration session are as follows:

- *Setup:* Session has been created and validated, but it has not been activated yet.

- *In Progress:* Session is activated; session is open and not finalized yet.

- *Approving:* Phase between "In Progress" and "Approved". The Finalize button has been clicked, but finalization has not completed yet.

- *Approved:* Session is finalized, ratings are approved, and session is complete.

- *Deactivated:* An "In Progress" session has been stopped. This status allows for changes to be made. Sessions must be reactivated to return to "In Progress" status.

It may be helpful to understand what validating and activating mean as well. After a session is created, it must be validated. The validation process checks to make sure the subjects have forms and the forms are in the calibration step. If validation is successful, the session may be activated. Activating a session makes it ready for the facilitators, owners, and participants to access to begin the calibration process.

Calibration Session Options

New sessions may be created, existing sessions may be cloned or deleted, and sessions may be exported.

The Create New, Export, and Filter options are shown in Figure 15-3. We will look at each option next.

Figure 15-3. *Manage Calibration Session Options*

Export Calibration Sessions

To export a calibration session, select one or multiple sessions and click the "Export" button. Click "Export All" to export all of the calibration sessions. The exported data is contained in an Excel workbook. There is a record for each subject which contains the basic information about the session as seen in the sample in Figure 15-4.

Session Name	Template	Status	Session Date	Planned Activation Date	Location	Participants	Facilitator	Owners	Subjects
Annual Calibration Review	Annual Calibration Review	Approved	12/31/19	1/1/18		crichardson|hmaigne|akuwa-1|patkins|ylu|ghill|pmoreira|akuwa|rbrunnert	twalker|sfadmin|cdolan	averrier|mcooper|vwagner|sgray|mt ang|mgoncalves|ebulanov|amillar|mtana	mshu
Annual Calibration Review	Annual Calibration Review	Approved	12/31/19	1/1/18		crichardson|hmaigne|akuwa-1|patkins|ylu|ghill|pmoreira|akuwa|rbrunnert	twalker|sfadmin|cdolan	averrier|mcooper|vwagner|sgray|mt ang|mgoncalves|ebulanov|amillar|mtana	jklein
Annual Calibration Review	Annual Calibration Review	Approved	12/31/19	1/1/18		crichardson|hmaigne|akuwa-1|patkins|ylu|ghill|pmoreira|akuwa|rbrunnert	twalker|sfadmin|cdolan	averrier|mcooper|vwagner|sgray|mt ang|mgoncalves|ebulanov|amillar|mtana	agao-1
Annual Calibration Review	Annual Calibration Review	Approved	12/31/19	1/1/18		crichardson|hmaigne|akuwa-1|patkins|ylu|ghill|pmoreira|akuwa|rbrunnert	twalker|sfadmin|cdolan	averrier|mcooper|vwagner|sgray|mt ang|mgoncalves|ebulanov|amillar|mtana	sthorn

Figure 15-4. *Calibration Session Export*

Filter Calibration Sessions

The Filter option may be used to avoid scrolling through multiple pages to find a specific session to manage. This is helpful in an organization with a large number of calibration sessions. Sessions can be filtered by name, status, facilitator, or number of subjects or participants. An example is shown in Figure 15-5.

Figure 15-5. *Advanced Filter to Find a Calibration Session*

Apply a filter to display the sessions that meet the selected criteria.

Search for Calibration Sessions

There is also a search option which can be used to find a session when a large number of sessions exist. Quickly find a session by typing part of a calibration session name in the search box and clicking "Go." Sessions that meet the criteria will display.

Now, let's create a new session!

Calibration Session Target Groups by Role

When creating a calibration session, you must identify which employees and ratings to calibrate and by whom. Role-based permissions are used to grant access to create calibration sessions. However, each of the roles creates the sessions using different means with different target groups. Details are shown in Table 15-1.

Table 15-1. *Calibration Session Creation Types and Targets*

Session Type	Role	Target Group	Where to Create the Session?
Single session	Admin	All employees	Admin Center ➤ Calibration ➤ Manage Calibration Sessions ➤ Create New
	Manager	Direct reports	Home ➤ Performance ➤ Team Overview ➤ Calibration button
		Direct reports and below	Home ➤ Calibration ➤ Create New
Multiple Sessions	Admin	All employees	Admin Center ➤ Calibration ➤ Mass Create Calibration Sessions

We will start by looking at how an admin would create a single calibration session.

A new session may be created by clicking the "Create New" button or cloning an existing session. Cloning a session will create a copy of an existing session that you may use as a starting point to rename and make updates on. During the session creation process, you will identify the time frame the session is applicable to and identify the calibration template being used. You will also designate users to

- Run the session (facilitator)

- Act as backup (co-facilitator)

- Own the session (owner)

- Provide input (participant)

- Be calibrated (subject)

- Have access to all session data for a calibration template (executive reviewer)

The creation process involves three tabs: Basic Info, People, and Validation.

Basic Info Tab

The Basic Info tab is seen in Figure 15-6.

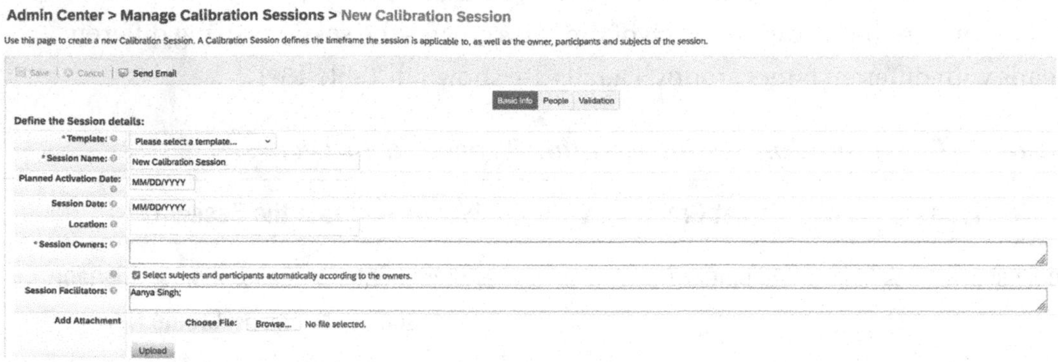

Admin Center > Manage Calibration Sessions > New Calibration Session

Use this page to create a new Calibration Session. A Calibration Session defines the timeframe the session is applicable to, as well as the owner, participants and subjects of the session.

Figure 15-6. *Basic Info Tab for a Calibration Session*

The Basic Info tab is used to name the session, identify the calibration template to associate the session with, and select the session owners and facilitators. Required fields are the session name, associated calibration template, and session owner(s).

A session owner would be a manager with more than two levels reporting to them. The default setting is "Select subjects and participants automatically according to the owners." When designating an owner, the direct reports of the owner automatically become the participants of the calibration session. Additionally, the direct reports of the participants become the subjects of the calibration session.

This setting will add the participants and subjects as session members in the People tab. Participants would be all users one level down from the owner. Subjects would include all users two levels down from the owner.

The admin's username defaults as the facilitator, but this may be changed. A second name added becomes the co-facilitator, but a co-facilitator is not required.

It is possible to upload one attachment which would be visible in the calibration session. Rating descriptions or distribution guidelines are examples of attachments that could be used.

Planned Activation Date is the date that the session is activated and ready for use. Session Date is the start date of the calibration session, and Location is where the session will take place. These three fields are optional. Save the tab with your entries and then go to the People tab.

People Tab

The People tab is used to add or edit participants and subjects for the session. The People tab is divided into three sections: User Search, Search Results, and Session Members. The User Search section is used to find users to add to the calibration session. The search results display in the middle panel. Users that are owners, participants, and subjects display in the Session Members panel on the far right. If the "Select subjects and participants automatically according to the owners" option is checked in the Basic Info tab, the Session Members panel will be populated as seen in Figure 15-7.

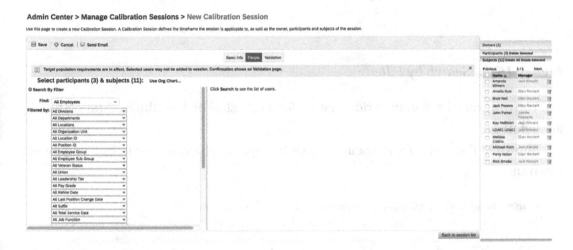

Figure 15-7. *People Tab of Manage Calibration Sessions*

However, any of these names may be removed or additional ones added. To add additional session subjects or participants, you may for search for users by filter, group, or org chart.

"Search by Filter" is the default search. The standard filters are Division, Department, Location, Name, Username, and Job Code. The custom calibration filters added to the data model will be available as filters as well. An example is shown in Figure 15-8.

Select participants (9) & subjects (59):
Use Org Chart...
Search By Filter
Find:
All Employees
Filtered by:
All Divisions
All Departments
All Locations
All Organization Unit
All Location ID
All Position ID
All Employee Group
All Employee Sub Group
All Veteran Status
All Union
All Leadership Tier
All Pay Grade
All Rehire Date
All Last Position Change Date
All Suffix
All Total Service Date
All Job Function
All Job Family
With:
First Name:
and
Last Name:
and
Username:
and
Job Code:
Using:
Starts With
Search By Group
Search

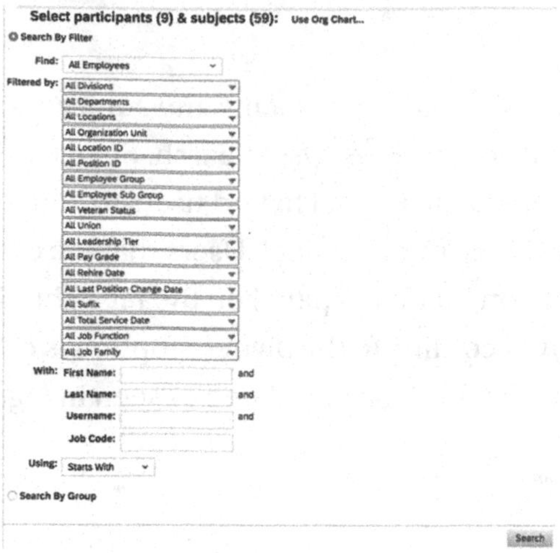

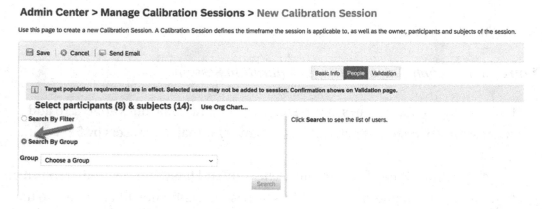

Figure 15-8. Search by Filter

You may refer back to the prior chapter for a refresher on how the calibration filters are defined.

Shown in Figure 15-9 is the Search by Group option which is used to find employees by group.

Admin Center > Manage Calibration Sessions > New Calibration Session
Use this page to create a new Calibration Session. A Calibration Session defines the timeframe the session is applicable to, as well as the owner, participants and subjects of the session.
Save
Cancel
Send Email
Basic Info
People
Validation
Target population requirements are in effect. Selected users may not be added to session. Confirmation shows on Validation page.
Select participants (8) & subjects (14):
Use Org Chart...
Search By Filter
Search By Group
Group
Choose a Group
Search
Click Search to see the list of users.

Figure 15-9. Search by Group

If you click the radio button for "Search by Group", you will be able to find employees using any existing groups as seen in Figure 15-10. You may also create new groups.

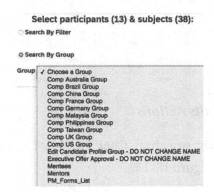

Figure 15-10. *Search by Group Option*

Based on the selections that had been made in the Search Results Fields tab in Manage Calibration Settings, additional display fields will be available by clicking the wheel icon as shown in Figure 15-11. The fields selected will then display as additional columns in the Search Results section of the screen as shown in the following. Any default return fields may be deselected as well.

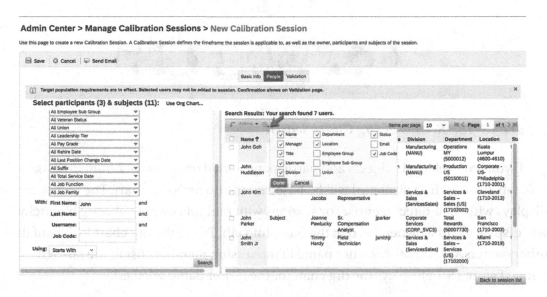

Figure 15-11. *Display Fields for the Search Results Section*

In the Search Results panel, select a user and click the "Actions" dropdown listing to add the name to the session members list as a participant or subject in the far-right panel of the tab. Figure 15-12 shows the search results table with the available actions.

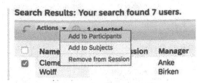

Figure 15-12. *Search Results Actions*

The last search option is by org chart. Click the "Use Org Chart..." link, and the org chart will display as seen in Figure 15-13.

Figure 15-13. *Results of Org Chart Search*

If you have selected subjects and participants based on the owner from the Basic Info tab, the org chart displayed will be based on the owner's org chart. The owner displays with their direct reports. For sessions with multiple owners, the org hierarchy will display the first owner listed in the Basic Info tab. To see the org chart for any of the other owners, click another owner name in the session members list in the far-right panel. Figure 15-14 displays the org chart for the owner name selected.

Figure 15-14. *Select Owner for Org Chart Search*

You may also search for anyone in the org chart to find a user to add as a participant or subject.

You may drill down in the org chart to lower levels. Each employee will have a "Take Action" link. Clicking the link will bring up options as seen in Figure 15-15.

Figure 15-15. *Add/Remove Users to/from a Session*

The "Take Action" option enables the employee to be added to the session as a "participant" or "subject" or "Not in Session." The "Not in Session" option will remove the user from the calibration session. The admin may also designate the entire organization of the user as subjects in the session.

In the Session Members panel as seen in Figure 15-16, names may be selected to remove. You may select one, many, or all names to remove from the session.

Figure 15-16. *Session Members as Seen in the People Tab*

If you wish to add or remove subjects or participants for a session already in progress, click the "Deactivate" button seen on the top of the page. While deactivated, the session cannot be accessed, and data cannot be edited. To resume the session after making updates, the session has to be validated and activated again.

There is also a Send Email button in the People tab. Clicking this button will display a screen used to create an email as shown in Figure 15-17. The owner and participant names default into the "Send to" address, but the entries may be modified.

Figure 15-17. *Send Email option in the People Tab*

The admin may send an email with any subject and message, and the recipients may also be updated.

Once you have made any changes, click the "Save" button, and we will be ready to go to the Validation tab.

Validation Tab

After entering the session info in the Basic Info tab, selecting who will be part of the calibration session in the People tab, and saving the session, the session must be validated.

This step must be completed in order to make the session ready for calibration. In the Validation tab, the system completes a series of checks that include verifying that every subject has a performance form and that each form is in the calibration step. Any errors are displayed and must be resolved before activating the session.

Common error and warning messages are shown in Table 15-2.

Table 15-2. *Validation Error and Warning Messages*

Error Message	Reason	Correction to Make
Subjects don't have forms	Subjects in session do not have a performance form.	Launch a form for the subject or remove the subject from the session.
Subjects have forms not yet routed to calibration	Forms exist for subjects, but they are not yet in the calibration step in the Performance route map.	Route forms to the calibration step or have users manually submit to the next step.
Subjects are in another session	Only an issue if the setting to allow an employee to be in only one session at a time is enabled.	Remove the subject from the session or change the global setting.
Warning Message	**Reason**	**Resolution**
Subjects have already been selected in other sessions	Subjects are in other sessions; the template may be different but has the same date range and data source.	Use different calibration templates with different data ranges or data sources or remove users from the session.
Users are inactive	Users are in inactive status	Remove the user from the session, change the setting to allow inactive users, or change the user to active status.

Warning messages will not cause validation to fail.

Figure 15-18 shows an example where validation fails because there are subjects without forms and forms have not been routed to the calibration step yet.

Admin Center > Manage Calibration Sessions > New Calibration Session

Use this page to create a new Calibration Session. A Calibration Session defines the timeframe the session is applicable to, as well as the owner, participants and subjects of the session.

Save	Cancel	Send Email	Activate			

| | | | | Basic Info | People | Validation |

⚠ **Validation Failed!**
11 subjects have forms not yet routed to calibration.   ⬅

Details:

Not yet routed to calibration (11) ⊟ Request Routing   Route Forms to Calibration

Subjects	Manager	Form Type	Form Status	Current Owner
Amanda Winters	Jack Kincaid	Performance	Mid-Year Review	Amanda Winters
Amelia Ruiz	Ellen Reckert	Performance	Mid-Year Review	Amelia Ruiz
Brett Neil	Ellen Reckert	Performance	Mid-Year Review	Brett Neil
Jack Powers	Ellen Reckert	Performance	Mid-Year Review	Jack Powers
John Parker	Joanne Pawlucky	Performance	Mid-Year Review	John Parker
Kay Holliston	Jack Kincaid	Performance	Mid-Year Review	Kay Holliston
LOA01 LOA01	Jack Kincaid	Performance	Mid-Year Review	LOA01 LOA01
Melissa Collins	Ellen Reckert	Performance	Mid-Year Review	Melissa Collins
Michael Roth	Jack Kincaid	Performance	Mid-Year Review	Michael Roth
Parry Nolan	Ellen Reckert	Performance	Mid-Year Review	Parry Nolan
Rick Smolla	Jack Kincaid	Performance	Mid-Year Review	Rick Smolla

Figure 15-18. *Validation Errors*

The "Route Forms to Calibration" button will move the forms to the calibration step. First, a popup will display if the auto routing email notification is enabled. The email is sent to the managers of the employees having their forms moved. An example of the email is shown in Figure 15-19.

Figure 15-19. *Email Notification of Form Routing*

The email may be modified prior to sending. A message will display when the notifications are successfully sent. Once the email is sent, the routing of the forms begins as seen in Figure 15-20.

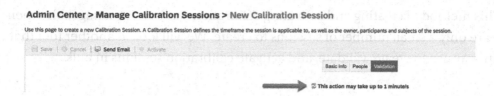

Admin Center > Manage Calibration Sessions > New Calibration Session

Use this page to create a new Calibration Session. A Calibration Session defines the timeframe the session is applicable to, as well as the owner, participants and subjects of the session.

Figure 15-20. *Forms Being Routed to the Calibration Step*

If there are no issues, you can successfully activate the session at this point. There will be a green banner containing "Validation finished. No problems found."

As seen in Figure 15-21, once the session is validated, it is ready to be activated.

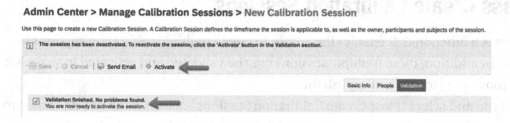

Admin Center > Manage Calibration Sessions > New Calibration Session

Use this page to create a new Calibration Session. A Calibration Session defines the timeframe the session is applicable to, as well as the owner, participants and subjects of the session.

Figure 15-21. *Successful Session Validation*

Activation

Once validated, click the "Activate" button. Activating a session makes it available for the calibration session to begin. As seen in Figure 15-22, a confirmation popup displays to verify activation. Once activated, an email may be sent to the facilitator, owner, and session participants. The recipients, prepopulated email subject, and message may be modified prior to sending. The session status is now "In Progress."

Figure 15-22. *Sequence to Validate a Session*

This method of creating and activating calibration sessions is manageable when there are only a small number of sessions to create. We will look at another tool that the admin may use to create, validate, and activate calibration sessions in bulk.

Mass Calibration Activities

Managing calibration sessions individually is labor intensive especially for an organization that needs to create hundreds of calibration sessions.

Mass Create Calibration Sessions

There is a function that enables the admin to create multiple calibration sessions at once. In addition, these multiple sessions may be validated and activated in mass. We will look at the tool to accomplish this.

Type and select "Mass Create Calibration Sessions" in the search bar. As shown in Figure 15-23, here, the mass creation activities may be performed. Using this feature assumes that the calibration settings have already been configured and the calibration template created.

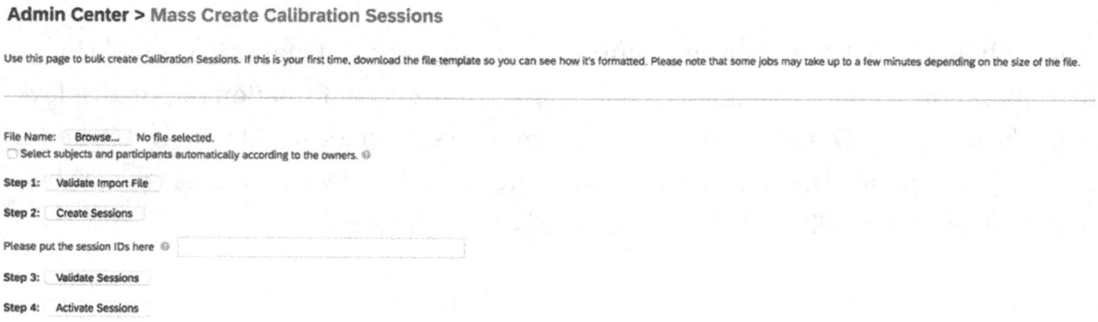

Admin Center > Mass Create Calibration Sessions

Use this page to bulk create Calibration Sessions. If this is your first time, download the file template so you can see how it's formatted. Please note that some jobs may take up to a few minutes depending on the size of the file.

File Name: Browse...   No file selected.
☐ Select subjects and participants automatically according to the owners. ⊙

Step 1:   Validate Import File

Step 2:   Create Sessions

Please put the session IDs here ⊙   [   ]

Step 3:   Validate Sessions

Step 4:   Activate Sessions

Figure 15-23. *Mass Create Calibration Sessions*

There are four steps to perform on this screen: Validate Import File, Create Sessions, Validate Sessions, and Activate Sessions. We will walk through each step.

Validate Import File

To start, the calibration file template must be downloaded. The template provides the file layout used to create the calibration sessions. Click "File Template" seen in the introductory text at the top of the screen and open the CSV file. The downloaded template is seen in Figure 15-24.

	A	B	C	D	E	F	G	H	I
1	Session Name	Template	Session Date	Activation Date	Location	Participant	Session Facilitator	Session Owner	Subject
2	Session Name	Template	Session Date	Planned Activation Date	Location	Participants	Facilitator	Owners	Subjects
3									
4									

Figure 15-24. *Calibration File Template*

The file columns represent the same fields that are used when creating a calibration session manually via Manage Calibration Sessions.

The first two header rows in the file template must remain intact. The first row contains columns which represent the session attributes. The second row contains the system column names.

Create a row on the file for each calibration session that you wish to create. Similar to creating the calibration session manually, the same fields are required: session name, the calibration template associated with the session, and the session owner.

Required Entries

The required entries on the file are

Column A – Session Name: Give each session a unique name.

Column B – Template: The calibration template to associate with the session.

Column G – Session Facilitator: If the facilitator is left blank, the system defaults the facilitator to the person who uploaded the file. If you wish to list a facilitator and co-facilitator, list each username in the same row separated by the bar delimiter "|".

Column H – Session Owner: Enter the username of the session owner. If there are multiple owners, list each in the same cell separated by the bar delimiter.

Figure 15-25 shows an example using two facilitators with multiple owners.

G	H
Session Facilitator	Session Owner
Facilitator	Owners
SFADMIN|HRMGR1	TESTSRMGR1|TESTSRMGR2|TESTMGR3

Figure 15-25. *Example of Multiple Facilitators and Owners*

Optional Entries

Column C (Session Date), column D (Activation Date), and column E (Location) are optional and may be left blank. The date format is based on the localized format of the user uploading the file. The file needs to use CSV format when uploading.

On the Mass Create Calibration Sessions screen is an option "Select subjects and participants automatically according to the owners." This is the same option found in the Basic Info tab when creating a session via Manage Calibration Sessions. By enabling this option, all of the managers reporting to the owner become participants in the session. Individual contributors reporting to the participants become the subjects. Enabling this option eliminates the need to individually identify the participants and subjects to include in a session. Therefore, no entries are added in the Participants and Subjects columns.

To replicate this option for mass session creation, leave the cells empty in the Participants (column F) and Subjects (column I) columns. You can have rows with participants and subjects listed on the file if the automatic selection of subjects and participants is enabled. In other words, you may include rows for sessions with no participants and no subjects and rows with participants and subjects for sessions when the "Select subjects and participants automatically according to the owners" is checked.

If you are building sessions that are not based on the owner's org hierarchy, the participants and subjects must be entered on the file in columns F and I:

Column F – Participants: Enter all of the participants in one cell separated by the bar delimiter.

Column I – Subjects: Enter all of the subjects in one cell separated by the bar delimiter.

Continue to add rows to the file for each unique calibration session you wish to create. You may create sessions that use different calibration templates.

Figure 15-26 shows an example of rows on the CSV file with subjects and participants populated.

A	B	C	D	E	F	G	H	I
Session Name	Template	Session Date	Activation Date	Location	Participant	Session Facilitator	Session Owner	Subject
Session Name	Template	Session Date	Planned Activation	Location	Participants	Facilitator	Owners	Subjects
Mass Test 1	Talent Review Calibration				mgoncalves|grodriques lmahoney		acatarino	lcarriao|pmoreira|rolivera|ccorreia|fgomes|mlombardi|flopes|ndias|asousa|lalves
Mass Test 2	Annual Calibration Review				lmazure|lthom|tgunter|bm anessis|nkeegan|lbromby	fcrawley|mtravers	omoscato	awilliams|ryang|jking|jadams|rsmith|acoe|
Mass Test 3	Annual Calibration Review					echang	ecamargo	
Mass Test 4	Annual Calibration Review					gmacdevitt	jking	
Mass Test 5	Talent Review Calibration					lmazure jpowers	srampal sstone|jroberts	

Figure 15-26. *Mass Create Upload File*

Once the file is populated and saved, it must be uploaded and validated as seen in Figure 15-27. Make sure the file name is listed and check the box next to "Select subjects and participants automatically according to the owners" if any of the file entries have owners and no participants and subjects. Click the Step 1 button, "Validate Import File".

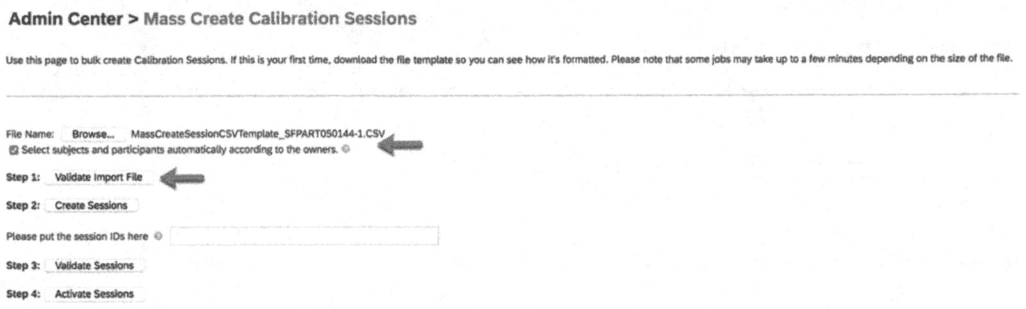

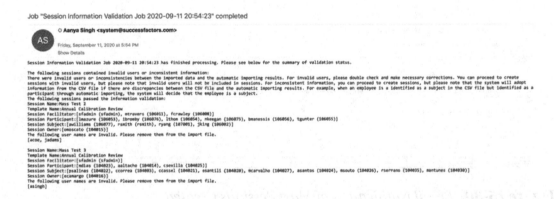

Figure 15-27. *Select a File and Validate*

After the file is validated, the admin will receive an email. If there are any issues, the email will contain validation errors. Figure 15-28 shows an example of an import that contains errors.

Figure 15-28. *Calibration Session Import Validation Email with Errors*

If there were any errors, the file must be corrected, saved, uploaded, and validated again.

Create Sessions

The admin will need to return to the Mass Create Calibration Sessions tool to create the sessions. Once the file is validated, the sessions may be created. Make sure the file name is listed and click the Step 2 button, "Create Sessions", as seen in Figure 15-29.

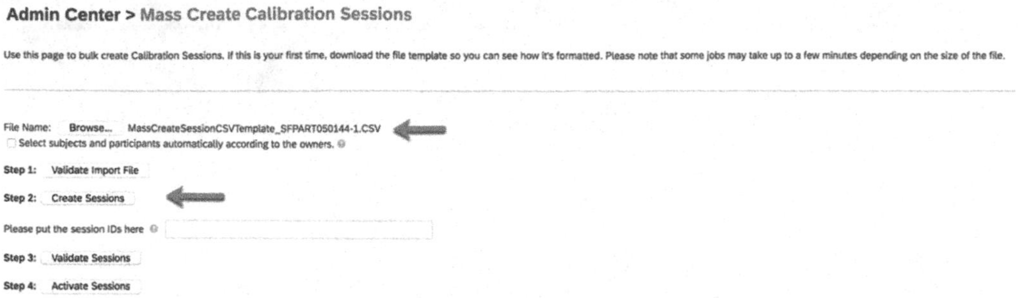

Figure 15-29. *Mass Create the Calibration Sessions*

The admin will receive an email as shown in Figure 15-30. The sessions have been created, and each shows a session ID which will need to be referenced when validating the sessions.

Figure 15-30. *Email Notification of Mass Sessions Created*

The status of each calibration session is now "Setup."

Validate Sessions

The admin will need to return to the Mass Create Calibration Sessions tool to validate the sessions. The subjects must have performance forms created and in the calibration step in order to validate successfully. Only "Setup" or "Deactivated" status sessions may be validated. Make sure the file name is listed along with the session IDs from the email from Step 2. Click the Step 3 button, "Validate Sessions". An example is shown in Figure 15-31.

Figure 15-31. *Validate Sessions*

The admin will receive an email with the status of the sessions. If there are no errors, as shown in Figure 15-32, the sessions are ready to be activated.

Figure 15-32. *Validation Successful Email*

Activate Sessions

The admin will need to return to the Mass Create Calibration Sessions tool to activate the sessions as seen in Figure 15-33. Make sure the file name is listed along with the session IDs from the email from Step 2. Click the Step 4 button, "Activate Sessions".

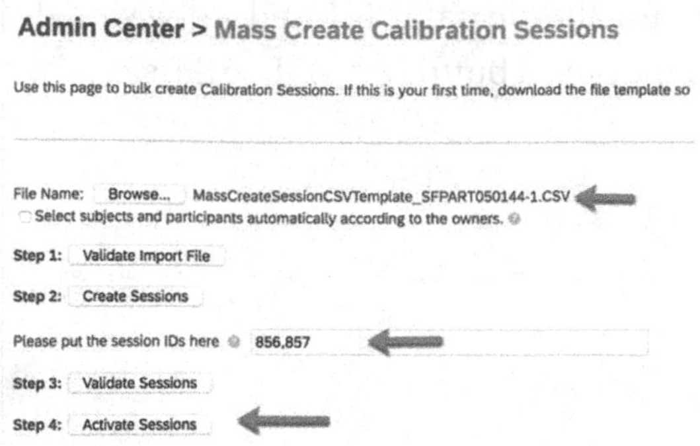

Admin Center > Mass Create Calibration Sessions

Use this page to bulk create Calibration Sessions. If this is your first time, download the file template so

File Name: Browse...   MassCreateSessionCSVTemplate_SFPART050144-1.CSV ⬅
          ☐ Select subjects and participants automatically according to the owners. ⓘ

Step 1:   Validate Import File

Step 2:   Create Sessions

Please put the session IDs here ⓘ   856,857 ⬅

Step 3:   Validate Sessions

Step 4:   Activate Sessions ⬅

Figure 15-33. *Activate Sessions*

An example of the email notification received by the admin for when sessions are activated is seen in Figure 15-34.

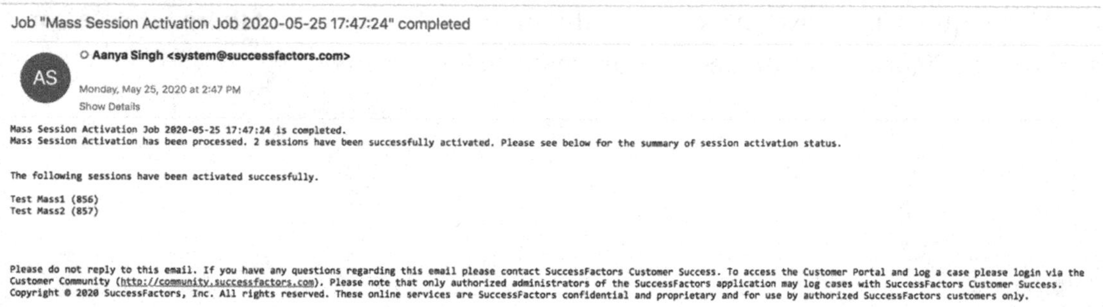

Job "Mass Session Activation Job 2020-05-25 17:47:24" completed

○ Aanya Singh <system@successfactors.com>
AS
Monday, May 25, 2020 at 2:47 PM
Show Details

Mass Session Activation Job 2020-05-25 17:47:24 is completed.
Mass Session Activation has been processed. 2 sessions have been successfully activated. Please see below for the summary of session activation status.

The following sessions have been activated successfully.

Test Mass1 (856)
Test Mass2 (857)

Please do not reply to this email. If you have any questions regarding this email please contact SuccessFactors Customer Success. To access the Customer Portal and log a case please login via the Customer Community (http://community.successfactors.com). Please note that only authorized administrators of the SuccessFactors application may log cases with SuccessFactors Customer Success. Copyright © 2020 SuccessFactors, Inc. All rights reserved. These online services are SuccessFactors confidential and proprietary and for use by authorized SuccessFactors customers only.

Figure 15-34. *Activation Email*

The status for the sessions is "In Progress," and calibration sessions may begin.

Other mass actions that may be performed are mass delete sessions and mass approve sessions. We will look at mass deletions next and leave the mass approve sessions discussion until after we walk through a calibration session.

Mass Delete Sessions

In a situation where calibration sessions need to be recreated, the existing sessions must first be deleted. It is possible to delete the sessions in bulk. Facilitators and co-facilitators may delete sessions as long as these calibration roles have the "Delete" permissions. The permissions to delete "In Progress" sessions and "Approved" sessions are set in the Permissions tab in Manage Calibration Settings.

Multiple sessions may be deleted at once by using the Home menu and selecting "Calibration". All the sessions that the facilitator has permission to will display as shown in Figure 15-35.

Figure 15-35. *Calibration Sessions with the Mass Delete Feature*

To mass delete sessions, the facilitator may select any or all sessions and click the trash can icon on the top-right side of the screen. A confirmation page will display as seen in Figure 15-36.

Delete Sessions

You are about to delete the following sessions all at once.
Please review the list before continue.

Annual Calibration Review	In Progress
Annual Calibration for Thompson	Approved
Best Run Annual Calibration	Approved
Best Run Talent Review Calibration	In Progress
Cust Overall Weighted	In Progress
Jährliches Kalibrierungsmeeting	Deactivated
Talent Potentialeinschätzung	Deactivated
Talent Review Calibration	In Progress

⚠ The following sessions cannot be deleted due to permission limitation.

2019 Review Cycle	In Progress
2020 Performance Review for Lesley Ellis	In Progress

Cancel   Continue

Figure 15-36. *Delete Sessions Confirmation*

Any sessions that cannot be deleted due to permissions will be listed as seen in the preceding figure. Upon confirmation, the sessions are deleted and removed from the session list.

The facilitator may also use "Manage Calibration Sessions" to delete multiple sessions as shown in Figure 15-37. However, each session must be selected and deleted individually.

Admin Center > Manage Calibration Sessions

Use this page to configure your Calibration Session. You can create a new session, clone(copy) or modify an existing one and delete a session that is not required. A Calibration Session defines the timeframe the session is applicable to, as well as the owner, participants and subjects of the session. You can have multiple active sessions.

Tip! Each Calibration Session generally groups employees with a similar background, allowing for a meaningful comparison.

	Session	Template Name	Status ↑	# of Subjects	# of Participants	Facilitator	Attachment
	Annual Calibration for Thompson	Annual Calibration Review	Approved	3	1	Aanya Singh, William Muller	
	Test Mass1	Annual Calibration Review	Approved	5	2	Aanya Singh, Eric Schwab	
	Best Run Annual Calibration	Best Run Pay x Performance	Approved	32	9	Aanya Singh, Angela Rice, Chung Tai, Dana Fiona Curtis, Eric Schwab, Grace Olivo Segura, Linda R. Simpson, Terry Vincent Taylor	
	Talent Potentialeinschätzung	Talent Review Calibration	Deactivated	12	4	Aanya Singh, Brigitte Kaiser, Fritz Winter, Heike Hartmann, Tanja Grupp	
	Jährliches Kalibrierungsmeeting	Best Run Pay x Performance	Deactivated	12	4	Aanya Singh, Brigitte Kaiser, Fritz Winter, Heike Hartmann, Tanja Grupp	

Figure 15-37. *Deletion of Sessions via Manage Calibration Sessions*

We have now seen how to create an individual calibration session, mass create calibration sessions, and mass delete calibration sessions. We will now learn the ways a manager may create sessions.

Manager Creates Sessions

There is an option to permit senior managers to create calibration sessions for their own teams.

"Enable Manager Calibration Session" would have to be enabled in the Global Settings tab of Manage Calibration Settings in order for this to work.

The manager would navigate to the Calibration page from the Home menu. As shown in Figure 15-38, the manager would see a "Create New" button to start a session directly on the calibration session screen.

Sessions Ask HR

Calibration

Sessions (0)   + Create New   Export   Export All

Session	Template Name	Status	# of Subjects	# of Particip...	Facilitator	My Role(s)	Session Date	Attachment
			No Data					

Items per page 10

Figure 15-38. *Calibration Session Screen*

The manager would have to select the calibration template that is linked to the performance form to be calibrated, name the session, and identify the number of levels to include as seen in Figure 15-39. For a manager with direct reports only, the only level option will be "Direct Reports."

Figure 15-39. *Manager New Session Creation*

In order for a session to be created, all of the subjects must have the performance forms associated with the calibration template launched, and each form must be in the calibration step.

Upon creation, the manager may go directly to the calibration session as seen in Figure 15-40.

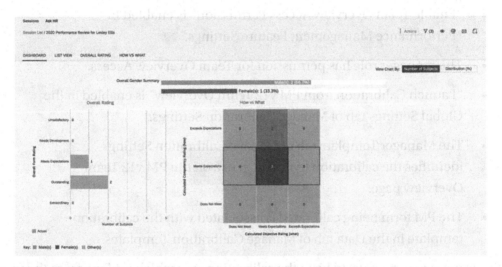

Figure 15-40. *Manager Created a Session*

The manager will also have the ability to delete their session by going back to the Sessions tab in Calibration as seen in Figure 15-41.

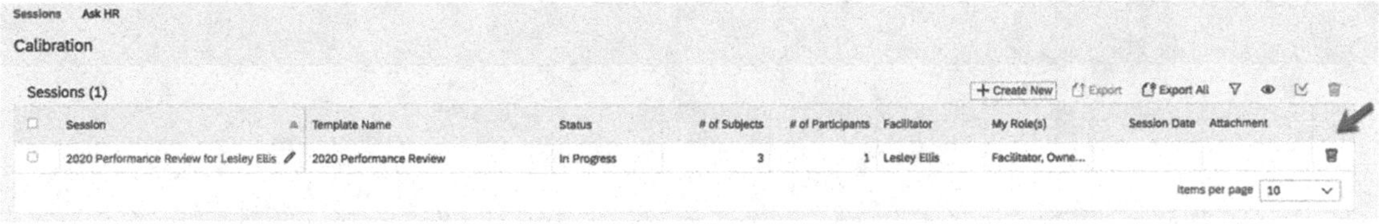

Session		Template Name	Status	# of Subjects	# of Participants	Facilitator	My Role(s)	Session Date	Attachment	
2020 Performance Review for Lesley Ellis		2020 Performance Review	In Progress	3	1	Lesley Ellis	Facilitator, Owne...			

Figure 15-41. *Manager Deletes a Calibration Session*

The manager would select the session and click the trash can icon. Upon confirmation, the session will be deleted.

Manager Creates Calibration Sessions in Team Overview

There is an additional feature that permits managers to create calibration sessions on the Team Overview page of Performance Management. This feature only permits sessions to be created for a manager's direct reports.

The following are required to use this feature:

- "Enable Team Overview Access Permission" is enabled in "Performance Management Feature Settings."

- The manager role has permission for Team Overview Access.

- "Launch Calibration from PM v12 Team Overview" is enabled in the Global Settings tab of Manage Calibration Settings.

- The Manager Template tab of Manage Calibration Settings identifies the calibration template to use on the PM v12 Team Overview page.

- The PM form being calibrated is associated with the calibration template in the Data tab of Manage Calibration Templates.

Performance forms have to be in the calibration step which is identical to the process for a manager creating a session directly in Calibration. The manager would go to Performance ➤ Team Overview. The Calibration button will appear on the top-right side of the screen as shown in Figure 15-42.

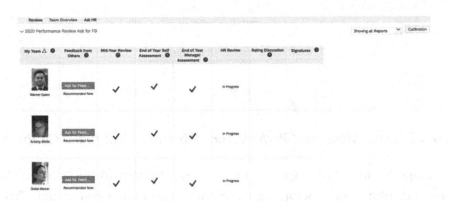

Figure 15-42. *Team Overview in Performance Management*

Clicking the "Calibration" button will open the calibration session as seen in Figure 15-43.

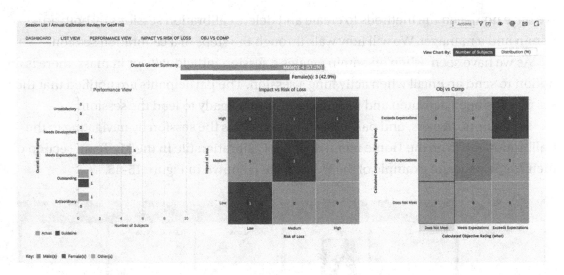

Figure 15-43. *Calibration Session Created via Team Overview*

If forms are not yet in the calibration step, an error message will display as shown in Figure 15-44.

Figure 15-44. Error Message if Performance Forms Are Not in the Calibration Step

The manager would need to go back into the performance forms to complete the review step and submit them before the calibration session may be created. This could also be accomplished in Team Overview.

Running a Calibration Session

We have now seen the methods to create and delete calibration sessions by both an admin and a manager. We will now walk through the steps of a calibration session.

As we have seen, when an admin creates a session individually or in mass, there is an option to send an email when activating a session. The participants are notified that the session has been activated and the facilitator is now ready to lead the session.

Facilitators, owners, and participants could access the session by navigating to the Calibration tab from the Home menu or to the Calibration tile in the My Team section of their home page. An example of the Home page is shown in Figure 15-45.

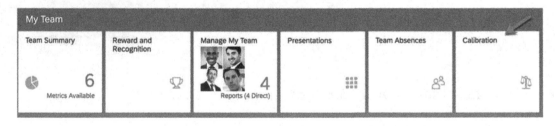

Figure 15-45. Calibration Tile for Managers

If a non-manager is participating in a calibration session, the Calibration tile will display by default in the My Specialty section of their home page. An example is shown in Figure 15-46.

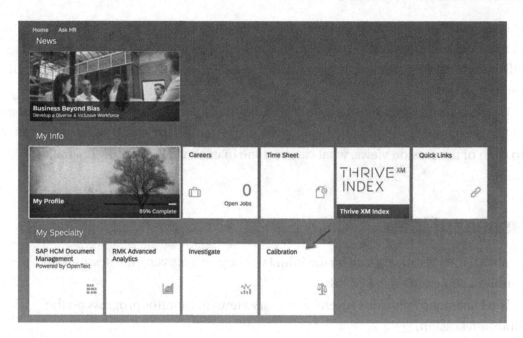

Figure 15-46. *Non-manager Calibration Tile*

Clicking the tile will take the user directly to the Calibration overview page. The Calibration overview screen will display with all sessions that a user has a role in. An example is shown in Figure 15-47.

Figure 15-47. *Session List for Facilitators, Owners, and Participants*

For participants, there most likely will only be one session, while a facilitator may have many sessions displayed.

The calibration role assigned to the user will dictate what they can do within the session. As a reminder, these permissions are set in the Permissions tab of Manage Calibration Settings.

A participant with read access will not be able to make any changes within the session.

The facilitator will moderate the session, make any rating changes, add comments, and mark each subject as discussed when completed. After saving the changes and confirming that the participants have no further updates, the facilitator will finalize the session.

The next series of session views will be from the facilitator's perspective. This means that the permissions will include Read, Write, Export, Finalize, and Delete. We will dive into each of the session views, what can be done in each view, and how to finalize a session.

Dashboard View

If enabled, the Dashboard will be the initial view upon accessing the session. An example is shown in Figure 15-48.

The Dashboard provides several summary views to monitor progress on the calibration session.

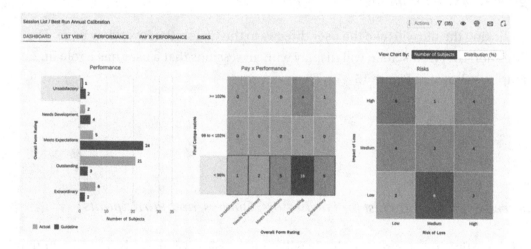

Figure 15-48. *Dashboard View of a Calibration Session*

Note   If gender indicators have been enabled in the calibration template, the overall gender summary displays at the top of the page once the session is finalized.

List View

Click the List View tab to see the subjects in a table-like format. An example of the List View tab of the session displays in Figure 15-49.

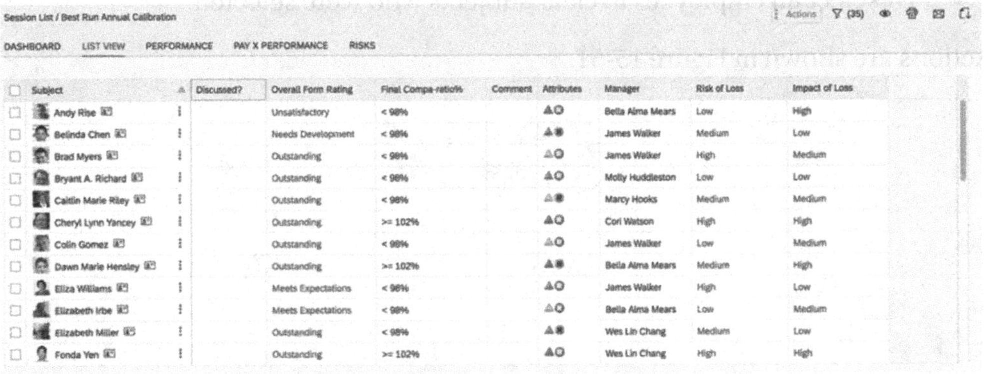

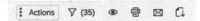

Figure 15-49. List View of a Calibration Session

Some of the columns that display and some of the features available are based on the selections made in "Manage Calibration Templates" and "Manage Calibration Settings."

For example, the Attributes column displays talent flags, and there is a quick card for each employee.

The Calibration toolbar as seen in Figure 15-50 is visible within each view.

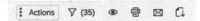

Figure 15-50. Calibration Toolbar

The options are Actions, Filter Options, Display Options, Print, Email, and Export. Additionally, the matrix views have the option to identify unrated subjects. These options are available for all view types.

Actions

The *Actions* button does not display on the Dashboard view and is not available when viewing approved sessions. The "Actions" button is not active until a subject is selected. In the List and Bin Views, a subject is selected by clicking the checkbox to the left of their name. For the Matrix View, click a subject within a cell to select. Multiple subjects may be selected for any of these views.

The actions performed on the selected subjects are as follows:

- Mark or unmark a subject as discussed.

- Analyze subjects side by side to view or update ratings.

- Deselect all employees to clear subjects who were selected.

Actions are shown in Figure 15-51.

Figure 15-51. *Actions*

Mark as Discussed

During the calibration session, the facilitator may present each subject for review. The subject's rating is updated or left unchanged. The facilitator may mark subjects as "discussed" when going through the session to keep track of who has been calibrated. The subject is selected and, using the Actions button, may be marked as discussed. An example of three subjects being selected and marked as discussed is shown in Figure 15-52.

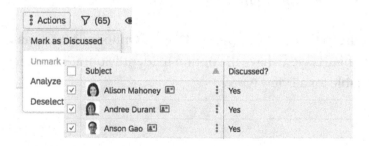

Figure 15-52. *Marking Subjects as Discussed*

In the List View, the "Discussed?" column will populate with "Yes" as seen in the preceding figure. This identifies subjects who have been reviewed. In the Bin View, subject names are grayed out when marked as discussed. An example is shown in Figure 15-53.

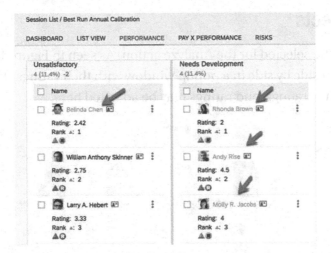

Figure 15-53. *Discussed Subjects in the Bin View*

In the Matrix View, the discussed subjects will be identified by a green checkmark icon next to their name. An example is shown in Figure 15-54.

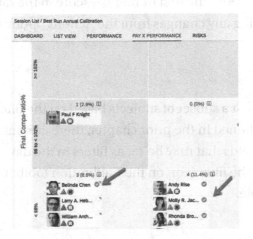

Figure 15-54. *Discussed Subjects in the Matrix View*

This is a helpful indicator when calibrating a large group of subjects. The indicator can keep track of which subjects have had their ratings reviewed and/or updated.

Any of the discussed subjects may also be changed to undiscussed. When selected, any discussed subjects will have the "Unmark as Discussed" action active. This option will remove the discussed indicators on all the views for the selected subjects.

Analyze Subjects

Any subjects may be selected for the Analyze action. As seen in Figure 15-55, the selected subjects are shown side by side in a popup window with their ratings. This provides a visual comparison of ratings, and ratings may be adjusted here.

Figure 15-55. *Analyze Subjects*

The unrated rating or "Too New to Rate" based on your rating scale is identified by the blank square that precedes the first numerical score in the rating scale. Click the "Save" button after making any changes from the Actions options.

Filter Options

Filter Options is used to list a subset of subjects based on the filter options set up in the data model. As mentioned in the prior chapter, there are standard filters and the custom01 to custom15 fields that may be set as filters in the data model. The filter fields are accessed by clicking the filter icon on the Calibration toolbar. Figure 15-56 displays the filter options available.

Figure 15-56. *Filter Options*

All employees who match the applied filter will display.

Display Options

Display options are identified by the eye icon and are used to add or remove data to or from the view. There are two tabs of display options. The hardcoded fields appear in the Other Options tab. First Name, Last Name, and Count are hardcoded and will always appear in the display options for a session as seen in Figure 15-57. If Quick card is enabled, it will be available in this tab as well.

Figure 15-57. *Display Options – Other Options*

Any display option fields defined in the Matrix Grid Classifier tool in Provisioning or set in Matrix Grid Report Icon Reconfiguration in the instance will be used in another tab of display options (Employee Attributes) as seen in Figure 15-58.

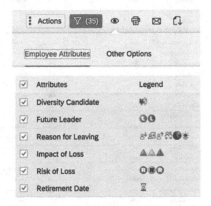

Figure 15-58. *Employee Attributes Display Options*

Deselect any field, and the Submit button will become active as seen in Figure 15-59.

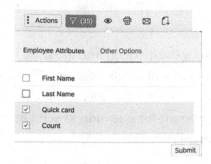

Figure 15-59. *Deselect Fields to Display*

Upon submission, the deselected fields will no longer display as columns on the view.

Print

The Print icon is used to print the view to a PDF as shown in Figure 15-60.

Best Run Annual Calibration

Subject	Discussed?	Overall Form Rating	Final Compa-ratio%	Comment	Attributes	Manager	Risk of Loss	Impact of Loss
Andy Rise		Unsatisfactory	< 98%		▲○	Bella Alma Mears	Low	High
Belinda Chen		Needs Development	< 98%		▲●	James Walker	Medium	Low
Brad Myers		Outstanding	< 98%		▲○	James Walker	High	Medium
Bryant A. Richard		Outstanding	< 98%		▲○	Molly Huddleston	Low	Low
Caitlin Marie Riley		Outstanding	< 98%		▲●	Marcy Hooks	Medium	Medium
Cheryl Lynn Yancey		Outstanding	>= 102%		▲○	Cori Watson	High	High
Colin Gomez		Outstanding	< 98%		▲○	James Walker	Low	Medium
Dawn Marie Hensley		Outstanding	>= 102%		▲●	Bella Alma Mears	Medium	High
Eliza Williams		Meets Expectations	< 98%		▲○	James Walker	High	Low
Elizabeth Irbe		Meets Expectations	< 98%		▲○	Bella Alma Mears	Low	Medium
Elizabeth Miller		Outstanding	< 98%		▲●	Wes Lin Chang	Medium	Low
Fonda Yen		Outstanding	>= 102%		▲○	Wes Lin Chang	High	High
James Reynolds		Outstanding	< 98%		▲○	Marcy Hooks	Low	High
Jennifer Lederman		Outstanding	< 98%		▲●	Marcy Hooks	Medium	Low
Jorge Gould		Extraordinary	< 98%		▲○	Molly Huddleston	High	Medium
Larry A. Hebert		Meets Expectations	< 98%		▲○	Wes Lin Chang	Low	High
Larry Griffin		Outstanding	< 98%		▲●	James Walker	Medium	Medium
Marcus Jones		Extraordinary	< 98%		▲○	Wes Lin Chang	High	Low
Marty Goodman		Extraordinary	< 98%		○▲○	Molly Huddleston	Low	Medium
Molly R. Jacobs		Outstanding	< 98%		▲●	Wes Lin Chang	Medium	Low
Paul F Knight		Outstanding	98 to < 102%		▲○	Bella Alma Mears	High	High
Philip A Fenimore		Outstanding	< 98%		▲○	Cori Watson	Low	Medium
Rhonda Brown		Needs Development	< 98%		▲●	Molly Huddleston	Medium	Low
Robbie Stephens		Meets Expectations	< 98%		▲○	Cori Watson	High	High
Samuel Juan Rodriguez		Extraordinary	>= 102%		▲○	Molly Huddleston	Low	High

Figure 15-60. *PDF Version of the List View*

Each view may be printed including the Dashboard.

Email

The Email icon creates a popup where an email may be crafted and sent. As seen in Figure 15-61, the owner and participants are defaulted in the "Send to" field but may be edited. The subject and message are required in order to send the email. The email does not send the session details or allow attachments.

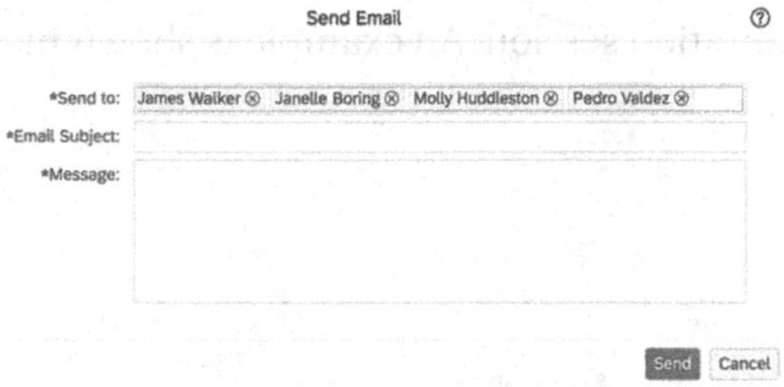

Send Email   ⑦

*Send to: James Walker ⊗   Janelle Boring ⊗   Molly Huddleston ⊗   Pedro Valdez ⊗

*Email Subject:

*Message:

Send   Cancel

Figure 15-61. *Send Email*

Export

The Export icon is used to download data from the session into Excel. There is a tab to represent each view of the session. An example is shown in Figure 15-62.

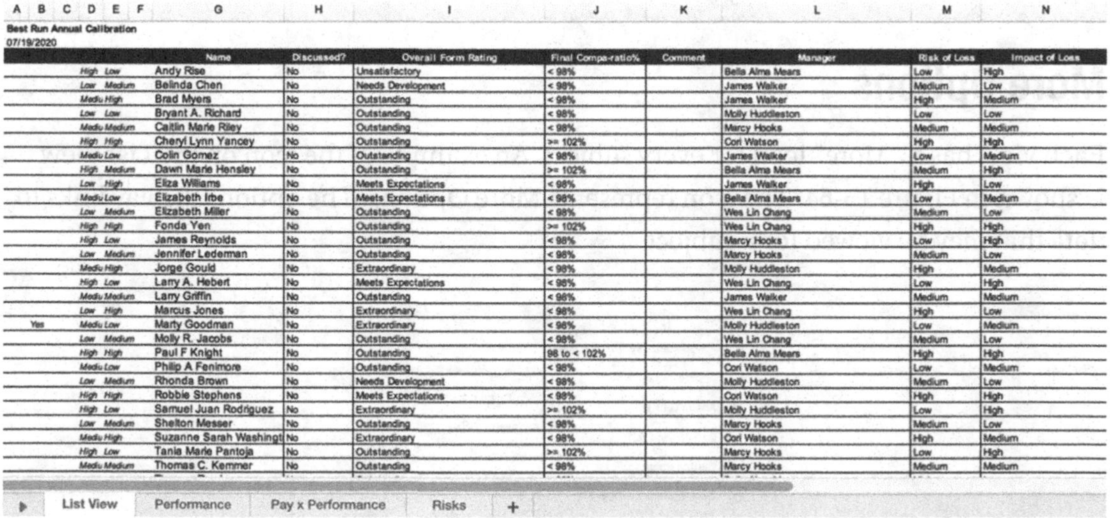

		Name	Discussed?	Overall Form Rating	Final Compa-ratio%	Comment	Manager	Risk of Loss	Impact of Loss
	High Low	Andy Rise	No	Unsatisfactory	< 98%		Bella Alma Mears	Low	High
	Low Medium	Belinda Chen	No	Needs Development	< 98%		James Walker	Medium	Low
	Mediu High	Brad Myers	No	Outstanding	< 98%		James Walker	High	Medium
	Low Low	Bryant A. Richard	No	Outstanding	< 98%		Molly Huddleston	Low	Low
	Mediu Medium	Caitlin Marie Riley	No	Outstanding	< 98%		Marcy Hooks	Medium	Medium
	High High	Cheryl Lynn Yancey	No	Outstanding	>= 102%		Cori Watson	High	High
	Mediu Low	Colin Gomez	No	Outstanding	< 98%		James Walker	Low	Medium
	High Medium	Dawn Marie Hensley	No	Outstanding	>= 102%		Bella Alma Mears	Medium	High
	Low High	Eliza Williams	No	Meets Expectations	< 98%		James Walker	High	Low
	Mediu Low	Elizabeth Irbe	No	Meets Expectations	< 98%		Bella Alma Mears	Low	Medium
	Low Medium	Elizabeth Miller	No	Outstanding	< 98%		Wes Lin Chang	Medium	Low
	High High	Fonda Yen	No	Outstanding	>= 102%		Wes Lin Chang	High	High
	High Low	James Reynolds	No	Outstanding	< 98%		Marcy Hooks	Low	High
	Low Medium	Jennifer Lederman	No	Outstanding	< 98%		Marcy Hooks	Medium	Low
	Mediu High	Jorge Gould	No	Extraordinary	< 98%		Molly Huddleston	High	Medium
	High Low	Larry A. Hebert	No	Meets Expectations	< 98%		Wes Lin Chang	Low	High
	Mediu Medium	Larry Griffin	No	Outstanding	< 98%		James Walker	Medium	Medium
	Low High	Marcus Jones	No	Extraordinary	< 98%		Wes Lin Chang	High	Low
Yes		Marty Goodman	No	Extraordinary	< 98%		Molly Huddleston	Low	Medium
	Low Medium	Molly R. Jacobs	No	Outstanding	< 98%		Wes Lin Chang	Medium	Low
	High High	Paul F Knight	No	Outstanding	98 to < 102%		Bella Alma Mears	High	High
	Mediu Low	Philip A Fenimore	No	Outstanding	< 98%		Cori Watson	Low	Medium
	Low Medium	Rhonda Brown	No	Needs Development	< 98%		Molly Huddleston	Medium	Low
	High High	Robbie Stephens	No	Meets Expectations	< 98%		Cori Watson	High	High
	High Low	Samuel Juan Rodriguez	No	Extraordinary	>= 102%		Molly Huddleston	Low	High
	Low Medium	Shelton Messer	No	Outstanding	< 98%		Marcy Hooks	Medium	Low
	Mediu High	Suzanne Sarah Washingt	No	Extraordinary	< 98%		Cori Watson	High	Medium
	High Low	Tania Marie Pantoja	No	Outstanding	>= 102%		Marcy Hooks	Low	High
	Mediu Medium	Thomas C. Kemmer	No	Outstanding	< 98%		Marcy Hooks	Medium	Medium

List View   Performance   Pay x Performance   Risks   +

Figure 15-62. *Export Session*

We have now reviewed the toolbar options. We will now explore some more features.

Unrated

In the Bin and Matrix Views, there is an additional toolbar option. There is an icon with a count to indicate the number of subjects without ratings. Clicking the icon will create a new bin, and a message will also display above the bins. The subjects will display in the bin by rating category, "Unrated" or "Too New to Rate." These subjects do not have a rating from their performance form, were rated "Too New to Rate," or had their rating removed during the calibration session. An example is shown in Figure 15-63.

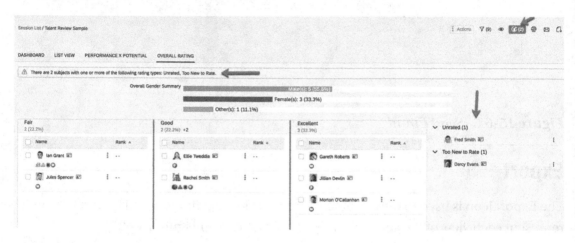

Figure 15-63. *Unrated Subjects*

More Options

Each view has a "More" icon for every subject. An example of the icon on the List View is shown in Figure 15-64. The icon represents More Options. The options display links to data that may be viewed for a subject.

Figure 15-64. *More Options*

Performance Forms

Based on the performance form template permissions, it may be possible to go into the performance form associated with the calibration template to make edits.

The additional links to data are based on the options selected in the Data tab of Manage Calibration Templates.

Calibration Talent Card

There is also an option to view the Calibration Talent Card as seen in Figure 15-65. The sections that display are based on the Calibration Talent Card configuration.

Figure 15-65. *Calibration Talent Card*

Additional Employee Data Access

Access to Employee Profile, Development, Learning Activities, and Achievements is available through the links, and each opens in a popup window. An example of a link to Employee Profile is shown in Figure 15-66.

Figure 15-66. *Employee Profile from a Calibration Session*

These links are helpful in providing additional information about the subjects to make informed decisions about rating changes.

Comment

In addition to the links to employee data, there is an option to add comments. When a calibration session is in progress, session participants with "Write" permission can add, edit, delete, and view comments. For those with "Read" permission, they may only view existing comments.

Clicking "Comment" will bring up a screen where it is possible to add and view any comments as seen in Figure 15-67. Each comment has a maximum of 4000 characters.

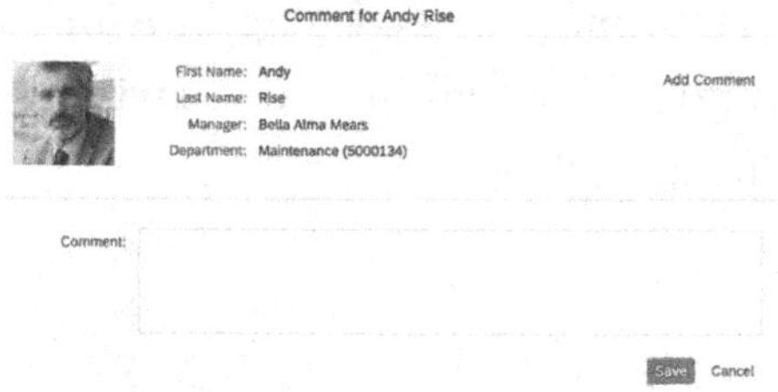

Figure 15-67. *Adding a Comment for a Subject*

After comments are entered and saved, the Comment column for the employee will display a comment bubble icon as seen in Figure 15-68.

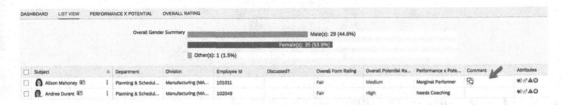

Figure 15-68. *Comment Exists for a Subject*

Clicking the comment icon will display the comment along with the source and date the comment was made. Only the comment creator may edit or delete the comment. An example is shown in Figure 15-69.

Figure 15-69. *View of Comments*

Comments are visible in any calibration session view except the Dashboard. The comments may be seen on the Subjects List page in Executive Review, in the Calibration History Portlet, in Employee Profile, an exported sessions and may be included in ad hoc reports.

Quick Card

The other option for more information on a subject is through their quick card.

Clicking the icon will open the card. An example is shown in Figure 15-70.

Figure 15-70. *View of an Employee's Quick Card*

Rating Updates

Each calibration view has a different method to update ratings. With the List View, ratings are updated via a dropdown listing as seen in Figure 15-71.

Figure 15-71. *Updating Ratings in the List View*

If "Enforce comments on rating change" is enabled in Manage Calibration Settings, a popup will force a comment to be entered prior to updating the rating as seen in Figure 15-72.

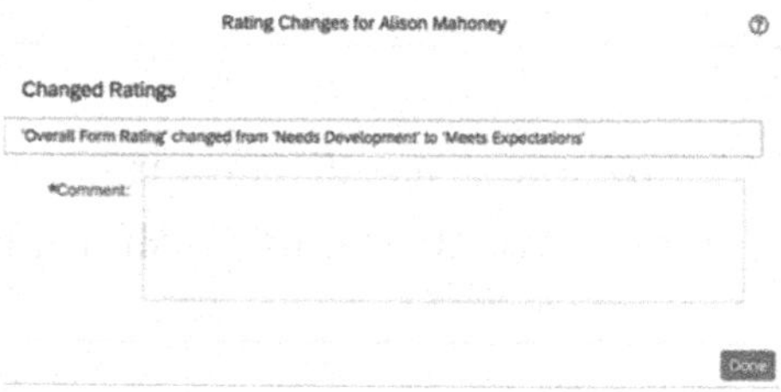

Figure 15-72. *Comment for Rating Changes*

We have now seen the features and functionality of List View. Click the next tab to see the Bin View. You will only have the Bin View if a view was configured with one calibration element.

Bin View

The Bin View is used to calibrate one rating source for the subjects. The rating source displayed is set in the Views tab of Manage Calibration Templates. As seen in Figure 15-73, subjects are placed in the bin (bucket) which represents their rating.

Figure 15-73. *Bin View of a Calibration Session*

Similar to the List View, the quick card will be available for each employee, and the More icon will have the same options to see additional employee information.

Bin View Rating Updates

Ratings are updated by selecting a subject and dragging their name to a different bin. You may move one subject or select several from the same bin to move to another bin.

Subjects may be ranked within a bin by moving their name up or down. This will populate ranking as seen in Figure 15-74.

Figure 15-74. Ranking Subjects Within a Bin

Each rating bucket shows the number of subjects it contains, the percentage of subjects in the bucket, and the number of subjects that need to be added or subtracted in order to meet the distribution guidelines. The distribution guidelines are set when creating the Bin View in Manage Calibration Templates. Figure 15-75 shows an example of the bins with their required subject totals.

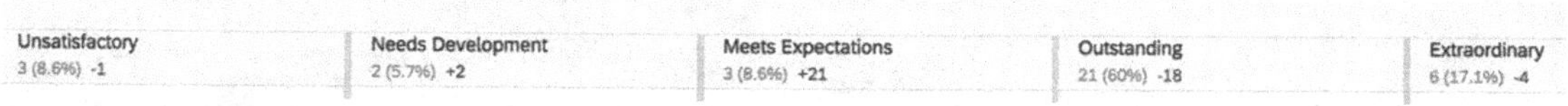

Unsatisfactory	Needs Development	Meets Expectations	Outstanding	Extraordinary
3 (8.6%) -1	2 (5.7%) +2	3 (8.6%) +21	21 (60%) -18	6 (17.1%) -4

Figure 15-75. Bin View with Distribution Guidelines

You are able to add more subjects to a bin than are permitted, since validation won't occur until you finalize the session. This means that you are able to save the changes, but at finalization, you will have to make updates that respect the guidelines.

When the bin holds exactly the number of subjects as expected in order to meet distribution guidelines, you will no longer see a plus or minus number at the top of the bin as seen in Figure 15-76.

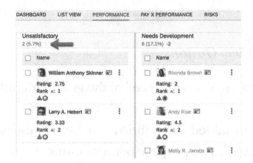

Figure 15-76. *Bin That Meets Distribution Guidelines*

Matrix View

The Matrix View, shown in Figure 15-77, is based on two ratings that form a 9-box. The subjects are placed in the grid based on the intersection of the two ratings. In this view, you may drag and drop subjects to other cells which updates the ratings.

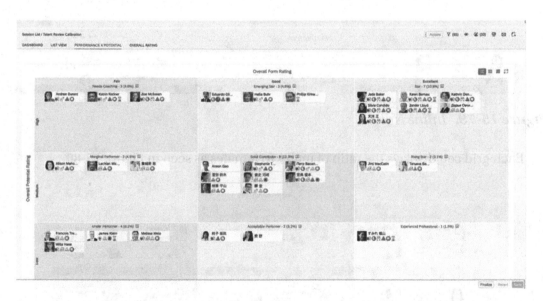

Figure 15-77. *Matrix View of a Calibration Session*

The Matrix View may display the subjects in the grid cells in several ways based on which of the four icons is selected as shown in Figure 15-78. View options are "Display Both Name and Photo," "Display Only Name," "Display Only Photo," or "Open Full Screen." New with the H1 2020 release, matrix views will now have the toolbar available in full screen mode.

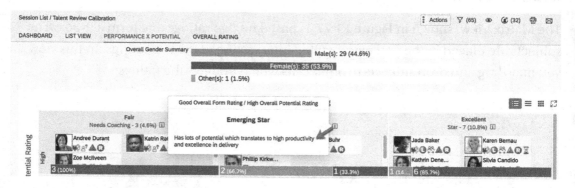

Figure 15-78. *Matrix View Options*

There is an information icon for each cell of the grid. It identifies the rating intersection values.

Any cell notes that were added when the Matrix View of the calibration template was created would display as well. The purpose of these inline notes is to give the calibration participants more information about what each matrix cell represents and to avoid unintentional bias.

An example is shown in Figure 15-79.

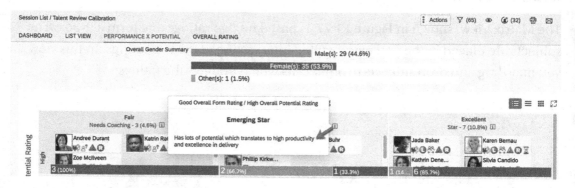

Figure 15-79. *Inline Notes*

Each grid cell displays the ratio of males to females as seen in Figure 15-80.

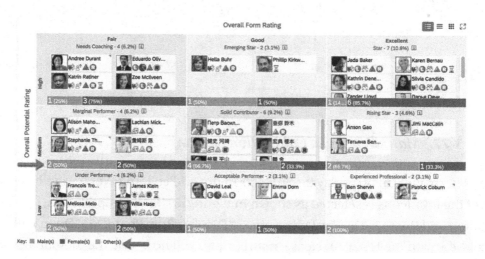

Figure 15-80. *Gender Ratio*

Similar to the "More" icon found on the other views, clicking the subject will display the options as seen in Figure 15-81.

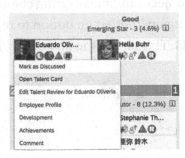

Figure 15-81. *More Options in the Matrix View*

Matrix View Rating Updates

To update any ratings, you may drag a name to another cell. If a compensation template is the data source for one of the axes, the drag and drop functionality is not possible. Using any of the views, save any updates made during the session. You may add comments and mark subjects as discussed as well.

A calibration session will have three buttons at the bottom of the view as shown in Figure 15-82. The buttons are "Finalize", "Revert", and "Save".

Figure 15-82. *Session Buttons*

Based on what is happening on the current screen, not all three will be active. For instance, after updating a rating, the "Revert" and "Save" buttons can be used. "Revert" only works on a change that has been made but not yet saved.

Calibration Alerts

Calibration alerts are used to point out situations where bias could impact the evaluation of some subjects or highlight scenarios where evaluators may have blind spots.

When a session is saved, if ratings of any subjects meet the trigger criteria in any of the calibration alert business rules, an Alerts popup message will display. There will be one message containing all of the alerts that were triggered. Each alert will identify the issue, identify all subjects impacted, and offer possible resolutions. The evaluators can then reexamine any of these subjects and make rating changes.

When the session is saved again, there is an option to regenerate the alerts. An example is seen in Figure 15-83. This allows the business rules to be evaluated again.

Figure 15-83. *Regenerate Alerts*

When regenerating the alerts, a popup will display as seen in Figure 15-84. Once completed, any remaining alerts will display.

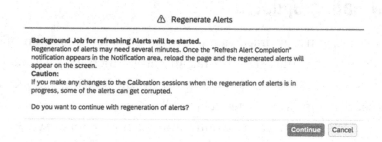

Figure 15-84. *Background Job Confirmation*

After the regeneration, alerts may have been removed or retained for some subjects and added for others. The evaluators should continue to reassess these subjects. Alerts may be cleared without changing ratings, but alerts of substance should be addressed. The session may be saved again, and the alerts may be regenerated again to see if any serious situations of bias remain. Once the evaluators feel that they have made all of the necessary changes, the facilitator should save the session and will be ready to finalize. We will review the finalization process once we look at one more calibration view.

Executive Review View

Executive Review is used by a senior HR or business executive to have a summarized view of the calibration sessions. All sessions tied to a calibration template will be included in the view, and the graphs from the calibration template's matrix views will be aggregated. The executive reviewer does not have to participate in any of the sessions to have access to this view. Anyone assigned to this role will have access to the sessions associated with the calibration template.

When the executive reviewer goes to Calibration from the Home menu, the Sessions tab will display along with an additional tab called Executive Review as seen in Figure 15-85.

Figure 15-85. *Executive Review Tab*

If the executive reviewer has been granted access to multiple calibration templates, each will be listed. This means all sessions that are based on the same calibration template will be part of the data that displays. If the Executive Reviewer role has calibration role access restricted by target population when creating the template, the graphs and filters respect the restriction.

Standard Graphs

When the executive reviewer clicks the name of a template, the aggregated data will display in the Standard Graphs section of the screen as seen in Figure 15-86.

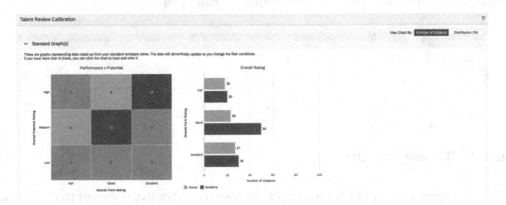

Figure 15-86. *Standard Graphs in Executive Review*

The graphs are based on the calibration template's matrix views. The chart view can be changed by clicking either the "Number of Subjects" or "Distribution (%)" button shown for "View Chart By."

There is a filter icon on the top-right side of the page. Data may be viewed using filter options as shown in Figure 15-87.

Figure 15-87. *Standard Graphs Filter Options*

Subjects List

There is a drilldown feature for the standard graphs which provides details of employees aggregated on this view. These details are displayed in Subjects List. Clicking a data point on any of the graphs creates a Subjects List view. An example is shown in Figure 15-88. The subjects listed are based on the data point selected on the chart. In the following example, everyone with an overall form rating of "Fair" displays.

Figure 15-88. *Subjects List*

Clicking the session name for a subject will take the executive reviewer to the specific calibration session with the detail information. All of the views from the session will be available. If the session is not finalized yet, the executive reviewer may update ratings.

The talent card and a link to Employee Profile are available for each subject on the list.

Similar to the views within a calibration session, there are filter and display options. The Subjects List may be printed as a PDF or exported as an Excel document.

On the Subjects List page, columns can be reordered or sorted, and the column widths can be adjusted. Display options can be set as well. All these adjustments are saved and remain effective after the Subjects List page is refreshed.

Sensitive Data Graphs

When the executive reviewer returns to the Standard Graphs page, they may scroll down to the Sensitive Data Graphs section as seen in Figure 15-89.

Figure 15-89. *Sensitive Data Graphs in Executive Review*

Each of the sensitive data points (Gender, Risk of Loss, Impact of Loss, and Reason for Leaving) can be charted against any rating sources used on the template's views.

Once the data source is selected from the dropdown listing, the graphs will populate as seen in Figure 15-90.

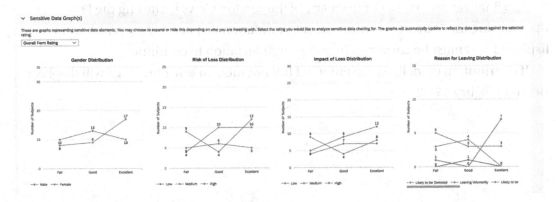

Figure 15-90. *Sensitive Data Graphs*

Changing the rating source from the calibration template will update the graphs. An example is shown in Figure 15-91.

761

Figure 15-91. *Change Sensitive Data Graphs Rating Source*

We have now seen a calibration session in progress. We have seen the features available for the views; and we have learned how to add comments, analyze subjects, and update ratings. We have also seen how the Executive Review tab works. Next, we will finalize our calibration session.

Finalize a Session

After all of the subjects have been discussed, their ratings reviewed, and any changes made and saved, the session may be finalized. Finalization closes out the session and applies the rating changes to the performance forms. This will also move the performance forms to the next step if enabled in the Advanced tab in Manage Calibration Templates. Any of the roles granted the "Finalize" permission in the Permissions tab of Manage Calibration Sessions may perform this action.

The finalization may occur from any of the session views including the Dashboard. After clicking the "Finalize" button, session validation will occur. Any errors will be displayed and must be corrected in order for finalization to continue.

If distribution guidelines are enforced but not met, an error message will display as shown in Figure 15-92.

Figure 15-92. *Guidelines Enforcement Error*

In a situation like this, ratings will have to be updated to meet the distribution guidelines. If the participants want to override the guidelines, the admin will have to disable the enforcement of guidelines in the calibration template. Any setting changes made in the calibration settings or template will apply to live sessions.

Once all errors are corrected, you may try to finalize the session again. If there are no errors, a confirmation popup will display as shown in Figure 15-93. Once finalization begins, it cannot be undone. Finalizing a session locks down all of the ratings and ends the session. The forms are sent to the next step of the performance review process with the updated ratings if this feature is enabled. Once a session is finalized, it is closed and cannot be edited.

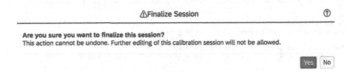

⚠Finalize Session   ⑦

Are you sure you want to finalize this session?
This action cannot be undone. Further editing of this calibration session will not be allowed.

Yes No

Figure 15-93. *Finalize Session Confirmation*

Confirm by clicking the "Yes" button; a popup will display as shown in Figure 15-94. The session is finalized, and the admin may send out a notification to owners and participants. The notification recipients, subject, and message may be modified prior to sending.

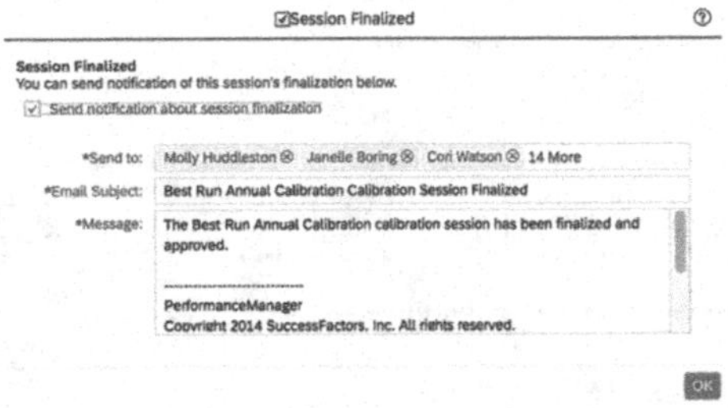

☑Session Finalized   ⑦

Session Finalized
You can send notification of this session's finalization below.
☑ Send notification about session finalization

*Send to:	Molly Huddleston ⊗ Janelle Boring ⊗ Cori Watson ⊗ 14 More
*Email Subject:	Best Run Annual Calibration Calibration Session Finalized
*Message:	The Best Run Annual Calibration calibration session has been finalized and approved.

PerformanceManager
Copyright 2014 SuccessFactors, Inc. All rights reserved.

OK

Figure 15-94. *Finalization Confirmation with Option to Send a Notification Email*

If emails have been sent, as shown in Figure 15-95, a popup confirms that the notifications were successfully sent.

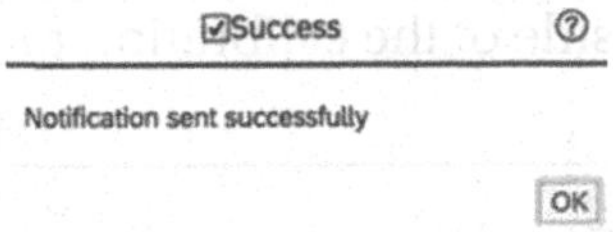

☑Success   ⑦

Notification sent successfully

OK

Figure 15-95. *Notification Sent Confirmation*

The owners and participants will receive an email notifying them that the calibration is now complete as seen in Figure 15-96.

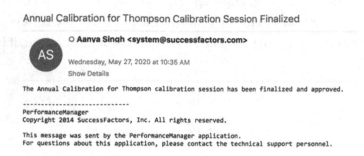

Figure 15-96. *Finalize Session Notification*

All managers who have employees with rating changes will receive an email which shows the original rating and the calibrated (final) rating. This will occur if this option is enabled in the Advanced tab of Manage Calibration Templates. Figure 15-97 shows an example of the notification.

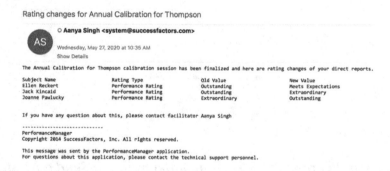

Figure 15-97. *Email Sent to Managers with Rating Changes*

If for some reason a rating needs to be changed after calibration, the admin may do so on an individual performance form. The form would need to be routed back to a step where the rating is editable, the change made, and then the form routed past the calibration step. This occurs outside of the calibration process.

Mass Approve Sessions

Any of the roles granted the "Finalize" permission in the Permissions tab of Manage Calibration Sessions may finalize sessions in bulk as well.

From the calibration session overview page, multiple sessions may be selected. Click the "Finalize" icon in the upper-right corner as seen in Figure 15-98.

Calibration
Sessions (15)
Session
Status
Finalize each session individually or finalize multiple sessions in one go.

***Figure 15-98.** Mass Finalization of Sessions*

A confirmation popup will display as seen in Figure 15-99.

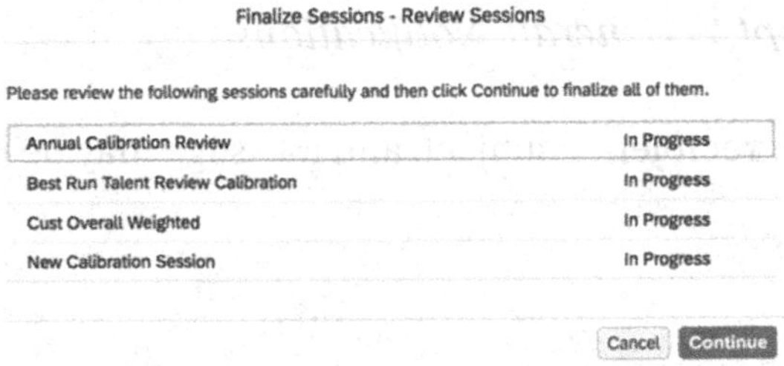
Finalize Sessions - Review Sessions
Please review the following sessions carefully and then click Continue to finalize all of them.
Annual Calibration Review
In Progress
Best Run Talent Review Calibration
In Progress
Cust Overall Weighted
In Progress
New Calibration Session
In Progress
Cancel
Continue

***Figure 15-99.** Confirmation to Finalize Sessions*

Any sessions with errors will display a warning icon. Clicking the icon will show the details of the issue as seen in Figure 15-100.

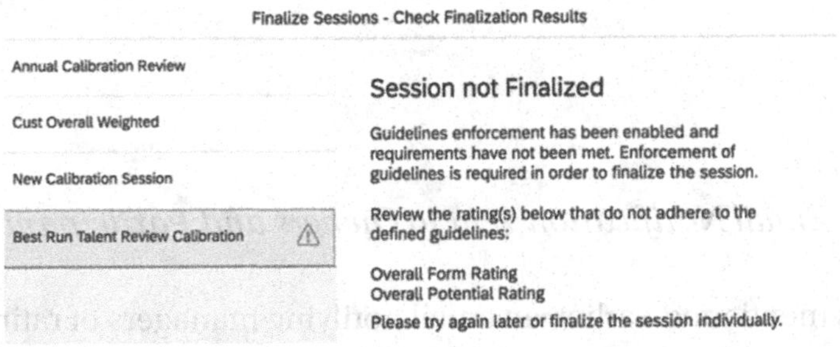
Finalize Sessions - Check Finalization Results
Annual Calibration Review
Cust Overall Weighted
New Calibration Session
Best Run Talent Review Calibration
Session not Finalized
Guidelines enforcement has been enabled and requirements have not been met. Enforcement of guidelines is required in order to finalize the session.
Review the rating(s) below that do not adhere to the defined guidelines:
Overall Form Rating
Overall Potential Rating
Please try again later or finalize the session individually.

***Figure 15-100.** Finalization Results*

If "Notify Calibration Participants of Session Finalization" has been enabled, any sessions without errors can generate an email to the owners and participants of the sessions as shown in Figure 15-101.

Figure 15-101. *Prompt to Generate Notifications*

Prior to sending, the recipients, subject, and message may be modified as seen in Figure 15-102.

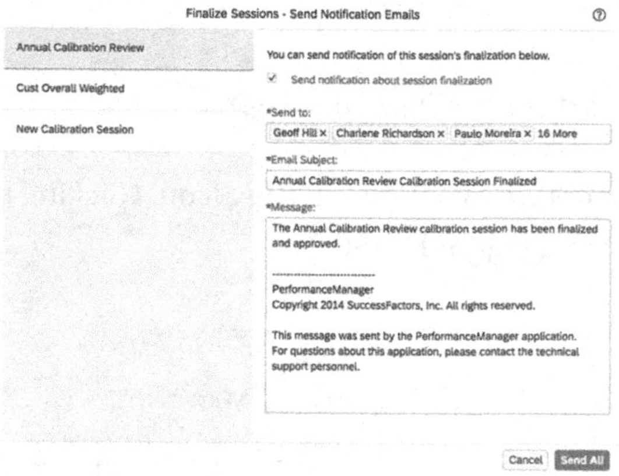

Figure 15-102. *Email Notification Sent to Owners and Participants*

If enabled, as mentioned earlier, an email notifying managers of rating changes at session finalization will be sent as well.

Sessions that have been successfully finalized will now have the status of "Approved".

We have now finalized sessions in mass, and we will look at some other features available.

Calibration Summary Tile

When we began our calibration session, we saw the Calibration tile available on the home page for managers and users who have a role in a calibration session. On the manager's home page, there will also be a To-Do tile called Team Calibration Summary. An example is shown in Figure 15-103.

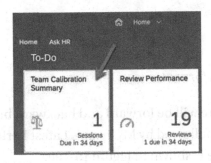

Figure 15-103. *Calibration To-Do Tile*

To see this tile, the participant of the session must be the manager of the subjects. The Team Calibration Summary tile will only display if the data source of the session comes from a performance form. Clicking the tile will display a review summary link. An example is shown in Figure 15-104.

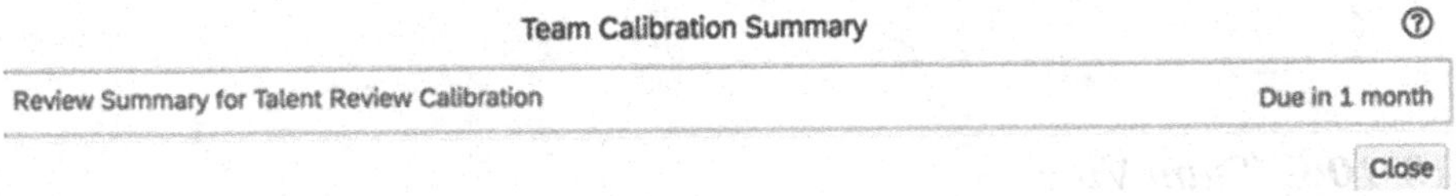

Team Calibration Summary	⑦
Review Summary for Talent Review Calibration	Due in 1 month
	Close

Figure 15-104. *To-Do Item*

After clicking the link, the manager will see a series of screens starting with an overview page. An example is shown in Figure 15-105. There will be Summary, Participants, and Subjects tabs.

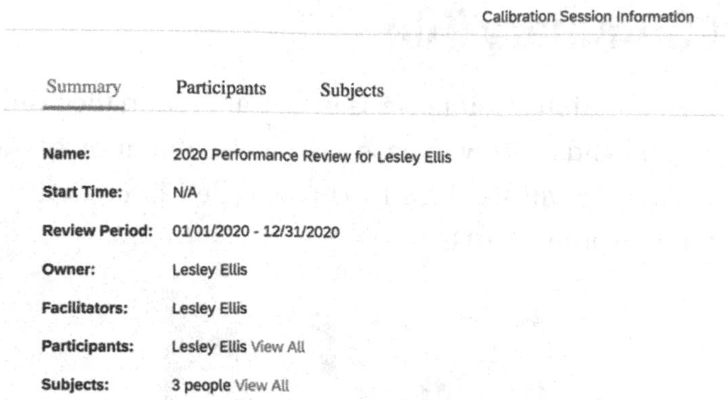

Calibration Session Information
Summary
Participants
Subjects
Name:
2020 Performance Review for Lesley Ellis
Start Time:
N/A
Review Period:
01/01/2020 - 12/31/2020
Owner:
Lesley Ellis
Facilitators:
Lesley Ellis
Participants:
Lesley Ellis View All
Subjects:
3 people View All

Figure 15-105. *Session Information*

In any of these tabs, there will be forward and backward buttons. Use the forward button to get to Team View, followed by My Team's Latest Performance and Performance History screens. An example is shown in Figure 15-106.

Team View
Lesley Ellis
Director Operations (US)
3 Direct Reports
3 Total
Click employee to review their performance form
Antony White
Business Development Lead
Greta Mercer
Resource Manager
Warner Gates
Finance Officer

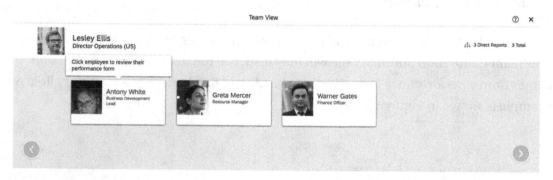

Figure 15-106. *Team View*

Clicking a name will display the user's talent card with options to go the goal plan, the development plan, achievements, activities, or the performance form. An example is shown in Figure 15-107.

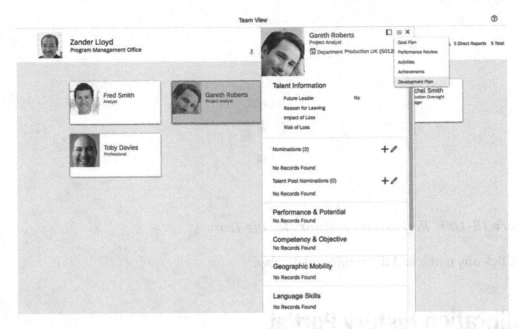

Figure 15-107. *Team View Options*

There are performance-related screens as well. The rating allocation for the team is shown in Figure 15-108.

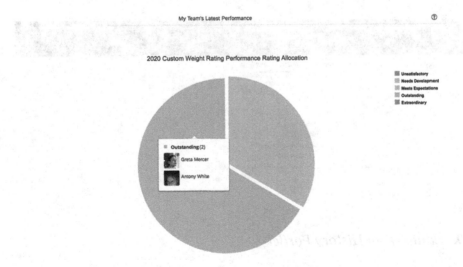

Figure 15-108. *Rating Allocation for the Team*

Moving to the final screen, performance history may be viewed for the team as well. An example is seen in Figure 15-109.

Figure 15-109. *Performance History for the Team*

Click any name and the rating will display.

Calibration History Portlet

If configured, the calibrated rating will display after finalization in People Profile as seen in Figure 15-110. Normally, this block would be visible to managers and HR managers and not to employees.

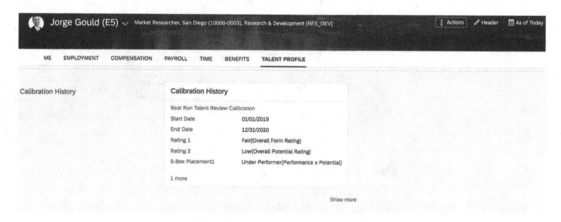

Figure 15-110. *Calibration History Portlet*

The calibration session name, dates, and ratings will show. Multiple calibration sessions will display, if available.

Reporting

During and after calibration sessions, calibration-related data may be reported on. There are no standard calibration reports, dashboards, or tiles available for reporting. Instead, you will need to create your own ad hoc reports.

The domains available when creating an ad hoc table are Calibration, Calibration Activity, and Calibration Org Chart Coverage. They are described in the following:

> *Calibration Reporting:* Includes information on the calibration template and session, along with details on the facilitators, participants, and subjects and ratings. Old and new ratings can be reported on.

> *Calibration Activity Reporting:* the same fields are available as the Calibration domain, but only reports on employees with rating changes.

> *Calibration Org Chart Coverage Reporting:* Includes similar fields as the Calibration and Calibration Activity domains but does not include ratings and change activity.

The ad hoc reports use snapshots of ratings at session activation, ratings changed and saved in an activated session, and ratings when the session is finalized. This differs from the rating in the session which is always the latest rating.

As a reminder, in order to create and run calibration reports, role-based permissions must be granted.

Conclusion

We hope this chapter has given you a thorough view of the main features and functions of the SAP SuccessFactors Calibration module. We demonstrated how a calibration session is created, individually and in mass. We have learned how a manager may create a session through the Calibration tab or through Team Overview in the Performance tab. We walked through a calibration session and saw the features for each view. We have finalized a session and seen the options for reporting on calibration activity. We hope you take away an understanding of the benefits of this module and how SAP SuccessFactors Calibration delivers an efficient system to see rating data from multiple sources in order to adjust ratings equitably and then update this data into its original source.

CHAPTER 16

Conclusion

We hope you have enjoyed this first volume covering the Talent Management modules and functions of SAP SuccessFactors! Let's take a moment to step back and review what we've learned along the way so we can understand how the modules covered thus far work together to provide a comprehensive talent management solution that provides real value to organizations and their employees.

In Chapter 1, we outlined the contents of the book and introduced key concepts such as an instance, Provisioning, role-based permissions, the search bar, and the user data file (UDF) which were referenced throughout the book. Chapter 2 began our deeper dive into the modules and functions of SAP SuccessFactors starting with Talent Profile. We looked at various standard portlets and blocks available for display in People Profile and also how to configure custom portlets. We walked through how to configure XML and conduct data imports and exports and wrapped up with a case study. Overall, this taught you how to store, organize, and display employee data relevant to Talent and for use in the various modules of SuccessFactors Talent.

Chapter 3 brought us to Job Profile Builder. You learned how to configure job profiles to suit your organization's specific requirements. Additionally, you learned how to populate the configured profiles with job-related data such as competencies to build a catalog of jobs. Overall, this taught you how to store, organize, and display job-related data relevant for talent management that can be used for the various modules of SuccessFactors Talent.

In Chapter 4, we started looking into the Goal Management module. We started with basic configurations, showing you how to download a sample goal plan from SuccessStore and then configure it online. We then jumped into how to perform more detailed configurations in the XML followed by a walk-through of the functionality as an end user. Chapter 5 then dove into alternative features of the module. We shared how to manage goal plans on a mass scale and introduced concepts like Goal Execution, group goals, team goals, and initiatives. Overall, these chapters instructed you how to configure

© Susan Traynor, Michael A. Wellens and Venki Krishnamoorthy 2021
S. Traynor et al., *SAP SuccessFactors Talent: Volume 1*, https://doi.org/10.1007/978-1-4842-6600-7_16

the system so that your organization can effectively log and track execution of goals on the individual employee level while still remaining relevant to high-level business objectives.

Chapters 6–13 took an in-depth look at the Performance Management module. In Chapters 6–10, you learned how to configure a Performance Management form and how to integrate those forms to other areas of Talent Management by bringing in goals, competencies, and development objectives. In Chapters 11 and 12, you learned how Ask for Feedback, Get Feedback, Add Modifier, and Add Signer features as well as the 360 form can provide feedback from a variety of sources rather than just managers. Chapter 13 took a look at a performance option that has started to become more common in the past few years: Continuous Performance Management. You learned how to set up the system so that managers and employees can have ongoing conversations tracked and assisted by the system. Furthermore, these could also be directly tied to goals within the goal plan. The key takeaway from these chapters was learning how the system tracks employee performance on a massive scale from a variety of sources either through a formal review cycle or other less formal means.

Chapters 14 and 15 covered Calibration. In these chapters, you learned how Calibration can be tied to performance forms or other talent data sources to allow collaborators to decide on finalized performance ratings, 9-box placements, and other talent field values for groups of individuals. You learned not only how to decide on the fields to be collectively rated but also how to involve different participants and potentially tie the calibration sessions to different stages in a route map. In summary, these chapters showed how the system can be used to fairly evaluate groups of employees by involving specific groups of evaluators to make important talent management decisions across the span of the talent suite.

In Volume 2, we will take a look at various employee development features as well as the Succession Management module. These will show you how SAP SuccessFactors allows you to easily identify the top talent you've been able to identify during the performance review process and develop them to fill key positions.

We hope this review has given you the opportunity now to step back from the details we covered in each chapter to realize the high-level business processes that these features and modules cohesively bring to life. It is fulfilling to see how the product, when properly implemented and used, can help employees and organizations set and track business and development goals collaboratively while providing rewarding career opportunities that help both the business and employees succeed. At the conclusion of the next volume, we will briefly talk about how to realize this potential business value through an implementation of a fully productive system.

Index

A

Add/remove modifier or signer
  actions, 545–546
  additional modifier, 548
  additional signers, 550
  confirmation, 546–547
  considerations, 544
  deselect, 545
  name searching, 546
  new steps, 547–548
  Performance Inbox, 546
  select stages, 545
  sign form, 549
  team overview, 549
  To-Do item, 548
  view modifiers/signers, 547
Alternate goal management
  concepts/features, 182
  custom calculations
    configure, 198–200
    view goal scores, end users, 200
  goal execution/alignment chart, 183
    configuration, 185, 188
    configuration permissions, 184–185
    email configuration, 190
    end user permission, 191–192
    fields, 186–188
    meeting agenda screen, 194
    prerequisites, 183

Provisioning settings, 184
  settings, 189
  specific fields, 193
  status report, 193
  use, 192–195
goal plan state, 195–196
  configure, 196–197
  use, 197–198
group goals, 201
  assigning end user
    permissions, 203
  configuring group goals, 202
  prerequisites for
    configuration, 201–202
  use, 204–206
initiatives, 213
  assigning end user
    permissions, 215–216
  configure, 214–215
  prerequisites for
    configuration, 213–214
  use, end user, 216–220
team goals
  assigning end user
    permissions, 208–209
  configure, 207–208
  prerequisites for
    configuration, 206–207
  use, end user, 209–213

775

© Susan Traynor, Michael A. Wellens and Venki Krishnamoorthy 2021
S. Traynor et al., *SAP SuccessFactors Talent: Volume 1*, https://doi.org/10.1007/978-1-4842-6600-7

X, Y, Z

Printed in the United States
by Baker & Taylor Publisher Services